THRIVING ON VAGUE OBJECTIVES

Other DILBERT Books from BOXTREE

BUSINESS BOOKS

The Dilbert Principle
TPB ISBN: 0-7522-2470-0
PB ISBN: 0-7522-7220-9

The Way of the Weasel
HB ISBN: 0-7522-6503-2
TPB ISBN: 0-7522-1559-0

The Dilbert Future
TPB ISBN: 0-7522-1161-7
PB ISBN: 0-7522-7221-7

Dogbert's Top Secret Management Handbook
ISBN: 0-7522-1148-X

The Joy of Work
TPB ISBN: 0-7522-1720-8

TREASURIES

Fugitive From the Cubicle Police
ISBN: 0-7522-2431-X

Seven Years of Highly Defective People
ISBN: 0-7522-2407-7

Dilbert Gives You the Business
ISBN: 0-7522-2394-1

Dilbert – A Treasury of Sunday Strips: Version 00
ISBN: 0-7522-7232-2

COLLECTIONS

Shave the Wale
ISBN: 0-7522-0849-7

When Did Ignorance Become a Point of View?
ISBN: 0-7522-2412-3

Bring Me the Head of Willy the Mailboy!
ISBN: 0-7522-0136-0

**Words You Don't Want to Hear During Your
Annual Performance Review**
ISBN: 0-7522-2422-0

Always Postpone Meetings with Time-Wasting Morons
ISBN: 0-7522-0854-3

When Body Language Goes Bad
ISBN: 0-7522-2491-3

Another Day In Cubicle Paradise
ISBN: 0-7522-2486-7

Random Acts of Management
ISBN: 0-7522-7174-1

Don't Step in the Leadership
ISBN: 0-7522-2389-5

I'm Not Anti-Business, I'm Anti-Idiot
ISBN: 0-7522-2379-8

Casual Day Has Gone Too Far
ISBN: 0-7522-1119-6

**Don't Stand Where the Comet
is Assumed to Strike Oil**
ISBN: 0-7522-2402-6

BEST OF DILBERT

The Best of Dilbert Volume 1
ISBN: 0-7522-6541-5

Best of Dilbert Volume 2
ISBN: 0-7522-1500-0

For ordering information, call +44 01625 677237

THRIVING ON VAGUE OBJECTIVES

A DILBERT BOOK
BY SCOTT ADAMS

BOXTREE

First published 2005 by Andrews McMeel Publishing, an Andrews McMeel Universal company,
4520 Main Street, Kansas City, Missouri 64111, USA

First published in Great Britain 2005 by Boxtree
an imprint of Pan Macmillan Ltd
Pan Macmillan, 20 New Wharf Road, London N1 9RR
Basingstoke and Oxford
Associated companies throughout the world
www.panmacmillan.com

ISBN 0 7522 2605 3

1 3 5 7 9 8 6 4 2

A CIP catalogue record for this book is available from
the British Library.

Printed by The Bath Press Ltd, Bath

Introduction

My publisher just informed me that I should finish writing the introduction to my book *Thriving on Vague Objectives*, "sooner." This guidance is based on the theory that sooner is better, and all things being equal, it's better to be better, especially if it's sooner.

My first impulse was to get literal and argue that everything is sooner than something else. Therefore, there's no real rush. But I can't do that because one of my other personality defects involves compulsive earliness. I don't mean that I'm merely punctual—generally considered a good trait. I mean I'm early to the point of being spectacularly annoying.

I'm the guy who shows up at your 7 p.m. party at 6:45 p.m., when the host and hostess are still unwashed and staring into their closets wishing they had shopped more. I've become quite the expert at making conversation with the appetizers until other humans arrive. It usually goes something like this:

> Me:
> "Hello, bean dip. The traffic wasn't bad. I guess I got here too early."
>
> Bean dip:
> (creepy silence)
>
> Me:
> "You look very brown. Have you been getting some sun?"
>
> Bean dip:
> (more creepy silence)
>
> Me:
> "Okay, be that way. Let's see how you like having this chip rammed into your torso.
> BUWHAHAHA!!! MMMPHPH! Gulp!"

That, in a nutshell, is everything you need to know about why I don't get invited to many parties.

So now I have this vague objective of writing the introduction "sooner." Ever since I received this logically unjustifiable objective ten minutes ago, I find it impossible to do anything else. I wish I could be tardy like normal people, but I just don't know how. I can't take a break until I am done. My bladder is the size of a small ottoman—damn you, delicious Diet Coke!—but I must finish this task before all the others that are not due "sooner." I worry that my body will get all backed up and poison my brain with urine. When you are semifamous like me, you hope that you won't die in a way that the newspapers find both humorous and easy to pun. Here's one to avoid: Pee-Brained Cartoonist Dies!

I prefer to die from a pulmonary thrombosis, or anything else that makes a lousy headline. I don't even know what a pulmonary thrombosis is, but it sounds bad. Oh God, the urine poisoning has begun. I'm not making any sense. How many words have I written? Wait, I don't recall that my editor mentioned a specific word-count objective for the introduction. Ha ha! More vagueness! But this time it works in my favor! I am done!

Speaking of done, our civilization is obviously about to self-destruct. And when it does, Dogbert will be there to take his rightful position as supreme overlord. If you would like to rule by his side, sign up for the free *Dilbert Newsletter* and automatically become part of Dogbert's New Ruling Class. The newsletter comes out approximately whenever I feel like it (if not "sooner"), which is about four times a year. To sign up, go to www.dilbert.com and follow the subscription instructions. If that doesn't work for some reason, send e-mail to newsletter@unitedmedia.com.

S. Adams

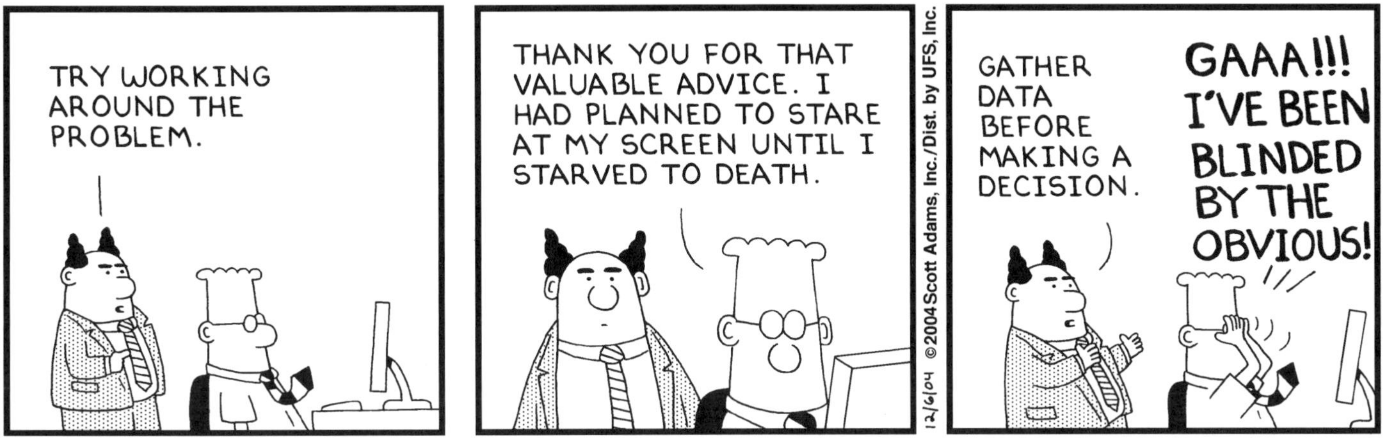
TRY WORKING AROUND THE PROBLEM.
THANK YOU FOR THAT VALUABLE ADVICE. I HAD PLANNED TO STARE AT MY SCREEN UNTIL I STARVED TO DEATH.
12/6/04 © 2004 Scott Adams, Inc./Dist. by UFS, Inc.
GATHER DATA BEFORE MAKING A DECISION.
GAAA!!! I'VE BEEN BLINDED BY THE OBVIOUS!

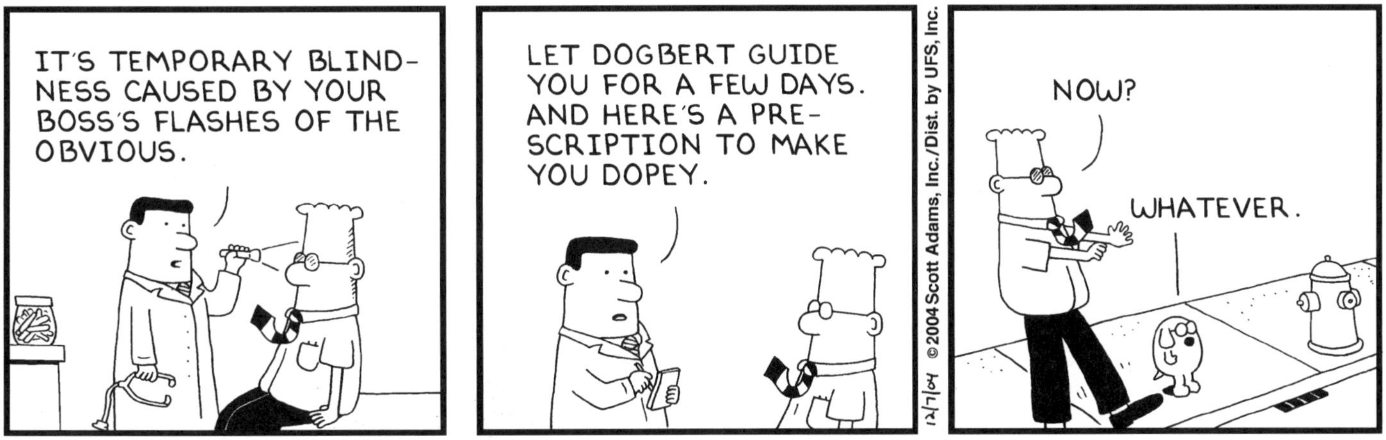
IT'S TEMPORARY BLINDNESS CAUSED BY YOUR BOSS'S FLASHES OF THE OBVIOUS.
LET DOGBERT GUIDE YOU FOR A FEW DAYS. AND HERE'S A PRESCRIPTION TO MAKE YOU DOPEY.
12/7/04 © 2004 Scott Adams, Inc./Dist. by UFS, Inc.
NOW?
WHATEVER.

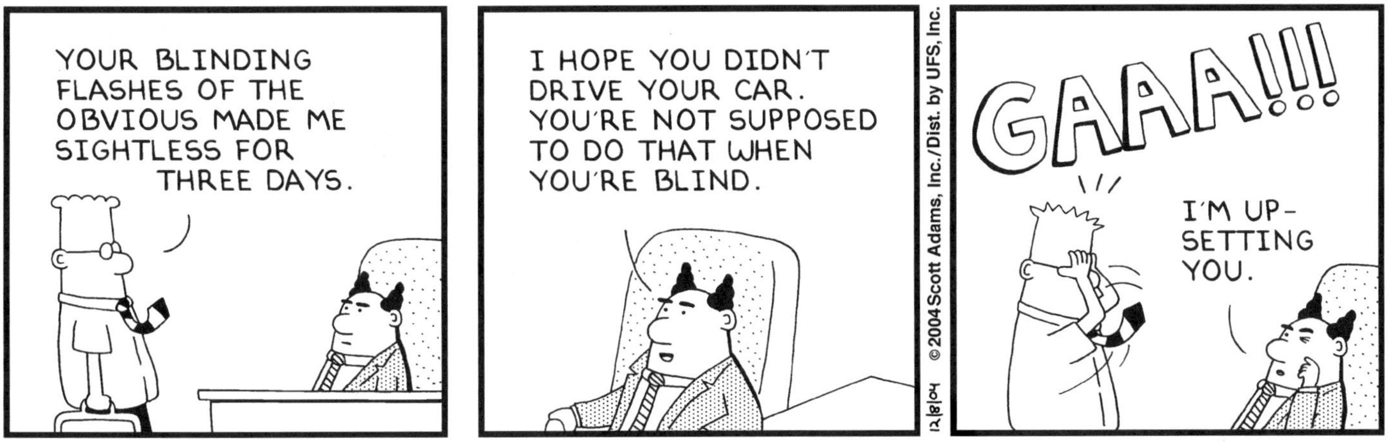
YOUR BLINDING FLASHES OF THE OBVIOUS MADE ME SIGHTLESS FOR THREE DAYS.
I HOPE YOU DIDN'T DRIVE YOUR CAR. YOU'RE NOT SUPPOSED TO DO THAT WHEN YOU'RE BLIND.
12/8/04 © 2004 Scott Adams, Inc./Dist. by UFS, Inc.
GAAA!!!
I'M UPSETTING YOU.

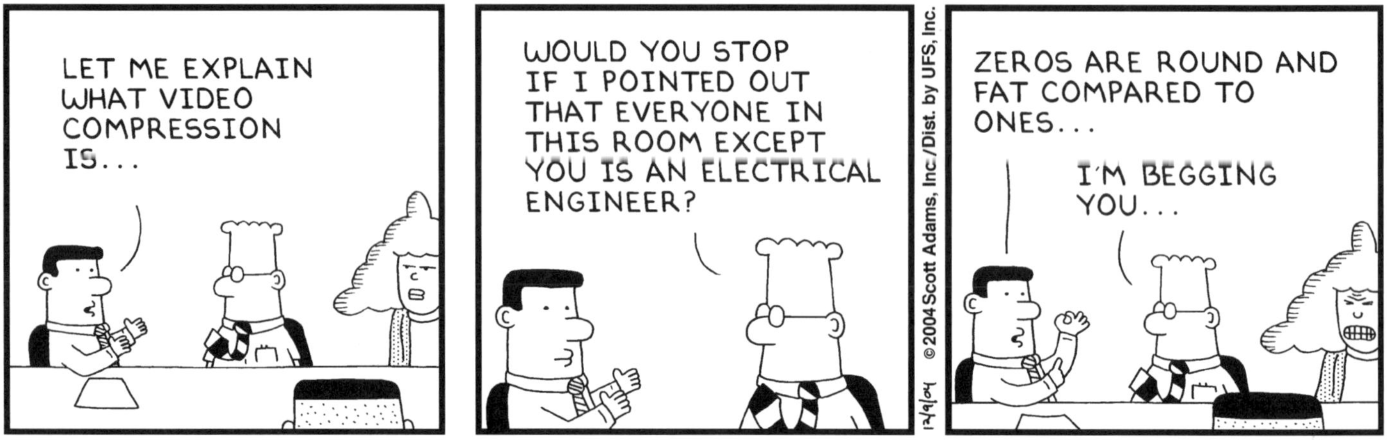
LET ME EXPLAIN WHAT VIDEO COMPRESSION IS...
WOULD YOU STOP IF I POINTED OUT THAT EVERYONE IN THIS ROOM EXCEPT YOU IS AN ELECTRICAL ENGINEER?
ZEROS ARE ROUND AND FAT COMPARED TO ONES...
I'M BEGGING YOU...
© 2004 Scott Adams, Inc./Dist. by UFS, Inc.
12/9/04

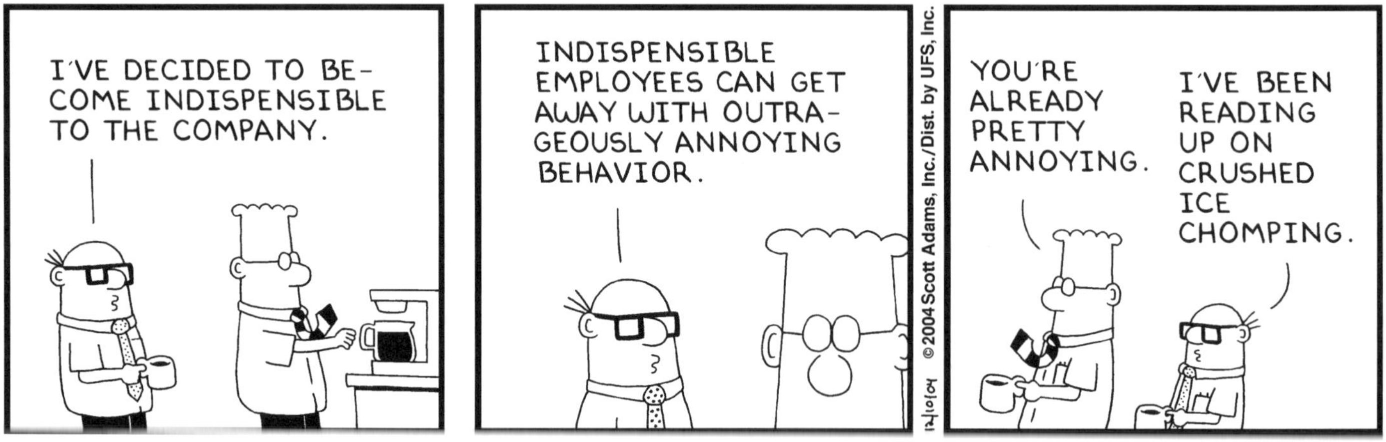
I'VE DECIDED TO BE-COME INDISPENSIBLE TO THE COMPANY.
INDISPENSIBLE EMPLOYEES CAN GET AWAY WITH OUTRA-GEOUSLY ANNOYING BEHAVIOR.
YOU'RE ALREADY PRETTY ANNOYING.
I'VE BEEN READING UP ON CRUSHED ICE CHOMPING.
© 2004 Scott Adams, Inc./Dist. by UFS, Inc.
12/10/04

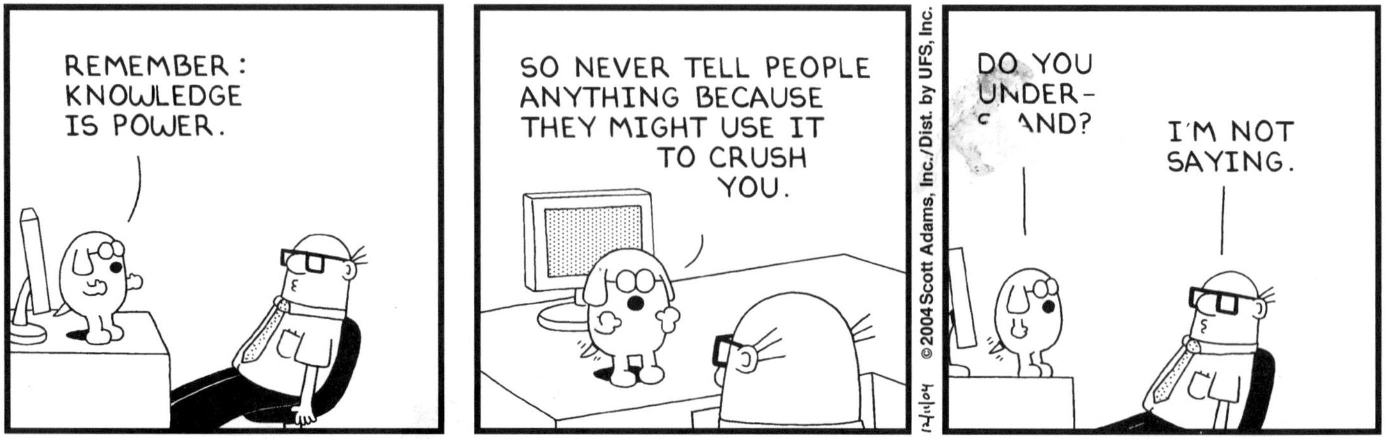
REMEMBER: KNOWLEDGE IS POWER.
SO NEVER TELL PEOPLE ANYTHING BECAUSE THEY MIGHT USE IT TO CRUSH YOU.
DO YOU UNDER-STAND?
I'M NOT SAYING.
© 2004 Scott Adams, Inc./Dist. by UFS, Inc.
12/11/04

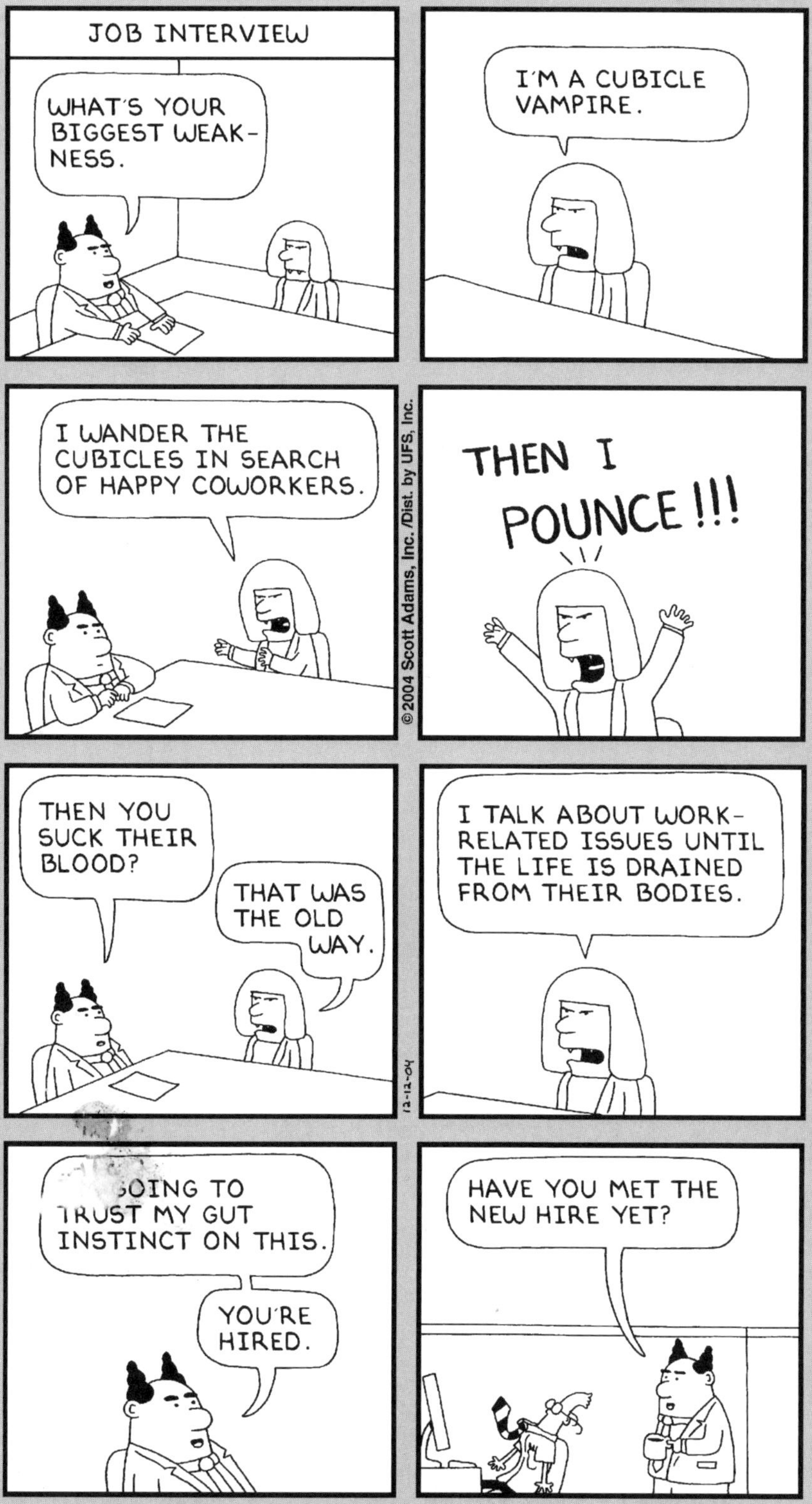
JOB INTERVIEW
WHAT'S YOUR BIGGEST WEAK- NESS.
I'M A CUBICLE VAMPIRE.
I WANDER THE CUBICLES IN SEARCH OF HAPPY COWORKERS.
©2004 Scott Adams, Inc./Dist. by UFS, Inc.
THEN I POUNCE!!!
THEN YOU SUCK THEIR BLOOD?
THAT WAS THE OLD WAY.
I TALK ABOUT WORK- RELATED ISSUES UNTIL THE LIFE IS DRAINED FROM THEIR BODIES.
12-12-04
GOING TO TRUST MY GUT INSTINCT ON THIS.
YOU'RE HIRED.
HAVE YOU MET THE NEW HIRE YET?

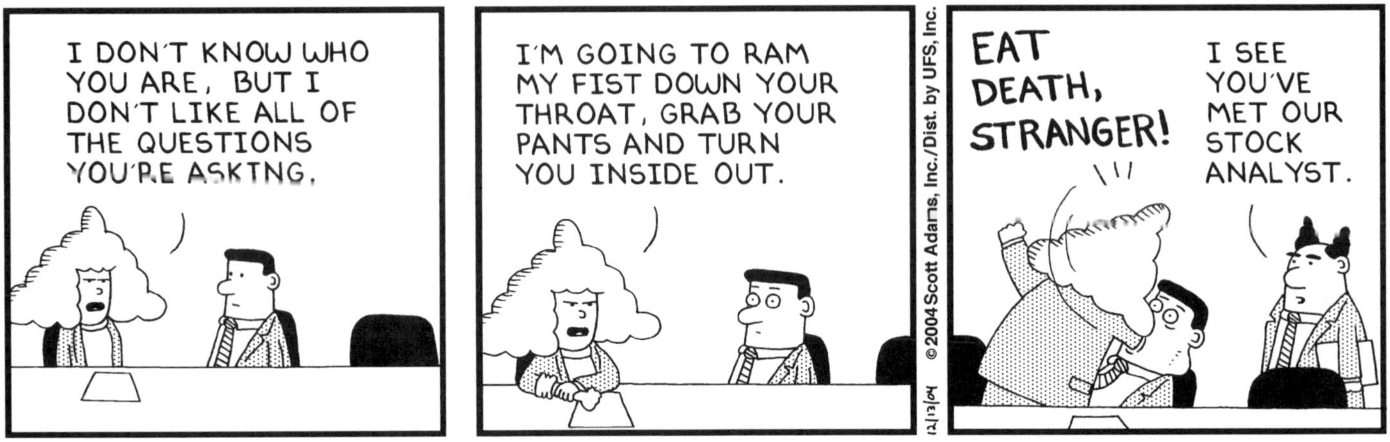
I DON'T KNOW WHO YOU ARE, BUT I DON'T LIKE ALL OF THE QUESTIONS YOU'RE ASKING.
I'M GOING TO RAM MY FIST DOWN YOUR THROAT, GRAB YOUR PANTS AND TURN YOU INSIDE OUT.
EAT DEATH, STRANGER!
I SEE YOU'VE MET OUR STOCK ANALYST.
12/13/04
© 2004 Scott Adams, Inc./Dist. by UFS, Inc.

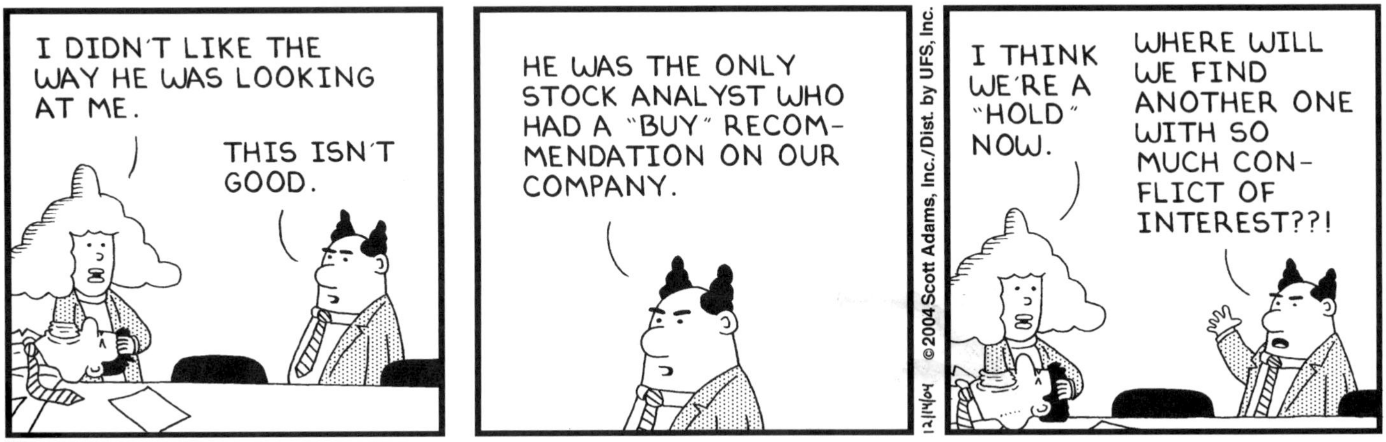
I DIDN'T LIKE THE WAY HE WAS LOOKING AT ME.
THIS ISN'T GOOD.
HE WAS THE ONLY STOCK ANALYST WHO HAD A "BUY" RECOMMENDATION ON OUR COMPANY.
I THINK WE'RE A "HOLD" NOW.
WHERE WILL WE FIND ANOTHER ONE WITH SO MUCH CONFLICT OF INTEREST??!
12/14/04
© 2004 Scott Adams, Inc./Dist. by UFS, Inc.

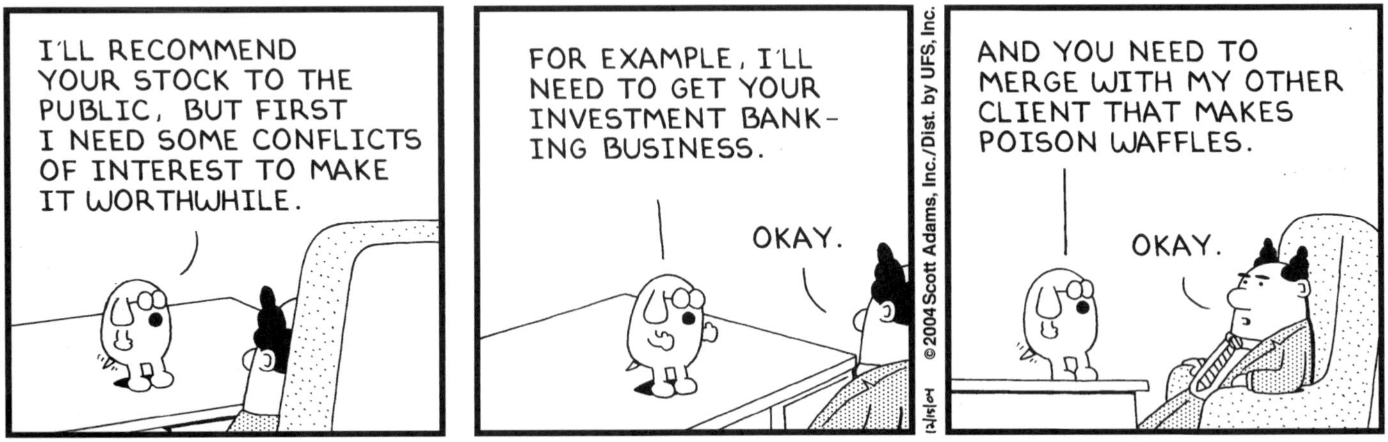
I'LL RECOMMEND YOUR STOCK TO THE PUBLIC, BUT FIRST I NEED SOME CONFLICTS OF INTEREST TO MAKE IT WORTHWHILE.
FOR EXAMPLE, I'LL NEED TO GET YOUR INVESTMENT BANKING BUSINESS.
OKAY.
AND YOU NEED TO MERGE WITH MY OTHER CLIENT THAT MAKES POISON WAFFLES.
OKAY.
12/15/04
© 2004 Scott Adams, Inc./Dist. by UFS, Inc.

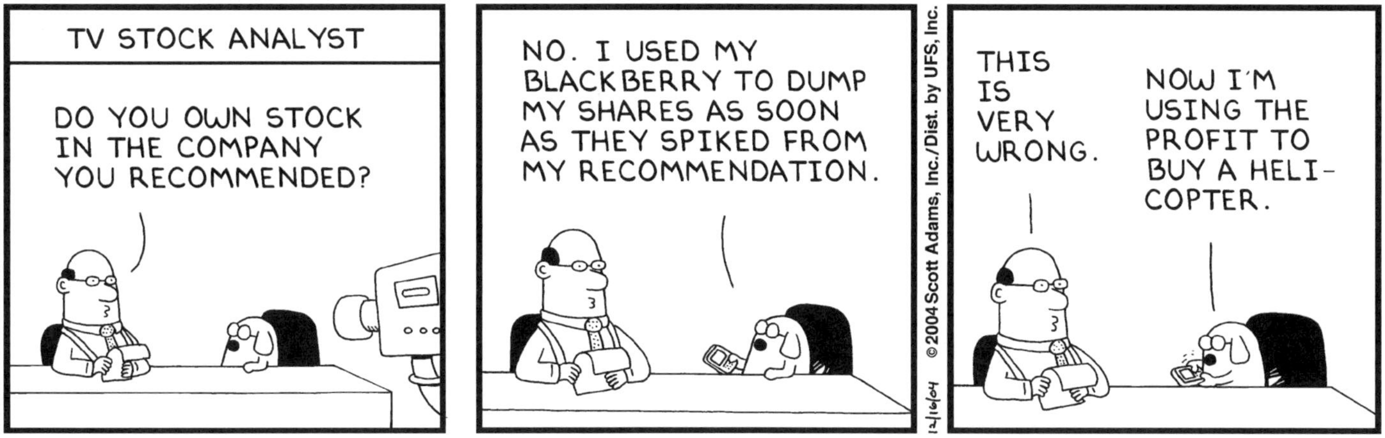
TV STOCK ANALYST
DO YOU OWN STOCK IN THE COMPANY YOU RECOMMENDED?
NO. I USED MY BLACKBERRY TO DUMP MY SHARES AS SOON AS THEY SPIKED FROM MY RECOMMENDATION.
THIS IS VERY WRONG.
NOW I'M USING THE PROFIT TO BUY A HELI-COPTER.

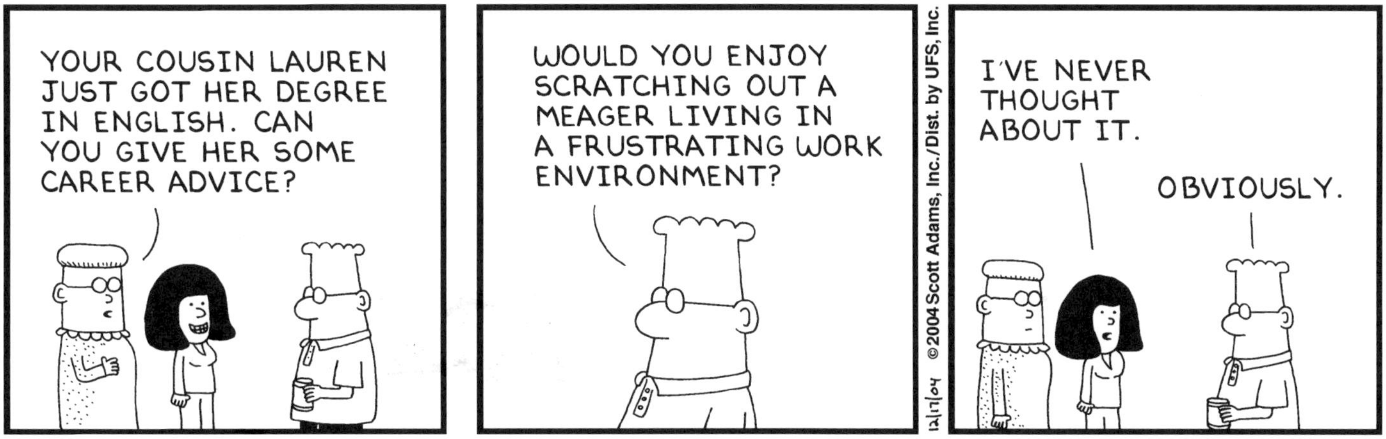
YOUR COUSIN LAUREN JUST GOT HER DEGREE IN ENGLISH. CAN YOU GIVE HER SOME CAREER ADVICE?
WOULD YOU ENJOY SCRATCHING OUT A MEAGER LIVING IN A FRUSTRATING WORK ENVIRONMENT?
I'VE NEVER THOUGHT ABOUT IT.
OBVIOUSLY.

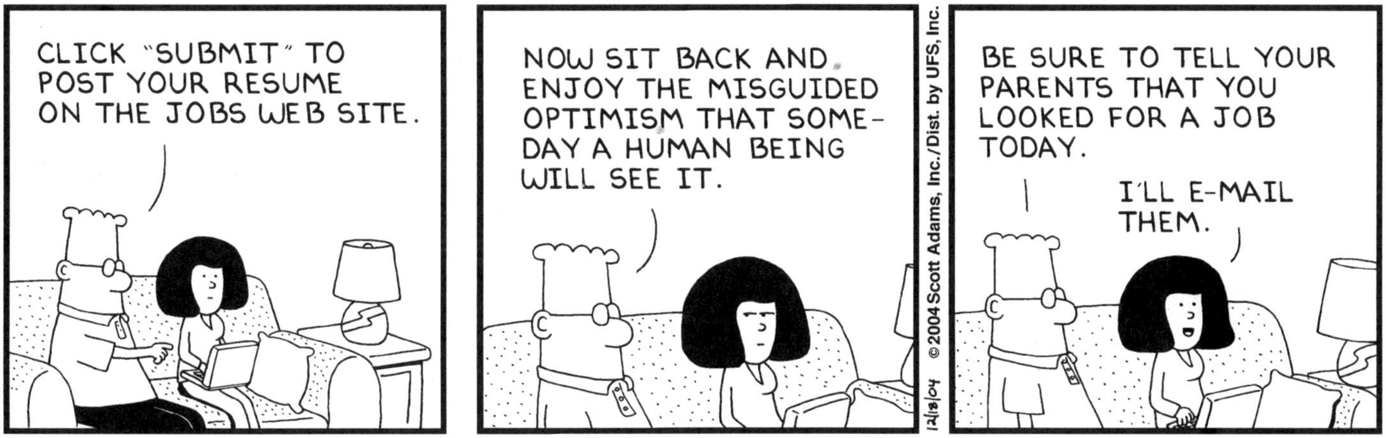
CLICK "SUBMIT" TO POST YOUR RESUME ON THE JOBS WEB SITE.
NOW SIT BACK AND ENJOY THE MISGUIDED OPTIMISM THAT SOME-DAY A HUMAN BEING WILL SEE IT.
BE SURE TO TELL YOUR PARENTS THAT YOU LOOKED FOR A JOB TODAY.
I'LL E-MAIL THEM.

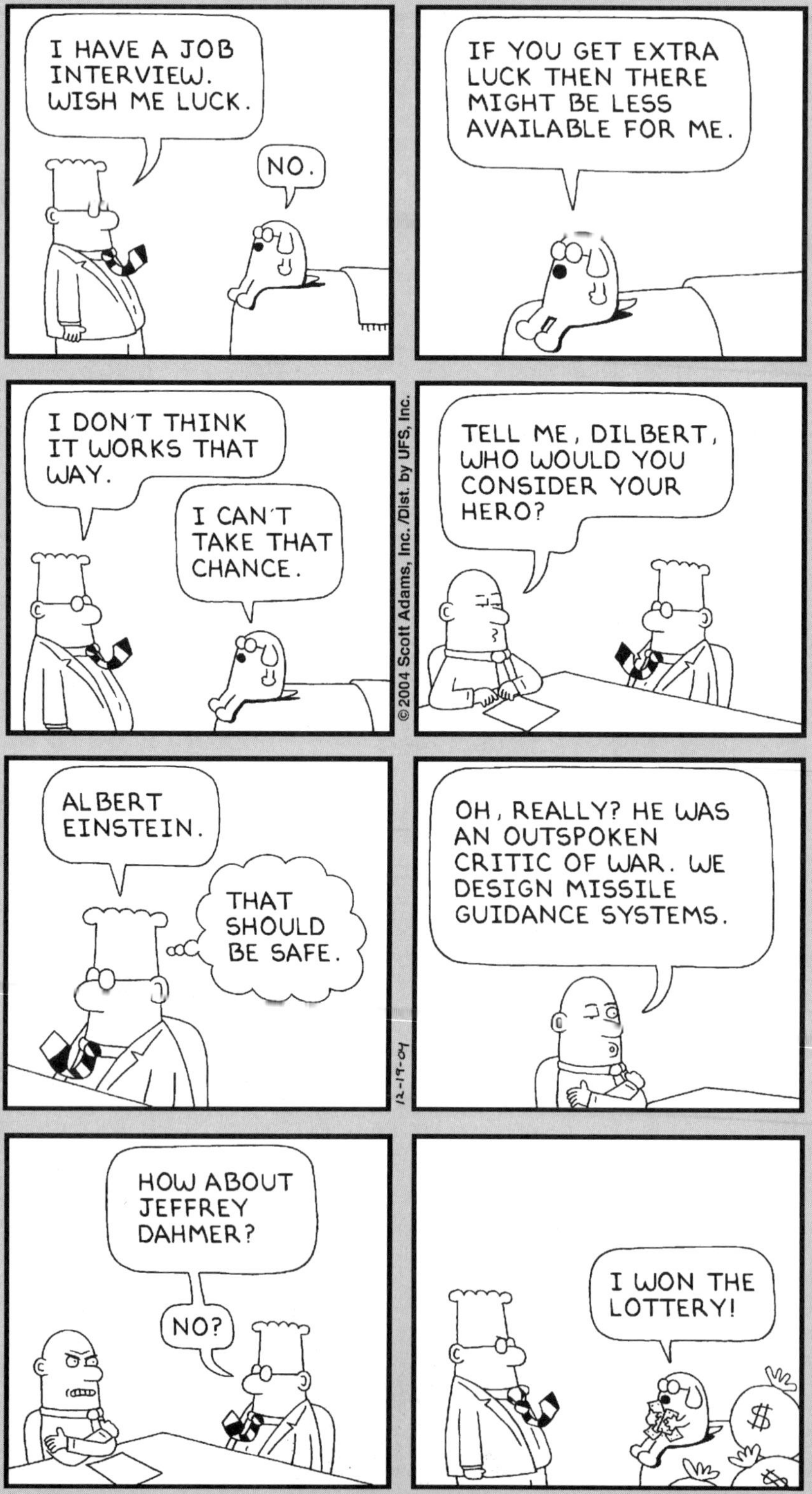
I HAVE A JOB INTERVIEW. WISH ME LUCK.
NO.
IF YOU GET EXTRA LUCK THEN THERE MIGHT BE LESS AVAILABLE FOR ME.
I DON'T THINK IT WORKS THAT WAY.
I CAN'T TAKE THAT CHANCE.
©2004 Scott Adams, Inc./Dist. by UFS, Inc.
TELL ME, DILBERT, WHO WOULD YOU CONSIDER YOUR HERO?
ALBERT EINSTEIN.
THAT SHOULD BE SAFE.
12-19-04
OH, REALLY? HE WAS AN OUTSPOKEN CRITIC OF WAR. WE DESIGN MISSILE GUIDANCE SYSTEMS.
HOW ABOUT JEFFREY DAHMER?
NO?
I WON THE LOTTERY!

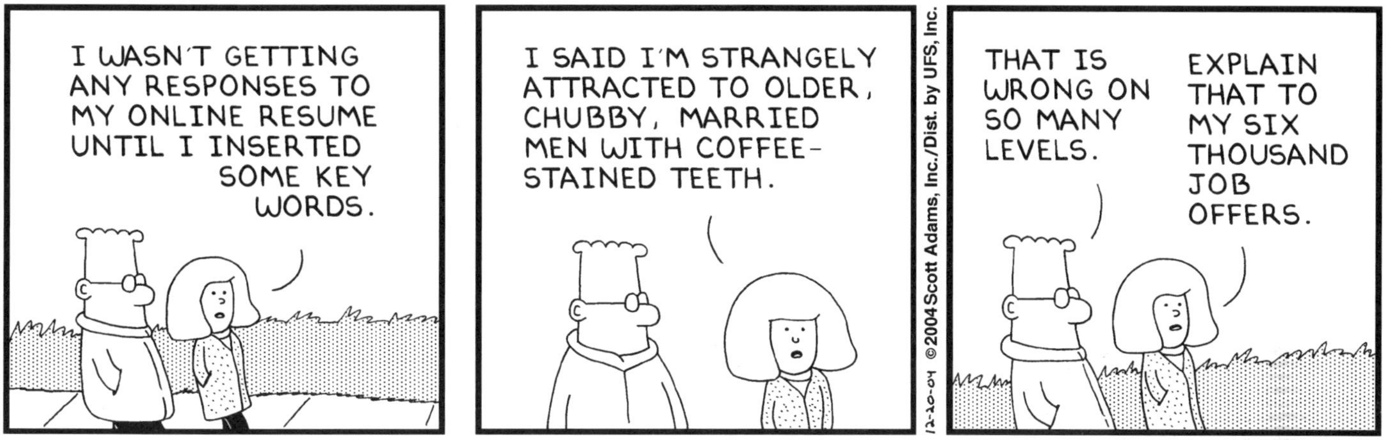
I WASN'T GETTING ANY RESPONSES TO MY ONLINE RESUME UNTIL I INSERTED SOME KEY WORDS.
I SAID I'M STRANGELY ATTRACTED TO OLDER, CHUBBY, MARRIED MEN WITH COFFEE-STAINED TEETH.
12-20-04 © 2004 Scott Adams, Inc./Dist. by UFS, Inc.
THAT IS WRONG ON SO MANY LEVELS.
EXPLAIN THAT TO MY SIX THOUSAND JOB OFFERS.

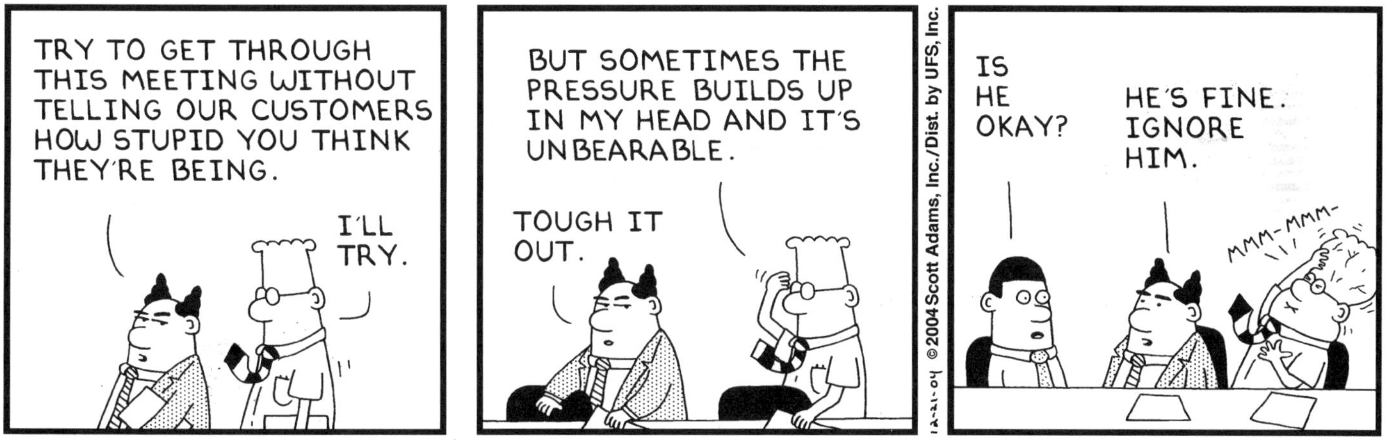
TRY TO GET THROUGH THIS MEETING WITHOUT TELLING OUR CUSTOMERS HOW STUPID YOU THINK THEY'RE BEING.
I'LL TRY.
BUT SOMETIMES THE PRESSURE BUILDS UP IN MY HEAD AND IT'S UNBEARABLE.
TOUGH IT OUT.
12-21-04 © 2004 Scott Adams, Inc./Dist. by UFS, Inc.
IS HE OKAY?
HE'S FINE. IGNORE HIM.
MMM-MMM-

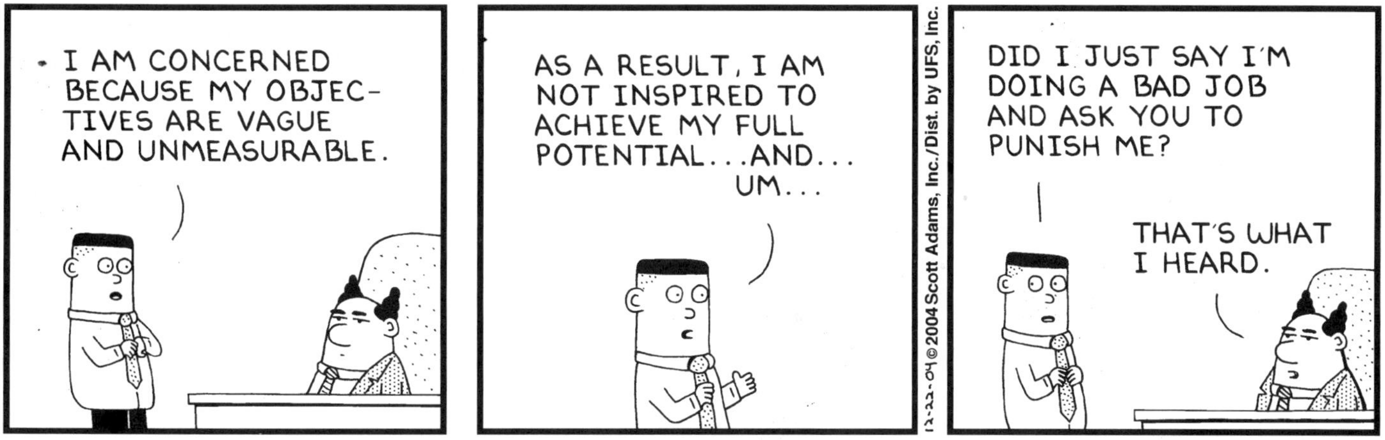
I AM CONCERNED BECAUSE MY OBJEC-TIVES ARE VAGUE AND UNMEASURABLE.
AS A RESULT, I AM NOT INSPIRED TO ACHIEVE MY FULL POTENTIAL...AND... UM...
12-22-04 © 2004 Scott Adams, Inc./Dist. by UFS, Inc.
DID I JUST SAY I'M DOING A BAD JOB AND ASK YOU TO PUNISH ME?
THAT'S WHAT I HEARD.

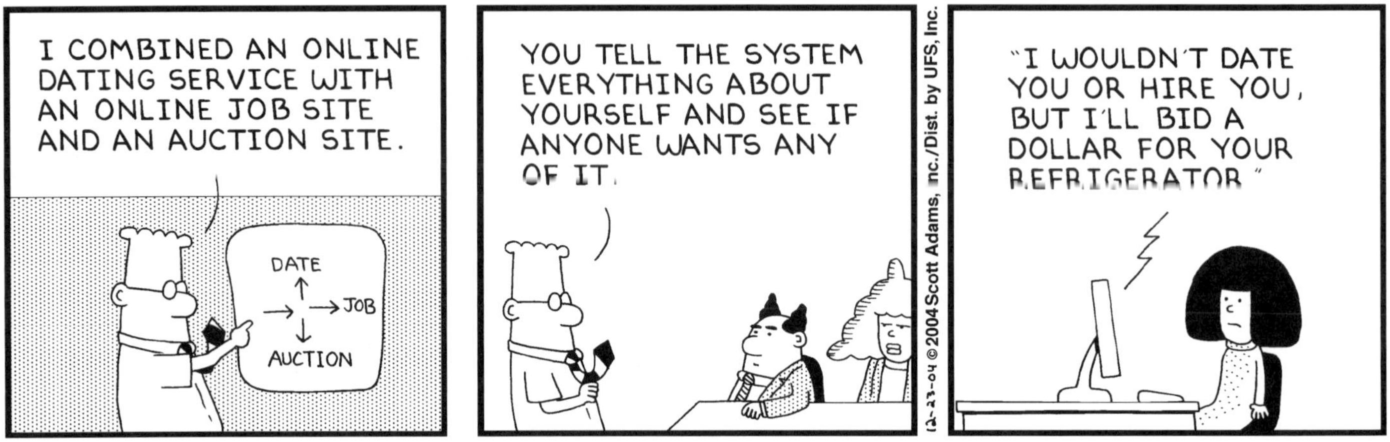
I COMBINED AN ONLINE DATING SERVICE WITH AN ONLINE JOB SITE AND AN AUCTION SITE.
DATE
JOB
AUCTION
YOU TELL THE SYSTEM EVERYTHING ABOUT YOURSELF AND SEE IF ANYONE WANTS ANY OF IT.
"I WOULDN'T DATE YOU OR HIRE YOU, BUT I'LL BID A DOLLAR FOR YOUR REFRIGERATOR."

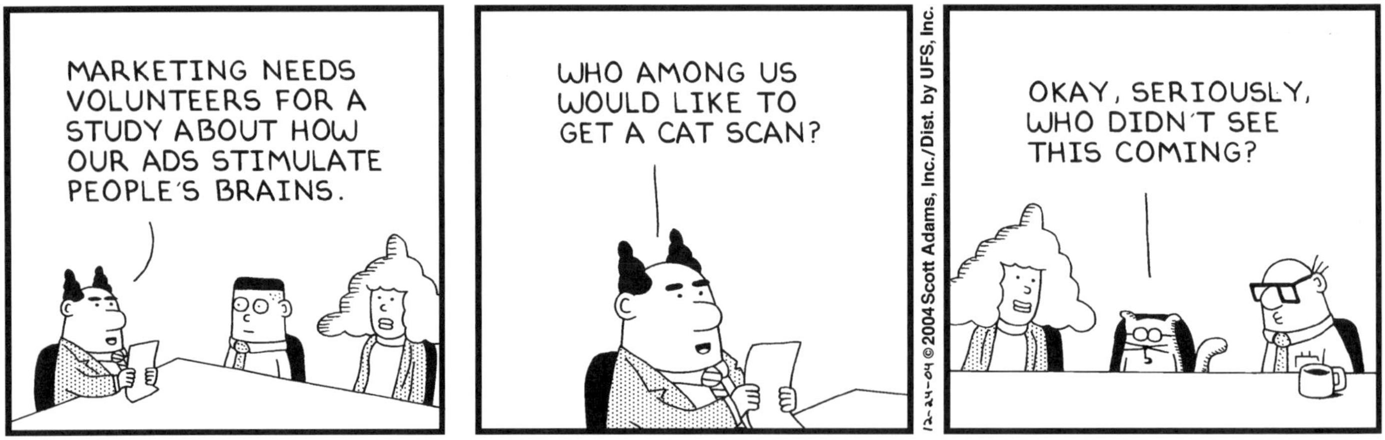
MARKETING NEEDS VOLUNTEERS FOR A STUDY ABOUT HOW OUR ADS STIMULATE PEOPLE'S BRAINS.
WHO AMONG US WOULD LIKE TO GET A CAT SCAN?
OKAY, SERIOUSLY, WHO DIDN'T SEE THIS COMING?

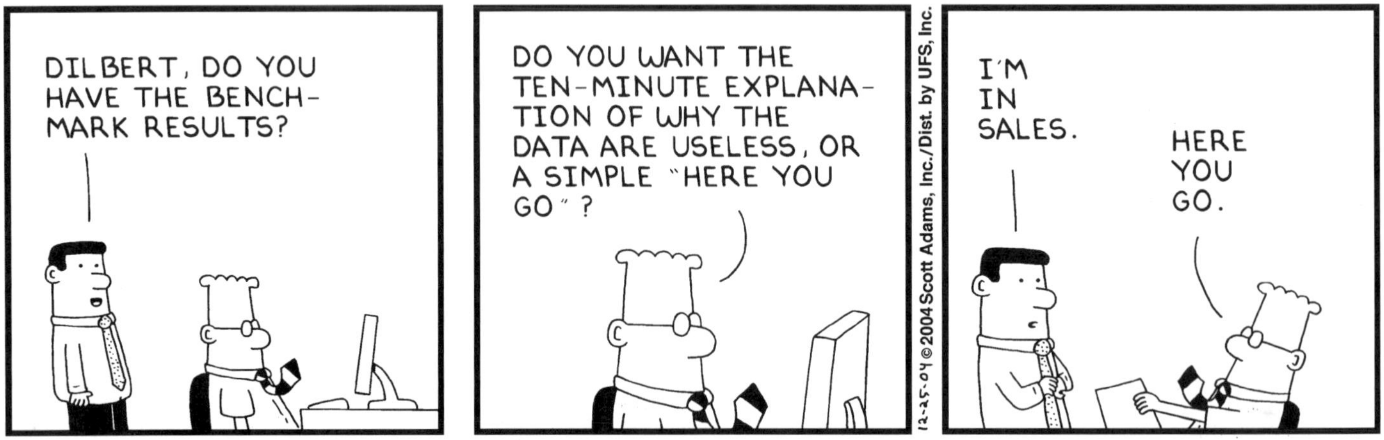
DILBERT, DO YOU HAVE THE BENCH-MARK RESULTS?
DO YOU WANT THE TEN-MINUTE EXPLANA-TION OF WHY THE DATA ARE USELESS, OR A SIMPLE "HERE YOU GO"?
I'M IN SALES.
HERE YOU GO.

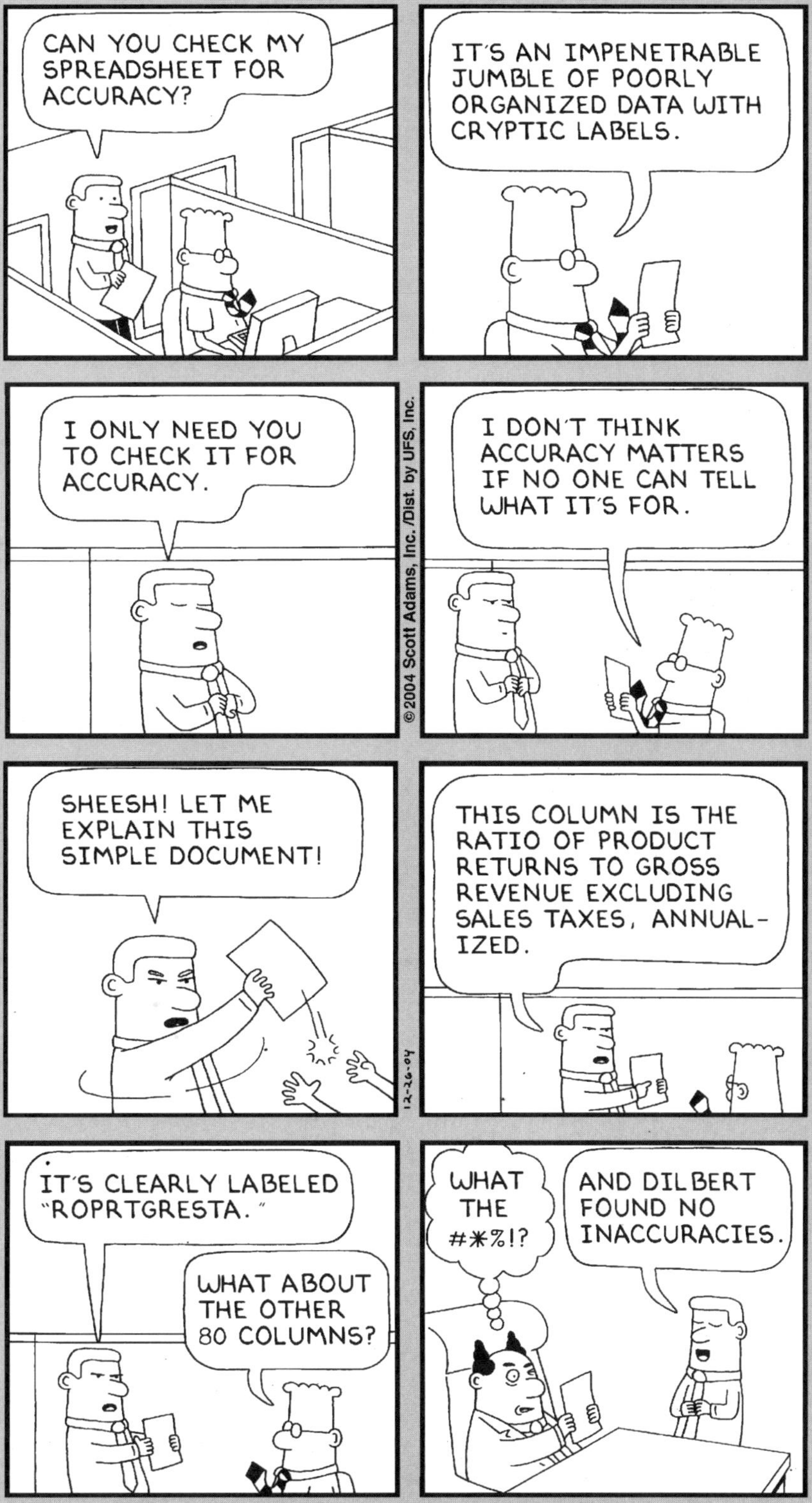
CAN YOU CHECK MY SPREADSHEET FOR ACCURACY?
IT'S AN IMPENETRABLE JUMBLE OF POORLY ORGANIZED DATA WITH CRYPTIC LABELS.
I ONLY NEED YOU TO CHECK IT FOR ACCURACY.
I DON'T THINK ACCURACY MATTERS IF NO ONE CAN TELL WHAT IT'S FOR.
SHEESH! LET ME EXPLAIN THIS SIMPLE DOCUMENT!
THIS COLUMN IS THE RATIO OF PRODUCT RETURNS TO GROSS REVENUE EXCLUDING SALES TAXES, ANNUALIZED.
IT'S CLEARLY LABELED "ROPRTGRESTA."
WHAT ABOUT THE OTHER 80 COLUMNS?
WHAT THE #*%!?
AND DILBERT FOUND NO INACCURACIES.
© 2004 Scott Adams, Inc. /Dist. by UFS, Inc.
12-26-04

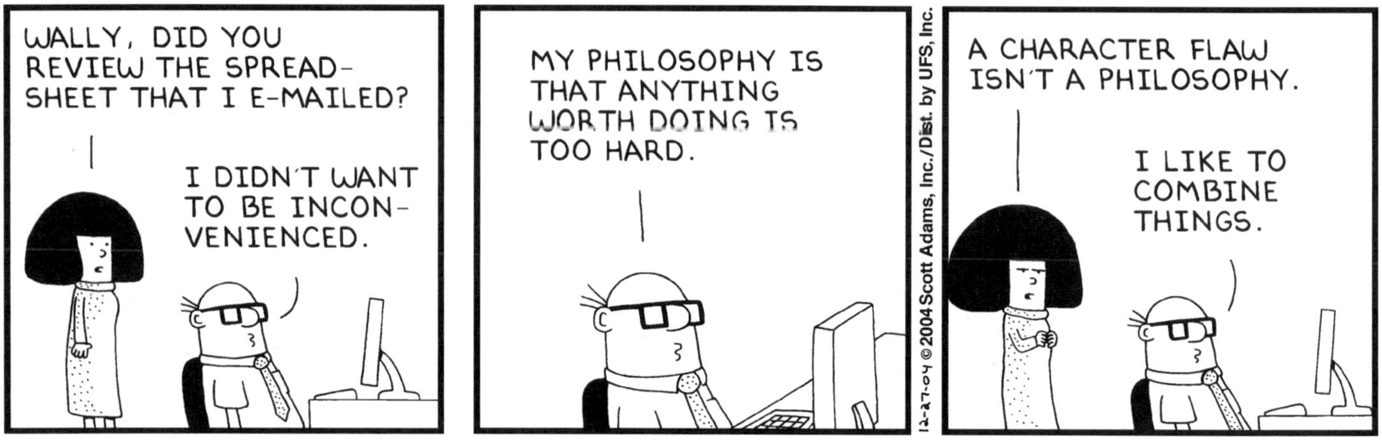
WALLY, DID YOU REVIEW THE SPREAD-SHEET THAT I E-MAILED?
I DIDN'T WANT TO BE INCON-VENIENCED.
MY PHILOSOPHY IS THAT ANYTHING WORTH DOING IS TOO HARD.
12-27-04 © 2004 Scott Adams, Inc./Dist. by UFS, Inc.
A CHARACTER FLAW ISN'T A PHILOSOPHY.
I LIKE TO COMBINE THINGS.

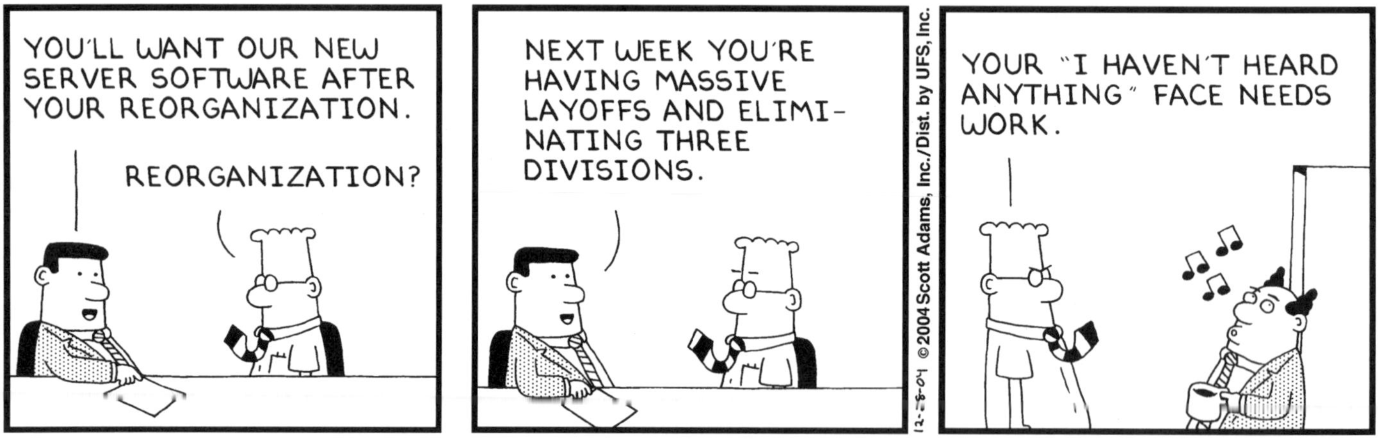
YOU'LL WANT OUR NEW SERVER SOFTWARE AFTER YOUR REORGANIZATION.
REORGANIZATION?
NEXT WEEK YOU'RE HAVING MASSIVE LAYOFFS AND ELIMI-NATING THREE DIVISIONS.
12-28-04 © 2004 Scott Adams, Inc./Dist. by UFS, Inc.
YOUR "I HAVEN'T HEARD ANYTHING" FACE NEEDS WORK.

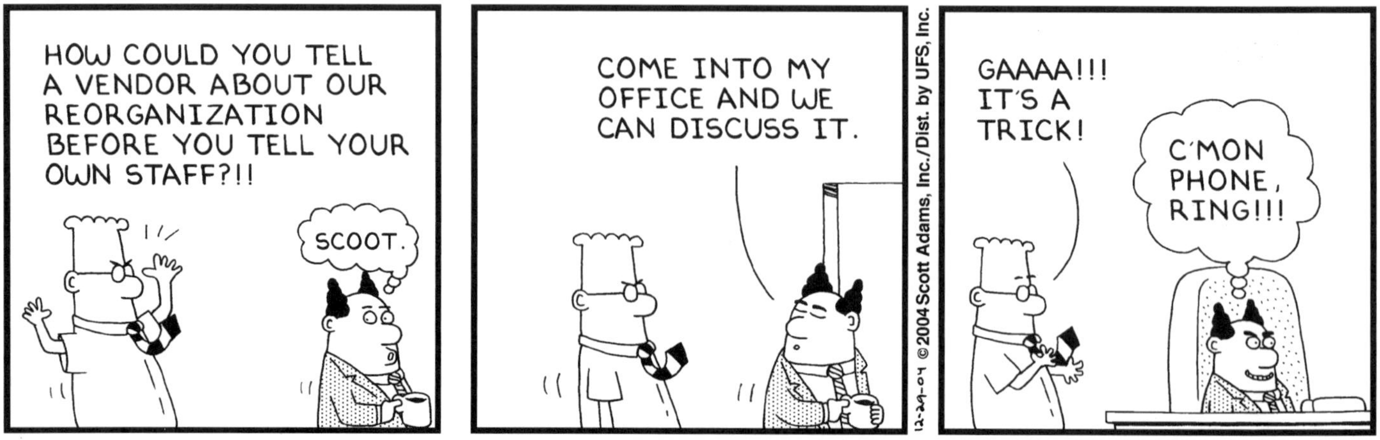
HOW COULD YOU TELL A VENDOR ABOUT OUR REORGANIZATION BEFORE YOU TELL YOUR OWN STAFF?!!
SCOOT.
COME INTO MY OFFICE AND WE CAN DISCUSS IT.
12-29-04 © 2004 Scott Adams, Inc./Dist. by UFS, Inc.
GAAAA!!! IT'S A TRICK!
C'MON PHONE, RING!!!

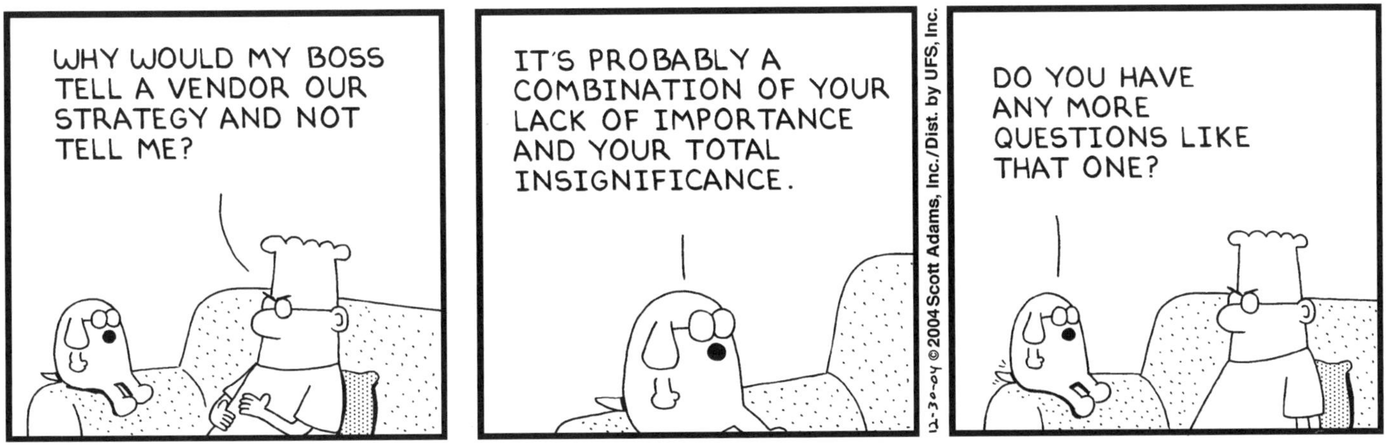
WHY WOULD MY BOSS TELL A VENDOR OUR STRATEGY AND NOT TELL ME?
IT'S PROBABLY A COMBINATION OF YOUR LACK OF IMPORTANCE AND YOUR TOTAL INSIGNIFICANCE.
12-30-04 © 2004 Scott Adams, Inc./Dist. by UFS, Inc.
DO YOU HAVE ANY MORE QUESTIONS LIKE THAT ONE?

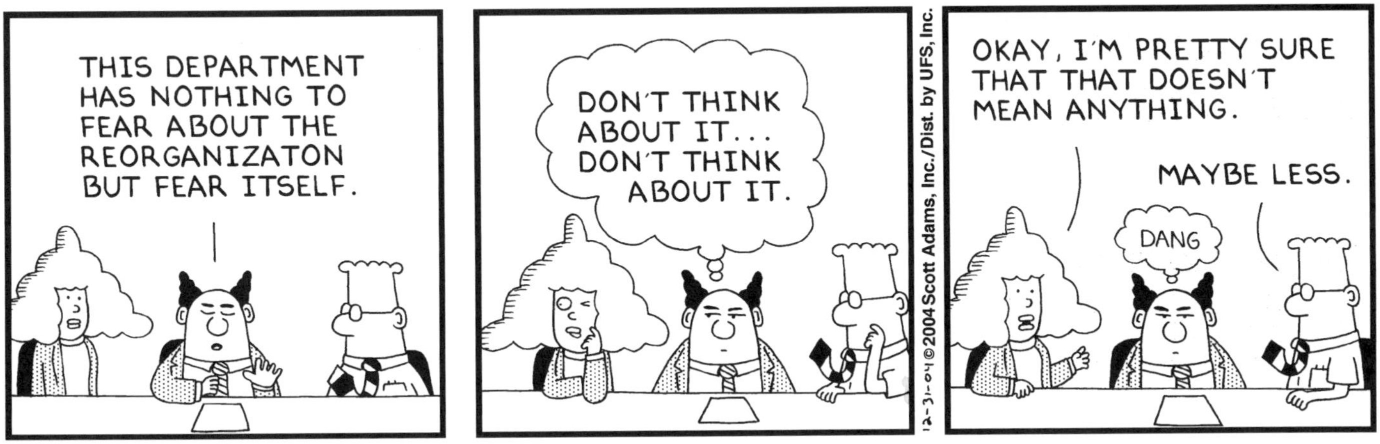
THIS DEPARTMENT HAS NOTHING TO FEAR ABOUT THE REORGANIZATON BUT FEAR ITSELF.
DON'T THINK ABOUT IT... DON'T THINK ABOUT IT.
12-31-04 © 2004 Scott Adams, Inc./Dist. by UFS, Inc.
OKAY, I'M PRETTY SURE THAT THAT DOESN'T MEAN ANYTHING.
DANG
MAYBE LESS.

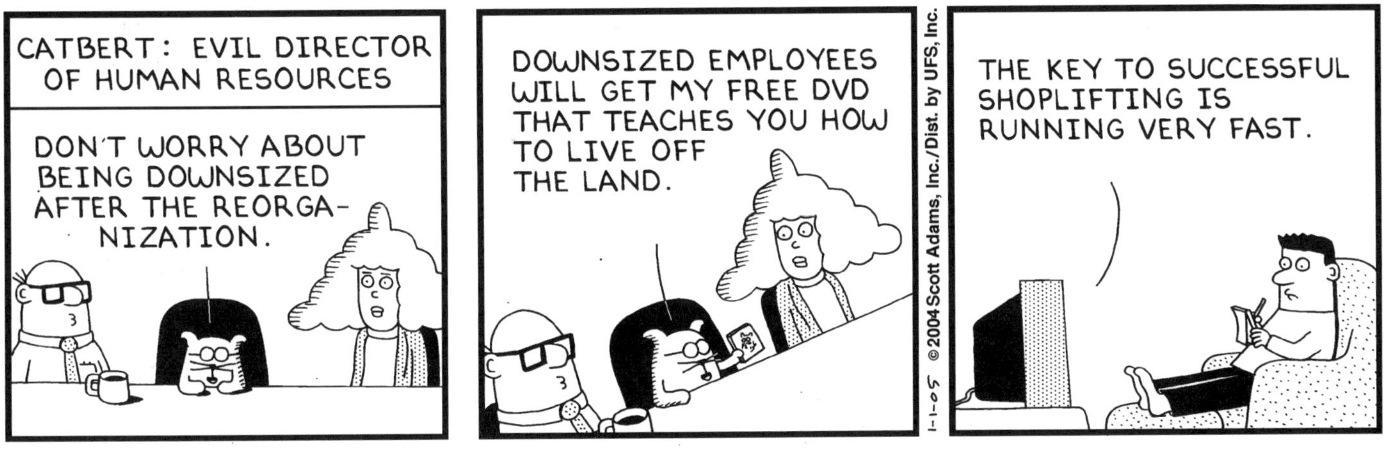
CATBERT: EVIL DIRECTOR OF HUMAN RESOURCES
DON'T WORRY ABOUT BEING DOWNSIZED AFTER THE REORGA-NIZATION.
DOWNSIZED EMPLOYEES WILL GET MY FREE DVD THAT TEACHES YOU HOW TO LIVE OFF THE LAND.
1-1-05 © 2004 Scott Adams, Inc./Dist. by UFS, Inc.
THE KEY TO SUCCESSFUL SHOPLIFTING IS RUNNING VERY FAST.

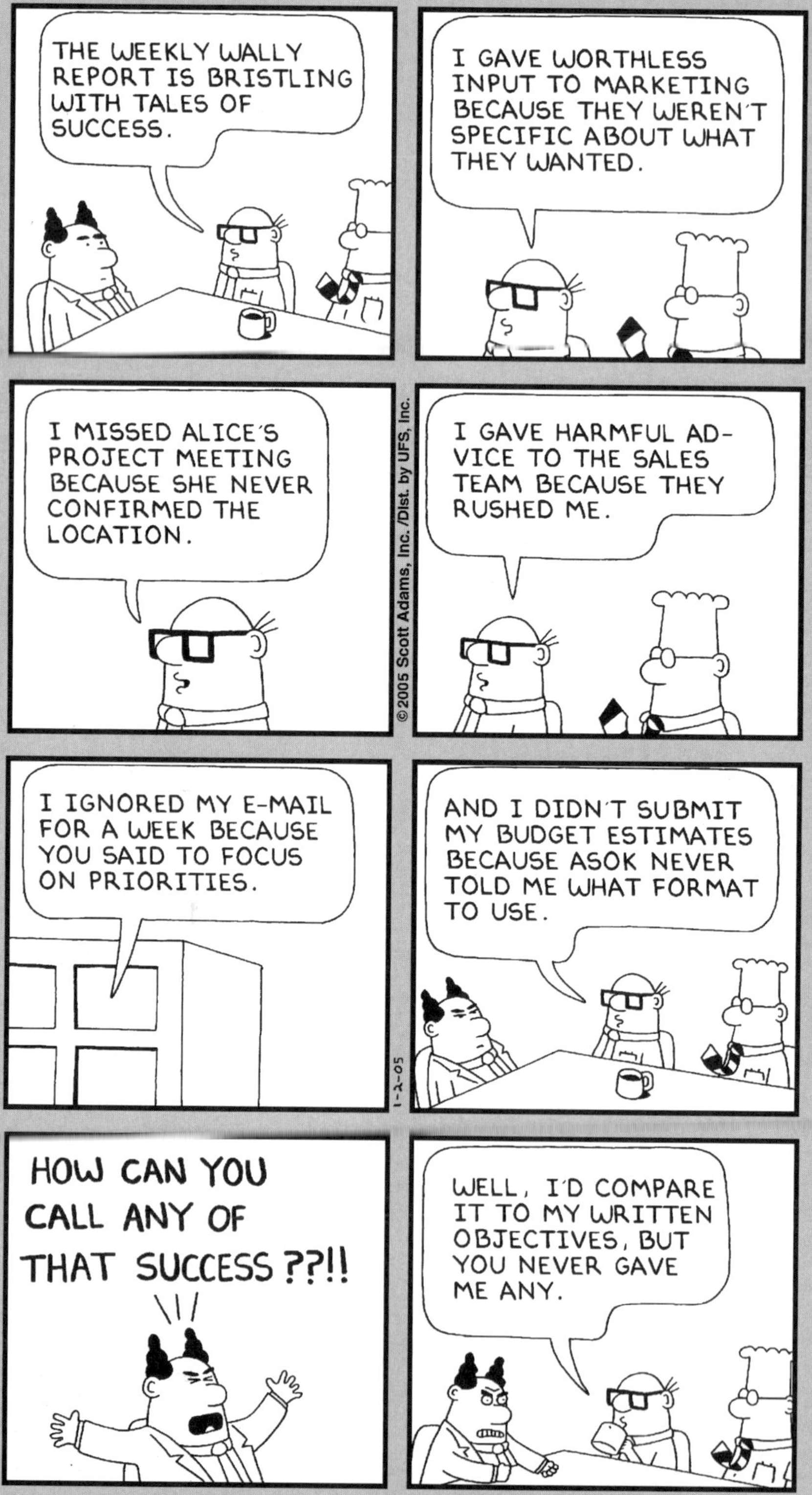
THE WEEKLY WALLY REPORT IS BRISTLING WITH TALES OF SUCCESS.
I GAVE WORTHLESS INPUT TO MARKETING BECAUSE THEY WEREN'T SPECIFIC ABOUT WHAT THEY WANTED.
I MISSED ALICE'S PROJECT MEETING BECAUSE SHE NEVER CONFIRMED THE LOCATION.
I GAVE HARMFUL ADVICE TO THE SALES TEAM BECAUSE THEY RUSHED ME.
©2005 Scott Adams, Inc./Dist. by UFS, Inc.
I IGNORED MY E-MAIL FOR A WEEK BECAUSE YOU SAID TO FOCUS ON PRIORITIES.
AND I DIDN'T SUBMIT MY BUDGET ESTIMATES BECAUSE ASOK NEVER TOLD ME WHAT FORMAT TO USE.
1-2-05
HOW CAN YOU CALL ANY OF THAT SUCCESS??!!
WELL, I'D COMPARE IT TO MY WRITTEN OBJECTIVES, BUT YOU NEVER GAVE ME ANY.

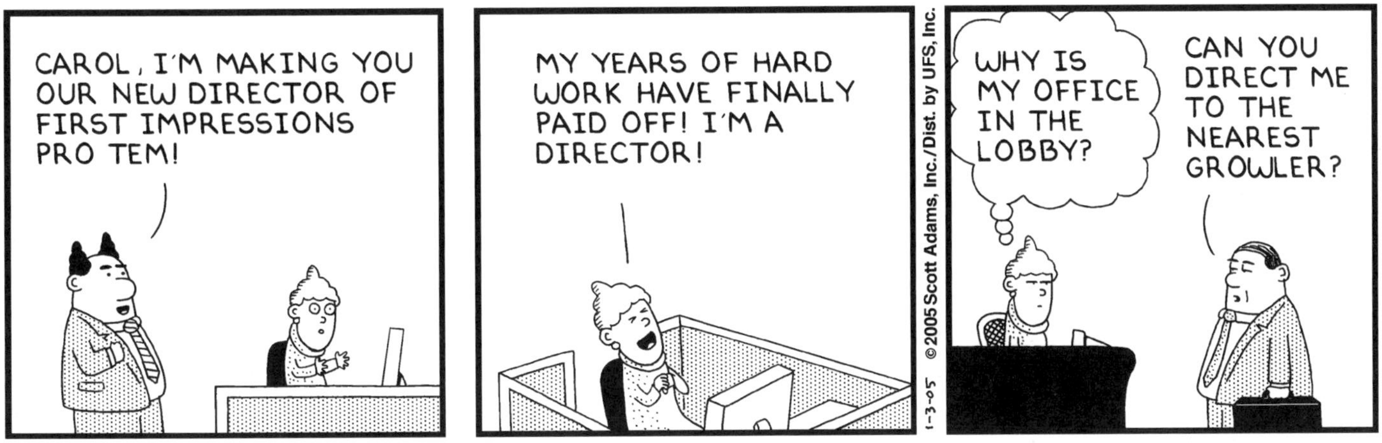
CAROL, I'M MAKING YOU OUR NEW DIRECTOR OF FIRST IMPRESSIONS PRO TEM!
MY YEARS OF HARD WORK HAVE FINALLY PAID OFF! I'M A DIRECTOR!
WHY IS MY OFFICE IN THE LOBBY?
CAN YOU DIRECT ME TO THE NEAREST GROWLER?
©2005 Scott Adams, Inc./Dist. by UFS, Inc.
1-3-05

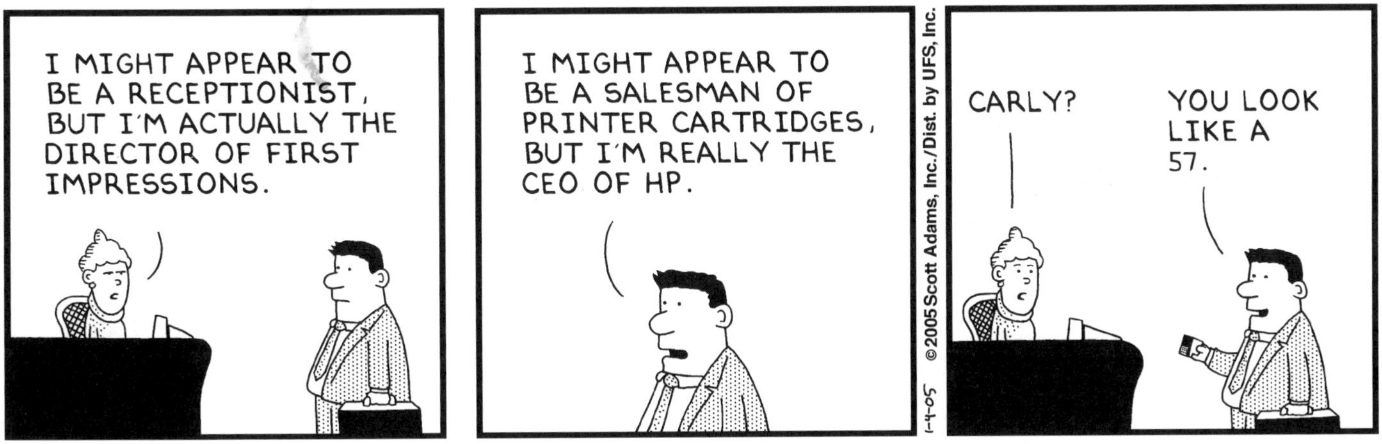
I MIGHT APPEAR TO BE A RECEPTIONIST, BUT I'M ACTUALLY THE DIRECTOR OF FIRST IMPRESSIONS.
I MIGHT APPEAR TO BE A SALESMAN OF PRINTER CARTRIDGES, BUT I'M REALLY THE CEO OF HP.
CARLY?
YOU LOOK LIKE A 57.
©2005 Scott Adams, Inc./Dist. by UFS, Inc.
1-4-05

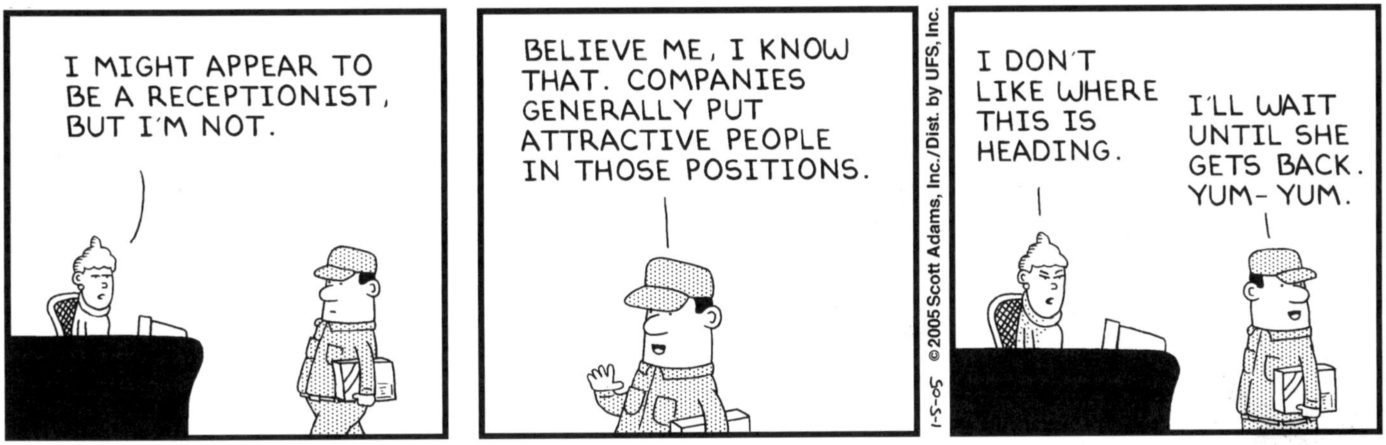
I MIGHT APPEAR TO BE A RECEPTIONIST, BUT I'M NOT.
BELIEVE ME, I KNOW THAT. COMPANIES GENERALLY PUT ATTRACTIVE PEOPLE IN THOSE POSITIONS.
I DON'T LIKE WHERE THIS IS HEADING.
I'LL WAIT UNTIL SHE GETS BACK. YUM-YUM.
©2005 Scott Adams, Inc./Dist. by UFS, Inc.
1-5-05

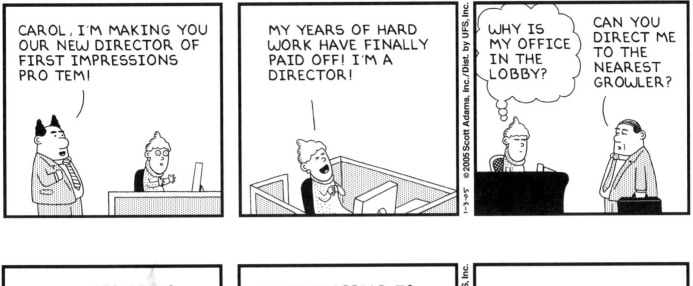

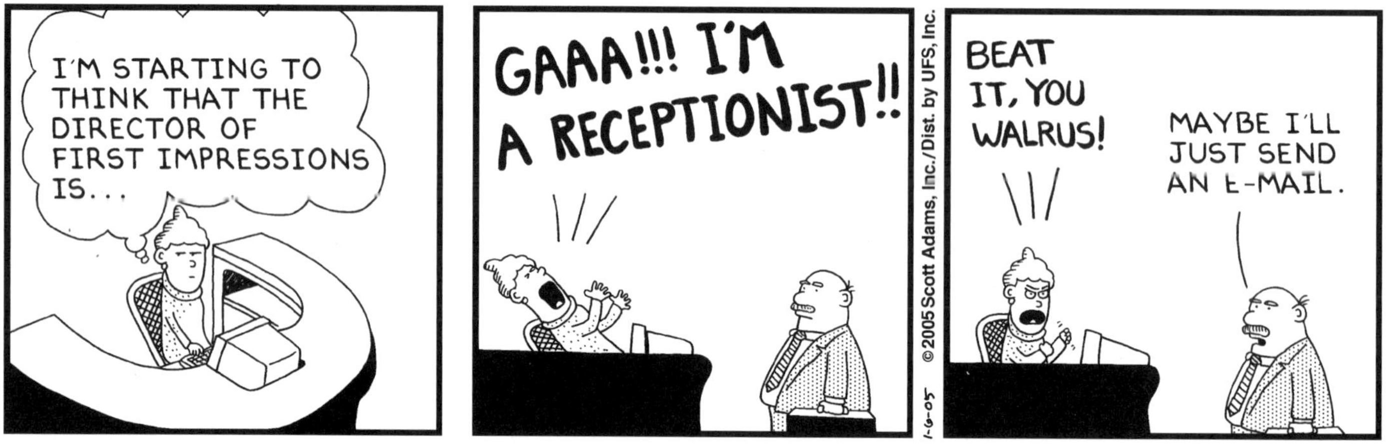
I'M STARTING TO THINK THAT THE DIRECTOR OF FIRST IMPRESSIONS IS...
GAAA!!! I'M A RECEPTIONIST!!
©2005 Scott Adams, Inc./Dist. by UFS, Inc.
1-6-05
BEAT IT, YOU WALRUS!
MAYBE I'LL JUST SEND AN E-MAIL.

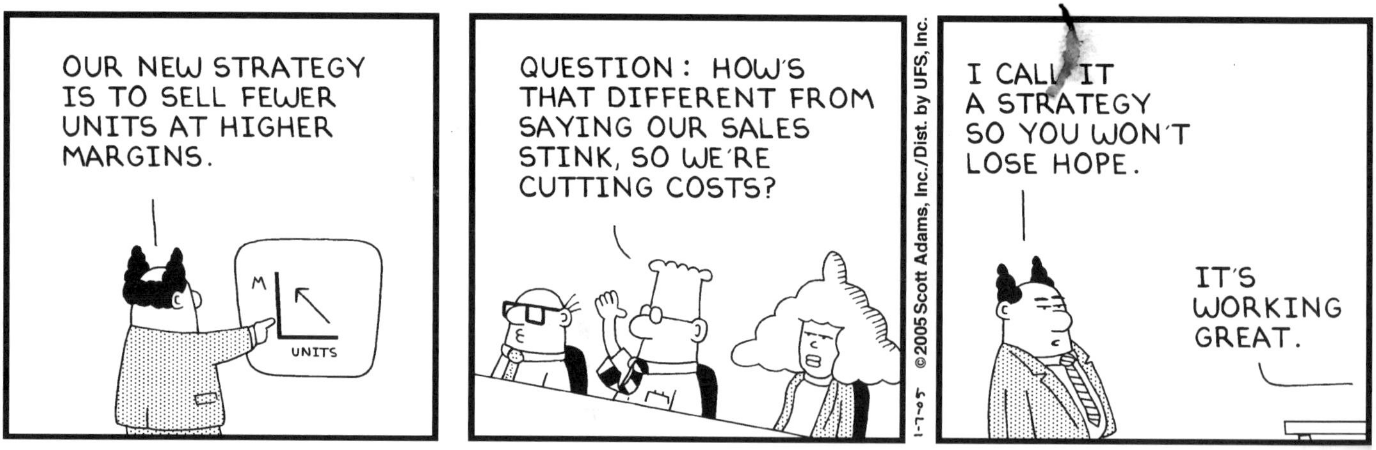
OUR NEW STRATEGY IS TO SELL FEWER UNITS AT HIGHER MARGINS.
M
UNITS
QUESTION: HOW'S THAT DIFFERENT FROM SAYING OUR SALES STINK, SO WE'RE CUTTING COSTS?
©2005 Scott Adams, Inc./Dist. by UFS, Inc.
1-7-05
I CALL IT A STRATEGY SO YOU WON'T LOSE HOPE.
IT'S WORKING GREAT.

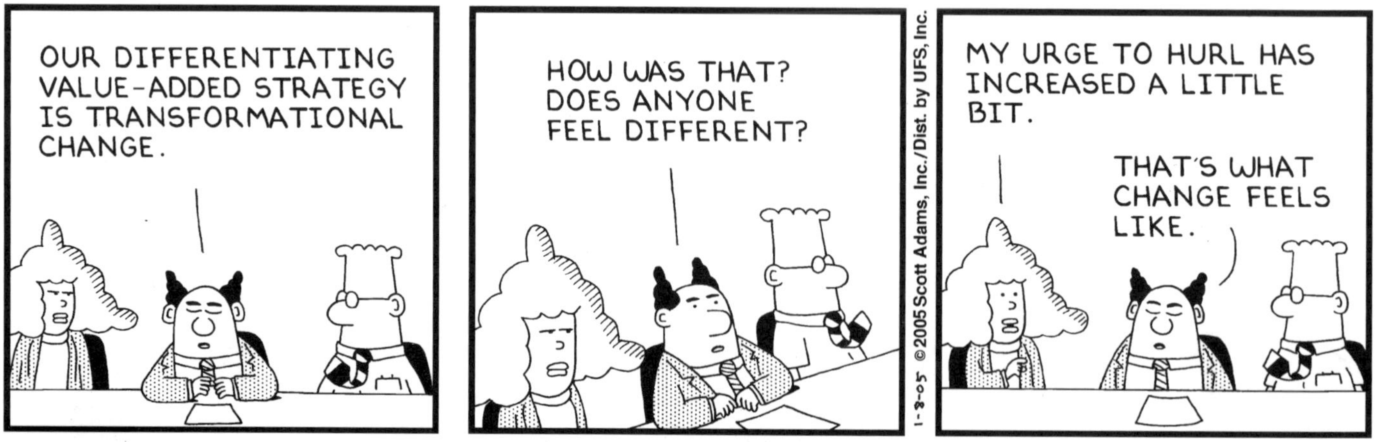
OUR DIFFERENTIATING VALUE-ADDED STRATEGY IS TRANSFORMATIONAL CHANGE.
HOW WAS THAT? DOES ANYONE FEEL DIFFERENT?
©2005 Scott Adams, Inc./Dist. by UFS, Inc.
1-8-05
MY URGE TO HURL HAS INCREASED A LITTLE BIT.
THAT'S WHAT CHANGE FEELS LIKE.

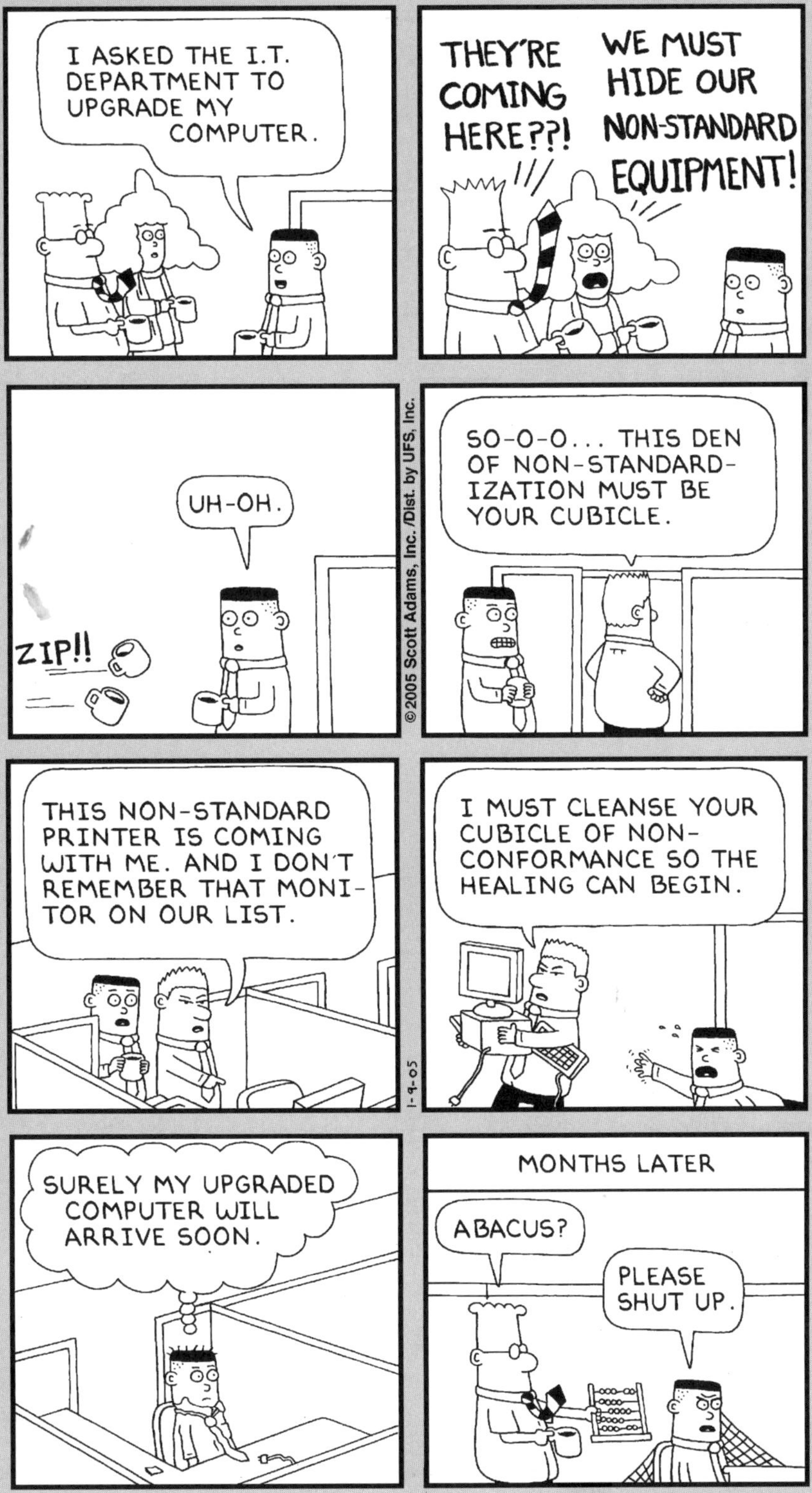
I ASKED THE I.T. DEPARTMENT TO UPGRADE MY COMPUTER.
THEY'RE COMING HERE??!
WE MUST HIDE OUR NON-STANDARD EQUIPMENT!
UH-OH.
ZIP!!
SO-O-O... THIS DEN OF NON-STANDARD-IZATION MUST BE YOUR CUBICLE.
THIS NON-STANDARD PRINTER IS COMING WITH ME. AND I DON'T REMEMBER THAT MONITOR ON OUR LIST.
I MUST CLEANSE YOUR CUBICLE OF NON-CONFORMANCE SO THE HEALING CAN BEGIN.
SURELY MY UPGRADED COMPUTER WILL ARRIVE SOON.
MONTHS LATER
ABACUS?
PLEASE SHUT UP.
©2005 Scott Adams, Inc./Dist. by UFS, Inc.
1-9-05

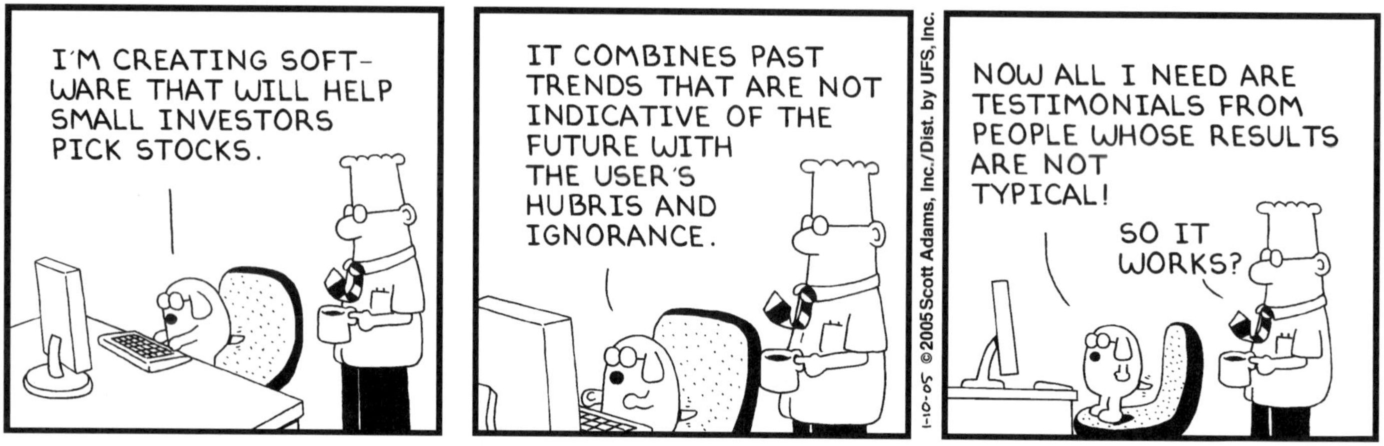
I'M CREATING SOFTWARE THAT WILL HELP SMALL INVESTORS PICK STOCKS.
IT COMBINES PAST TRENDS THAT ARE NOT INDICATIVE OF THE FUTURE WITH THE USER'S HUBRIS AND IGNORANCE.
1-10-05 ©2005 Scott Adams, Inc./Dist. by UFS, Inc.
NOW ALL I NEED ARE TESTIMONIALS FROM PEOPLE WHOSE RESULTS ARE NOT TYPICAL!
SO IT WORKS?

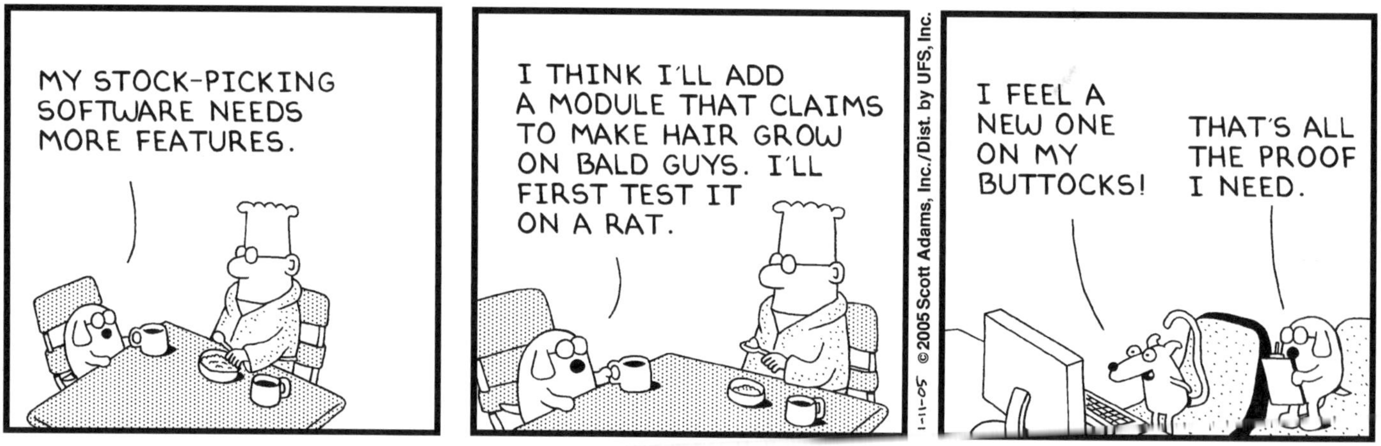
MY STOCK-PICKING SOFTWARE NEEDS MORE FEATURES.
I THINK I'LL ADD A MODULE THAT CLAIMS TO MAKE HAIR GROW ON BALD GUYS. I'LL FIRST TEST IT ON A RAT.
1-11-05 ©2005 Scott Adams, Inc./Dist. by UFS, Inc.
I FEEL A NEW ONE ON MY BUTTOCKS!
THAT'S ALL THE PROOF I NEED.

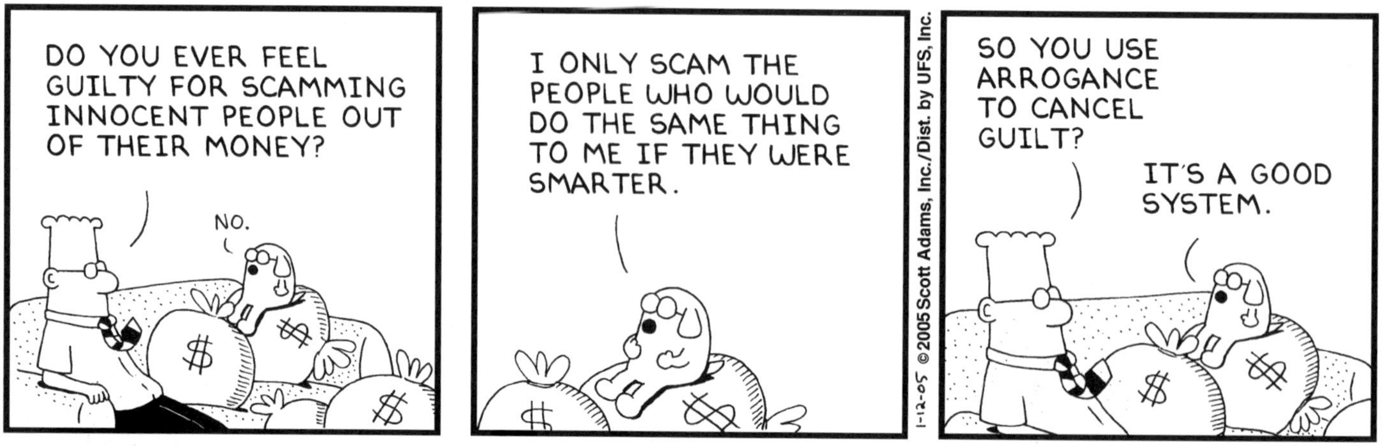
DO YOU EVER FEEL GUILTY FOR SCAMMING INNOCENT PEOPLE OUT OF THEIR MONEY?
NO.
I ONLY SCAM THE PEOPLE WHO WOULD DO THE SAME THING TO ME IF THEY WERE SMARTER.
1-12-05 ©2005 Scott Adams, Inc./Dist. by UFS, Inc.
SO YOU USE ARROGANCE TO CANCEL GUILT?
IT'S A GOOD SYSTEM.

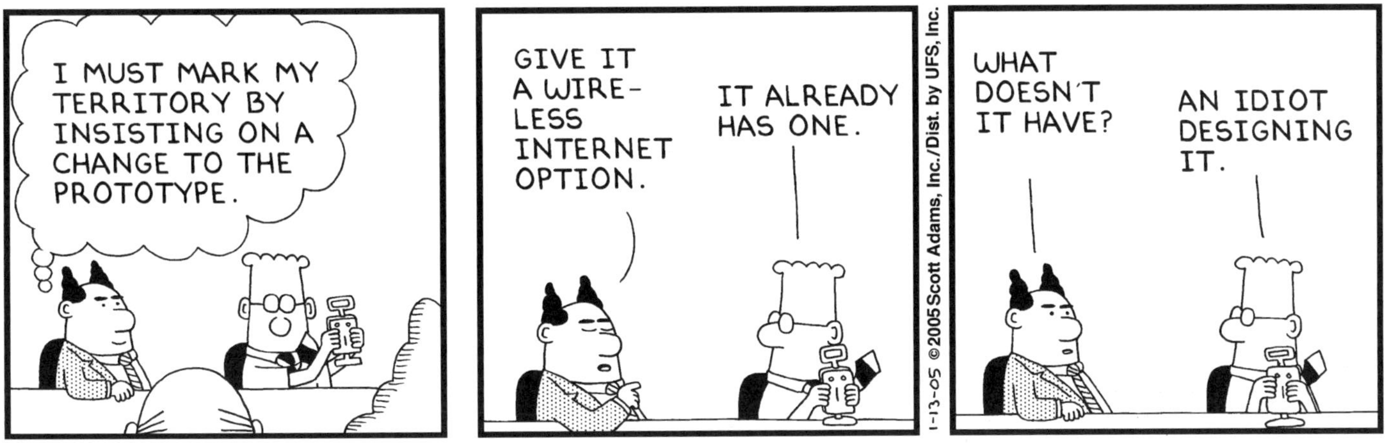
I MUST MARK MY TERRITORY BY INSISTING ON A CHANGE TO THE PROTOTYPE.
GIVE IT A WIRE-LESS INTERNET OPTION.
IT ALREADY HAS ONE.
1-13-05 ©2005 Scott Adams, Inc./Dist. by UFS, Inc.
WHAT DOESN'T IT HAVE?
AN IDIOT DESIGNING IT.

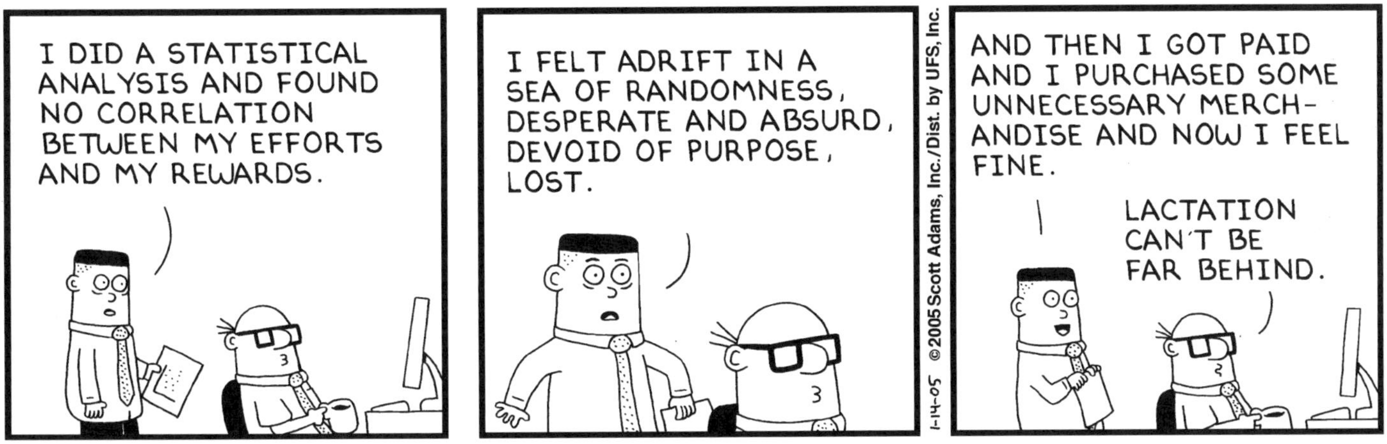
I DID A STATISTICAL ANALYSIS AND FOUND NO CORRELATION BETWEEN MY EFFORTS AND MY REWARDS.
I FELT ADRIFT IN A SEA OF RANDOMNESS, DESPERATE AND ABSURD, DEVOID OF PURPOSE, LOST.
1-14-05 ©2005 Scott Adams, Inc./Dist. by UFS, Inc.
AND THEN I GOT PAID AND I PURCHASED SOME UNNECESSARY MERCH-ANDISE AND NOW I FEEL FINE.
LACTATION CAN'T BE FAR BEHIND.

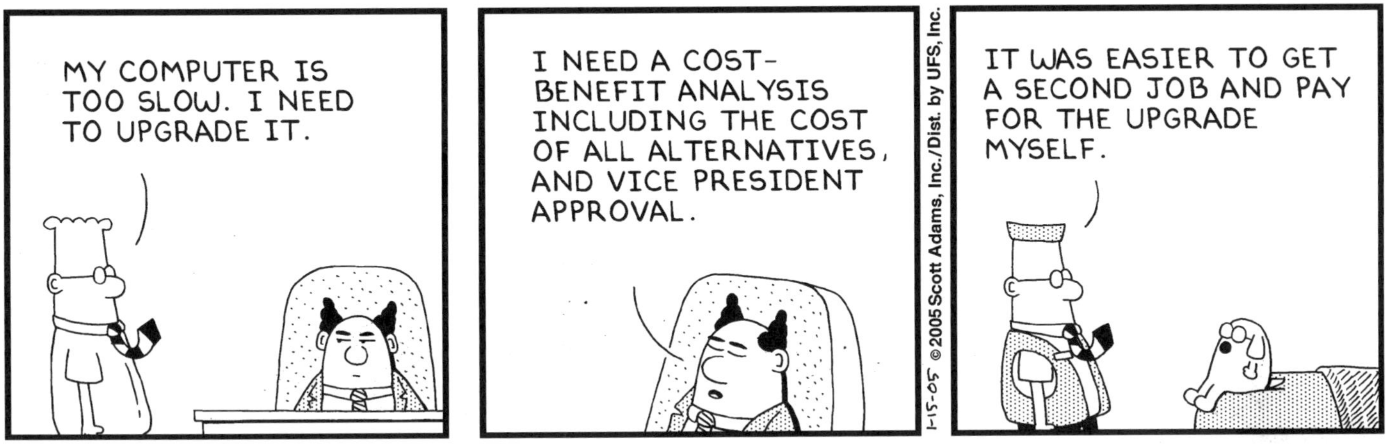
MY COMPUTER IS TOO SLOW. I NEED TO UPGRADE IT.
I NEED A COST-BENEFIT ANALYSIS INCLUDING THE COST OF ALL ALTERNATIVES, AND VICE PRESIDENT APPROVAL.
1-15-05 ©2005 Scott Adams, Inc./Dist. by UFS, Inc.
IT WAS EASIER TO GET A SECOND JOB AND PAY FOR THE UPGRADE MYSELF.

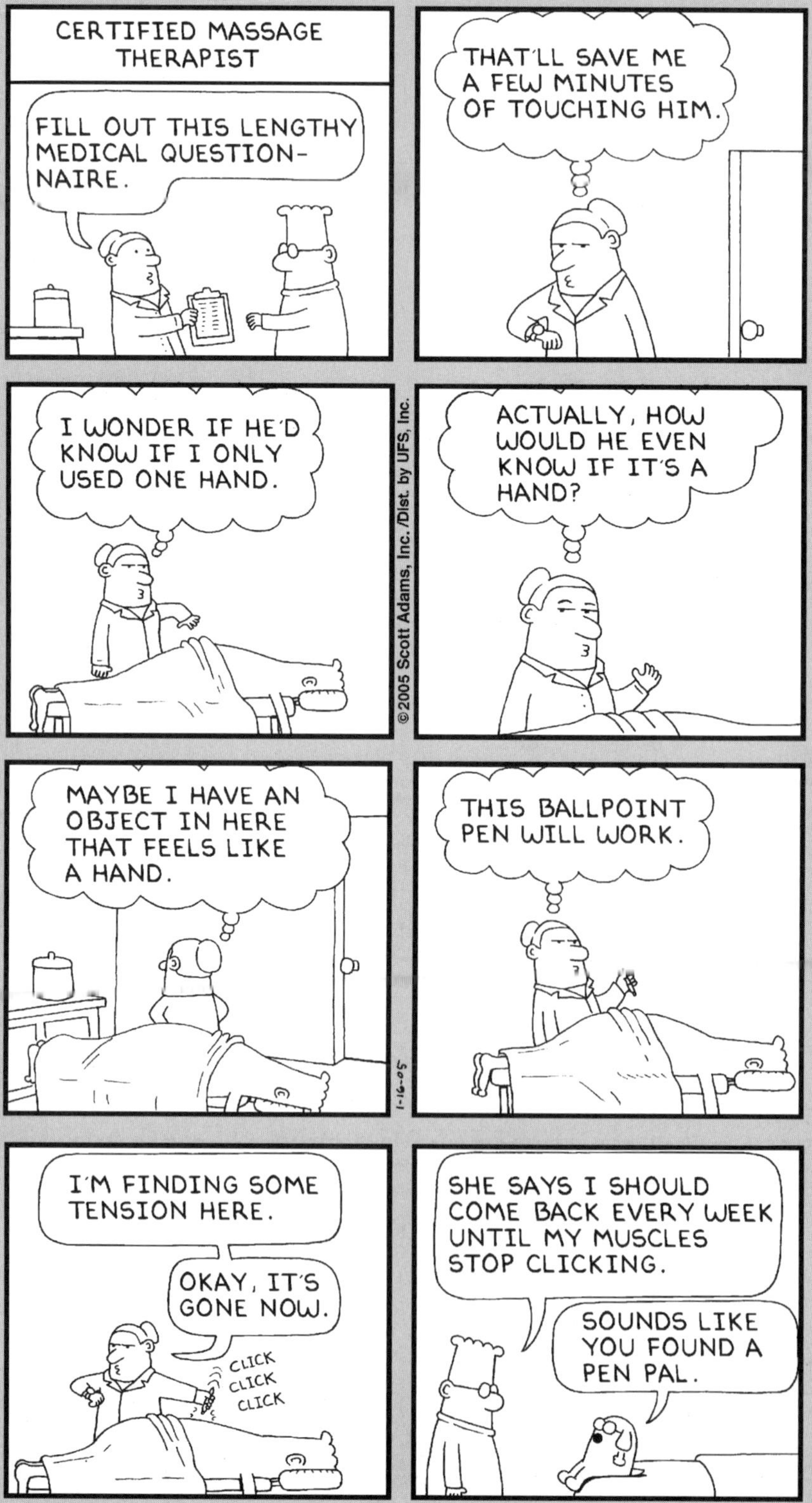
CERTIFIED MASSAGE THERAPIST
FILL OUT THIS LENGTHY MEDICAL QUESTION-NAIRE.
THAT'LL SAVE ME A FEW MINUTES OF TOUCHING HIM.
I WONDER IF HE'D KNOW IF I ONLY USED ONE HAND.
ACTUALLY, HOW WOULD HE EVEN KNOW IF IT'S A HAND?
MAYBE I HAVE AN OBJECT IN HERE THAT FEELS LIKE A HAND.
THIS BALLPOINT PEN WILL WORK.
I'M FINDING SOME TENSION HERE.
OKAY, IT'S GONE NOW.
CLICK CLICK CLICK
SHE SAYS I SHOULD COME BACK EVERY WEEK UNTIL MY MUSCLES STOP CLICKING.
SOUNDS LIKE YOU FOUND A PEN PAL.
©2005 Scott Adams, Inc./Dist. by UFS, Inc.
1-16-05

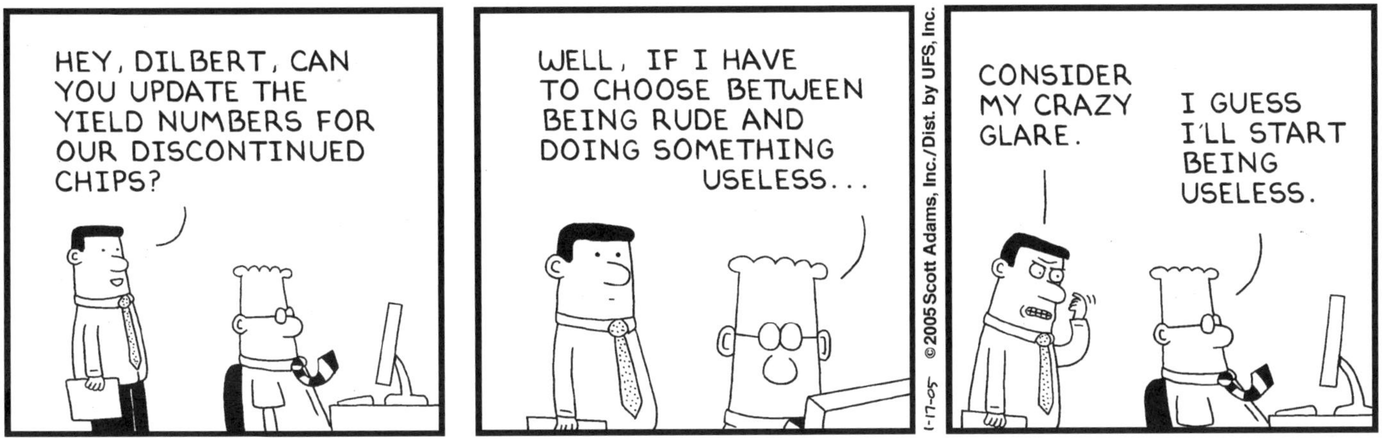
HEY, DILBERT, CAN YOU UPDATE THE YIELD NUMBERS FOR OUR DISCONTINUED CHIPS?
WELL, IF I HAVE TO CHOOSE BETWEEN BEING RUDE AND DOING SOMETHING USELESS...
© 2005 Scott Adams, Inc./Dist. by UFS, Inc.
1-17-05
CONSIDER MY CRAZY GLARE.
I GUESS I'LL START BEING USELESS.

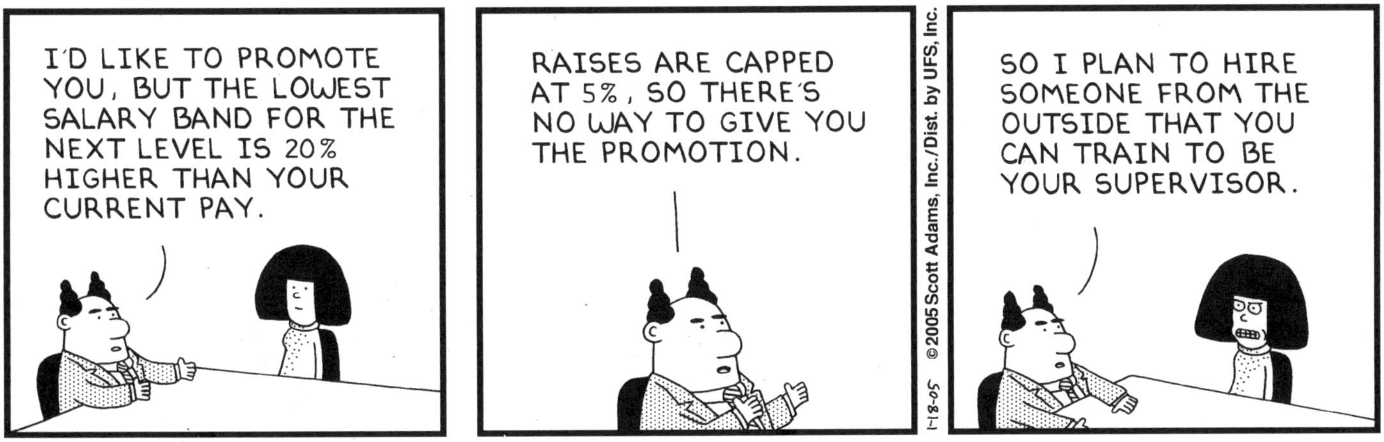
I'D LIKE TO PROMOTE YOU, BUT THE LOWEST SALARY BAND FOR THE NEXT LEVEL IS 20% HIGHER THAN YOUR CURRENT PAY.
RAISES ARE CAPPED AT 5%, SO THERE'S NO WAY TO GIVE YOU THE PROMOTION.
© 2005 Scott Adams, Inc./Dist. by UFS, Inc.
1-18-05
SO I PLAN TO HIRE SOMEONE FROM THE OUTSIDE THAT YOU CAN TRAIN TO BE YOUR SUPERVISOR.

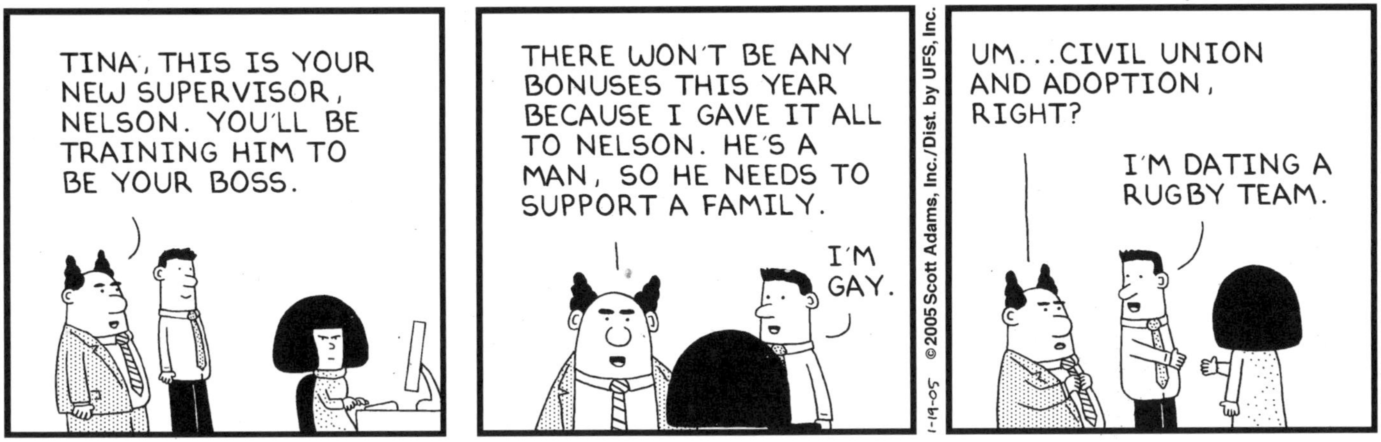
TINA, THIS IS YOUR NEW SUPERVISOR, NELSON. YOU'LL BE TRAINING HIM TO BE YOUR BOSS.
THERE WON'T BE ANY BONUSES THIS YEAR BECAUSE I GAVE IT ALL TO NELSON. HE'S A MAN, SO HE NEEDS TO SUPPORT A FAMILY.
I'M GAY.
© 2005 Scott Adams, Inc./Dist. by UFS, Inc.
1-19-05
UM...CIVIL UNION AND ADOPTION, RIGHT?
I'M DATING A RUGBY TEAM.

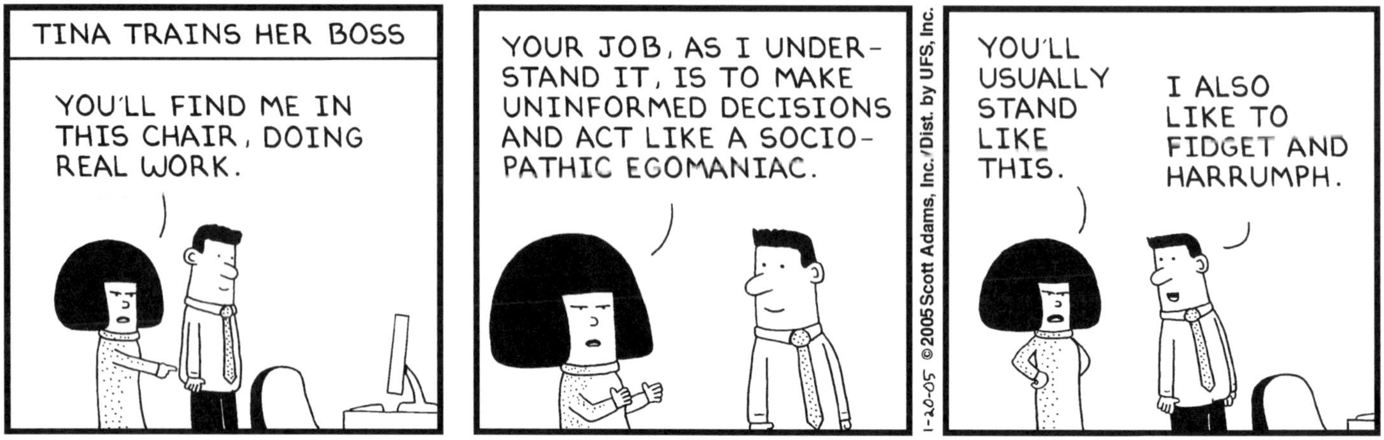
TINA TRAINS HER BOSS
YOU'LL FIND ME IN THIS CHAIR, DOING REAL WORK.
YOUR JOB, AS I UNDERSTAND IT, IS TO MAKE UNINFORMED DECISIONS AND ACT LIKE A SOCIOPATHIC EGOMANIAC.
1-20-05 ©2005 Scott Adams, Inc./Dist. by UFS, Inc.
YOU'LL USUALLY STAND LIKE THIS.
I ALSO LIKE TO FIDGET AND HARRUMPH.

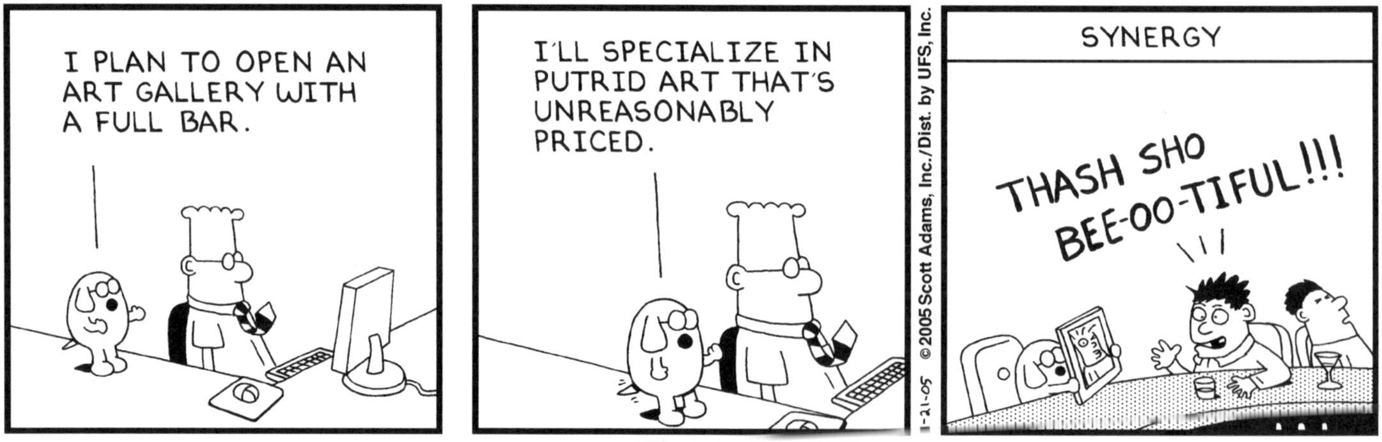
I PLAN TO OPEN AN ART GALLERY WITH A FULL BAR.
I'LL SPECIALIZE IN PUTRID ART THAT'S UNREASONABLY PRICED.
1-21-05 ©2005 Scott Adams, Inc./Dist. by UFS, Inc.
SYNERGY
THASH SHO BEE-OO-TIFUL!!!

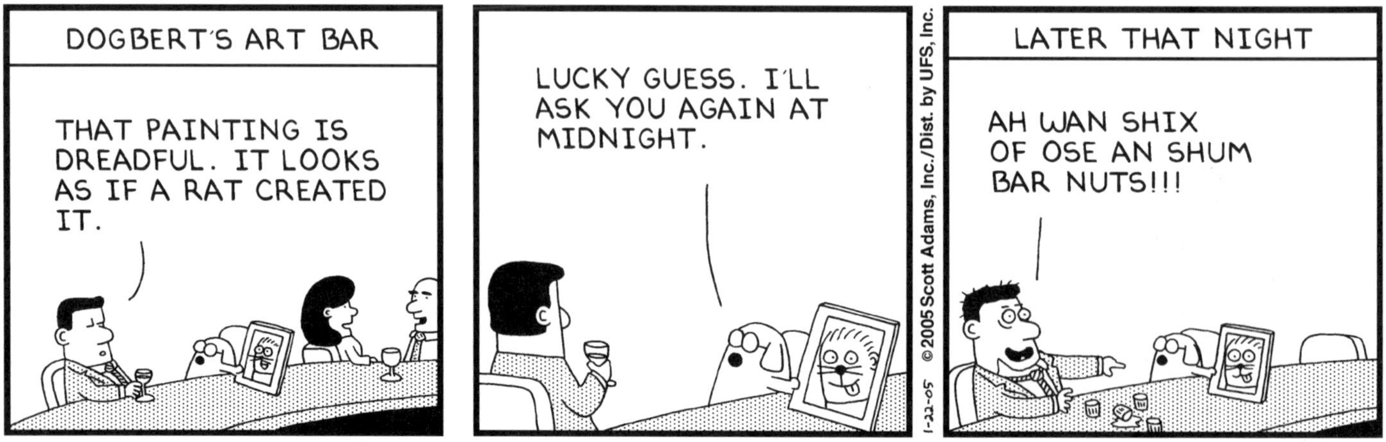
DOGBERT'S ART BAR
THAT PAINTING IS DREADFUL. IT LOOKS AS IF A RAT CREATED IT.
LUCKY GUESS. I'LL ASK YOU AGAIN AT MIDNIGHT.
1-22-05 ©2005 Scott Adams, Inc./Dist. by UFS, Inc.
LATER THAT NIGHT
AH WAN SHIX OF OSE AN SHUM BAR NUTS!!!

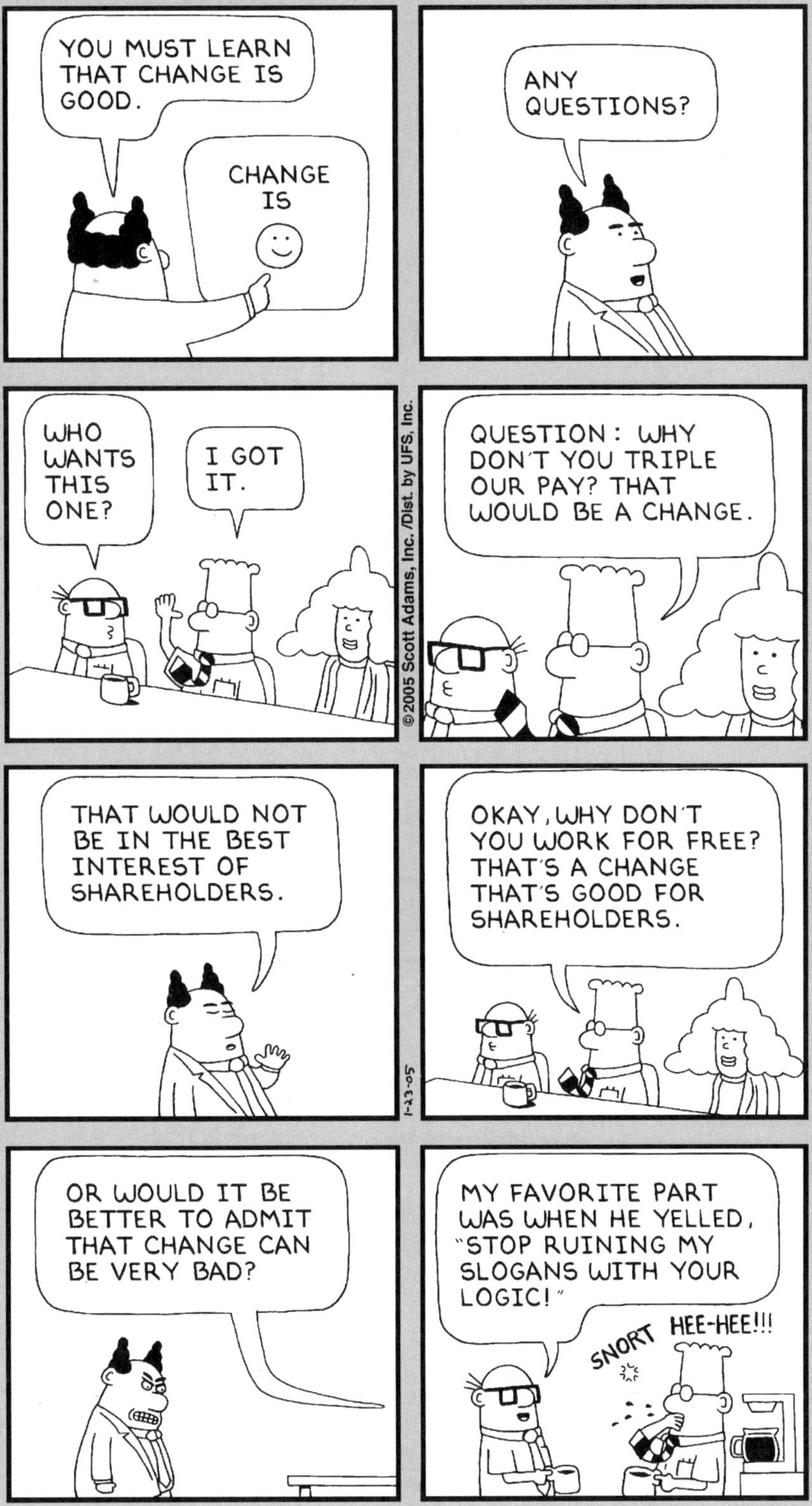

YOU MUST LEARN THAT CHANGE IS GOOD.
CHANGE IS
ANY QUESTIONS?
WHO WANTS THIS ONE?
I GOT IT.
QUESTION: WHY DON'T YOU TRIPLE OUR PAY? THAT WOULD BE A CHANGE.
©2005 Scott Adams, Inc. /Dist. by UFS, Inc.
THAT WOULD NOT BE IN THE BEST INTEREST OF SHAREHOLDERS.
OKAY, WHY DON'T YOU WORK FOR FREE? THAT'S A CHANGE THAT'S GOOD FOR SHAREHOLDERS.
1-23-05
OR WOULD IT BE BETTER TO ADMIT THAT CHANGE CAN BE VERY BAD?
MY FAVORITE PART WAS WHEN HE YELLED, "STOP RUINING MY SLOGANS WITH YOUR LOGIC!"
SNORT
HEE-HEE!!!

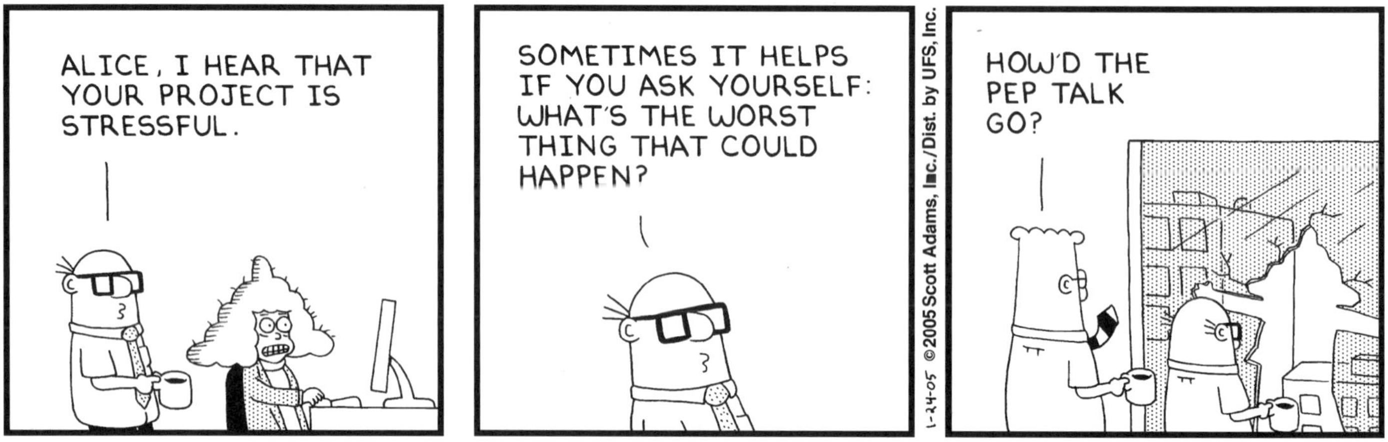
ALICE, I HEAR THAT YOUR PROJECT IS STRESSFUL.
SOMETIMES IT HELPS IF YOU ASK YOURSELF: WHAT'S THE WORST THING THAT COULD HAPPEN?
© 2005 Scott Adams, Inc./Dist. by UFS, Inc.
HOW'D THE PEP TALK GO?

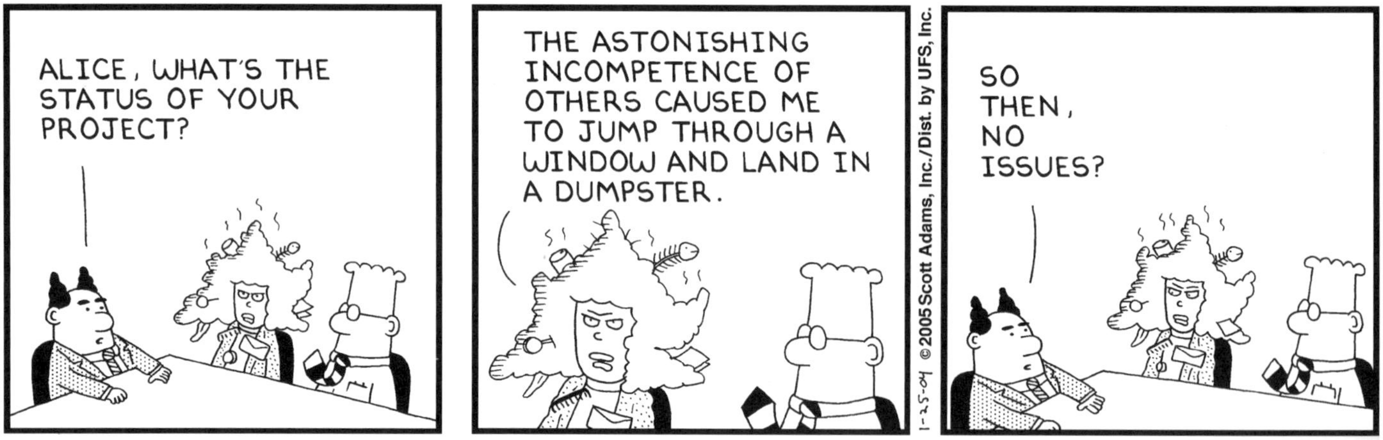
ALICE, WHAT'S THE STATUS OF YOUR PROJECT?
THE ASTONISHING INCOMPETENCE OF OTHERS CAUSED ME TO JUMP THROUGH A WINDOW AND LAND IN A DUMPSTER.
© 2005 Scott Adams, Inc./Dist. by UFS, Inc.
SO THEN, NO ISSUES?

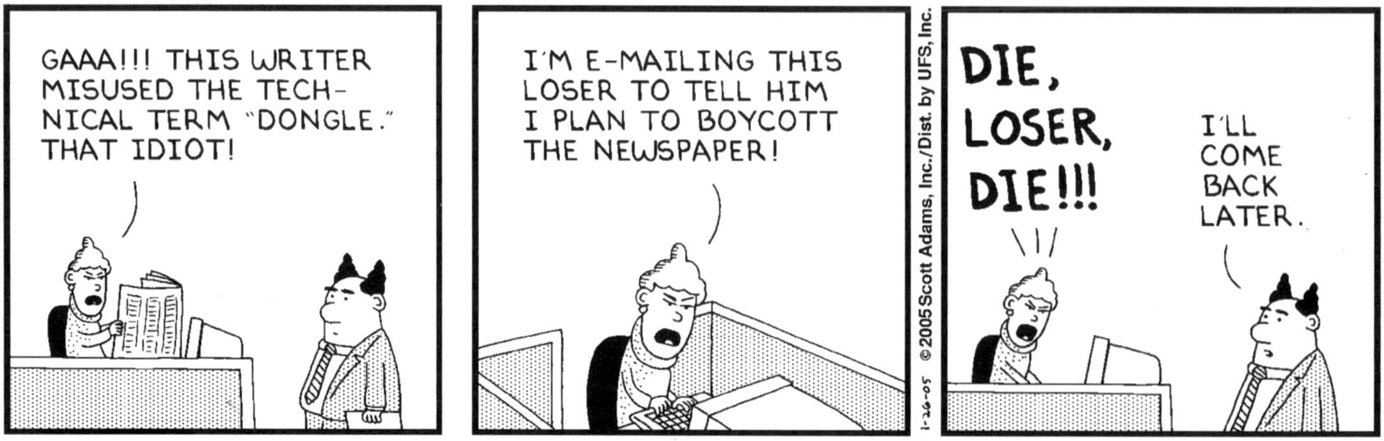
GAAA!!! THIS WRITER MISUSED THE TECH-NICAL TERM "DONGLE." THAT IDIOT!
I'M E-MAILING THIS LOSER TO TELL HIM I PLAN TO BOYCOTT THE NEWSPAPER!
© 2005 Scott Adams, Inc./Dist. by UFS, Inc.
DIE, LOSER, DIE!!!
I'LL COME BACK LATER.

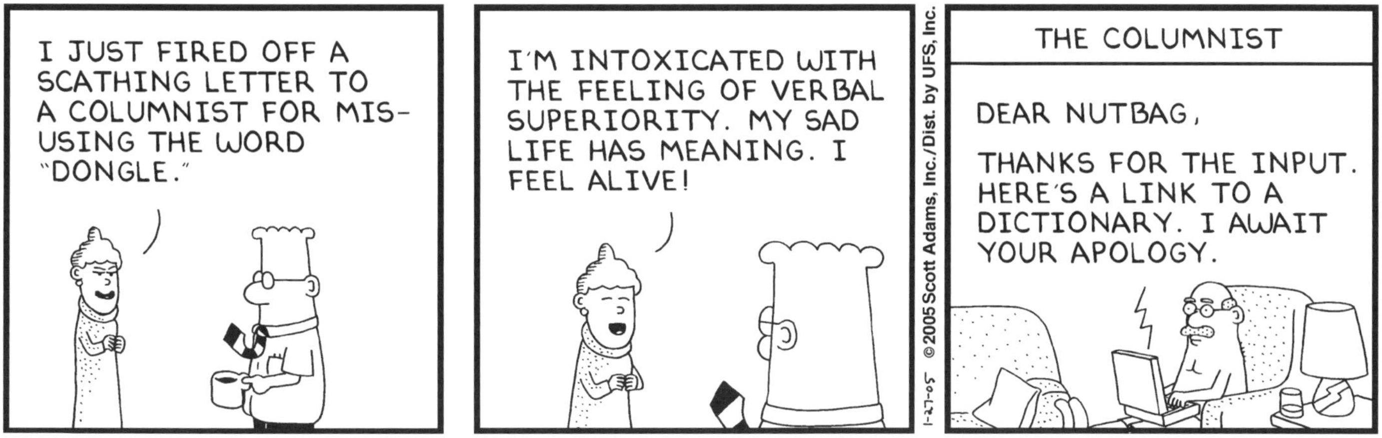
I JUST FIRED OFF A SCATHING LETTER TO A COLUMNIST FOR MIS-USING THE WORD "DONGLE."
I'M INTOXICATED WITH THE FEELING OF VERBAL SUPERIORITY. MY SAD LIFE HAS MEANING. I FEEL ALIVE!
1-27-05 © 2005 Scott Adams, Inc./Dist. by UFS, Inc.
THE COLUMNIST
DEAR NUTBAG,
THANKS FOR THE INPUT. HERE'S A LINK TO A DICTIONARY. I AWAIT YOUR APOLOGY.

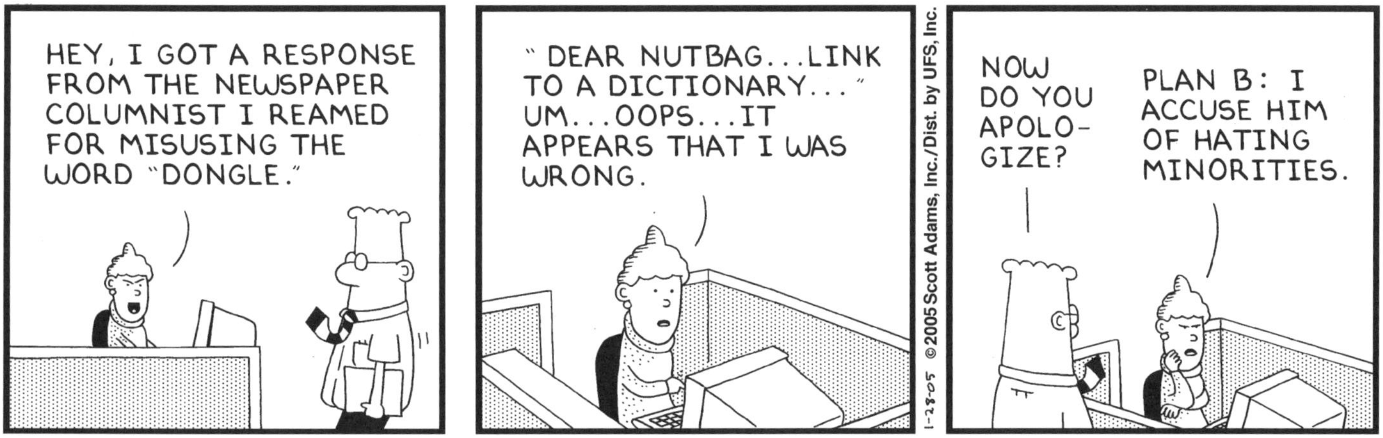
HEY, I GOT A RESPONSE FROM THE NEWSPAPER COLUMNIST I REAMED FOR MISUSING THE WORD "DONGLE."
" DEAR NUTBAG...LINK TO A DICTIONARY... " UM...OOPS...IT APPEARS THAT I WAS WRONG.
1-28-05 © 2005 Scott Adams, Inc./Dist. by UFS, Inc.
NOW DO YOU APOLO-GIZE?
PLAN B: I ACCUSE HIM OF HATING MINORITIES.

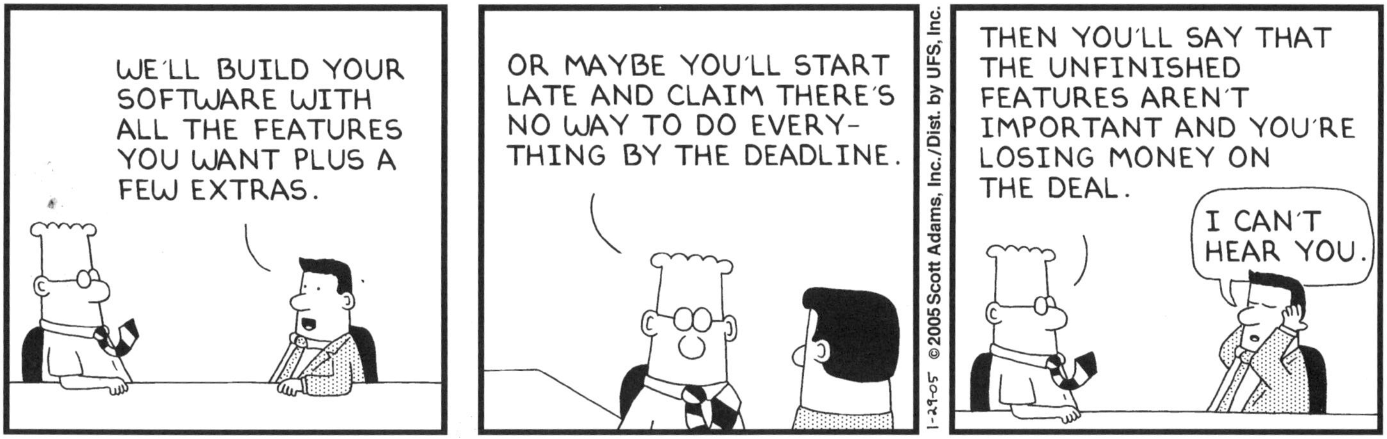
WE'LL BUILD YOUR SOFTWARE WITH ALL THE FEATURES YOU WANT PLUS A FEW EXTRAS.
OR MAYBE YOU'LL START LATE AND CLAIM THERE'S NO WAY TO DO EVERY-THING BY THE DEADLINE.
1-29-05 © 2005 Scott Adams, Inc./Dist. by UFS, Inc.
THEN YOU'LL SAY THAT THE UNFINISHED FEATURES AREN'T IMPORTANT AND YOU'RE LOSING MONEY ON THE DEAL.
I CAN'T HEAR YOU.

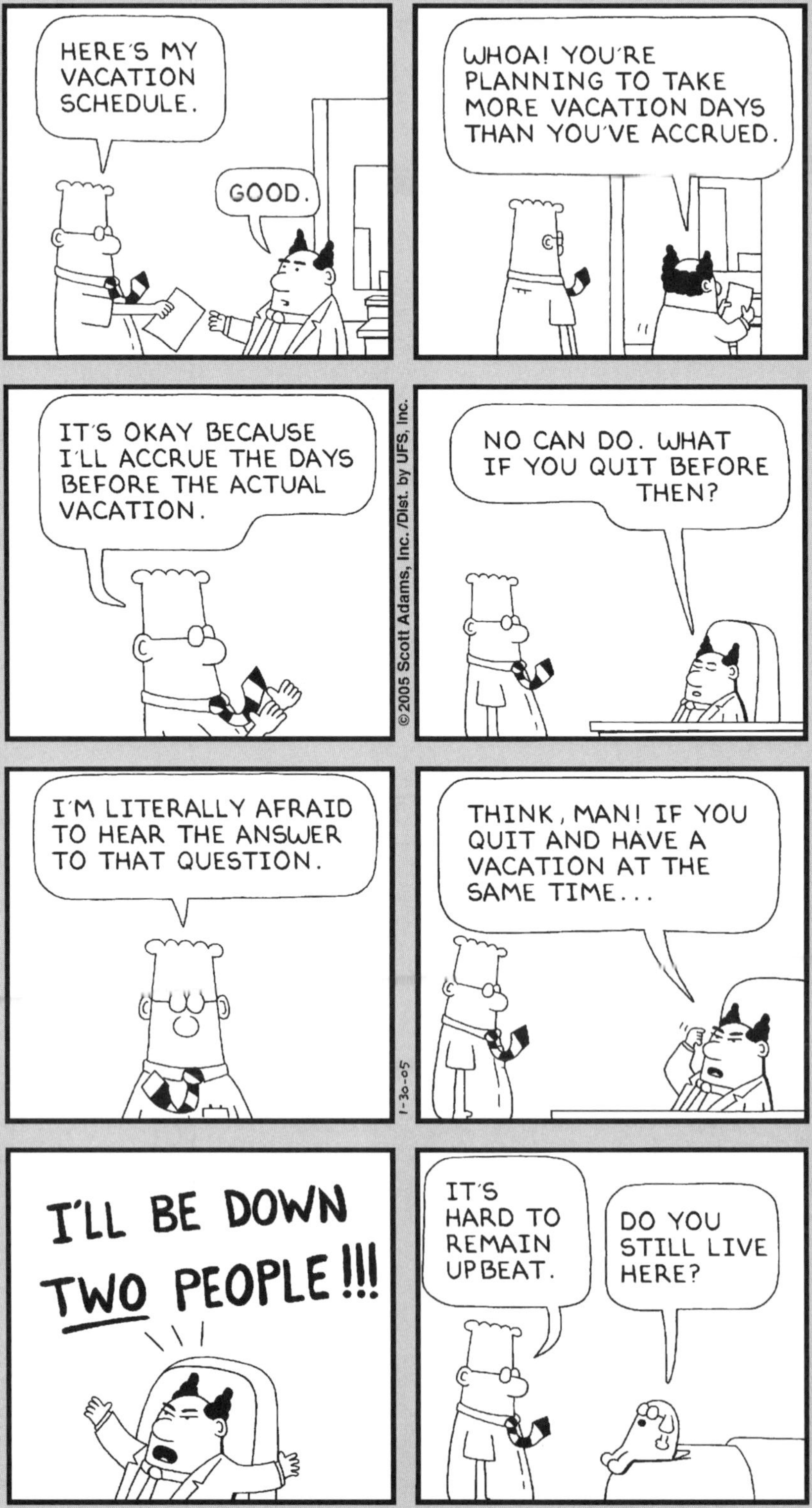
HERE'S MY VACATION SCHEDULE.
GOOD.
WHOA! YOU'RE PLANNING TO TAKE MORE VACATION DAYS THAN YOU'VE ACCRUED.
IT'S OKAY BECAUSE I'LL ACCRUE THE DAYS BEFORE THE ACTUAL VACATION.
NO CAN DO. WHAT IF YOU QUIT BEFORE THEN?
I'M LITERALLY AFRAID TO HEAR THE ANSWER TO THAT QUESTION.
THINK, MAN! IF YOU QUIT AND HAVE A VACATION AT THE SAME TIME...
I'LL BE DOWN TWO PEOPLE!!!
IT'S HARD TO REMAIN UPBEAT.
DO YOU STILL LIVE HERE?
©2005 Scott Adams, Inc. /Dist. by UFS, Inc.
1-30-05

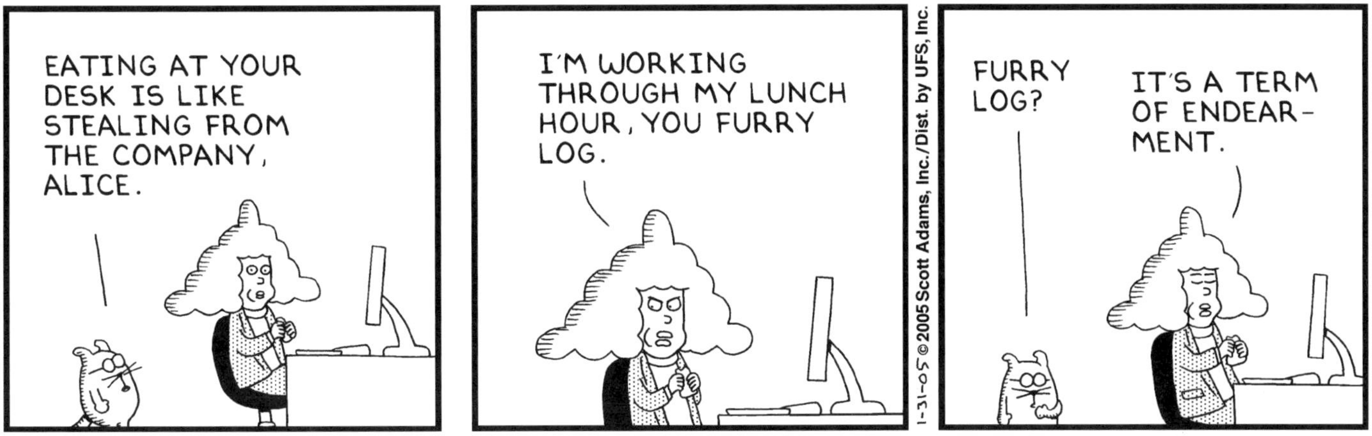
EATING AT YOUR DESK IS LIKE STEALING FROM THE COMPANY, ALICE.
I'M WORKING THROUGH MY LUNCH HOUR, YOU FURRY LOG.
1-31-05 © 2005 Scott Adams, Inc./Dist. by UFS, Inc.
FURRY LOG?
IT'S A TERM OF ENDEAR-MENT.

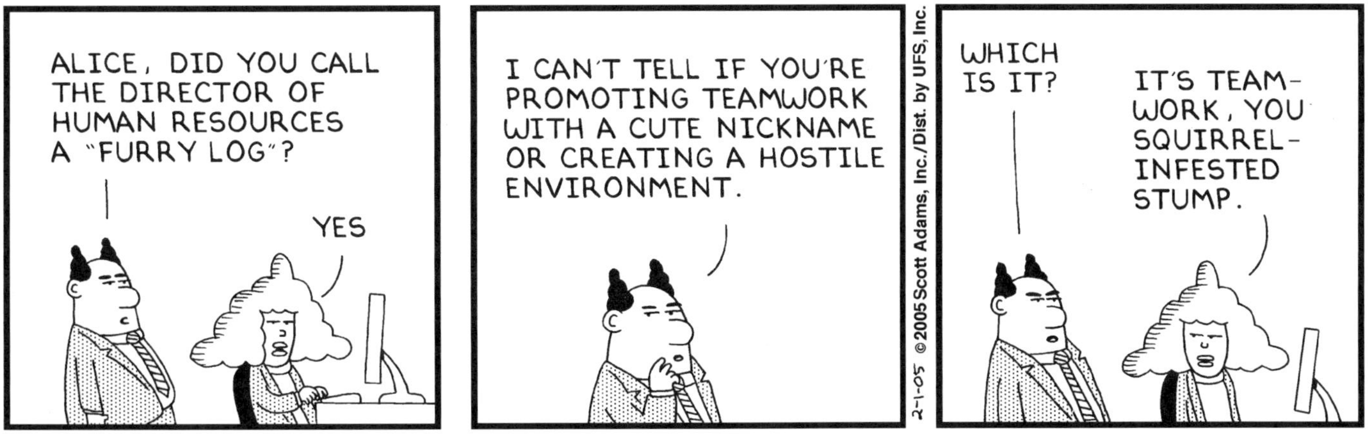
ALICE, DID YOU CALL THE DIRECTOR OF HUMAN RESOURCES A "FURRY LOG"?
YES
I CAN'T TELL IF YOU'RE PROMOTING TEAMWORK WITH A CUTE NICKNAME OR CREATING A HOSTILE ENVIRONMENT.
2-1-05 © 2005 Scott Adams, Inc./Dist. by UFS, Inc.
WHICH IS IT?
IT'S TEAM-WORK, YOU SQUIRREL-INFESTED STUMP.

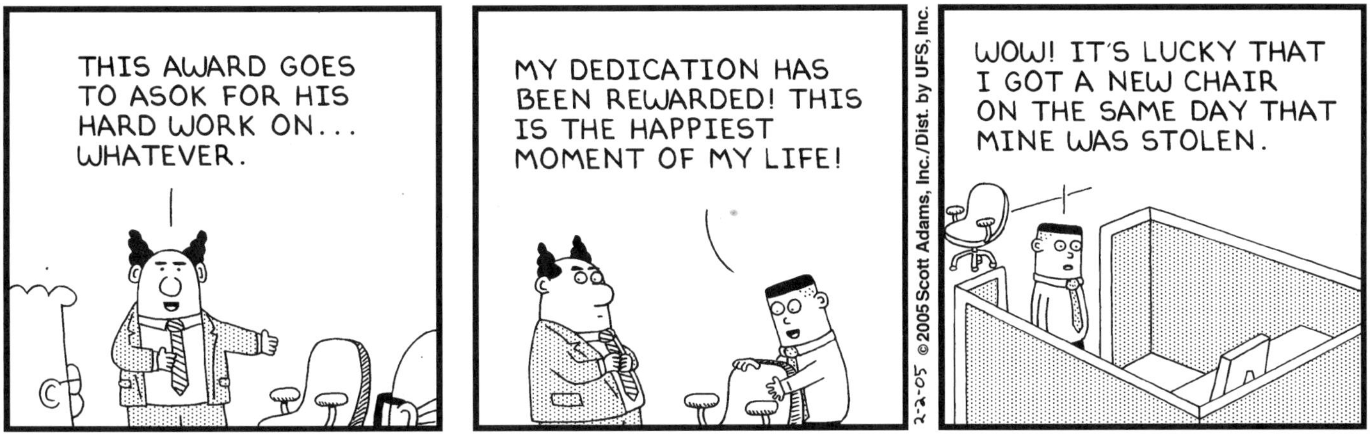
THIS AWARD GOES TO ASOK FOR HIS HARD WORK ON... WHATEVER.
MY DEDICATION HAS BEEN REWARDED! THIS IS THE HAPPIEST MOMENT OF MY LIFE!
2-2-05 © 2005 Scott Adams, Inc./Dist. by UFS, Inc.
WOW! IT'S LUCKY THAT I GOT A NEW CHAIR ON THE SAME DAY THAT MINE WAS STOLEN.

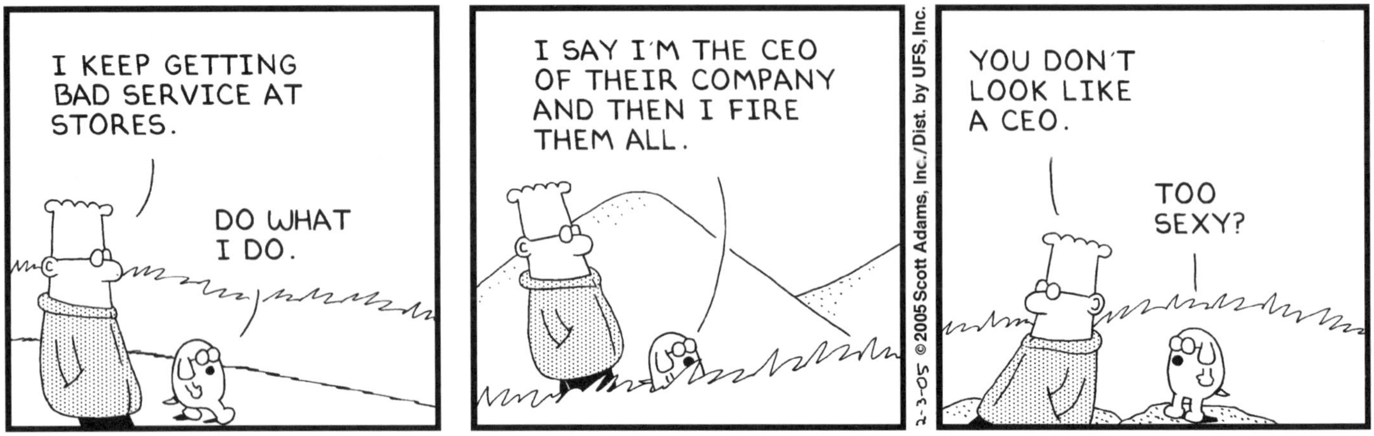
I KEEP GETTING BAD SERVICE AT STORES.
DO WHAT I DO.
I SAY I'M THE CEO OF THEIR COMPANY AND THEN I FIRE THEM ALL.
2-3-05 © 2005 Scott Adams, Inc./Dist. by UFS, Inc.
YOU DON'T LOOK LIKE A CEO.
TOO SEXY?

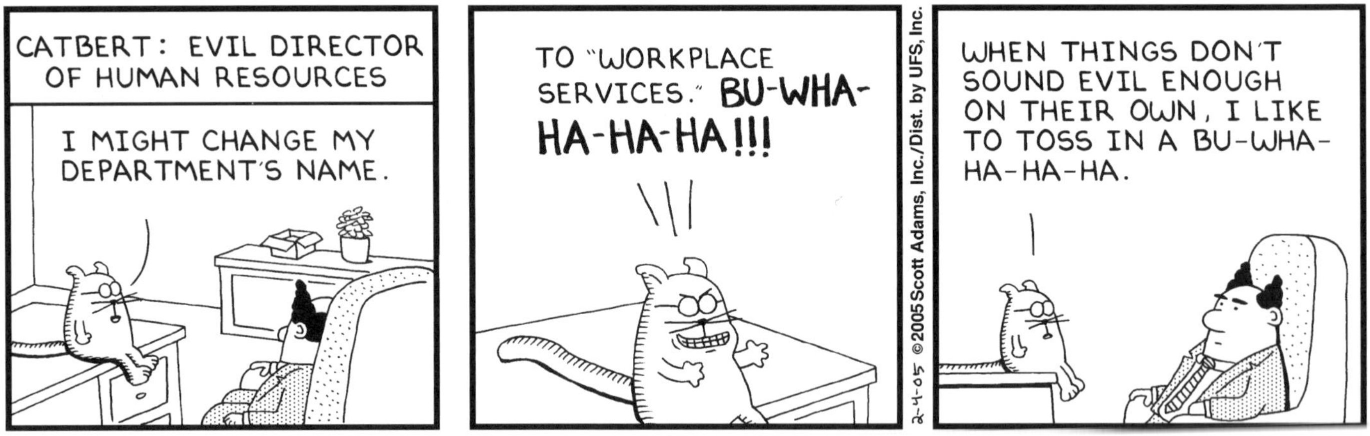
CATBERT: EVIL DIRECTOR OF HUMAN RESOURCES
I MIGHT CHANGE MY DEPARTMENT'S NAME.
TO "WORKPLACE SERVICES." BU-WHA-HA-HA-HA!!!
2-4-05 © 2005 Scott Adams, Inc./Dist. by UFS, Inc.
WHEN THINGS DON'T SOUND EVIL ENOUGH ON THEIR OWN, I LIKE TO TOSS IN A BU-WHA-HA-HA-HA.

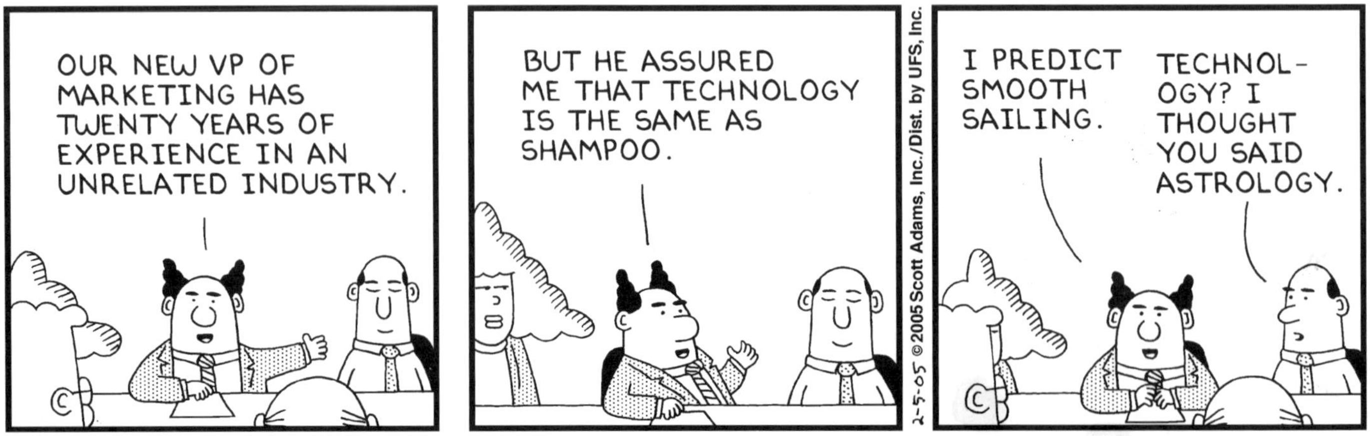
OUR NEW VP OF MARKETING HAS TWENTY YEARS OF EXPERIENCE IN AN UNRELATED INDUSTRY.
BUT HE ASSURED ME THAT TECHNOLOGY IS THE SAME AS SHAMPOO.
2-5-05 © 2005 Scott Adams, Inc./Dist. by UFS, Inc.
I PREDICT SMOOTH SAILING.
TECHNOLOGY? I THOUGHT YOU SAID ASTROLOGY.

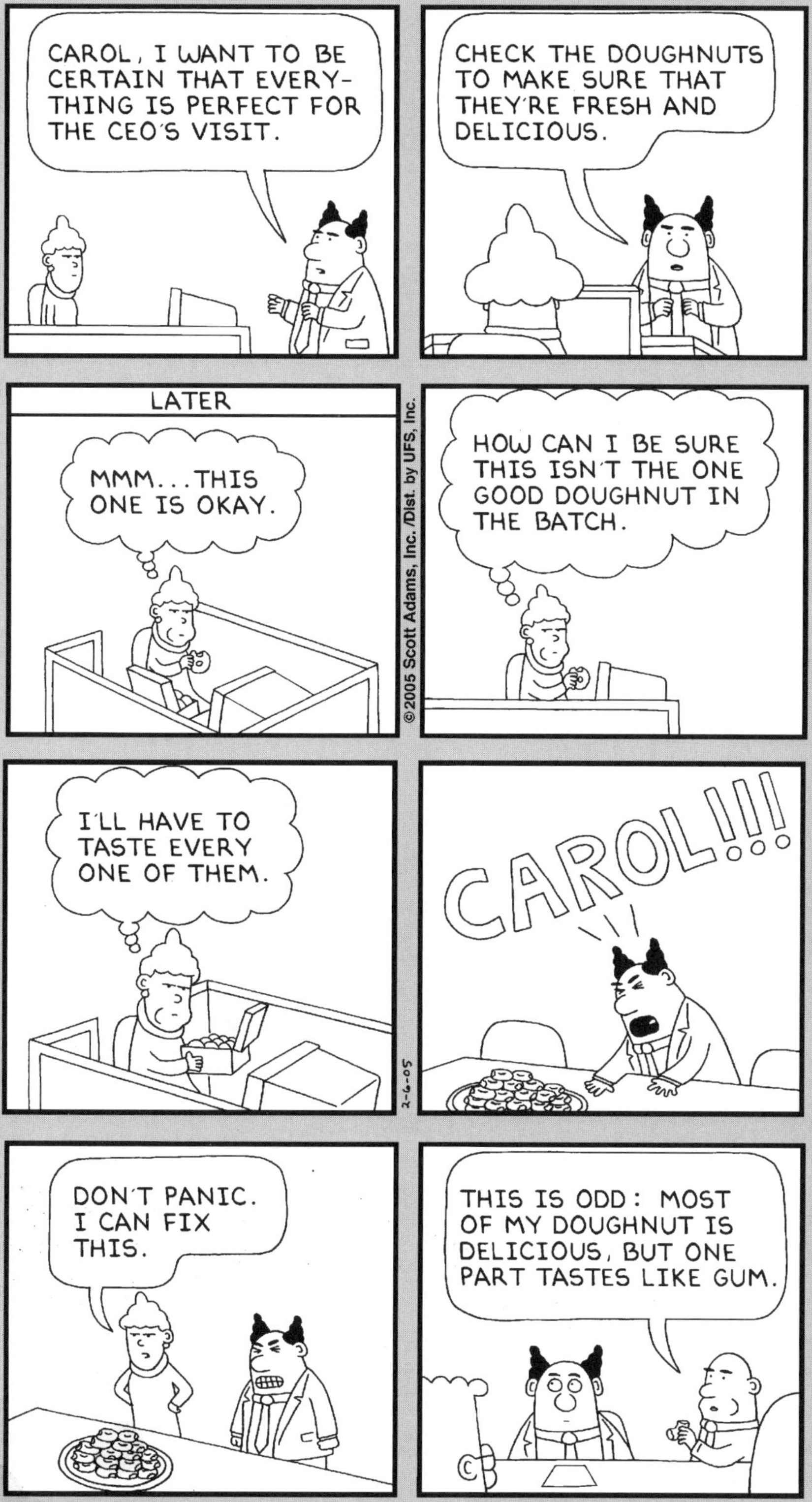
CAROL, I WANT TO BE CERTAIN THAT EVERY-THING IS PERFECT FOR THE CEO'S VISIT.
CHECK THE DOUGHNUTS TO MAKE SURE THAT THEY'RE FRESH AND DELICIOUS.
LATER
MMM...THIS ONE IS OKAY.
©2005 Scott Adams, Inc. /Dist. by UFS, Inc.
HOW CAN I BE SURE THIS ISN'T THE ONE GOOD DOUGHNUT IN THE BATCH.
I'LL HAVE TO TASTE EVERY ONE OF THEM.
2-6-05
CAROL!!!
DON'T PANIC. I CAN FIX THIS.
THIS IS ODD: MOST OF MY DOUGHNUT IS DELICIOUS, BUT ONE PART TASTES LIKE GUM.

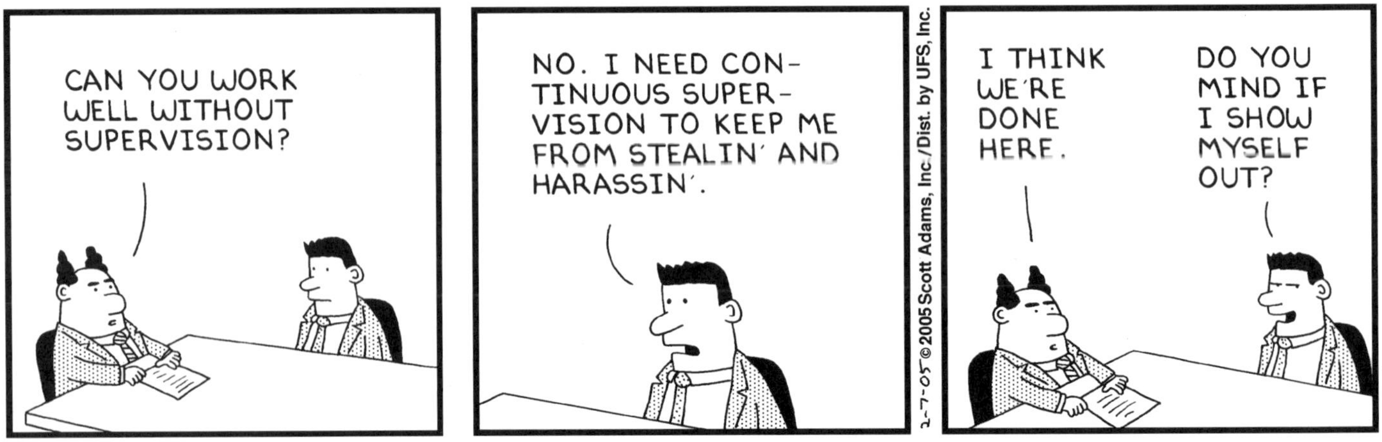
CAN YOU WORK WELL WITHOUT SUPERVISION?
NO. I NEED CONTINUOUS SUPERVISION TO KEEP ME FROM STEALIN' AND HARASSIN'.
2-7-05 © 2005 Scott Adams, Inc./Dist. by UFS, Inc.
I THINK WE'RE DONE HERE.
DO YOU MIND IF I SHOW MYSELF OUT?

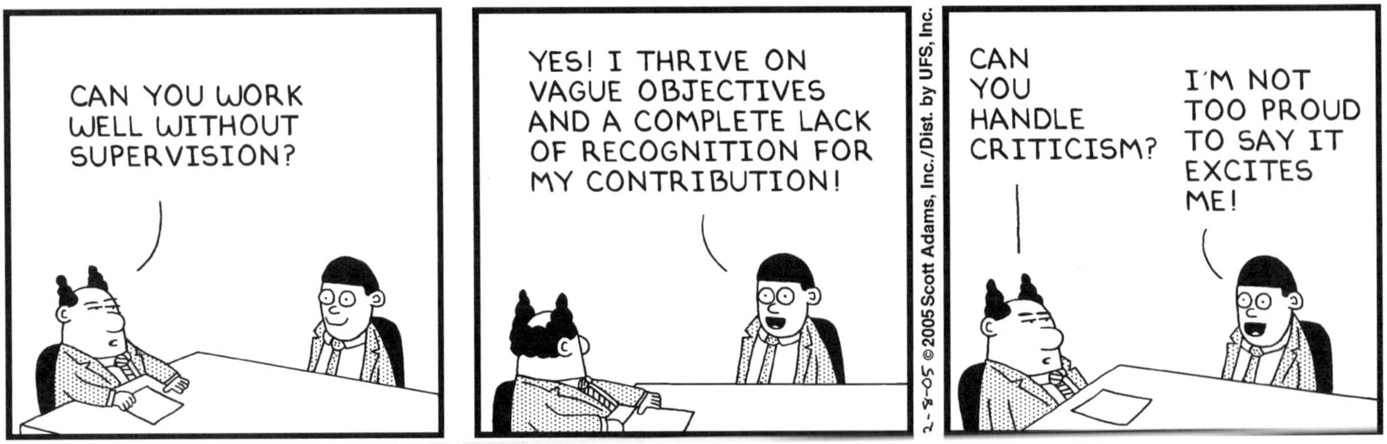
CAN YOU WORK WELL WITHOUT SUPERVISION?
YES! I THRIVE ON VAGUE OBJECTIVES AND A COMPLETE LACK OF RECOGNITION FOR MY CONTRIBUTION!
2-8-05 © 2005 Scott Adams, Inc./Dist. by UFS, Inc.
CAN YOU HANDLE CRITICISM?
I'M NOT TOO PROUD TO SAY IT EXCITES ME!

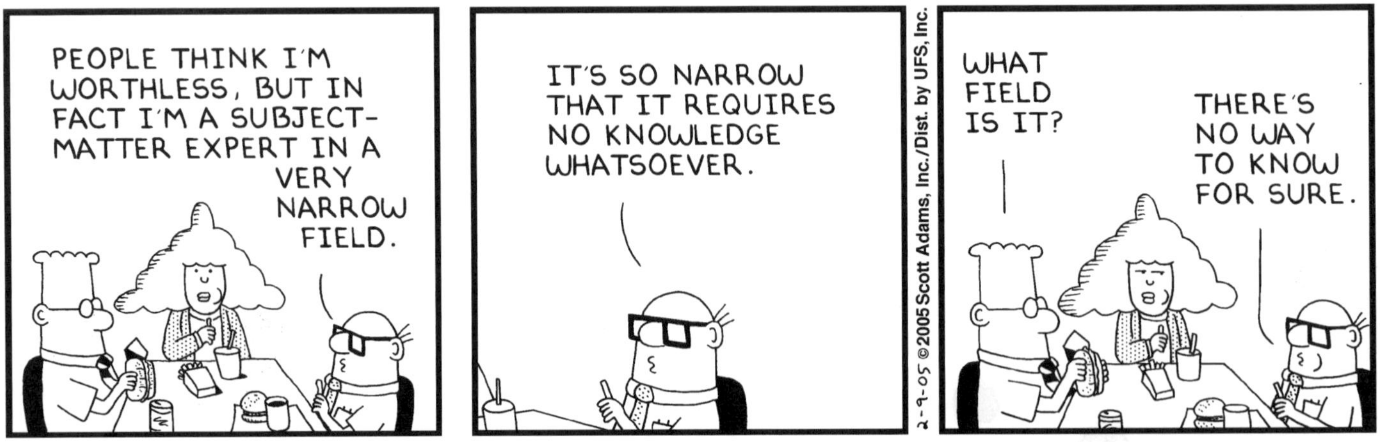
PEOPLE THINK I'M WORTHLESS, BUT IN FACT I'M A SUBJECT-MATTER EXPERT IN A VERY NARROW FIELD.
IT'S SO NARROW THAT IT REQUIRES NO KNOWLEDGE WHATSOEVER.
2-9-05 © 2005 Scott Adams, Inc./Dist. by UFS, Inc.
WHAT FIELD IS IT?
THERE'S NO WAY TO KNOW FOR SURE.

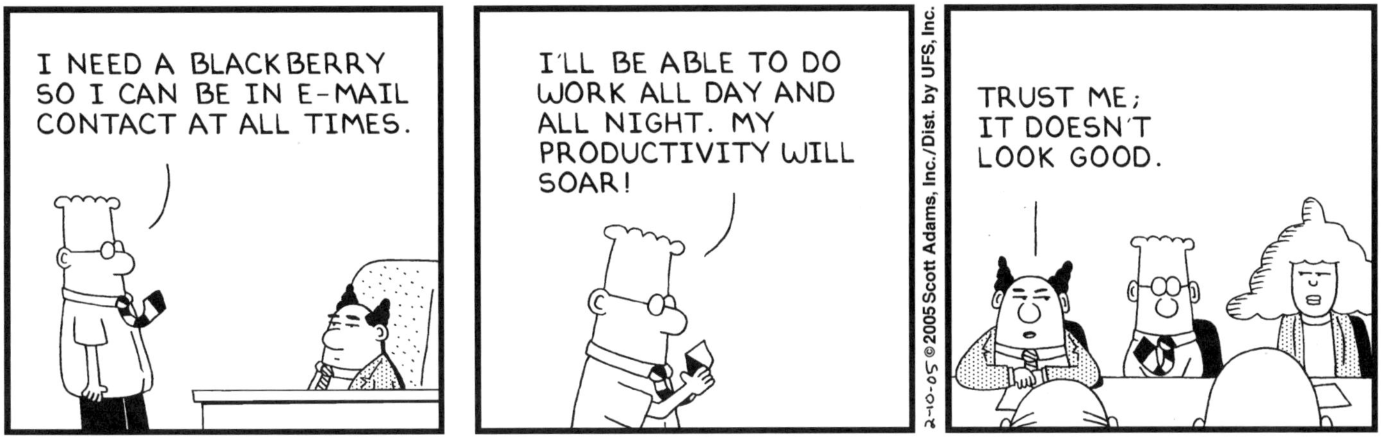
I NEED A BLACKBERRY SO I CAN BE IN E-MAIL CONTACT AT ALL TIMES.
I'LL BE ABLE TO DO WORK ALL DAY AND ALL NIGHT. MY PRODUCTIVITY WILL SOAR!
2-10-05 © 2005 Scott Adams, Inc./Dist. by UFS, Inc.
TRUST ME; IT DOESN'T LOOK GOOD.

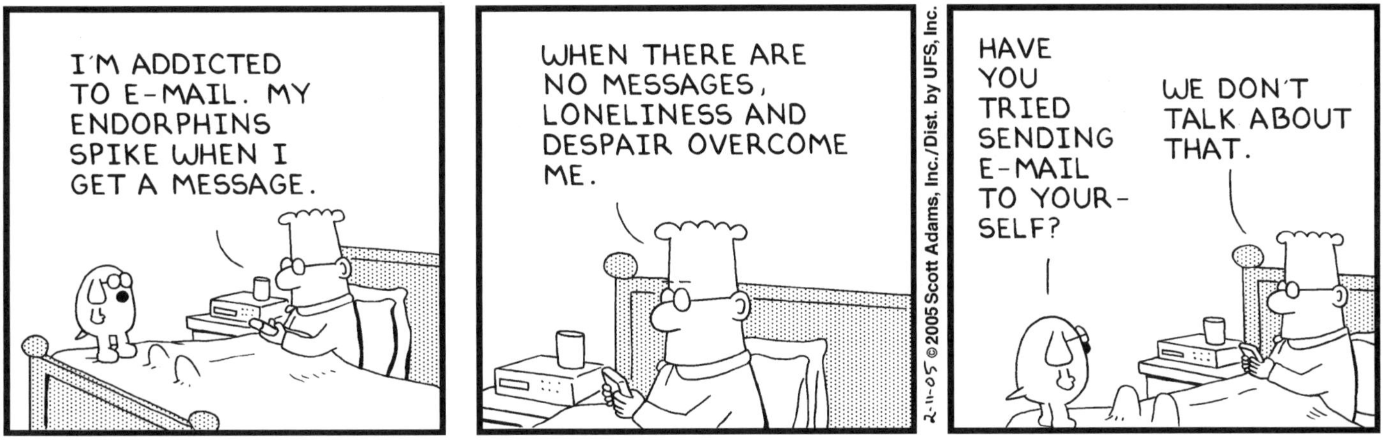
I'M ADDICTED TO E-MAIL. MY ENDORPHINS SPIKE WHEN I GET A MESSAGE.
WHEN THERE ARE NO MESSAGES, LONELINESS AND DESPAIR OVERCOME ME.
2-11-05 © 2005 Scott Adams, Inc./Dist. by UFS, Inc.
HAVE YOU TRIED SENDING E-MAIL TO YOUR-SELF?
WE DON'T TALK ABOUT THAT.

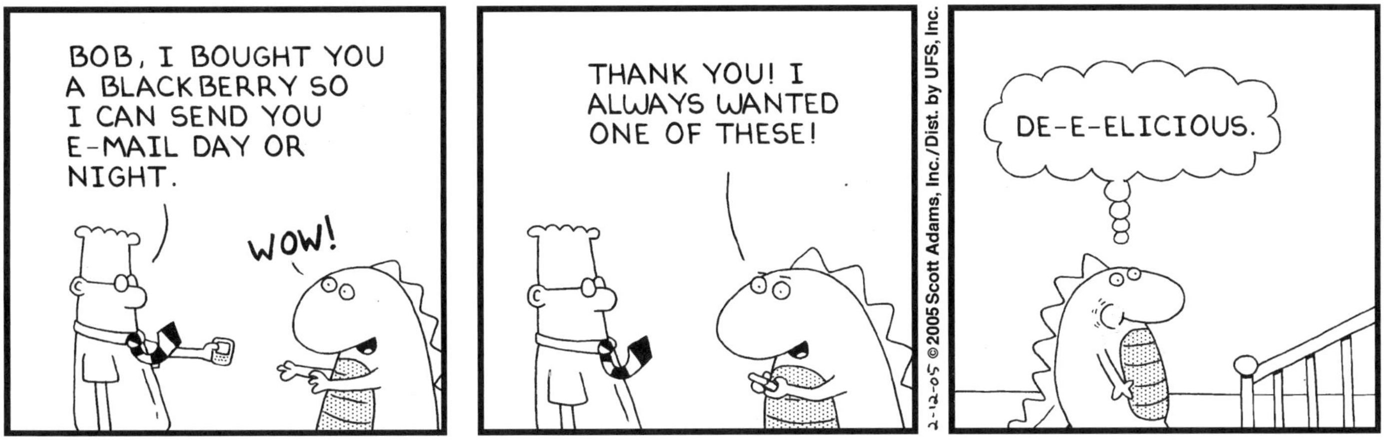
BOB, I BOUGHT YOU A BLACKBERRY SO I CAN SEND YOU E-MAIL DAY OR NIGHT.
WOW!
THANK YOU! I ALWAYS WANTED ONE OF THESE!
2-12-05 © 2005 Scott Adams, Inc./Dist. by UFS, Inc.
DE-E-ELICIOUS.

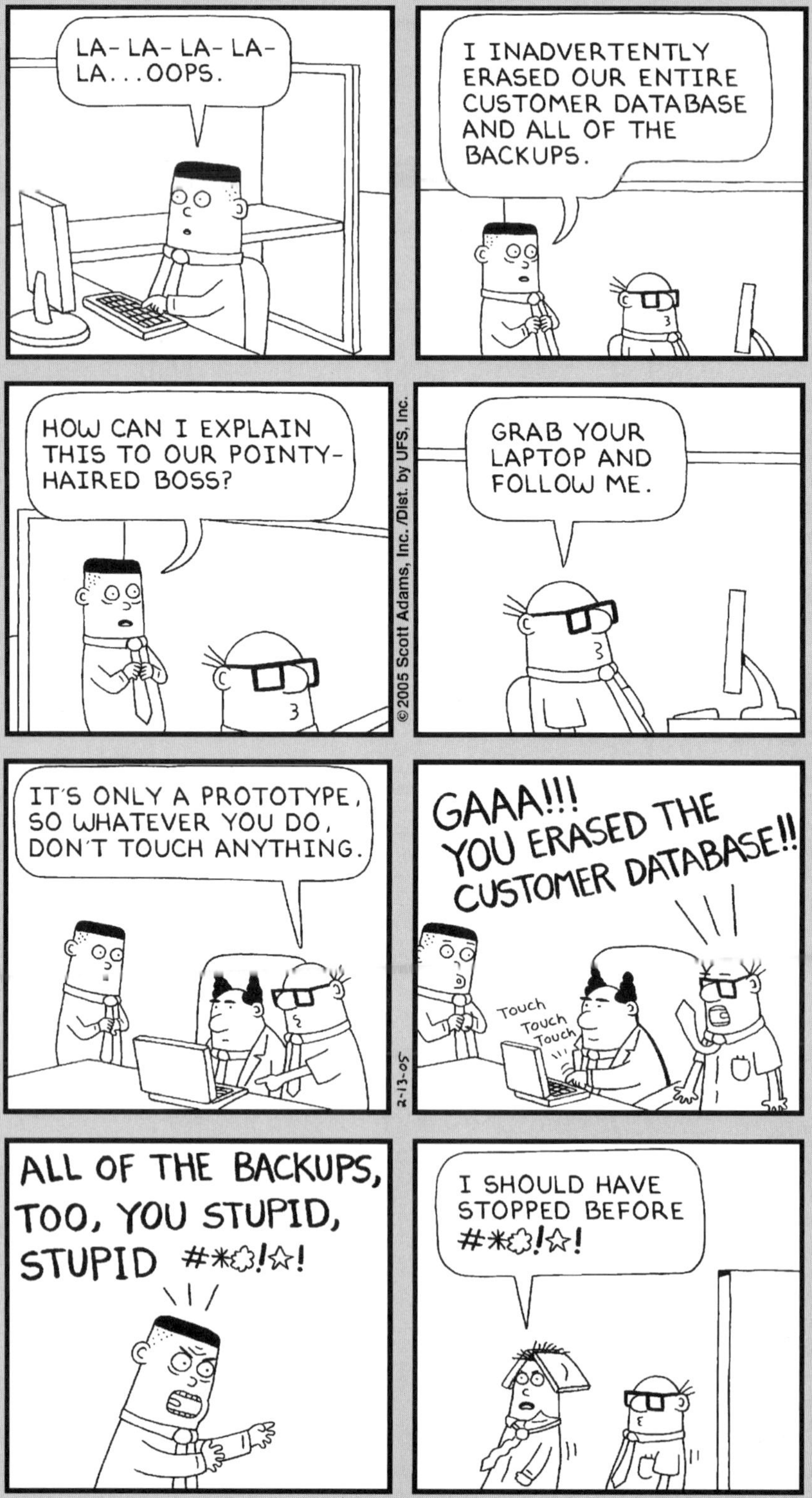
LA- LA- LA- LA- LA...OOPS.
I INADVERTENTLY ERASED OUR ENTIRE CUSTOMER DATABASE AND ALL OF THE BACKUPS.
HOW CAN I EXPLAIN THIS TO OUR POINTY-HAIRED BOSS?
GRAB YOUR LAPTOP AND FOLLOW ME.
© 2005 Scott Adams, Inc. /Dist. by UFS, Inc.
IT'S ONLY A PROTOTYPE, SO WHATEVER YOU DO, DON'T TOUCH ANYTHING.
GAAA!!! YOU ERASED THE CUSTOMER DATABASE!!
Touch Touch Touch
2-13-05
ALL OF THE BACKUPS, TOO, YOU STUPID, STUPID #*✿!☆!
I SHOULD HAVE STOPPED BEFORE #*✿!☆!

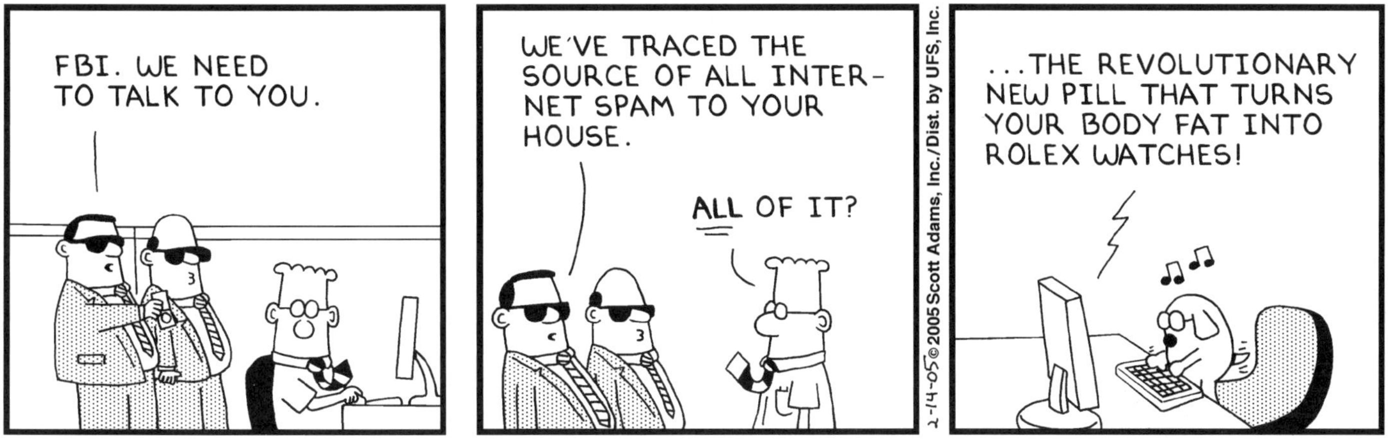
FBI. WE NEED TO TALK TO YOU.
WE'VE TRACED THE SOURCE OF ALL INTERNET SPAM TO YOUR HOUSE.
ALL OF IT?
2-14-05 © 2005 Scott Adams, Inc./Dist. by UFS, Inc.
...THE REVOLUTIONARY NEW PILL THAT TURNS YOUR BODY FAT INTO ROLEX WATCHES!

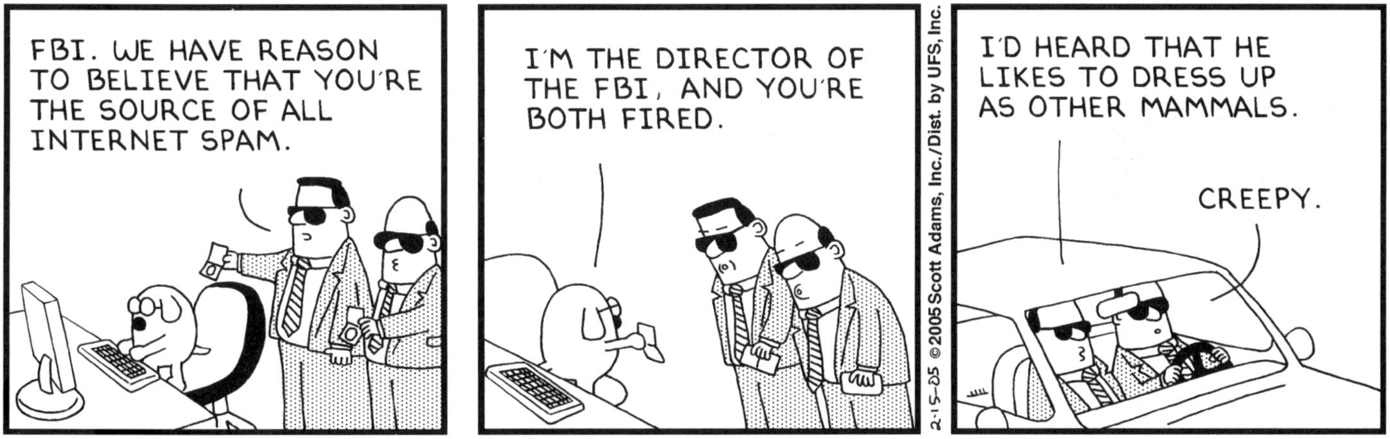
FBI. WE HAVE REASON TO BELIEVE THAT YOU'RE THE SOURCE OF ALL INTERNET SPAM.
I'M THE DIRECTOR OF THE FBI, AND YOU'RE BOTH FIRED.
2-15-05 © 2005 Scott Adams, Inc./Dist. by UFS, Inc.
I'D HEARD THAT HE LIKES TO DRESS UP AS OTHER MAMMALS.
CREEPY.

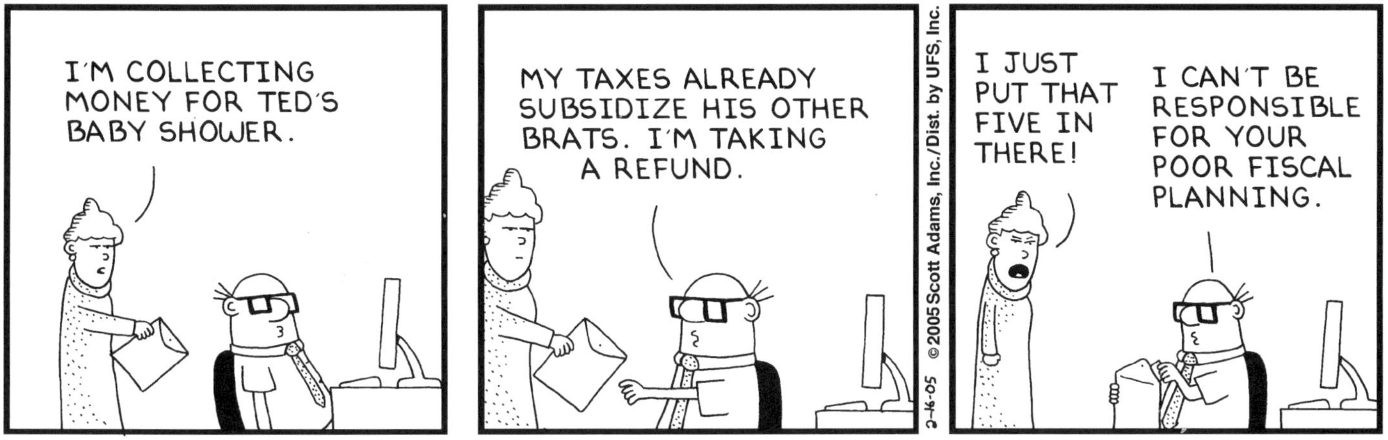
I'M COLLECTING MONEY FOR TED'S BABY SHOWER.
MY TAXES ALREADY SUBSIDIZE HIS OTHER BRATS. I'M TAKING A REFUND.
2-16-05 © 2005 Scott Adams, Inc./Dist. by UFS, Inc.
I JUST PUT THAT FIVE IN THERE!
I CAN'T BE RESPONSIBLE FOR YOUR POOR FISCAL PLANNING.

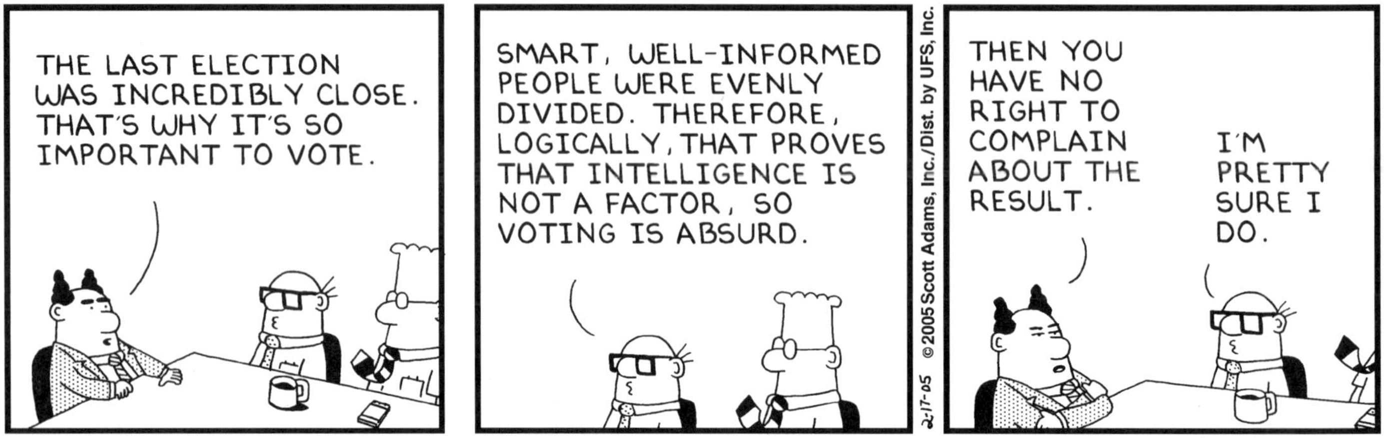
THE LAST ELECTION WAS INCREDIBLY CLOSE. THAT'S WHY IT'S SO IMPORTANT TO VOTE.
SMART, WELL-INFORMED PEOPLE WERE EVENLY DIVIDED. THEREFORE, LOGICALLY, THAT PROVES THAT INTELLIGENCE IS NOT A FACTOR, SO VOTING IS ABSURD.
2-17-05 © 2005 Scott Adams, Inc./Dist. by UFS, Inc.
THEN YOU HAVE NO RIGHT TO COMPLAIN ABOUT THE RESULT.
I'M PRETTY SURE I DO.

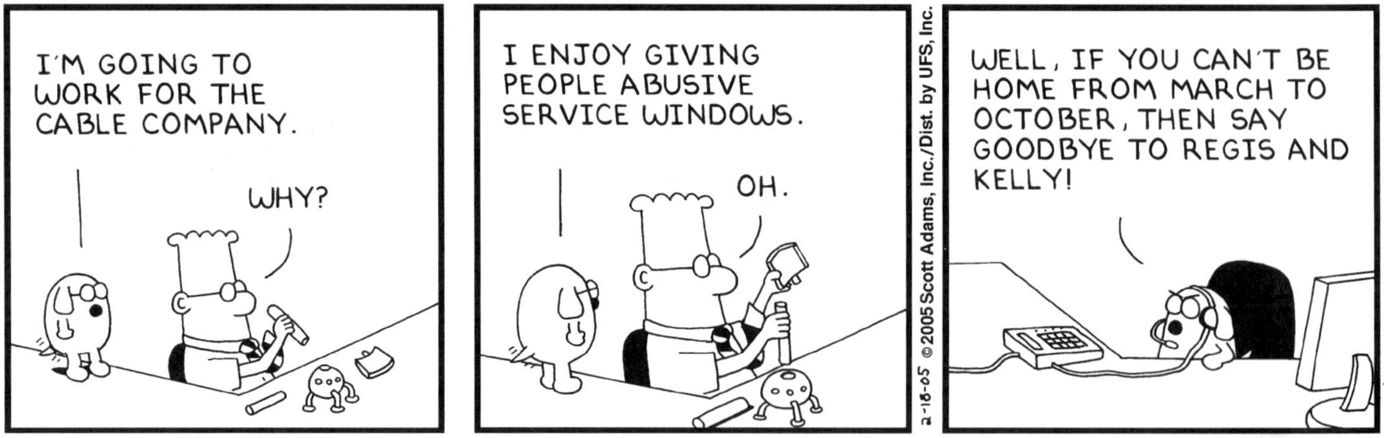
I'M GOING TO WORK FOR THE CABLE COMPANY.
WHY?
I ENJOY GIVING PEOPLE ABUSIVE SERVICE WINDOWS.
OH.
2-18-05 © 2005 Scott Adams, Inc./Dist. by UFS, Inc.
WELL, IF YOU CAN'T BE HOME FROM MARCH TO OCTOBER, THEN SAY GOODBYE TO REGIS AND KELLY!

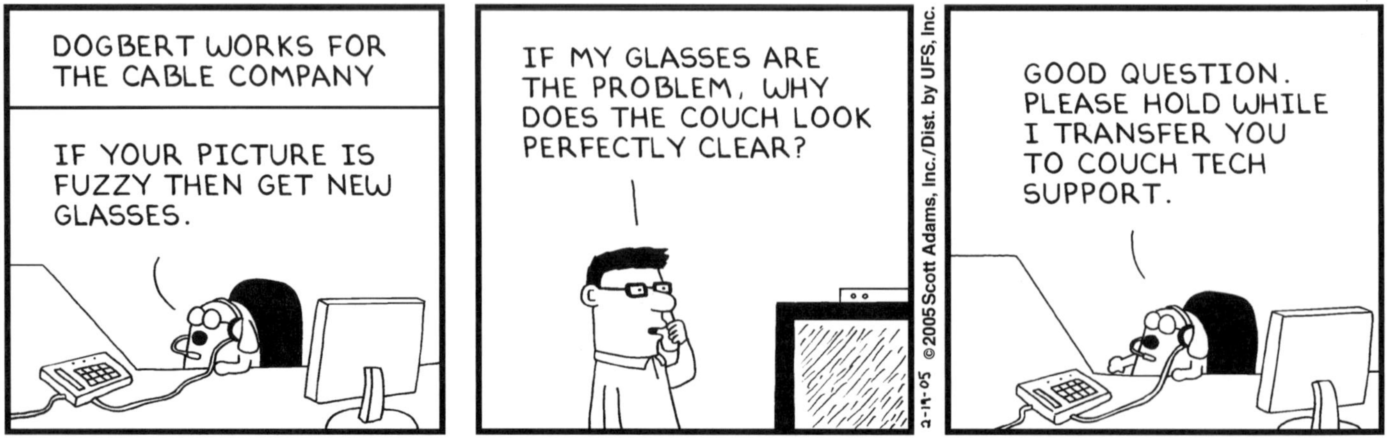
DOGBERT WORKS FOR THE CABLE COMPANY
IF YOUR PICTURE IS FUZZY THEN GET NEW GLASSES.
IF MY GLASSES ARE THE PROBLEM, WHY DOES THE COUCH LOOK PERFECTLY CLEAR?
2-19-05 © 2005 Scott Adams, Inc./Dist. by UFS, Inc.
GOOD QUESTION. PLEASE HOLD WHILE I TRANSFER YOU TO COUCH TECH SUPPORT.

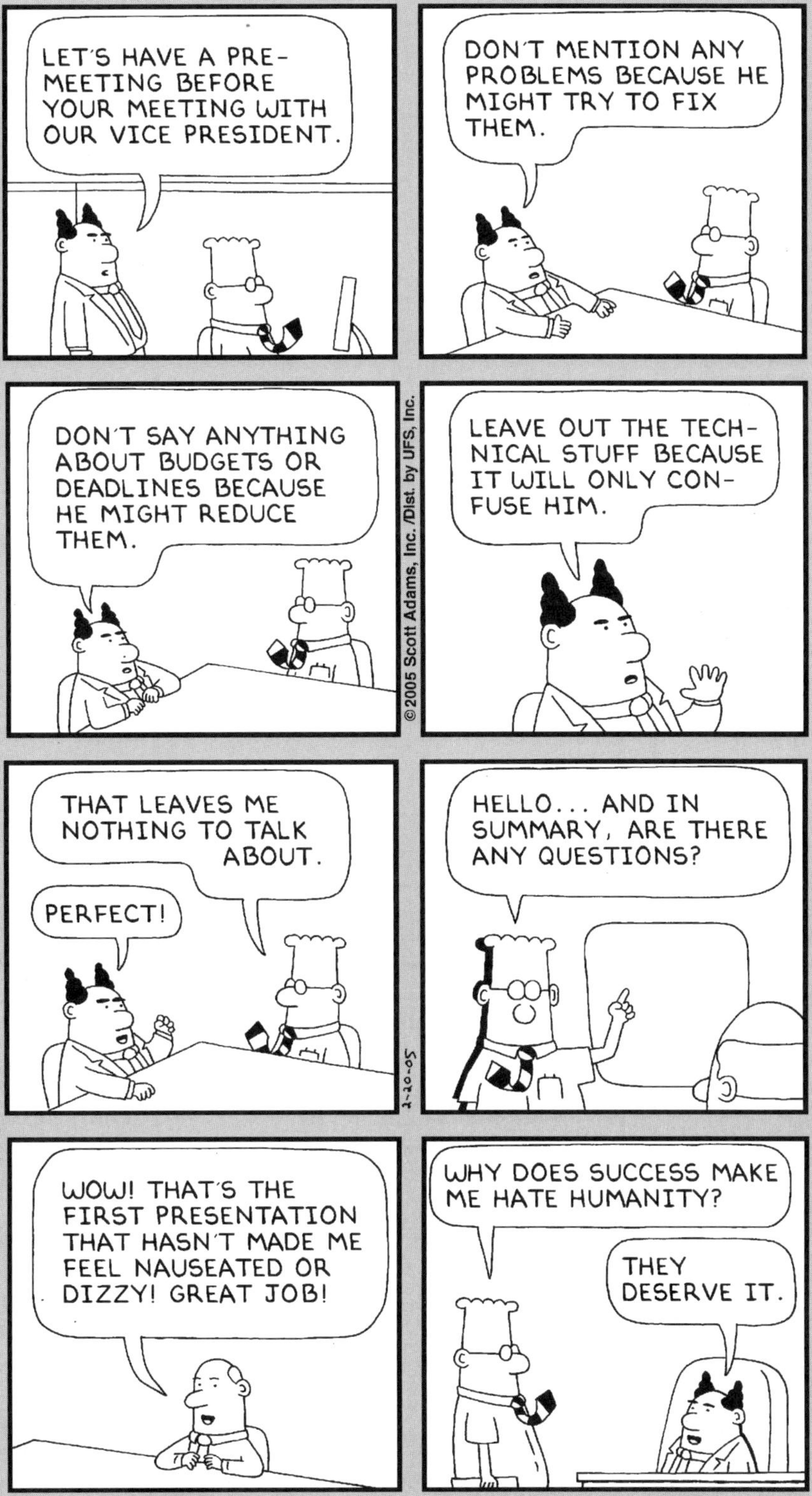
LET'S HAVE A PRE-MEETING BEFORE YOUR MEETING WITH OUR VICE PRESIDENT.
DON'T MENTION ANY PROBLEMS BECAUSE HE MIGHT TRY TO FIX THEM.
DON'T SAY ANYTHING ABOUT BUDGETS OR DEADLINES BECAUSE HE MIGHT REDUCE THEM.
LEAVE OUT THE TECHNICAL STUFF BECAUSE IT WILL ONLY CONFUSE HIM.
THAT LEAVES ME NOTHING TO TALK ABOUT.
PERFECT!
HELLO... AND IN SUMMARY, ARE THERE ANY QUESTIONS?
WOW! THAT'S THE FIRST PRESENTATION THAT HASN'T MADE ME FEEL NAUSEATED OR DIZZY! GREAT JOB!
WHY DOES SUCCESS MAKE ME HATE HUMANITY?
THEY DESERVE IT.
©2005 Scott Adams, Inc./Dist. by UFS, Inc.
1-20-05

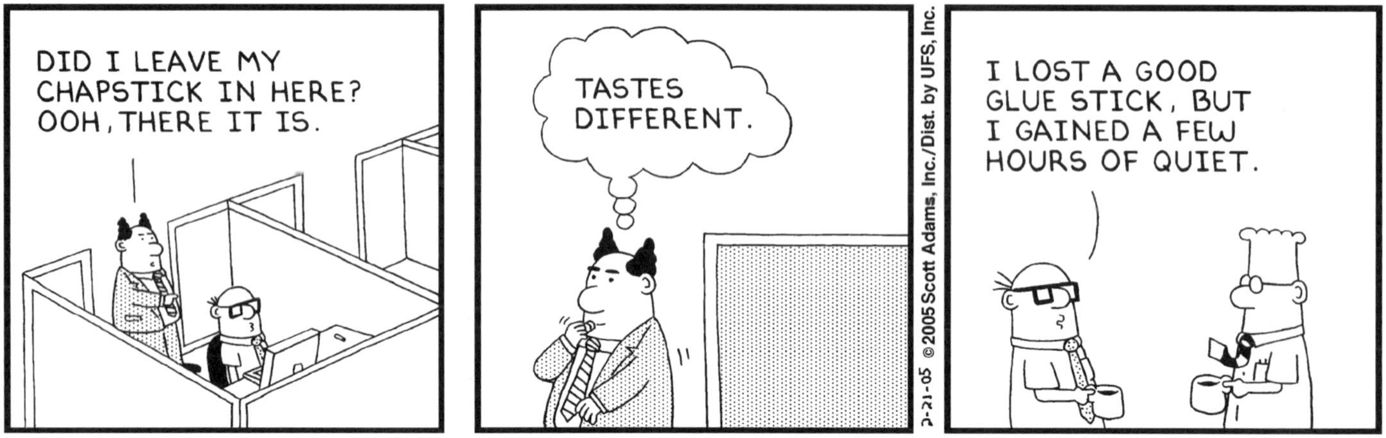
DID I LEAVE MY CHAPSTICK IN HERE? OOH, THERE IT IS.
TASTES DIFFERENT.
©2005 Scott Adams, Inc./Dist. by UFS, Inc.
I LOST A GOOD GLUE STICK, BUT I GAINED A FEW HOURS OF QUIET.

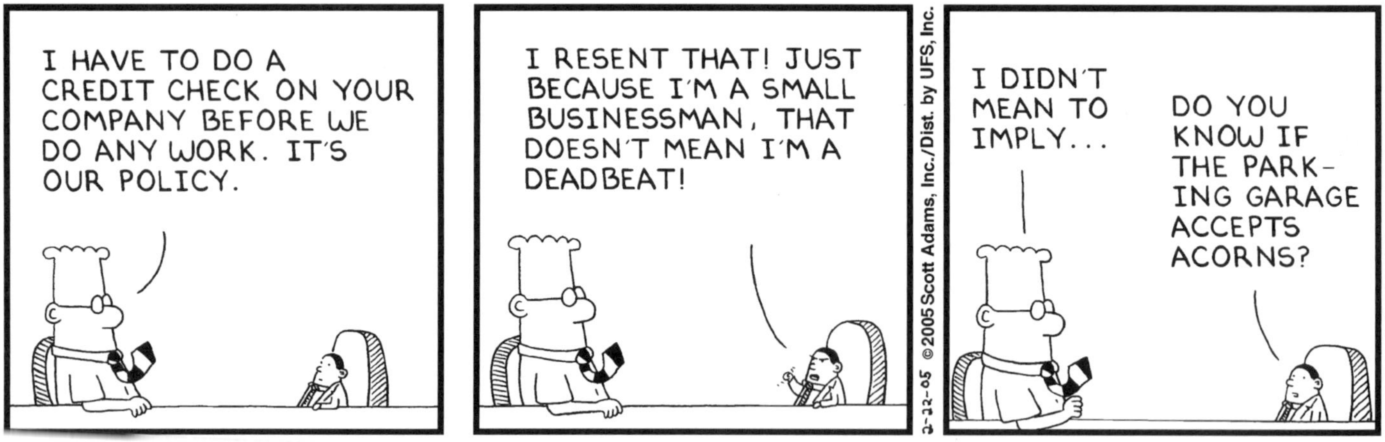
I HAVE TO DO A CREDIT CHECK ON YOUR COMPANY BEFORE WE DO ANY WORK. IT'S OUR POLICY.
I RESENT THAT! JUST BECAUSE I'M A SMALL BUSINESSMAN, THAT DOESN'T MEAN I'M A DEADBEAT!
©2005 Scott Adams, Inc./Dist. by UFS, Inc.
I DIDN'T MEAN TO IMPLY...
DO YOU KNOW IF THE PARK-ING GARAGE ACCEPTS ACORNS?

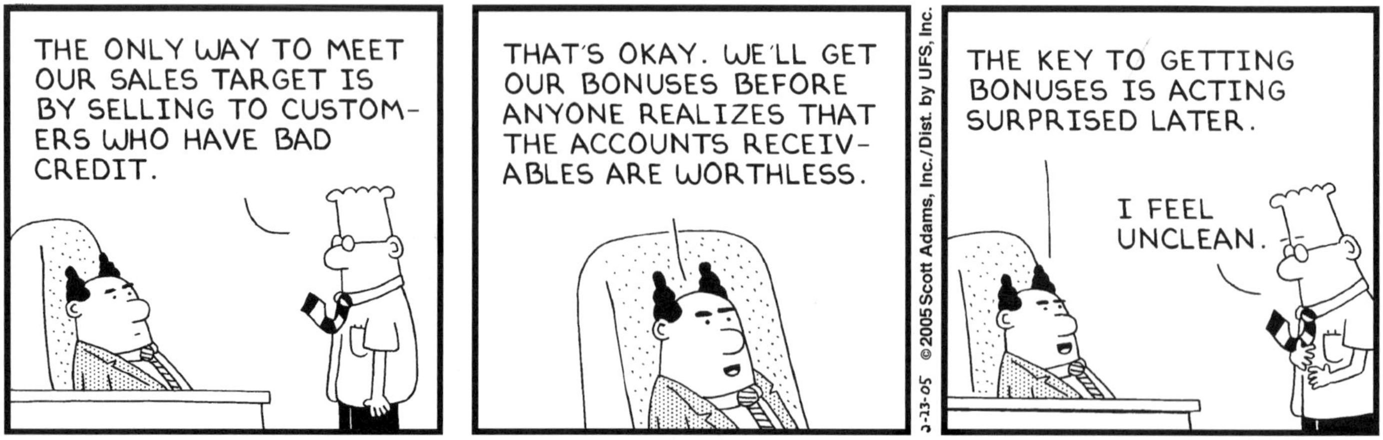
THE ONLY WAY TO MEET OUR SALES TARGET IS BY SELLING TO CUSTOM-ERS WHO HAVE BAD CREDIT.
THAT'S OKAY. WE'LL GET OUR BONUSES BEFORE ANYONE REALIZES THAT THE ACCOUNTS RECEIV-ABLES ARE WORTHLESS.
©2005 Scott Adams, Inc./Dist. by UFS, Inc.
THE KEY TO GETTING BONUSES IS ACTING SURPRISED LATER.
I FEEL UNCLEAN.

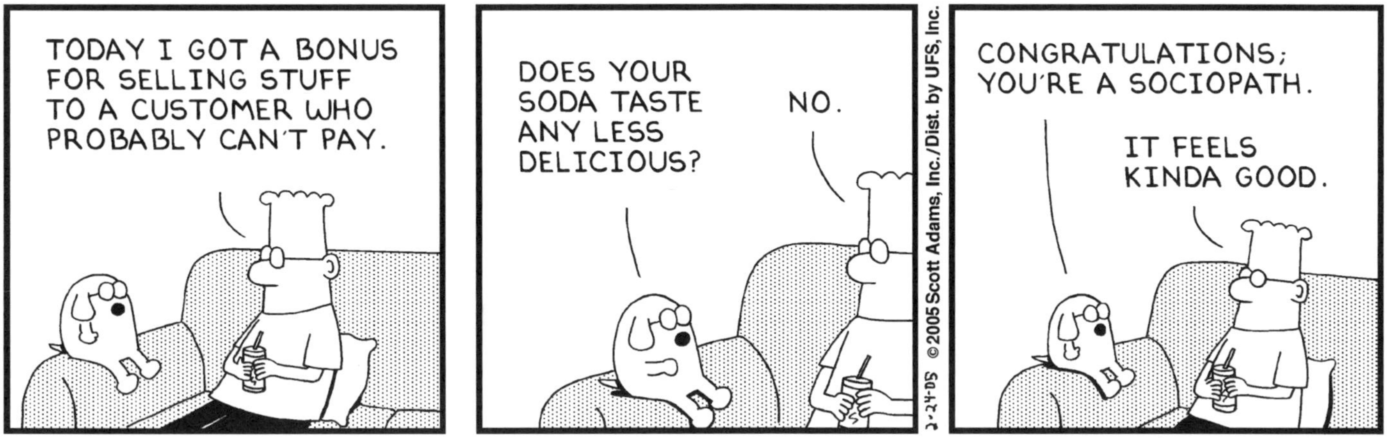
TODAY I GOT A BONUS FOR SELLING STUFF TO A CUSTOMER WHO PROBABLY CAN'T PAY.
DOES YOUR SODA TASTE ANY LESS DELICIOUS?
NO.
2-24-05 © 2005 Scott Adams, Inc./Dist. by UFS, Inc.
CONGRATULATIONS; YOU'RE A SOCIOPATH.
IT FEELS KINDA GOOD.

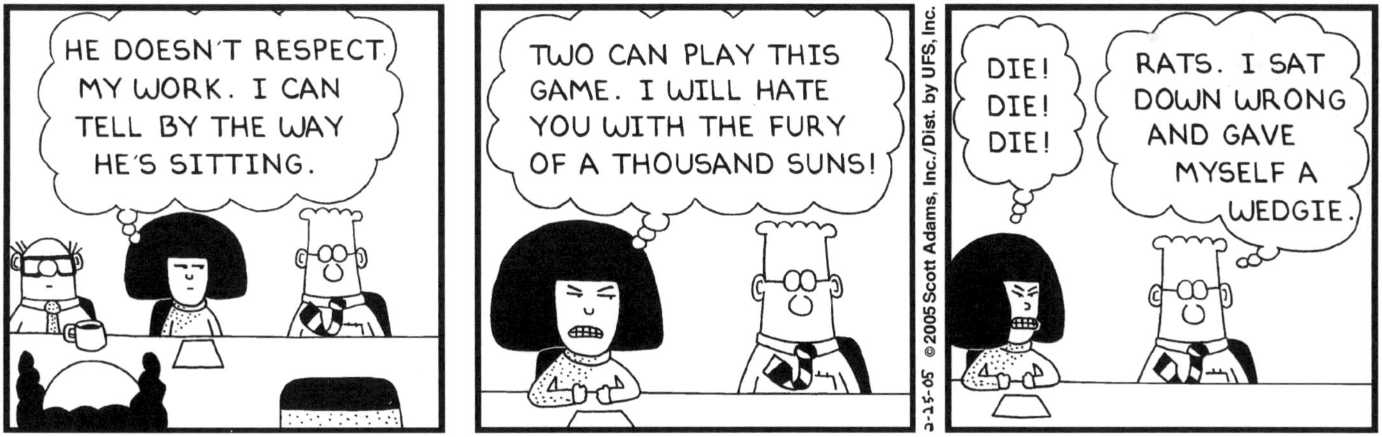
HE DOESN'T RESPECT MY WORK. I CAN TELL BY THE WAY HE'S SITTING.
TWO CAN PLAY THIS GAME. I WILL HATE YOU WITH THE FURY OF A THOUSAND SUNS!
2-25-05 © 2005 Scott Adams, Inc./Dist. by UFS, Inc.
DIE! DIE! DIE!
RATS. I SAT DOWN WRONG AND GAVE MYSELF A WEDGIE.

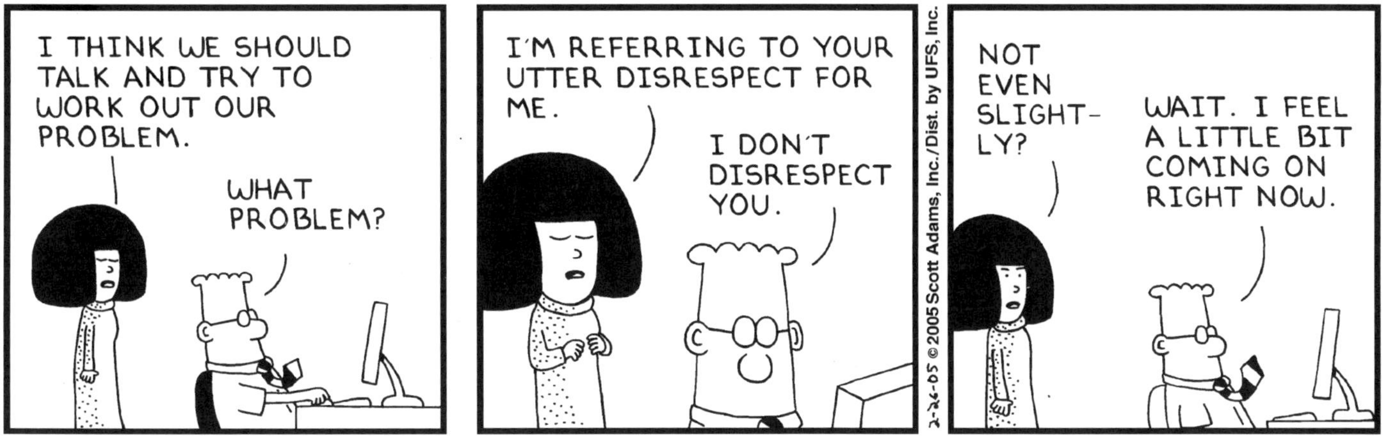
I THINK WE SHOULD TALK AND TRY TO WORK OUT OUR PROBLEM.
WHAT PROBLEM?
I'M REFERRING TO YOUR UTTER DISRESPECT FOR ME.
I DON'T DISRESPECT YOU.
2-26-05 © 2005 Scott Adams, Inc./Dist. by UFS, Inc.
NOT EVEN SLIGHT-LY?
WAIT. I FEEL A LITTLE BIT COMING ON RIGHT NOW.

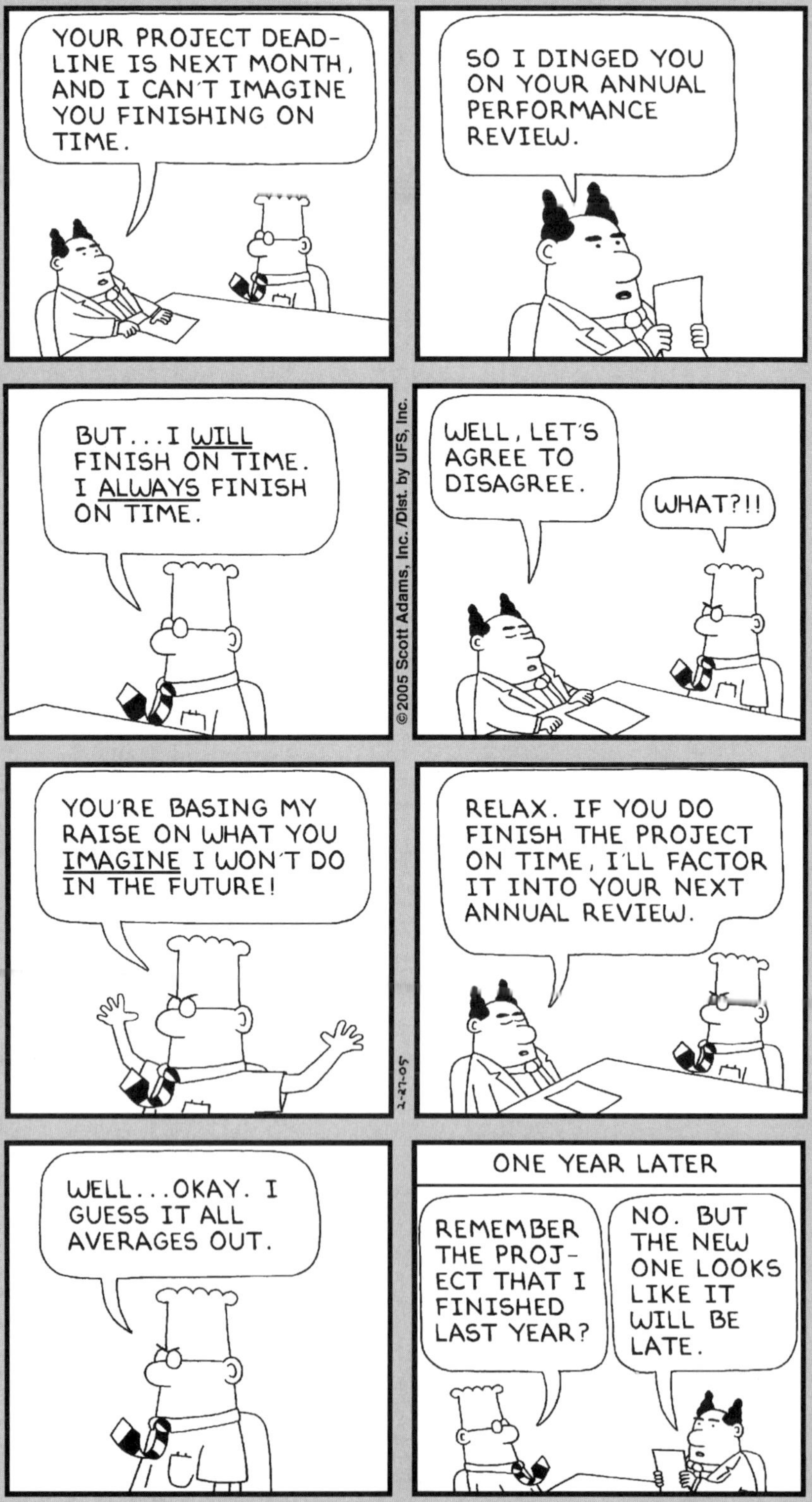
YOUR PROJECT DEAD-LINE IS NEXT MONTH, AND I CAN'T IMAGINE YOU FINISHING ON TIME.
SO I DINGED YOU ON YOUR ANNUAL PERFORMANCE REVIEW.
BUT...I WILL FINISH ON TIME. I ALWAYS FINISH ON TIME.
WELL, LET'S AGREE TO DISAGREE.
WHAT?!!
YOU'RE BASING MY RAISE ON WHAT YOU IMAGINE I WON'T DO IN THE FUTURE!
RELAX. IF YOU DO FINISH THE PROJECT ON TIME, I'LL FACTOR IT INTO YOUR NEXT ANNUAL REVIEW.
WELL...OKAY. I GUESS IT ALL AVERAGES OUT.
ONE YEAR LATER
REMEMBER THE PROJ-ECT THAT I FINISHED LAST YEAR?
NO. BUT THE NEW ONE LOOKS LIKE IT WILL BE LATE.
2-27-05

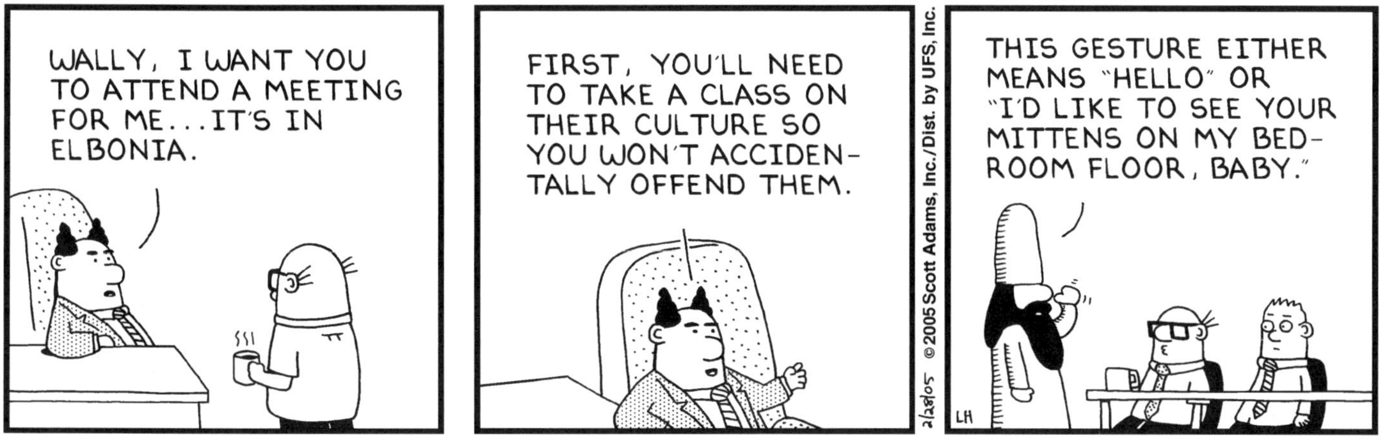
WALLY, I WANT YOU TO ATTEND A MEETING FOR ME...IT'S IN ELBONIA.
FIRST, YOU'LL NEED TO TAKE A CLASS ON THEIR CULTURE SO YOU WON'T ACCIDENTALLY OFFEND THEM.
2/28/05 © 2005 Scott Adams, Inc./Dist. by UFS, Inc.
THIS GESTURE EITHER MEANS "HELLO" OR "I'D LIKE TO SEE YOUR MITTENS ON MY BEDROOM FLOOR, BABY."

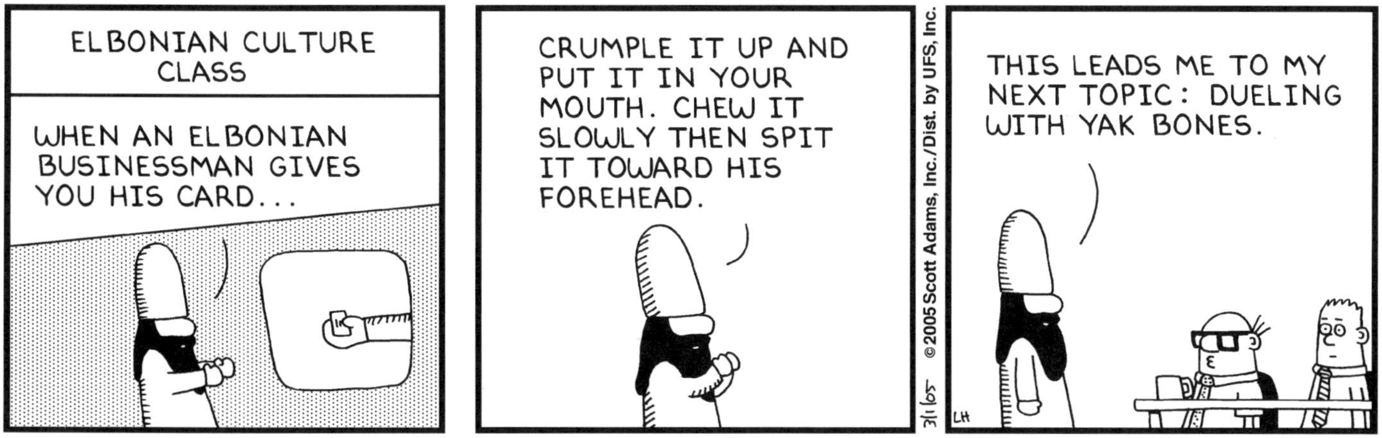
ELBONIAN CULTURE CLASS
WHEN AN ELBONIAN BUSINESSMAN GIVES YOU HIS CARD...
CRUMPLE IT UP AND PUT IT IN YOUR MOUTH. CHEW IT SLOWLY THEN SPIT IT TOWARD HIS FOREHEAD.
3/1/05 © 2005 Scott Adams, Inc./Dist. by UFS, Inc.
THIS LEADS ME TO MY NEXT TOPIC: DUELING WITH YAK BONES.

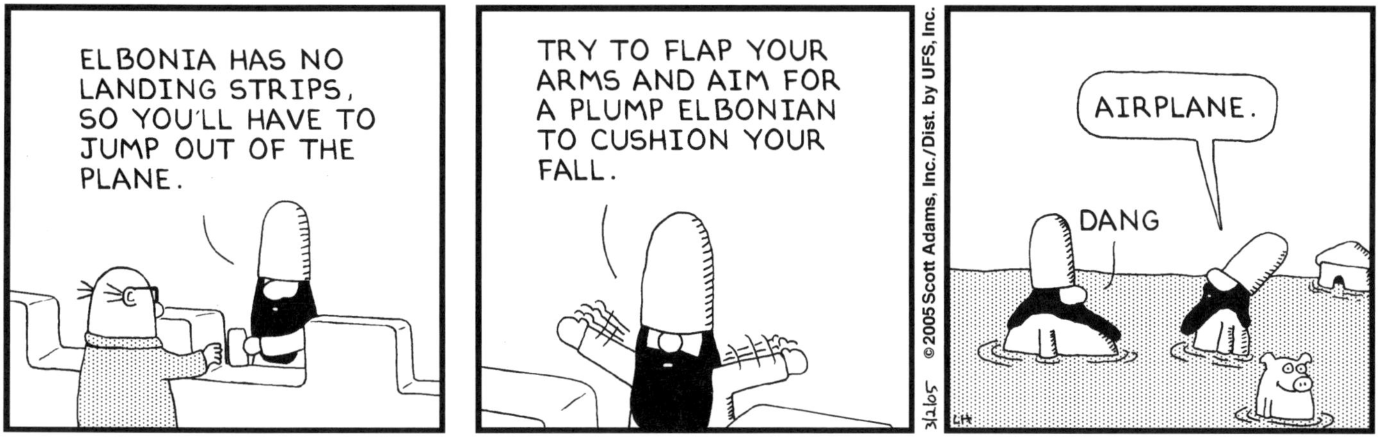
ELBONIA HAS NO LANDING STRIPS, SO YOU'LL HAVE TO JUMP OUT OF THE PLANE.
TRY TO FLAP YOUR ARMS AND AIM FOR A PLUMP ELBONIAN TO CUSHION YOUR FALL.
3/2/05 © 2005 Scott Adams, Inc./Dist. by UFS, Inc.
AIRPLANE.
DANG

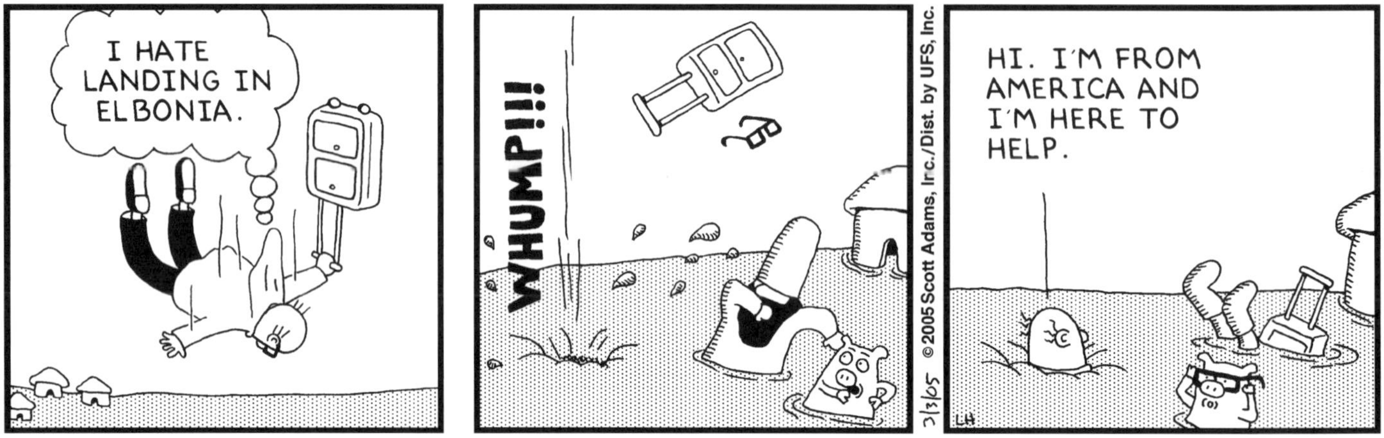
I HATE LANDING IN ELBONIA.
WHUMP!!!
3/3/05 © 2005 Scott Adams, Inc./Dist. by UFS, Inc.
HI. I'M FROM AMERICA AND I'M HERE TO HELP.

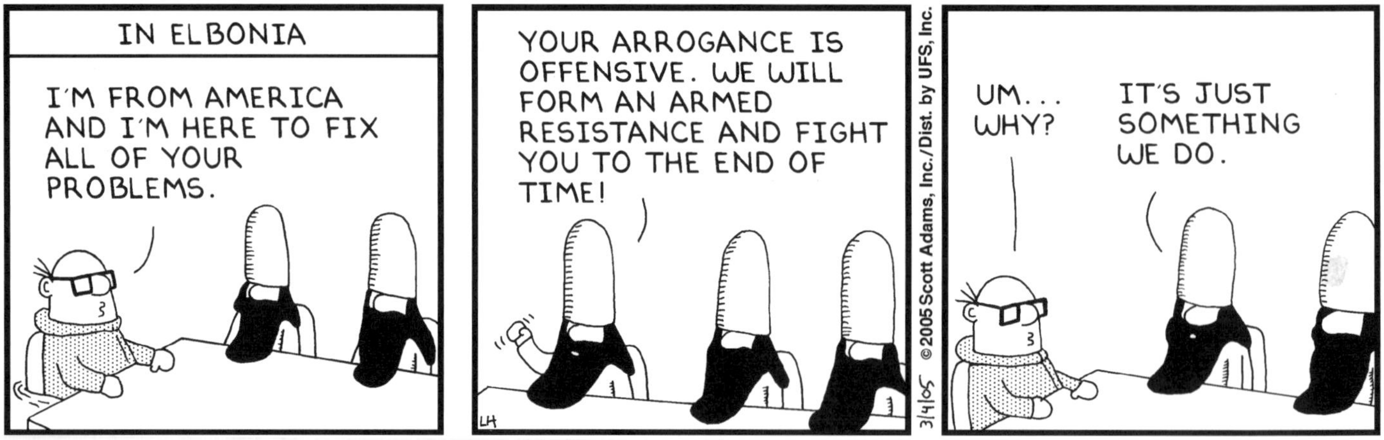
IN ELBONIA
I'M FROM AMERICA AND I'M HERE TO FIX ALL OF YOUR PROBLEMS.
YOUR ARROGANCE IS OFFENSIVE. WE WILL FORM AN ARMED RESISTANCE AND FIGHT YOU TO THE END OF TIME!
3/4/05 © 2005 Scott Adams, Inc./Dist. by UFS, Inc.
UM... WHY?
IT'S JUST SOMETHING WE DO.

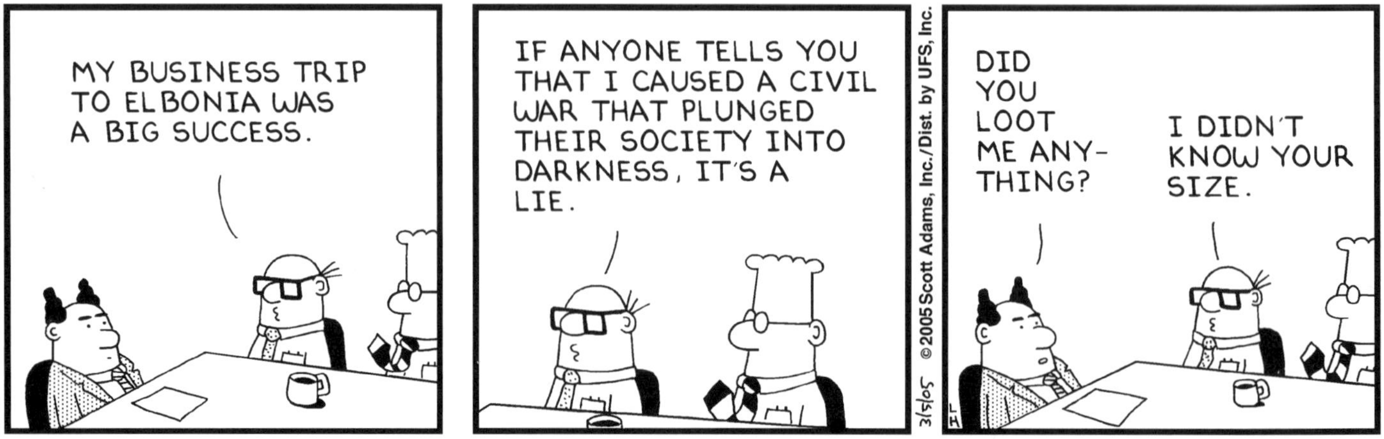
MY BUSINESS TRIP TO ELBONIA WAS A BIG SUCCESS.
IF ANYONE TELLS YOU THAT I CAUSED A CIVIL WAR THAT PLUNGED THEIR SOCIETY INTO DARKNESS, IT'S A LIE.
3/5/05 © 2005 Scott Adams, Inc./Dist. by UFS, Inc.
DID YOU LOOT ME ANY-THING?
I DIDN'T KNOW YOUR SIZE.

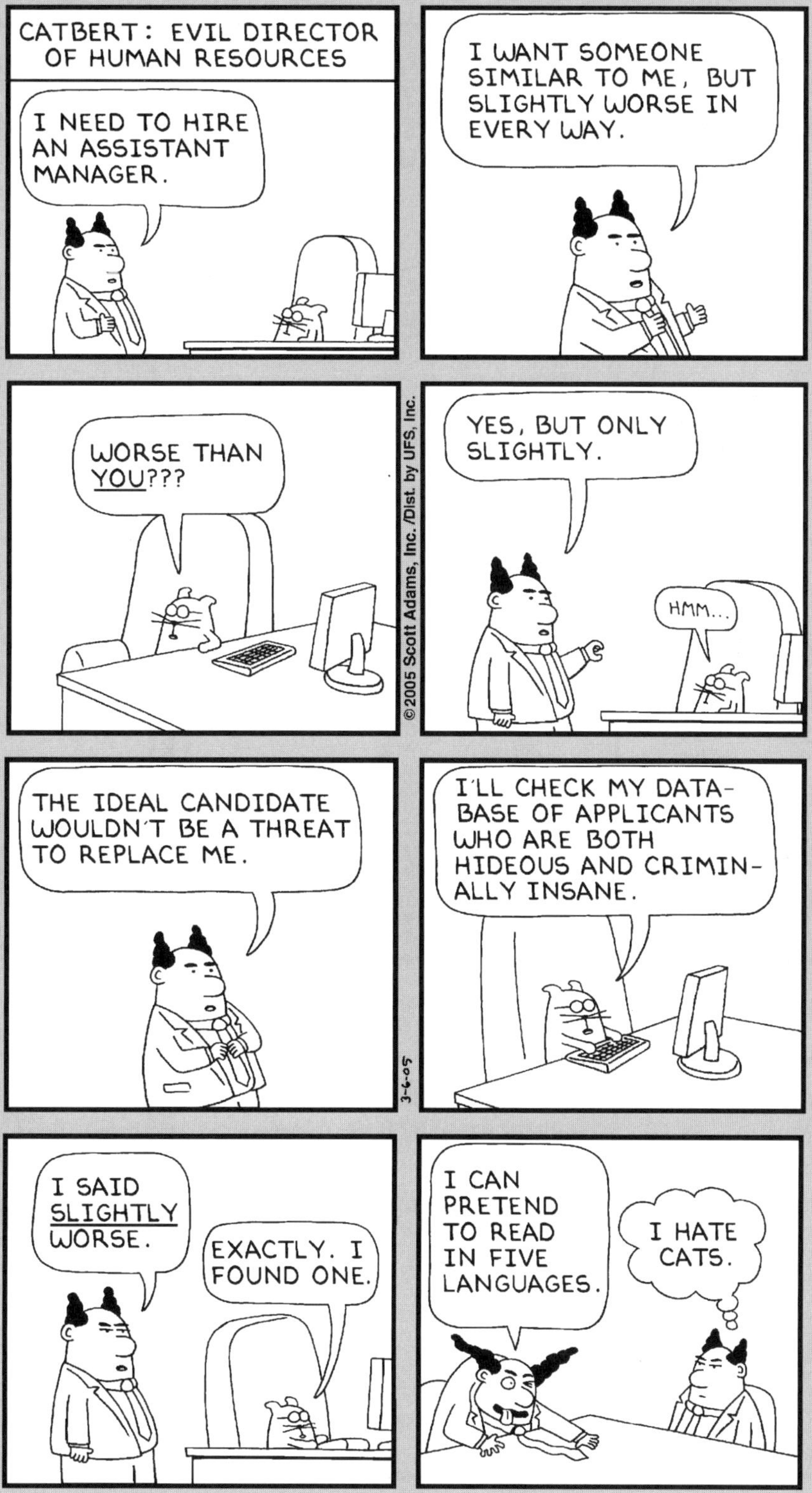
CATBERT: EVIL DIRECTOR OF HUMAN RESOURCES
I NEED TO HIRE AN ASSISTANT MANAGER.
I WANT SOMEONE SIMILAR TO ME, BUT SLIGHTLY WORSE IN EVERY WAY.
WORSE THAN YOU???
YES, BUT ONLY SLIGHTLY.
HMM...
©2005 Scott Adams, Inc. /Dist. by UFS, Inc.
THE IDEAL CANDIDATE WOULDN'T BE A THREAT TO REPLACE ME.
I'LL CHECK MY DATA-BASE OF APPLICANTS WHO ARE BOTH HIDEOUS AND CRIMIN-ALLY INSANE.
3-6-05
I SAID SLIGHTLY WORSE.
EXACTLY. I FOUND ONE.
I CAN PRETEND TO READ IN FIVE LANGUAGES.
I HATE CATS.

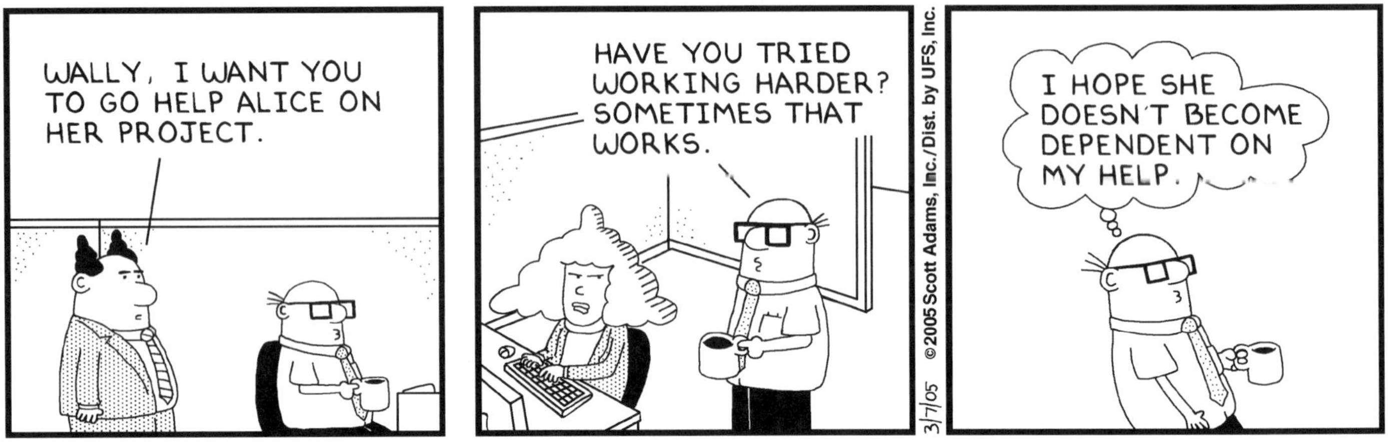
WALLY, I WANT YOU TO GO HELP ALICE ON HER PROJECT.
HAVE YOU TRIED WORKING HARDER? SOMETIMES THAT WORKS.
I HOPE SHE DOESN'T BECOME DEPENDENT ON MY HELP.
©2005 Scott Adams, Inc./Dist. by UFS, Inc.
3/7/05

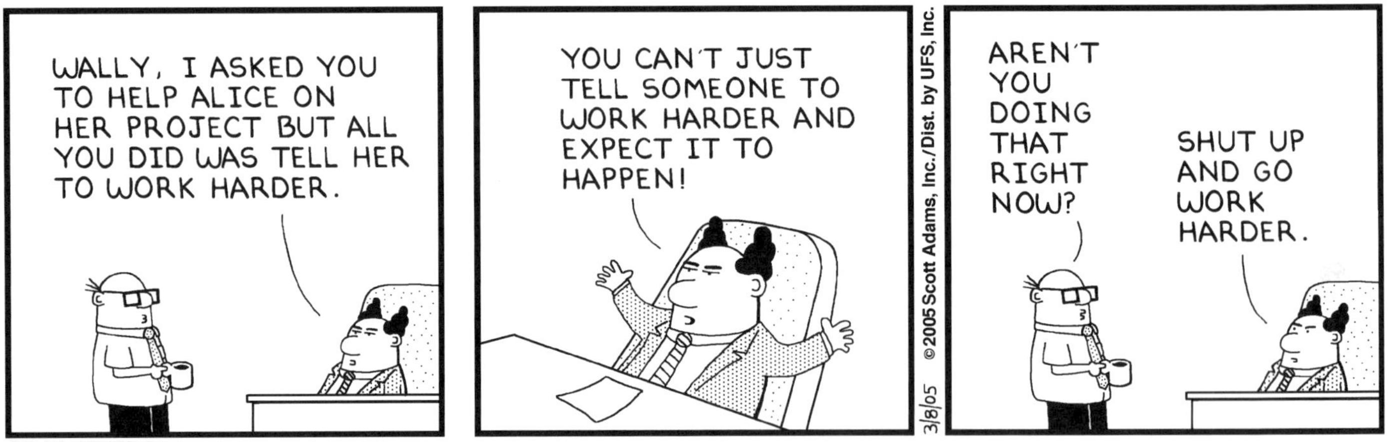
WALLY, I ASKED YOU TO HELP ALICE ON HER PROJECT BUT ALL YOU DID WAS TELL HER TO WORK HARDER.
YOU CAN'T JUST TELL SOMEONE TO WORK HARDER AND EXPECT IT TO HAPPEN!
AREN'T YOU DOING THAT RIGHT NOW?
SHUT UP AND GO WORK HARDER.
©2005 Scott Adams, Inc./Dist. by UFS, Inc.
3/8/05

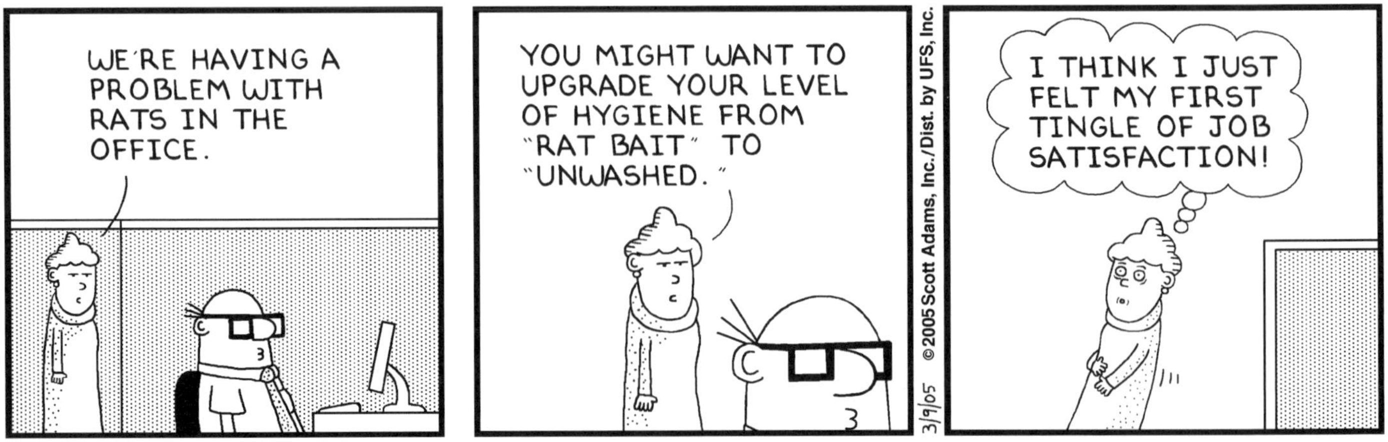
WE'RE HAVING A PROBLEM WITH RATS IN THE OFFICE.
YOU MIGHT WANT TO UPGRADE YOUR LEVEL OF HYGIENE FROM "RAT BAIT" TO "UNWASHED."
I THINK I JUST FELT MY FIRST TINGLE OF JOB SATISFACTION!
©2005 Scott Adams, Inc./Dist. by UFS, Inc.
3/9/05

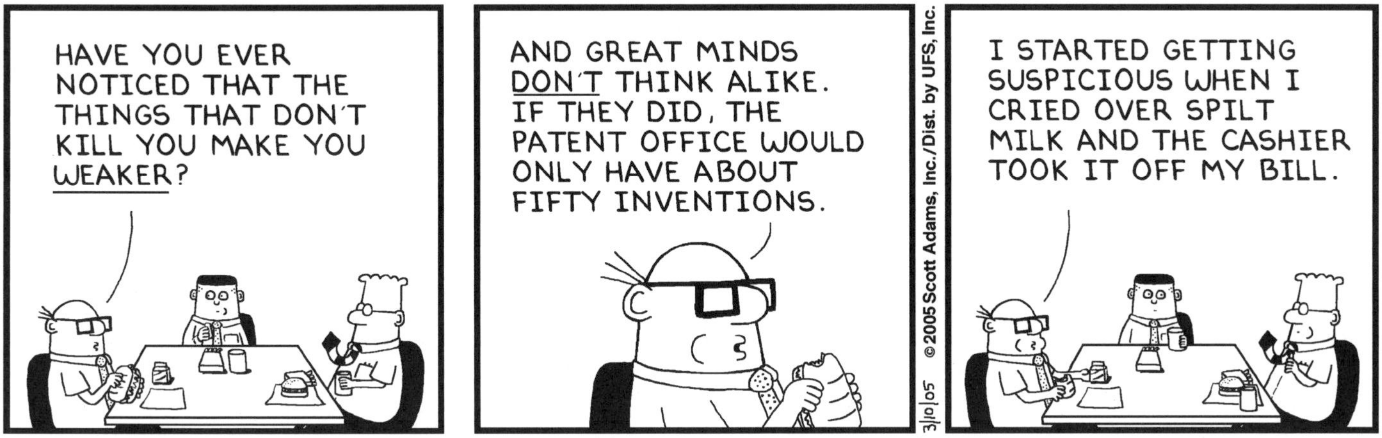
HAVE YOU EVER NOTICED THAT THE THINGS THAT DON'T KILL YOU MAKE YOU WEAKER?
AND GREAT MINDS DON'T THINK ALIKE. IF THEY DID, THE PATENT OFFICE WOULD ONLY HAVE ABOUT FIFTY INVENTIONS.
3/10/05 ©2005 Scott Adams, Inc./Dist. by UFS, Inc.
I STARTED GETTING SUSPICIOUS WHEN I CRIED OVER SPILT MILK AND THE CASHIER TOOK IT OFF MY BILL.

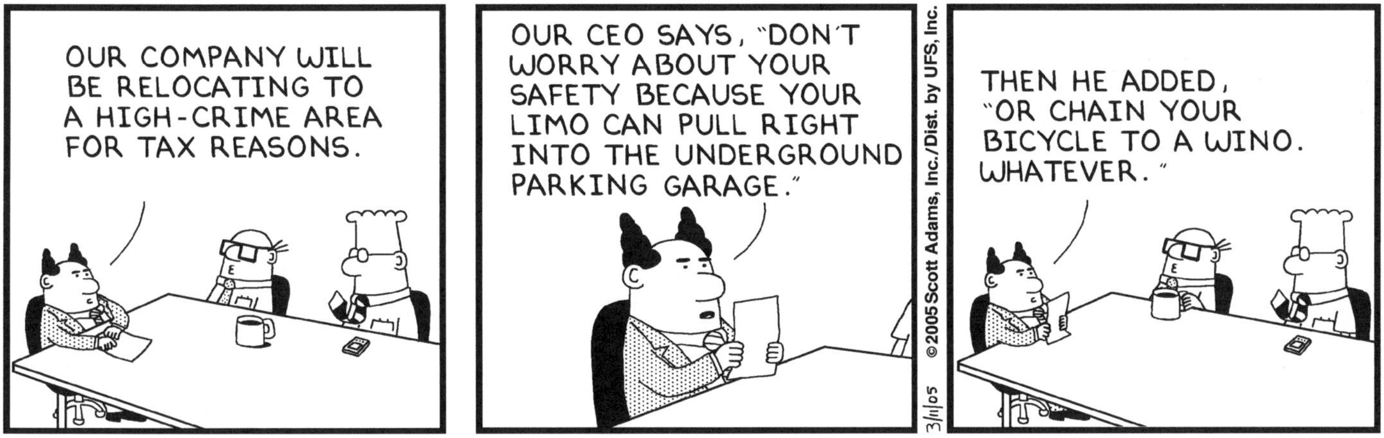
OUR COMPANY WILL BE RELOCATING TO A HIGH-CRIME AREA FOR TAX REASONS.
OUR CEO SAYS, "DON'T WORRY ABOUT YOUR SAFETY BECAUSE YOUR LIMO CAN PULL RIGHT INTO THE UNDERGROUND PARKING GARAGE."
3/11/05 ©2005 Scott Adams, Inc./Dist. by UFS, Inc.
THEN HE ADDED, "OR CHAIN YOUR BICYCLE TO A WINO. WHATEVER."

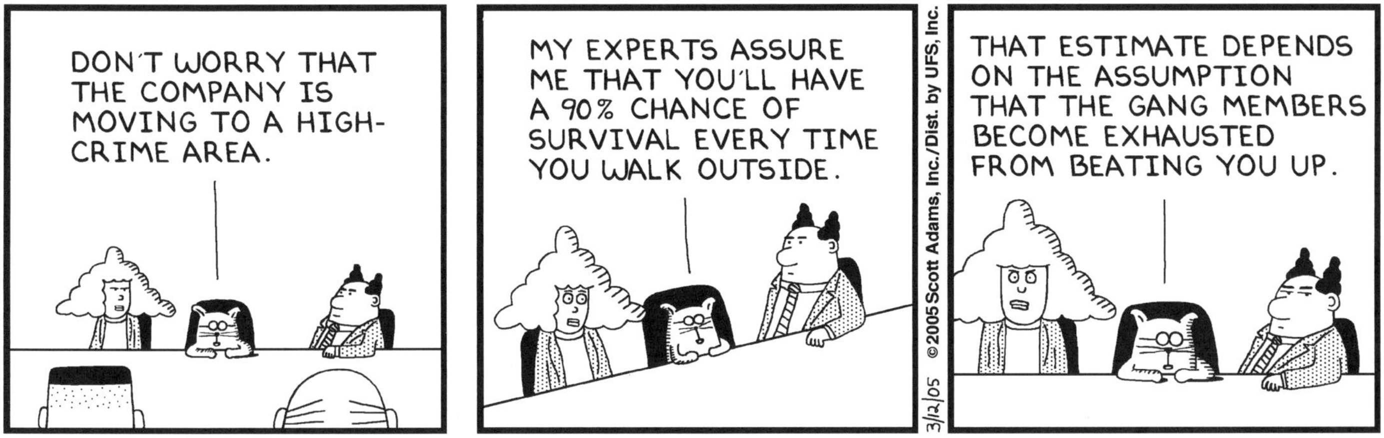
DON'T WORRY THAT THE COMPANY IS MOVING TO A HIGH-CRIME AREA.
MY EXPERTS ASSURE ME THAT YOU'LL HAVE A 90% CHANCE OF SURVIVAL EVERY TIME YOU WALK OUTSIDE.
3/12/05 ©2005 Scott Adams, Inc./Dist. by UFS, Inc.
THAT ESTIMATE DEPENDS ON THE ASSUMPTION THAT THE GANG MEMBERS BECOME EXHAUSTED FROM BEATING YOU UP.

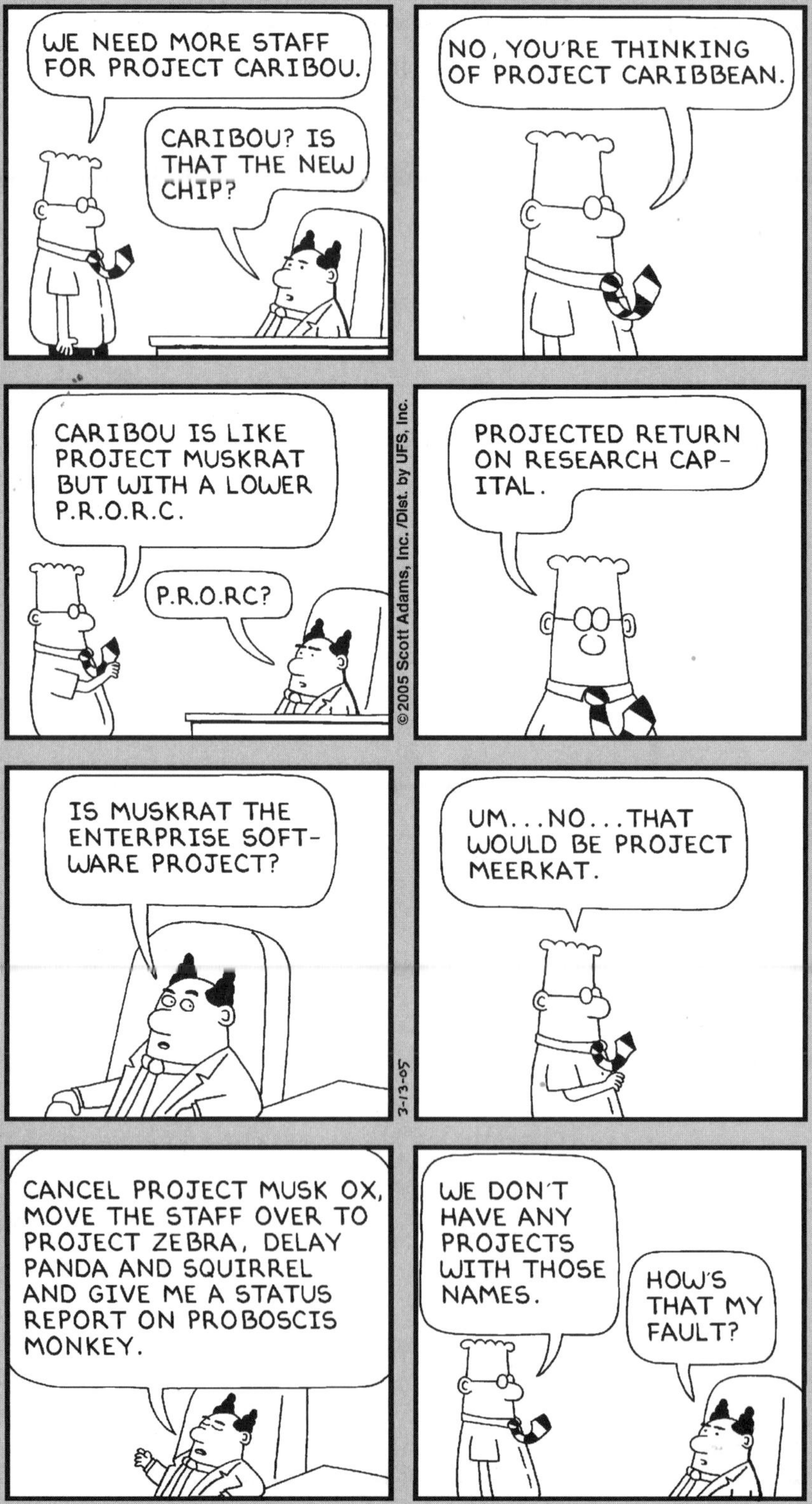
WE NEED MORE STAFF FOR PROJECT CARIBOU.
CARIBOU? IS THAT THE NEW CHIP?
NO, YOU'RE THINKING OF PROJECT CARIBBEAN.
CARIBOU IS LIKE PROJECT MUSKRAT BUT WITH A LOWER P.R.O.R.C.
P.R.O.RC?
PROJECTED RETURN ON RESEARCH CAP-ITAL.
©2005 Scott Adams, Inc./Dist. by UFS, Inc.
IS MUSKRAT THE ENTERPRISE SOFT-WARE PROJECT?
UM...NO...THAT WOULD BE PROJECT MEERKAT.
3-13-05
CANCEL PROJECT MUSK OX, MOVE THE STAFF OVER TO PROJECT ZEBRA, DELAY PANDA AND SQUIRREL AND GIVE ME A STATUS REPORT ON PROBOSCIS MONKEY.
WE DON'T HAVE ANY PROJECTS WITH THOSE NAMES.
HOW'S THAT MY FAULT?

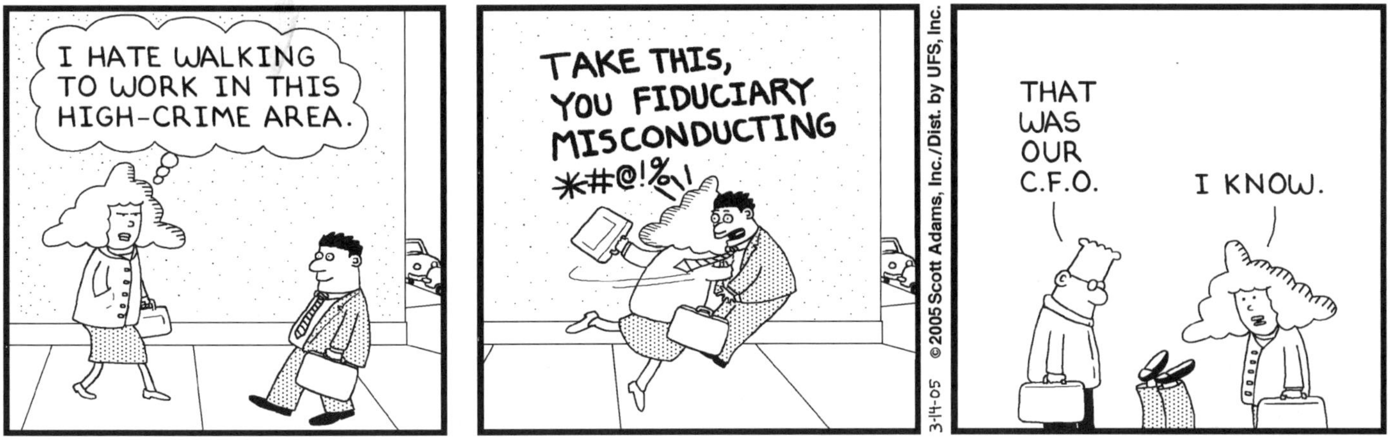
I HATE WALKING TO WORK IN THIS HIGH-CRIME AREA.
TAKE THIS, YOU FIDUCIARY MISCONDUCTING *#@!%
3-14-05 ©2005 Scott Adams, Inc./Dist. by UFS, Inc.
THAT WAS OUR C.F.O.
I KNOW.

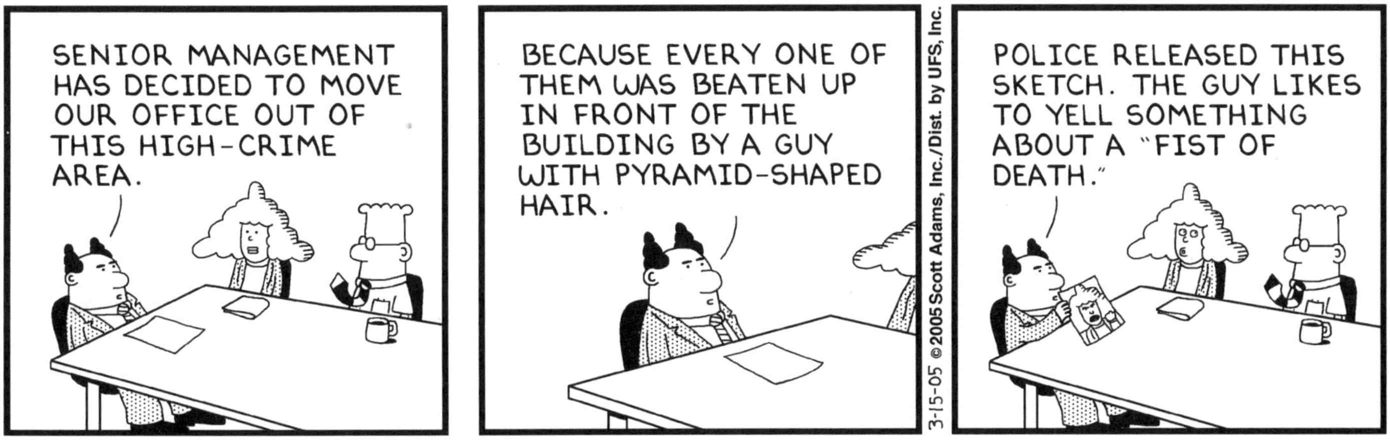
SENIOR MANAGEMENT HAS DECIDED TO MOVE OUR OFFICE OUT OF THIS HIGH-CRIME AREA.
BECAUSE EVERY ONE OF THEM WAS BEATEN UP IN FRONT OF THE BUILDING BY A GUY WITH PYRAMID-SHAPED HAIR.
3-15-05 ©2005 Scott Adams, Inc./Dist. by UFS, Inc.
POLICE RELEASED THIS SKETCH. THE GUY LIKES TO YELL SOMETHING ABOUT A "FIST OF DEATH."

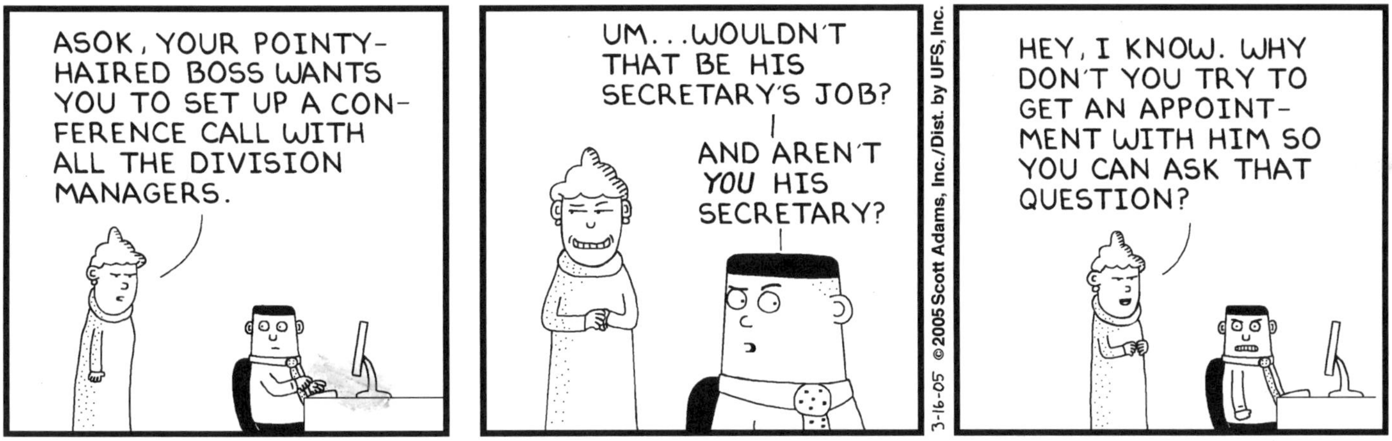
ASOK, YOUR POINTY-HAIRED BOSS WANTS YOU TO SET UP A CONFERENCE CALL WITH ALL THE DIVISION MANAGERS.
UM...WOULDN'T THAT BE HIS SECRETARY'S JOB?
AND AREN'T *YOU* HIS SECRETARY?
3-16-05 ©2005 Scott Adams, Inc./Dist. by UFS, Inc.
HEY, I KNOW. WHY DON'T YOU TRY TO GET AN APPOINTMENT WITH HIM SO YOU CAN ASK THAT QUESTION?

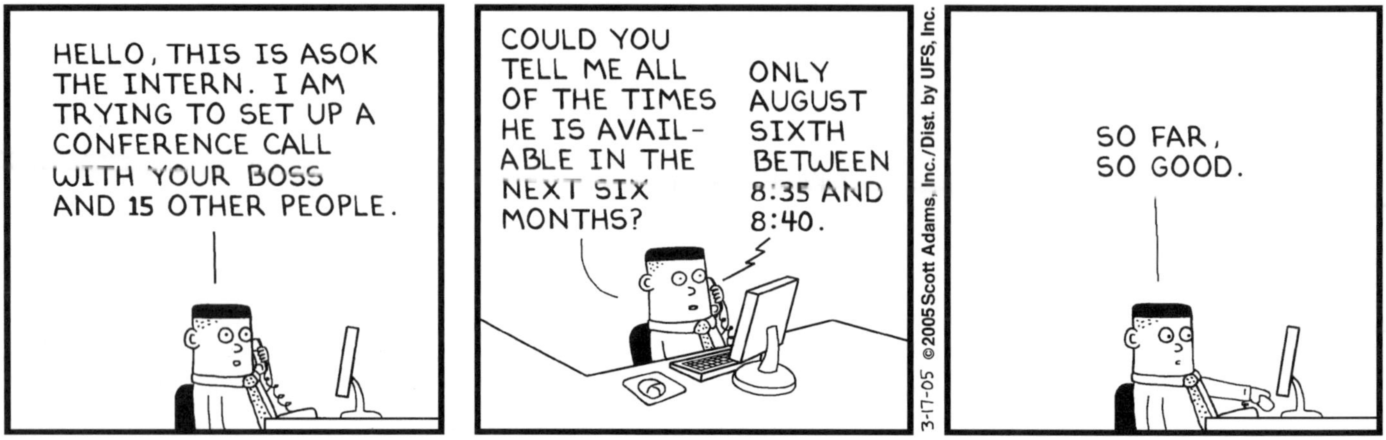
HELLO, THIS IS ASOK THE INTERN. I AM TRYING TO SET UP A CONFERENCE CALL WITH YOUR BOSS AND 15 OTHER PEOPLE.
COULD YOU TELL ME ALL OF THE TIMES HE IS AVAIL-ABLE IN THE NEXT SIX MONTHS?
ONLY AUGUST SIXTH BETWEEN 8:35 AND 8:40.
3-17-05 ©2005 Scott Adams, Inc./Dist. by UFS, Inc.
SO FAR, SO GOOD.

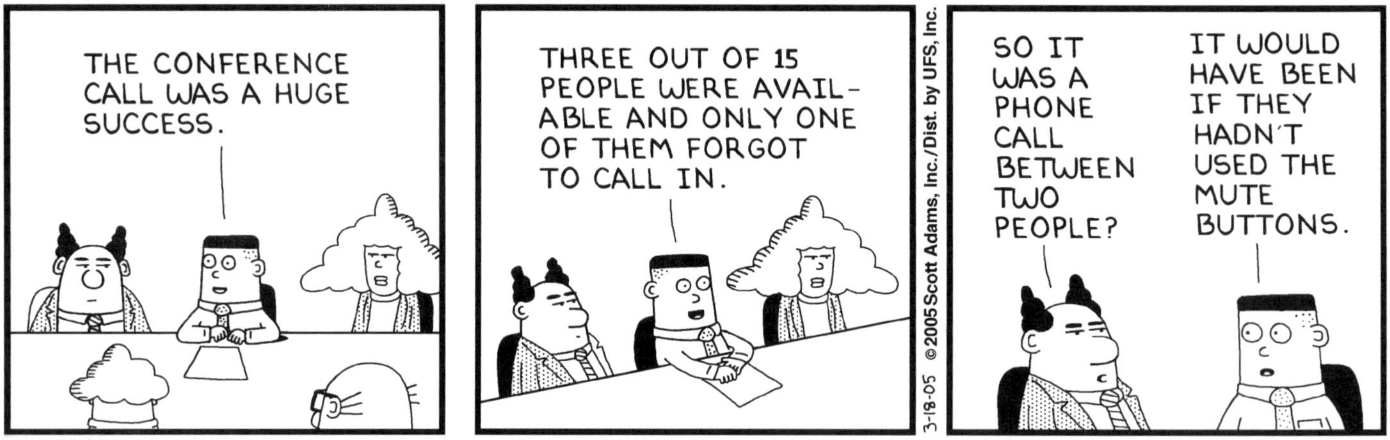
THE CONFERENCE CALL WAS A HUGE SUCCESS.
THREE OUT OF 15 PEOPLE WERE AVAIL-ABLE AND ONLY ONE OF THEM FORGOT TO CALL IN.
3-18-05 ©2005 Scott Adams, Inc./Dist. by UFS, Inc.
SO IT WAS A PHONE CALL BETWEEN TWO PEOPLE?
IT WOULD HAVE BEEN IF THEY HADN'T USED THE MUTE BUTTONS.

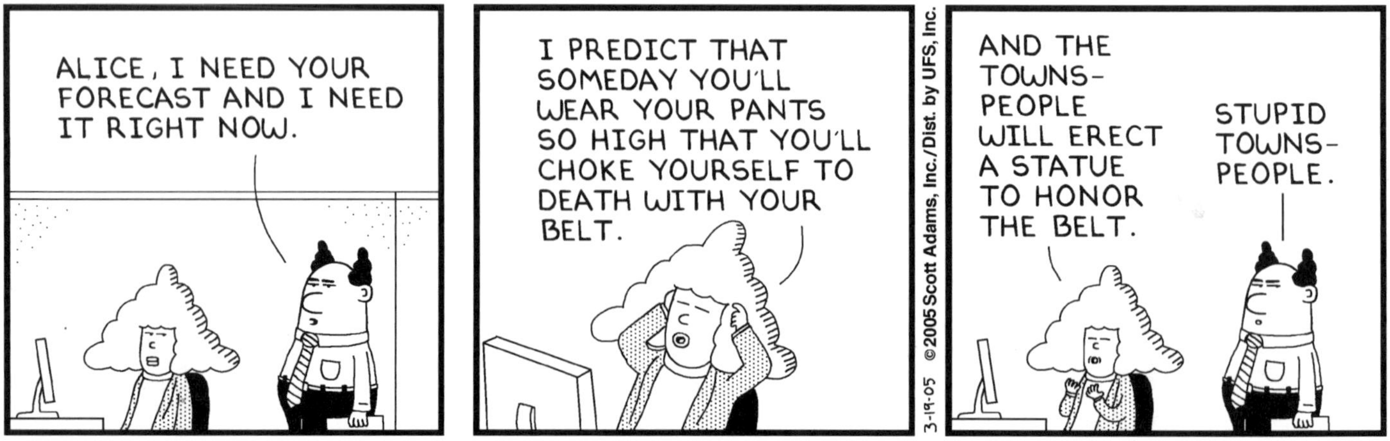
ALICE, I NEED YOUR FORECAST AND I NEED IT RIGHT NOW.
I PREDICT THAT SOMEDAY YOU'LL WEAR YOUR PANTS SO HIGH THAT YOU'LL CHOKE YOURSELF TO DEATH WITH YOUR BELT.
3-19-05 ©2005 Scott Adams, Inc./Dist. by UFS, Inc.
AND THE TOWNS-PEOPLE WILL ERECT A STATUE TO HONOR THE BELT.
STUPID TOWNS-PEOPLE.

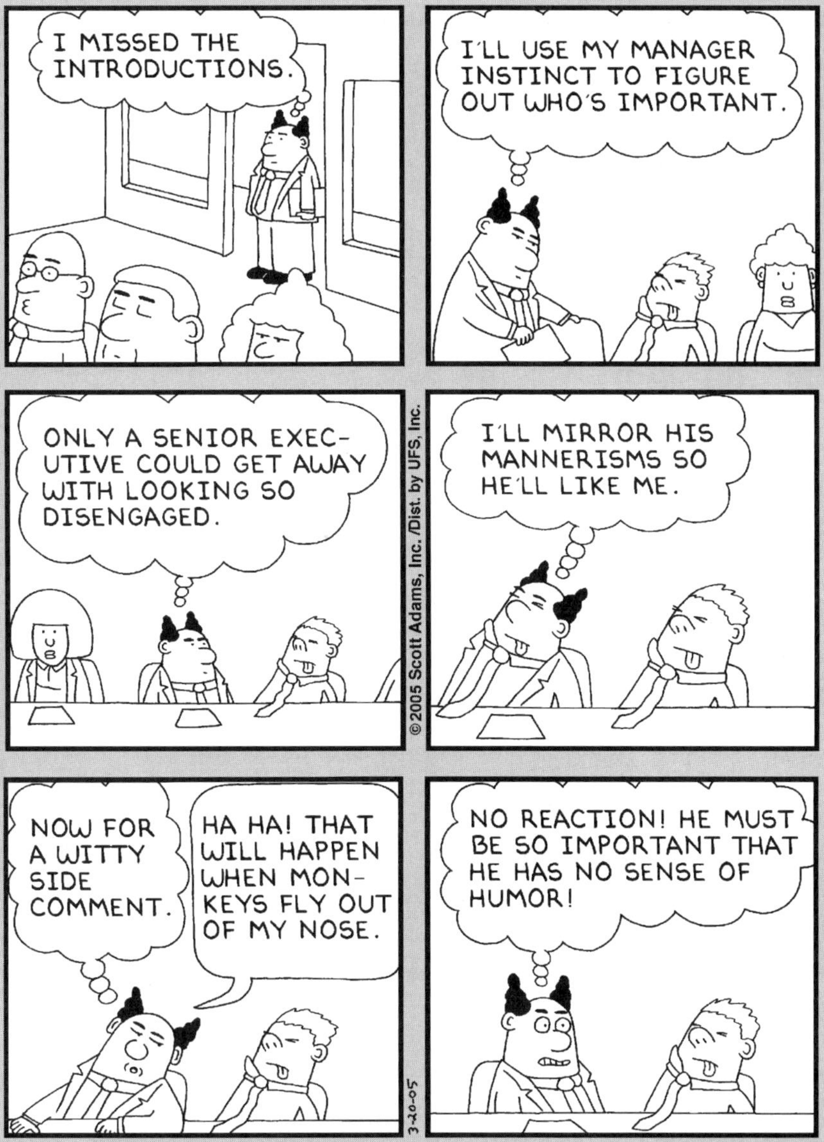

I MISSED THE INTRODUCTIONS.
I'LL USE MY MANAGER INSTINCT TO FIGURE OUT WHO'S IMPORTANT.
ONLY A SENIOR EXECUTIVE COULD GET AWAY WITH LOOKING SO DISENGAGED.
I'LL MIRROR HIS MANNERISMS SO HE'LL LIKE ME.
NOW FOR A WITTY SIDE COMMENT.
HA HA! THAT WILL HAPPEN WHEN MONKEYS FLY OUT OF MY NOSE.
NO REACTION! HE MUST BE SO IMPORTANT THAT HE HAS NO SENSE OF HUMOR!
©2005 Scott Adams, Inc./Dist. by UFS, Inc.
3-20-05

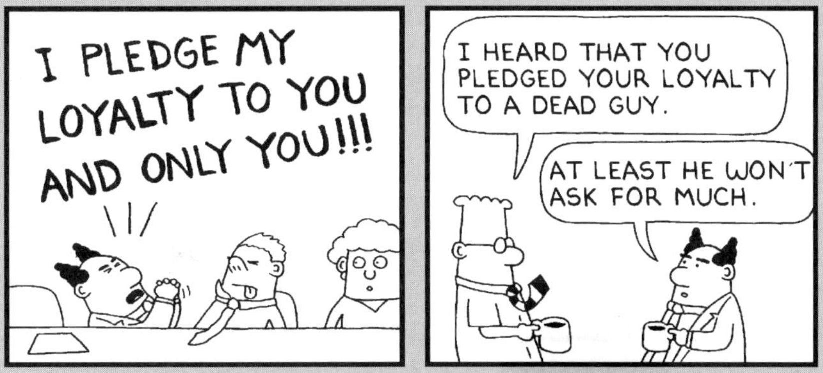

I PLEDGE MY LOYALTY TO YOU AND ONLY YOU!!!
I HEARD THAT YOU PLEDGED YOUR LOYALTY TO A DEAD GUY.
AT LEAST HE WON'T ASK FOR MUCH.

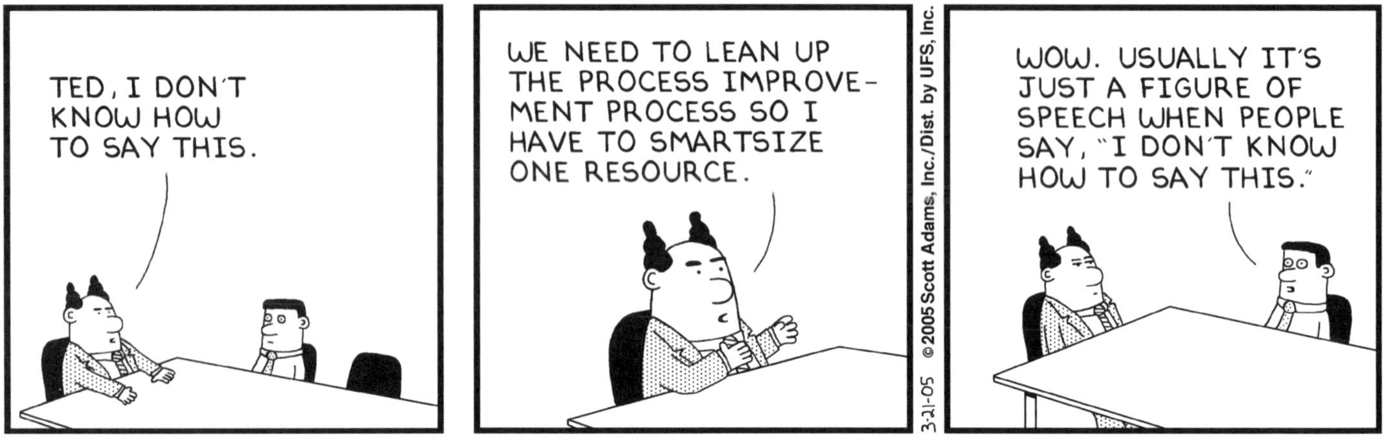
TED, I DON'T KNOW HOW TO SAY THIS.
WE NEED TO LEAN UP THE PROCESS IMPROVEMENT PROCESS SO I HAVE TO SMARTSIZE ONE RESOURCE.
3-21-05 ©2005 Scott Adams, Inc./Dist. by UFS, Inc.
WOW. USUALLY IT'S JUST A FIGURE OF SPEECH WHEN PEOPLE SAY, "I DON'T KNOW HOW TO SAY THIS."

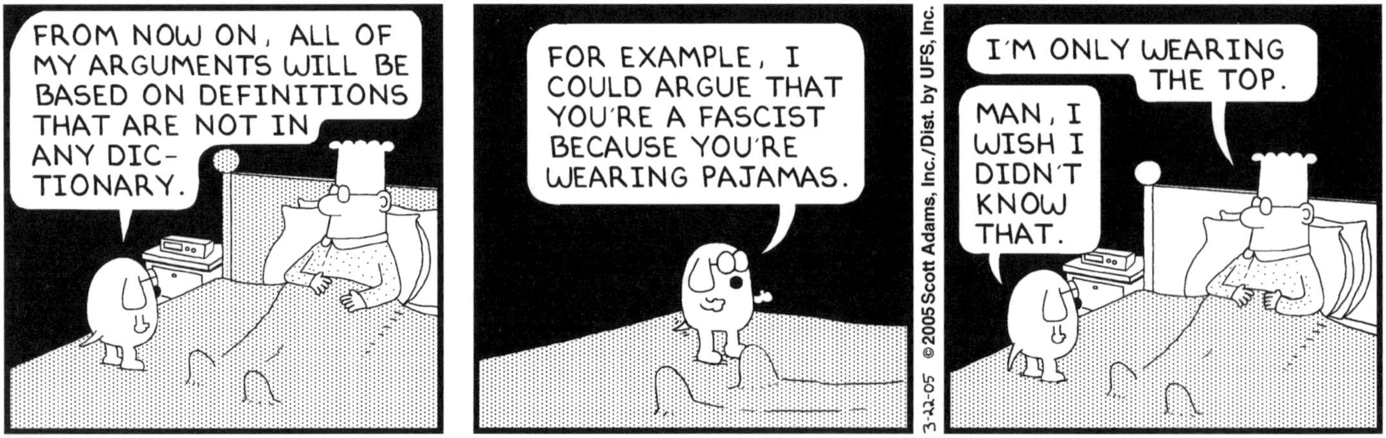
FROM NOW ON, ALL OF MY ARGUMENTS WILL BE BASED ON DEFINITIONS THAT ARE NOT IN ANY DICTIONARY.
FOR EXAMPLE, I COULD ARGUE THAT YOU'RE A FASCIST BECAUSE YOU'RE WEARING PAJAMAS.
3-22-05 ©2005 Scott Adams, Inc./Dist. by UFS, Inc.
I'M ONLY WEARING THE TOP.
MAN, I WISH I DIDN'T KNOW THAT.

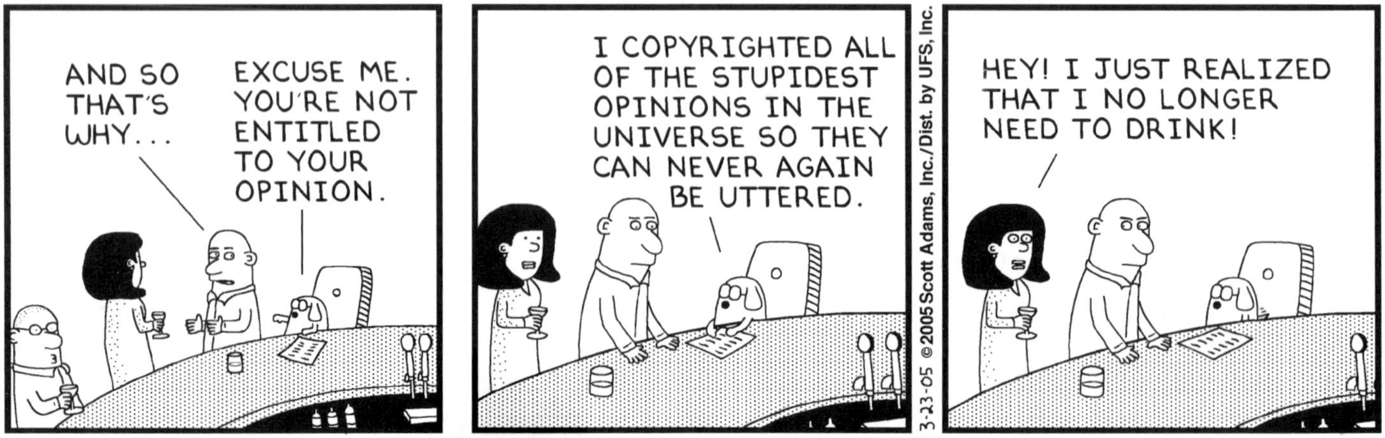
AND SO THAT'S WHY...
EXCUSE ME. YOU'RE NOT ENTITLED TO YOUR OPINION.
I COPYRIGHTED ALL OF THE STUPIDEST OPINIONS IN THE UNIVERSE SO THEY CAN NEVER AGAIN BE UTTERED.
3-23-05 ©2005 Scott Adams, Inc./Dist. by UFS, Inc.
HEY! I JUST REALIZED THAT I NO LONGER NEED TO DRINK!

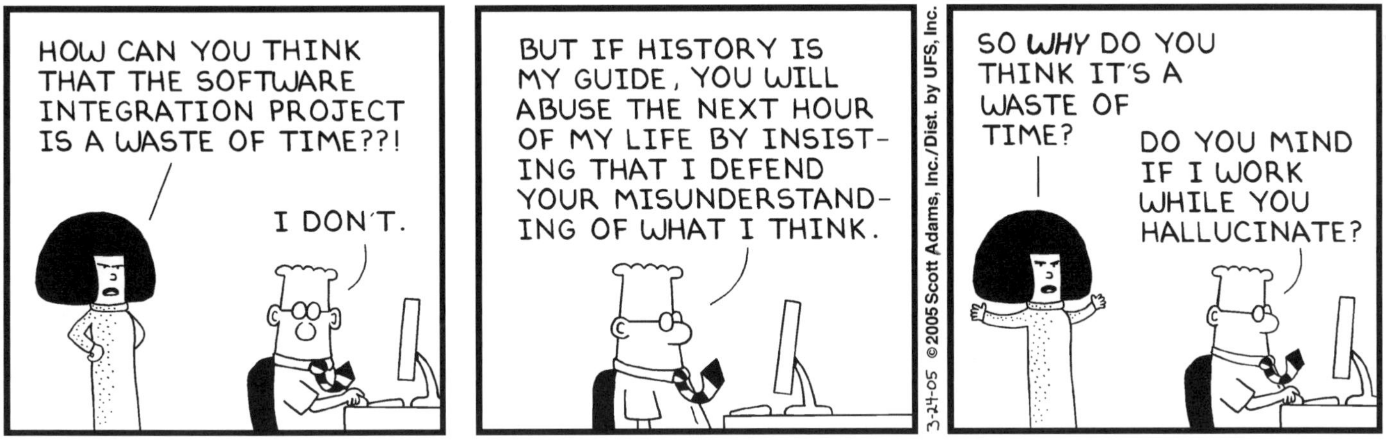
HOW CAN YOU THINK THAT THE SOFTWARE INTEGRATION PROJECT IS A WASTE OF TIME??!
I DON'T.
BUT IF HISTORY IS MY GUIDE, YOU WILL ABUSE THE NEXT HOUR OF MY LIFE BY INSISTING THAT I DEFEND YOUR MISUNDERSTANDING OF WHAT I THINK.
3-24-05 ©2005 Scott Adams, Inc./Dist. by UFS, Inc.
SO **WHY** DO YOU THINK IT'S A WASTE OF TIME?
DO YOU MIND IF I WORK WHILE YOU HALLUCINATE?

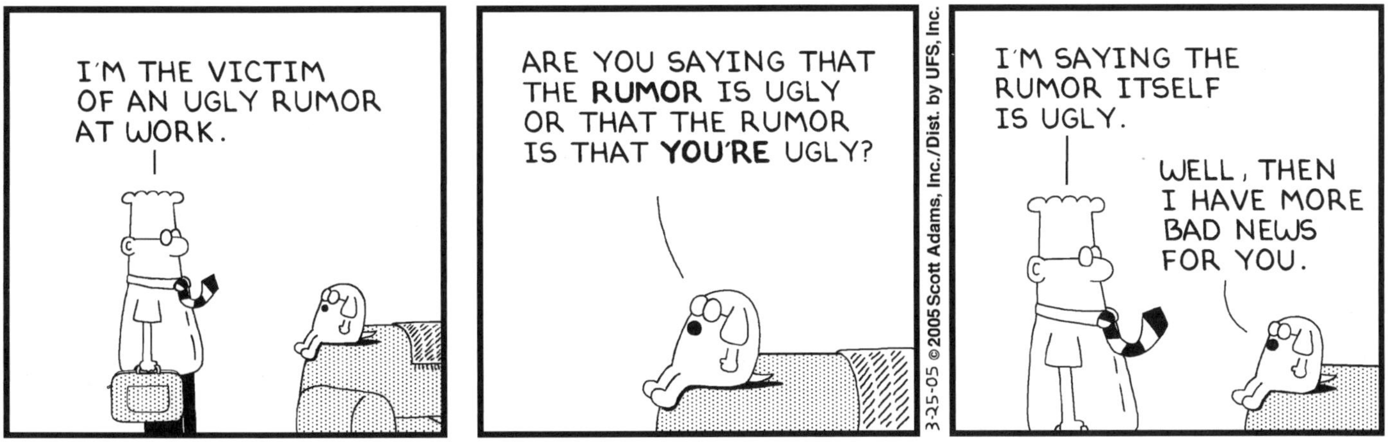
I'M THE VICTIM OF AN UGLY RUMOR AT WORK.
ARE YOU SAYING THAT THE **RUMOR** IS UGLY OR THAT THE RUMOR IS THAT **YOU'RE** UGLY?
3-25-05 ©2005 Scott Adams, Inc./Dist. by UFS, Inc.
I'M SAYING THE RUMOR ITSELF IS UGLY.
WELL, THEN I HAVE MORE BAD NEWS FOR YOU.

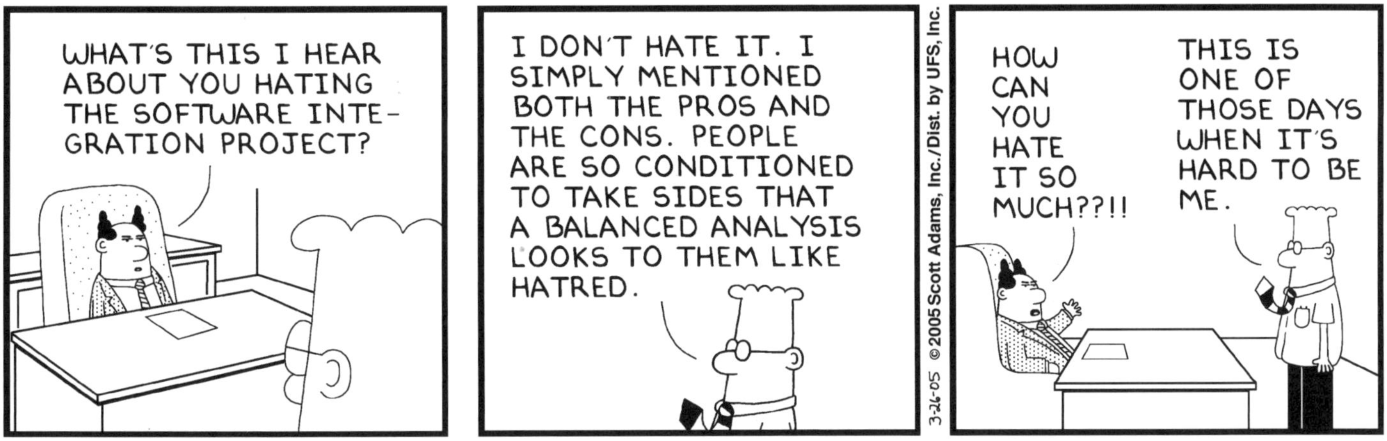
WHAT'S THIS I HEAR ABOUT YOU HATING THE SOFTWARE INTEGRATION PROJECT?
I DON'T HATE IT. I SIMPLY MENTIONED BOTH THE PROS AND THE CONS. PEOPLE ARE SO CONDITIONED TO TAKE SIDES THAT A BALANCED ANALYSIS LOOKS TO THEM LIKE HATRED.
3-26-05 ©2005 Scott Adams, Inc./Dist. by UFS, Inc.
HOW CAN YOU HATE IT SO MUCH??!!
THIS IS ONE OF THOSE DAYS WHEN IT'S HARD TO BE ME.

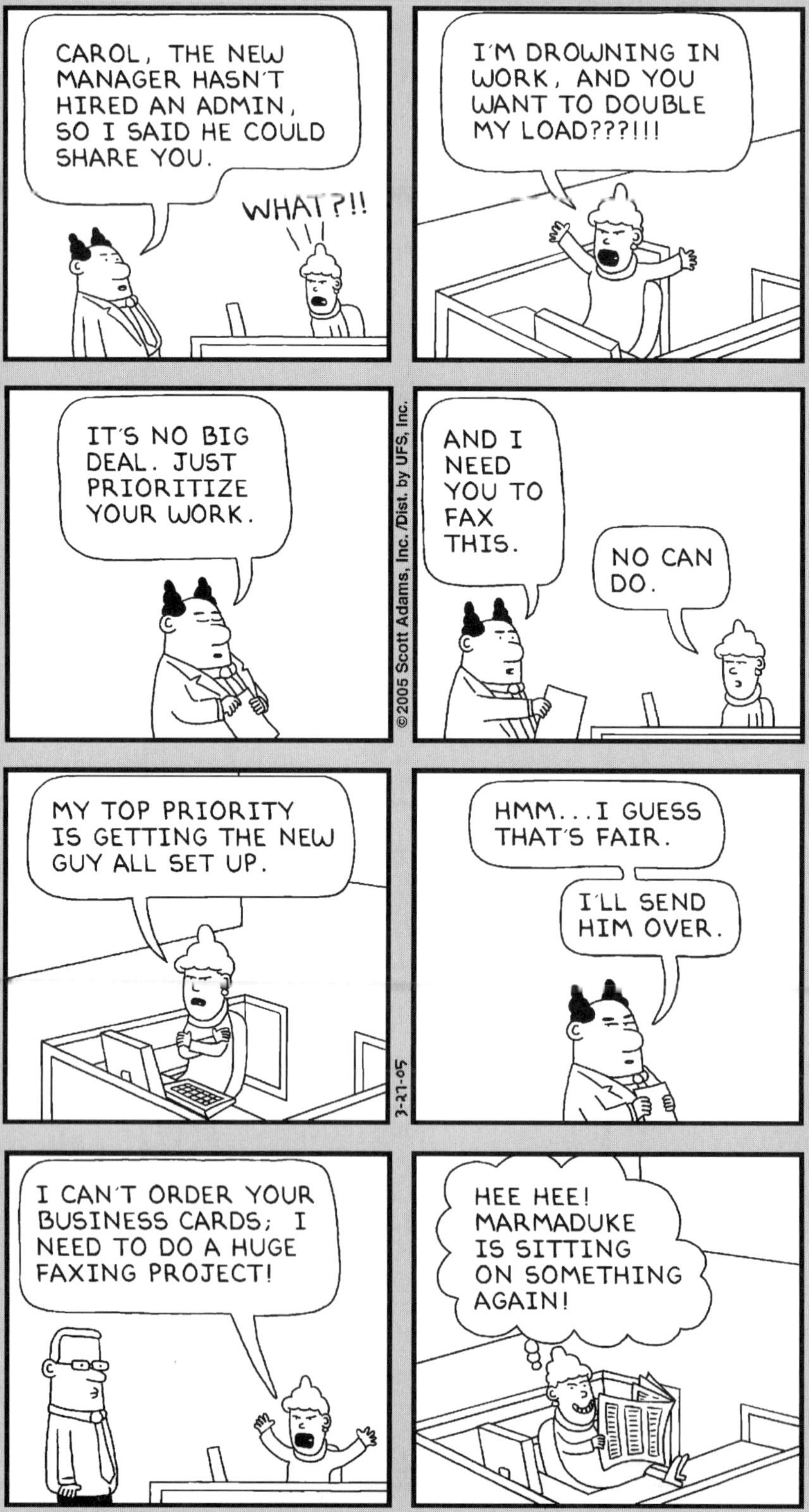

CAROL, THE NEW MANAGER HASN'T HIRED AN ADMIN, SO I SAID HE COULD SHARE YOU.
WHAT?!!
I'M DROWNING IN WORK, AND YOU WANT TO DOUBLE MY LOAD???!!!
IT'S NO BIG DEAL. JUST PRIORITIZE YOUR WORK.
©2005 Scott Adams, Inc. /Dist. by UFS, Inc.
AND I NEED YOU TO FAX THIS.
NO CAN DO.
MY TOP PRIORITY IS GETTING THE NEW GUY ALL SET UP.
3-21-05
HMM...I GUESS THAT'S FAIR.
I'LL SEND HIM OVER.
I CAN'T ORDER YOUR BUSINESS CARDS; I NEED TO DO A HUGE FAXING PROJECT!
HEE HEE! MARMADUKE IS SITTING ON SOMETHING AGAIN!

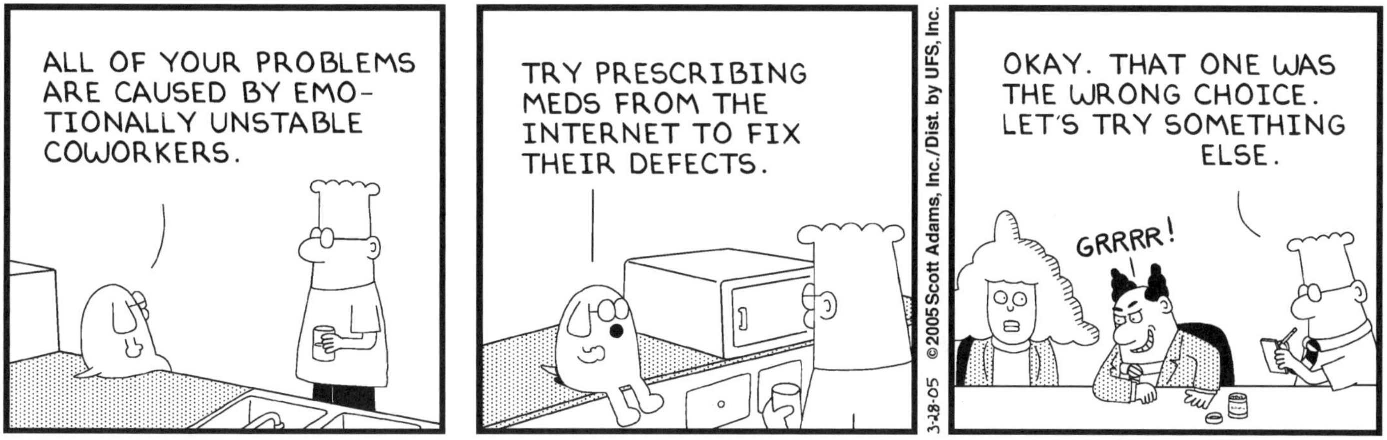
ALL OF YOUR PROBLEMS ARE CAUSED BY EMO-TIONALLY UNSTABLE COWORKERS.
TRY PRESCRIBING MEDS FROM THE INTERNET TO FIX THEIR DEFECTS.
3-28-05 ©2005 Scott Adams, Inc./Dist. by UFS, Inc.
OKAY. THAT ONE WAS THE WRONG CHOICE. LET'S TRY SOMETHING ELSE.
GRRRR!

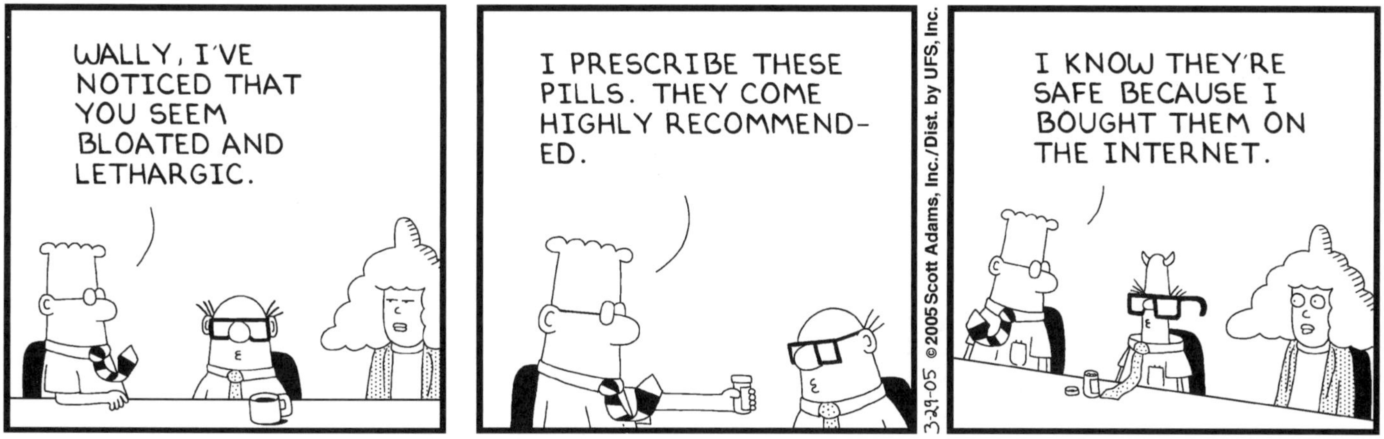
WALLY, I'VE NOTICED THAT YOU SEEM BLOATED AND LETHARGIC.
I PRESCRIBE THESE PILLS. THEY COME HIGHLY RECOMMEND-ED.
3-29-05 ©2005 Scott Adams, Inc./Dist. by UFS, Inc.
I KNOW THEY'RE SAFE BECAUSE I BOUGHT THEM ON THE INTERNET.

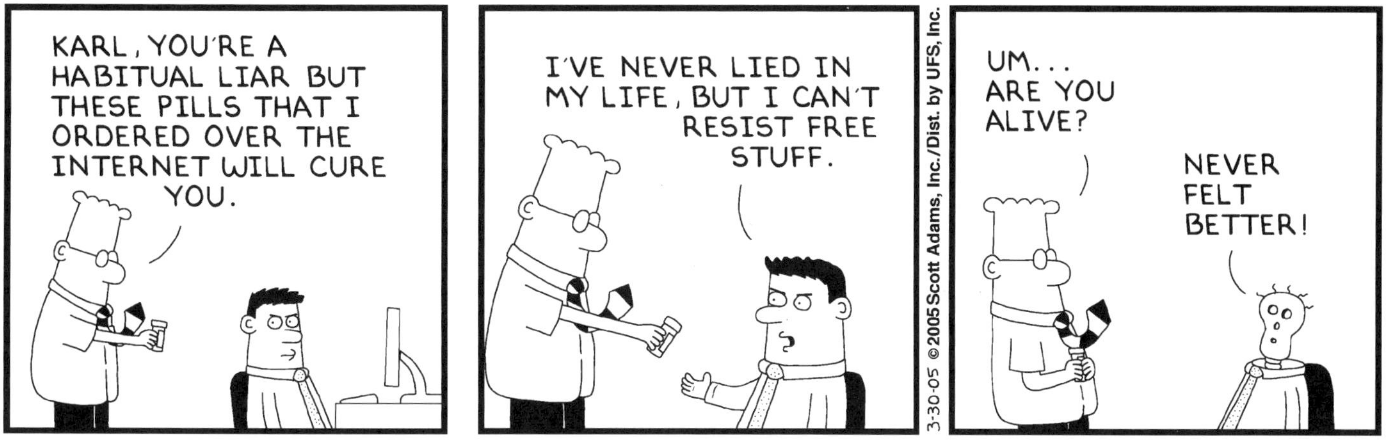
KARL, YOU'RE A HABITUAL LIAR BUT THESE PILLS THAT I ORDERED OVER THE INTERNET WILL CURE YOU.
I'VE NEVER LIED IN MY LIFE, BUT I CAN'T RESIST FREE STUFF.
3-30-05 ©2005 Scott Adams, Inc./Dist. by UFS, Inc.
UM... ARE YOU ALIVE?
NEVER FELT BETTER!

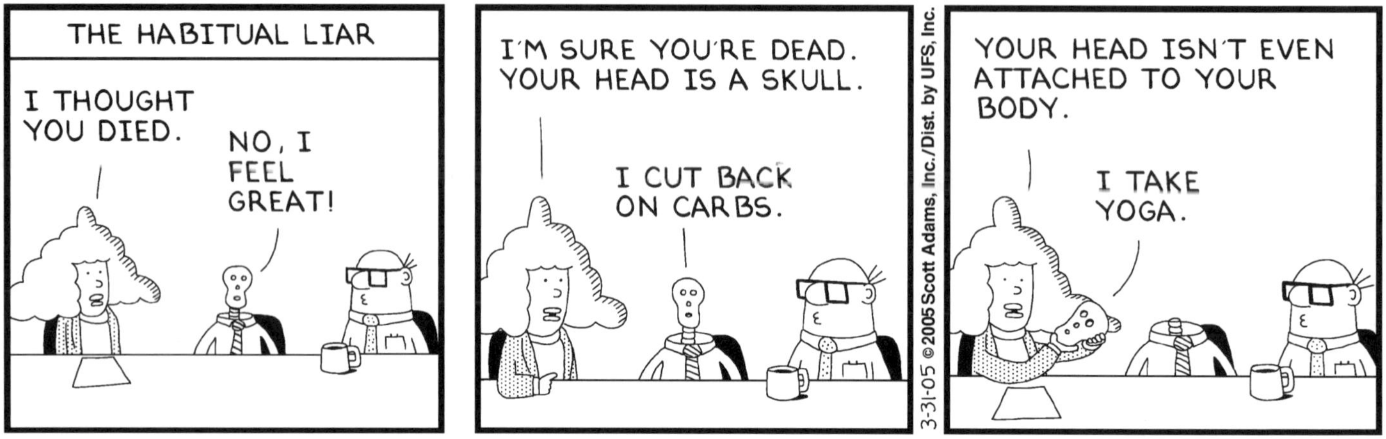
THE HABITUAL LIAR
I THOUGHT YOU DIED.
NO, I FEEL GREAT!
I'M SURE YOU'RE DEAD. YOUR HEAD IS A SKULL.
I CUT BACK ON CARBS.
3-31-05 © 2005 Scott Adams, Inc./Dist. by UFS, Inc.
YOUR HEAD ISN'T EVEN ATTACHED TO YOUR BODY.
I TAKE YOGA.

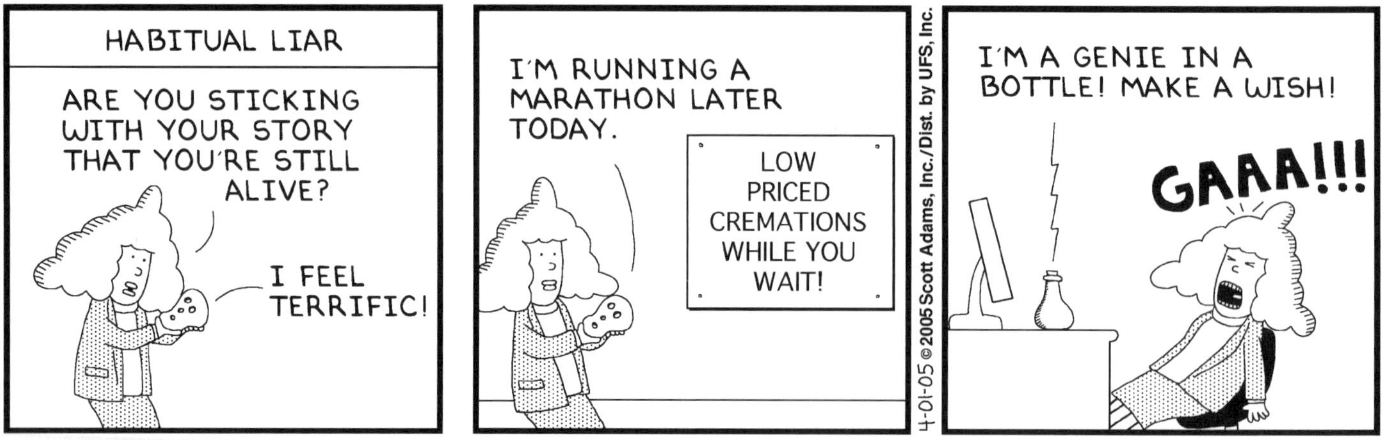
HABITUAL LIAR
ARE YOU STICKING WITH YOUR STORY THAT YOU'RE STILL ALIVE?
I FEEL TERRIFIC!
I'M RUNNING A MARATHON LATER TODAY.
LOW PRICED CREMATIONS WHILE YOU WAIT!
4-01-05 © 2005 Scott Adams, Inc./Dist. by UFS, Inc.
I'M A GENIE IN A BOTTLE! MAKE A WISH!
GAAA!!!

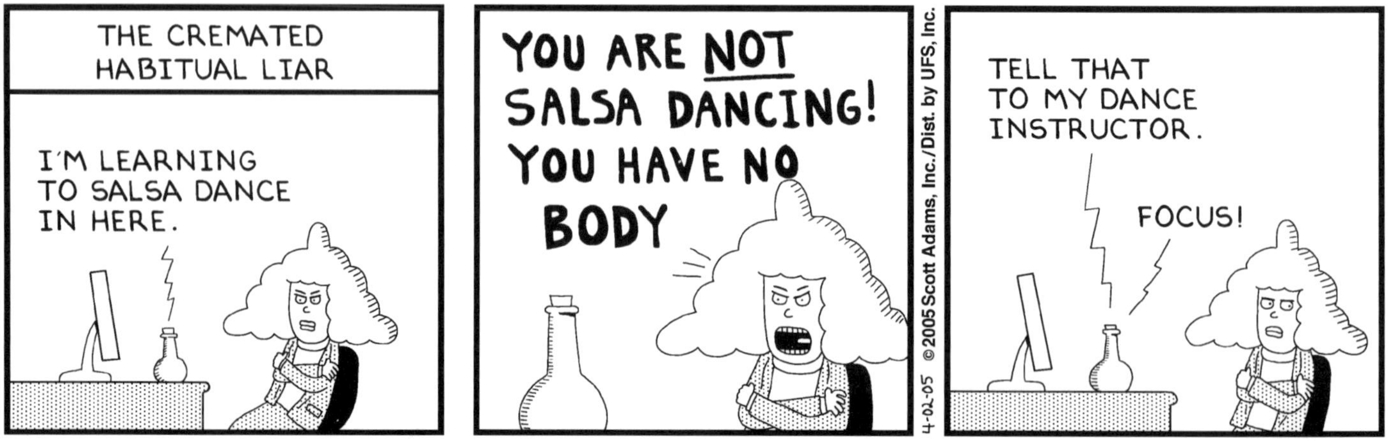
THE CREMATED HABITUAL LIAR
I'M LEARNING TO SALSA DANCE IN HERE.
YOU ARE NOT SALSA DANCING! YOU HAVE NO BODY
4-02-05 © 2005 Scott Adams, Inc./Dist. by UFS, Inc.
TELL THAT TO MY DANCE INSTRUCTOR.
FOCUS!

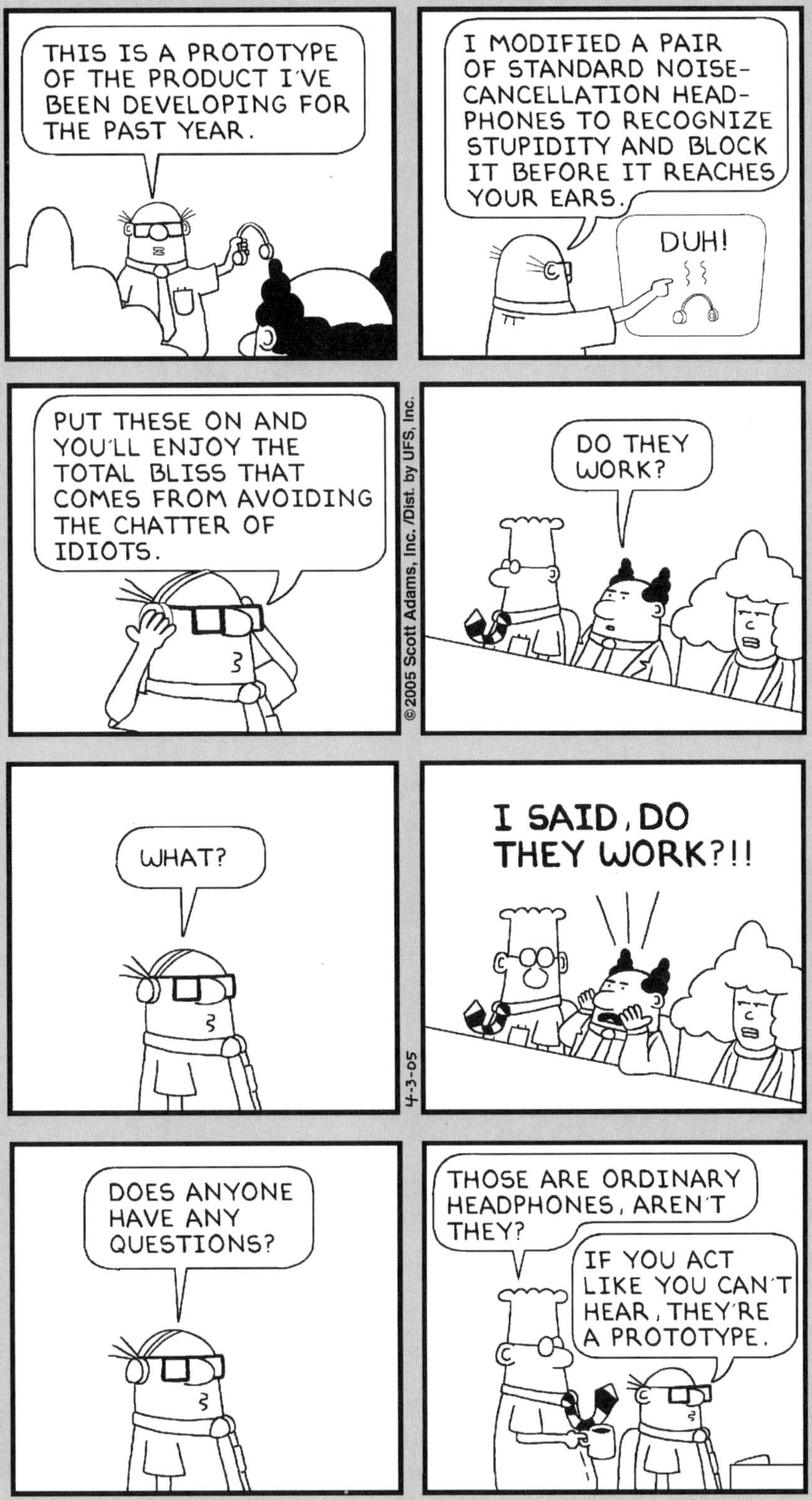
THIS IS A PROTOTYPE OF THE PRODUCT I'VE BEEN DEVELOPING FOR THE PAST YEAR.
I MODIFIED A PAIR OF STANDARD NOISE-CANCELLATION HEAD-PHONES TO RECOGNIZE STUPIDITY AND BLOCK IT BEFORE IT REACHES YOUR EARS.
DUH!
PUT THESE ON AND YOU'LL ENJOY THE TOTAL BLISS THAT COMES FROM AVOIDING THE CHATTER OF IDIOTS.
DO THEY WORK?
WHAT?
I SAID, DO THEY WORK?!!
DOES ANYONE HAVE ANY QUESTIONS?
THOSE ARE ORDINARY HEADPHONES, AREN'T THEY?
IF YOU ACT LIKE YOU CAN'T HEAR, THEY'RE A PROTOTYPE.
©2005 Scott Adams, Inc./Dist. by UFS, Inc.
4-3-05

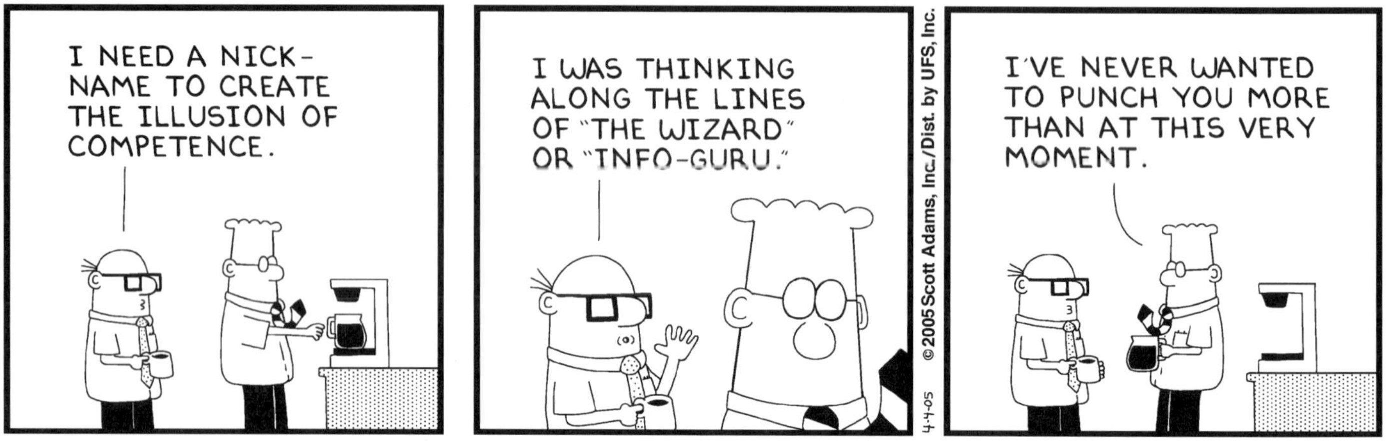
I NEED A NICK-NAME TO CREATE THE ILLUSION OF COMPETENCE.
I WAS THINKING ALONG THE LINES OF "THE WIZARD" OR "INFO-GURU."
©2005 Scott Adams, Inc./Dist. by UFS, Inc.
4-4-05
I'VE NEVER WANTED TO PUNCH YOU MORE THAN AT THIS VERY MOMENT.

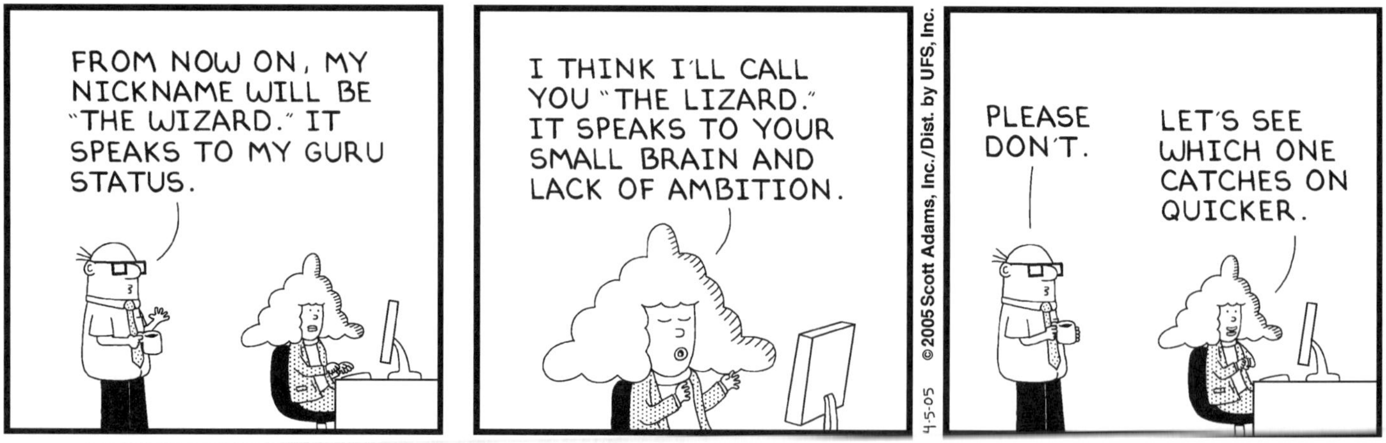
FROM NOW ON, MY NICKNAME WILL BE "THE WIZARD." IT SPEAKS TO MY GURU STATUS.
I THINK I'LL CALL YOU "THE LIZARD." IT SPEAKS TO YOUR SMALL BRAIN AND LACK OF AMBITION.
©2005 Scott Adams, Inc./Dist. by UFS, Inc.
4-5-05
PLEASE DON'T.
LET'S SEE WHICH ONE CATCHES ON QUICKER.

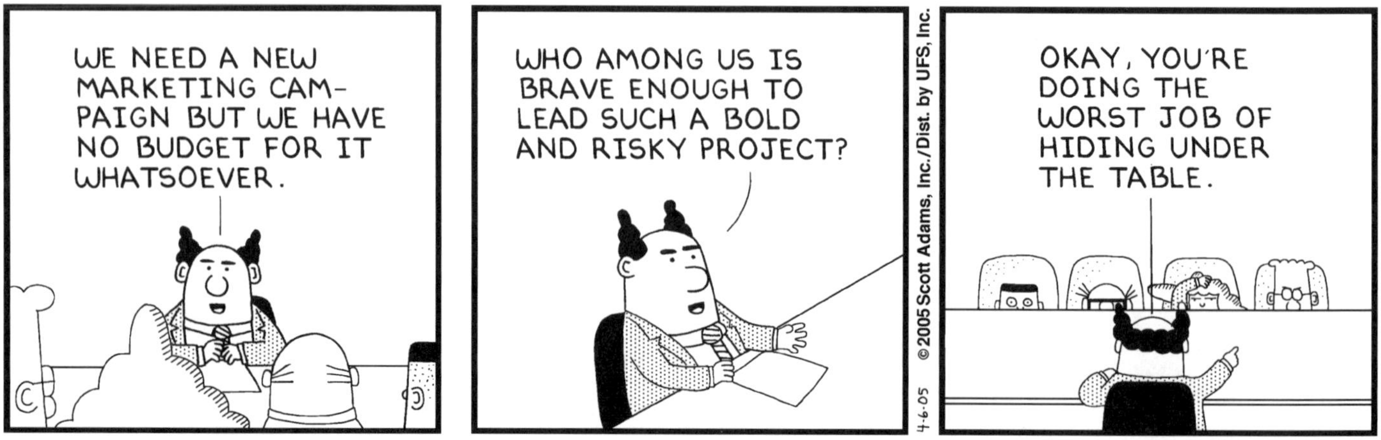
WE NEED A NEW MARKETING CAM-PAIGN BUT WE HAVE NO BUDGET FOR IT WHATSOEVER.
WHO AMONG US IS BRAVE ENOUGH TO LEAD SUCH A BOLD AND RISKY PROJECT?
©2005 Scott Adams, Inc./Dist. by UFS, Inc.
4-6-05
OKAY, YOU'RE DOING THE WORST JOB OF HIDING UNDER THE TABLE.

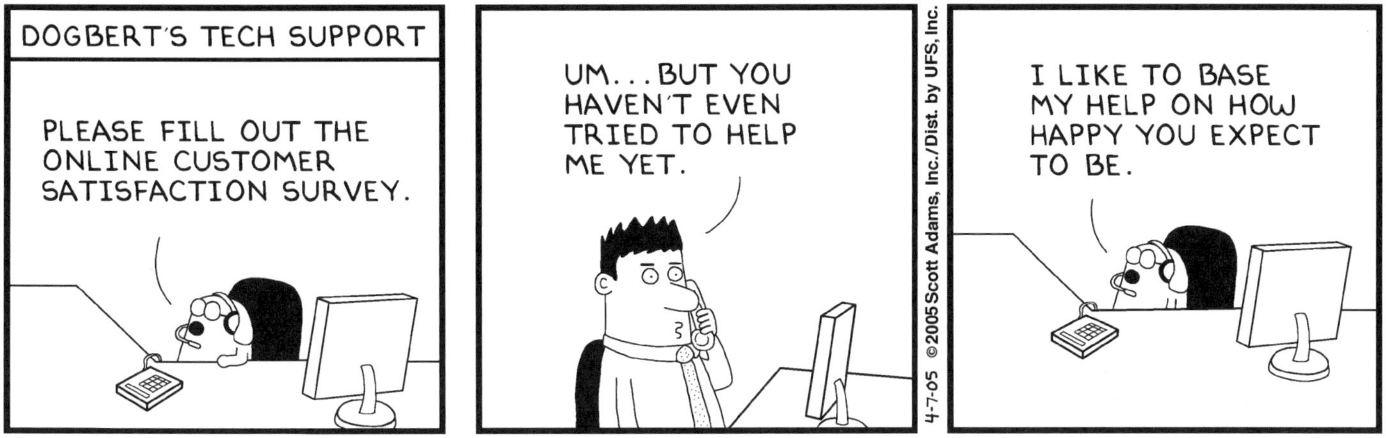
DOGBERT'S TECH SUPPORT
PLEASE FILL OUT THE ONLINE CUSTOMER SATISFACTION SURVEY.
UM... BUT YOU HAVEN'T EVEN TRIED TO HELP ME YET.
4-7-05 ©2005 Scott Adams, Inc./Dist. by UFS, Inc.
I LIKE TO BASE MY HELP ON HOW HAPPY YOU EXPECT TO BE.

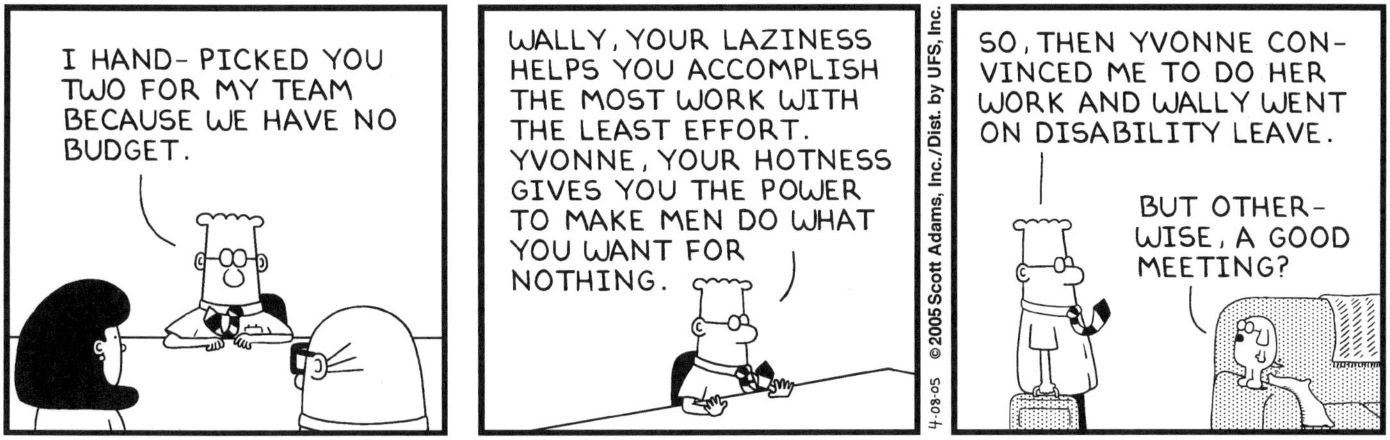
I HAND-PICKED YOU TWO FOR MY TEAM BECAUSE WE HAVE NO BUDGET.
WALLY, YOUR LAZINESS HELPS YOU ACCOMPLISH THE MOST WORK WITH THE LEAST EFFORT. YVONNE, YOUR HOTNESS GIVES YOU THE POWER TO MAKE MEN DO WHAT YOU WANT FOR NOTHING.
4-08-05 ©2005 Scott Adams, Inc./Dist. by UFS, Inc.
SO, THEN YVONNE CONVINCED ME TO DO HER WORK AND WALLY WENT ON DISABILITY LEAVE.
BUT OTHERWISE, A GOOD MEETING?

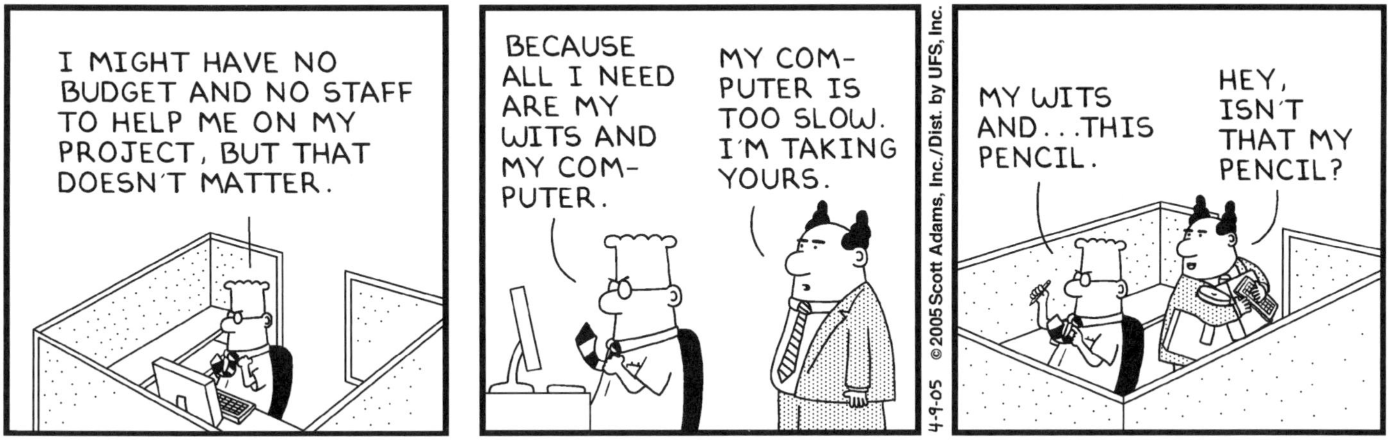
I MIGHT HAVE NO BUDGET AND NO STAFF TO HELP ME ON MY PROJECT, BUT THAT DOESN'T MATTER.
BECAUSE ALL I NEED ARE MY WITS AND MY COMPUTER.
MY COMPUTER IS TOO SLOW. I'M TAKING YOURS.
4-9-05 ©2005 Scott Adams, Inc./Dist. by UFS, Inc.
MY WITS AND... THIS PENCIL.
HEY, ISN'T THAT MY PENCIL?

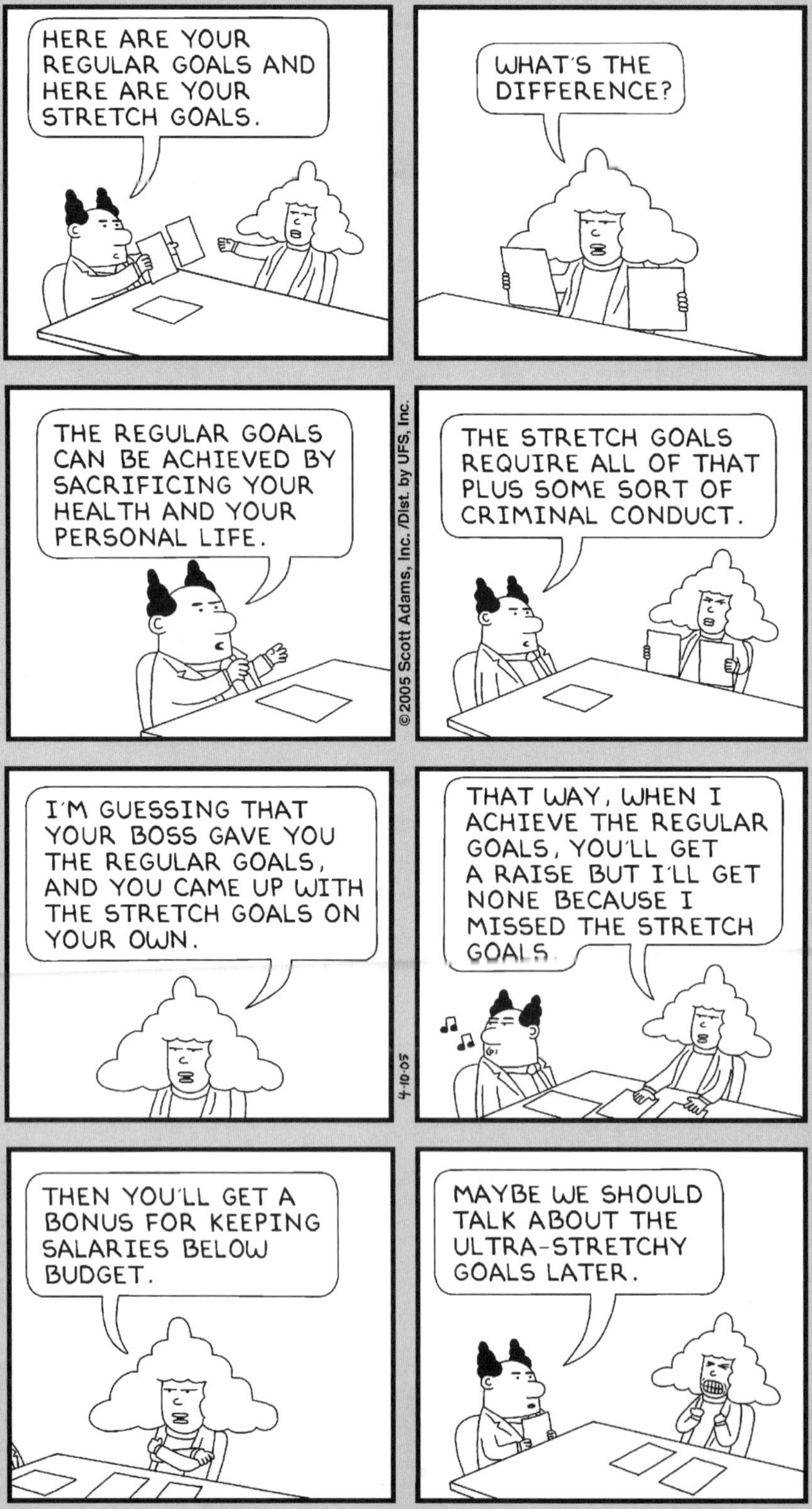
HERE ARE YOUR REGULAR GOALS AND HERE ARE YOUR STRETCH GOALS.
WHAT'S THE DIFFERENCE?
THE REGULAR GOALS CAN BE ACHIEVED BY SACRIFICING YOUR HEALTH AND YOUR PERSONAL LIFE.
THE STRETCH GOALS REQUIRE ALL OF THAT PLUS SOME SORT OF CRIMINAL CONDUCT.
©2005 Scott Adams, Inc. /Dist. by UFS, Inc.
I'M GUESSING THAT YOUR BOSS GAVE YOU THE REGULAR GOALS, AND YOU CAME UP WITH THE STRETCH GOALS ON YOUR OWN.
THAT WAY, WHEN I ACHIEVE THE REGULAR GOALS, YOU'LL GET A RAISE BUT I'LL GET NONE BECAUSE I MISSED THE STRETCH GOALS.
4-10-05
THEN YOU'LL GET A BONUS FOR KEEPING SALARIES BELOW BUDGET.
MAYBE WE SHOULD TALK ABOUT THE ULTRA-STRETCHY GOALS LATER.

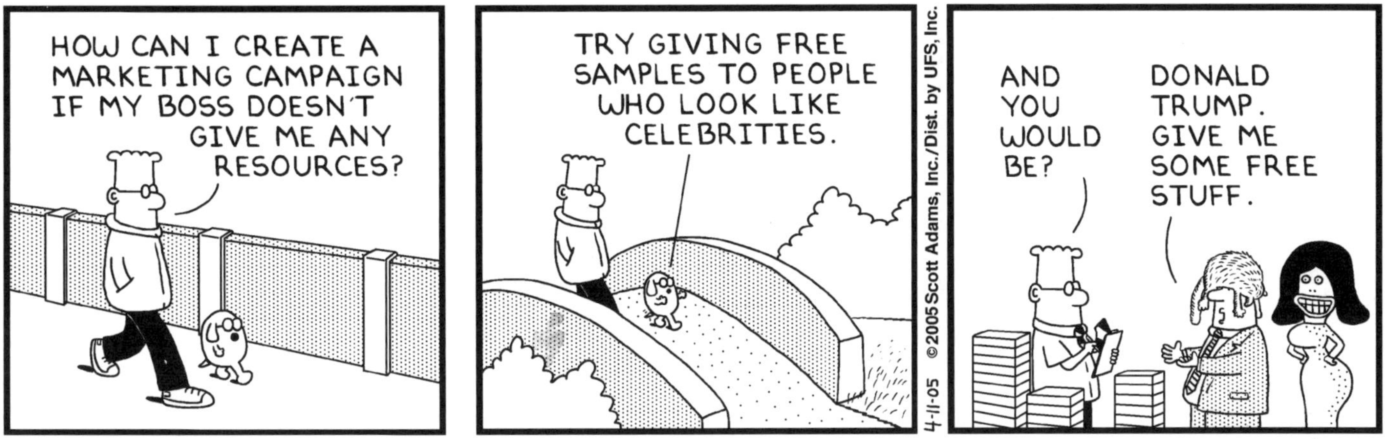
HOW CAN I CREATE A MARKETING CAMPAIGN IF MY BOSS DOESN'T GIVE ME ANY RESOURCES?
TRY GIVING FREE SAMPLES TO PEOPLE WHO LOOK LIKE CELEBRITIES.
4-11-05 ©2005 Scott Adams, Inc./Dist. by UFS, Inc.
AND YOU WOULD BE?
DONALD TRUMP. GIVE ME SOME FREE STUFF.

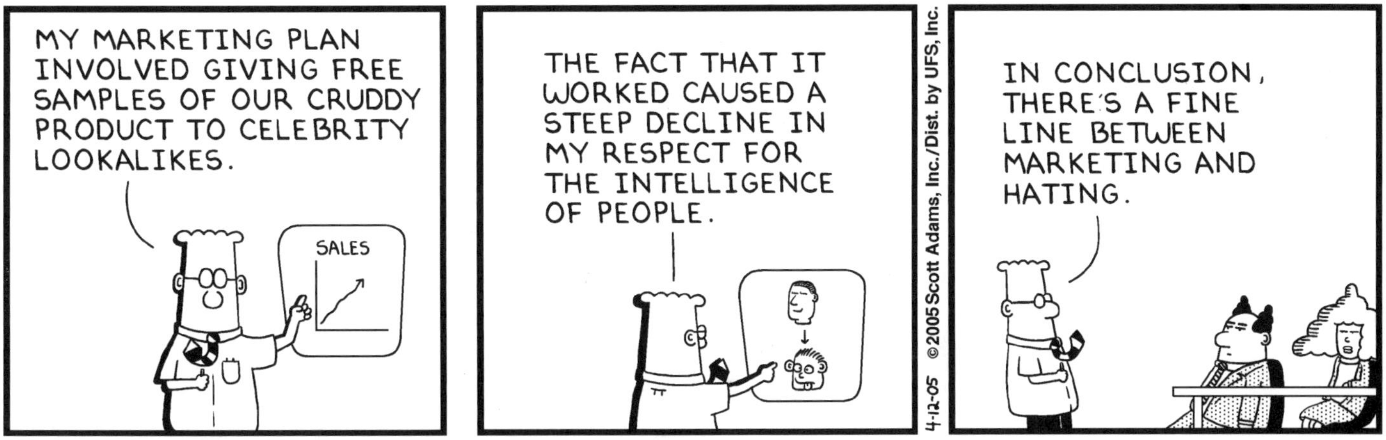
MY MARKETING PLAN INVOLVED GIVING FREE SAMPLES OF OUR CRUDDY PRODUCT TO CELEBRITY LOOKALIKES.
SALES
THE FACT THAT IT WORKED CAUSED A STEEP DECLINE IN MY RESPECT FOR THE INTELLIGENCE OF PEOPLE.
4-12-05 ©2005 Scott Adams, Inc./Dist. by UFS, Inc.
IN CONCLUSION, THERE'S A FINE LINE BETWEEN MARKETING AND HATING.

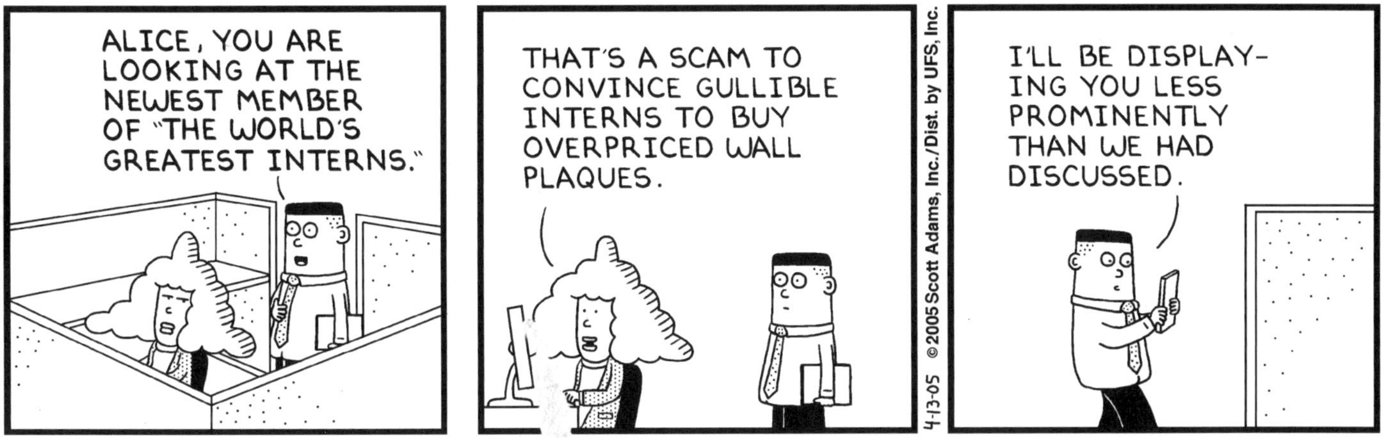
ALICE, YOU ARE LOOKING AT THE NEWEST MEMBER OF "THE WORLD'S GREATEST INTERNS."
THAT'S A SCAM TO CONVINCE GULLIBLE INTERNS TO BUY OVERPRICED WALL PLAQUES.
4-13-05 ©2005 Scott Adams, Inc./Dist. by UFS, Inc.
I'LL BE DISPLAY-ING YOU LESS PROMINENTLY THAN WE HAD DISCUSSED.

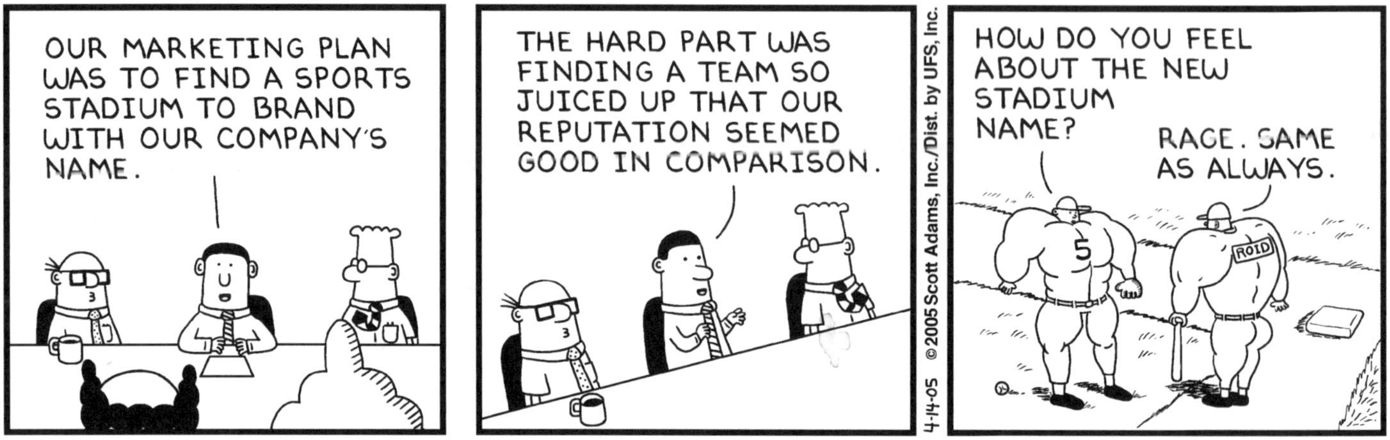
OUR MARKETING PLAN WAS TO FIND A SPORTS STADIUM TO BRAND WITH OUR COMPANY'S NAME.
THE HARD PART WAS FINDING A TEAM SO JUICED UP THAT OUR REPUTATION SEEMED GOOD IN COMPARISON.
4-14-05 © 2005 Scott Adams, Inc./Dist. by UFS, Inc.
HOW DO YOU FEEL ABOUT THE NEW STADIUM NAME?
RAGE. SAME AS ALWAYS.
5
ROID

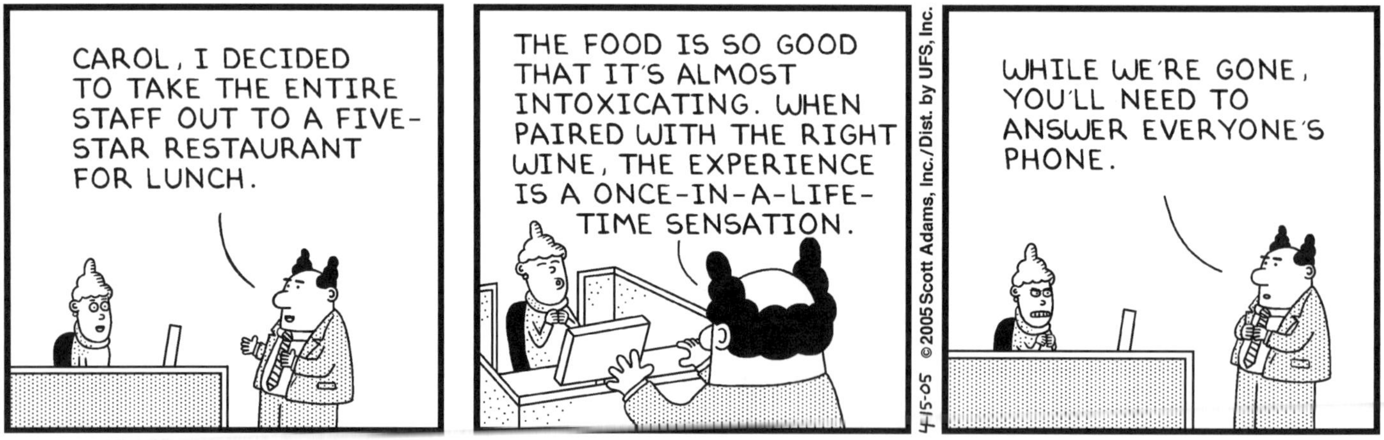
CAROL, I DECIDED TO TAKE THE ENTIRE STAFF OUT TO A FIVE-STAR RESTAURANT FOR LUNCH.
THE FOOD IS SO GOOD THAT IT'S ALMOST INTOXICATING. WHEN PAIRED WITH THE RIGHT WINE, THE EXPERIENCE IS A ONCE-IN-A-LIFE-TIME SENSATION.
4-15-05 © 2005 Scott Adams, Inc./Dist. by UFS, Inc.
WHILE WE'RE GONE, YOU'LL NEED TO ANSWER EVERYONE'S PHONE.

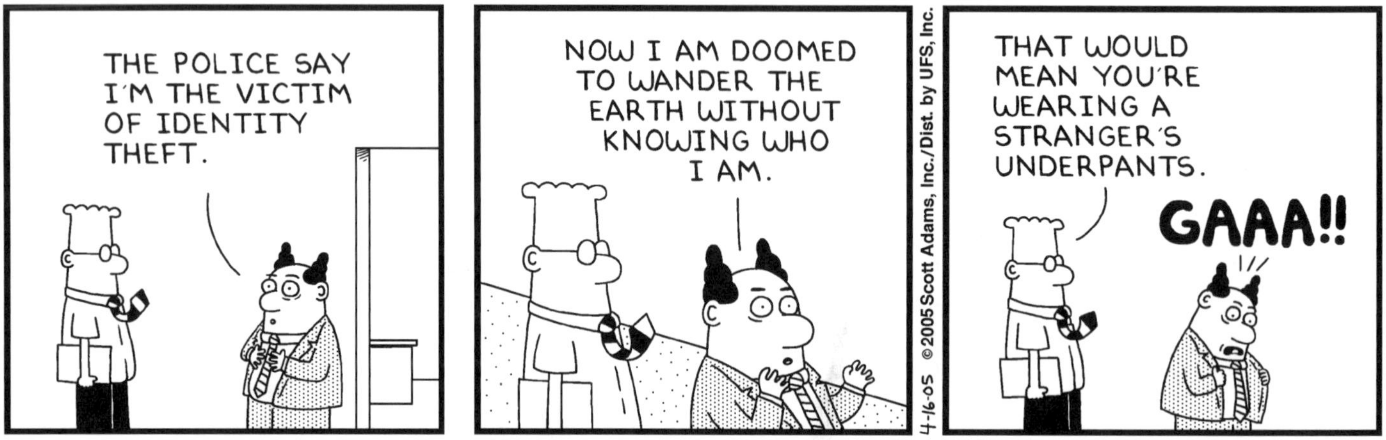
THE POLICE SAY I'M THE VICTIM OF IDENTITY THEFT.
NOW I AM DOOMED TO WANDER THE EARTH WITHOUT KNOWING WHO I AM.
4-16-05 © 2005 Scott Adams, Inc./Dist. by UFS, Inc.
THAT WOULD MEAN YOU'RE WEARING A STRANGER'S UNDERPANTS.
GAAA!!

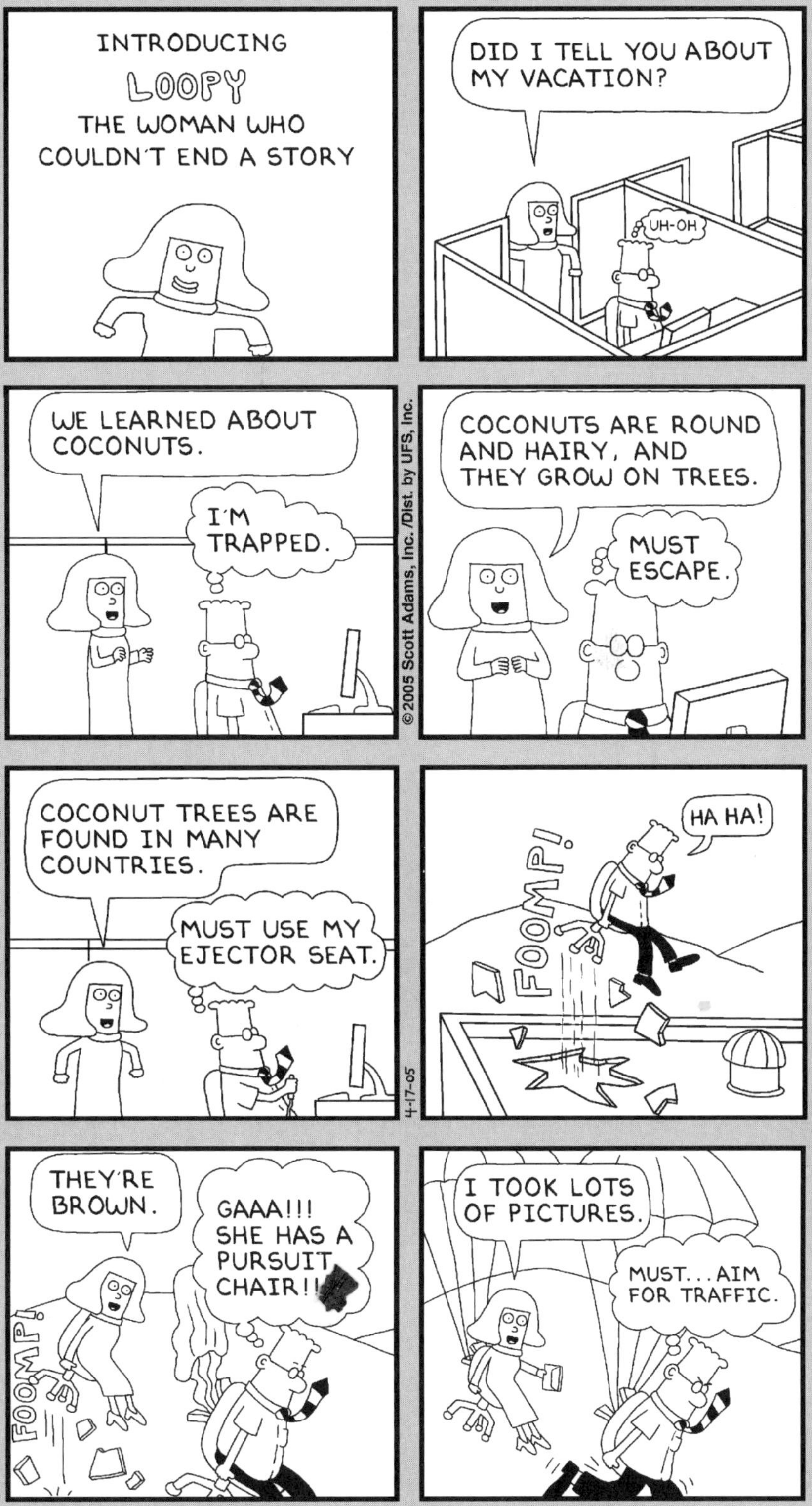
INTRODUCING
LOOPY
THE WOMAN WHO COULDN'T END A STORY
DID I TELL YOU ABOUT MY VACATION?
UH-OH
WE LEARNED ABOUT COCONUTS.
I'M TRAPPED.
© 2005 Scott Adams, Inc. /Dist. by UFS, Inc.
COCONUTS ARE ROUND AND HAIRY, AND THEY GROW ON TREES.
MUST ESCAPE.
COCONUT TREES ARE FOUND IN MANY COUNTRIES.
MUST USE MY EJECTOR SEAT.
4-17-05
HA HA!
FOOMP!
THEY'RE BROWN.
GAAA!!! SHE HAS A PURSUIT CHAIR!!
FOOMP!
I TOOK LOTS OF PICTURES.
MUST...AIM FOR TRAFFIC.

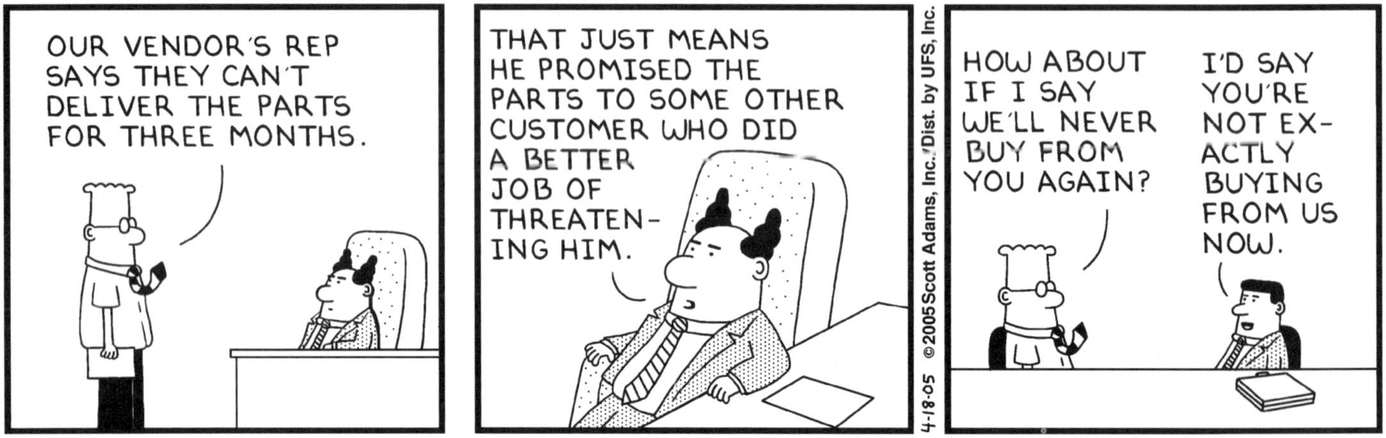
OUR VENDOR'S REP SAYS THEY CAN'T DELIVER THE PARTS FOR THREE MONTHS.
THAT JUST MEANS HE PROMISED THE PARTS TO SOME OTHER CUSTOMER WHO DID A BETTER JOB OF THREATEN- ING HIM.
4-18-05 ©2005 Scott Adams, Inc./Dist. by UFS, Inc.
HOW ABOUT IF I SAY WE'LL NEVER BUY FROM YOU AGAIN?
I'D SAY YOU'RE NOT EX- ACTLY BUYING FROM US NOW.

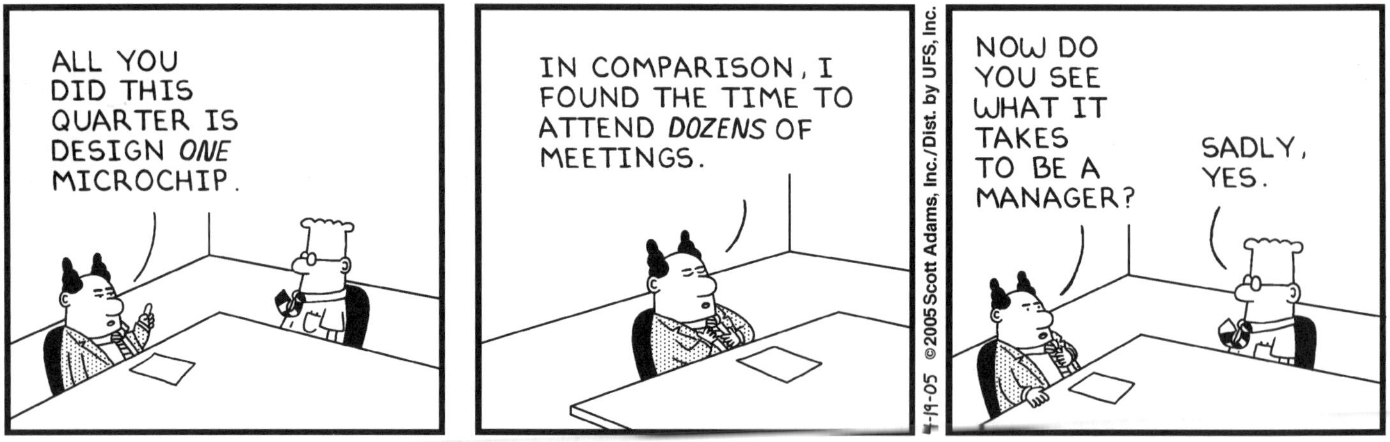
ALL YOU DID THIS QUARTER IS DESIGN *ONE* MICROCHIP.
IN COMPARISON, I FOUND THE TIME TO ATTEND *DOZENS* OF MEETINGS.
4-19-05 ©2005 Scott Adams, Inc./Dist. by UFS, Inc.
NOW DO YOU SEE WHAT IT TAKES TO BE A MANAGER?
SADLY, YES.

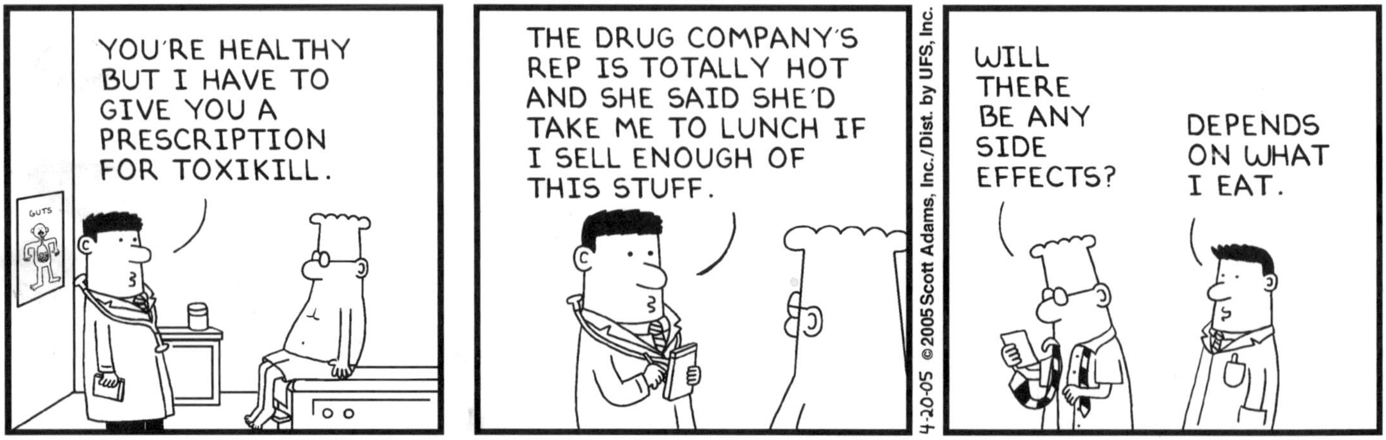
YOU'RE HEALTHY BUT I HAVE TO GIVE YOU A PRESCRIPTION FOR TOXIKILL.
GUTS
THE DRUG COMPANY'S REP IS TOTALLY HOT AND SHE SAID SHE'D TAKE ME TO LUNCH IF I SELL ENOUGH OF THIS STUFF.
4-20-05 ©2005 Scott Adams, Inc./Dist. by UFS, Inc.
WILL THERE BE ANY SIDE EFFECTS?
DEPENDS ON WHAT I EAT.

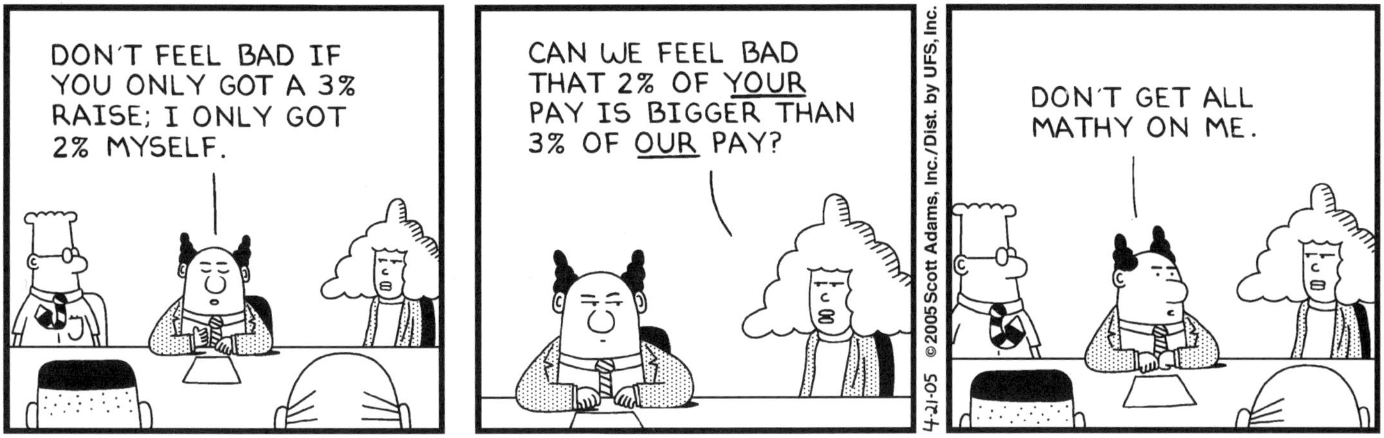
DON'T FEEL BAD IF YOU ONLY GOT A 3% RAISE; I ONLY GOT 2% MYSELF.
CAN WE FEEL BAD THAT 2% OF YOUR PAY IS BIGGER THAN 3% OF OUR PAY?
DON'T GET ALL MATHY ON ME.
4-21-05 © 2005 Scott Adams, Inc./Dist. by UFS, Inc.

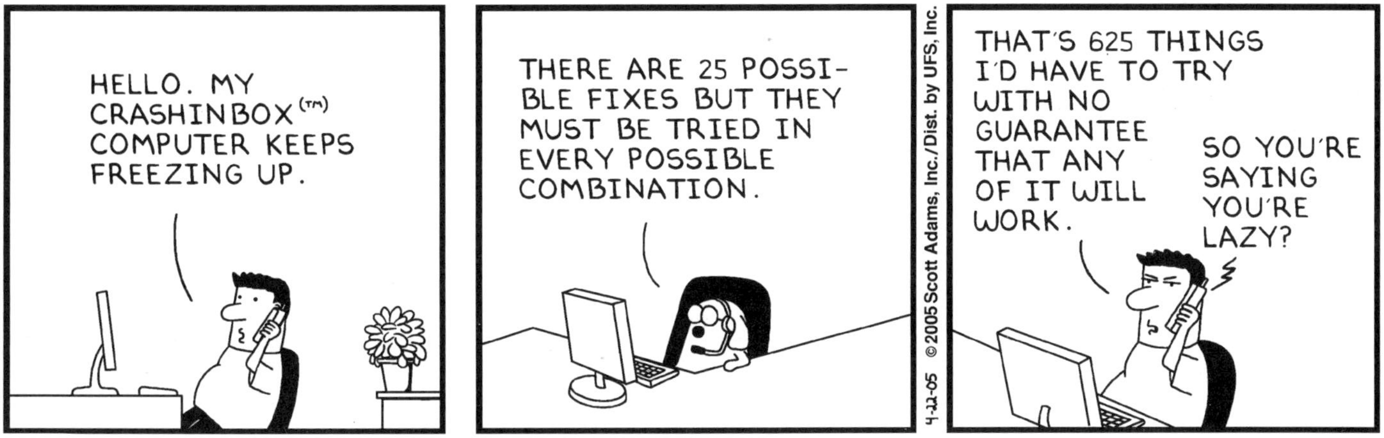
HELLO. MY CRASHINBOX(TM) COMPUTER KEEPS FREEZING UP.
THERE ARE 25 POSSIBLE FIXES BUT THEY MUST BE TRIED IN EVERY POSSIBLE COMBINATION.
THAT'S 625 THINGS I'D HAVE TO TRY WITH NO GUARANTEE THAT ANY OF IT WILL WORK.
SO YOU'RE SAYING YOU'RE LAZY?
4-22-05 © 2005 Scott Adams, Inc./Dist. by UFS, Inc.

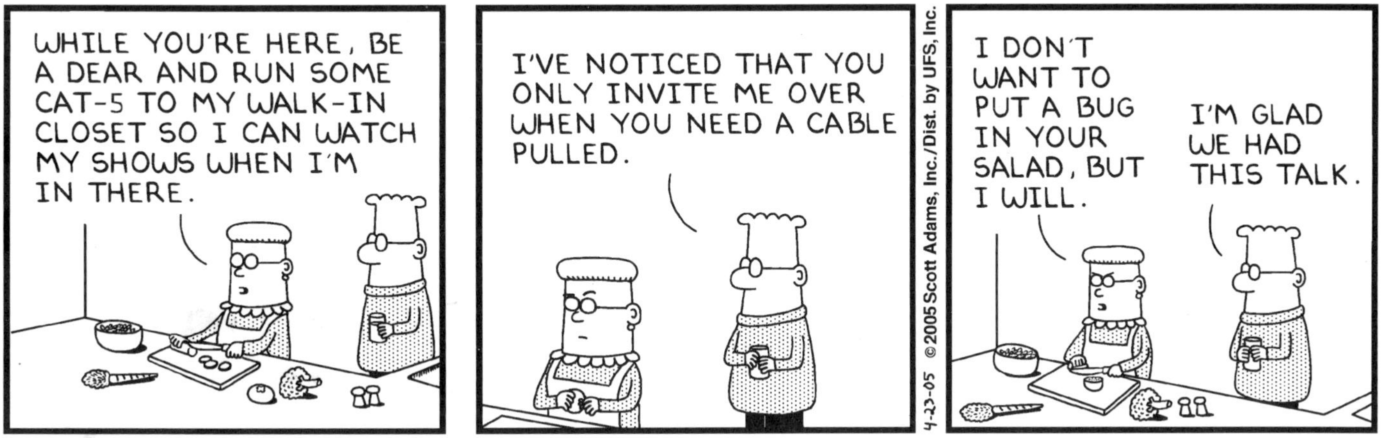
WHILE YOU'RE HERE, BE A DEAR AND RUN SOME CAT-5 TO MY WALK-IN CLOSET SO I CAN WATCH MY SHOWS WHEN I'M IN THERE.
I'VE NOTICED THAT YOU ONLY INVITE ME OVER WHEN YOU NEED A CABLE PULLED.
I DON'T WANT TO PUT A BUG IN YOUR SALAD, BUT I WILL.
I'M GLAD WE HAD THIS TALK.
4-23-05 © 2005 Scott Adams, Inc./Dist. by UFS, Inc.

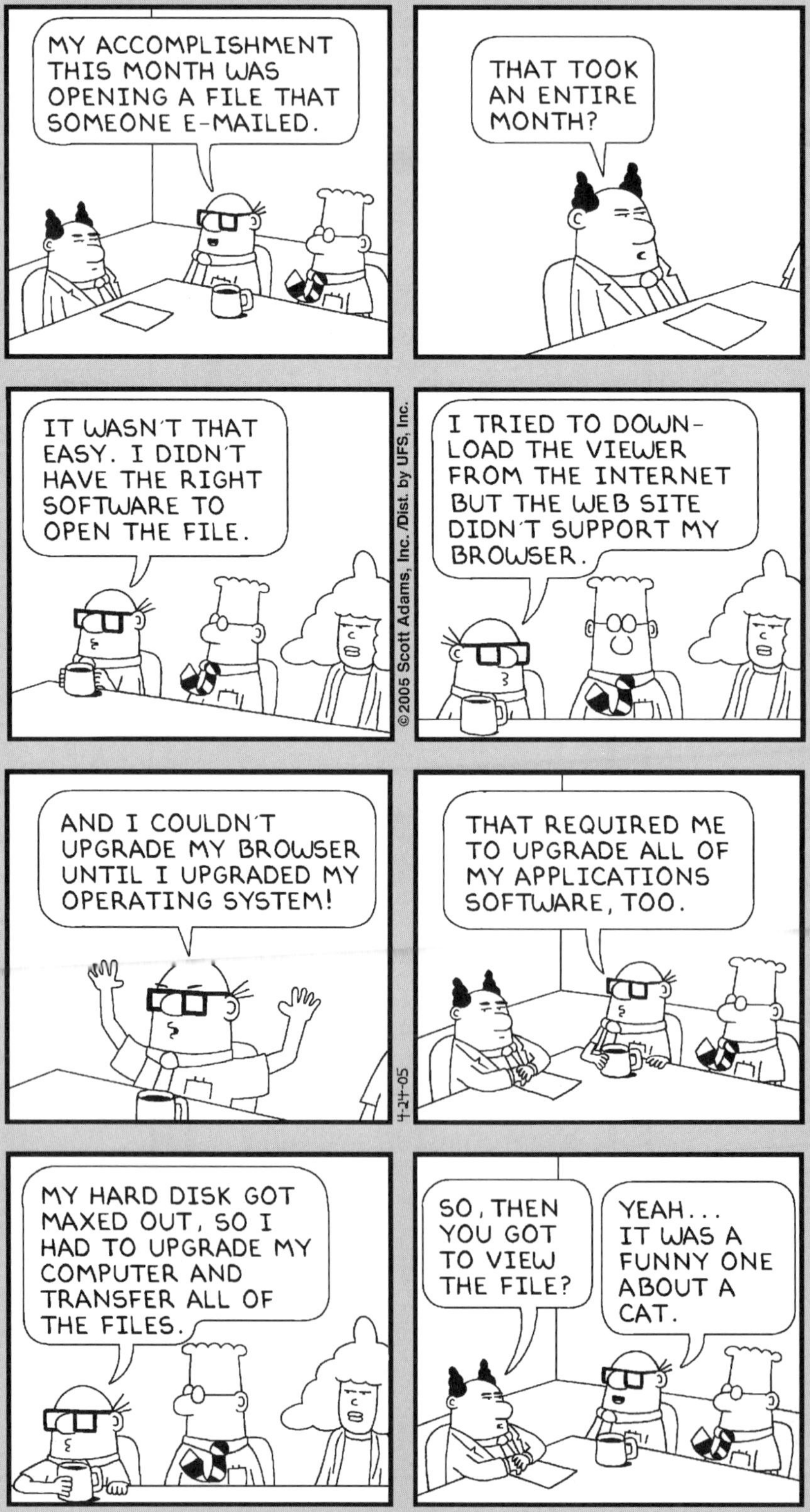
MY ACCOMPLISHMENT THIS MONTH WAS OPENING A FILE THAT SOMEONE E-MAILED.
THAT TOOK AN ENTIRE MONTH?
IT WASN'T THAT EASY. I DIDN'T HAVE THE RIGHT SOFTWARE TO OPEN THE FILE.
I TRIED TO DOWN-LOAD THE VIEWER FROM THE INTERNET BUT THE WEB SITE DIDN'T SUPPORT MY BROWSER.
AND I COULDN'T UPGRADE MY BROWSER UNTIL I UPGRADED MY OPERATING SYSTEM!
THAT REQUIRED ME TO UPGRADE ALL OF MY APPLICATIONS SOFTWARE, TOO.
MY HARD DISK GOT MAXED OUT, SO I HAD TO UPGRADE MY COMPUTER AND TRANSFER ALL OF THE FILES.
SO, THEN YOU GOT TO VIEW THE FILE?
YEAH... IT WAS A FUNNY ONE ABOUT A CAT.
©2005 Scott Adams, Inc./Dist. by UFS, Inc.
4-24-05

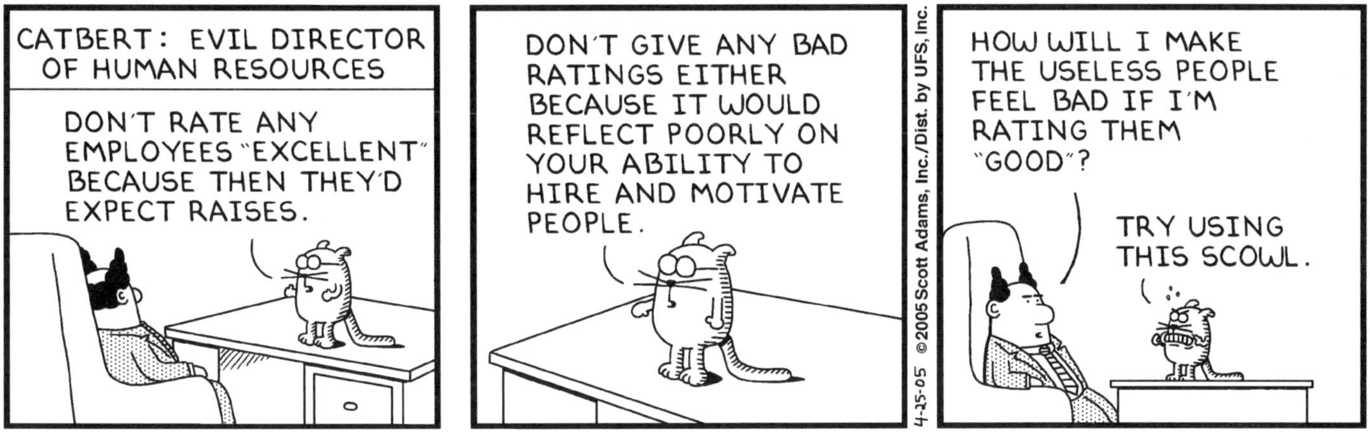
CATBERT: EVIL DIRECTOR OF HUMAN RESOURCES
DON'T RATE ANY EMPLOYEES "EXCELLENT" BECAUSE THEN THEY'D EXPECT RAISES.
DON'T GIVE ANY BAD RATINGS EITHER BECAUSE IT WOULD REFLECT POORLY ON YOUR ABILITY TO HIRE AND MOTIVATE PEOPLE.
4-25-05 © 2005 Scott Adams, Inc./Dist. by UFS, Inc.
HOW WILL I MAKE THE USELESS PEOPLE FEEL BAD IF I'M RATING THEM "GOOD"?
TRY USING THIS SCOWL.

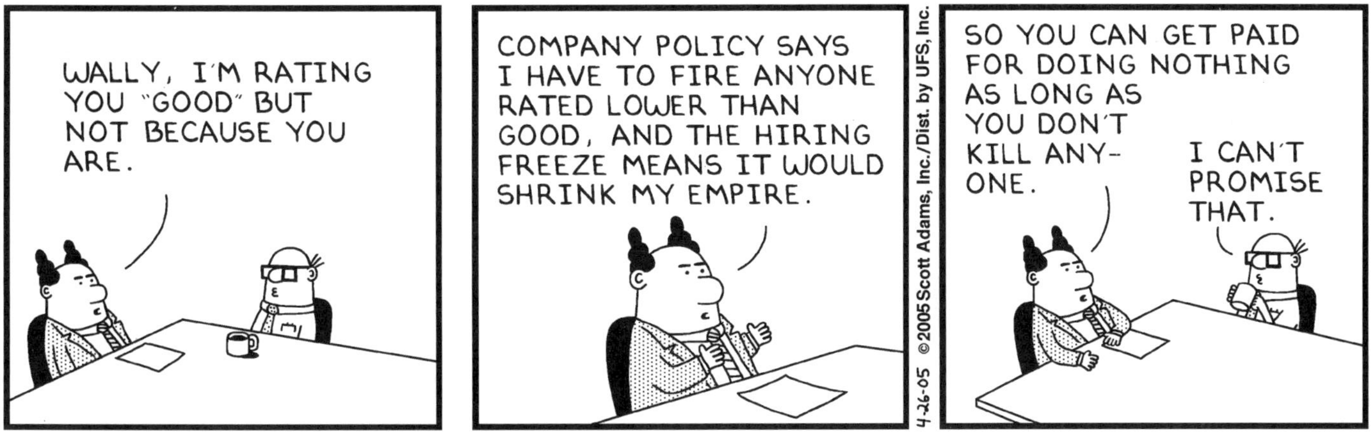
WALLY, I'M RATING YOU "GOOD" BUT NOT BECAUSE YOU ARE.
COMPANY POLICY SAYS I HAVE TO FIRE ANYONE RATED LOWER THAN GOOD, AND THE HIRING FREEZE MEANS IT WOULD SHRINK MY EMPIRE.
4-26-05 © 2005 Scott Adams, Inc./Dist. by UFS, Inc.
SO YOU CAN GET PAID FOR DOING NOTHING AS LONG AS YOU DON'T KILL ANY-ONE.
I CAN'T PROMISE THAT.

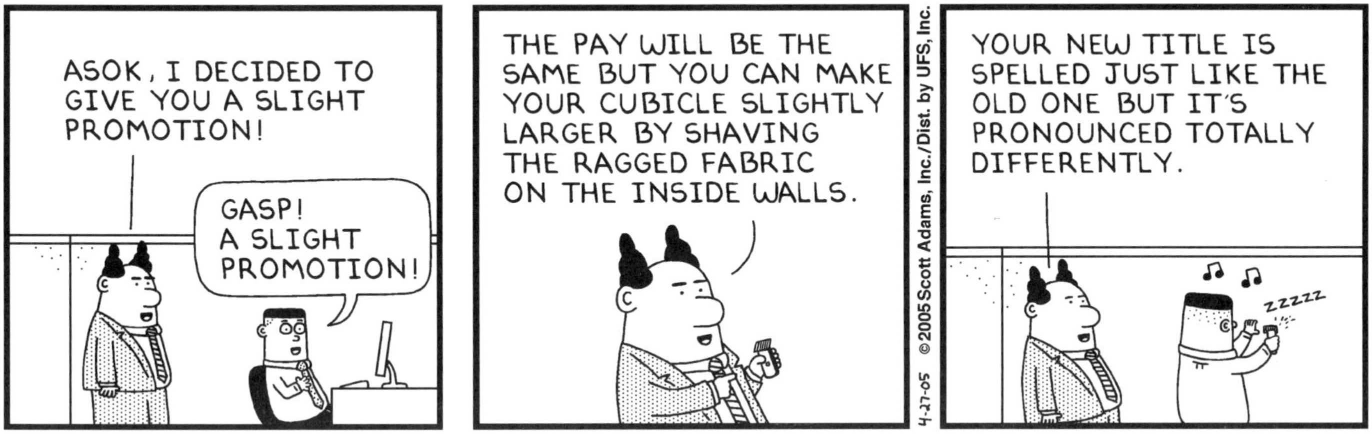
ASOK, I DECIDED TO GIVE YOU A SLIGHT PROMOTION!
GASP! A SLIGHT PROMOTION!
THE PAY WILL BE THE SAME BUT YOU CAN MAKE YOUR CUBICLE SLIGHTLY LARGER BY SHAVING THE RAGGED FABRIC ON THE INSIDE WALLS.
4-27-05 © 2005 Scott Adams, Inc./Dist. by UFS, Inc.
YOUR NEW TITLE IS SPELLED JUST LIKE THE OLD ONE BUT IT'S PRONOUNCED TOTALLY DIFFERENTLY.
ZZZZZ

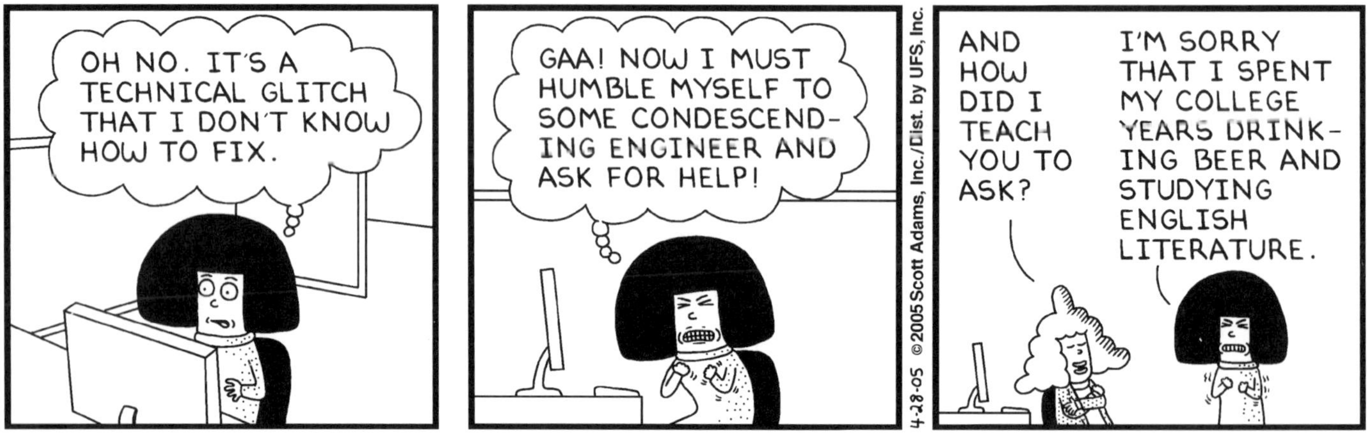
OH NO. IT'S A TECHNICAL GLITCH THAT I DON'T KNOW HOW TO FIX.
GAA! NOW I MUST HUMBLE MYSELF TO SOME CONDESCEND-ING ENGINEER AND ASK FOR HELP!
4-28-05 © 2005 Scott Adams, Inc./Dist. by UFS, Inc.
AND HOW DID I TEACH YOU TO ASK?
I'M SORRY THAT I SPENT MY COLLEGE YEARS DRINK-ING BEER AND STUDYING ENGLISH LITERATURE.

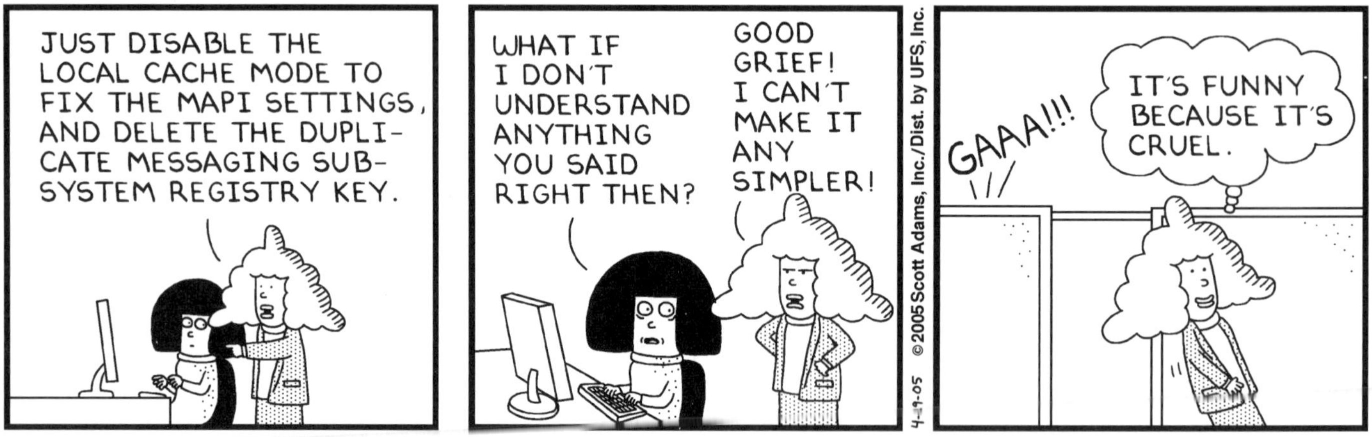
JUST DISABLE THE LOCAL CACHE MODE TO FIX THE MAPI SETTINGS, AND DELETE THE DUPLI-CATE MESSAGING SUB-SYSTEM REGISTRY KEY.
WHAT IF I DON'T UNDERSTAND ANYTHING YOU SAID RIGHT THEN?
GOOD GRIEF! I CAN'T MAKE IT ANY SIMPLER!
© 2005 Scott Adams, Inc./Dist. by UFS, Inc.
GAAA!!!
IT'S FUNNY BECAUSE IT'S CRUEL.

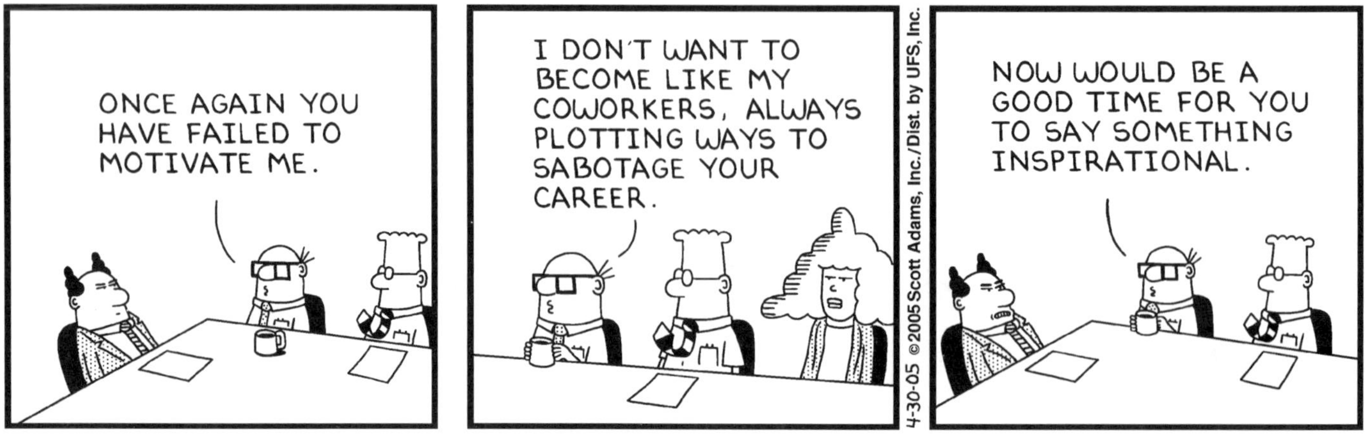
ONCE AGAIN YOU HAVE FAILED TO MOTIVATE ME.
I DON'T WANT TO BECOME LIKE MY COWORKERS, ALWAYS PLOTTING WAYS TO SABOTAGE YOUR CAREER.
4-30-05 © 2005 Scott Adams, Inc./Dist. by UFS, Inc.
NOW WOULD BE A GOOD TIME FOR YOU TO SAY SOMETHING INSPIRATIONAL.

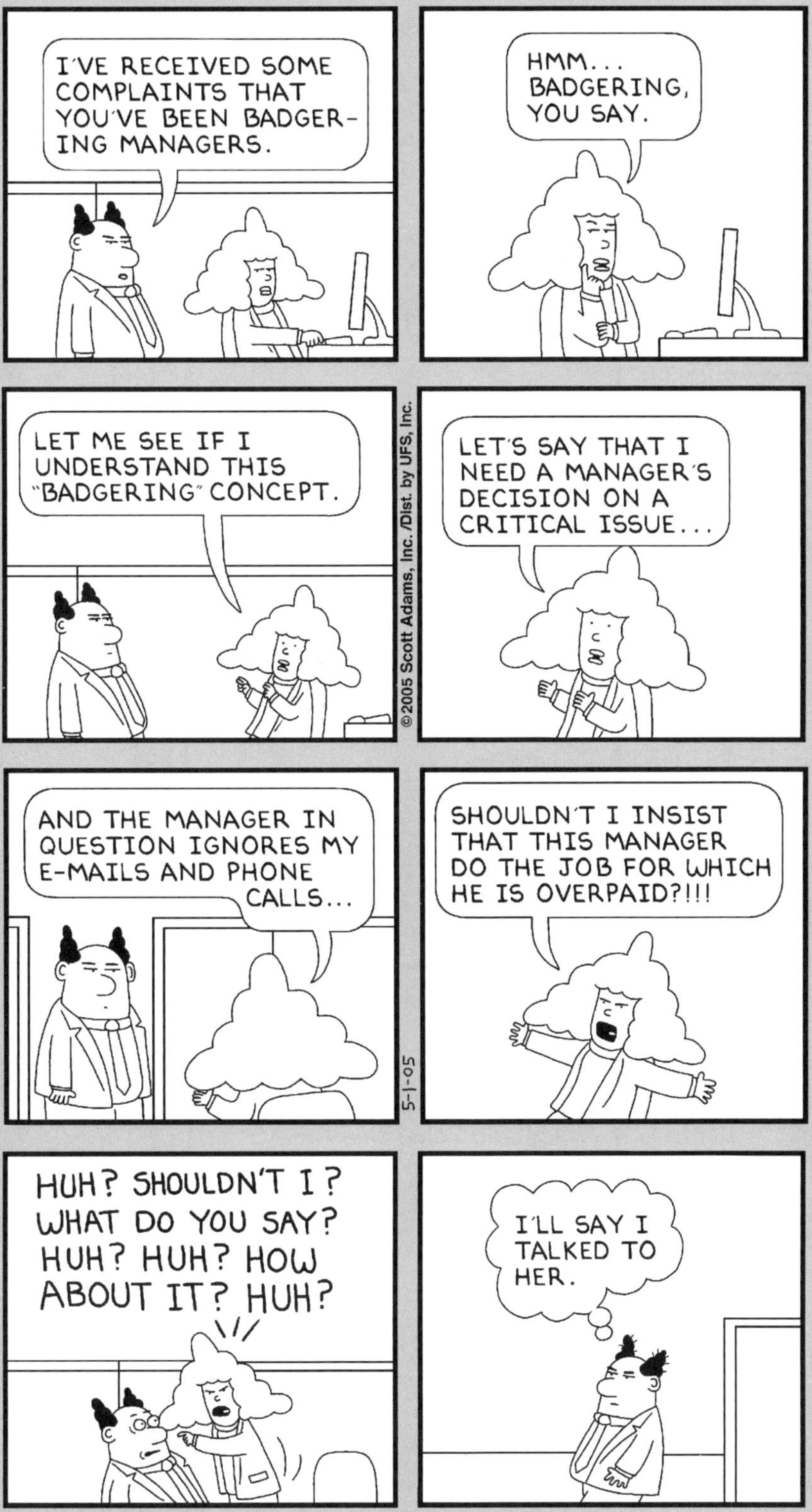
I'VE RECEIVED SOME COMPLAINTS THAT YOU'VE BEEN BADGERING MANAGERS.
HMM... BADGERING, YOU SAY.
LET ME SEE IF I UNDERSTAND THIS "BADGERING" CONCEPT.
LET'S SAY THAT I NEED A MANAGER'S DECISION ON A CRITICAL ISSUE...
AND THE MANAGER IN QUESTION IGNORES MY E-MAILS AND PHONE CALLS...
SHOULDN'T I INSIST THAT THIS MANAGER DO THE JOB FOR WHICH HE IS OVERPAID?!!!
HUH? SHOULDN'T I? WHAT DO YOU SAY? HUH? HUH? HOW ABOUT IT? HUH?
I'LL SAY I TALKED TO HER.
© 2005 Scott Adams, Inc. /Dist. by UFS, Inc.
5-1-05

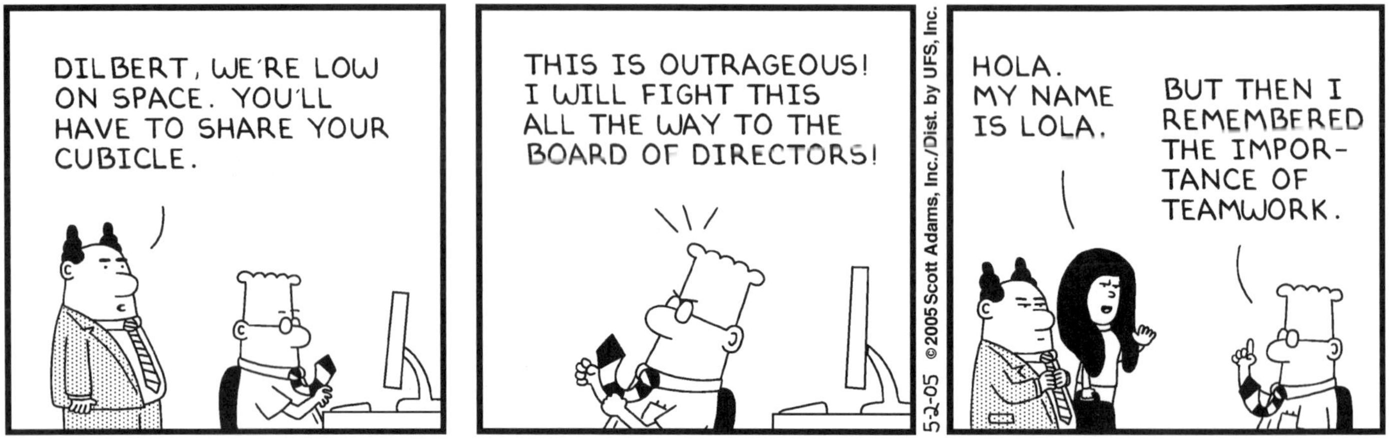
DILBERT, WE'RE LOW ON SPACE. YOU'LL HAVE TO SHARE YOUR CUBICLE.
THIS IS OUTRAGEOUS! I WILL FIGHT THIS ALL THE WAY TO THE BOARD OF DIRECTORS!
HOLA. MY NAME IS LOLA.
BUT THEN I REMEMBERED THE IMPORTANCE OF TEAMWORK.
5-2-05 © 2005 Scott Adams, Inc./Dist. by UFS, Inc.

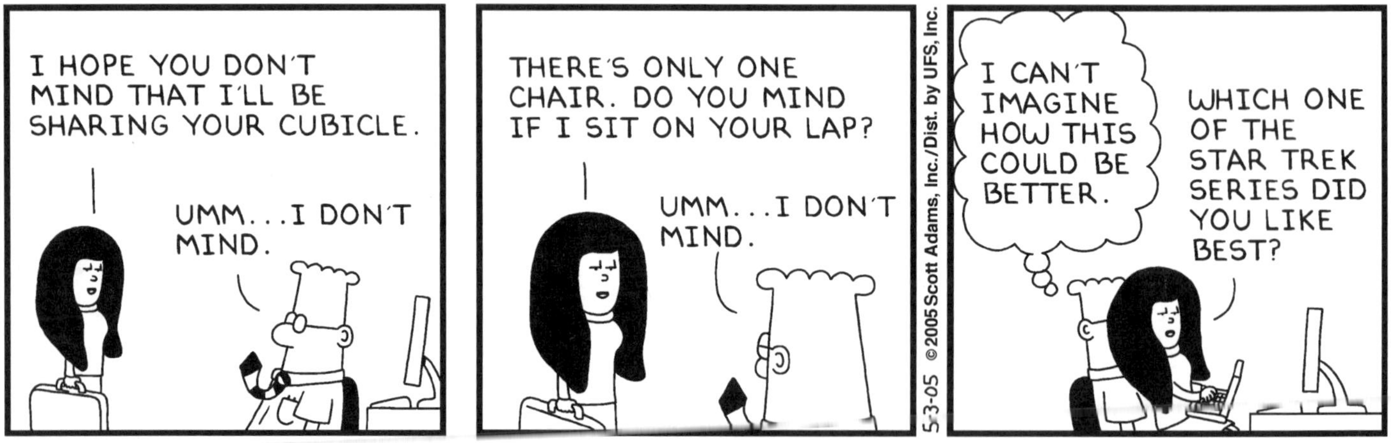
I HOPE YOU DON'T MIND THAT I'LL BE SHARING YOUR CUBICLE.
UMM...I DON'T MIND.
THERE'S ONLY ONE CHAIR. DO YOU MIND IF I SIT ON YOUR LAP?
UMM...I DON'T MIND.
I CAN'T IMAGINE HOW THIS COULD BE BETTER.
WHICH ONE OF THE STAR TREK SERIES DID YOU LIKE BEST?
5-3-05 © 2005 Scott Adams, Inc./Dist. by UFS, Inc.

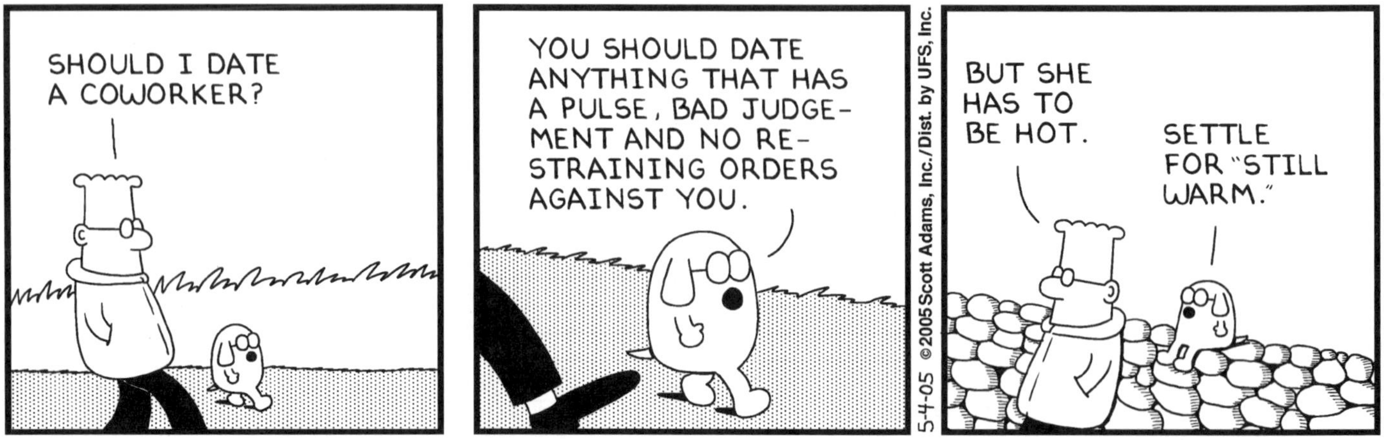
SHOULD I DATE A COWORKER?
YOU SHOULD DATE ANYTHING THAT HAS A PULSE, BAD JUDGEMENT AND NO RESTRAINING ORDERS AGAINST YOU.
BUT SHE HAS TO BE HOT.
SETTLE FOR "STILL WARM."
5-4-05 © 2005 Scott Adams, Inc./Dist. by UFS, Inc.

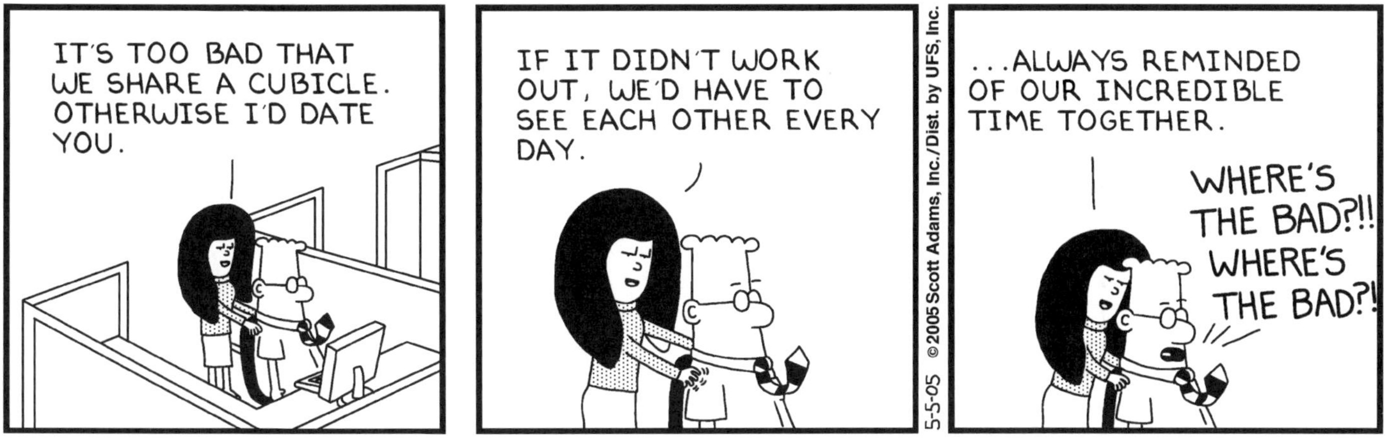
IT'S TOO BAD THAT WE SHARE A CUBICLE. OTHERWISE I'D DATE YOU.
IF IT DIDN'T WORK OUT, WE'D HAVE TO SEE EACH OTHER EVERY DAY.
...ALWAYS REMINDED OF OUR INCREDIBLE TIME TOGETHER.
WHERE'S THE BAD?!! WHERE'S THE BAD?!
5-5-05 © 2005 Scott Adams, Inc./Dist. by UFS, Inc.

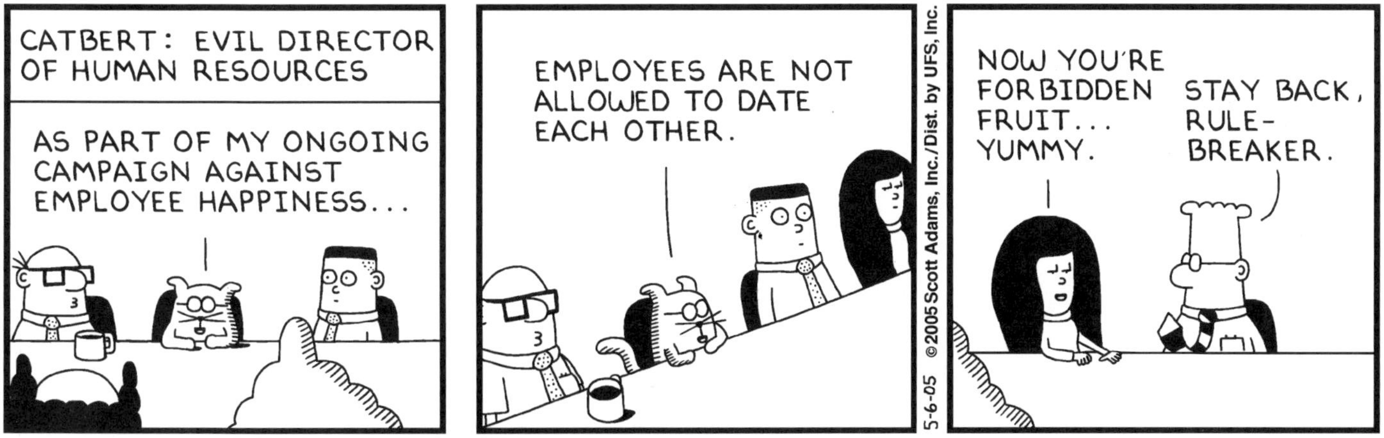
CATBERT: EVIL DIRECTOR OF HUMAN RESOURCES
AS PART OF MY ONGOING CAMPAIGN AGAINST EMPLOYEE HAPPINESS...
EMPLOYEES ARE NOT ALLOWED TO DATE EACH OTHER.
NOW YOU'RE FORBIDDEN FRUIT... YUMMY.
STAY BACK, RULE-BREAKER.
5-6-05 © 2005 Scott Adams, Inc./Dist. by UFS, Inc.

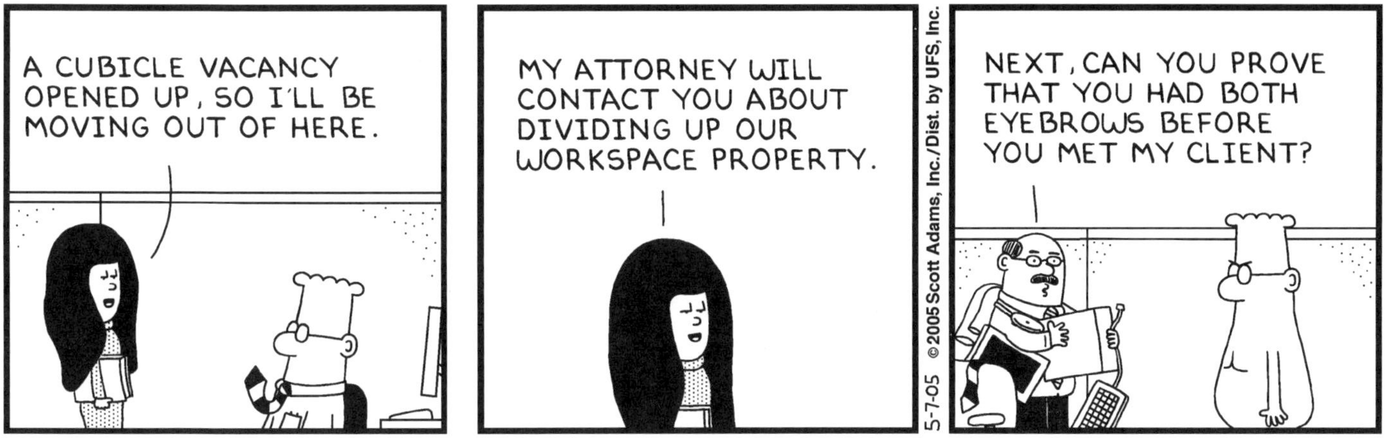
A CUBICLE VACANCY OPENED UP, SO I'LL BE MOVING OUT OF HERE.
MY ATTORNEY WILL CONTACT YOU ABOUT DIVIDING UP OUR WORKSPACE PROPERTY.
NEXT, CAN YOU PROVE THAT YOU HAD BOTH EYEBROWS BEFORE YOU MET MY CLIENT?
5-7-05 © 2005 Scott Adams, Inc./Dist. by UFS, Inc.

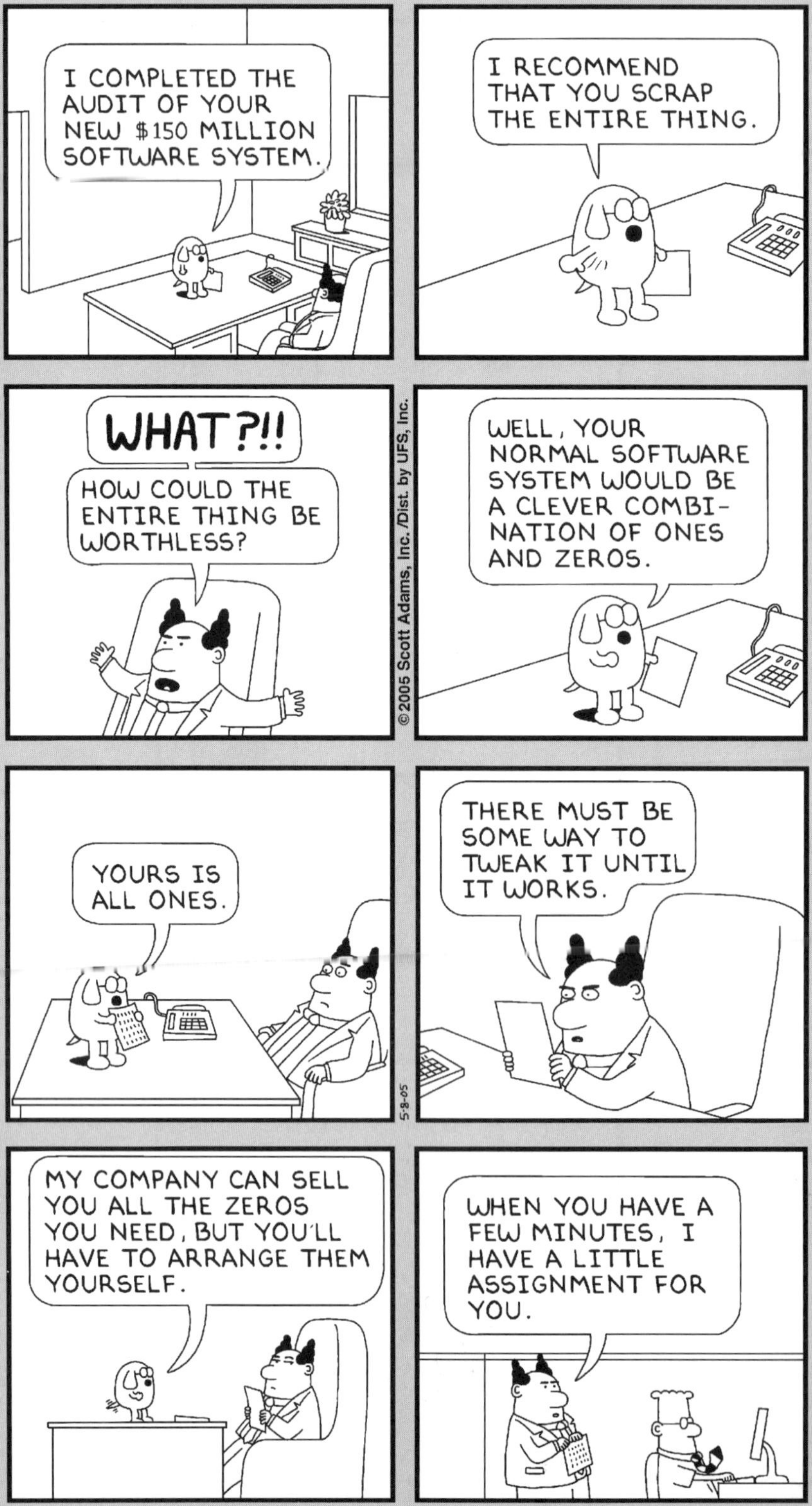
I COMPLETED THE AUDIT OF YOUR NEW $150 MILLION SOFTWARE SYSTEM.
I RECOMMEND THAT YOU SCRAP THE ENTIRE THING.
WHAT?!!
HOW COULD THE ENTIRE THING BE WORTHLESS?
WELL, YOUR NORMAL SOFTWARE SYSTEM WOULD BE A CLEVER COMBI-NATION OF ONES AND ZEROS.
YOURS IS ALL ONES.
THERE MUST BE SOME WAY TO TWEAK IT UNTIL IT WORKS.
MY COMPANY CAN SELL YOU ALL THE ZEROS YOU NEED, BUT YOU'LL HAVE TO ARRANGE THEM YOURSELF.
WHEN YOU HAVE A FEW MINUTES, I HAVE A LITTLE ASSIGNMENT FOR YOU.
©2005 Scott Adams, Inc./Dist. by UFS, Inc.
5-8-05

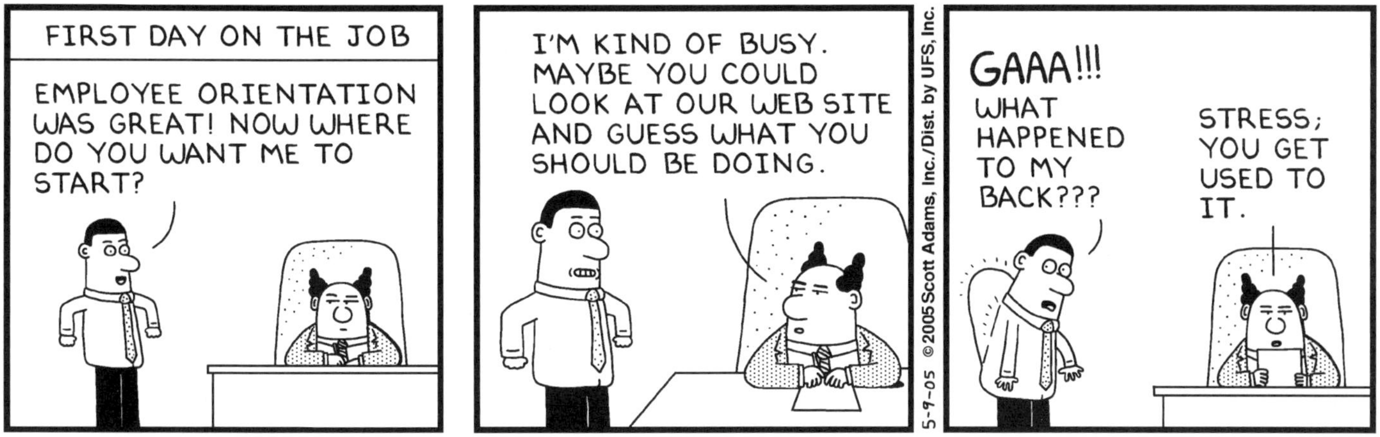
FIRST DAY ON THE JOB
EMPLOYEE ORIENTATION WAS GREAT! NOW WHERE DO YOU WANT ME TO START?
I'M KIND OF BUSY. MAYBE YOU COULD LOOK AT OUR WEB SITE AND GUESS WHAT YOU SHOULD BE DOING.
5-9-05 © 2005 Scott Adams, Inc./Dist. by UFS, Inc.
GAAA!!! WHAT HAPPENED TO MY BACK???
STRESS; YOU GET USED TO IT.

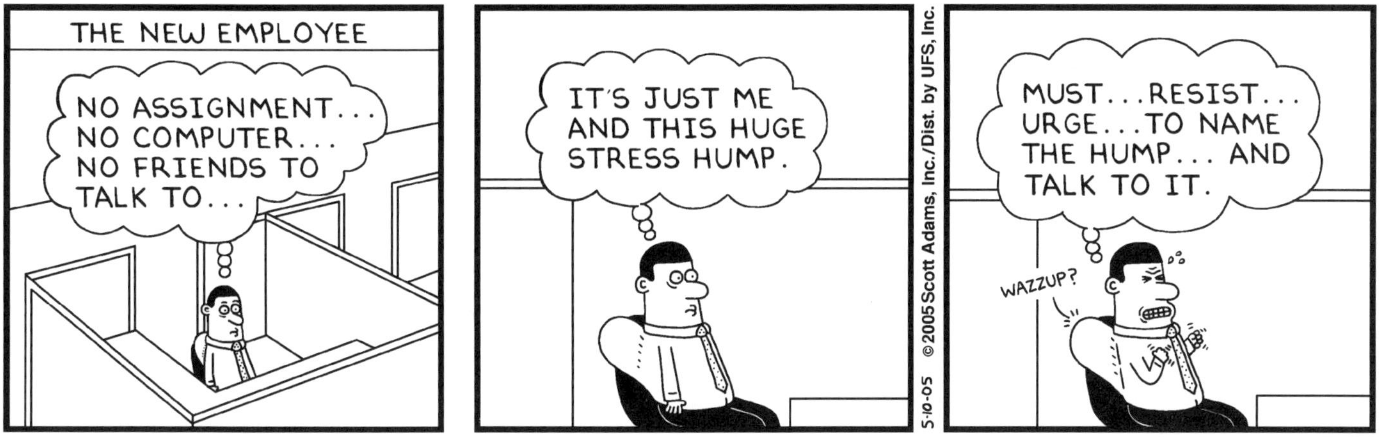
THE NEW EMPLOYEE
NO ASSIGNMENT... NO COMPUTER... NO FRIENDS TO TALK TO...
IT'S JUST ME AND THIS HUGE STRESS HUMP.
5-10-05 © 2005 Scott Adams, Inc./Dist. by UFS, Inc.
MUST... RESIST... URGE... TO NAME THE HUMP... AND TALK TO IT.
WAZZUP?

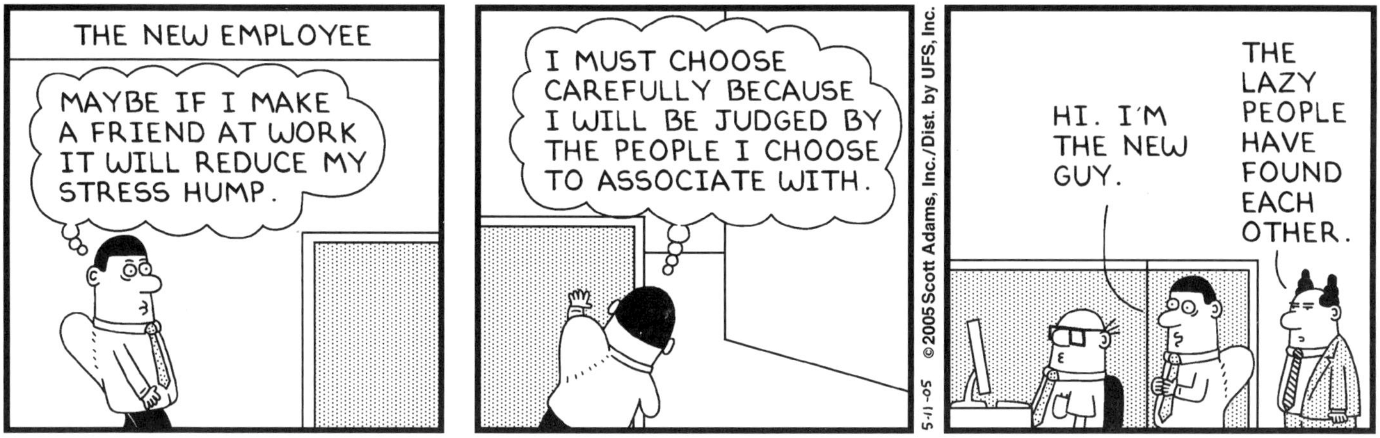
THE NEW EMPLOYEE
MAYBE IF I MAKE A FRIEND AT WORK IT WILL REDUCE MY STRESS HUMP.
I MUST CHOOSE CAREFULLY BECAUSE I WILL BE JUDGED BY THE PEOPLE I CHOOSE TO ASSOCIATE WITH.
5-11-05 © 2005 Scott Adams, Inc./Dist. by UFS, Inc.
HI. I'M THE NEW GUY.
THE LAZY PEOPLE HAVE FOUND EACH OTHER.

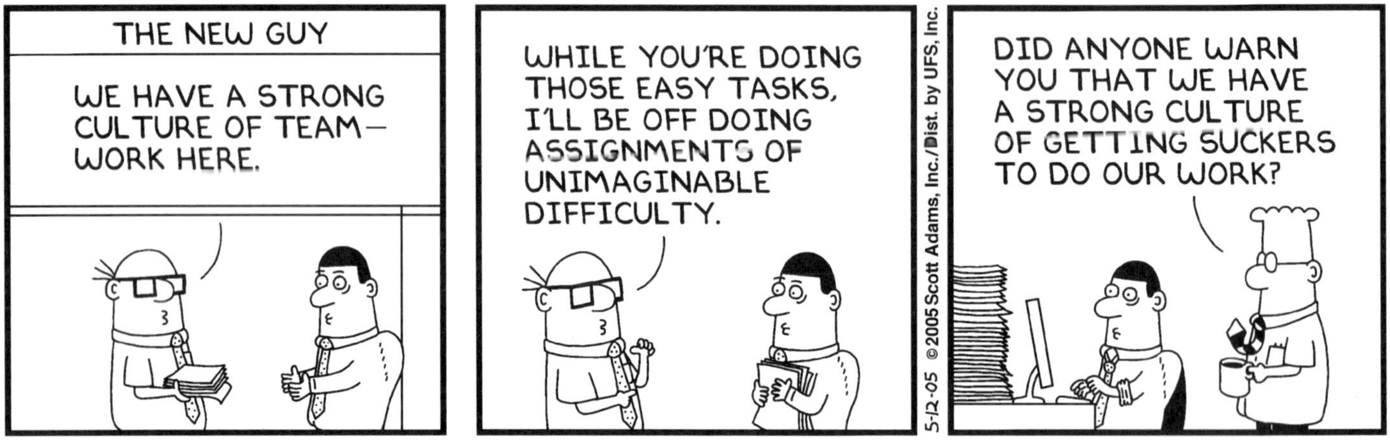
THE NEW GUY
WE HAVE A STRONG CULTURE OF TEAM-WORK HERE.
WHILE YOU'RE DOING THOSE EASY TASKS, I'LL BE OFF DOING ASSIGNMENTS OF UNIMAGINABLE DIFFICULTY.
5-12-05 © 2005 Scott Adams, Inc./Dist. by UFS, Inc.
DID ANYONE WARN YOU THAT WE HAVE A STRONG CULTURE OF GETTING SUCKERS TO DO OUR WORK?

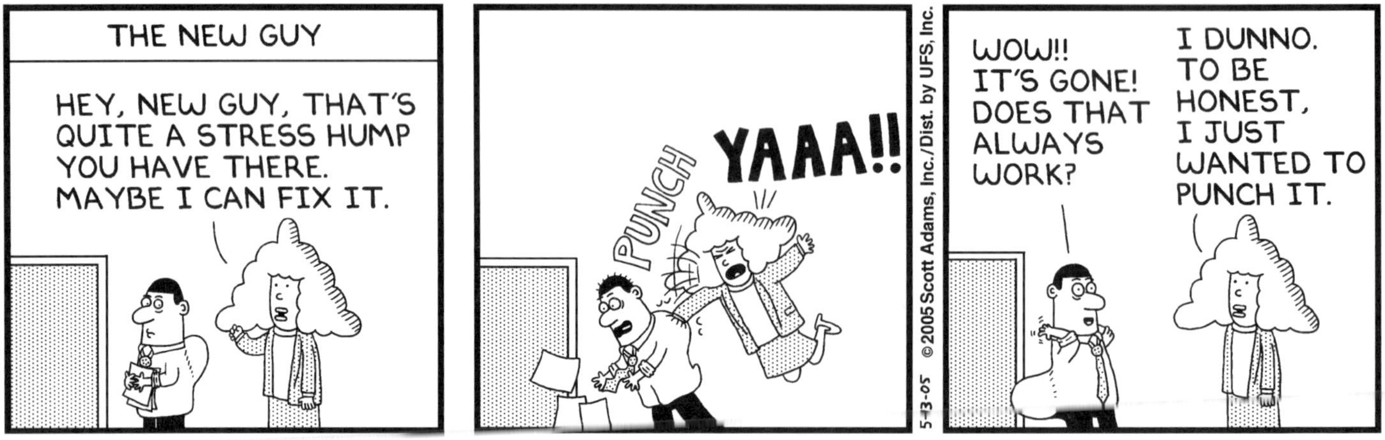
THE NEW GUY
HEY, NEW GUY, THAT'S QUITE A STRESS HUMP YOU HAVE THERE. MAYBE I CAN FIX IT.
PUNCH
YAAA!!
5-13-05 © 2005 Scott Adams, Inc./Dist. by UFS, Inc.
WOW!! IT'S GONE! DOES THAT ALWAYS WORK?
I DUNNO. TO BE HONEST, I JUST WANTED TO PUNCH IT.

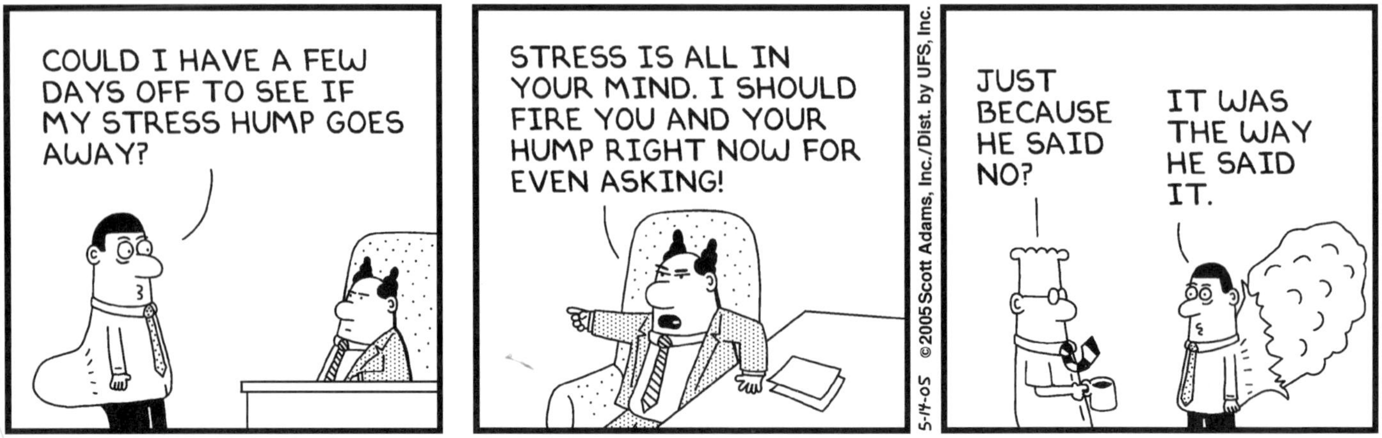
COULD I HAVE A FEW DAYS OFF TO SEE IF MY STRESS HUMP GOES AWAY?
STRESS IS ALL IN YOUR MIND. I SHOULD FIRE YOU AND YOUR HUMP RIGHT NOW FOR EVEN ASKING!
5-14-05 © 2005 Scott Adams, Inc./Dist. by UFS, Inc.
JUST BECAUSE HE SAID NO?
IT WAS THE WAY HE SAID IT.

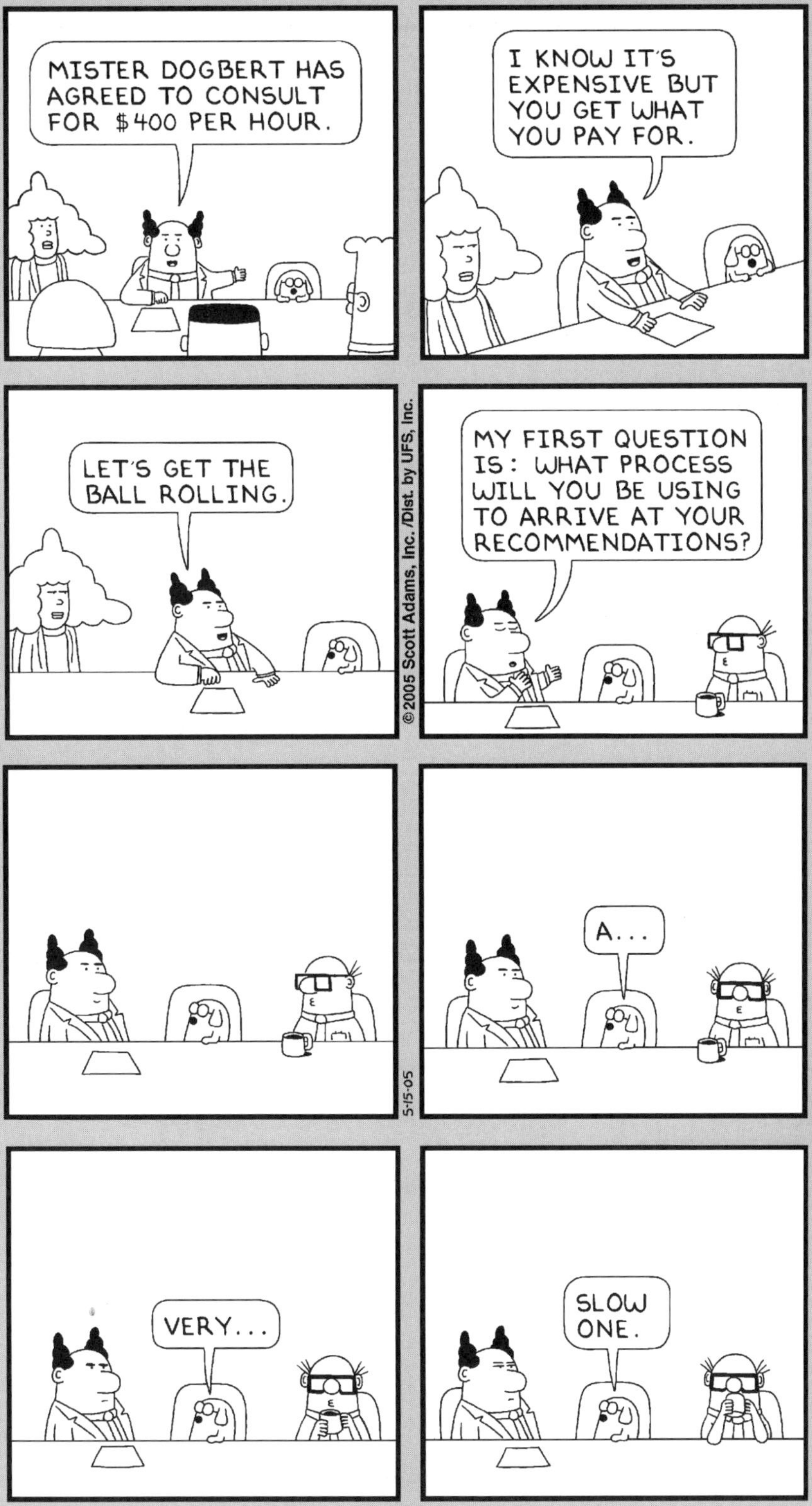
MISTER DOGBERT HAS AGREED TO CONSULT FOR $400 PER HOUR.
I KNOW IT'S EXPENSIVE BUT YOU GET WHAT YOU PAY FOR.
LET'S GET THE BALL ROLLING.
MY FIRST QUESTION IS: WHAT PROCESS WILL YOU BE USING TO ARRIVE AT YOUR RECOMMENDATIONS?
A...
VERY...
SLOW ONE.
©2005 Scott Adams, Inc. /Dist. by UFS, Inc.
5-15-05

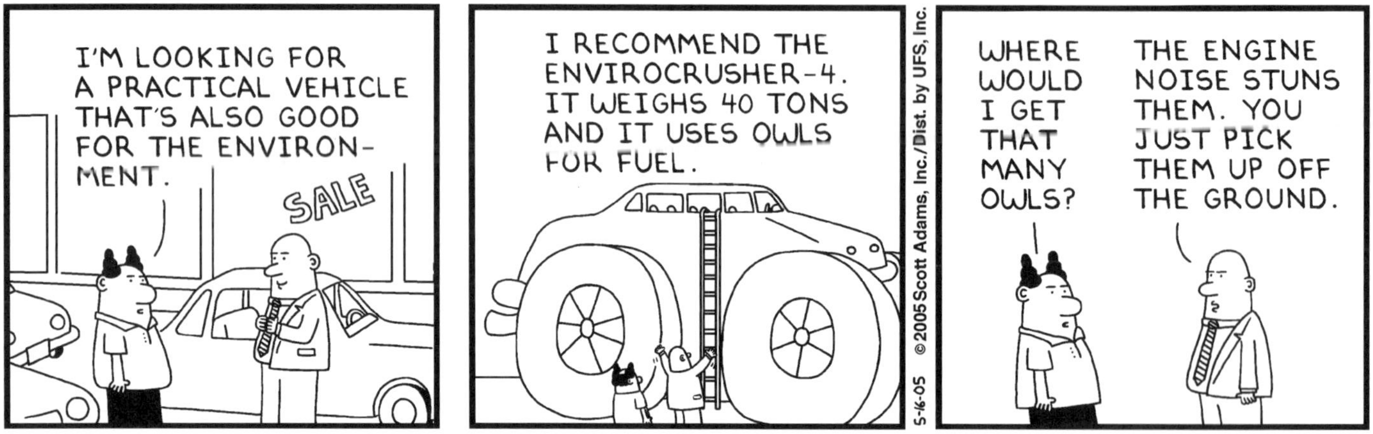
I'M LOOKING FOR A PRACTICAL VEHICLE THAT'S ALSO GOOD FOR THE ENVIRON-MENT.
SALE
I RECOMMEND THE ENVIROCRUSHER-4. IT WEIGHS 40 TONS AND IT USES OWLS FOR FUEL.
5-6-05 © 2005 Scott Adams, Inc./Dist. by UFS, Inc.
WHERE WOULD I GET THAT MANY OWLS?
THE ENGINE NOISE STUNS THEM. YOU JUST PICK THEM UP OFF THE GROUND.

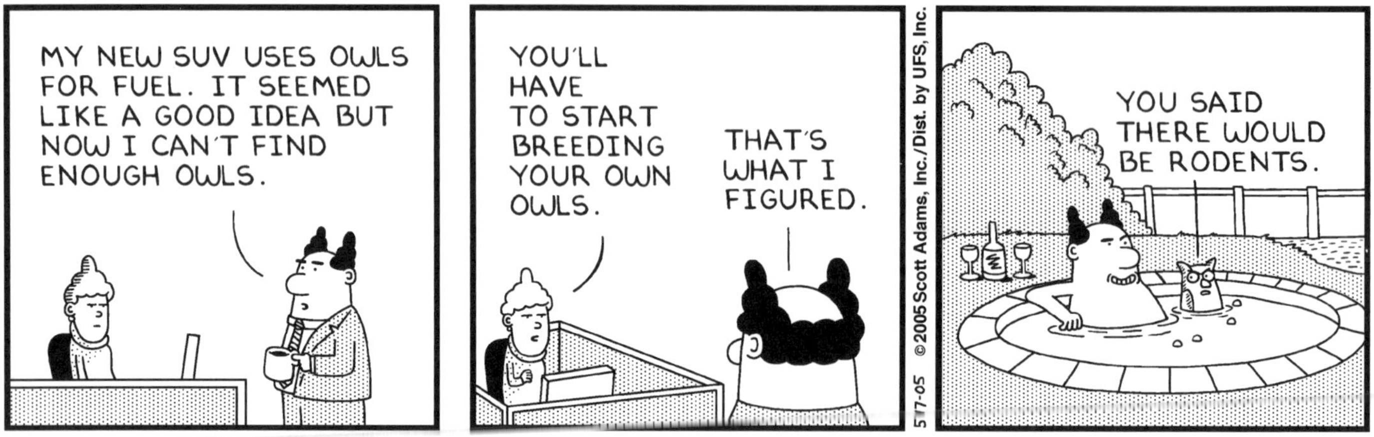
MY NEW SUV USES OWLS FOR FUEL. IT SEEMED LIKE A GOOD IDEA BUT NOW I CAN'T FIND ENOUGH OWLS.
YOU'LL HAVE TO START BREEDING YOUR OWN OWLS.
THAT'S WHAT I FIGURED.
5-7-05 © 2005 Scott Adams, Inc./Dist. by UFS, Inc.
YOU SAID THERE WOULD BE RODENTS.

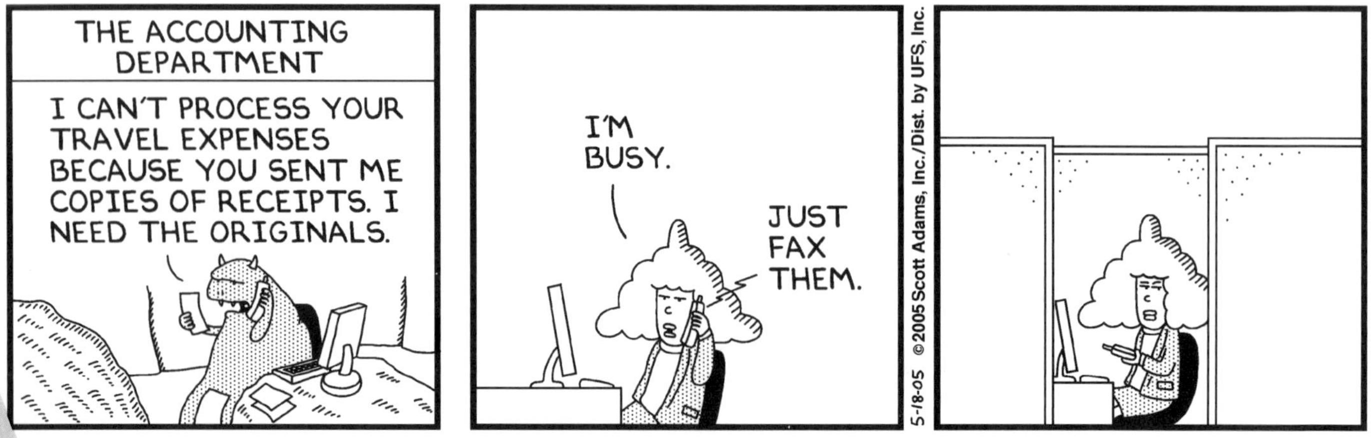
THE ACCOUNTING DEPARTMENT
I CAN'T PROCESS YOUR TRAVEL EXPENSES BECAUSE YOU SENT ME COPIES OF RECEIPTS. I NEED THE ORIGINALS.
I'M BUSY.
JUST FAX THEM.
5-8-05 © 2005 Scott Adams, Inc./Dist. by UFS, Inc.

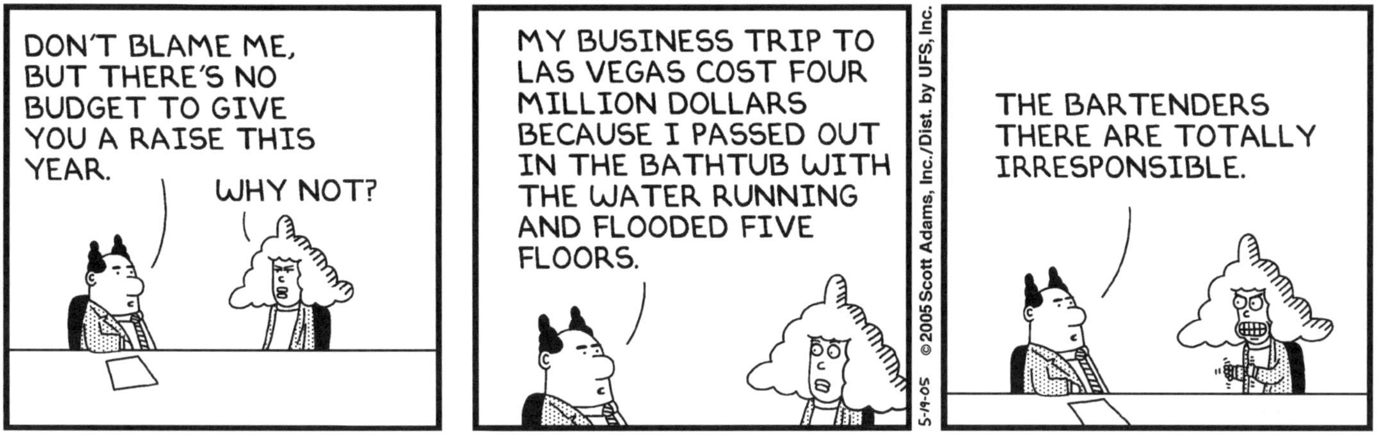
DON'T BLAME ME, BUT THERE'S NO BUDGET TO GIVE YOU A RAISE THIS YEAR.
WHY NOT?
MY BUSINESS TRIP TO LAS VEGAS COST FOUR MILLION DOLLARS BECAUSE I PASSED OUT IN THE BATHTUB WITH THE WATER RUNNING AND FLOODED FIVE FLOORS.
5-19-05 ©2005 Scott Adams, Inc./Dist. by UFS, Inc.
THE BARTENDERS THERE ARE TOTALLY IRRESPONSIBLE.

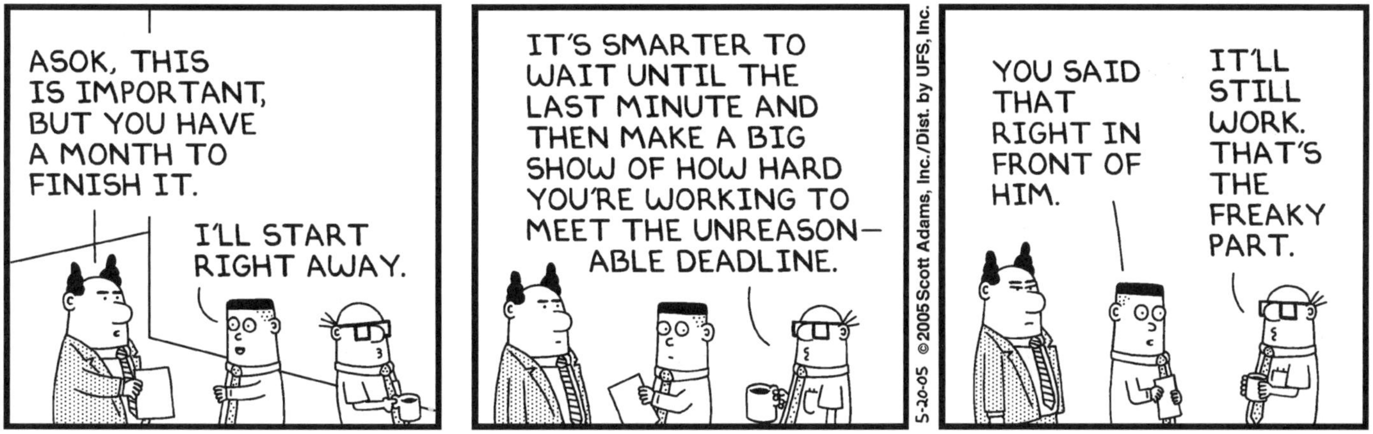
ASOK, THIS IS IMPORTANT, BUT YOU HAVE A MONTH TO FINISH IT.
I'LL START RIGHT AWAY.
IT'S SMARTER TO WAIT UNTIL THE LAST MINUTE AND THEN MAKE A BIG SHOW OF HOW HARD YOU'RE WORKING TO MEET THE UNREASON- ABLE DEADLINE.
5-20-05 ©2005 Scott Adams, Inc./Dist. by UFS, Inc.
YOU SAID THAT RIGHT IN FRONT OF HIM.
IT'LL STILL WORK. THAT'S THE FREAKY PART.

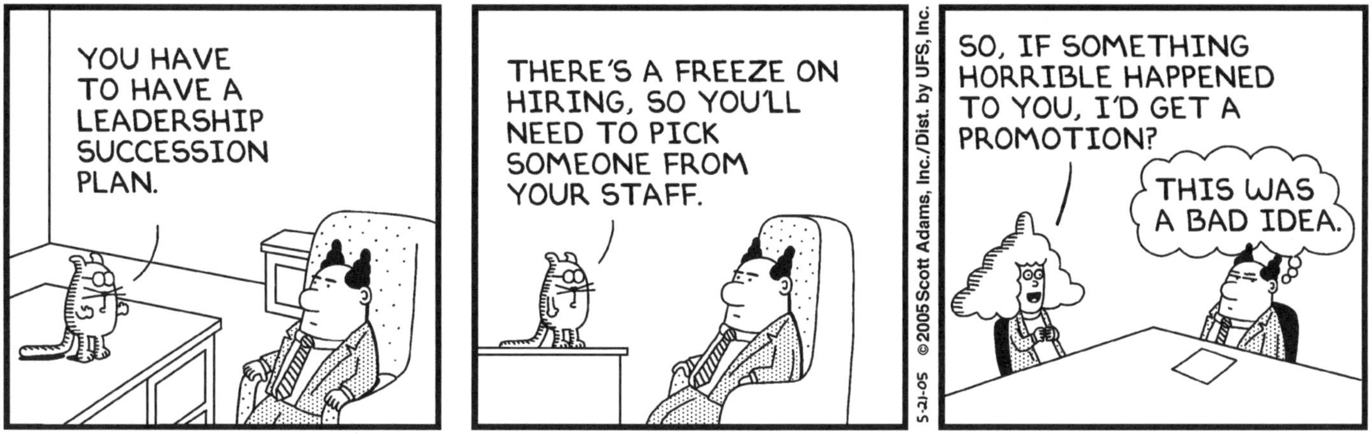
YOU HAVE TO HAVE A LEADERSHIP SUCCESSION PLAN.
THERE'S A FREEZE ON HIRING, SO YOU'LL NEED TO PICK SOMEONE FROM YOUR STAFF.
5-21-05 ©2005 Scott Adams, Inc./Dist. by UFS, Inc.
SO, IF SOMETHING HORRIBLE HAPPENED TO YOU, I'D GET A PROMOTION?
THIS WAS A BAD IDEA.

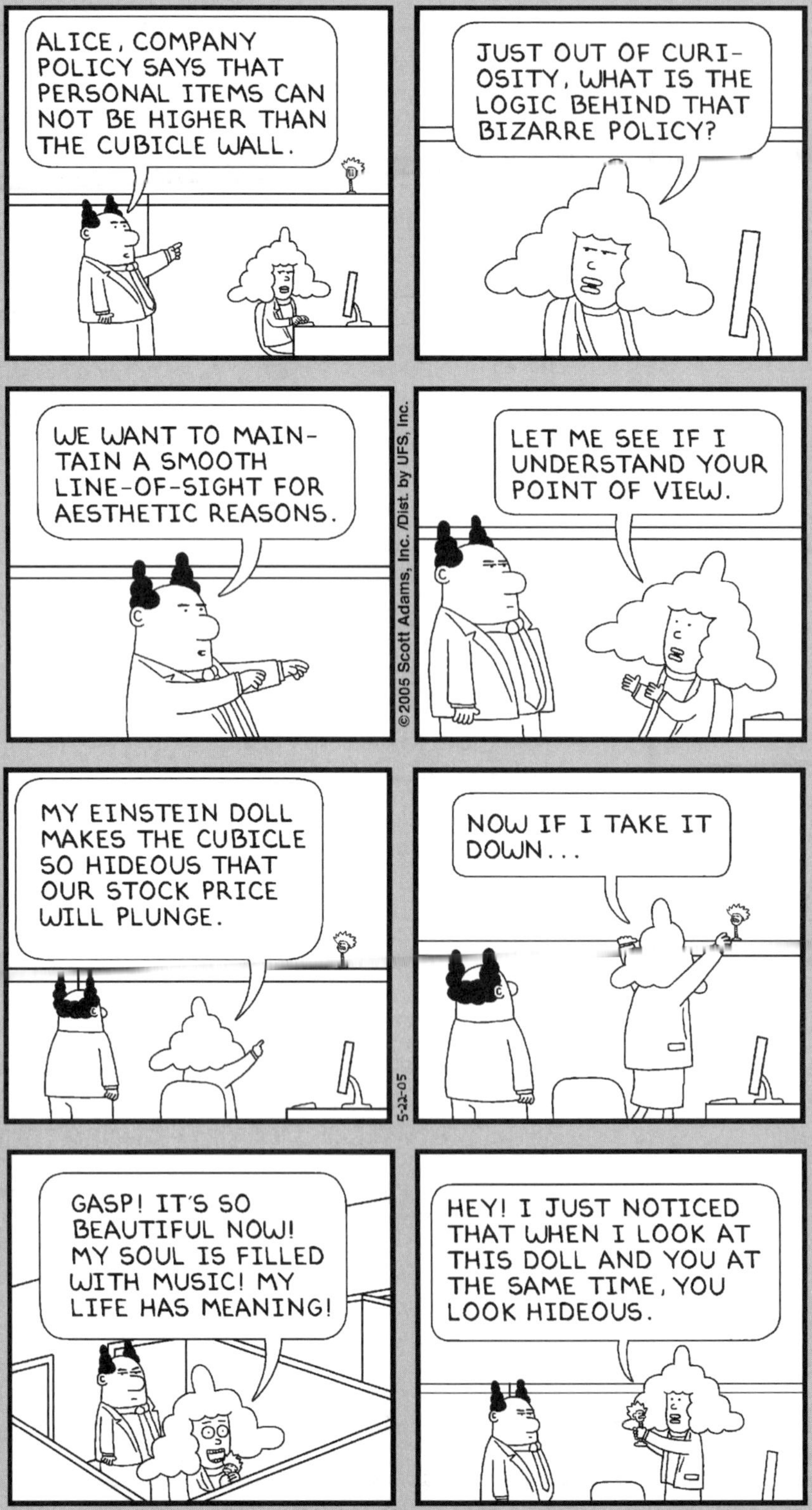
ALICE, COMPANY POLICY SAYS THAT PERSONAL ITEMS CAN NOT BE HIGHER THAN THE CUBICLE WALL.
JUST OUT OF CURI-OSITY, WHAT IS THE LOGIC BEHIND THAT BIZARRE POLICY?
WE WANT TO MAIN-TAIN A SMOOTH LINE-OF-SIGHT FOR AESTHETIC REASONS.
LET ME SEE IF I UNDERSTAND YOUR POINT OF VIEW.
MY EINSTEIN DOLL MAKES THE CUBICLE SO HIDEOUS THAT OUR STOCK PRICE WILL PLUNGE.
NOW IF I TAKE IT DOWN...
GASP! IT'S SO BEAUTIFUL NOW! MY SOUL IS FILLED WITH MUSIC! MY LIFE HAS MEANING!
HEY! I JUST NOTICED THAT WHEN I LOOK AT THIS DOLL AND YOU AT THE SAME TIME, YOU LOOK HIDEOUS.
©2005 Scott Adams, Inc. /Dist. by UFS, Inc.
5-22-05

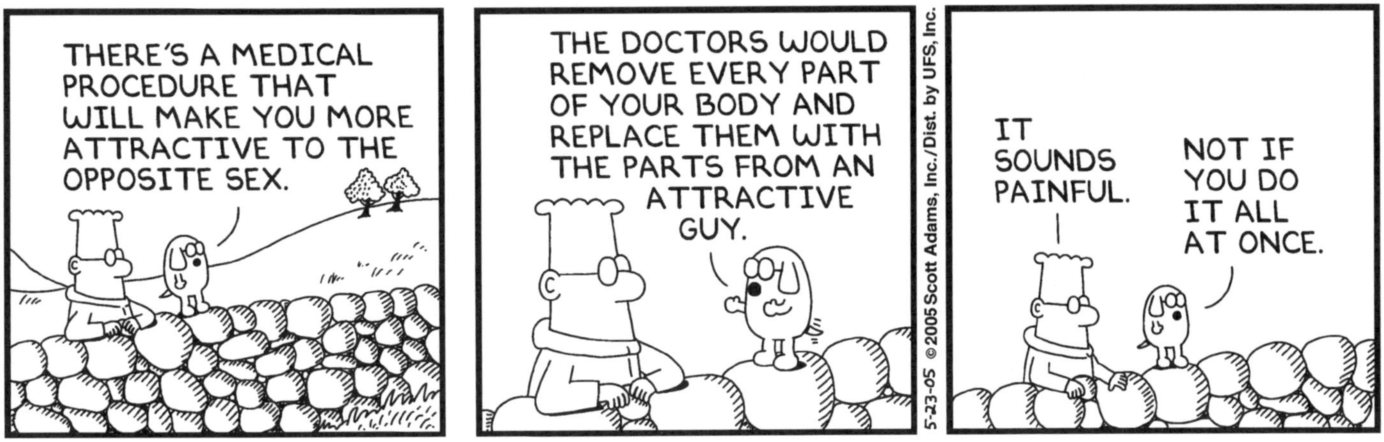
THERE'S A MEDICAL PROCEDURE THAT WILL MAKE YOU MORE ATTRACTIVE TO THE OPPOSITE SEX.
THE DOCTORS WOULD REMOVE EVERY PART OF YOUR BODY AND REPLACE THEM WITH THE PARTS FROM AN ATTRACTIVE GUY.
5-23-05 © 2005 Scott Adams, Inc./Dist. by UFS, Inc.
IT SOUNDS PAINFUL.
NOT IF YOU DO IT ALL AT ONCE.

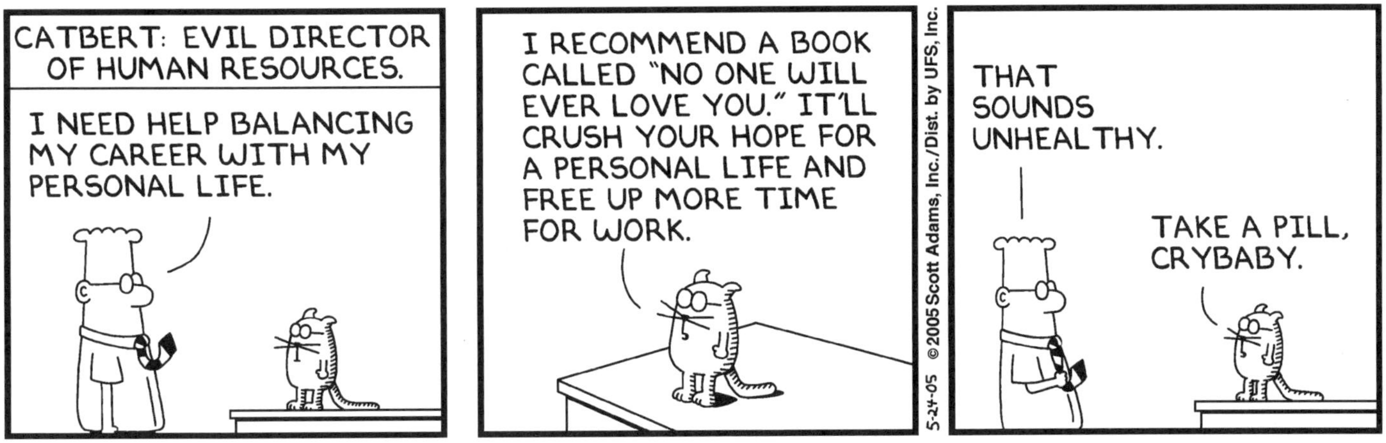
CATBERT: EVIL DIRECTOR OF HUMAN RESOURCES.
I NEED HELP BALANCING MY CAREER WITH MY PERSONAL LIFE.
I RECOMMEND A BOOK CALLED "NO ONE WILL EVER LOVE YOU." IT'LL CRUSH YOUR HOPE FOR A PERSONAL LIFE AND FREE UP MORE TIME FOR WORK.
5-24-05 © 2005 Scott Adams, Inc./Dist. by UFS, Inc.
THAT SOUNDS UNHEALTHY.
TAKE A PILL, CRYBABY.

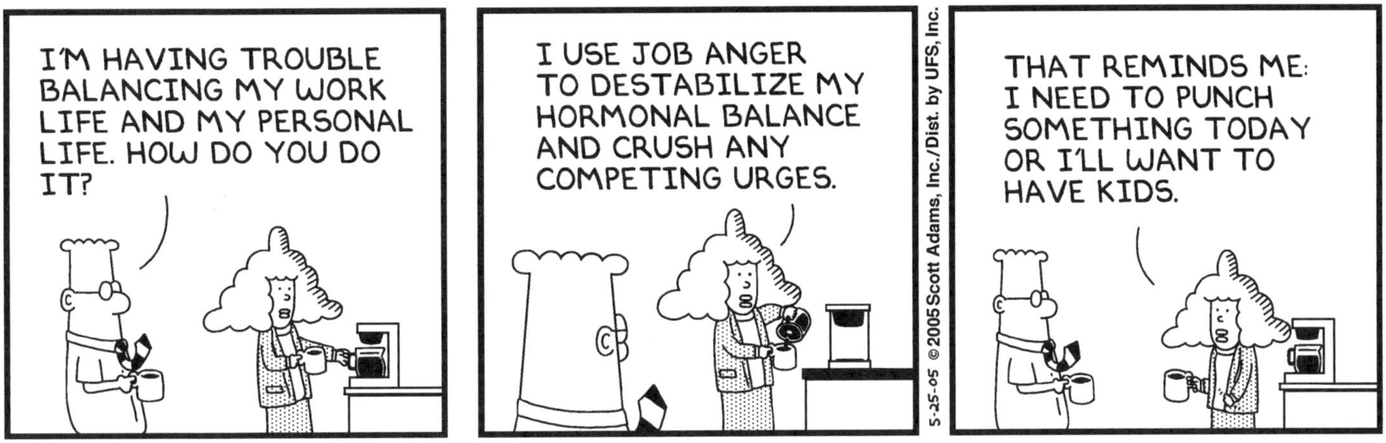
I'M HAVING TROUBLE BALANCING MY WORK LIFE AND MY PERSONAL LIFE. HOW DO YOU DO IT?
I USE JOB ANGER TO DESTABILIZE MY HORMONAL BALANCE AND CRUSH ANY COMPETING URGES.
5-25-05 © 2005 Scott Adams, Inc./Dist. by UFS, Inc.
THAT REMINDS ME: I NEED TO PUNCH SOMETHING TODAY OR I'LL WANT TO HAVE KIDS.

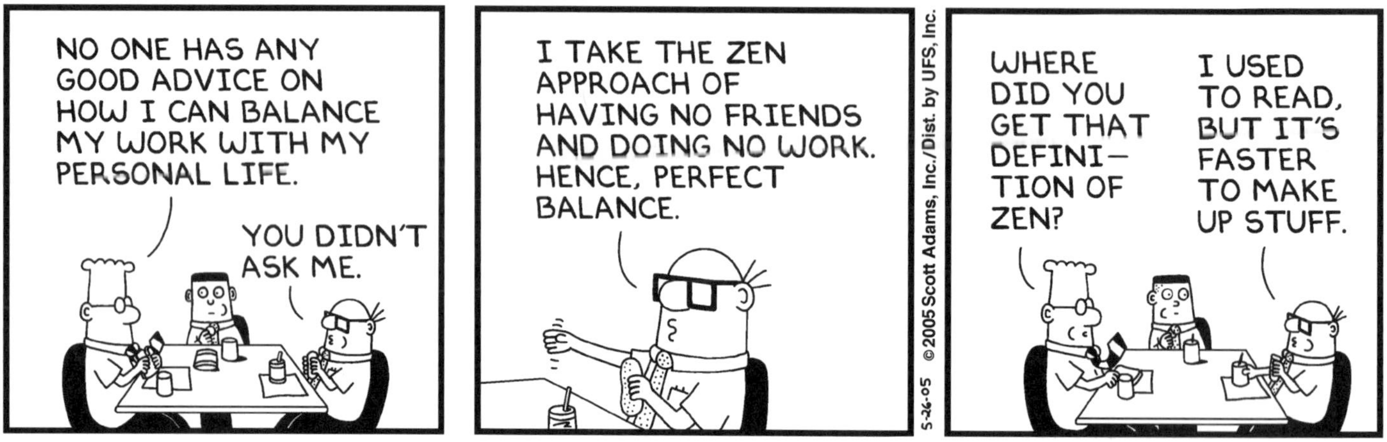
NO ONE HAS ANY GOOD ADVICE ON HOW I CAN BALANCE MY WORK WITH MY PERSONAL LIFE.
YOU DIDN'T ASK ME.
I TAKE THE ZEN APPROACH OF HAVING NO FRIENDS AND DOING NO WORK. HENCE, PERFECT BALANCE.
5-26-05 © 2005 Scott Adams, Inc./Dist. by UFS, Inc.
WHERE DID YOU GET THAT DEFINI-TION OF ZEN?
I USED TO READ, BUT IT'S FASTER TO MAKE UP STUFF.

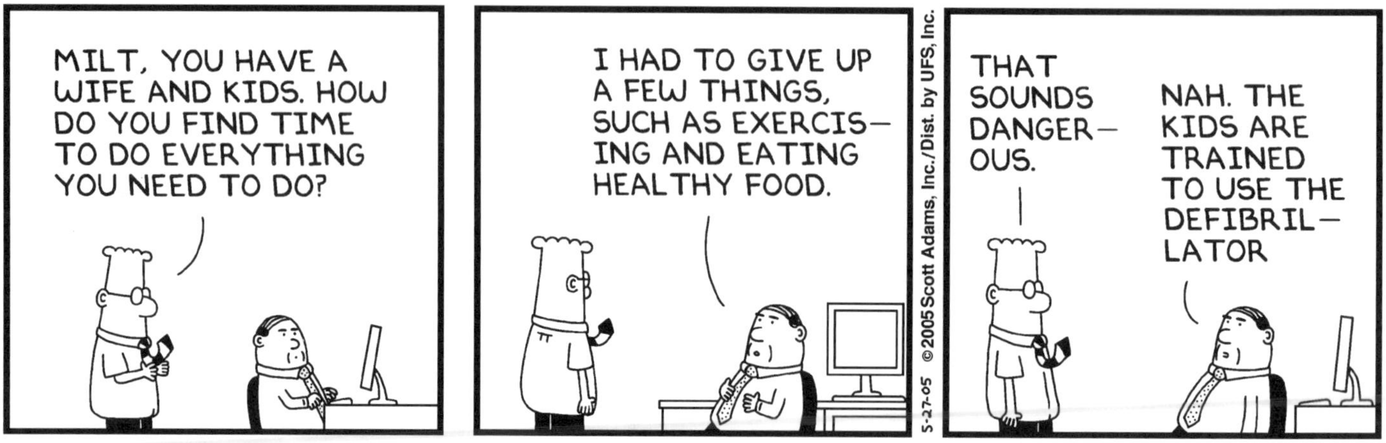
MILT, YOU HAVE A WIFE AND KIDS. HOW DO YOU FIND TIME TO DO EVERYTHING YOU NEED TO DO?
I HAD TO GIVE UP A FEW THINGS, SUCH AS EXERCIS-ING AND EATING HEALTHY FOOD.
5-27-05 © 2005 Scott Adams, Inc./Dist. by UFS, Inc.
THAT SOUNDS DANGER-OUS.
NAH. THE KIDS ARE TRAINED TO USE THE DEFIBRIL-LATOR

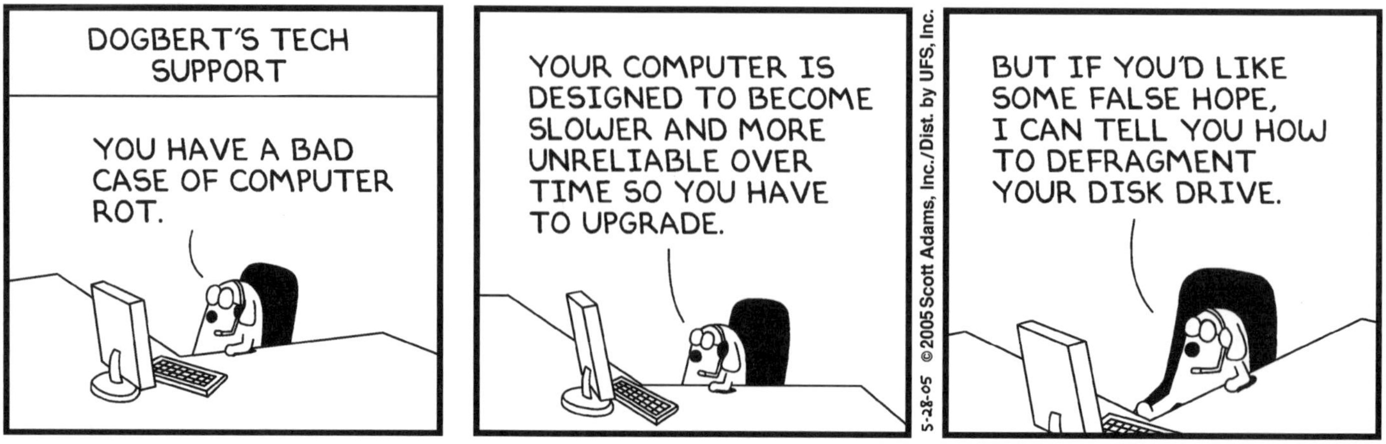
DOGBERT'S TECH SUPPORT
YOU HAVE A BAD CASE OF COMPUTER ROT.
YOUR COMPUTER IS DESIGNED TO BECOME SLOWER AND MORE UNRELIABLE OVER TIME SO YOU HAVE TO UPGRADE.
5-28-05 © 2005 Scott Adams, Inc./Dist. by UFS, Inc.
BUT IF YOU'D LIKE SOME FALSE HOPE, I CAN TELL YOU HOW TO DEFRAGMENT YOUR DISK DRIVE.

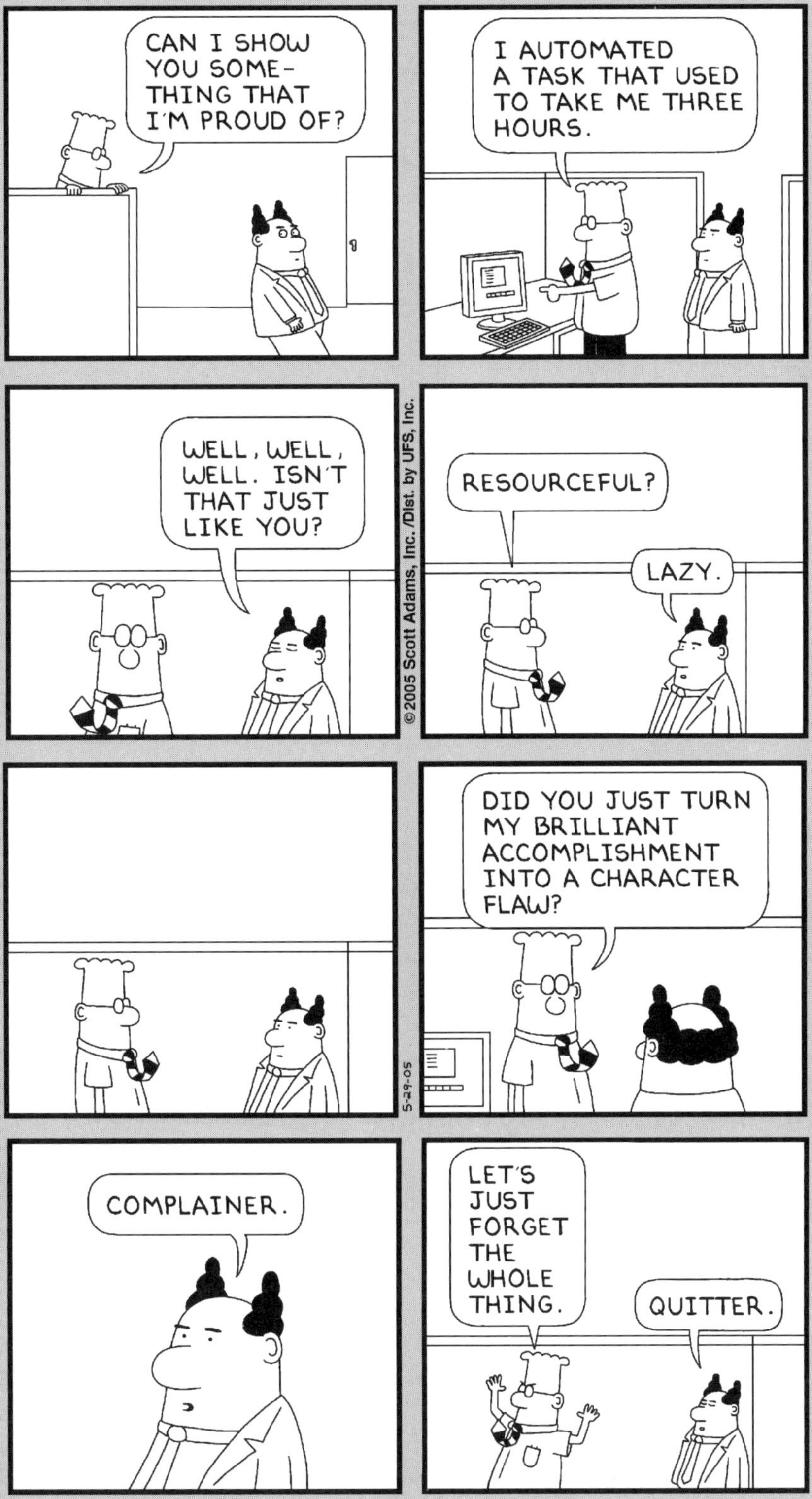
CAN I SHOW YOU SOMETHING THAT I'M PROUD OF?
I AUTOMATED A TASK THAT USED TO TAKE ME THREE HOURS.
WELL, WELL, WELL. ISN'T THAT JUST LIKE YOU?
RESOURCEFUL?
LAZY.
DID YOU JUST TURN MY BRILLIANT ACCOMPLISHMENT INTO A CHARACTER FLAW?
COMPLAINER.
LET'S JUST FORGET THE WHOLE THING.
QUITTER.
©2005 Scott Adams, Inc. /Dist. by UFS, Inc.
5-29-05

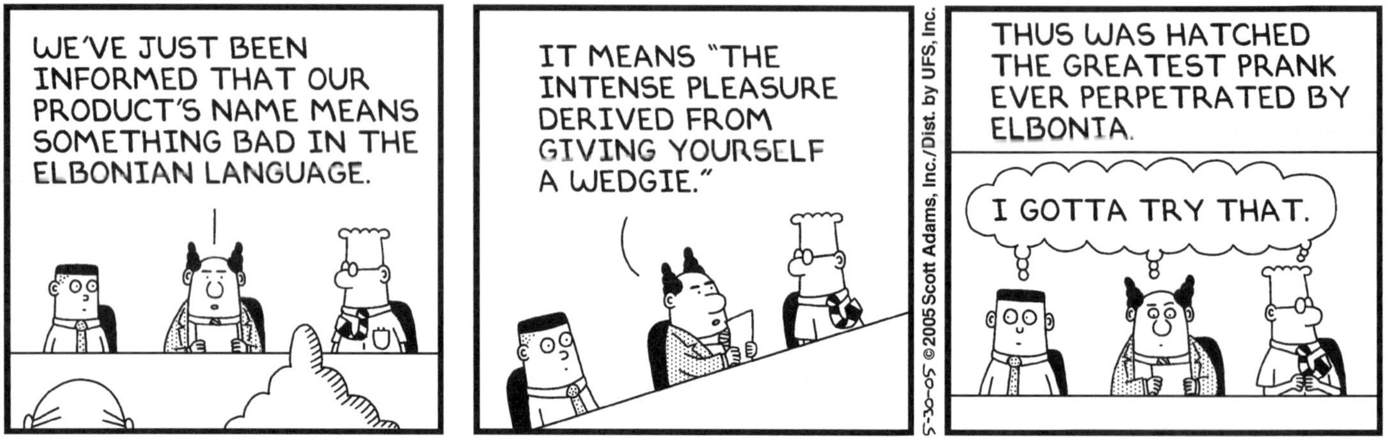
WE'VE JUST BEEN INFORMED THAT OUR PRODUCT'S NAME MEANS SOMETHING BAD IN THE ELBONIAN LANGUAGE.
IT MEANS "THE INTENSE PLEASURE DERIVED FROM GIVING YOURSELF A WEDGIE."
5-30-05 ©2005 Scott Adams, Inc./Dist. by UFS, Inc.
THUS WAS HATCHED THE GREATEST PRANK EVER PERPETRATED BY ELBONIA.
I GOTTA TRY THAT.

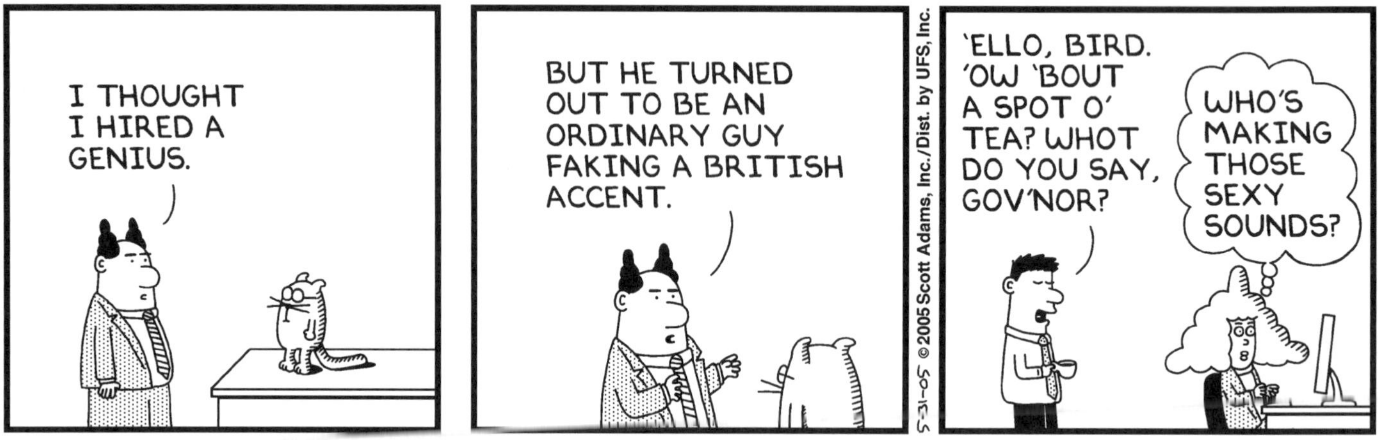
I THOUGHT I HIRED A GENIUS.
BUT HE TURNED OUT TO BE AN ORDINARY GUY FAKING A BRITISH ACCENT.
5-31-05 ©2005 Scott Adams, Inc./Dist. by UFS, Inc.
'ELLO, BIRD. 'OW 'BOUT A SPOT O' TEA? WHOT DO YOU SAY, GOV'NOR?
WHO'S MAKING THOSE SEXY SOUNDS?

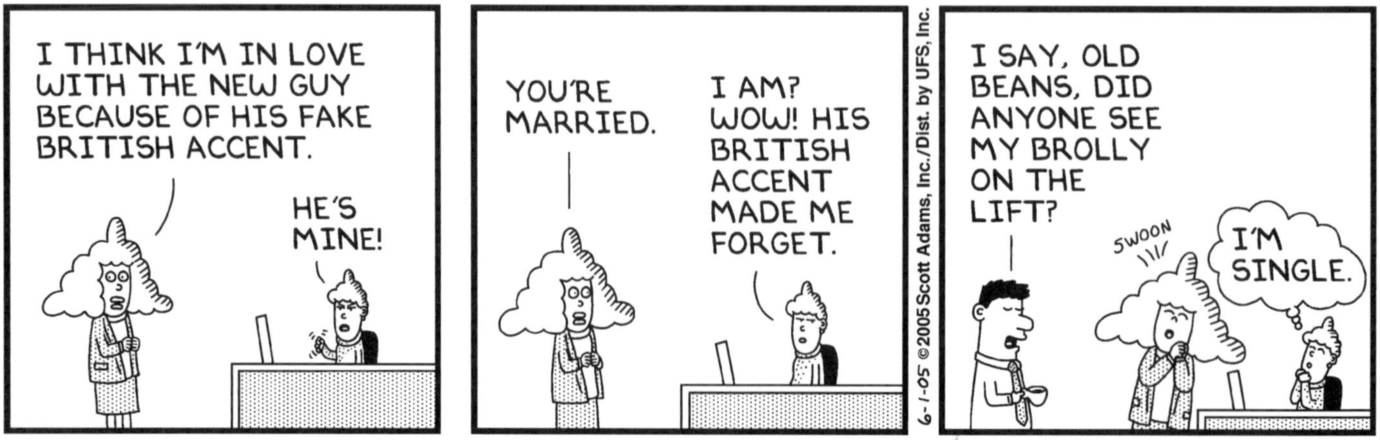
I THINK I'M IN LOVE WITH THE NEW GUY BECAUSE OF HIS FAKE BRITISH ACCENT.
HE'S MINE!
YOU'RE MARRIED.
I AM? WOW! HIS BRITISH ACCENT MADE ME FORGET.
6-1-05 ©2005 Scott Adams, Inc./Dist. by UFS, Inc.
I SAY, OLD BEANS, DID ANYONE SEE MY BROLLY ON THE LIFT?
SWOON
I'M SINGLE.

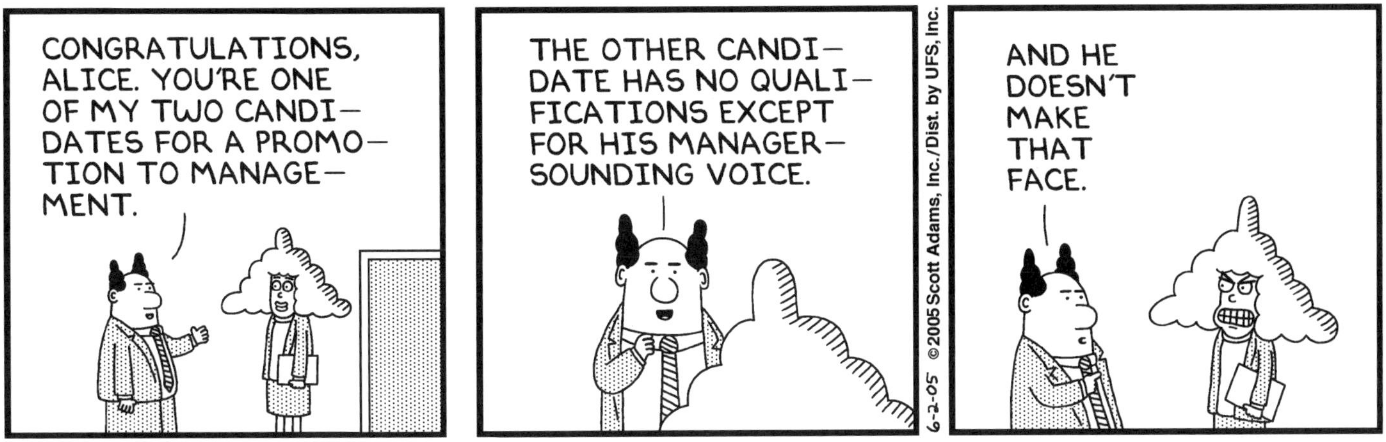
CONGRATULATIONS, ALICE. YOU'RE ONE OF MY TWO CANDI- DATES FOR A PROMO- TION TO MANAGE- MENT.
THE OTHER CANDI- DATE HAS NO QUALI- FICATIONS EXCEPT FOR HIS MANAGER- SOUNDING VOICE.
6-2-05 ©2005 Scott Adams, Inc./Dist. by UFS, Inc.
AND HE DOESN'T MAKE THAT FACE.

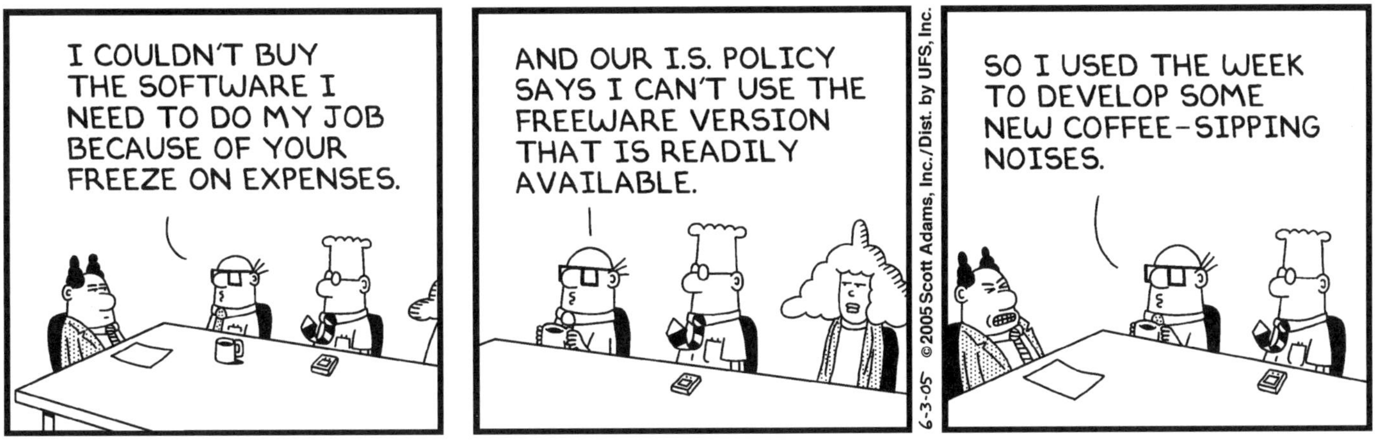
I COULDN'T BUY THE SOFTWARE I NEED TO DO MY JOB BECAUSE OF YOUR FREEZE ON EXPENSES.
AND OUR I.S. POLICY SAYS I CAN'T USE THE FREEWARE VERSION THAT IS READILY AVAILABLE.
6-3-05 ©2005 Scott Adams, Inc./Dist. by UFS, Inc.
SO I USED THE WEEK TO DEVELOP SOME NEW COFFEE-SIPPING NOISES.

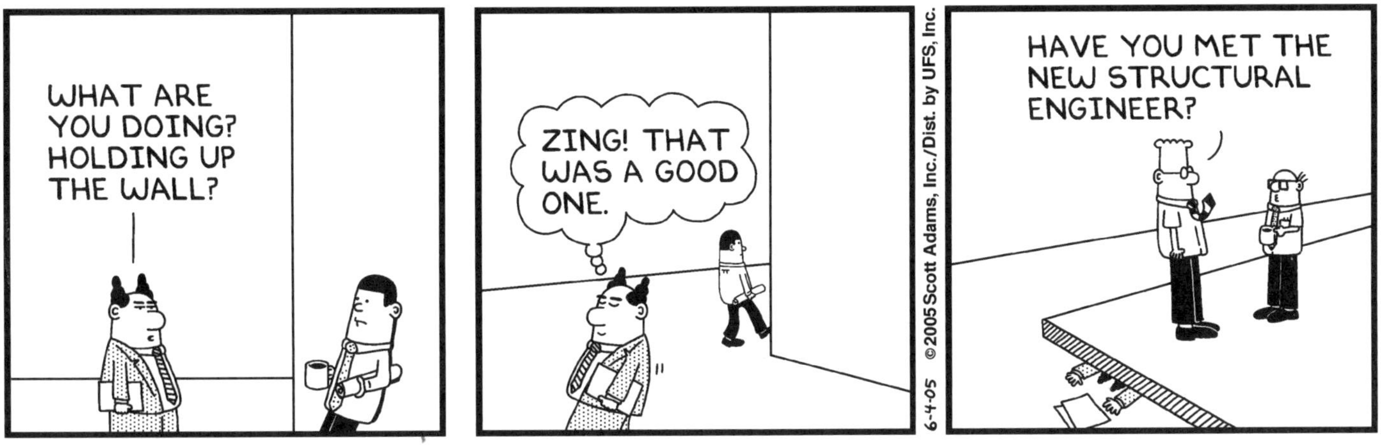
WHAT ARE YOU DOING? HOLDING UP THE WALL?
ZING! THAT WAS A GOOD ONE.
6-4-05 ©2005 Scott Adams, Inc./Dist. by UFS, Inc.
HAVE YOU MET THE NEW STRUCTURAL ENGINEER?

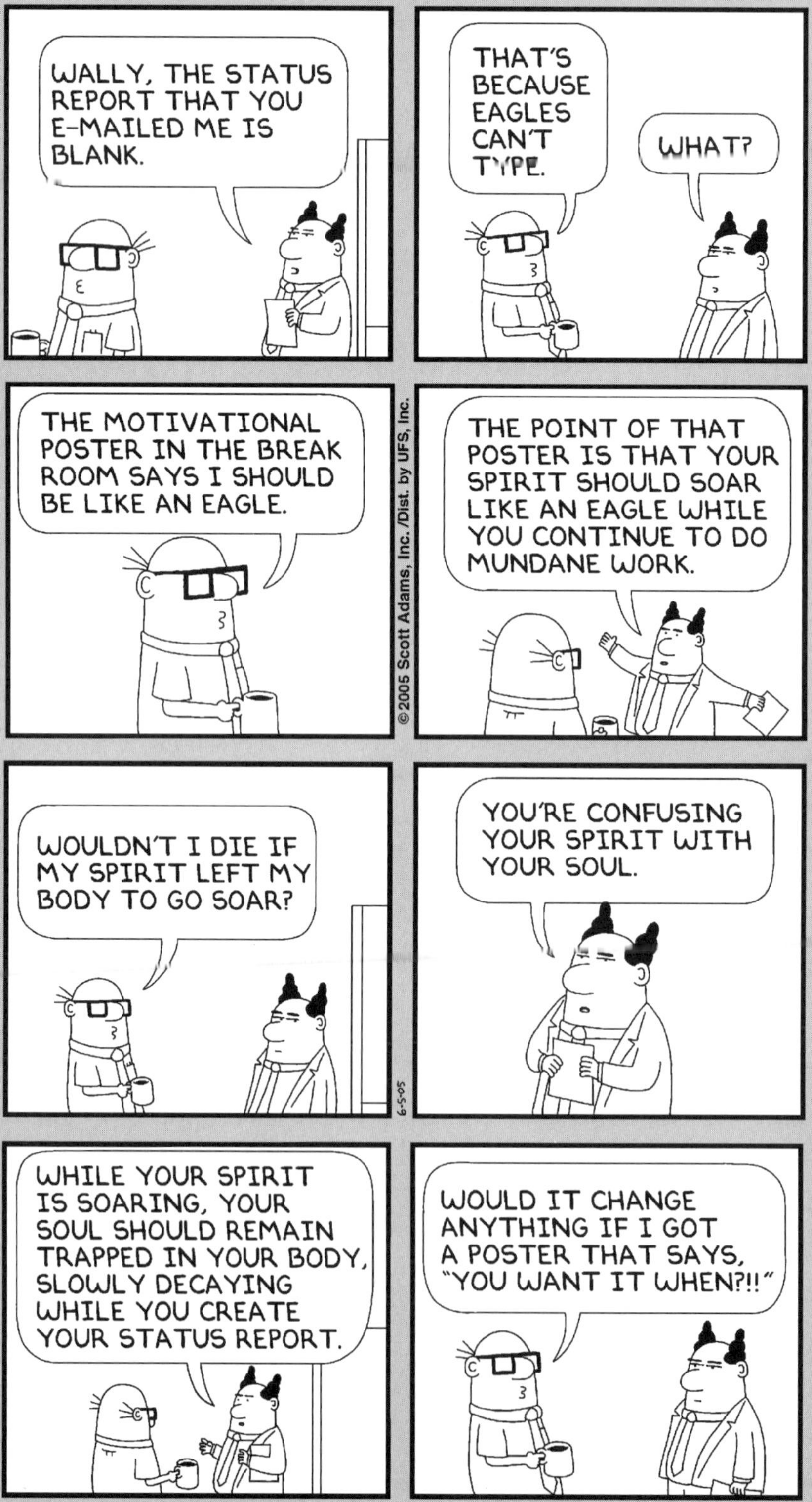
WALLY, THE STATUS REPORT THAT YOU E-MAILED ME IS BLANK.
THAT'S BECAUSE EAGLES CAN'T TYPE.
WHAT?
THE MOTIVATIONAL POSTER IN THE BREAK ROOM SAYS I SHOULD BE LIKE AN EAGLE.
THE POINT OF THAT POSTER IS THAT YOUR SPIRIT SHOULD SOAR LIKE AN EAGLE WHILE YOU CONTINUE TO DO MUNDANE WORK.
WOULDN'T I DIE IF MY SPIRIT LEFT MY BODY TO GO SOAR?
YOU'RE CONFUSING YOUR SPIRIT WITH YOUR SOUL.
WHILE YOUR SPIRIT IS SOARING, YOUR SOUL SHOULD REMAIN TRAPPED IN YOUR BODY, SLOWLY DECAYING WHILE YOU CREATE YOUR STATUS REPORT.
WOULD IT CHANGE ANYTHING IF I GOT A POSTER THAT SAYS, "YOU WANT IT WHEN?!!"
©2005 Scott Adams, Inc. /Dist. by UFS, Inc.
6-5-05

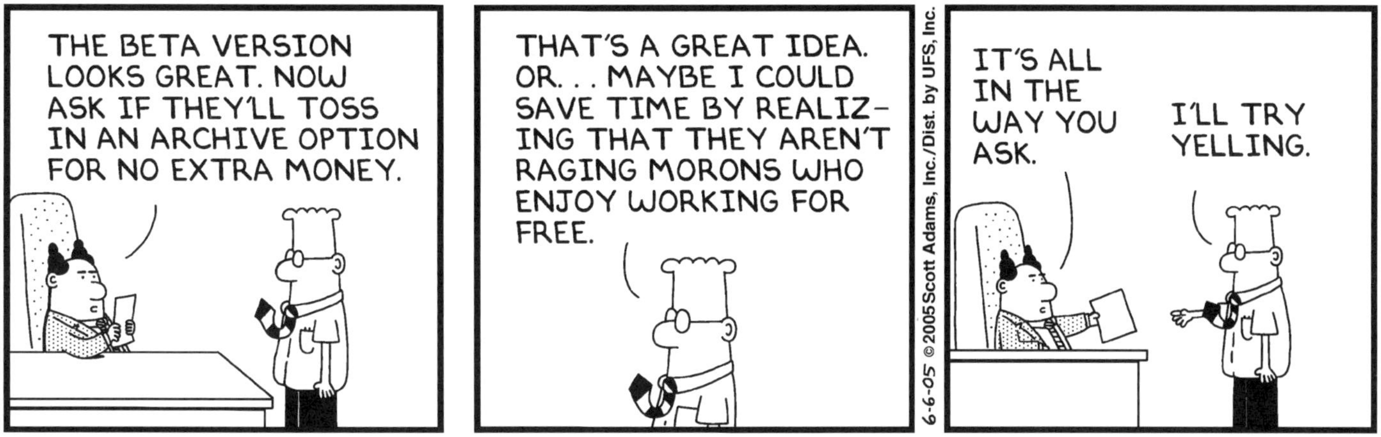
THE BETA VERSION LOOKS GREAT. NOW ASK IF THEY'LL TOSS IN AN ARCHIVE OPTION FOR NO EXTRA MONEY.
THAT'S A GREAT IDEA. OR. . . MAYBE I COULD SAVE TIME BY REALIZ-ING THAT THEY AREN'T RAGING MORONS WHO ENJOY WORKING FOR FREE.
6-6-05 ©2005 Scott Adams, Inc./Dist. by UFS, Inc.
IT'S ALL IN THE WAY YOU ASK.
I'LL TRY YELLING.

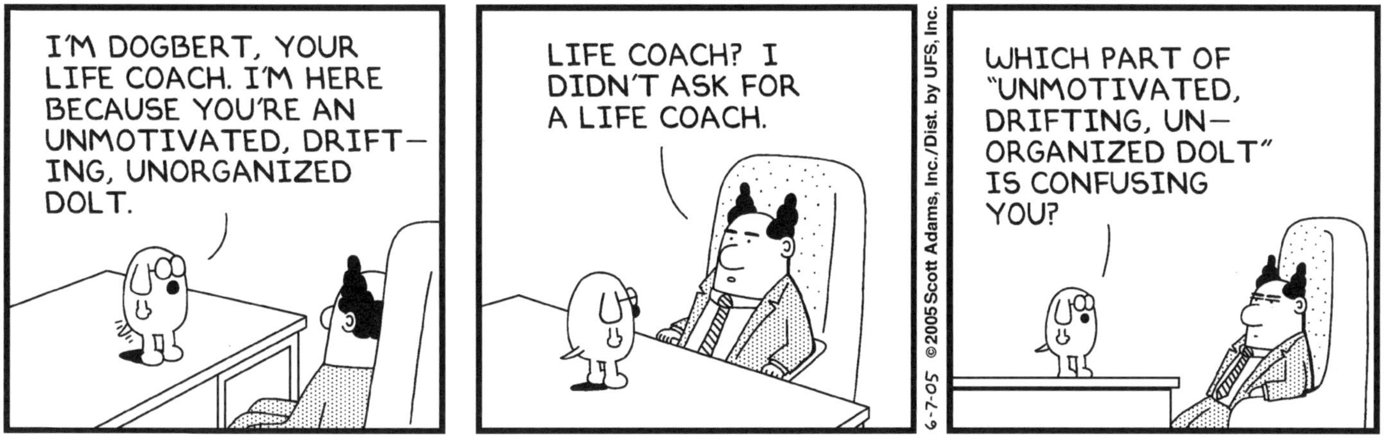
I'M DOGBERT, YOUR LIFE COACH. I'M HERE BECAUSE YOU'RE AN UNMOTIVATED, DRIFT-ING, UNORGANIZED DOLT.
LIFE COACH? I DIDN'T ASK FOR A LIFE COACH.
6-7-05 ©2005 Scott Adams, Inc./Dist. by UFS, Inc.
WHICH PART OF "UNMOTIVATED, DRIFTING, UN-ORGANIZED DOLT" IS CONFUSING YOU?

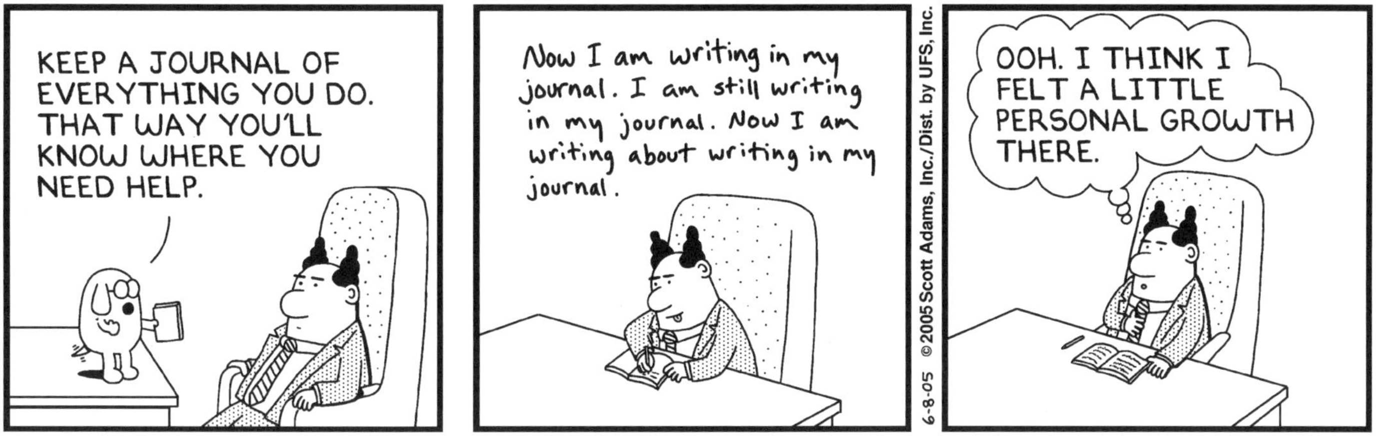
KEEP A JOURNAL OF EVERYTHING YOU DO. THAT WAY YOU'LL KNOW WHERE YOU NEED HELP.
Now I am writing in my journal. I am still writing in my journal. Now I am writing about writing in my journal.
6-8-05 ©2005 Scott Adams, Inc./Dist. by UFS, Inc.
OOH. I THINK I FELT A LITTLE PERSONAL GROWTH THERE.

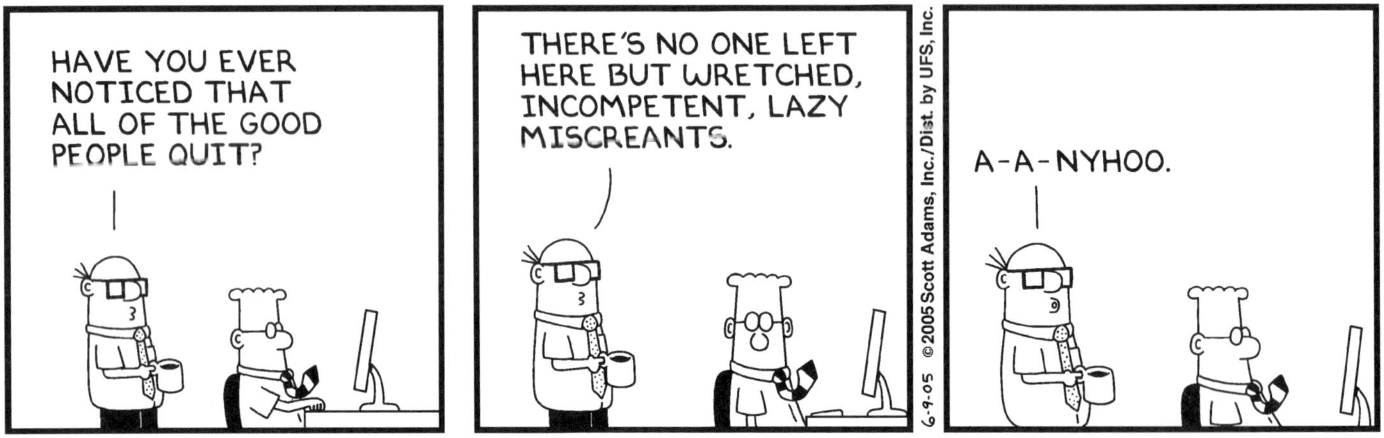
HAVE YOU EVER NOTICED THAT ALL OF THE GOOD PEOPLE QUIT?
THERE'S NO ONE LEFT HERE BUT WRETCHED, INCOMPETENT, LAZY MISCREANTS.
6-9-05 © 2005 Scott Adams, Inc./Dist. by UFS, Inc.
A-A-NYHOO.

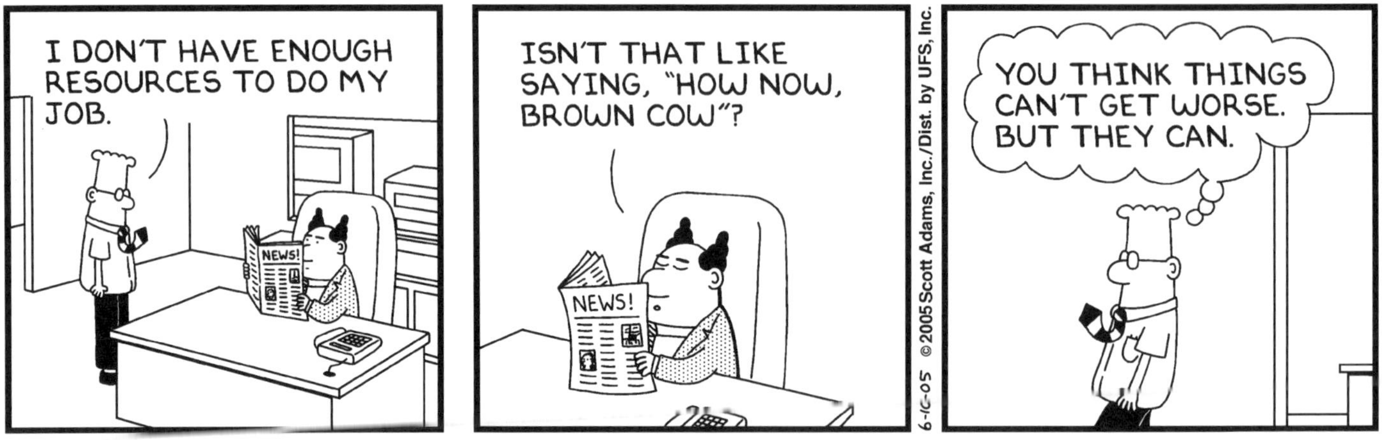
I DON'T HAVE ENOUGH RESOURCES TO DO MY JOB.
NEWS!
ISN'T THAT LIKE SAYING, "HOW NOW, BROWN COW"?
NEWS!
6-10-05 © 2005 Scott Adams, Inc./Dist. by UFS, Inc.
YOU THINK THINGS CAN'T GET WORSE. BUT THEY CAN.

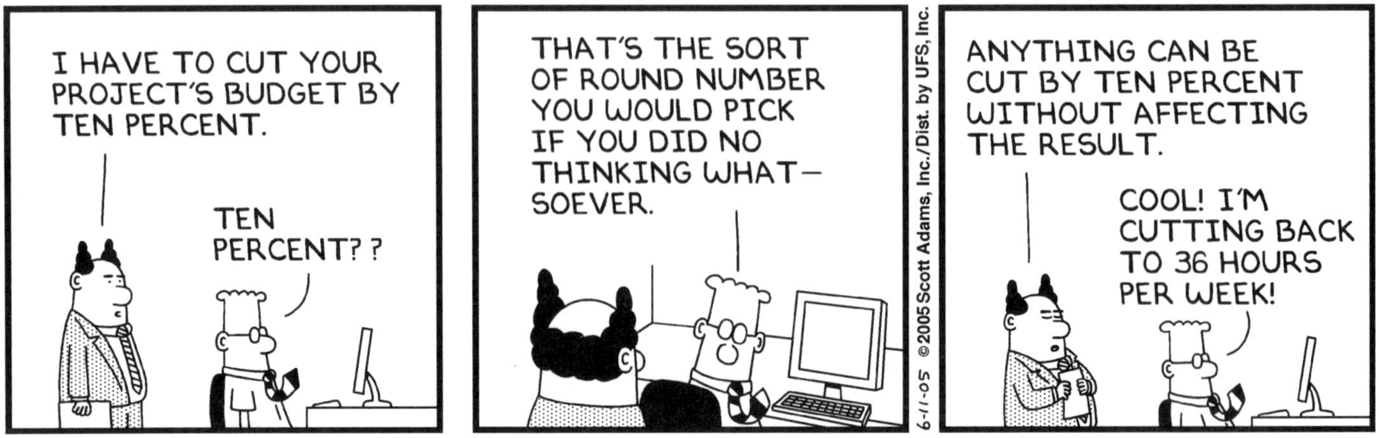
I HAVE TO CUT YOUR PROJECT'S BUDGET BY TEN PERCENT.
TEN PERCENT??
THAT'S THE SORT OF ROUND NUMBER YOU WOULD PICK IF YOU DID NO THINKING WHAT-SOEVER.
6-11-05 © 2005 Scott Adams, Inc./Dist. by UFS, Inc.
ANYTHING CAN BE CUT BY TEN PERCENT WITHOUT AFFECTING THE RESULT.
COOL! I'M CUTTING BACK TO 36 HOURS PER WEEK!

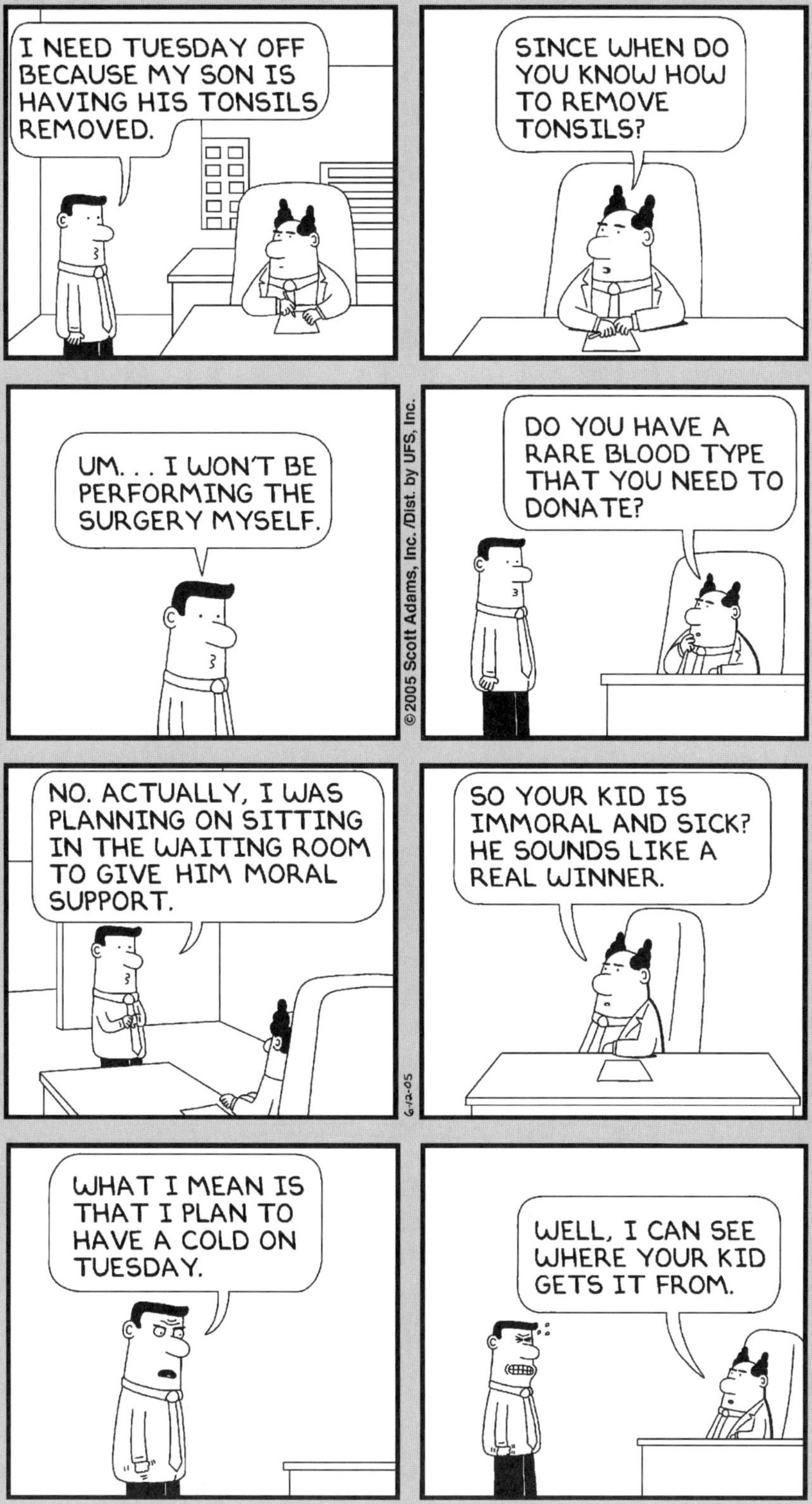
I NEED TUESDAY OFF BECAUSE MY SON IS HAVING HIS TONSILS REMOVED.
SINCE WHEN DO YOU KNOW HOW TO REMOVE TONSILS?
UM. . . I WON'T BE PERFORMING THE SURGERY MYSELF.
DO YOU HAVE A RARE BLOOD TYPE THAT YOU NEED TO DONATE?
NO. ACTUALLY, I WAS PLANNING ON SITTING IN THE WAITING ROOM TO GIVE HIM MORAL SUPPORT.
SO YOUR KID IS IMMORAL AND SICK? HE SOUNDS LIKE A REAL WINNER.
WHAT I MEAN IS THAT I PLAN TO HAVE A COLD ON TUESDAY.
WELL, I CAN SEE WHERE YOUR KID GETS IT FROM.
©2005 Scott Adams, Inc./Dist. by UFS, Inc.
6-12-05

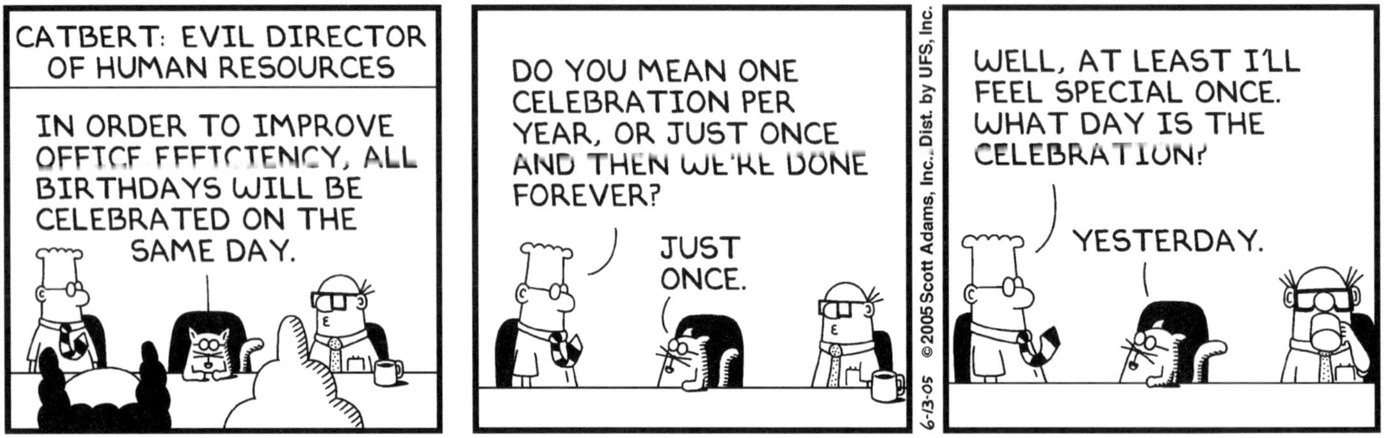
CATBERT: EVIL DIRECTOR OF HUMAN RESOURCES
IN ORDER TO IMPROVE OFFICE EFFICIENCY, ALL BIRTHDAYS WILL BE CELEBRATED ON THE SAME DAY.
DO YOU MEAN ONE CELEBRATION PER YEAR, OR JUST ONCE AND THEN WE'RE DONE FOREVER?
JUST ONCE.
6-13-05 © 2005 Scott Adams, Inc./Dist. by UFS, Inc.
WELL, AT LEAST I'LL FEEL SPECIAL ONCE. WHAT DAY IS THE CELEBRATION?
YESTERDAY.

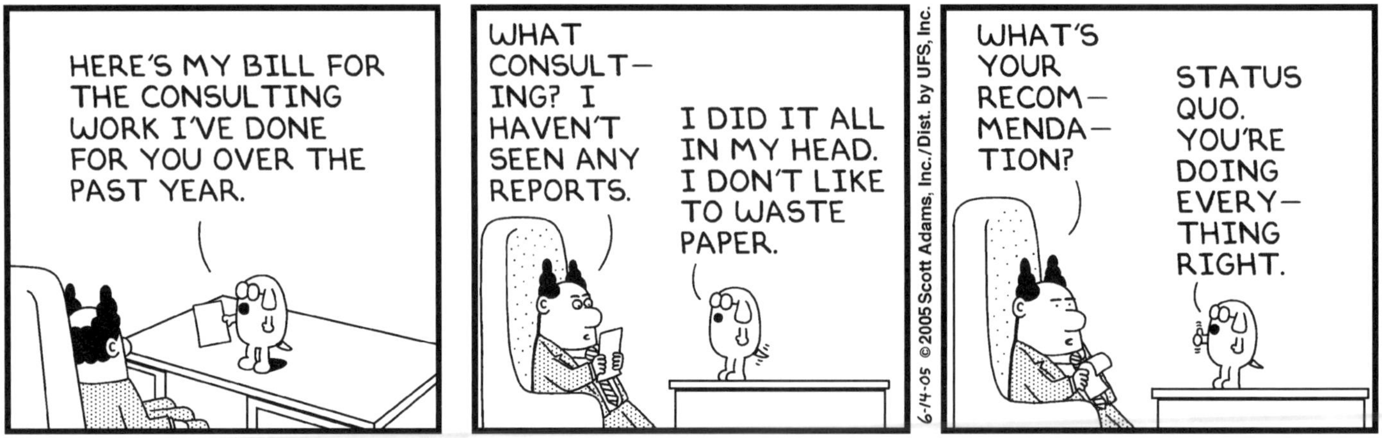
HERE'S MY BILL FOR THE CONSULTING WORK I'VE DONE FOR YOU OVER THE PAST YEAR.
WHAT CONSULTING? I HAVEN'T SEEN ANY REPORTS.
I DID IT ALL IN MY HEAD. I DON'T LIKE TO WASTE PAPER.
6-14-05 © 2005 Scott Adams, Inc./Dist. by UFS, Inc.
WHAT'S YOUR RECOMMENDATION?
STATUS QUO. YOU'RE DOING EVERYTHING RIGHT.

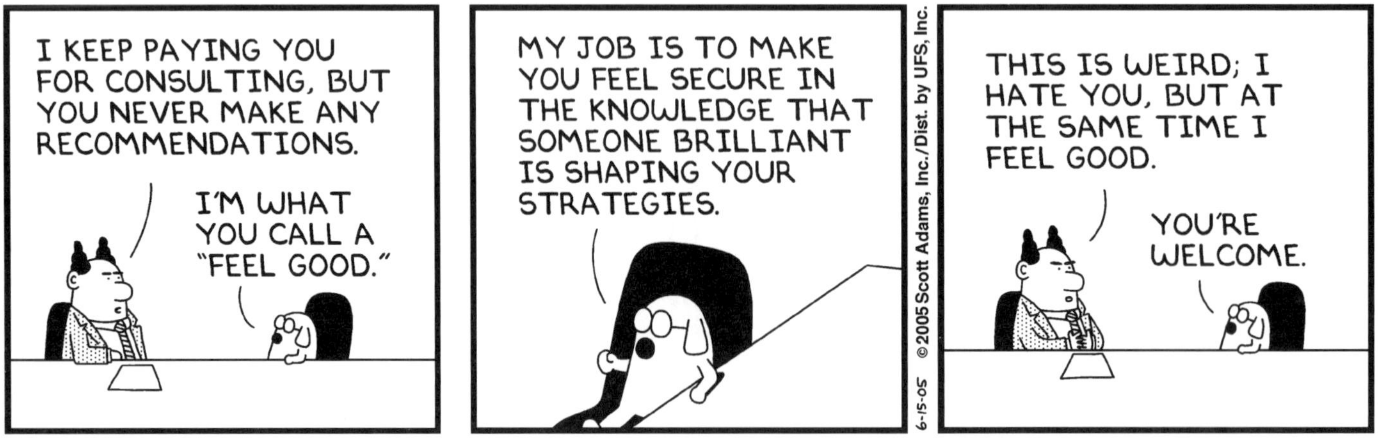
I KEEP PAYING YOU FOR CONSULTING, BUT YOU NEVER MAKE ANY RECOMMENDATIONS.
I'M WHAT YOU CALL A "FEEL GOOD."
MY JOB IS TO MAKE YOU FEEL SECURE IN THE KNOWLEDGE THAT SOMEONE BRILLIANT IS SHAPING YOUR STRATEGIES.
6-15-05 © 2005 Scott Adams, Inc./Dist. by UFS, Inc.
THIS IS WEIRD; I HATE YOU, BUT AT THE SAME TIME I FEEL GOOD.
YOU'RE WELCOME.

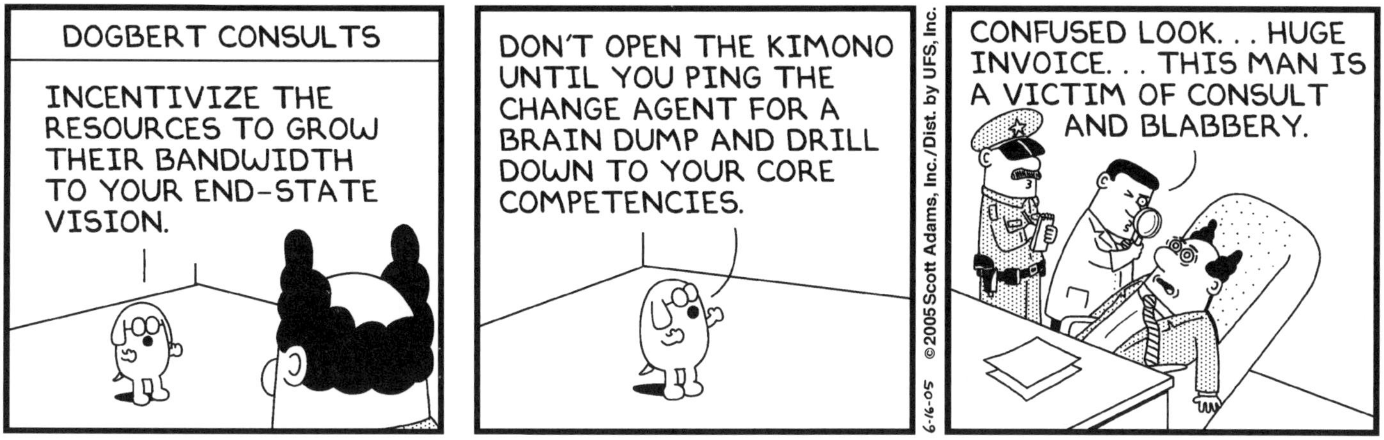
DOGBERT CONSULTS
INCENTIVIZE THE RESOURCES TO GROW THEIR BANDWIDTH TO YOUR END-STATE VISION.
DON'T OPEN THE KIMONO UNTIL YOU PING THE CHANGE AGENT FOR A BRAIN DUMP AND DRILL DOWN TO YOUR CORE COMPETENCIES.
6-16-05 © 2005 Scott Adams, Inc./Dist. by UFS, Inc.
CONFUSED LOOK. . . HUGE INVOICE. . . THIS MAN IS A VICTIM OF CONSULT AND BLABBERY.

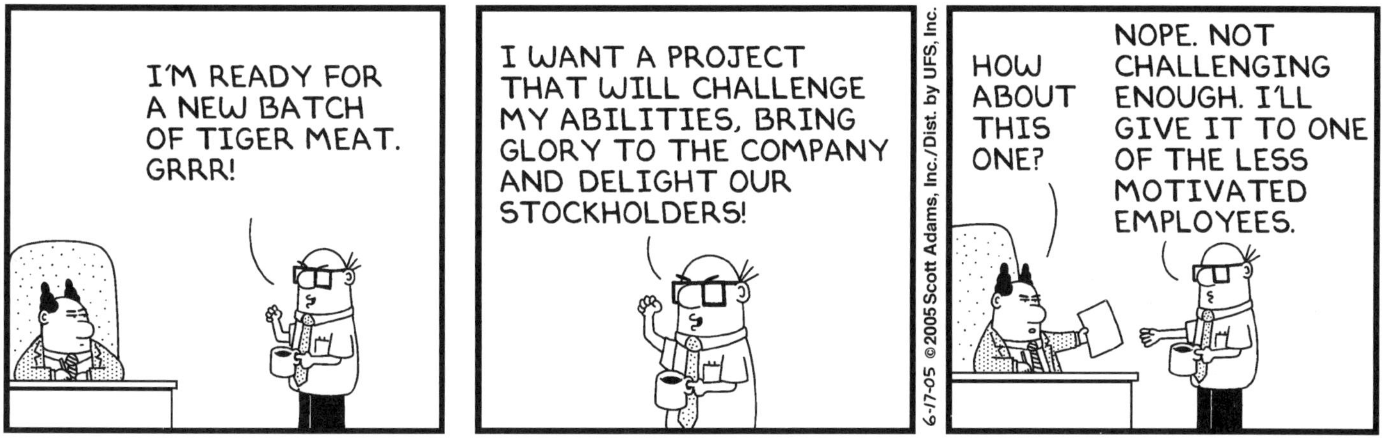
I'M READY FOR A NEW BATCH OF TIGER MEAT. GRRR!
I WANT A PROJECT THAT WILL CHALLENGE MY ABILITIES, BRING GLORY TO THE COMPANY AND DELIGHT OUR STOCKHOLDERS!
6-17-05 © 2005 Scott Adams, Inc./Dist. by UFS, Inc.
HOW ABOUT THIS ONE?
NOPE. NOT CHALLENGING ENOUGH. I'LL GIVE IT TO ONE OF THE LESS MOTIVATED EMPLOYEES.

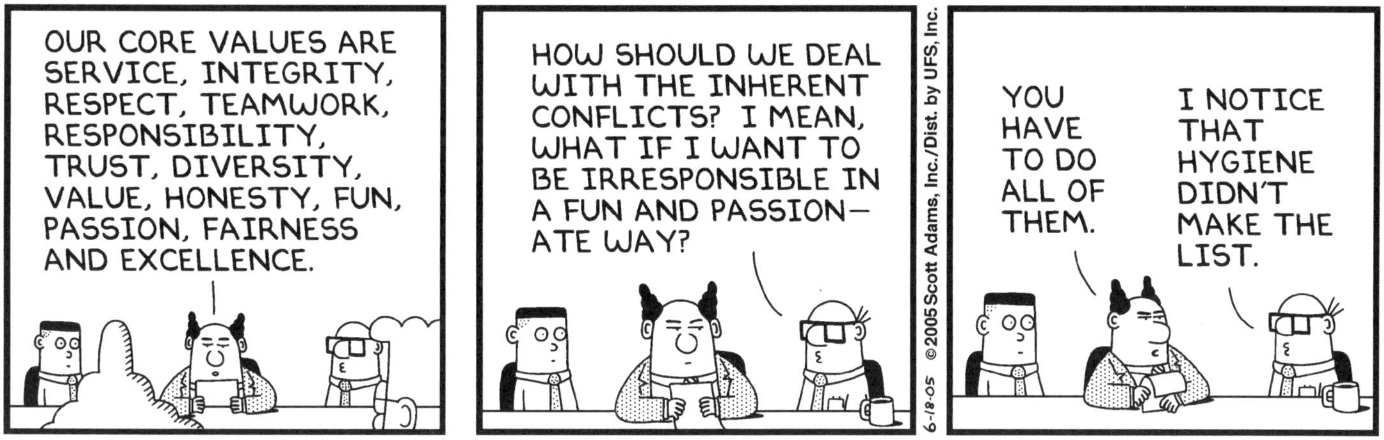
OUR CORE VALUES ARE SERVICE, INTEGRITY, RESPECT, TEAMWORK, RESPONSIBILITY, TRUST, DIVERSITY, VALUE, HONESTY, FUN, PASSION, FAIRNESS AND EXCELLENCE.
HOW SHOULD WE DEAL WITH THE INHERENT CONFLICTS? I MEAN, WHAT IF I WANT TO BE IRRESPONSIBLE IN A FUN AND PASSION-ATE WAY?
6-18-05 © 2005 Scott Adams, Inc./Dist. by UFS, Inc.
YOU HAVE TO DO ALL OF THEM.
I NOTICE THAT HYGIENE DIDN'T MAKE THE LIST.

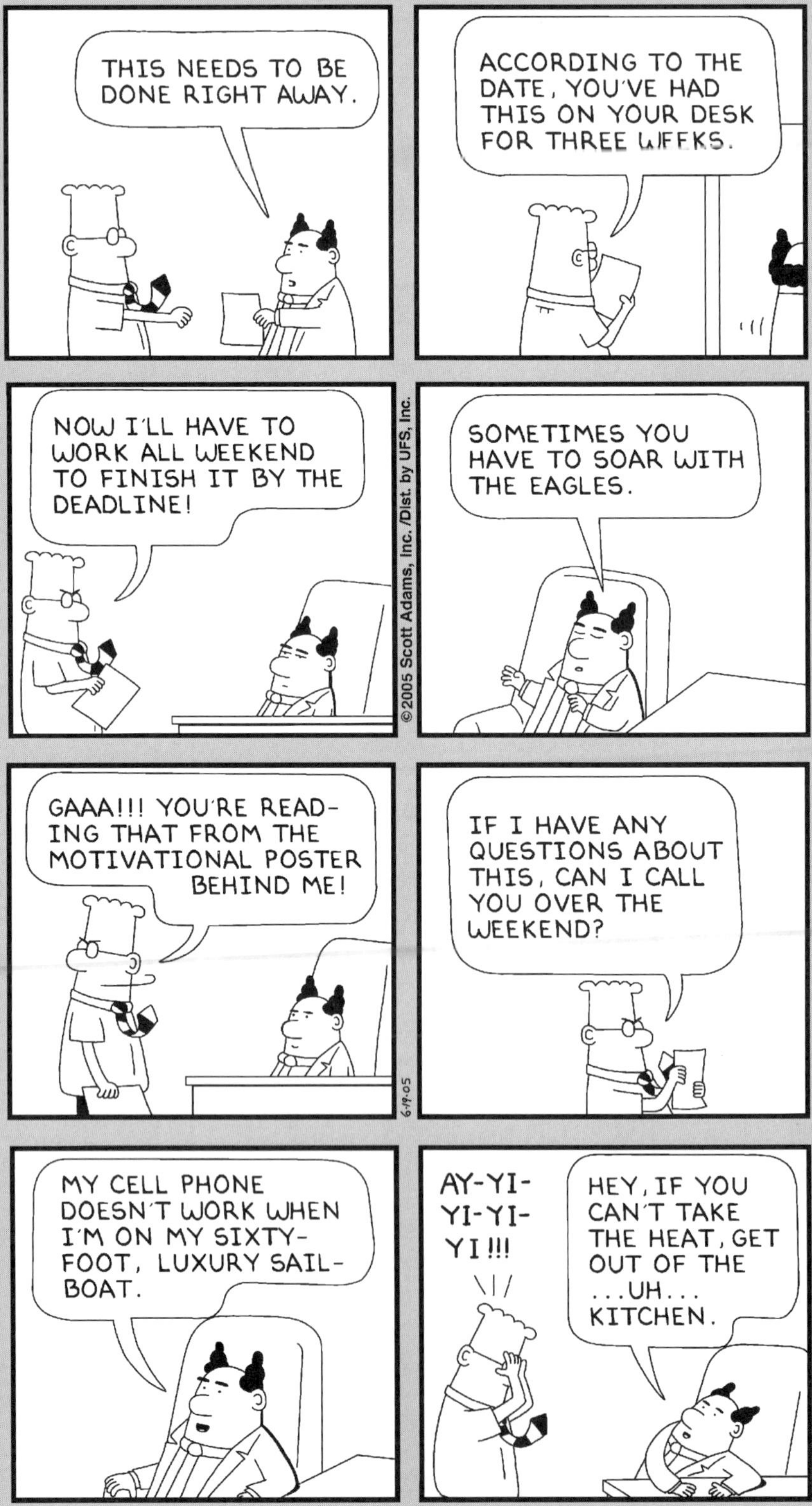
THIS NEEDS TO BE DONE RIGHT AWAY.
ACCORDING TO THE DATE, YOU'VE HAD THIS ON YOUR DESK FOR THREE WEEKS.
NOW I'LL HAVE TO WORK ALL WEEKEND TO FINISH IT BY THE DEADLINE!
SOMETIMES YOU HAVE TO SOAR WITH THE EAGLES.
©2005 Scott Adams, Inc. /Dist. by UFS, Inc.
GAAA!!! YOU'RE READING THAT FROM THE MOTIVATIONAL POSTER BEHIND ME!
IF I HAVE ANY QUESTIONS ABOUT THIS, CAN I CALL YOU OVER THE WEEKEND?
6-19-05
MY CELL PHONE DOESN'T WORK WHEN I'M ON MY SIXTY-FOOT, LUXURY SAILBOAT.
AY-YI-YI-YI-YI!!!
HEY, IF YOU CAN'T TAKE THE HEAT, GET OUT OF THE ...UH... KITCHEN.

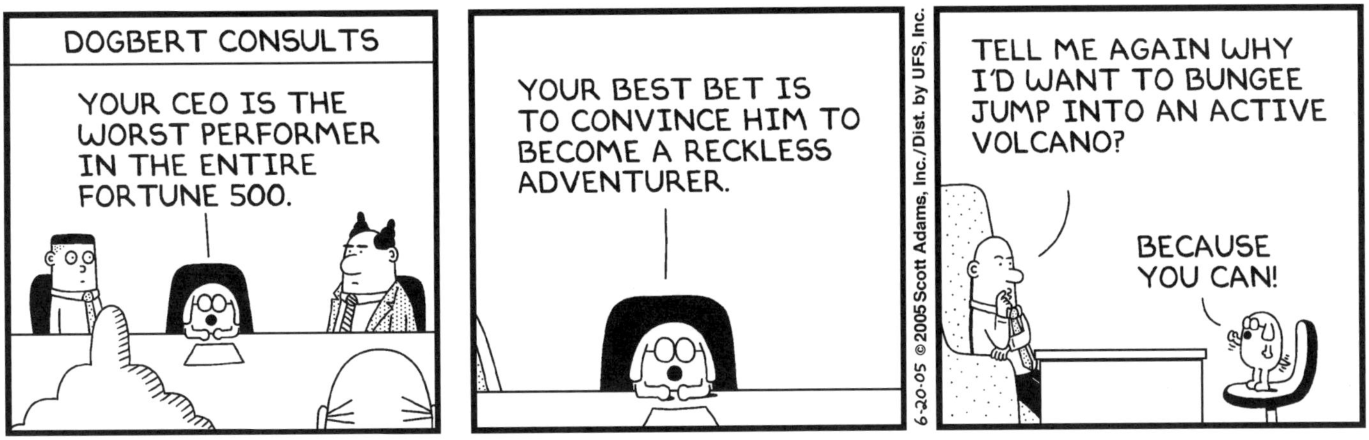
DOGBERT CONSULTS
YOUR CEO IS THE WORST PERFORMER IN THE ENTIRE FORTUNE 500.
YOUR BEST BET IS TO CONVINCE HIM TO BECOME A RECKLESS ADVENTURER.
6-20-05 © 2005 Scott Adams, Inc./Dist. by UFS, Inc.
TELL ME AGAIN WHY I'D WANT TO BUNGEE JUMP INTO AN ACTIVE VOLCANO?
BECAUSE YOU CAN!

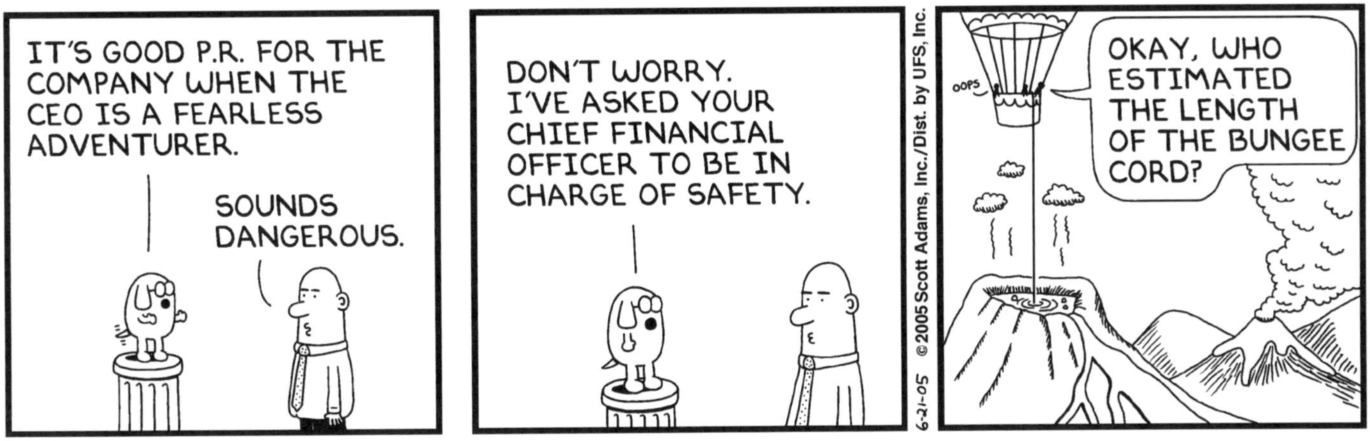
IT'S GOOD P.R. FOR THE COMPANY WHEN THE CEO IS A FEARLESS ADVENTURER.
SOUNDS DANGEROUS.
DON'T WORRY. I'VE ASKED YOUR CHIEF FINANCIAL OFFICER TO BE IN CHARGE OF SAFETY.
6-21-05 © 2005 Scott Adams, Inc./Dist. by UFS, Inc.
OOPS
OKAY, WHO ESTIMATED THE LENGTH OF THE BUNGEE CORD?

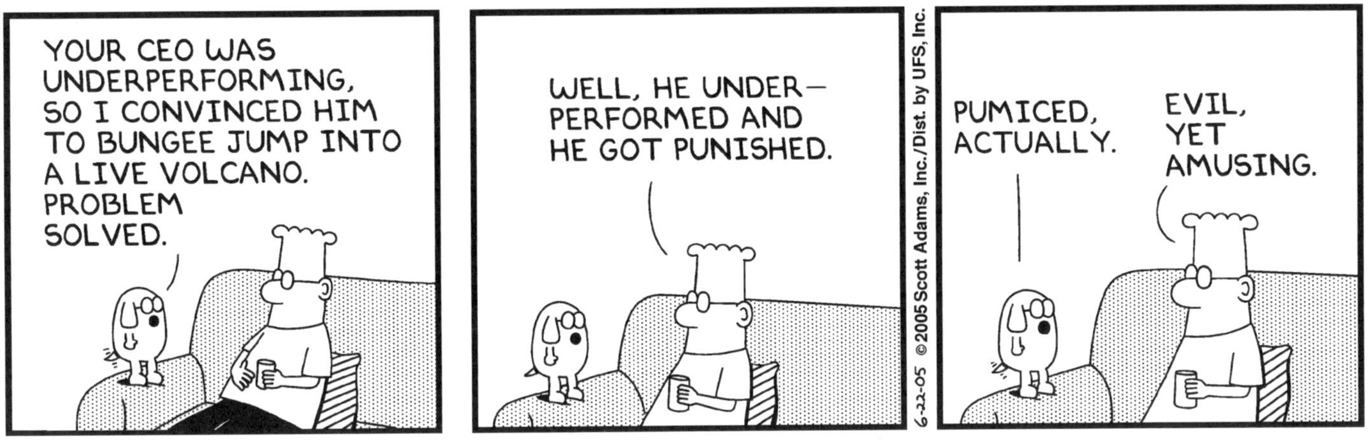
YOUR CEO WAS UNDERPERFORMING, SO I CONVINCED HIM TO BUNGEE JUMP INTO A LIVE VOLCANO. PROBLEM SOLVED.
WELL, HE UNDER-PERFORMED AND HE GOT PUNISHED.
6-22-05 © 2005 Scott Adams, Inc./Dist. by UFS, Inc.
PUMICED, ACTUALLY.
EVIL, YET AMUSING.

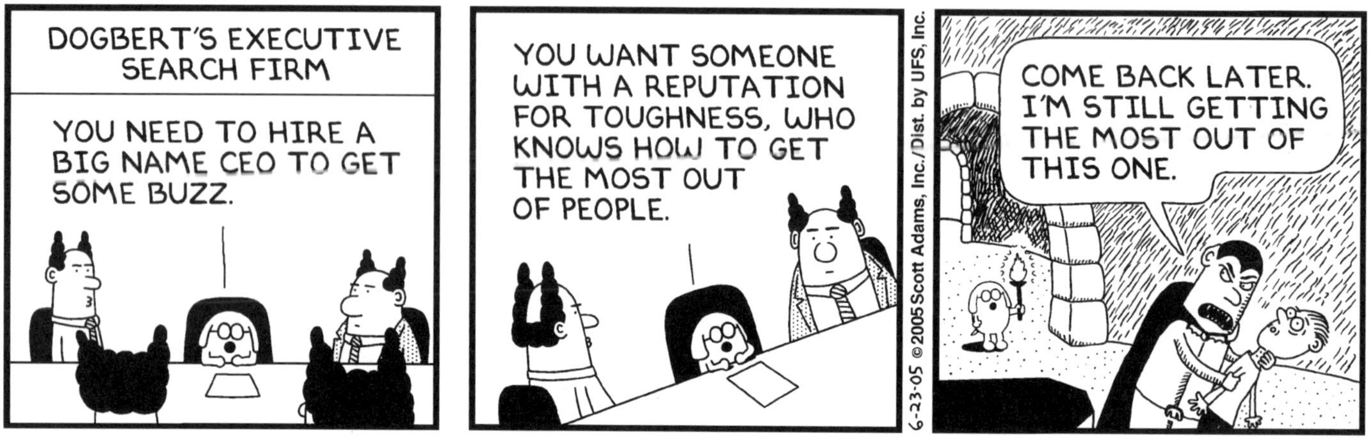
DOGBERT'S EXECUTIVE SEARCH FIRM
YOU NEED TO HIRE A BIG NAME CEO TO GET SOME BUZZ.
YOU WANT SOMEONE WITH A REPUTATION FOR TOUGHNESS, WHO KNOWS HOW TO GET THE MOST OUT OF PEOPLE.
6-23-05 © 2005 Scott Adams, Inc./Dist. by UFS, Inc.
COME BACK LATER. I'M STILL GETTING THE MOST OUT OF THIS ONE.

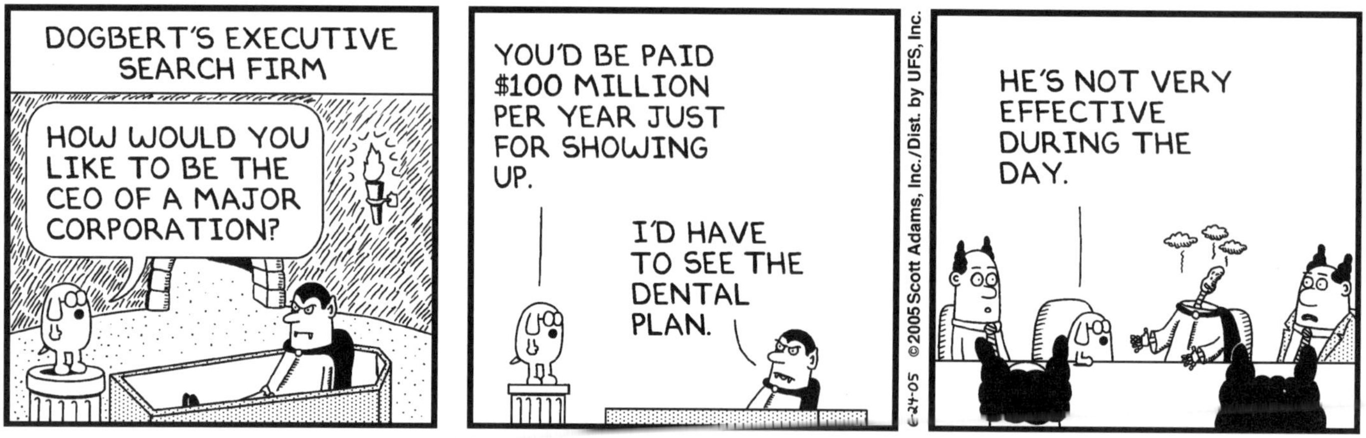
DOGBERT'S EXECUTIVE SEARCH FIRM
HOW WOULD YOU LIKE TO BE THE CEO OF A MAJOR CORPORATION?
YOU'D BE PAID $100 MILLION PER YEAR JUST FOR SHOWING UP.
I'D HAVE TO SEE THE DENTAL PLAN.
6-24-05 © 2005 Scott Adams, Inc./Dist. by UFS, Inc.
HE'S NOT VERY EFFECTIVE DURING THE DAY.

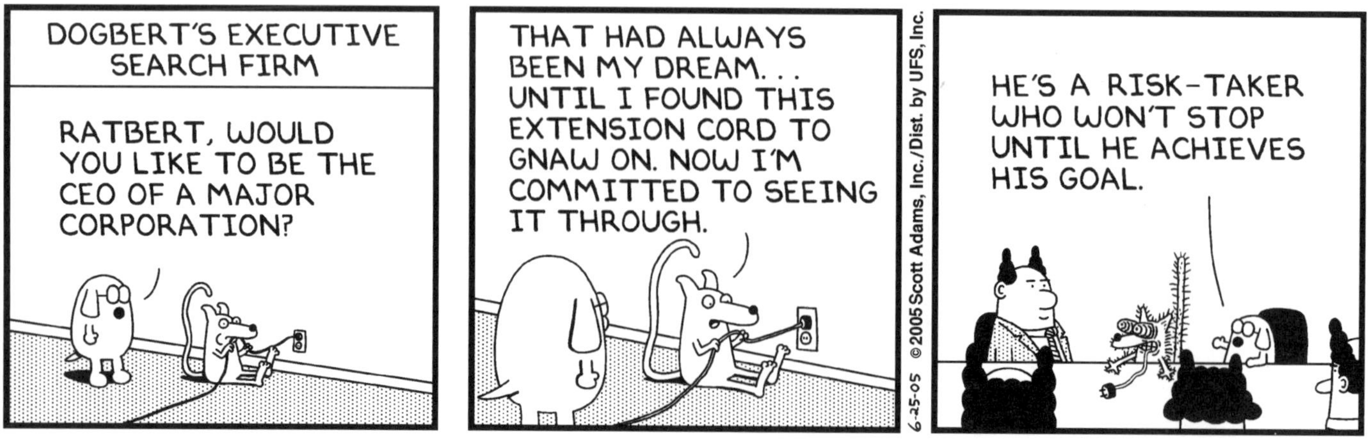
DOGBERT'S EXECUTIVE SEARCH FIRM
RATBERT, WOULD YOU LIKE TO BE THE CEO OF A MAJOR CORPORATION?
THAT HAD ALWAYS BEEN MY DREAM. . . UNTIL I FOUND THIS EXTENSION CORD TO GNAW ON. NOW I'M COMMITTED TO SEEING IT THROUGH.
6-25-05 © 2005 Scott Adams, Inc./Dist. by UFS, Inc.
HE'S A RISK-TAKER WHO WON'T STOP UNTIL HE ACHIEVES HIS GOAL.

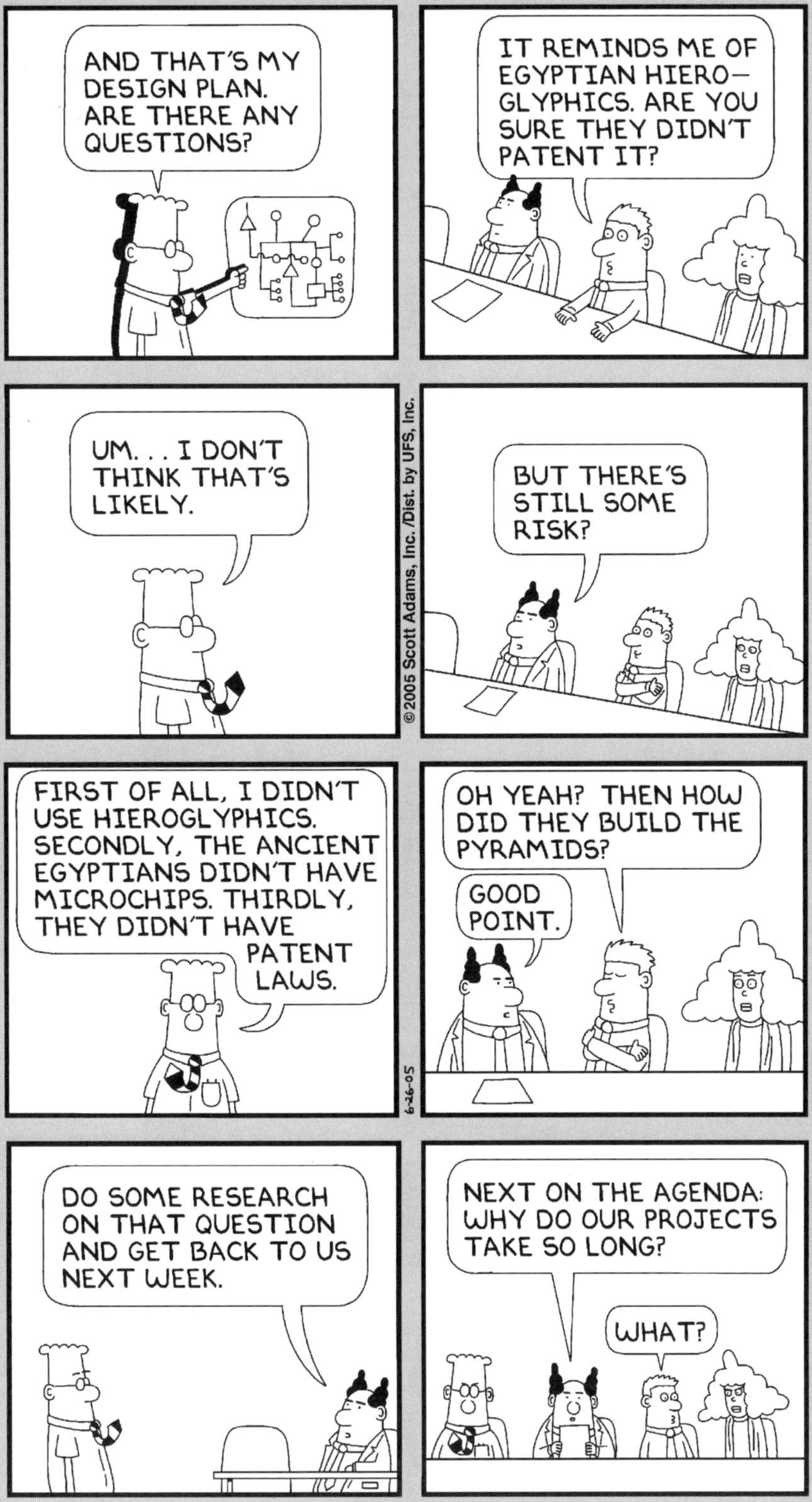
AND THAT'S MY DESIGN PLAN. ARE THERE ANY QUESTIONS?
IT REMINDS ME OF EGYPTIAN HIERO-GLYPHICS. ARE YOU SURE THEY DIDN'T PATENT IT?
UM. . . I DON'T THINK THAT'S LIKELY.
BUT THERE'S STILL SOME RISK?
FIRST OF ALL, I DIDN'T USE HIEROGLYPHICS. SECONDLY, THE ANCIENT EGYPTIANS DIDN'T HAVE MICROCHIPS. THIRDLY, THEY DIDN'T HAVE PATENT LAWS.
OH YEAH? THEN HOW DID THEY BUILD THE PYRAMIDS?
GOOD POINT.
DO SOME RESEARCH ON THAT QUESTION AND GET BACK TO US NEXT WEEK.
NEXT ON THE AGENDA: WHY DO OUR PROJECTS TAKE SO LONG?
WHAT?
©2005 Scott Adams, Inc./Dist. by UFS, Inc.
6-26-05

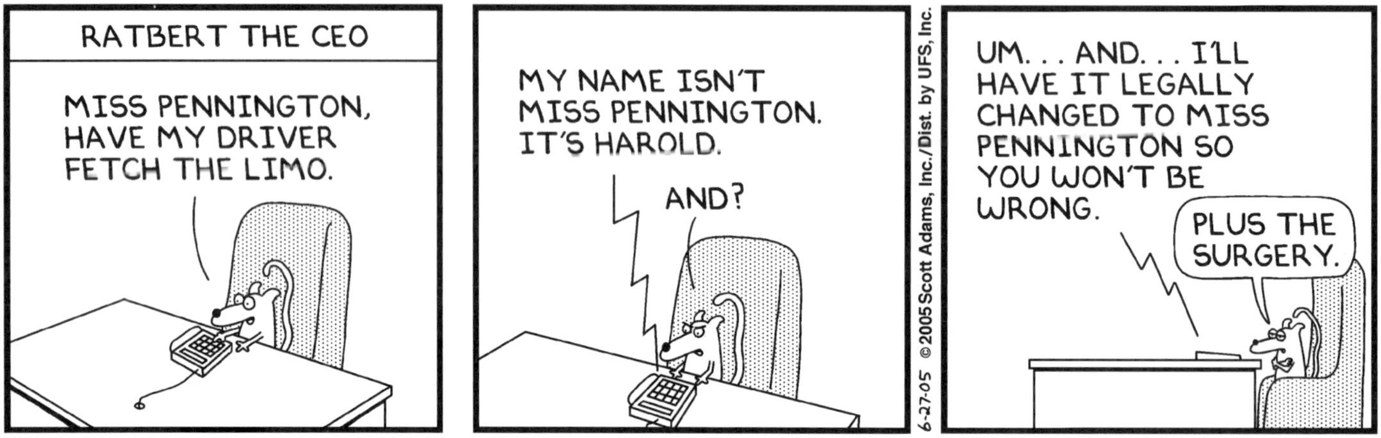
RATBERT THE CEO
MISS PENNINGTON, HAVE MY DRIVER FETCH THE LIMO.
MY NAME ISN'T MISS PENNINGTON. IT'S HAROLD.
AND?
UM. . . AND. . . I'LL HAVE IT LEGALLY CHANGED TO MISS PENNINGTON SO YOU WON'T BE WRONG.
PLUS THE SURGERY.
6-27-05 © 2005 Scott Adams, Inc./Dist. by UFS, Inc.

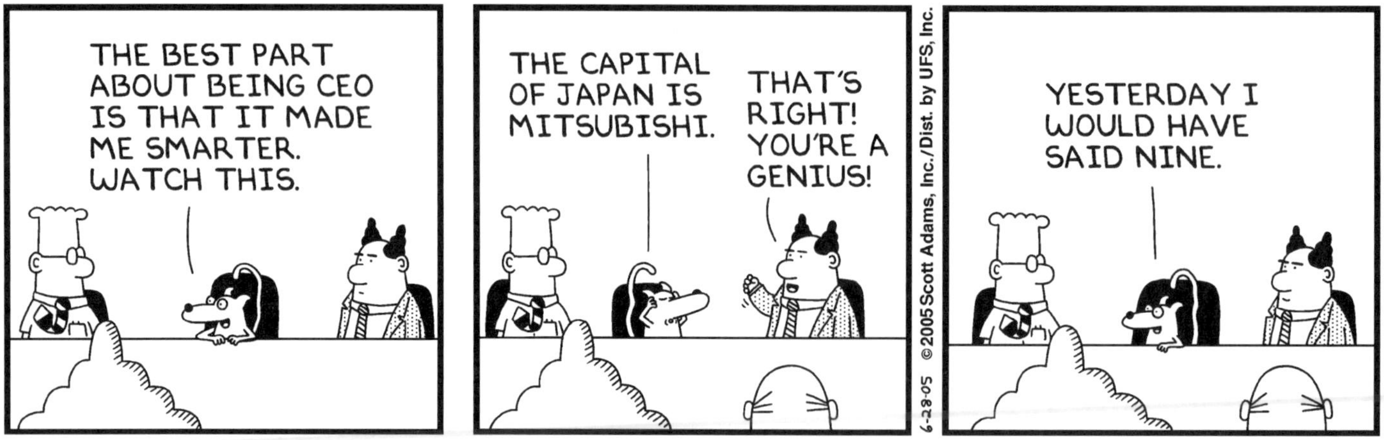
THE BEST PART ABOUT BEING CEO IS THAT IT MADE ME SMARTER. WATCH THIS.
THE CAPITAL OF JAPAN IS MITSUBISHI.
THAT'S RIGHT! YOU'RE A GENIUS!
YESTERDAY I WOULD HAVE SAID NINE.
6-28-05 © 2005 Scott Adams, Inc./Dist. by UFS, Inc.

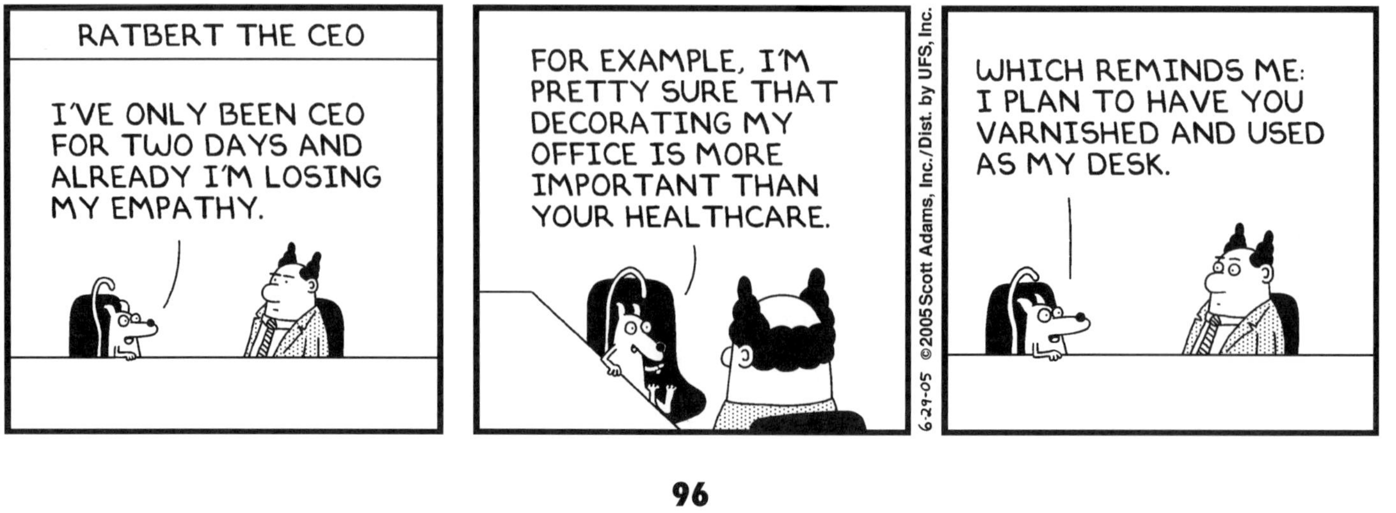
RATBERT THE CEO
I'VE ONLY BEEN CEO FOR TWO DAYS AND ALREADY I'M LOSING MY EMPATHY.
FOR EXAMPLE, I'M PRETTY SURE THAT DECORATING MY OFFICE IS MORE IMPORTANT THAN YOUR HEALTHCARE.
WHICH REMINDS ME: I PLAN TO HAVE YOU VARNISHED AND USED AS MY DESK.
6-29-05 © 2005 Scott Adams, Inc./Dist. by UFS, Inc.

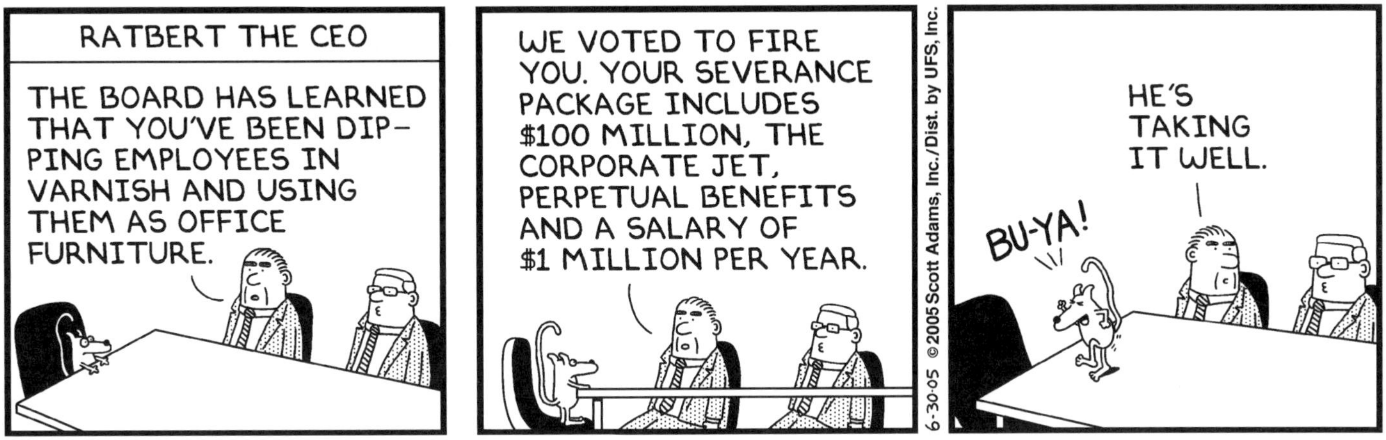
RATBERT THE CEO
THE BOARD HAS LEARNED THAT YOU'VE BEEN DIP-PING EMPLOYEES IN VARNISH AND USING THEM AS OFFICE FURNITURE.
WE VOTED TO FIRE YOU. YOUR SEVERANCE PACKAGE INCLUDES $100 MILLION, THE CORPORATE JET, PERPETUAL BENEFITS AND A SALARY OF $1 MILLION PER YEAR.
6-30-05 © 2005 Scott Adams, Inc./Dist. by UFS, Inc.
BU-YA!
HE'S TAKING IT WELL.

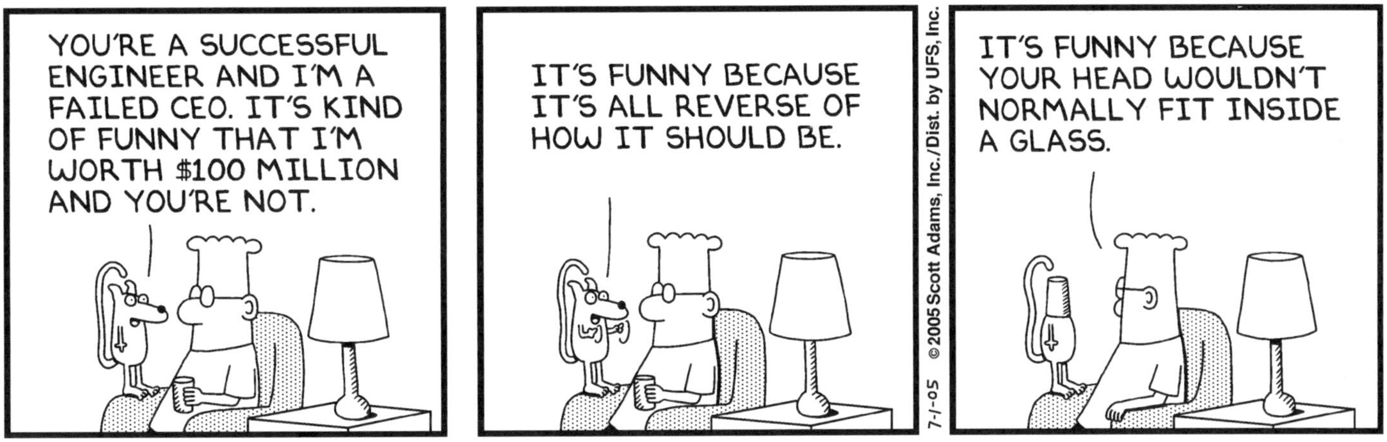
YOU'RE A SUCCESSFUL ENGINEER AND I'M A FAILED CEO. IT'S KIND OF FUNNY THAT I'M WORTH $100 MILLION AND YOU'RE NOT.
IT'S FUNNY BECAUSE IT'S ALL REVERSE OF HOW IT SHOULD BE.
7-1-05 © 2005 Scott Adams, Inc./Dist. by UFS, Inc.
IT'S FUNNY BECAUSE YOUR HEAD WOULDN'T NORMALLY FIT INSIDE A GLASS.

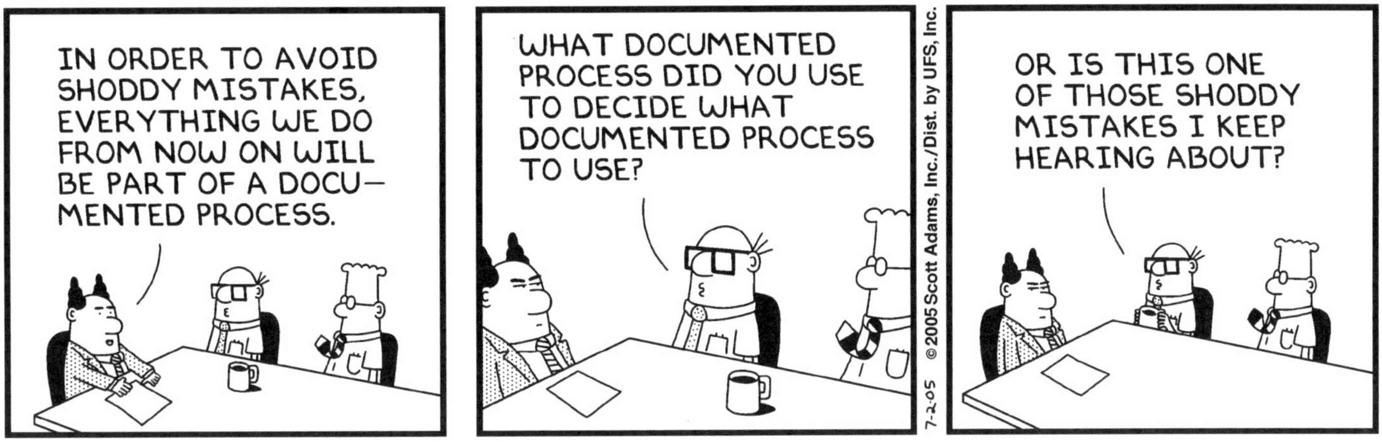
IN ORDER TO AVOID SHODDY MISTAKES, EVERYTHING WE DO FROM NOW ON WILL BE PART OF A DOCU-MENTED PROCESS.
WHAT DOCUMENTED PROCESS DID YOU USE TO DECIDE WHAT DOCUMENTED PROCESS TO USE?
7-2-05 © 2005 Scott Adams, Inc./Dist. by UFS, Inc.
OR IS THIS ONE OF THOSE SHODDY MISTAKES I KEEP HEARING ABOUT?

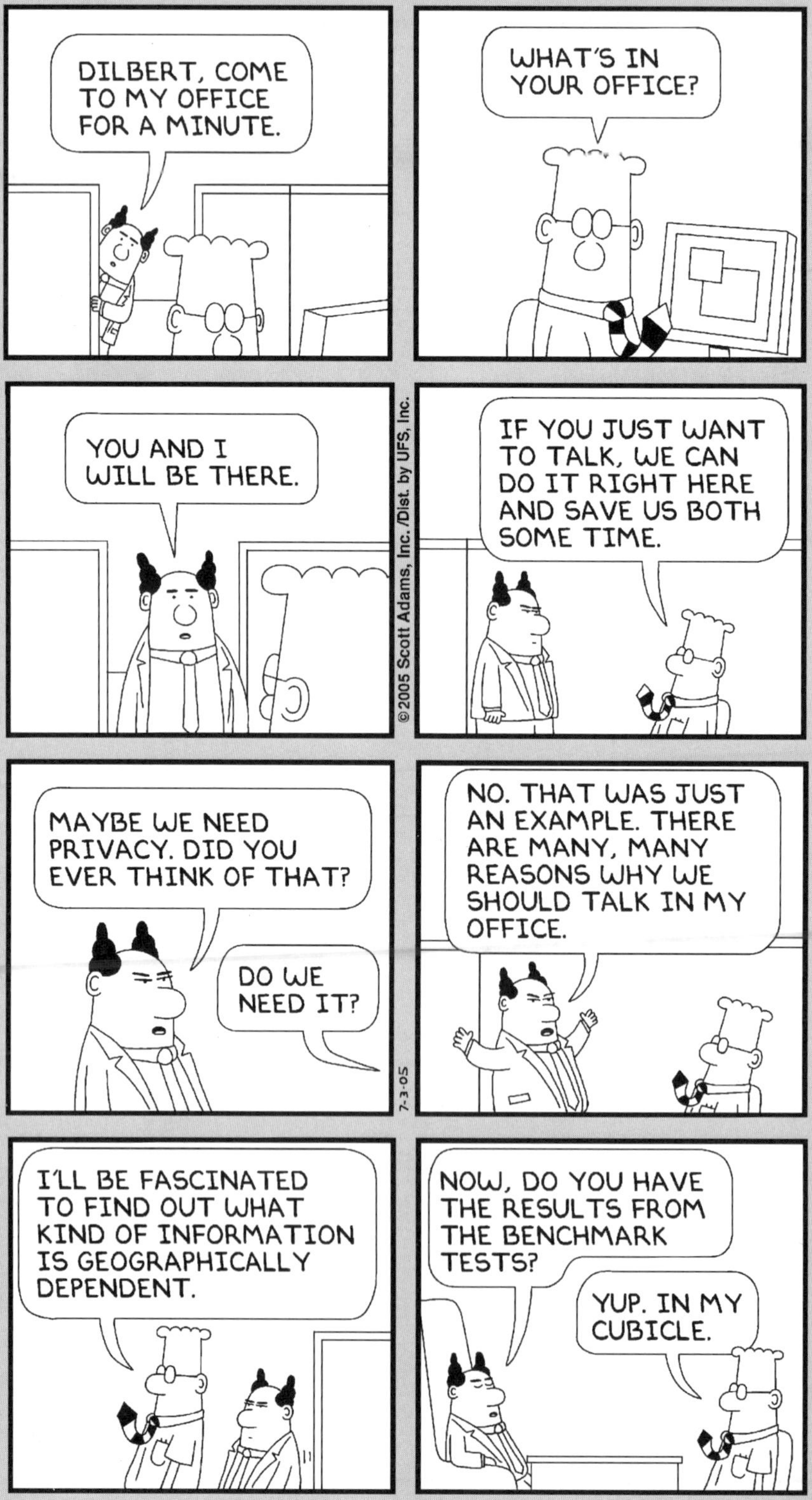
DILBERT, COME TO MY OFFICE FOR A MINUTE.
WHAT'S IN YOUR OFFICE?
YOU AND I WILL BE THERE.
IF YOU JUST WANT TO TALK, WE CAN DO IT RIGHT HERE AND SAVE US BOTH SOME TIME.
MAYBE WE NEED PRIVACY. DID YOU EVER THINK OF THAT?
DO WE NEED IT?
NO. THAT WAS JUST AN EXAMPLE. THERE ARE MANY, MANY REASONS WHY WE SHOULD TALK IN MY OFFICE.
I'LL BE FASCINATED TO FIND OUT WHAT KIND OF INFORMATION IS GEOGRAPHICALLY DEPENDENT.
NOW, DO YOU HAVE THE RESULTS FROM THE BENCHMARK TESTS?
YUP. IN MY CUBICLE.
©2005 Scott Adams, Inc./Dist. by UFS, Inc.
7-3-05

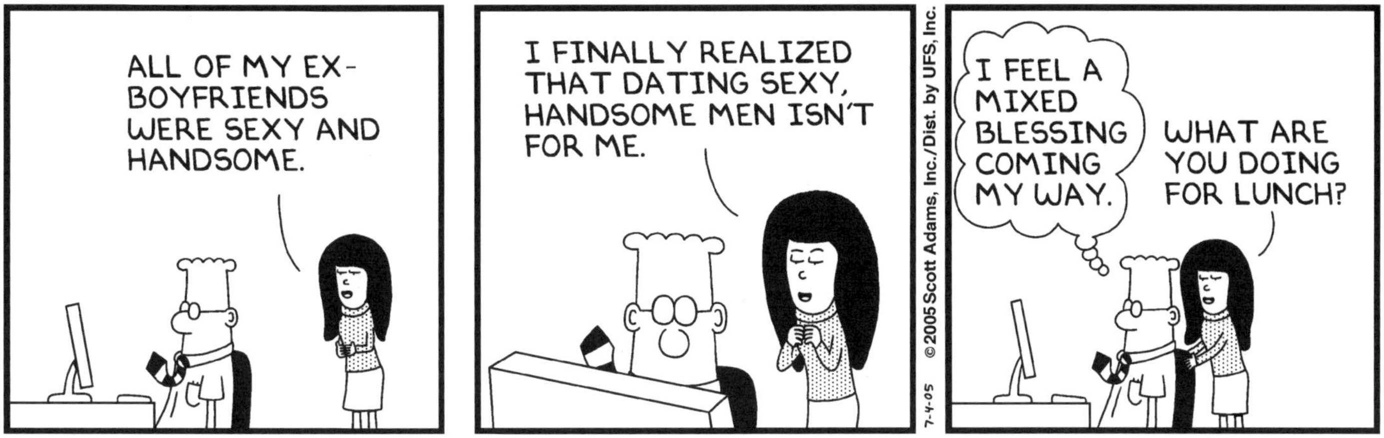
ALL OF MY EX-BOYFRIENDS WERE SEXY AND HANDSOME.
I FINALLY REALIZED THAT DATING SEXY, HANDSOME MEN ISN'T FOR ME.
7-4-05 ©2005 Scott Adams, Inc./Dist. by UFS, Inc.
I FEEL A MIXED BLESSING COMING MY WAY.
WHAT ARE YOU DOING FOR LUNCH?

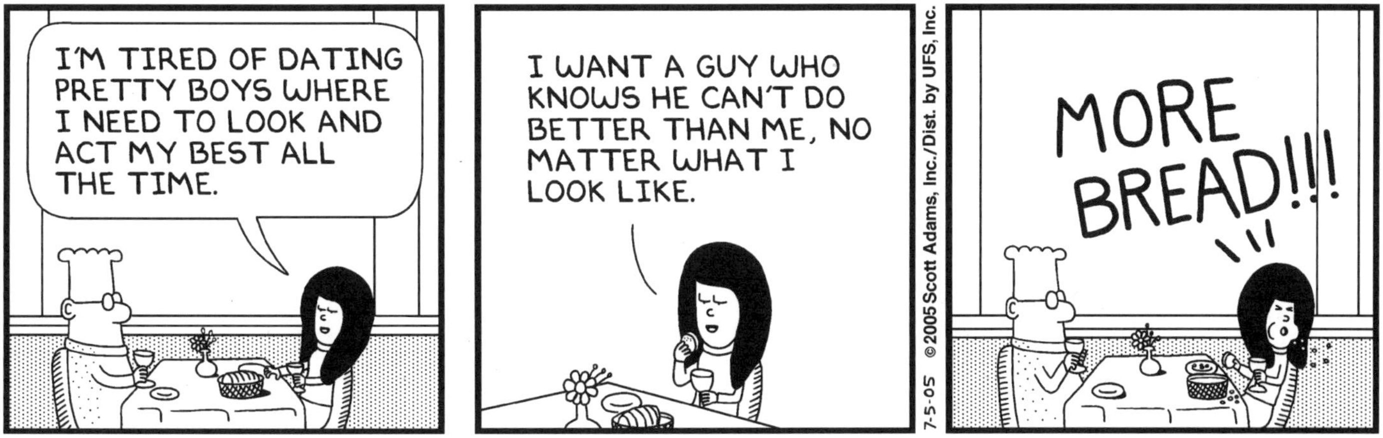
I'M TIRED OF DATING PRETTY BOYS WHERE I NEED TO LOOK AND ACT MY BEST ALL THE TIME.
I WANT A GUY WHO KNOWS HE CAN'T DO BETTER THAN ME, NO MATTER WHAT I LOOK LIKE.
7-5-05 ©2005 Scott Adams, Inc./Dist. by UFS, Inc.
MORE BREAD!!!

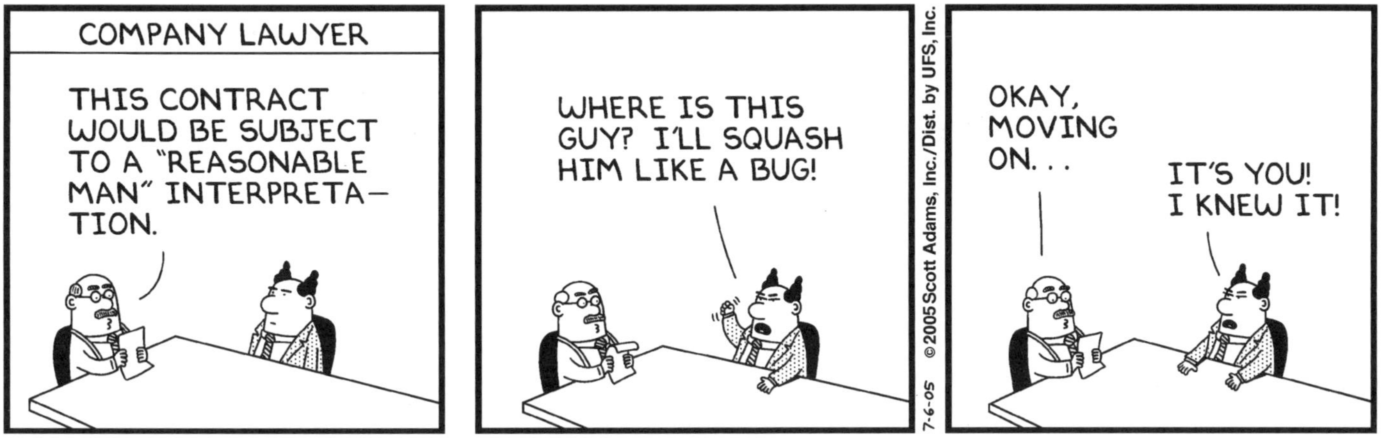
COMPANY LAWYER
THIS CONTRACT WOULD BE SUBJECT TO A "REASONABLE MAN" INTERPRETA-TION.
WHERE IS THIS GUY? I'LL SQUASH HIM LIKE A BUG!
7-6-05 ©2005 Scott Adams, Inc./Dist. by UFS, Inc.
OKAY, MOVING ON. . .
IT'S YOU! I KNEW IT!

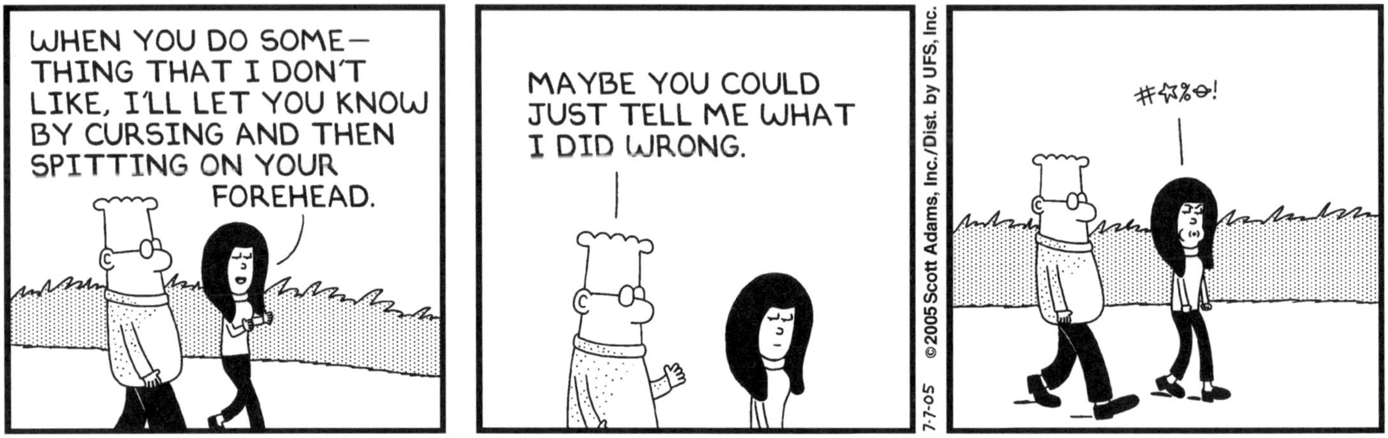
WHEN YOU DO SOME-THING THAT I DON'T LIKE, I'LL LET YOU KNOW BY CURSING AND THEN SPITTING ON YOUR FOREHEAD.
MAYBE YOU COULD JUST TELL ME WHAT I DID WRONG.
7-7-05 ©2005 Scott Adams, Inc./Dist. by UFS, Inc.

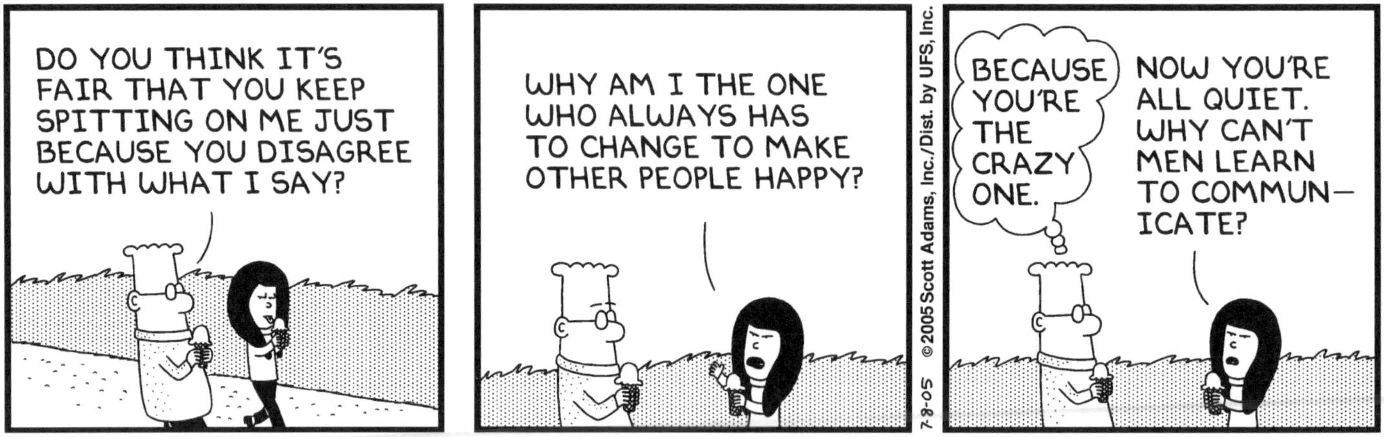
DO YOU THINK IT'S FAIR THAT YOU KEEP SPITTING ON ME JUST BECAUSE YOU DISAGREE WITH WHAT I SAY?
WHY AM I THE ONE WHO ALWAYS HAS TO CHANGE TO MAKE OTHER PEOPLE HAPPY?
7-8-05 ©2005 Scott Adams, Inc./Dist. by UFS, Inc.
BECAUSE YOU'RE THE CRAZY ONE.
NOW YOU'RE ALL QUIET. WHY CAN'T MEN LEARN TO COMMUN-ICATE?

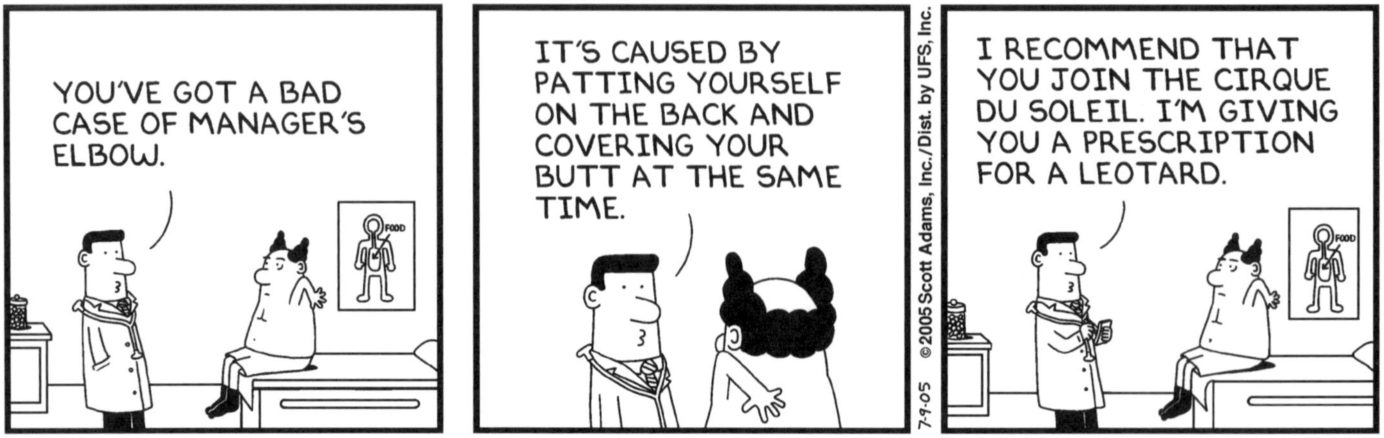
YOU'VE GOT A BAD CASE OF MANAGER'S ELBOW.
FOOD
IT'S CAUSED BY PATTING YOURSELF ON THE BACK AND COVERING YOUR BUTT AT THE SAME TIME.
7-9-05 ©2005 Scott Adams, Inc./Dist. by UFS, Inc.
I RECOMMEND THAT YOU JOIN THE CIRQUE DU SOLEIL. I'M GIVING YOU A PRESCRIPTION FOR A LEOTARD.
FOOD

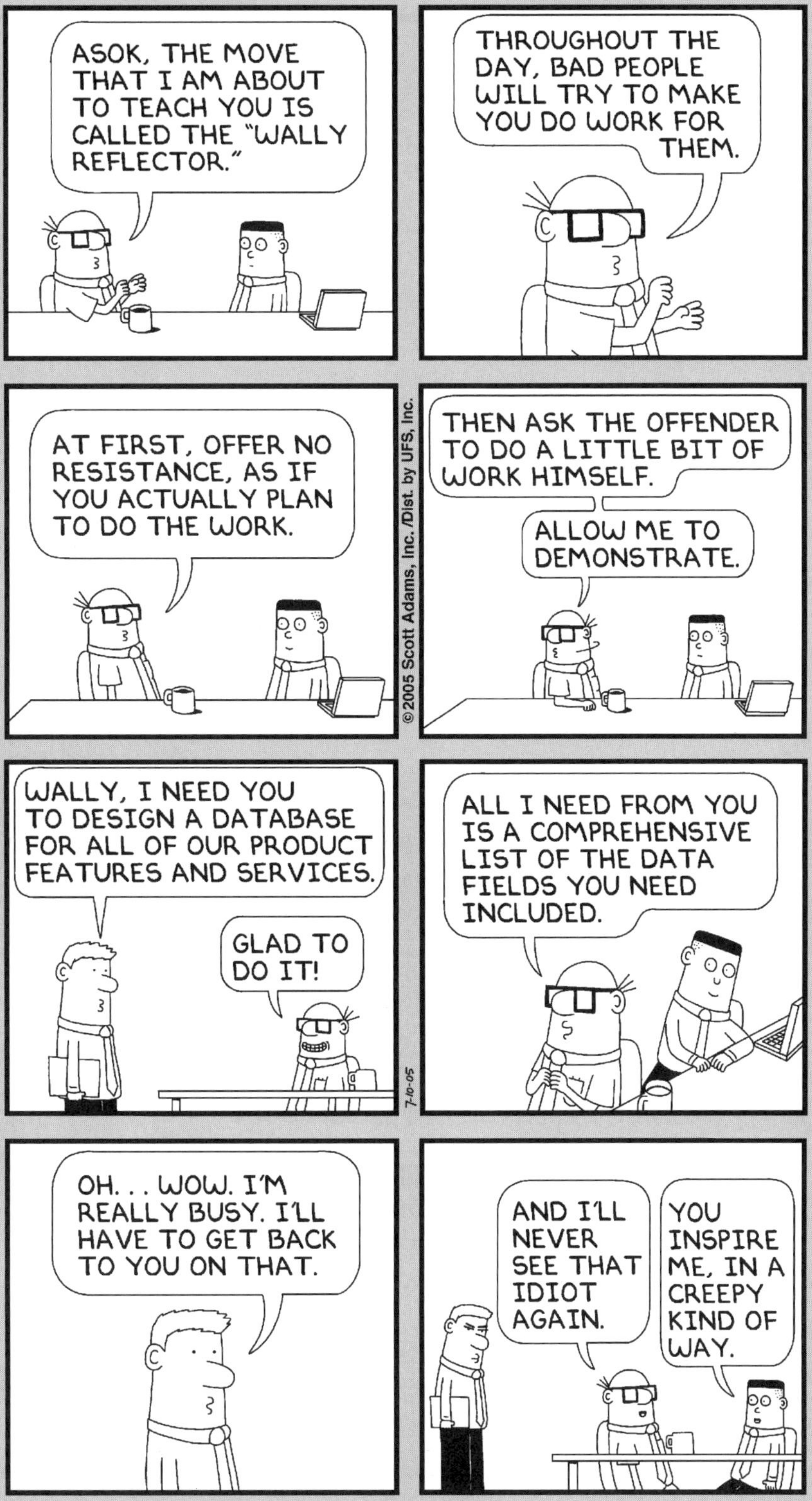
ASOK, THE MOVE THAT I AM ABOUT TO TEACH YOU IS CALLED THE "WALLY REFLECTOR."
THROUGHOUT THE DAY, BAD PEOPLE WILL TRY TO MAKE YOU DO WORK FOR THEM.
AT FIRST, OFFER NO RESISTANCE, AS IF YOU ACTUALLY PLAN TO DO THE WORK.
THEN ASK THE OFFENDER TO DO A LITTLE BIT OF WORK HIMSELF.
ALLOW ME TO DEMONSTRATE.
©2005 Scott Adams, Inc. /Dist. by UFS, Inc.
WALLY, I NEED YOU TO DESIGN A DATABASE FOR ALL OF OUR PRODUCT FEATURES AND SERVICES.
GLAD TO DO IT!
7-10-05
ALL I NEED FROM YOU IS A COMPREHENSIVE LIST OF THE DATA FIELDS YOU NEED INCLUDED.
OH... WOW. I'M REALLY BUSY. I'LL HAVE TO GET BACK TO YOU ON THAT.
AND I'LL NEVER SEE THAT IDIOT AGAIN.
YOU INSPIRE ME, IN A CREEPY KIND OF WAY.

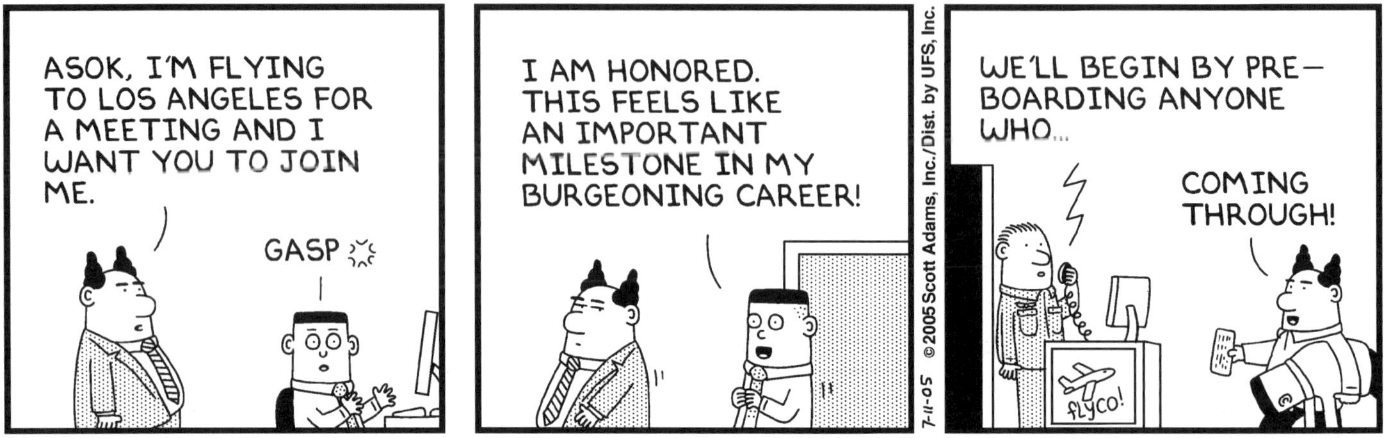
ASOK, I'M FLYING TO LOS ANGELES FOR A MEETING AND I WANT YOU TO JOIN ME.
GASP
I AM HONORED. THIS FEELS LIKE AN IMPORTANT MILESTONE IN MY BURGEONING CAREER!
7-11-05 © 2005 Scott Adams, Inc./Dist. by UFS, Inc.
WE'LL BEGIN BY PRE-BOARDING ANYONE WHO...
COMING THROUGH!
FLYCO!

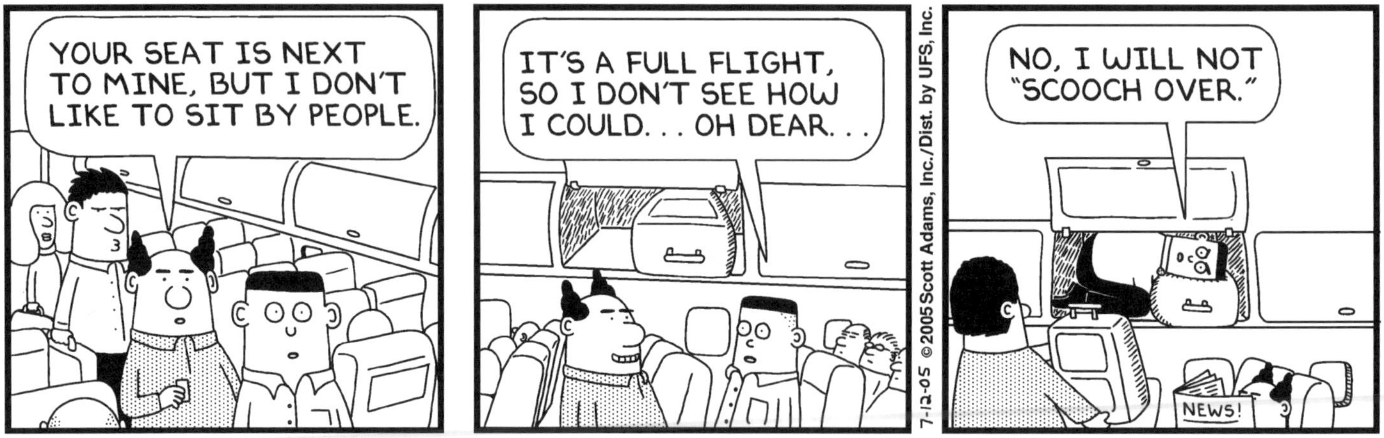
YOUR SEAT IS NEXT TO MINE, BUT I DON'T LIKE TO SIT BY PEOPLE.
IT'S A FULL FLIGHT, SO I DON'T SEE HOW I COULD. . . OH DEAR. . .
7-12-05 © 2005 Scott Adams, Inc./Dist. by UFS, Inc.
NO, I WILL NOT "SCOOCH OVER."
NEWS!

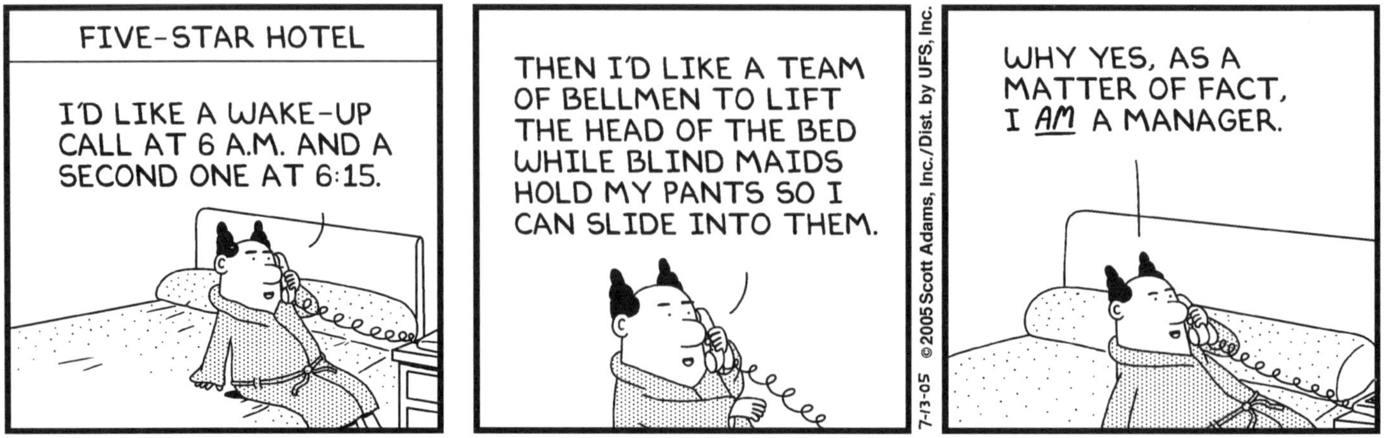
FIVE-STAR HOTEL
I'D LIKE A WAKE-UP CALL AT 6 A.M. AND A SECOND ONE AT 6:15.
THEN I'D LIKE A TEAM OF BELLMEN TO LIFT THE HEAD OF THE BED WHILE BLIND MAIDS HOLD MY PANTS SO I CAN SLIDE INTO THEM.
7-13-05 © 2005 Scott Adams, Inc./Dist. by UFS, Inc.
WHY YES, AS A MATTER OF FACT, I AM A MANAGER.

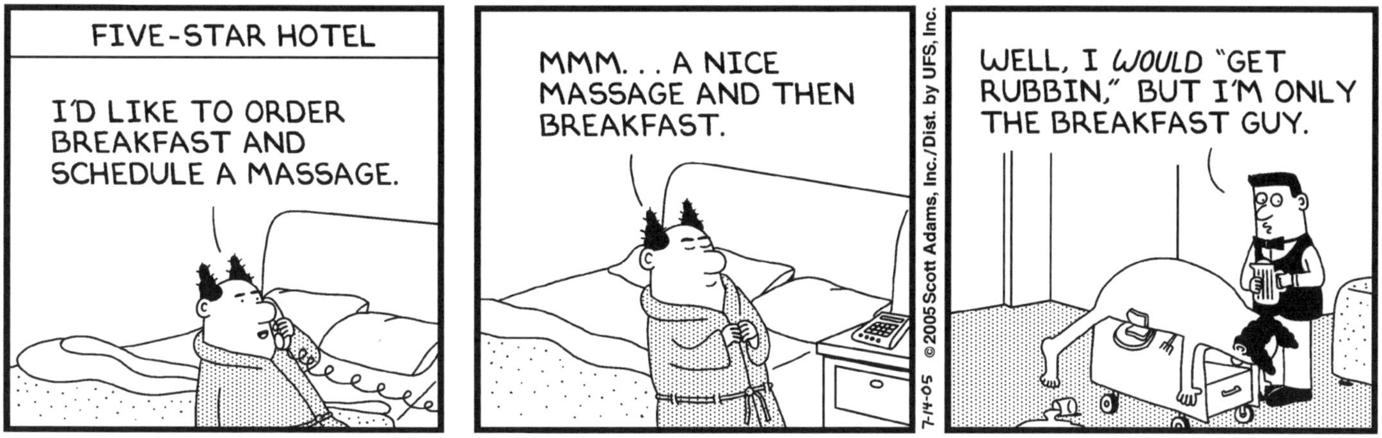
FIVE-STAR HOTEL
I'D LIKE TO ORDER BREAKFAST AND SCHEDULE A MASSAGE.
MMM. . . A NICE MASSAGE AND THEN BREAKFAST.
7-14-05 ©2005 Scott Adams, Inc./Dist. by UFS, Inc.
WELL, I *WOULD* "GET RUBBIN," BUT I'M ONLY THE BREAKFAST GUY.

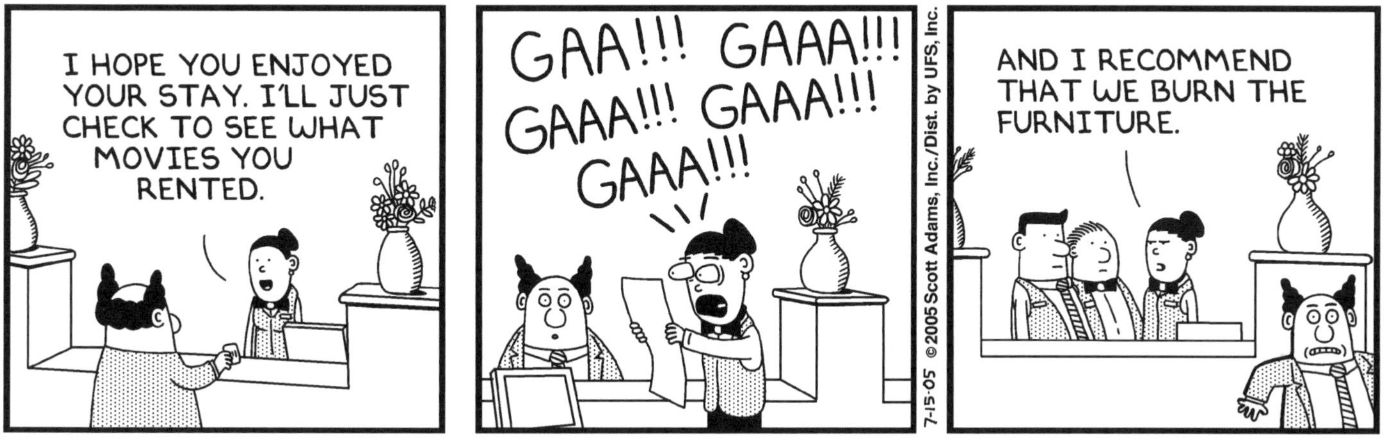
I HOPE YOU ENJOYED YOUR STAY. I'LL JUST CHECK TO SEE WHAT MOVIES YOU RENTED.
GAA!!! GAAA!!! GAAA!!! GAAA!!! GAAA!!!
7-15-05 ©2005 Scott Adams, Inc./Dist. by UFS, Inc.
AND I RECOMMEND THAT WE BURN THE FURNITURE.

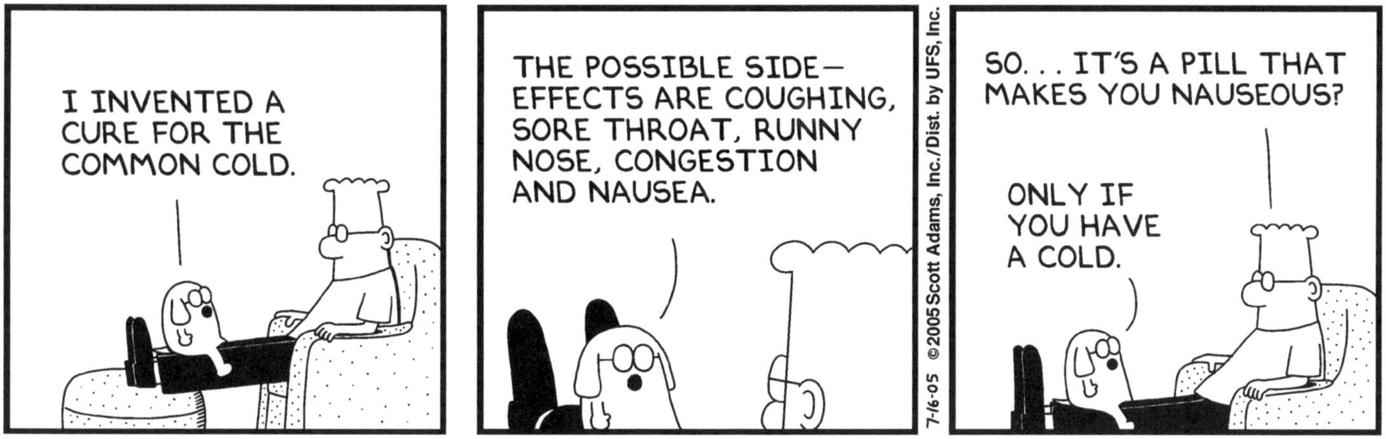
I INVENTED A CURE FOR THE COMMON COLD.
THE POSSIBLE SIDE-EFFECTS ARE COUGHING, SORE THROAT, RUNNY NOSE, CONGESTION AND NAUSEA.
7-16-05 ©2005 Scott Adams, Inc./Dist. by UFS, Inc.
SO. . . IT'S A PILL THAT MAKES YOU NAUSEOUS?
ONLY IF YOU HAVE A COLD.

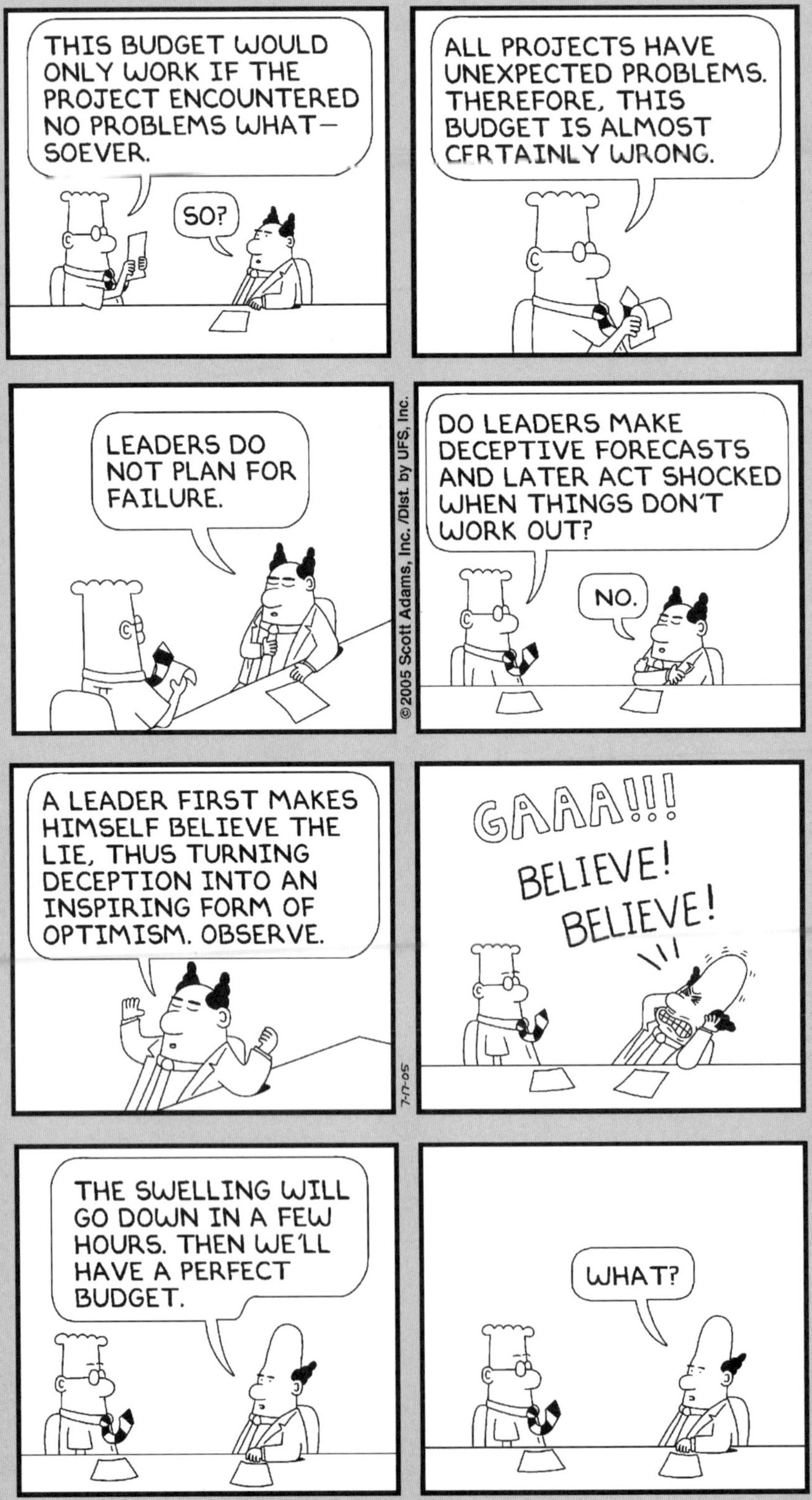
THIS BUDGET WOULD ONLY WORK IF THE PROJECT ENCOUNTERED NO PROBLEMS WHAT-SOEVER.
SO?
ALL PROJECTS HAVE UNEXPECTED PROBLEMS. THEREFORE, THIS BUDGET IS ALMOST CERTAINLY WRONG.
LEADERS DO NOT PLAN FOR FAILURE.
DO LEADERS MAKE DECEPTIVE FORECASTS AND LATER ACT SHOCKED WHEN THINGS DON'T WORK OUT?
NO.
©2005 Scott Adams, Inc./Dist. by UFS, Inc.
A LEADER FIRST MAKES HIMSELF BELIEVE THE LIE, THUS TURNING DECEPTION INTO AN INSPIRING FORM OF OPTIMISM. OBSERVE.
7-17-05
GAAA!!!
BELIEVE!
BELIEVE!
THE SWELLING WILL GO DOWN IN A FEW HOURS. THEN WE'LL HAVE A PERFECT BUDGET.
WHAT?

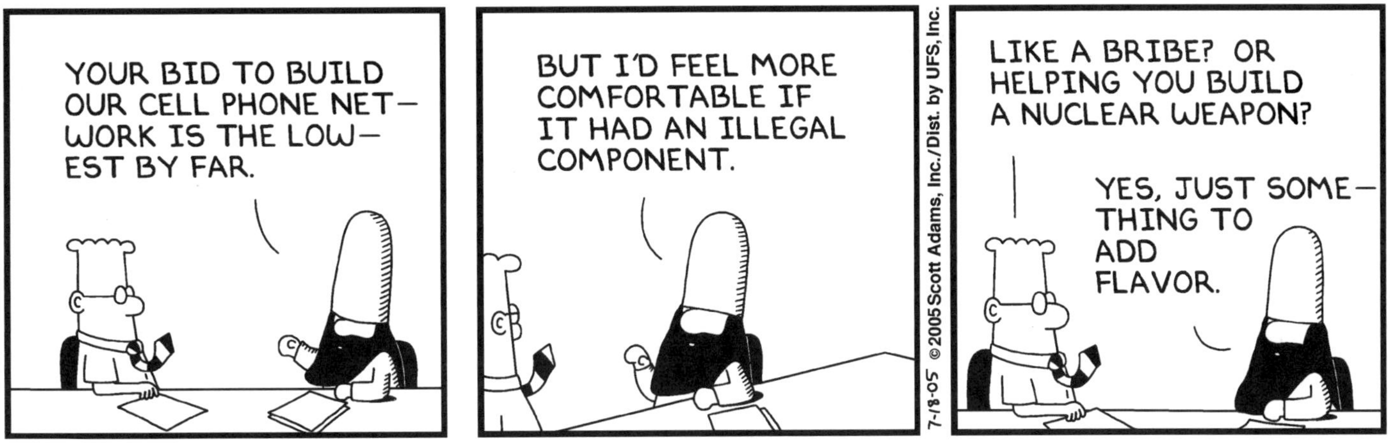
YOUR BID TO BUILD OUR CELL PHONE NET–WORK IS THE LOW–EST BY FAR.
BUT I'D FEEL MORE COMFORTABLE IF IT HAD AN ILLEGAL COMPONENT.
7-18-05 © 2005 Scott Adams, Inc./Dist. by UFS, Inc.
LIKE A BRIBE? OR HELPING YOU BUILD A NUCLEAR WEAPON?
YES, JUST SOME–THING TO ADD FLAVOR.

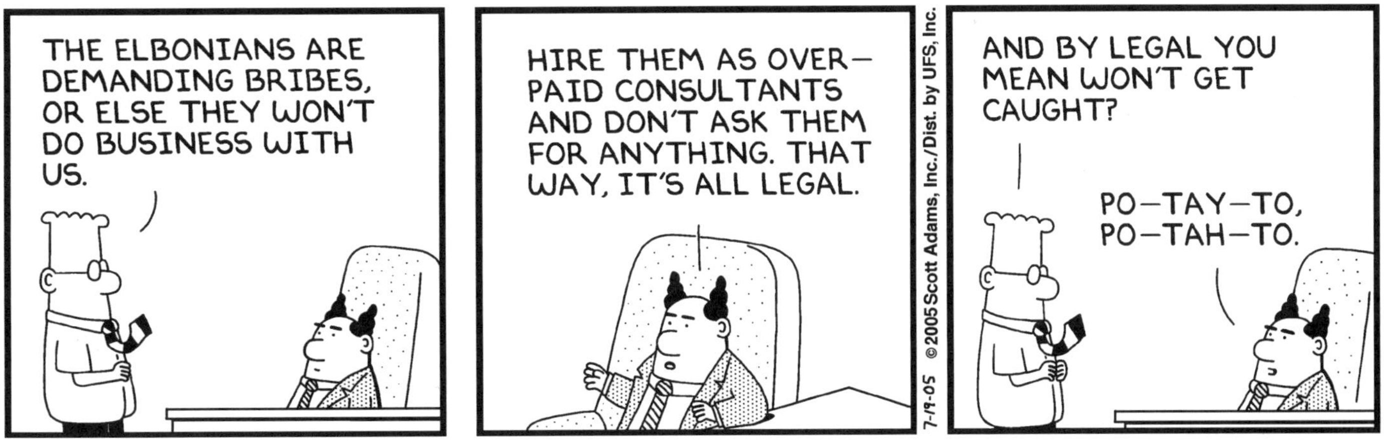
THE ELBONIANS ARE DEMANDING BRIBES, OR ELSE THEY WON'T DO BUSINESS WITH US.
HIRE THEM AS OVER–PAID CONSULTANTS AND DON'T ASK THEM FOR ANYTHING. THAT WAY, IT'S ALL LEGAL.
7-19-05 © 2005 Scott Adams, Inc./Dist. by UFS, Inc.
AND BY LEGAL YOU MEAN WON'T GET CAUGHT?
PO–TAY–TO, PO–TAH–TO.

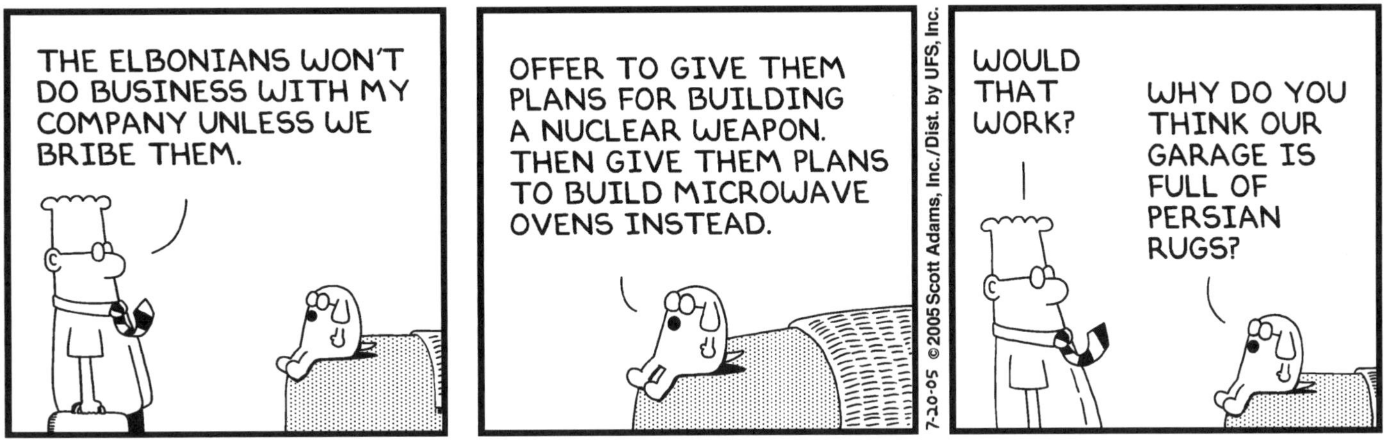
THE ELBONIANS WON'T DO BUSINESS WITH MY COMPANY UNLESS WE BRIBE THEM.
OFFER TO GIVE THEM PLANS FOR BUILDING A NUCLEAR WEAPON. THEN GIVE THEM PLANS TO BUILD MICROWAVE OVENS INSTEAD.
7-20-05 © 2005 Scott Adams, Inc./Dist. by UFS, Inc.
WOULD THAT WORK?
WHY DO YOU THINK OUR GARAGE IS FULL OF PERSIAN RUGS?

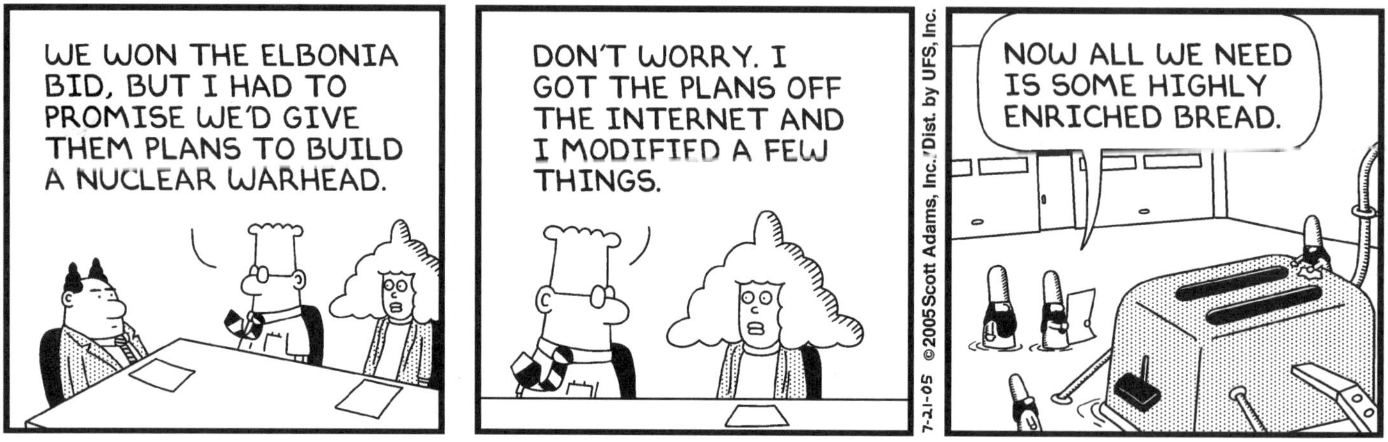
WE WON THE ELBONIA BID, BUT I HAD TO PROMISE WE'D GIVE THEM PLANS TO BUILD A NUCLEAR WARHEAD.
DON'T WORRY. I GOT THE PLANS OFF THE INTERNET AND I MODIFIED A FEW THINGS.
7-21-05 ©2005 Scott Adams, Inc./Dist. by UFS, Inc.
NOW ALL WE NEED IS SOME HIGHLY ENRICHED BREAD.

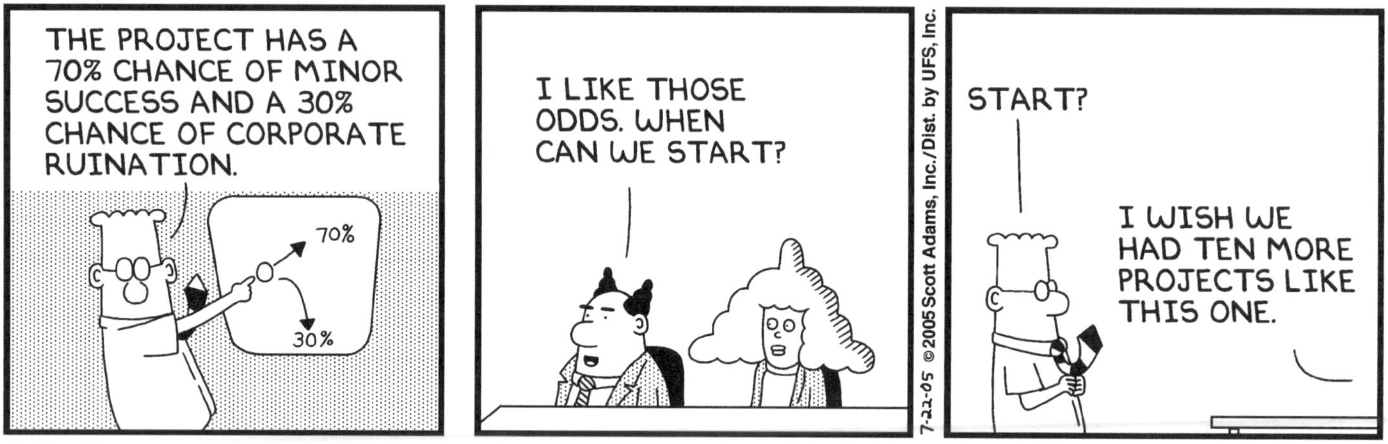
THE PROJECT HAS A 70% CHANCE OF MINOR SUCCESS AND A 30% CHANCE OF CORPORATE RUINATION.
70%
30%
I LIKE THOSE ODDS. WHEN CAN WE START?
7-22-05 ©2005 Scott Adams, Inc./Dist. by UFS, Inc.
START?
I WISH WE HAD TEN MORE PROJECTS LIKE THIS ONE.

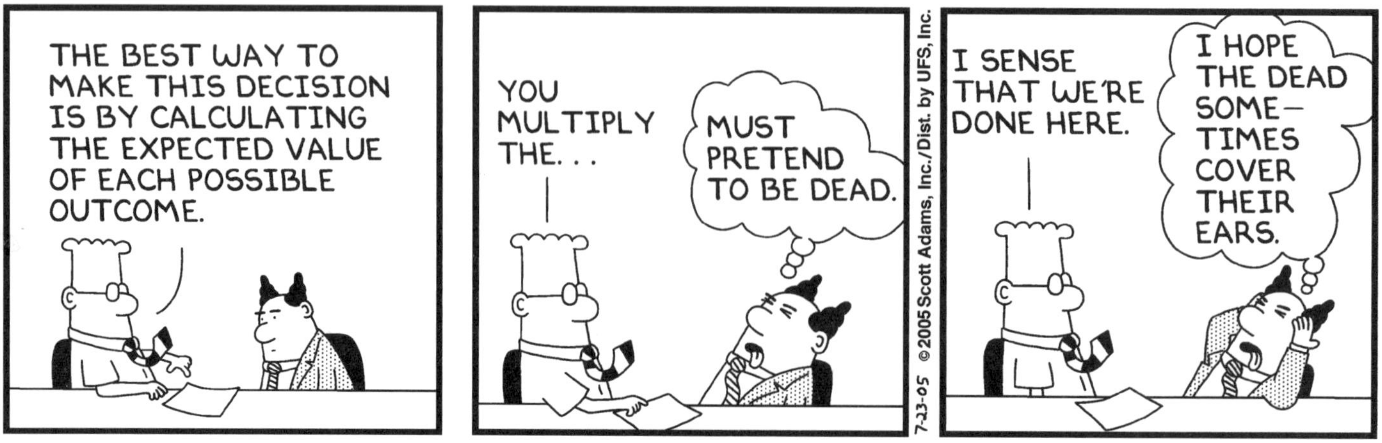
THE BEST WAY TO MAKE THIS DECISION IS BY CALCULATING THE EXPECTED VALUE OF EACH POSSIBLE OUTCOME.
YOU MULTIPLY THE. . .
MUST PRETEND TO BE DEAD.
7-23-05 ©2005 Scott Adams, Inc./Dist. by UFS, Inc.
I SENSE THAT WE'RE DONE HERE.
I HOPE THE DEAD SOME-TIMES COVER THEIR EARS.

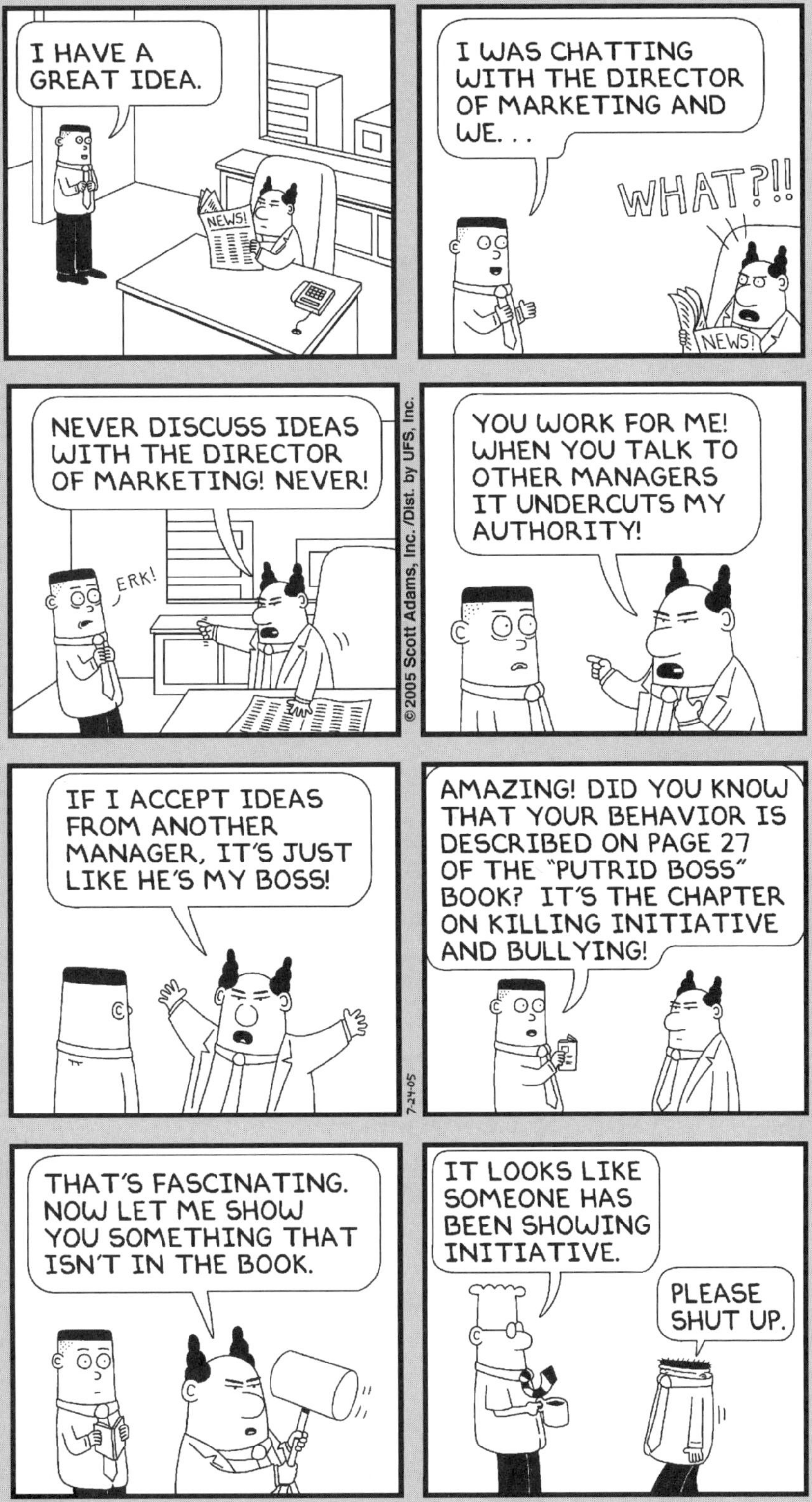
I HAVE A GREAT IDEA.
NEWS!
I WAS CHATTING WITH THE DIRECTOR OF MARKETING AND WE. . .
WHAT?!!
NEWS!
NEVER DISCUSS IDEAS WITH THE DIRECTOR OF MARKETING! NEVER!
ERK!
YOU WORK FOR ME! WHEN YOU TALK TO OTHER MANAGERS IT UNDERCUTS MY AUTHORITY!
IF I ACCEPT IDEAS FROM ANOTHER MANAGER, IT'S JUST LIKE HE'S MY BOSS!
AMAZING! DID YOU KNOW THAT YOUR BEHAVIOR IS DESCRIBED ON PAGE 27 OF THE "PUTRID BOSS" BOOK? IT'S THE CHAPTER ON KILLING INITIATIVE AND BULLYING!
THAT'S FASCINATING. NOW LET ME SHOW YOU SOMETHING THAT ISN'T IN THE BOOK.
IT LOOKS LIKE SOMEONE HAS BEEN SHOWING INITIATIVE.
PLEASE SHUT UP.
7-24-05

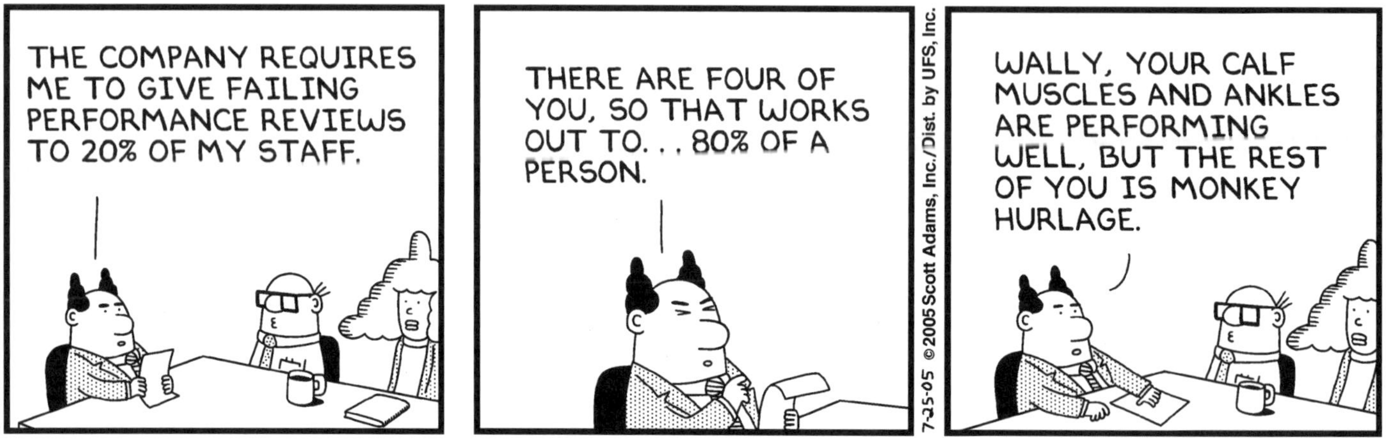
THE COMPANY REQUIRES ME TO GIVE FAILING PERFORMANCE REVIEWS TO 20% OF MY STAFF.
THERE ARE FOUR OF YOU, SO THAT WORKS OUT TO. . . 80% OF A PERSON.
7-25-05 ©2005 Scott Adams, Inc./Dist. by UFS, Inc.
WALLY, YOUR CALF MUSCLES AND ANKLES ARE PERFORMING WELL, BUT THE REST OF YOU IS MONKEY HURLAGE.

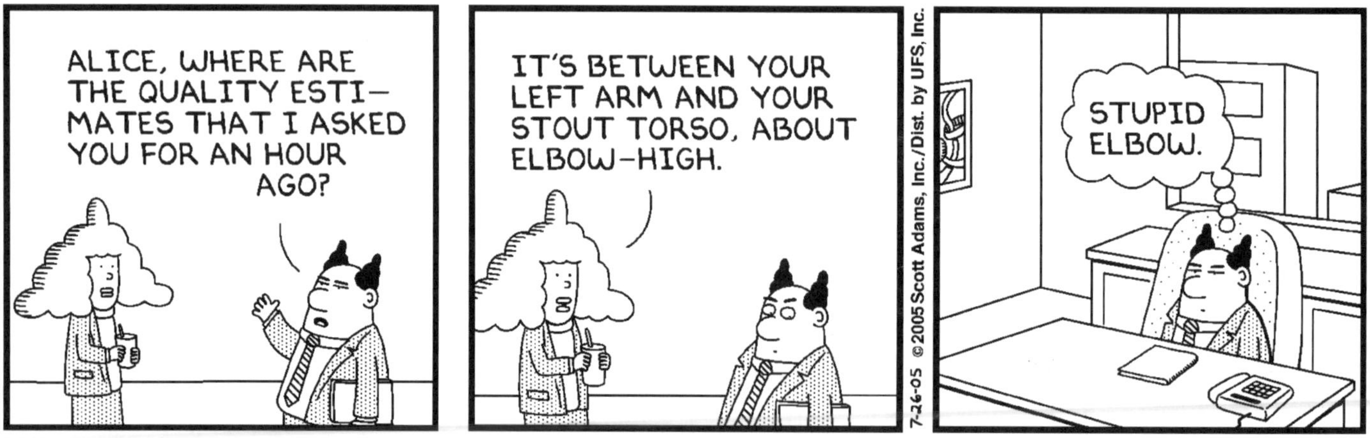
ALICE, WHERE ARE THE QUALITY ESTI– MATES THAT I ASKED YOU FOR AN HOUR AGO?
IT'S BETWEEN YOUR LEFT ARM AND YOUR STOUT TORSO, ABOUT ELBOW–HIGH.
7-26-05 ©2005 Scott Adams, Inc./Dist. by UFS, Inc.
STUPID ELBOW.

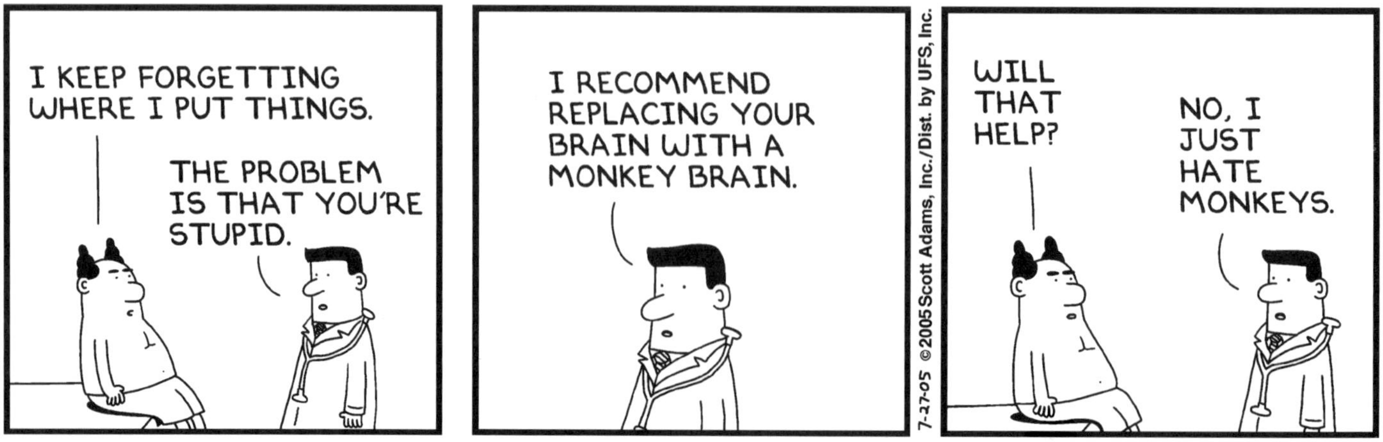
I KEEP FORGETTING WHERE I PUT THINGS.
THE PROBLEM IS THAT YOU'RE STUPID.
I RECOMMEND REPLACING YOUR BRAIN WITH A MONKEY BRAIN.
7-27-05 ©2005 Scott Adams, Inc./Dist. by UFS, Inc.
WILL THAT HELP?
NO, I JUST HATE MONKEYS.

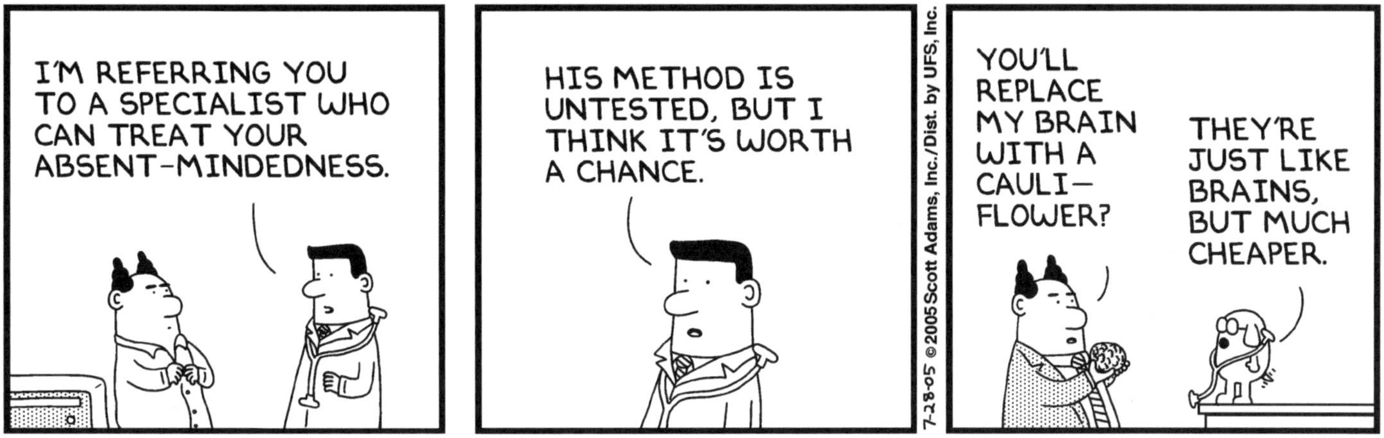
I'M REFERRING YOU TO A SPECIALIST WHO CAN TREAT YOUR ABSENT-MINDEDNESS.
HIS METHOD IS UNTESTED, BUT I THINK IT'S WORTH A CHANCE.
7-28-05 ©2005 Scott Adams, Inc./Dist. by UFS, Inc.
YOU'LL REPLACE MY BRAIN WITH A CAULI-FLOWER?
THEY'RE JUST LIKE BRAINS, BUT MUCH CHEAPER.

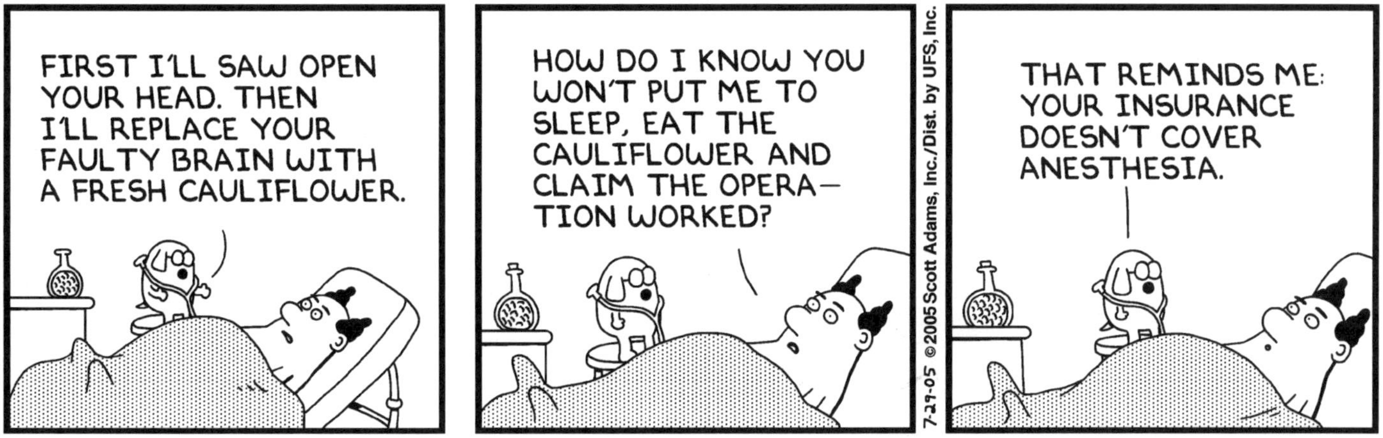
FIRST I'LL SAW OPEN YOUR HEAD. THEN I'LL REPLACE YOUR FAULTY BRAIN WITH A FRESH CAULIFLOWER.
HOW DO I KNOW YOU WON'T PUT ME TO SLEEP, EAT THE CAULIFLOWER AND CLAIM THE OPERA-TION WORKED?
7-29-05 ©2005 Scott Adams, Inc./Dist. by UFS, Inc.
THAT REMINDS ME: YOUR INSURANCE DOESN'T COVER ANESTHESIA.

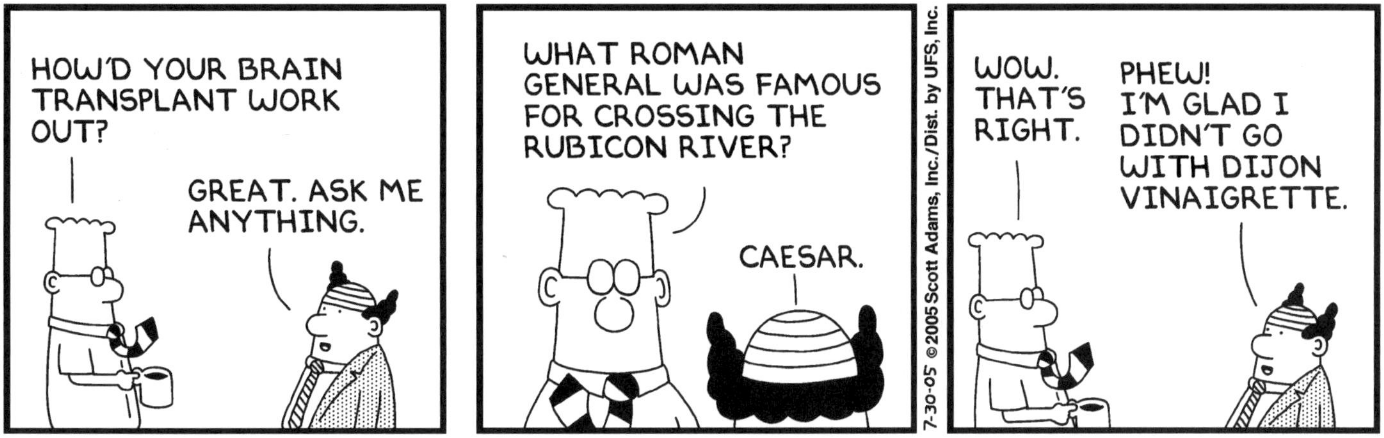
HOW'D YOUR BRAIN TRANSPLANT WORK OUT?
GREAT. ASK ME ANYTHING.
WHAT ROMAN GENERAL WAS FAMOUS FOR CROSSING THE RUBICON RIVER?
CAESAR.
7-30-05 ©2005 Scott Adams, Inc./Dist. by UFS, Inc.
WOW. THAT'S RIGHT.
PHEW! I'M GLAD I DIDN'T GO WITH DIJON VINAIGRETTE.

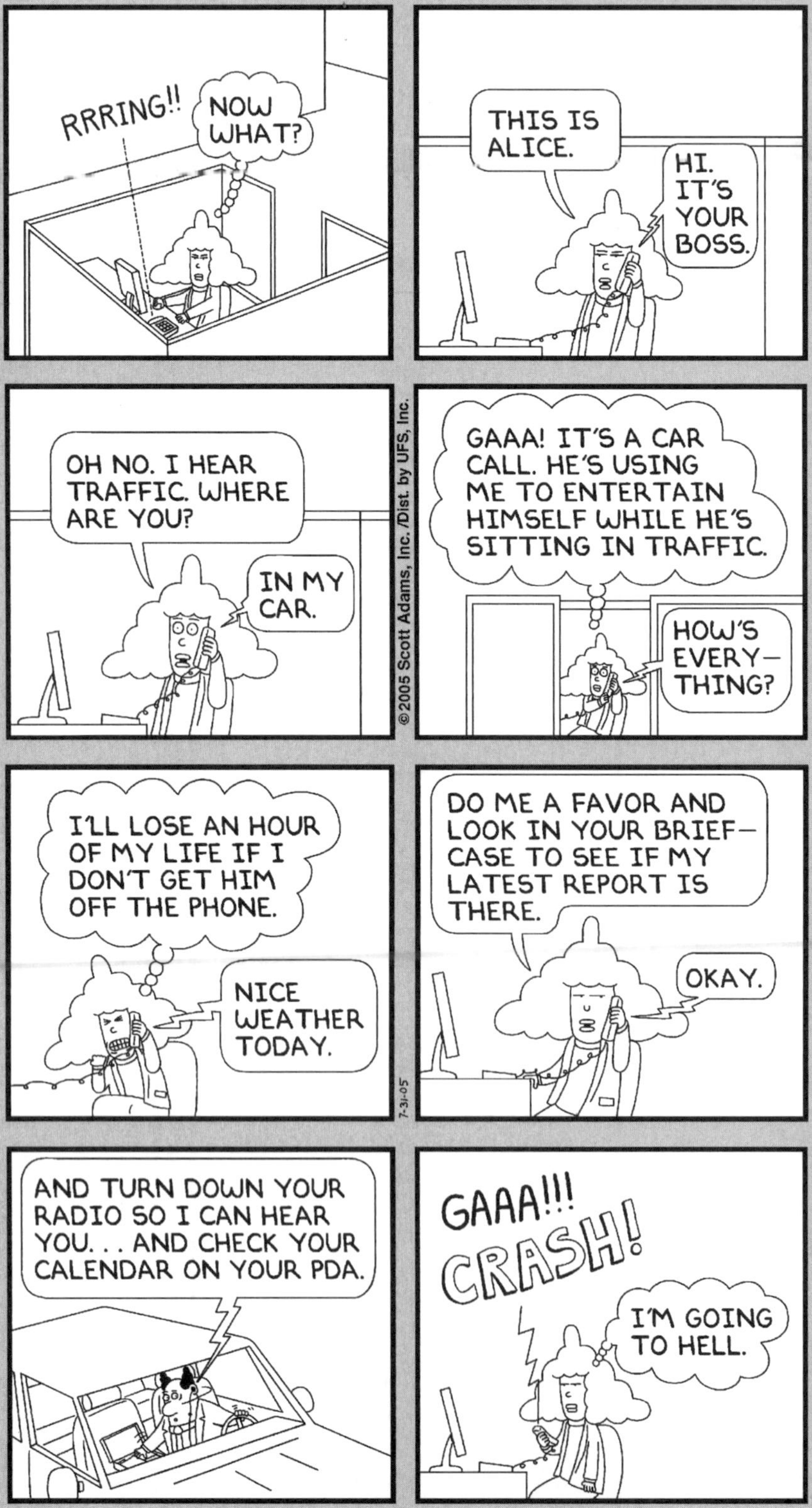
RRRING!!
NOW WHAT?
THIS IS ALICE.
HI. IT'S YOUR BOSS.
OH NO. I HEAR TRAFFIC. WHERE ARE YOU?
IN MY CAR.
GAAA! IT'S A CAR CALL. HE'S USING ME TO ENTERTAIN HIMSELF WHILE HE'S SITTING IN TRAFFIC.
HOW'S EVERY-THING?
I'LL LOSE AN HOUR OF MY LIFE IF I DON'T GET HIM OFF THE PHONE.
NICE WEATHER TODAY.
DO ME A FAVOR AND LOOK IN YOUR BRIEF-CASE TO SEE IF MY LATEST REPORT IS THERE.
OKAY.
AND TURN DOWN YOUR RADIO SO I CAN HEAR YOU. . . AND CHECK YOUR CALENDAR ON YOUR PDA.
GAAA!!!
CRASH!
I'M GOING TO HELL.
©2005 Scott Adams, Inc./Dist. by UFS, Inc.
7-31-05

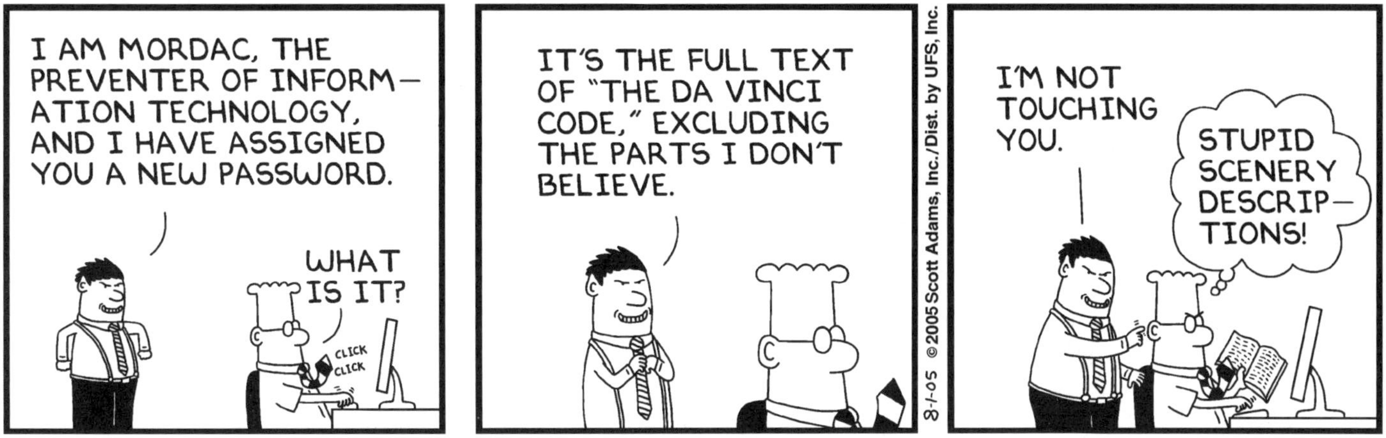
I AM MORDAC, THE PREVENTER OF INFORM-ATION TECHNOLOGY, AND I HAVE ASSIGNED YOU A NEW PASSWORD.
WHAT IS IT?
CLICK CLICK
IT'S THE FULL TEXT OF "THE DA VINCI CODE," EXCLUDING THE PARTS I DON'T BELIEVE.
8-1-05 © 2005 Scott Adams, Inc./Dist. by UFS, Inc.
I'M NOT TOUCHING YOU.
STUPID SCENERY DESCRIP-TIONS!

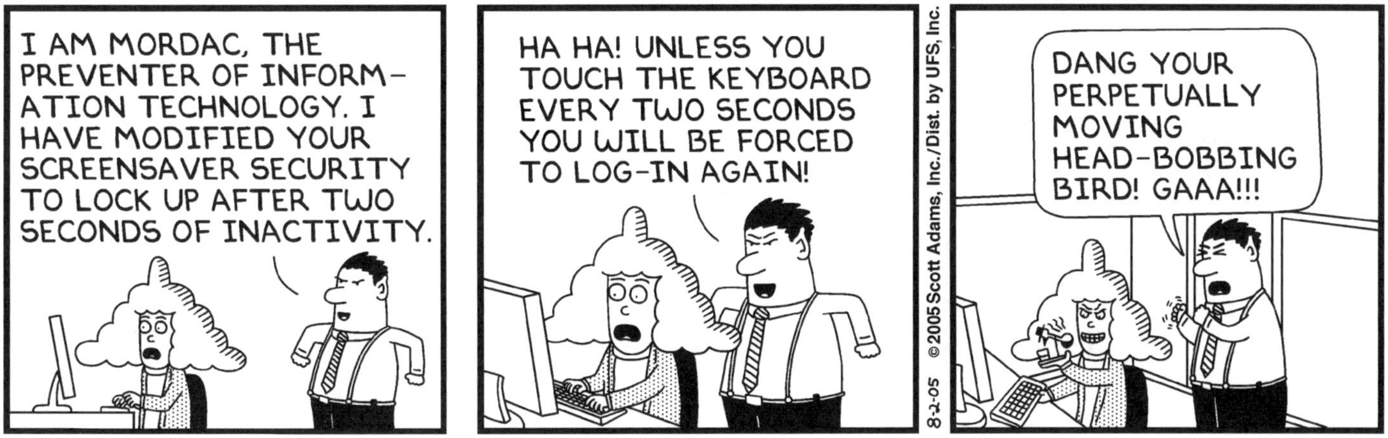
I AM MORDAC, THE PREVENTER OF INFORM-ATION TECHNOLOGY. I HAVE MODIFIED YOUR SCREENSAVER SECURITY TO LOCK UP AFTER TWO SECONDS OF INACTIVITY.
HA HA! UNLESS YOU TOUCH THE KEYBOARD EVERY TWO SECONDS YOU WILL BE FORCED TO LOG-IN AGAIN!
8-2-05 © 2005 Scott Adams, Inc./Dist. by UFS, Inc.
DANG YOUR PERPETUALLY MOVING HEAD-BOBBING BIRD! GAAA!!!

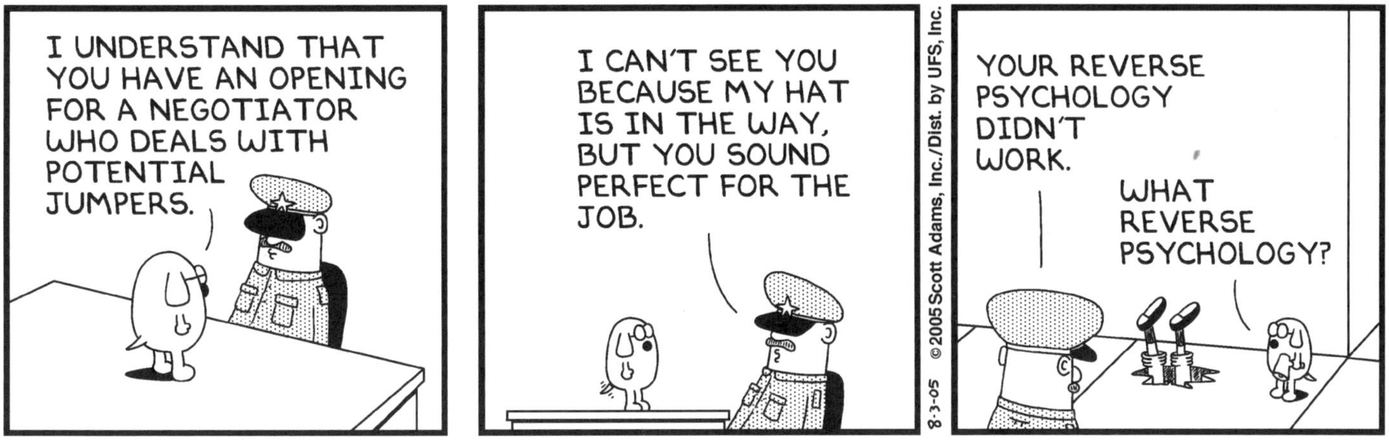
I UNDERSTAND THAT YOU HAVE AN OPENING FOR A NEGOTIATOR WHO DEALS WITH POTENTIAL JUMPERS.
I CAN'T SEE YOU BECAUSE MY HAT IS IN THE WAY, BUT YOU SOUND PERFECT FOR THE JOB.
8-3-05 © 2005 Scott Adams, Inc./Dist. by UFS, Inc.
YOUR REVERSE PSYCHOLOGY DIDN'T WORK.
WHAT REVERSE PSYCHOLOGY?

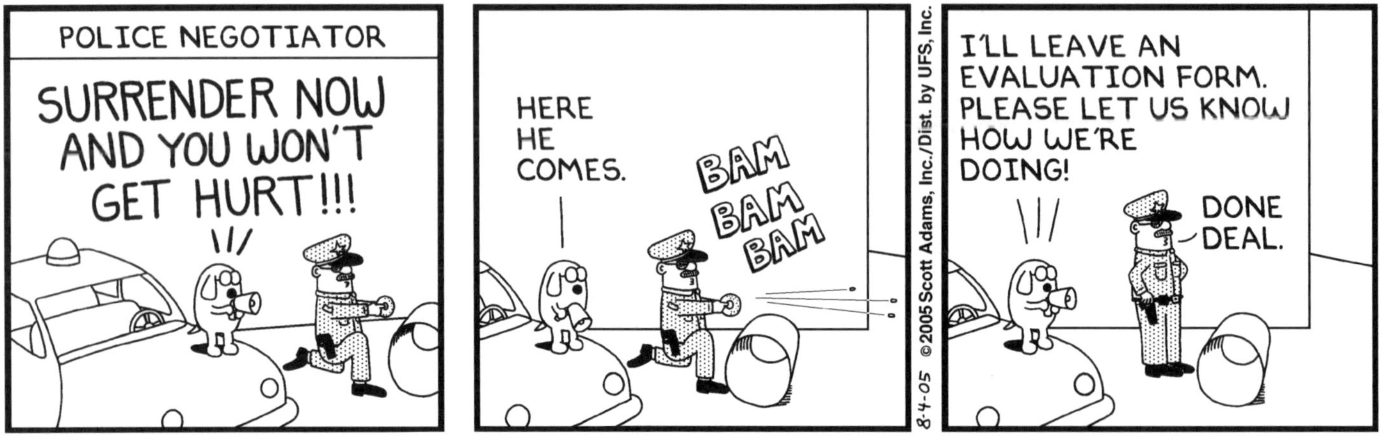
POLICE NEGOTIATOR
SURRENDER NOW AND YOU WON'T GET HURT!!!
HERE HE COMES.
BAM BAM BAM
8-4-05 ©2005 Scott Adams, Inc./Dist. by UFS, Inc.
I'LL LEAVE AN EVALUATION FORM. PLEASE LET US KNOW HOW WE'RE DOING!
DONE DEAL.

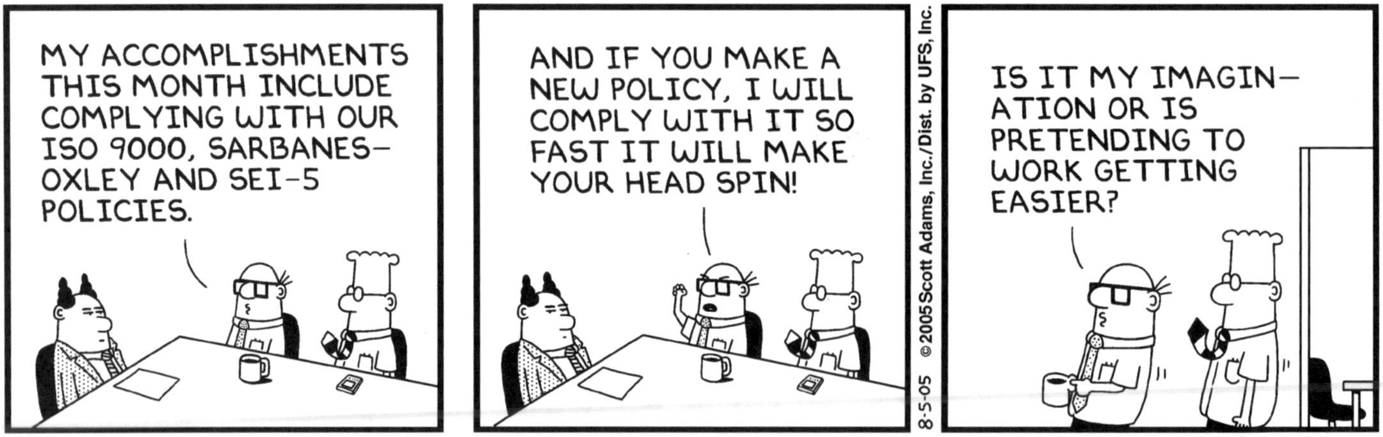
MY ACCOMPLISHMENTS THIS MONTH INCLUDE COMPLYING WITH OUR ISO 9000, SARBANES-OXLEY AND SEI-5 POLICIES.
AND IF YOU MAKE A NEW POLICY, I WILL COMPLY WITH IT SO FAST IT WILL MAKE YOUR HEAD SPIN!
8-5-05 ©2005 Scott Adams, Inc./Dist. by UFS, Inc.
IS IT MY IMAGIN-ATION OR IS PRETENDING TO WORK GETTING EASIER?

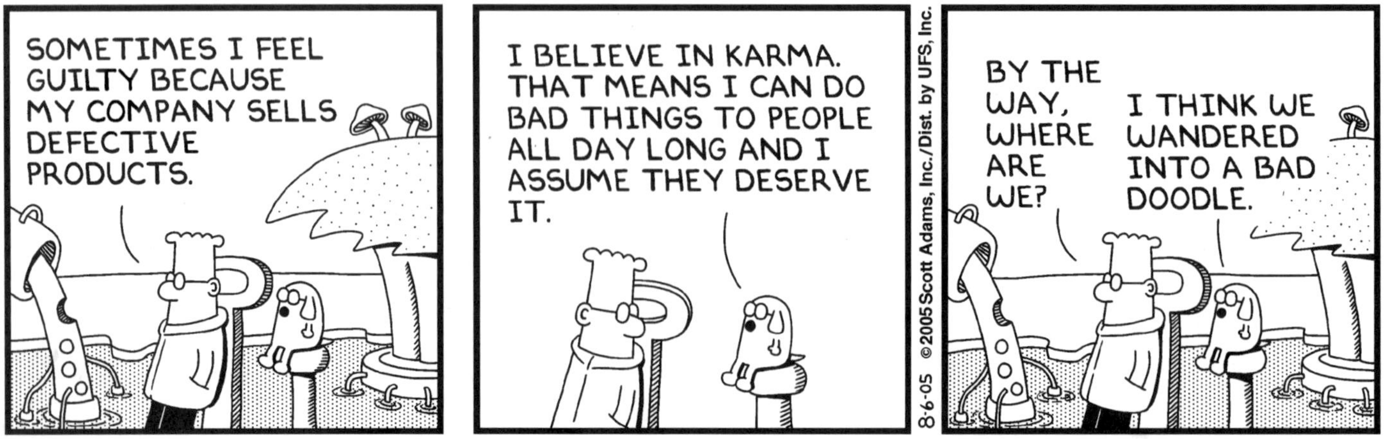
SOMETIMES I FEEL GUILTY BECAUSE MY COMPANY SELLS DEFECTIVE PRODUCTS.
I BELIEVE IN KARMA. THAT MEANS I CAN DO BAD THINGS TO PEOPLE ALL DAY LONG AND I ASSUME THEY DESERVE IT.
8-6-05 ©2005 Scott Adams, Inc./Dist. by UFS, Inc.
BY THE WAY, WHERE ARE WE?
I THINK WE WANDERED INTO A BAD DOODLE.

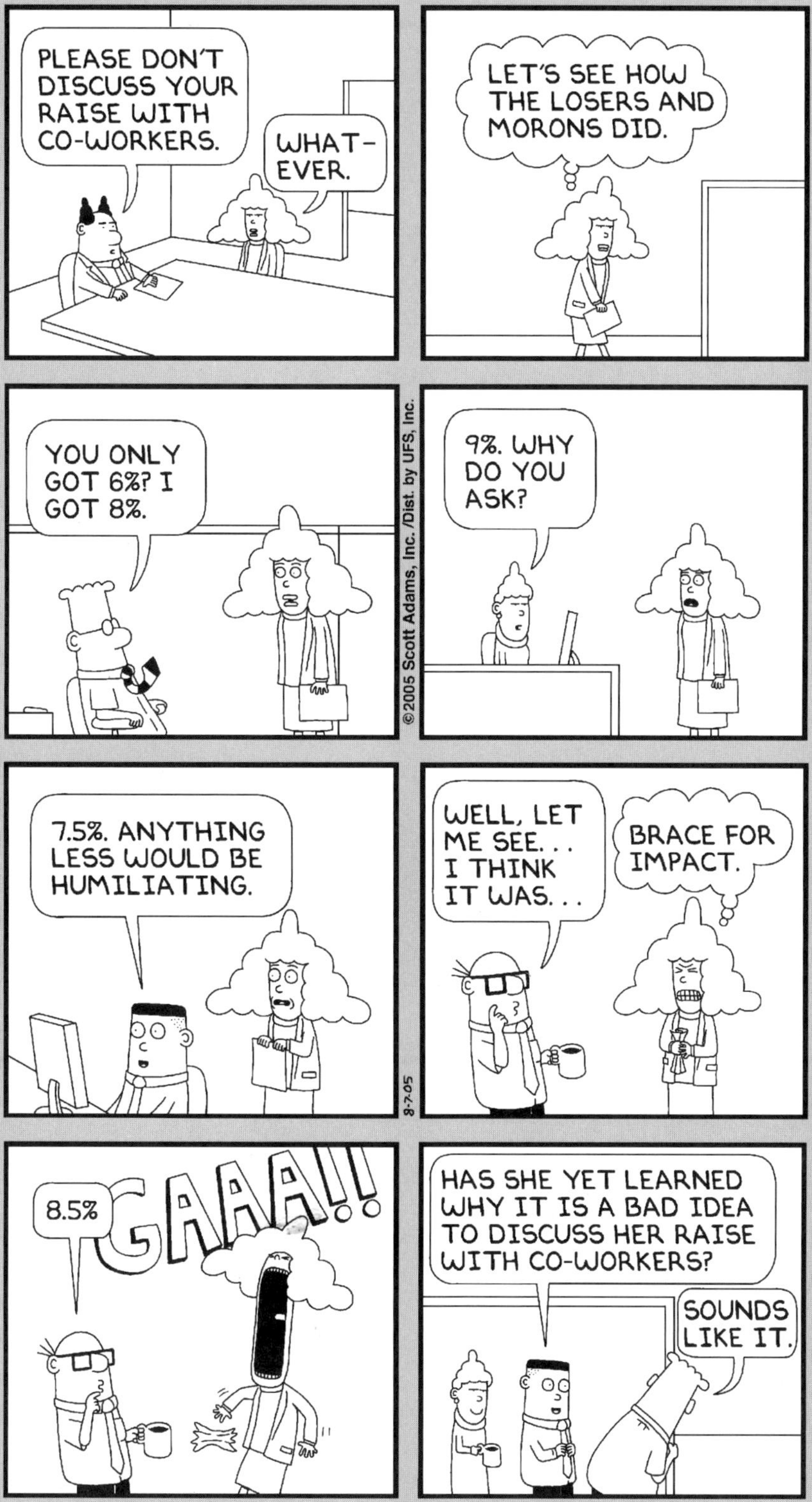
PLEASE DON'T DISCUSS YOUR RAISE WITH CO-WORKERS.
WHAT-EVER.
LET'S SEE HOW THE LOSERS AND MORONS DID.
YOU ONLY GOT 6%? I GOT 8%.
9%. WHY DO YOU ASK?
7.5%. ANYTHING LESS WOULD BE HUMILIATING.
WELL, LET ME SEE. . . I THINK IT WAS. . .
BRACE FOR IMPACT.
8.5%
GAAA!!
HAS SHE YET LEARNED WHY IT IS A BAD IDEA TO DISCUSS HER RAISE WITH CO-WORKERS?
SOUNDS LIKE IT.
©2005 Scott Adams, Inc./Dist. by UFS, Inc.
9-7-05

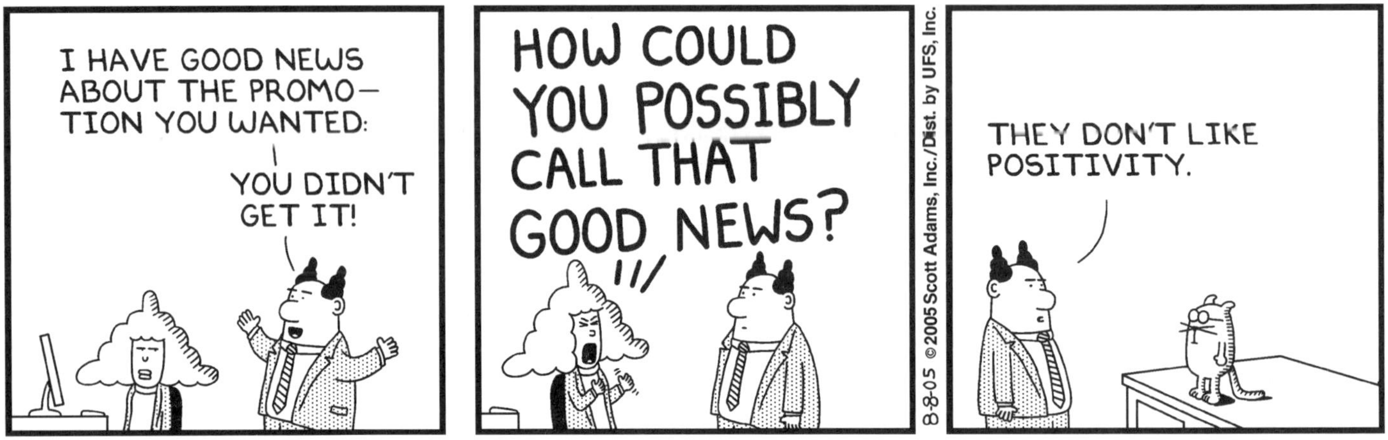
I HAVE GOOD NEWS ABOUT THE PROMOTION YOU WANTED:
YOU DIDN'T GET IT!
HOW COULD YOU POSSIBLY CALL THAT GOOD NEWS?
8-8-05 © 2005 Scott Adams, Inc./Dist. by UFS, Inc.
THEY DON'T LIKE POSITIVITY.

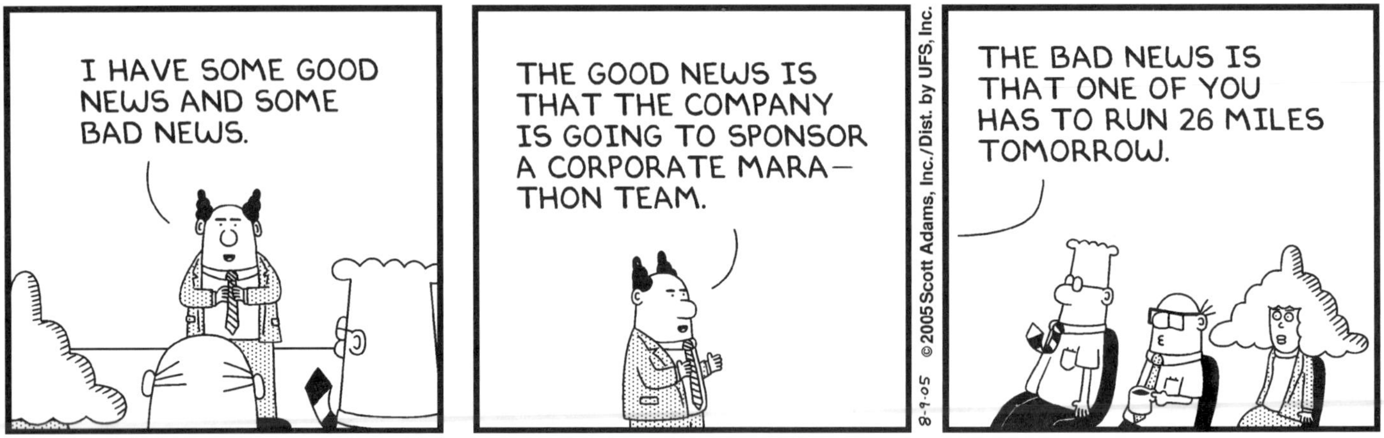
I HAVE SOME GOOD NEWS AND SOME BAD NEWS.
THE GOOD NEWS IS THAT THE COMPANY IS GOING TO SPONSOR A CORPORATE MARATHON TEAM.
8-9-05 © 2005 Scott Adams, Inc./Dist. by UFS, Inc.
THE BAD NEWS IS THAT ONE OF YOU HAS TO RUN 26 MILES TOMORROW.

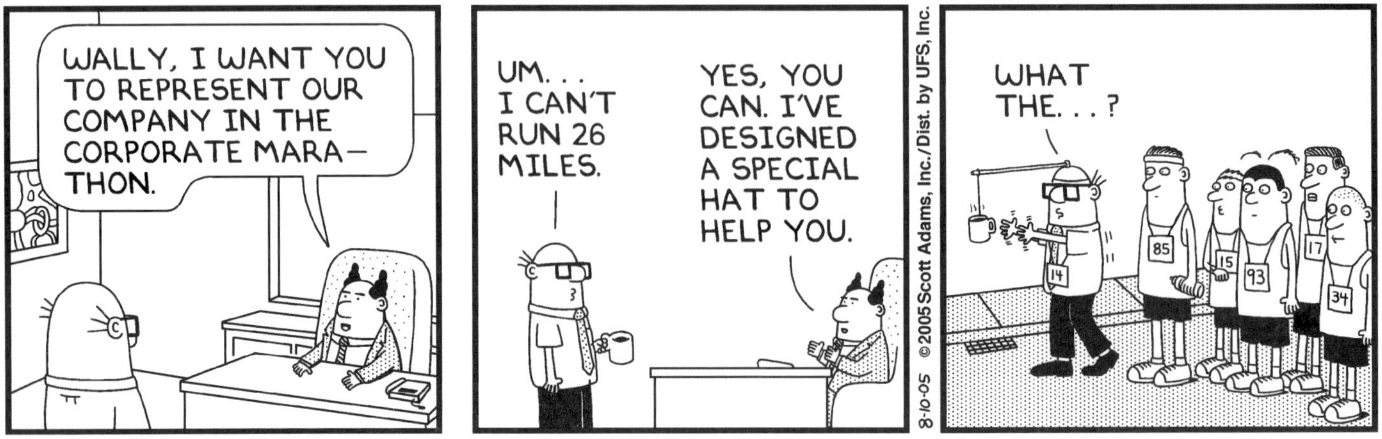
WALLY, I WANT YOU TO REPRESENT OUR COMPANY IN THE CORPORATE MARATHON.
UM... I CAN'T RUN 26 MILES.
YES, YOU CAN. I'VE DESIGNED A SPECIAL HAT TO HELP YOU.
8-10-05 © 2005 Scott Adams, Inc./Dist. by UFS, Inc.
WHAT THE...?
14
85
15
93
17
34

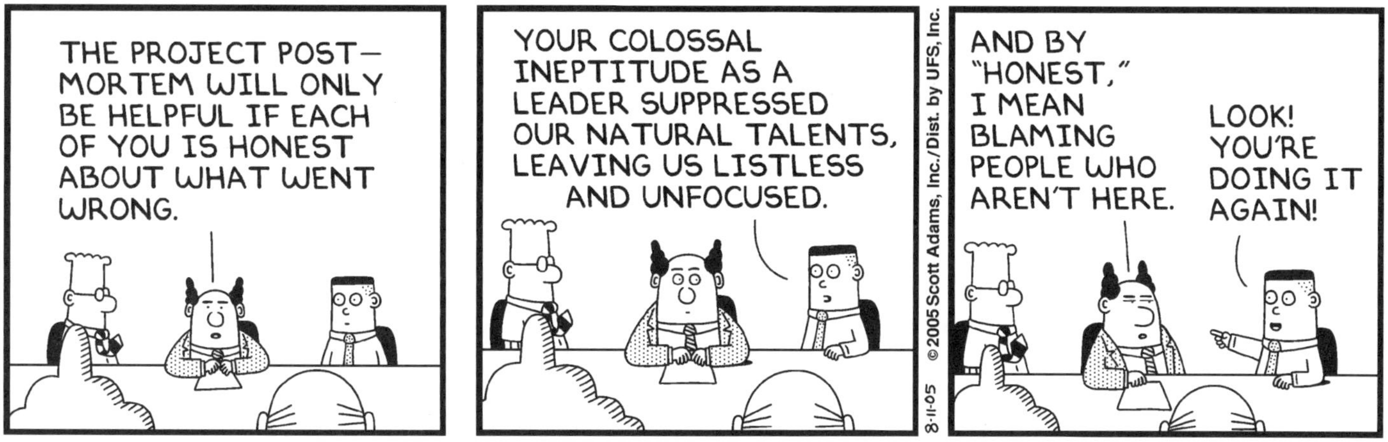
THE PROJECT POST-MORTEM WILL ONLY BE HELPFUL IF EACH OF YOU IS HONEST ABOUT WHAT WENT WRONG.
YOUR COLOSSAL INEPTITUDE AS A LEADER SUPPRESSED OUR NATURAL TALENTS, LEAVING US LISTLESS AND UNFOCUSED.
8-11-05 ©2005 Scott Adams, Inc./Dist. by UFS, Inc.
AND BY "HONEST," I MEAN BLAMING PEOPLE WHO AREN'T HERE.
LOOK! YOU'RE DOING IT AGAIN!

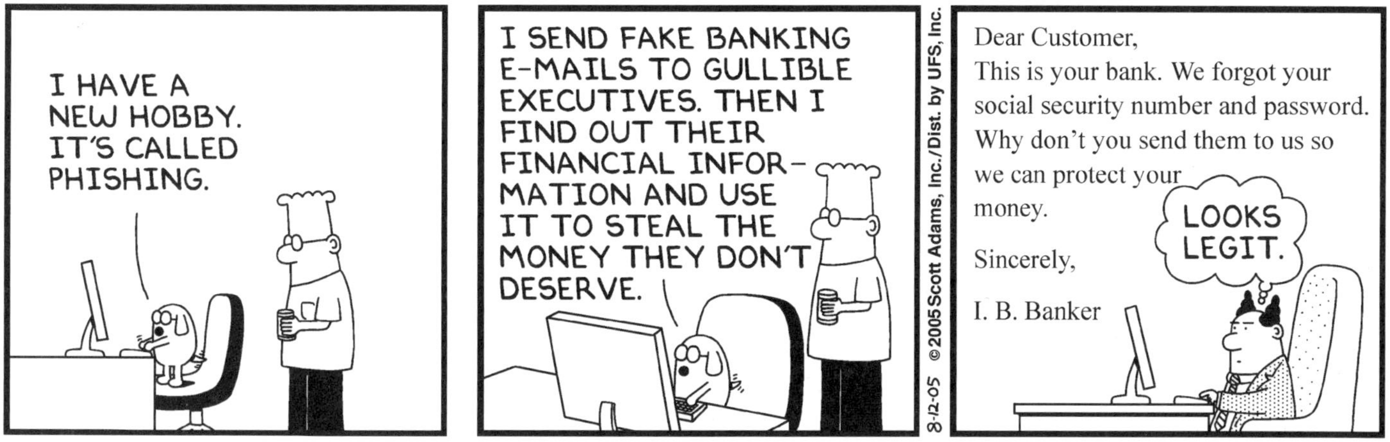
I HAVE A NEW HOBBY. IT'S CALLED PHISHING.
I SEND FAKE BANKING E-MAILS TO GULLIBLE EXECUTIVES. THEN I FIND OUT THEIR FINANCIAL INFORMATION AND USE IT TO STEAL THE MONEY THEY DON'T DESERVE.
8-12-05 ©2005 Scott Adams, Inc./Dist. by UFS, Inc.
Dear Customer,
This is your bank. We forgot your social security number and password. Why don't you send them to us so we can protect your money.
Sincerely,
I. B. Banker
LOOKS LEGIT.

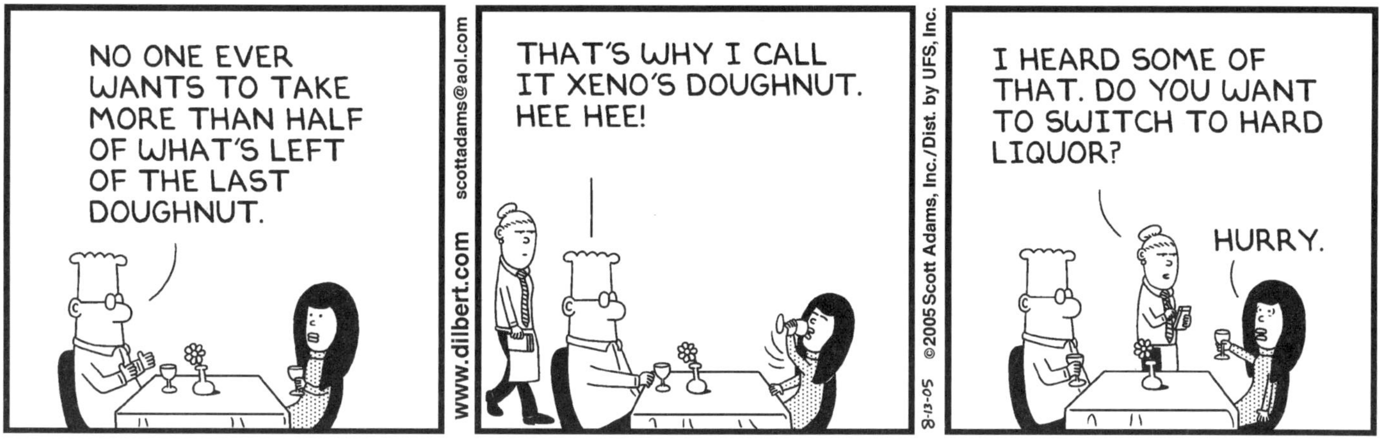
NO ONE EVER WANTS TO TAKE MORE THAN HALF OF WHAT'S LEFT OF THE LAST DOUGHNUT.
www.dilbert.com scottadams@aol.com
THAT'S WHY I CALL IT XENO'S DOUGHNUT. HEE HEE!
8-13-05 ©2005 Scott Adams, Inc./Dist. by UFS, Inc.
I HEARD SOME OF THAT. DO YOU WANT TO SWITCH TO HARD LIQUOR?
HURRY.

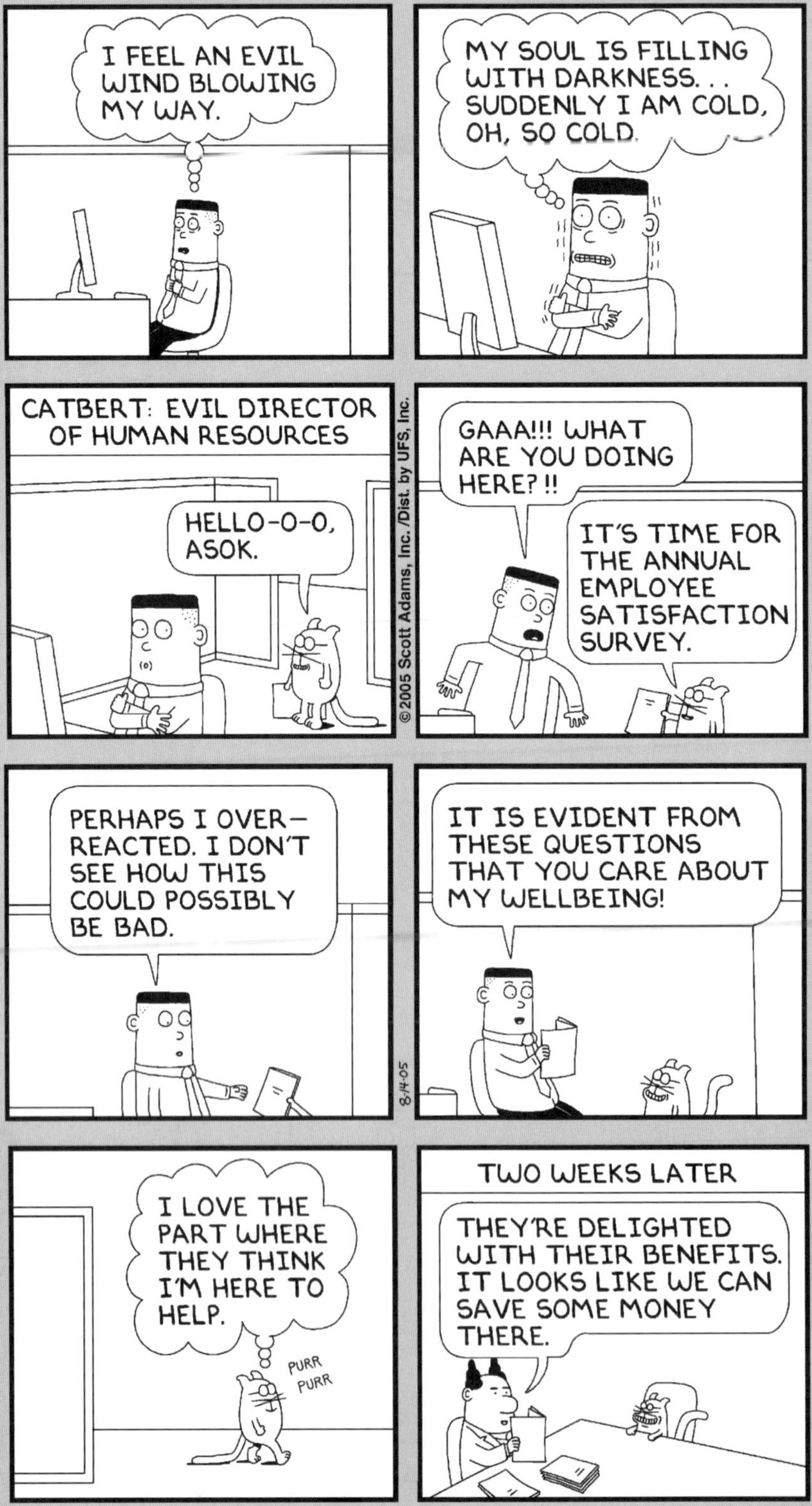
I FEEL AN EVIL WIND BLOWING MY WAY.
MY SOUL IS FILLING WITH DARKNESS. . . SUDDENLY I AM COLD, OH, SO COLD.
CATBERT: EVIL DIRECTOR OF HUMAN RESOURCES
HELLO-O-O, ASOK.
GAAA!!! WHAT ARE YOU DOING HERE? !!
IT'S TIME FOR THE ANNUAL EMPLOYEE SATISFACTION SURVEY.
PERHAPS I OVER— REACTED. I DON'T SEE HOW THIS COULD POSSIBLY BE BAD.
IT IS EVIDENT FROM THESE QUESTIONS THAT YOU CARE ABOUT MY WELLBEING!
I LOVE THE PART WHERE THEY THINK I'M HERE TO HELP.
PURR PURR
TWO WEEKS LATER
THEY'RE DELIGHTED WITH THEIR BENEFITS. IT LOOKS LIKE WE CAN SAVE SOME MONEY THERE.
©2005 Scott Adams, Inc./Dist. by UFS, Inc.
8-14-05

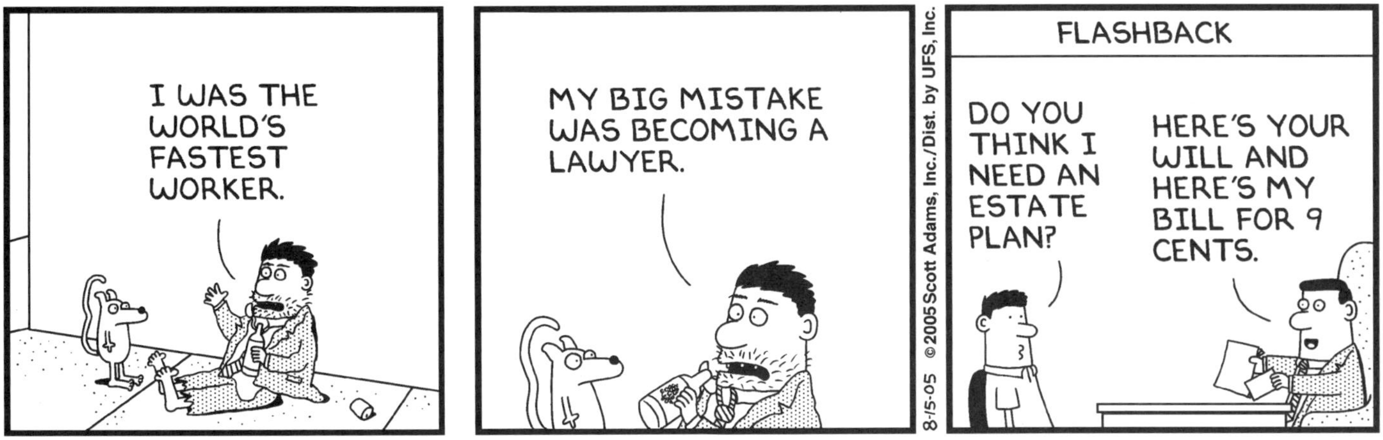
I WAS THE WORLD'S FASTEST WORKER.
MY BIG MISTAKE WAS BECOMING A LAWYER.
8-15-05 © 2005 Scott Adams, Inc./Dist. by UFS, Inc.
FLASHBACK
DO YOU THINK I NEED AN ESTATE PLAN?
HERE'S YOUR WILL AND HERE'S MY BILL FOR 9 CENTS.

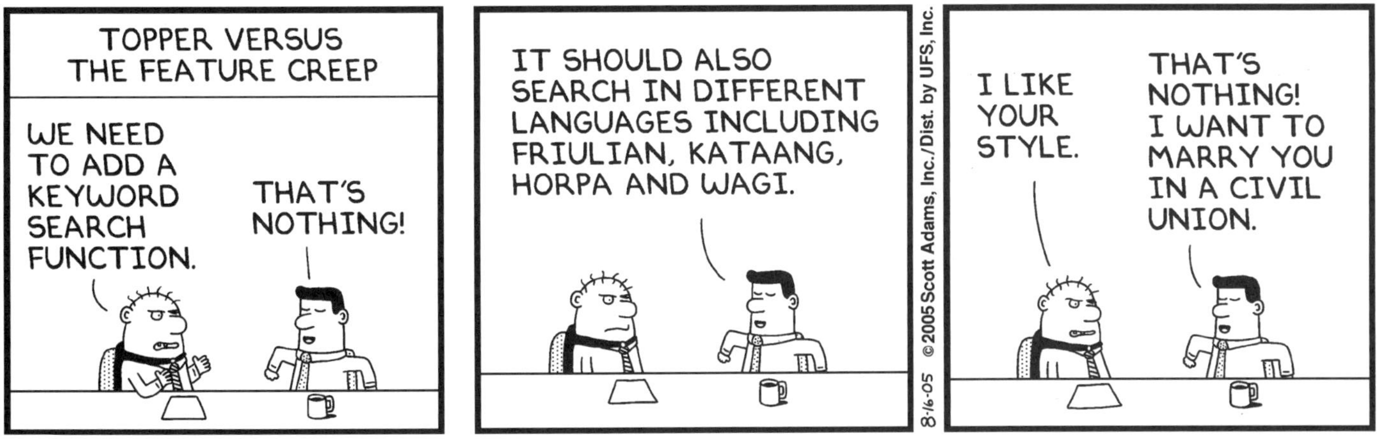
TOPPER VERSUS THE FEATURE CREEP
WE NEED TO ADD A KEYWORD SEARCH FUNCTION.
THAT'S NOTHING!
IT SHOULD ALSO SEARCH IN DIFFERENT LANGUAGES INCLUDING FRIULIAN, KATAANG, HORPA AND WAGI.
8-16-05 © 2005 Scott Adams, Inc./Dist. by UFS, Inc.
I LIKE YOUR STYLE.
THAT'S NOTHING! I WANT TO MARRY YOU IN A CIVIL UNION.

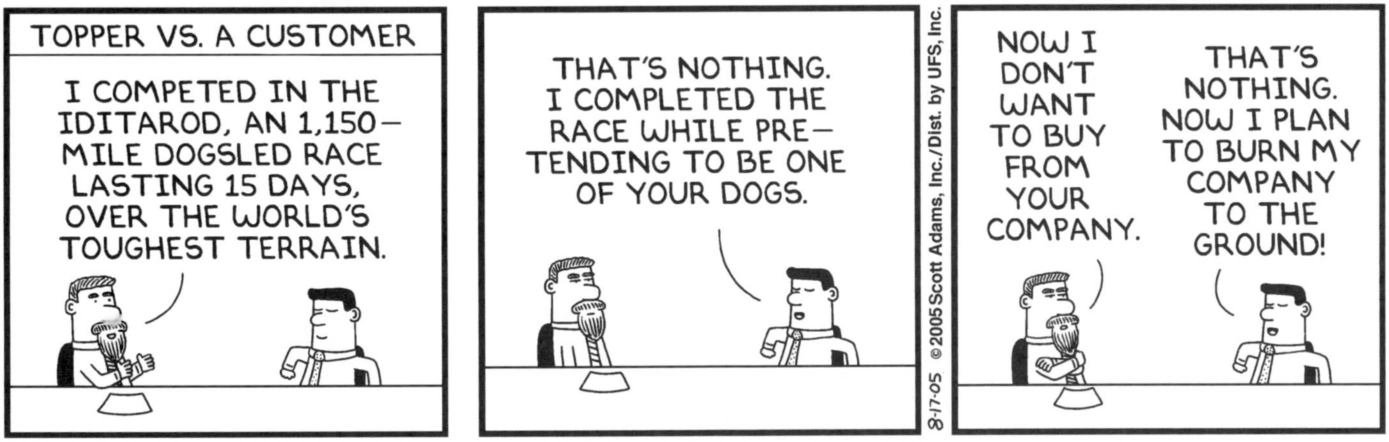
TOPPER VS. A CUSTOMER
I COMPETED IN THE IDITAROD, AN 1,150-MILE DOGSLED RACE LASTING 15 DAYS, OVER THE WORLD'S TOUGHEST TERRAIN.
THAT'S NOTHING. I COMPLETED THE RACE WHILE PRETENDING TO BE ONE OF YOUR DOGS.
8-17-05 © 2005 Scott Adams, Inc./Dist. by UFS, Inc.
NOW I DON'T WANT TO BUY FROM YOUR COMPANY.
THAT'S NOTHING. NOW I PLAN TO BURN MY COMPANY TO THE GROUND!

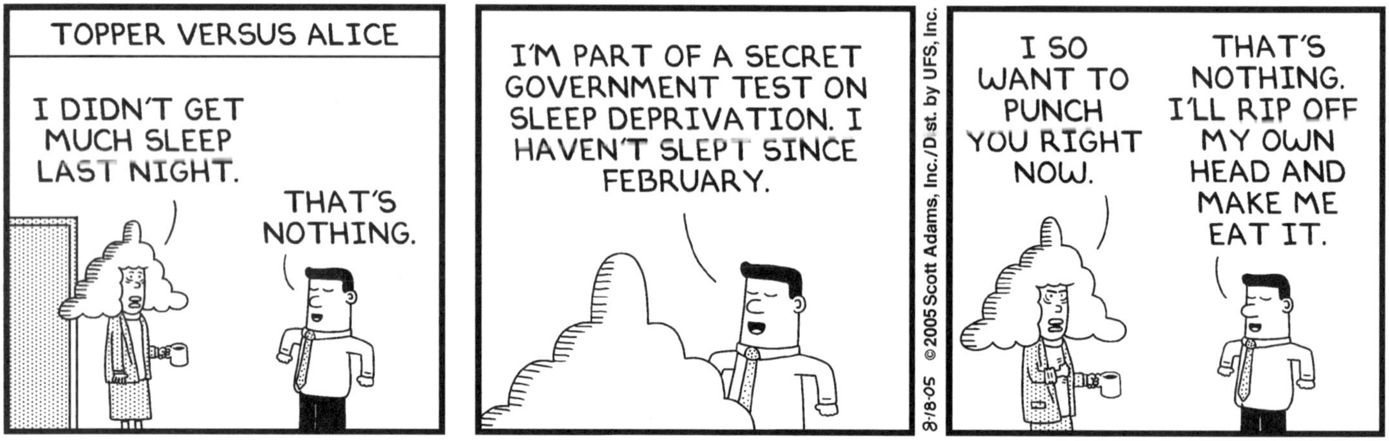
TOPPER VERSUS ALICE
I DIDN'T GET MUCH SLEEP LAST NIGHT.
THAT'S NOTHING.
I'M PART OF A SECRET GOVERNMENT TEST ON SLEEP DEPRIVATION. I HAVEN'T SLEPT SINCE FEBRUARY.
8-8-05 © 2005 Scott Adams, Inc./Dist. by UFS, Inc.
I SO WANT TO PUNCH YOU RIGHT NOW.
THAT'S NOTHING. I'LL RIP OFF MY OWN HEAD AND MAKE ME EAT IT.

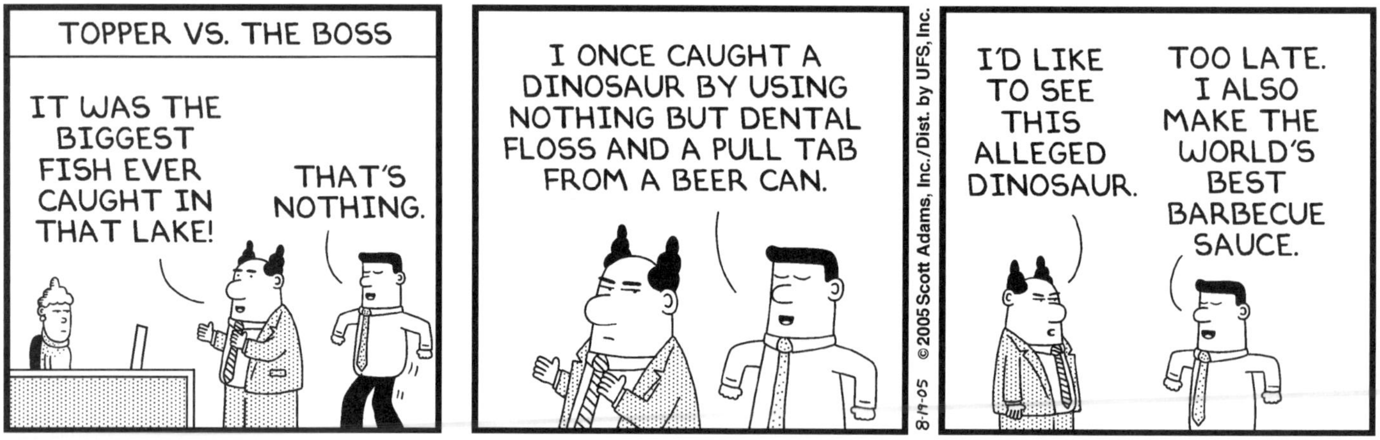
TOPPER VS. THE BOSS
IT WAS THE BIGGEST FISH EVER CAUGHT IN THAT LAKE!
THAT'S NOTHING.
I ONCE CAUGHT A DINOSAUR BY USING NOTHING BUT DENTAL FLOSS AND A PULL TAB FROM A BEER CAN.
8-19-05 © 2005 Scott Adams, Inc./Dist. by UFS, Inc.
I'D LIKE TO SEE THIS ALLEGED DINOSAUR.
TOO LATE. I ALSO MAKE THE WORLD'S BEST BARBECUE SAUCE.

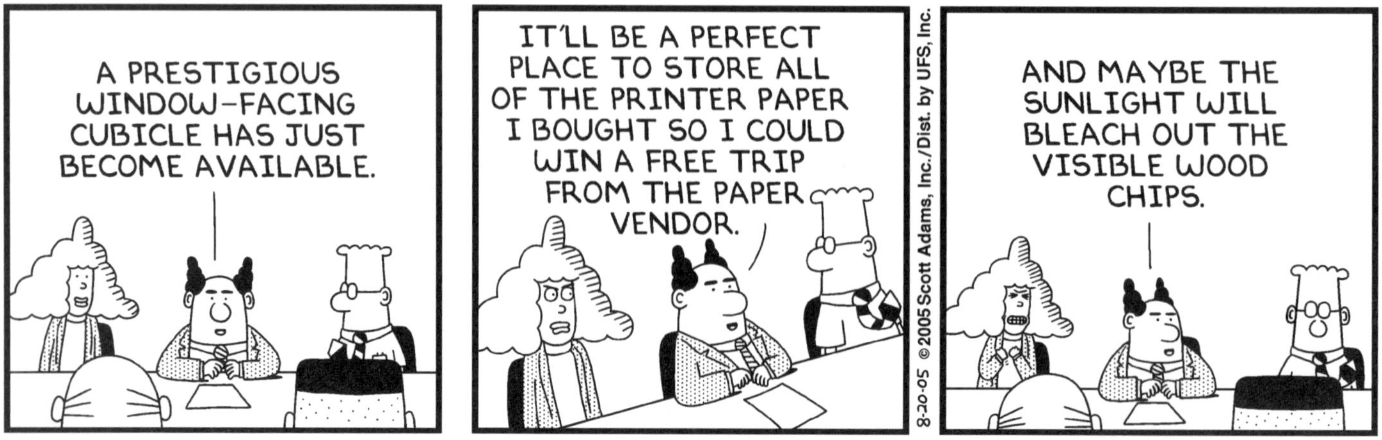
A PRESTIGIOUS WINDOW-FACING CUBICLE HAS JUST BECOME AVAILABLE.
IT'LL BE A PERFECT PLACE TO STORE ALL OF THE PRINTER PAPER I BOUGHT SO I COULD WIN A FREE TRIP FROM THE PAPER VENDOR.
8-20-05 © 2005 Scott Adams, Inc./Dist. by UFS, Inc.
AND MAYBE THE SUNLIGHT WILL BLEACH OUT THE VISIBLE WOOD CHIPS.

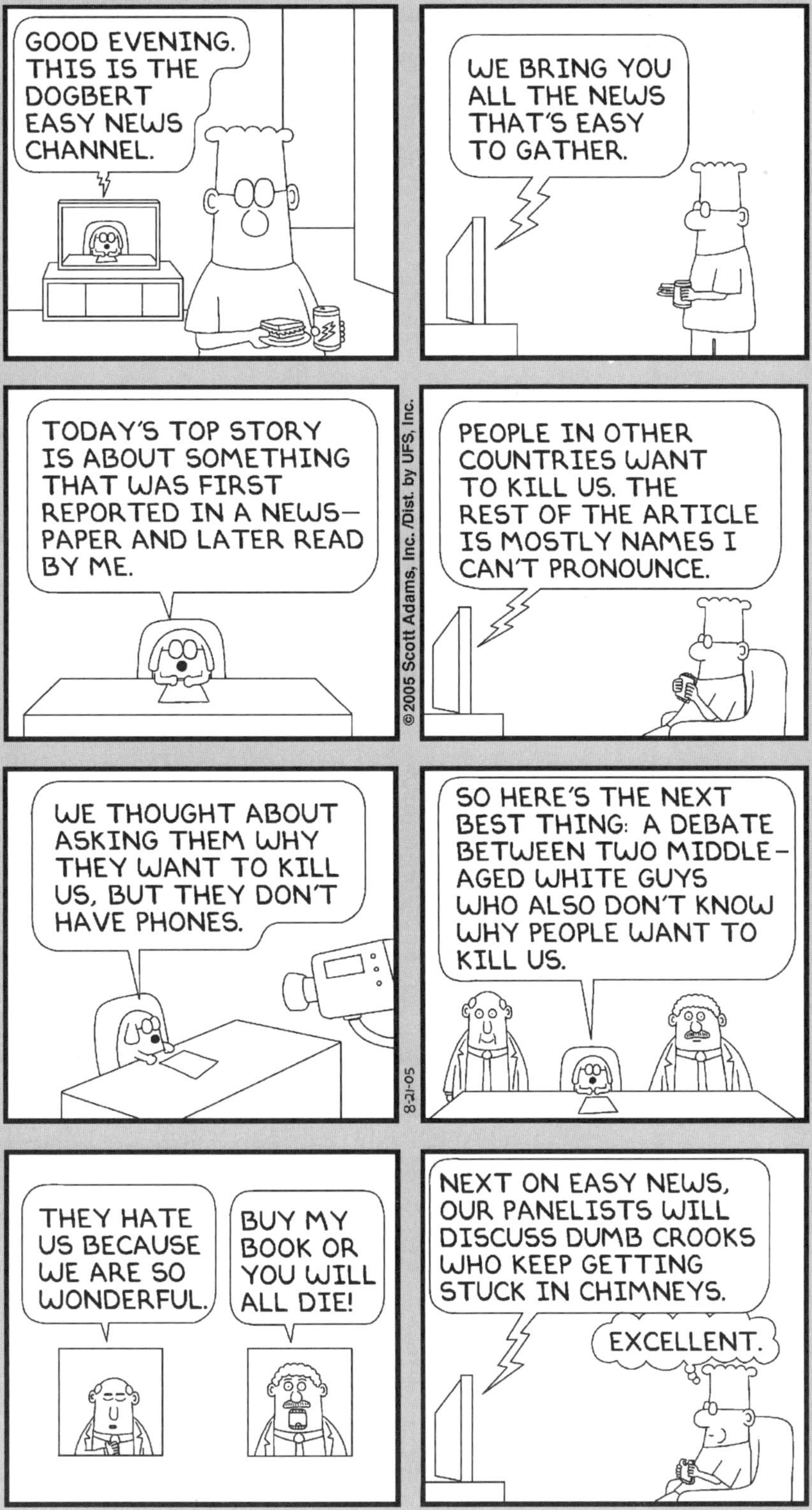
GOOD EVENING. THIS IS THE DOGBERT EASY NEWS CHANNEL.
WE BRING YOU ALL THE NEWS THAT'S EASY TO GATHER.
TODAY'S TOP STORY IS ABOUT SOMETHING THAT WAS FIRST REPORTED IN A NEWS-PAPER AND LATER READ BY ME.
PEOPLE IN OTHER COUNTRIES WANT TO KILL US. THE REST OF THE ARTICLE IS MOSTLY NAMES I CAN'T PRONOUNCE.
©2005 Scott Adams, Inc./Dist. by UFS, Inc.
WE THOUGHT ABOUT ASKING THEM WHY THEY WANT TO KILL US, BUT THEY DON'T HAVE PHONES.
SO HERE'S THE NEXT BEST THING: A DEBATE BETWEEN TWO MIDDLE-AGED WHITE GUYS WHO ALSO DON'T KNOW WHY PEOPLE WANT TO KILL US.
8-21-05
THEY HATE US BECAUSE WE ARE SO WONDERFUL.
BUY MY BOOK OR YOU WILL ALL DIE!
NEXT ON EASY NEWS, OUR PANELISTS WILL DISCUSS DUMB CROOKS WHO KEEP GETTING STUCK IN CHIMNEYS.
EXCELLENT.

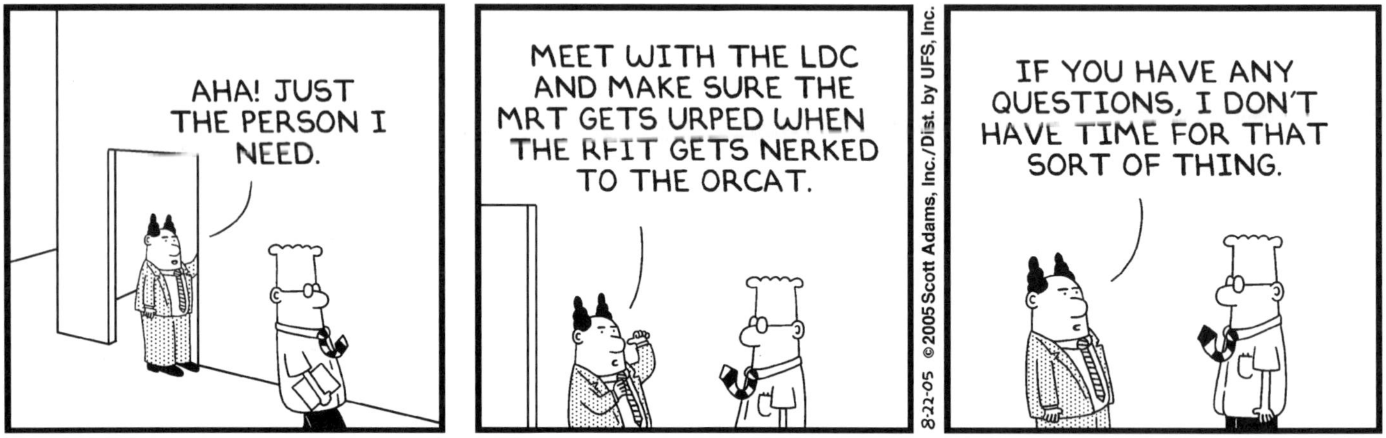
AHA! JUST THE PERSON I NEED.
MEET WITH THE LDC AND MAKE SURE THE MRT GETS URPED WHEN THE RFIT GETS NERKED TO THE ORCAT.
IF YOU HAVE ANY QUESTIONS, I DON'T HAVE TIME FOR THAT SORT OF THING.
8-22-05 ©2005 Scott Adams, Inc./Dist. by UFS, Inc.

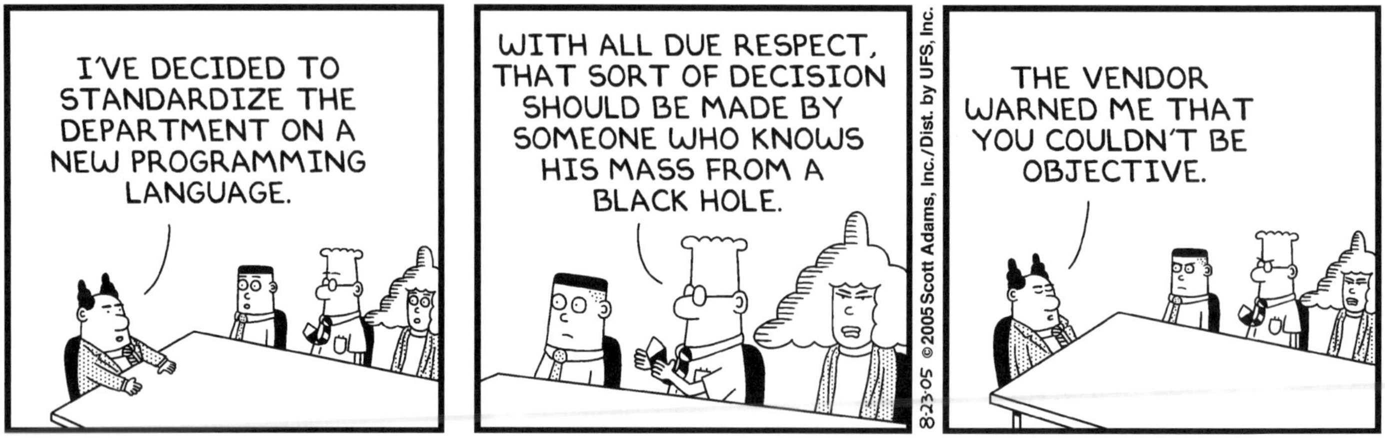
I'VE DECIDED TO STANDARDIZE THE DEPARTMENT ON A NEW PROGRAMMING LANGUAGE.
WITH ALL DUE RESPECT, THAT SORT OF DECISION SHOULD BE MADE BY SOMEONE WHO KNOWS HIS MASS FROM A BLACK HOLE.
THE VENDOR WARNED ME THAT YOU COULDN'T BE OBJECTIVE.
8-23-05 ©2005 Scott Adams, Inc./Dist. by UFS, Inc.

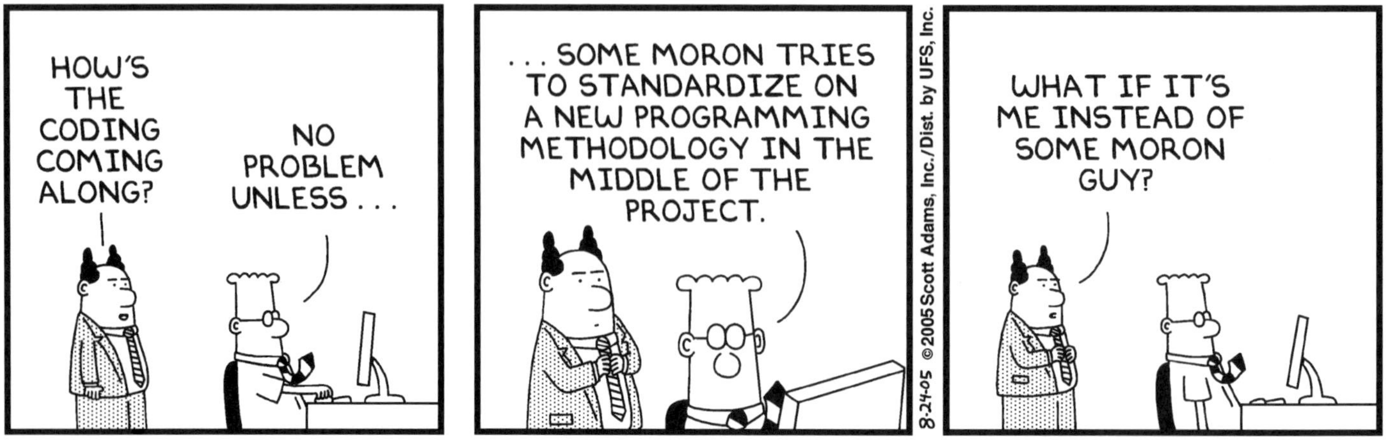
HOW'S THE CODING COMING ALONG?
NO PROBLEM UNLESS . . .
. . . SOME MORON TRIES TO STANDARDIZE ON A NEW PROGRAMMING METHODOLOGY IN THE MIDDLE OF THE PROJECT.
WHAT IF IT'S ME INSTEAD OF SOME MORON GUY?
8-24-05 ©2005 Scott Adams, Inc./Dist. by UFS, Inc.

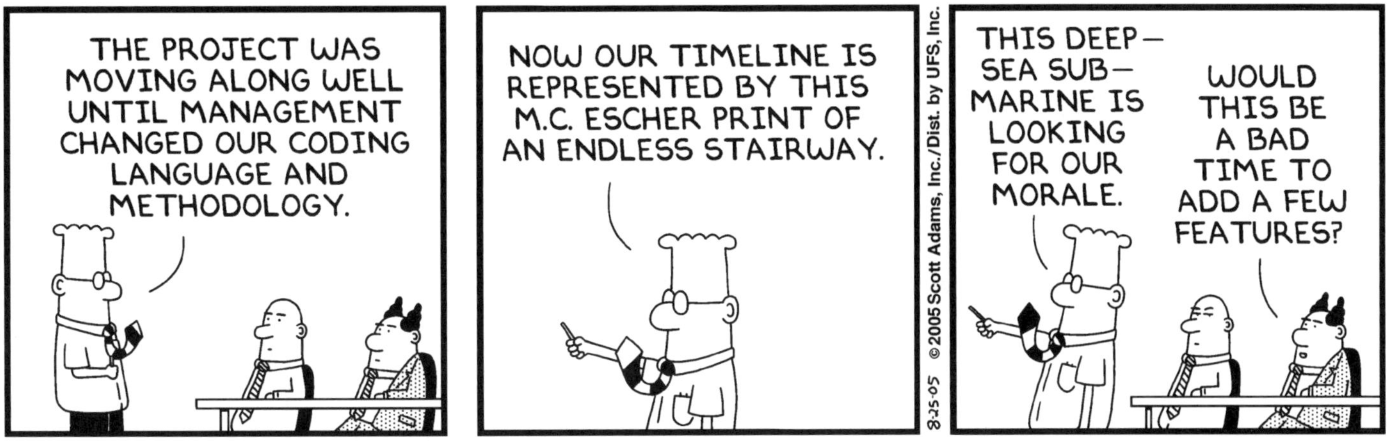
THE PROJECT WAS MOVING ALONG WELL UNTIL MANAGEMENT CHANGED OUR CODING LANGUAGE AND METHODOLOGY.
NOW OUR TIMELINE IS REPRESENTED BY THIS M.C. ESCHER PRINT OF AN ENDLESS STAIRWAY.
8-25-05 ©2005 Scott Adams, Inc./Dist. by UFS, Inc.
THIS DEEP-SEA SUB-MARINE IS LOOKING FOR OUR MORALE.
WOULD THIS BE A BAD TIME TO ADD A FEW FEATURES?

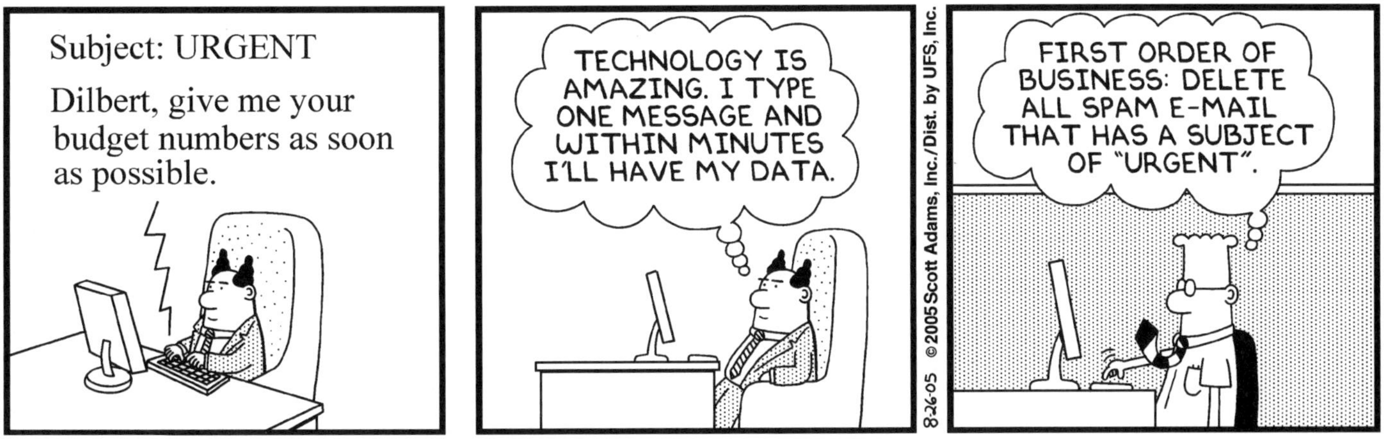
Subject: URGENT
Dilbert, give me your budget numbers as soon as possible.
TECHNOLOGY IS AMAZING. I TYPE ONE MESSAGE AND WITHIN MINUTES I'LL HAVE MY DATA.
8-26-05 ©2005 Scott Adams, Inc./Dist. by UFS, Inc.
FIRST ORDER OF BUSINESS: DELETE ALL SPAM E-MAIL THAT HAS A SUBJECT OF "URGENT".

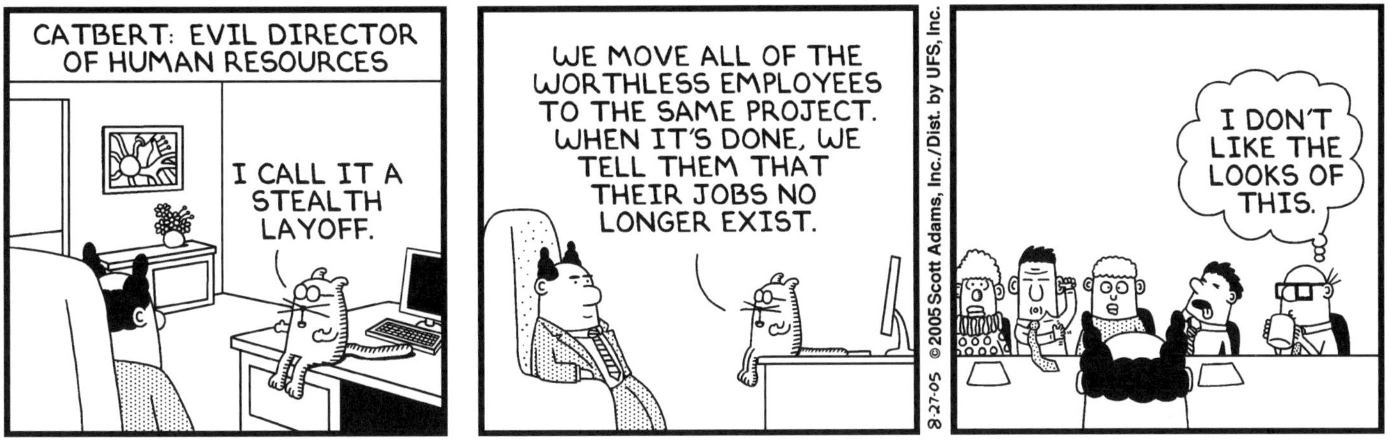
CATBERT: EVIL DIRECTOR OF HUMAN RESOURCES
I CALL IT A STEALTH LAYOFF.
WE MOVE ALL OF THE WORTHLESS EMPLOYEES TO THE SAME PROJECT. WHEN IT'S DONE, WE TELL THEM THAT THEIR JOBS NO LONGER EXIST.
8-27-05 ©2005 Scott Adams, Inc./Dist. by UFS, Inc.
I DON'T LIKE THE LOOKS OF THIS.

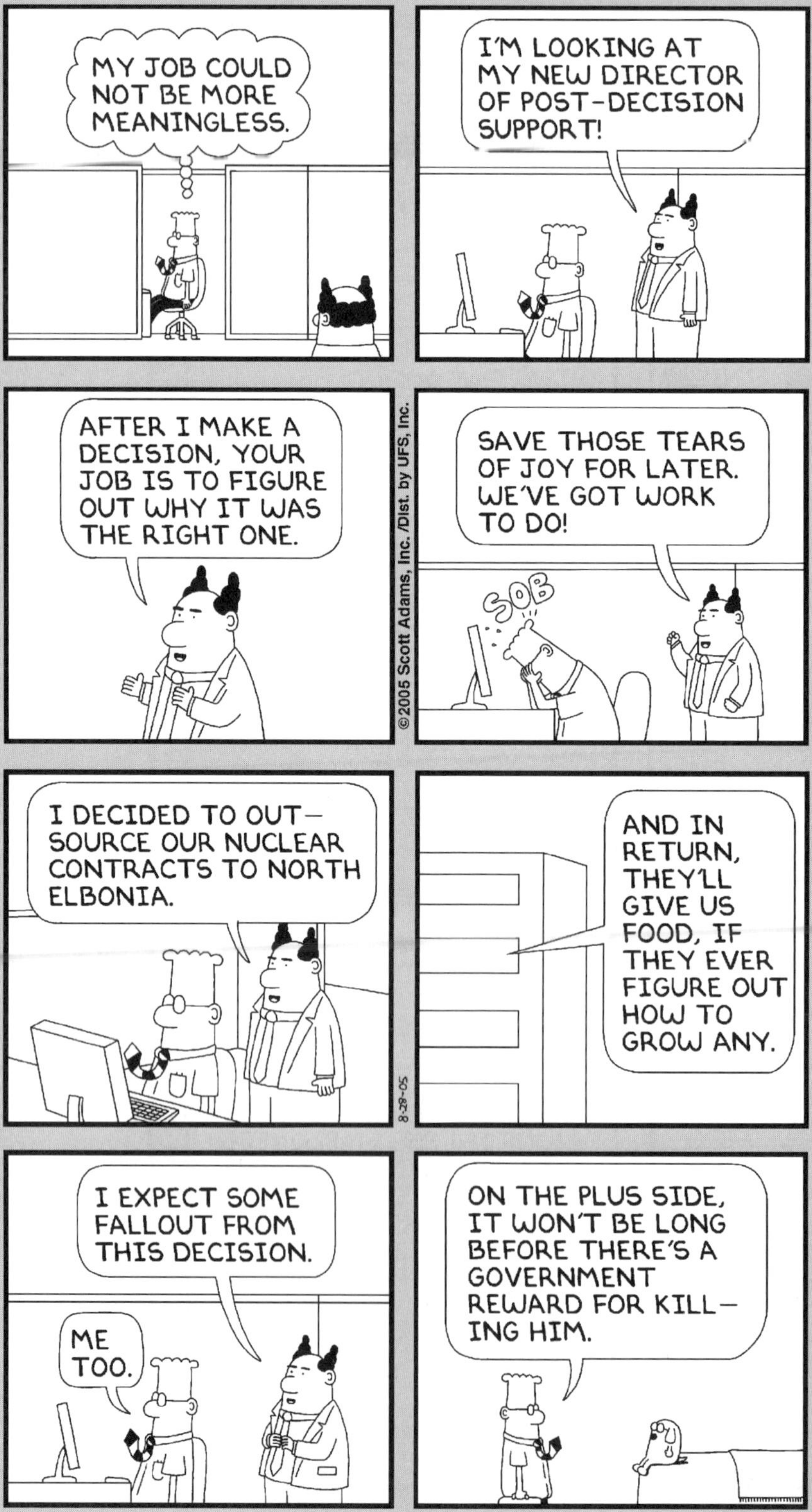

MY JOB COULD NOT BE MORE MEANINGLESS.
I'M LOOKING AT MY NEW DIRECTOR OF POST-DECISION SUPPORT!
AFTER I MAKE A DECISION, YOUR JOB IS TO FIGURE OUT WHY IT WAS THE RIGHT ONE.
SAVE THOSE TEARS OF JOY FOR LATER. WE'VE GOT WORK TO DO!
SOB
©2005 Scott Adams, Inc./Dist. by UFS, Inc.
I DECIDED TO OUT-SOURCE OUR NUCLEAR CONTRACTS TO NORTH ELBONIA.
AND IN RETURN, THEY'LL GIVE US FOOD, IF THEY EVER FIGURE OUT HOW TO GROW ANY.
8-29-05
I EXPECT SOME FALLOUT FROM THIS DECISION.
ME TOO.
ON THE PLUS SIDE, IT WON'T BE LONG BEFORE THERE'S A GOVERNMENT REWARD FOR KILL-ING HIM.

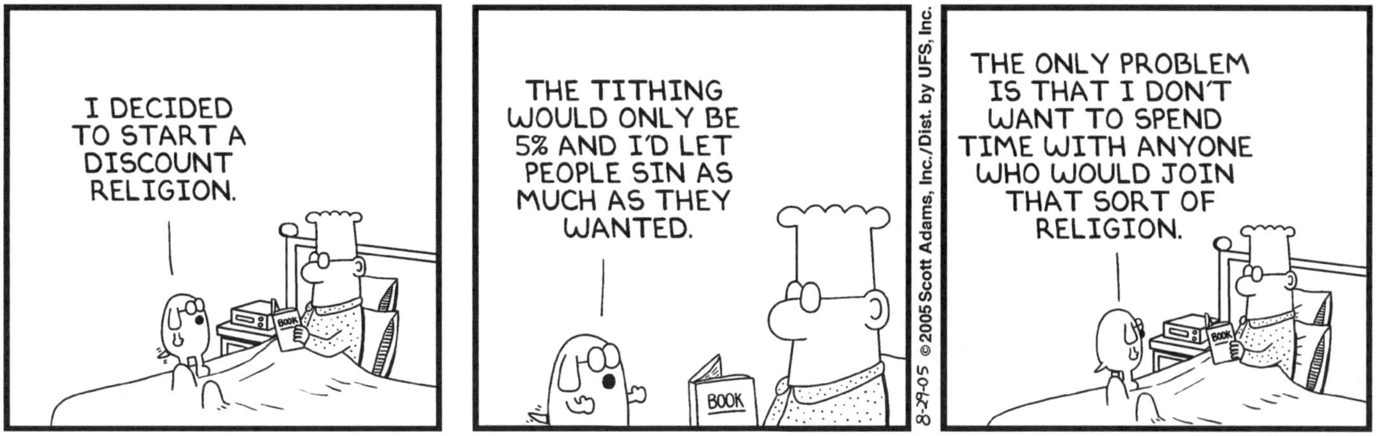
I DECIDED TO START A DISCOUNT RELIGION.
THE TITHING WOULD ONLY BE 5% AND I'D LET PEOPLE SIN AS MUCH AS THEY WANTED.
BOOK
8-29-05 © 2005 Scott Adams, Inc./Dist. by UFS, Inc.
THE ONLY PROBLEM IS THAT I DON'T WANT TO SPEND TIME WITH ANYONE WHO WOULD JOIN THAT SORT OF RELIGION.

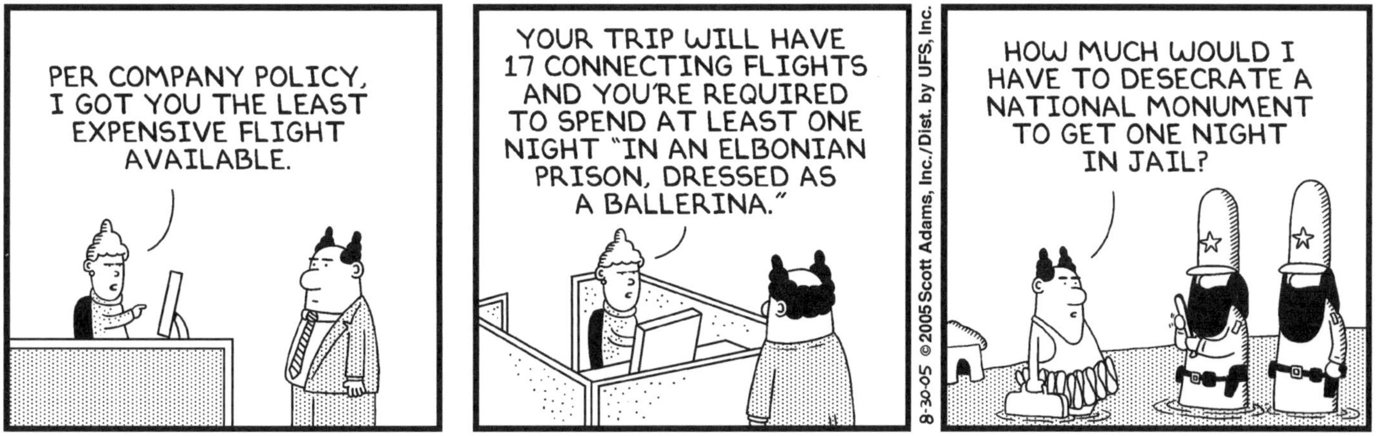
PER COMPANY POLICY, I GOT YOU THE LEAST EXPENSIVE FLIGHT AVAILABLE.
YOUR TRIP WILL HAVE 17 CONNECTING FLIGHTS AND YOU'RE REQUIRED TO SPEND AT LEAST ONE NIGHT "IN AN ELBONIAN PRISON, DRESSED AS A BALLERINA."
8-30-05 © 2005 Scott Adams, Inc./Dist. by UFS, Inc.
HOW MUCH WOULD I HAVE TO DESECRATE A NATIONAL MONUMENT TO GET ONE NIGHT IN JAIL?

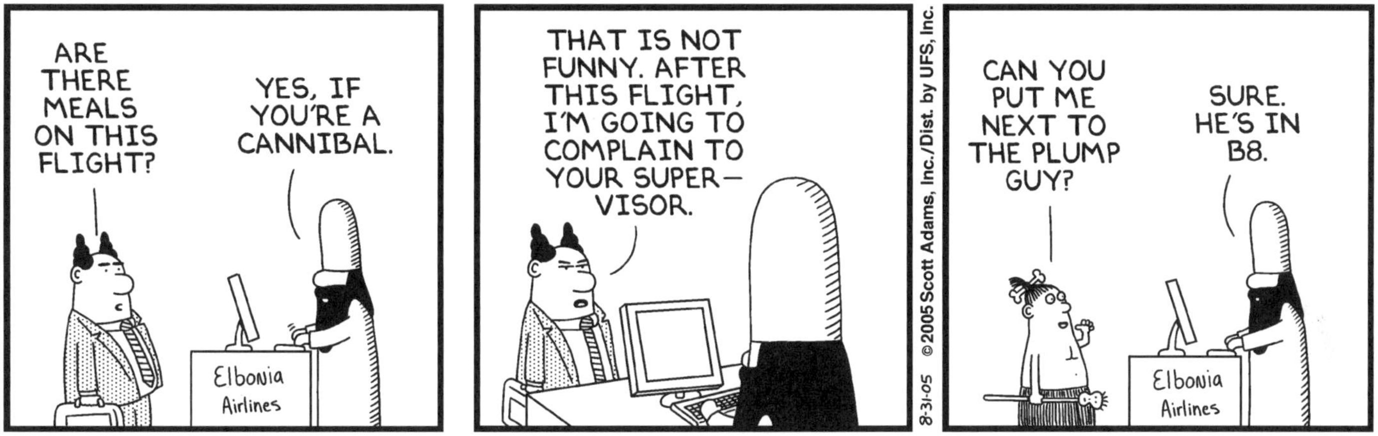
ARE THERE MEALS ON THIS FLIGHT?
YES, IF YOU'RE A CANNIBAL.
Elbonia Airlines
THAT IS NOT FUNNY. AFTER THIS FLIGHT, I'M GOING TO COMPLAIN TO YOUR SUPER-VISOR.
8-31-05 © 2005 Scott Adams, Inc./Dist. by UFS, Inc.
CAN YOU PUT ME NEXT TO THE PLUMP GUY?
SURE. HE'S IN B8.
Elbonia Airlines

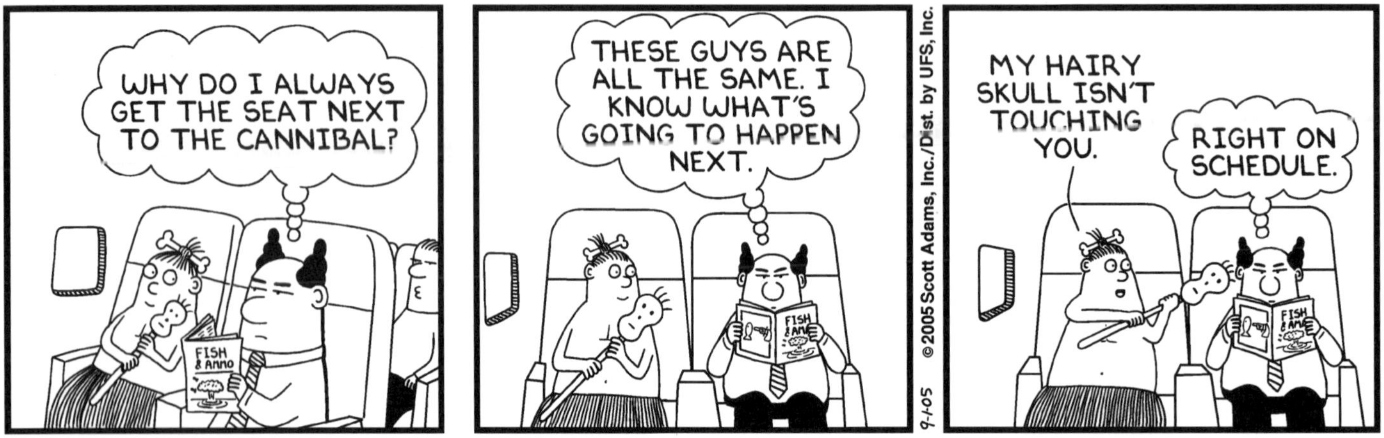
WHY DO I ALWAYS GET THE SEAT NEXT TO THE CANNIBAL?
THESE GUYS ARE ALL THE SAME. I KNOW WHAT'S GOING TO HAPPEN NEXT.
MY HAIRY SKULL ISN'T TOUCHING YOU.
RIGHT ON SCHEDULE.
FISH & AMMO
9-1-05
© 2005 Scott Adams, Inc./Dist. by UFS, Inc.

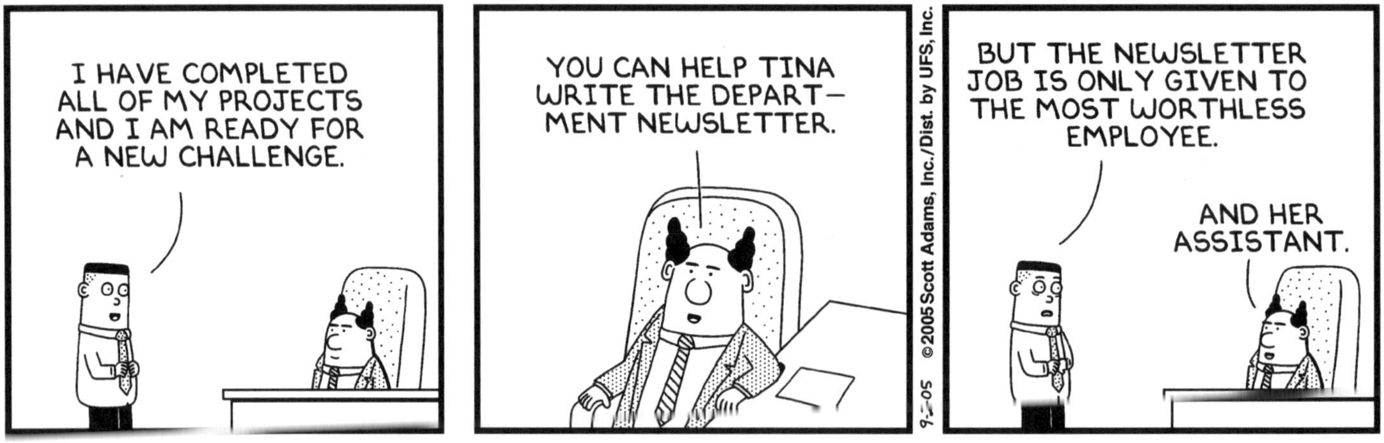
I HAVE COMPLETED ALL OF MY PROJECTS AND I AM READY FOR A NEW CHALLENGE.
YOU CAN HELP TINA WRITE THE DEPART-MENT NEWSLETTER.
BUT THE NEWSLETTER JOB IS ONLY GIVEN TO THE MOST WORTHLESS EMPLOYEE.
AND HER ASSISTANT.
© 2005 Scott Adams, Inc./Dist. by UFS, Inc.

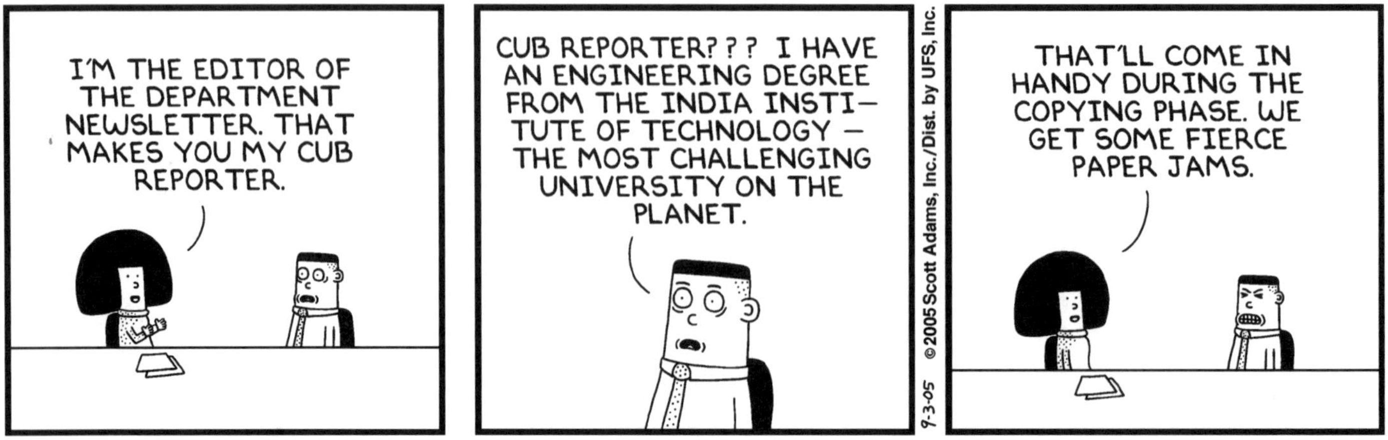
I'M THE EDITOR OF THE DEPARTMENT NEWSLETTER. THAT MAKES YOU MY CUB REPORTER.
CUB REPORTER??? I HAVE AN ENGINEERING DEGREE FROM THE INDIA INSTI-TUTE OF TECHNOLOGY — THE MOST CHALLENGING UNIVERSITY ON THE PLANET.
THAT'LL COME IN HANDY DURING THE COPYING PHASE. WE GET SOME FIERCE PAPER JAMS.
9-3-05
© 2005 Scott Adams, Inc./Dist. by UFS, Inc.

THE TROUBLE STARTED WHEN YOU INSISTED ON GIVING INSPIRA-TIONAL NAMES TO THE CONFERENCE ROOMS.
I SCHEDULED A PROJECT MEETING FOR THE "QUALITY" ROOM AND NO ONE KNEW WHERE TO GO.
SOME PEOPLE ENDED UP IN THE "TEAMWORK" ROOM WHILE OTHERS WENT TO THE "EXCEL-LENCE" ROOM.
©2005 Scott Adams, Inc./Dist. by UFS, Inc.
BY THE TIME WE SORTED IT ALL OUT, SOMEONE ELSE WAS SCHEDULED TO USE OUR CONFERENCE ROOM.
THEN IT TOOK THREE WEEKS TO SCHEDULE ANOTHER MEETING WHEN EVERYONE COULD MAKE IT.
9-4-05
BUT HALF OF THE TEAM WENT TO THE "ACTION" ROOM AND SAT THERE WHILE WE WAITED FOR THEM IN THE "GOOD PLANNING" ROOM.
I THOUGHT THIS WAS THE BUDGET MEETING.

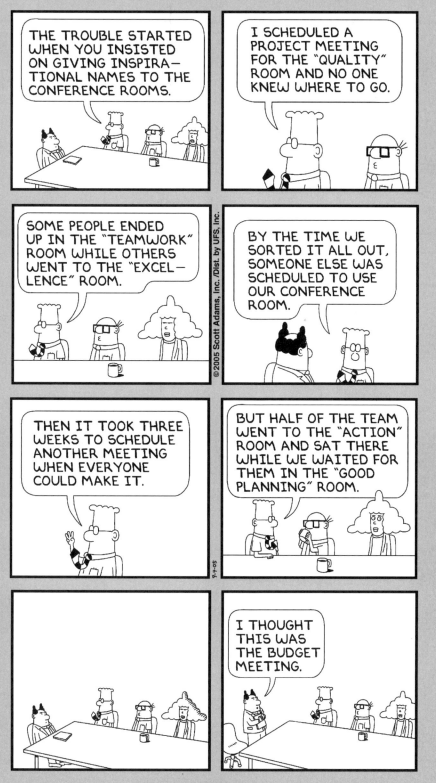

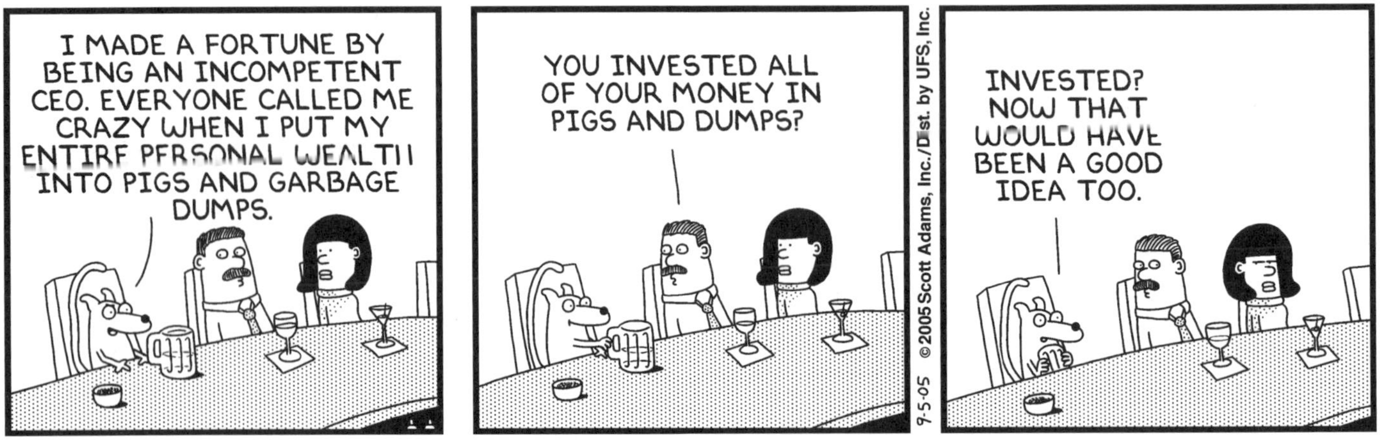
I MADE A FORTUNE BY BEING AN INCOMPETENT CEO. EVERYONE CALLED ME CRAZY WHEN I PUT MY ENTIRE PERSONAL WEALTH INTO PIGS AND GARBAGE DUMPS.
YOU INVESTED ALL OF YOUR MONEY IN PIGS AND DUMPS?
INVESTED? NOW THAT WOULD HAVE BEEN A GOOD IDEA TOO.
9-5-05 © 2005 Scott Adams, Inc./Dist. by UFS, Inc.

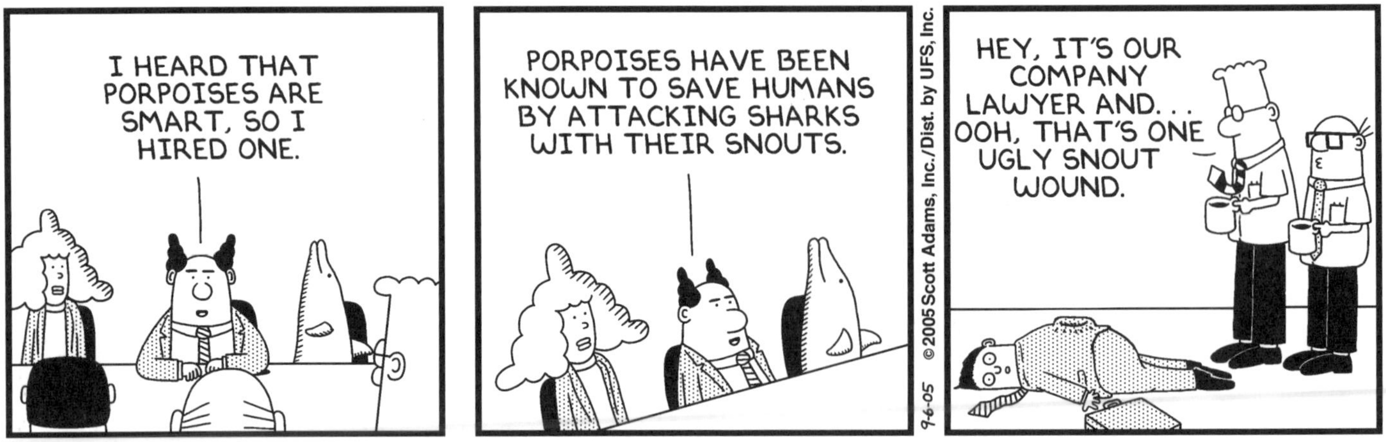
I HEARD THAT PORPOISES ARE SMART, SO I HIRED ONE.
PORPOISES HAVE BEEN KNOWN TO SAVE HUMANS BY ATTACKING SHARKS WITH THEIR SNOUTS.
HEY, IT'S OUR COMPANY LAWYER AND. . . OOH, THAT'S ONE UGLY SNOUT WOUND.
9-6-05 © 2005 Scott Adams, Inc./Dist. by UFS, Inc.

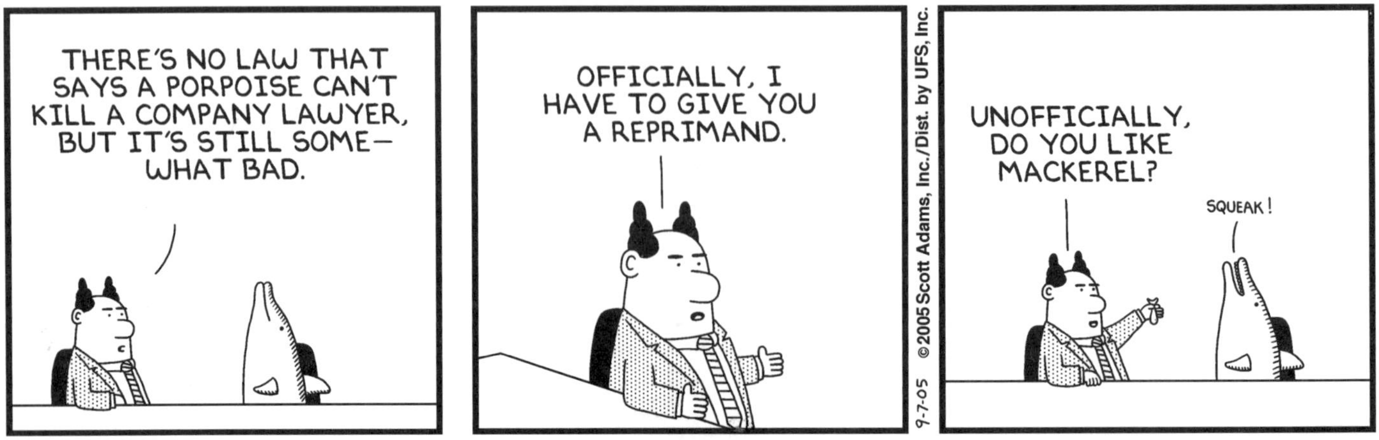
THERE'S NO LAW THAT SAYS A PORPOISE CAN'T KILL A COMPANY LAWYER, BUT IT'S STILL SOME-WHAT BAD.
OFFICIALLY, I HAVE TO GIVE YOU A REPRIMAND.
UNOFFICIALLY, DO YOU LIKE MACKEREL?
SQUEAK!
9-7-05 © 2005 Scott Adams, Inc./Dist. by UFS, Inc.

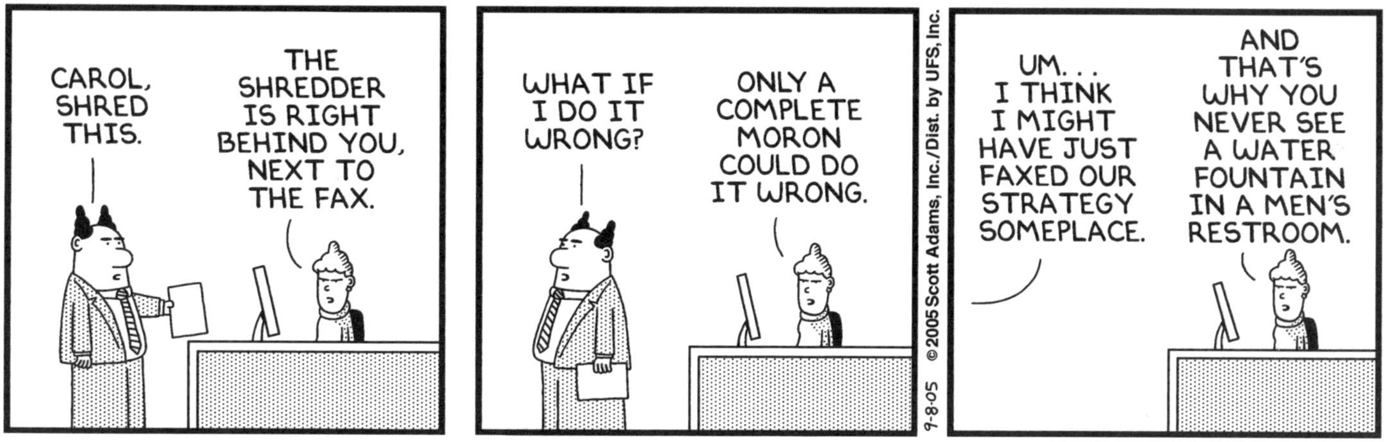
CAROL, SHRED THIS.
THE SHREDDER IS RIGHT BEHIND YOU, NEXT TO THE FAX.
WHAT IF I DO IT WRONG?
ONLY A COMPLETE MORON COULD DO IT WRONG.
9-8-05 © 2005 Scott Adams, Inc./Dist. by UFS, Inc.
UM... I THINK I MIGHT HAVE JUST FAXED OUR STRATEGY SOMEPLACE.
AND THAT'S WHY YOU NEVER SEE A WATER FOUNTAIN IN A MEN'S RESTROOM.

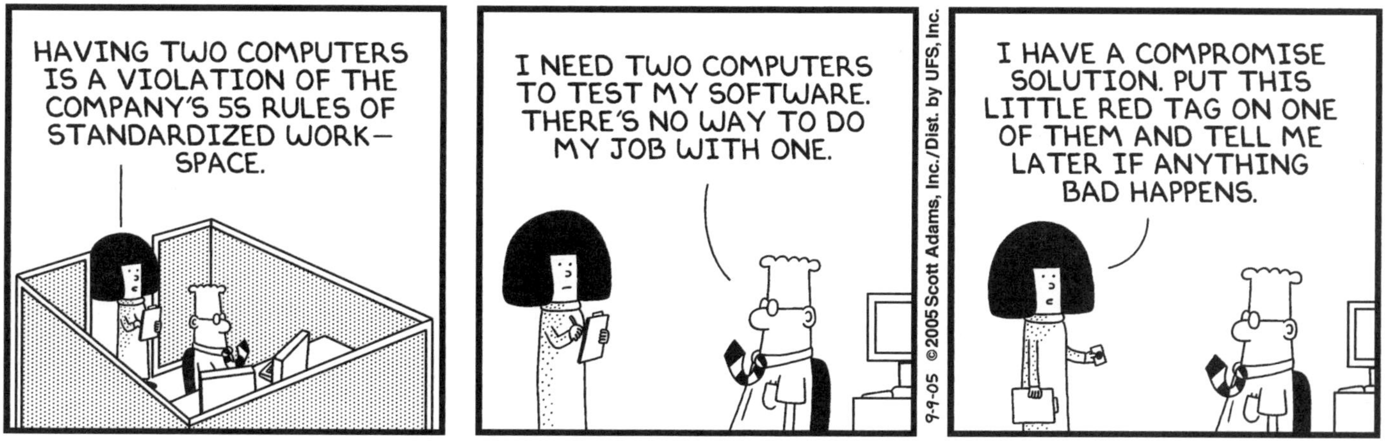
HAVING TWO COMPUTERS IS A VIOLATION OF THE COMPANY'S 5S RULES OF STANDARDIZED WORK-SPACE.
I NEED TWO COMPUTERS TO TEST MY SOFTWARE. THERE'S NO WAY TO DO MY JOB WITH ONE.
9-9-05 © 2005 Scott Adams, Inc./Dist. by UFS, Inc.
I HAVE A COMPROMISE SOLUTION. PUT THIS LITTLE RED TAG ON ONE OF THEM AND TELL ME LATER IF ANYTHING BAD HAPPENS.

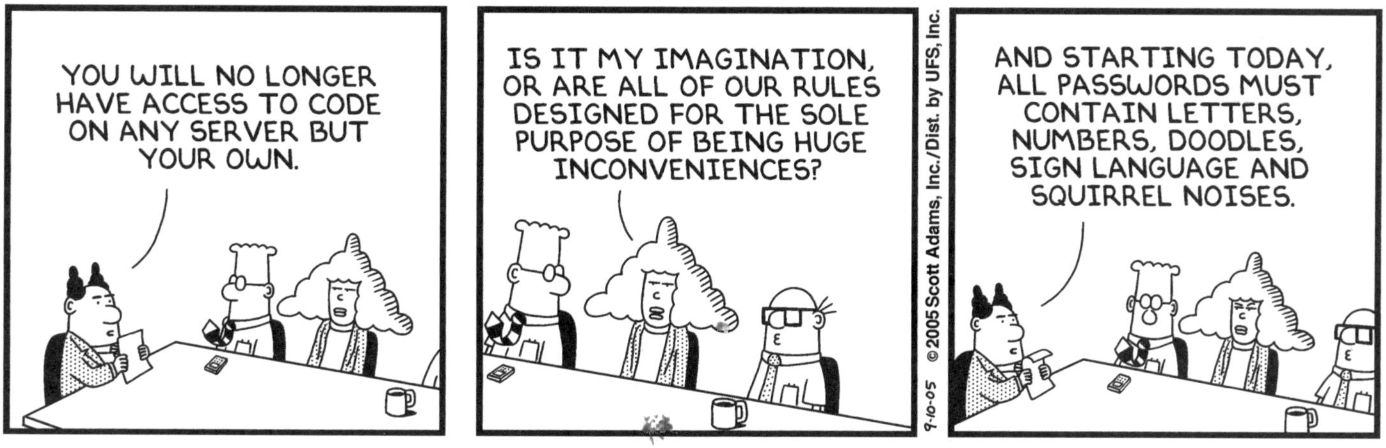
YOU WILL NO LONGER HAVE ACCESS TO CODE ON ANY SERVER BUT YOUR OWN.
IS IT MY IMAGINATION, OR ARE ALL OF OUR RULES DESIGNED FOR THE SOLE PURPOSE OF BEING HUGE INCONVENIENCES?
9-10-05 © 2005 Scott Adams, Inc./Dist. by UFS, Inc.
AND STARTING TODAY, ALL PASSWORDS MUST CONTAIN LETTERS, NUMBERS, DOODLES, SIGN LANGUAGE AND SQUIRREL NOISES.

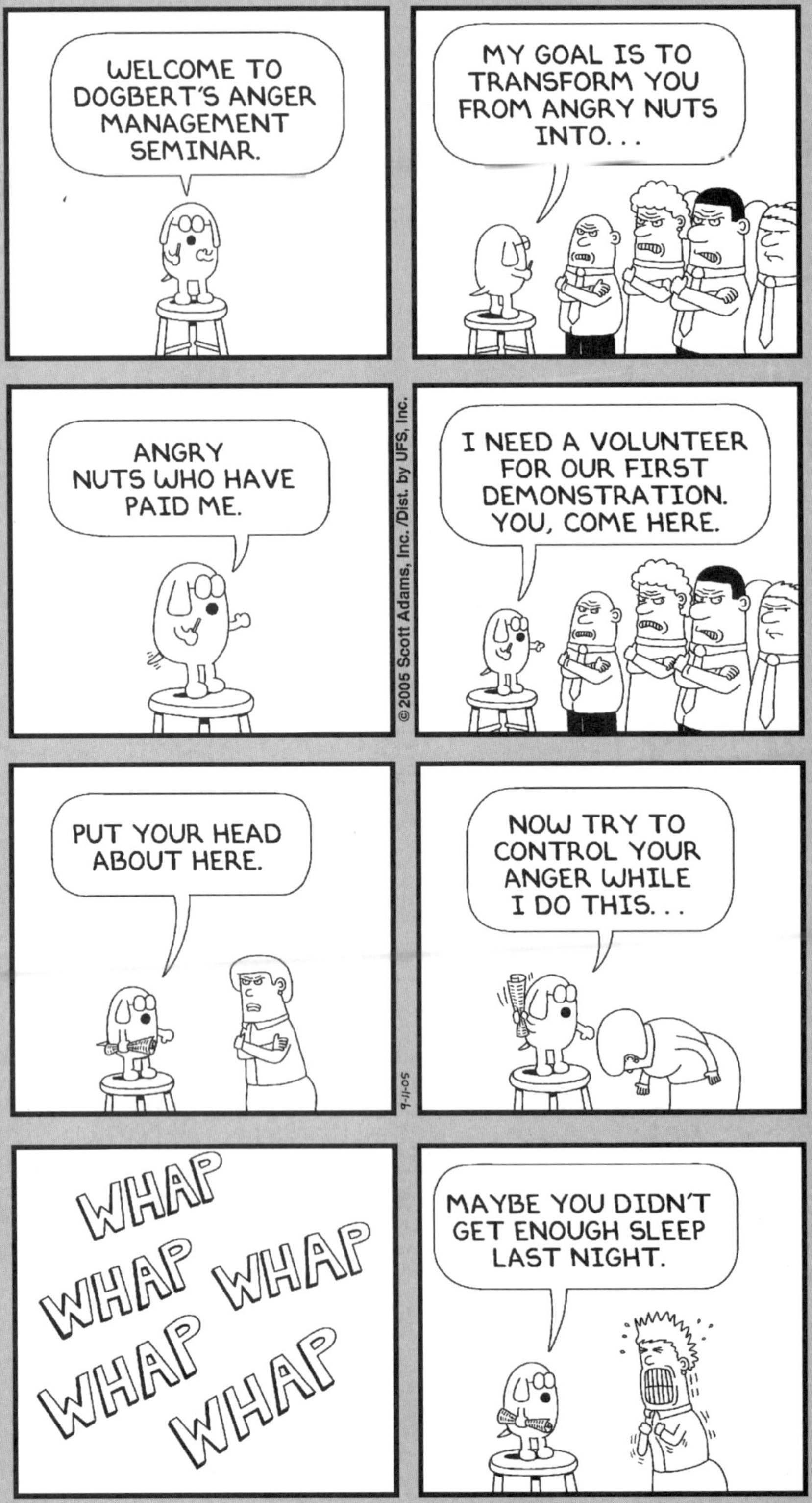
WELCOME TO DOGBERT'S ANGER MANAGEMENT SEMINAR.
MY GOAL IS TO TRANSFORM YOU FROM ANGRY NUTS INTO. . .
ANGRY NUTS WHO HAVE PAID ME.
I NEED A VOLUNTEER FOR OUR FIRST DEMONSTRATION. YOU, COME HERE.
PUT YOUR HEAD ABOUT HERE.
NOW TRY TO CONTROL YOUR ANGER WHILE I DO THIS. . .
WHAP WHAP WHAP WHAP WHAP WHAP
MAYBE YOU DIDN'T GET ENOUGH SLEEP LAST NIGHT.
©2005 Scott Adams, Inc./Dist. by UFS, Inc.
9-11-05

CONTENTS

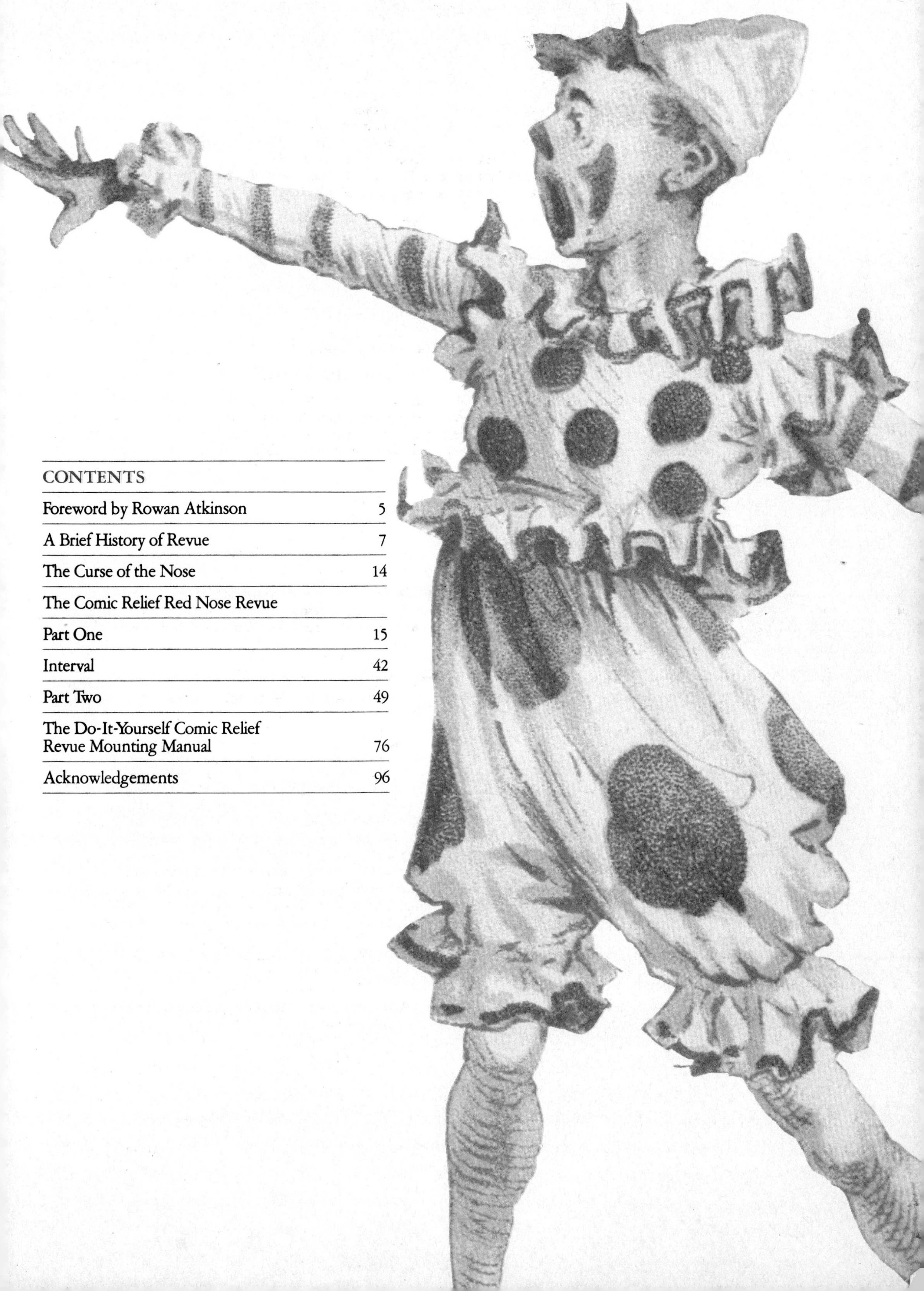

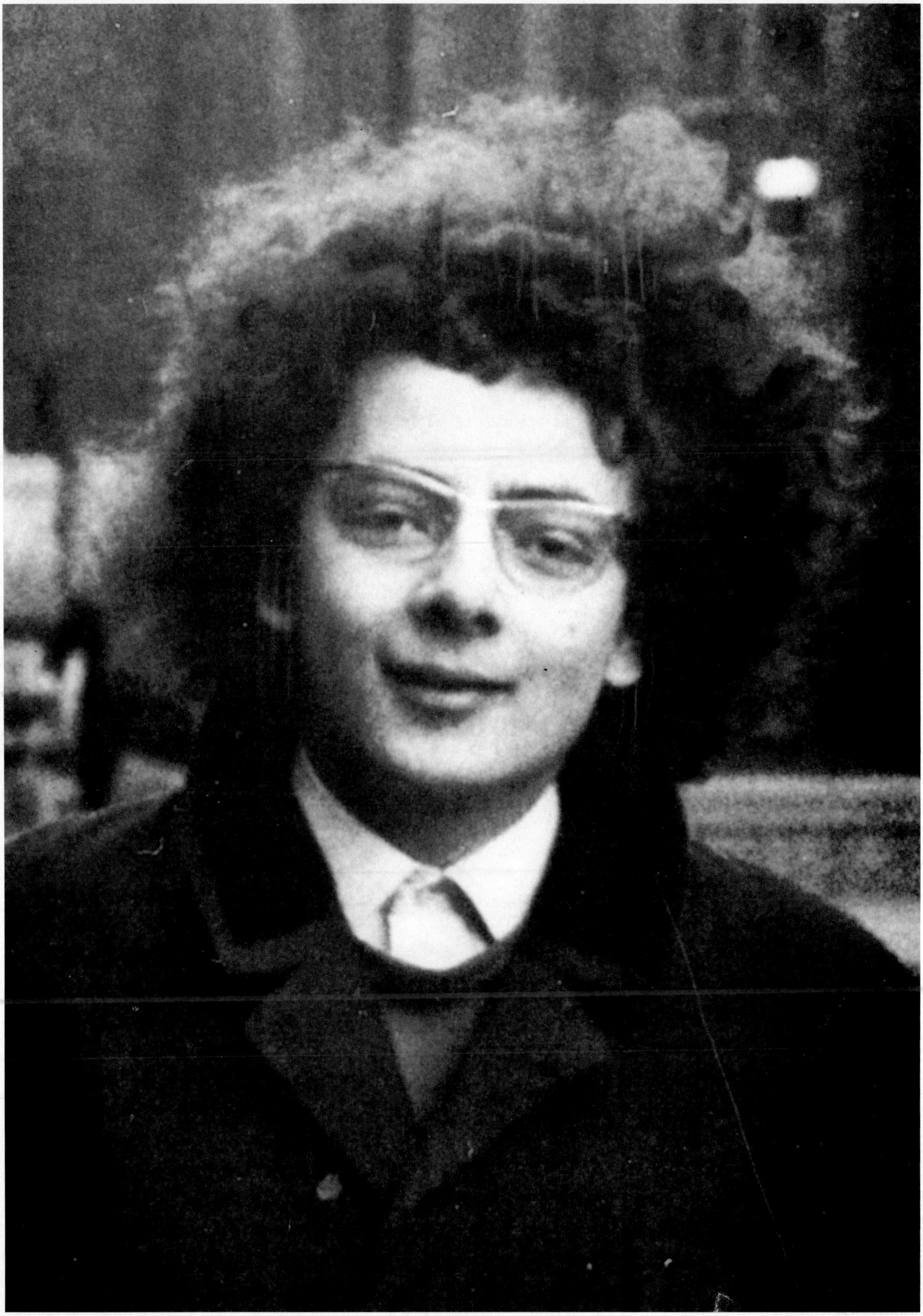

The Author of the Damn Foreword

A FOREWORD BY ROWAN ATKINSON

Dear Reader,

Thanks a lot for buying this book. It's a very important book indeed to us at Comic Relief. For one, it contains some of the greatest sketches written over the last 30 years – the best sketches we've done, the sketches that inspired us to do the best sketches we've done, and the sketches we pinched gags from in order to do the best sketches we've done.

But what makes it most special is that it is a **MAGICAL MONEY-MAKING BOOK.**

The original inspiration was not only to give you a classic sketch compendium, but also to give you a text you can actually perform for Comic Relief – so in the end, our dream was that we not only get the cash from the book, but the cash from performances of the revue that you do, thus spinning a huge web of dosh enough to do good works from the tip of Mozambique to the top of John o' Groats.

So, if you can put on **ANY VERSION** of the revue this book contains – all of it, some of it, just the clean bits, just the dirty bits,

. . . at **ANY TIME** – March 10, the night of Red Nose Day 2, or the weekend before, or the weekend after, or any day from then on, Christmas, high summer, low autumn,

. . . in **ANY PLACE,** from the Royal National Theatre to your school gym, from the Royal Shakespeare Company to the back of your garage,

then **I BEG YOU,** on bended knee, with my nose touching the ground, and my fists beating against the hard gravel – **DO IT, AND SEND US THE PROFITS YOU MAKE.**

All the writers of these sketches have given them free for performance, and it would be wonderful if together we could create a huge new revenue for Comic Relief and its work in Africa and the U.K.

I hope you'll agree it's a cracking good read – even the stupid extra bits at the beginning and end. In fact, the only thing I must apologise for is that this damn foreword is so serious. Still, someone had to write the worst page, eh?

Ever Yours, with a shiny, slightly smelly red nose, and high hopes that money will come rolling in,

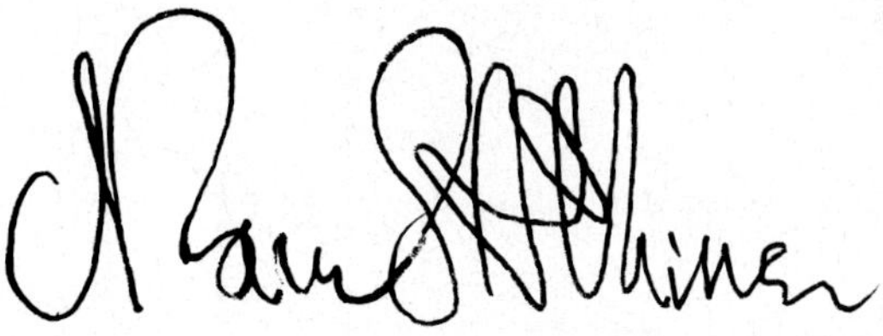

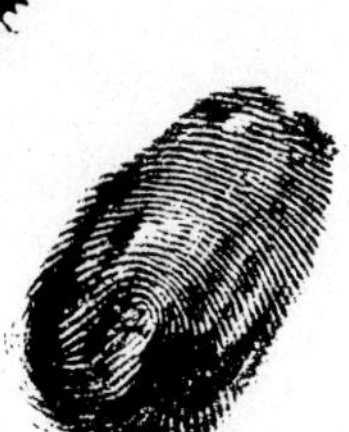

Rowan Atkinson.

PS. Editors – please leave this foreword as it is. It's got a very serious message. Do not, I repeat, do not try to pep it up by publishing that stupid picture of me on my first day at University. It would be childish and churlish.

All profits from performances of this revue should be sent to
Comic Relief, c/o Peat Marwick McLintock, P.O. Box 678, London EC47 8AF
and a special certificate of Red Nose worthiness will be rushed to all contributors

St Biddulph

St Biddulph was an early British saint, who was arrested in a time of persecution and sentenced to death for his beliefs. In order to cheer up those with whom he was imprisoned, Biddulph, a cheery soul and one much given to japes and larks and merriments, decided to stage a revue for the weekend before their execution. At first it was hard getting enthusiasm up (but isn't it always, eh???!!!) but it was soon discovered that one of the martyrs had a very amusing walk and another one of them did a stunning impression of the head guard which had them all rolling around in their cells. As you might expect, what with all the torture and stuff going on, the first night had to be cancelled owing to lack of rehearsal time, but finally the revue, entitled *Laugh Till You Die!*, was staged on the day of the execution.

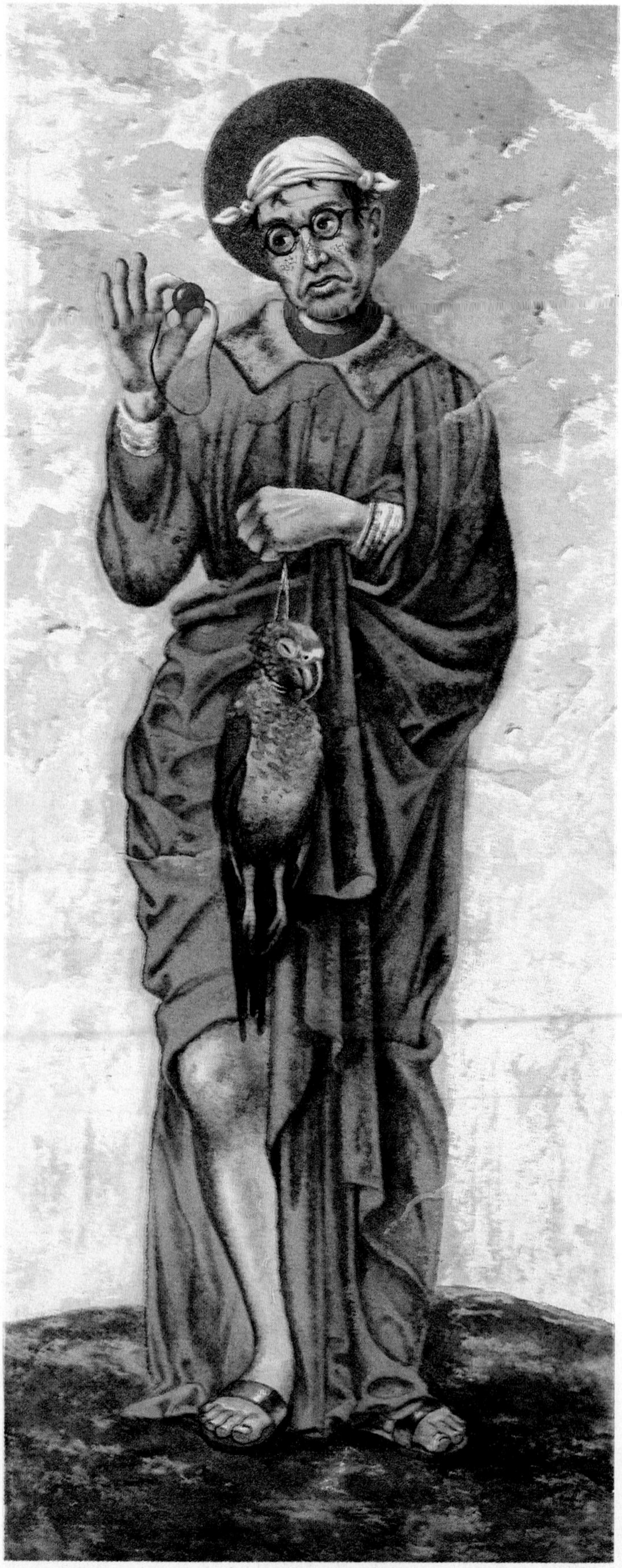

Unfortunately, it was not a success, and it was rightly said of all the members of the cast that they died twice that day.

It was because of the spectacular lack of success of the revue that St Biddulph is the patron saint of all revues. And because this book contains a revue that he blesses its contents.

Amen

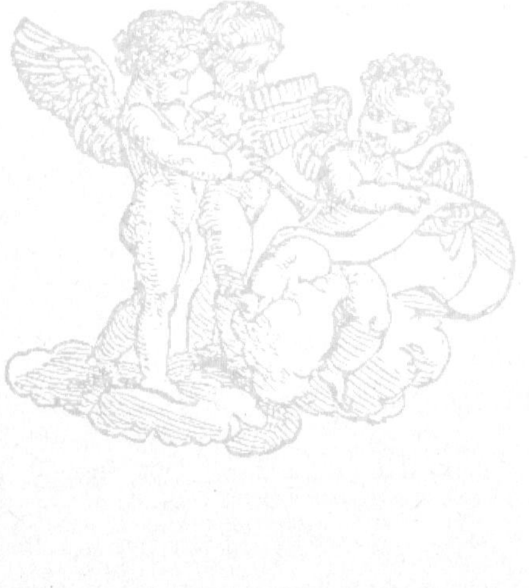

A BRIEF HISTORY OF REVUE

by Simon Turt (Associate Member of The Friends of Ned Sherrin Ltd)

THE BIRTH OF REVUE

Comedy began in Ancient Greece, when Archimedes, leaping in and out of his bath in the course of his work on hydraulics, suddenly formulated the idea of the willy joke.

The first revue proper was put on at the Amphitheatre at Marathon in 490 BC. It was directed by Pericles and starred Sophocles, Plato, Aristotle, Socrates and a very pretty girl who (Herodotus tells us) sang a serious song in the middle of the first half. After the production, she got a job at Corfu Rep and was never heard of again.

The revue – *What Is Truth!* – was the first to take the form of a series of sketches (or 'dialogues') and is famous for its classic routines: 'The Nature of Justice', 'Courage and Beauty Examined', 'What Do We Mean When We Talk of Virtue?' and 'Is Death Real and If So Has This Parrot Experienced It?'

During the show, the zany group of young philosophers were not only uproariously funny (although this was, admittedly, due mainly to their pathetic attempts at dancing) but in the second half went on to lay down the foundations of modern thermodynamics, expound the principles of solid geometry, measure the distance to the sun and invent hummus.

Unfortunately, the only review that has come down to us (*The Iliad*, Book XII, Lines 392–3) reads:

> stunningly predictable,
> O! for a Jonathan Miller amongst this lot.

While *What Is Truth!* is unquestionably the forerunner of modern revue, it was at first unpopular with audiences.

Each performance ran for 30 days with one 15-minute interval. This was due mainly to two crucial technical problems. (1) Since the show took place in the open air, the blackouts between the sketches arrived extremely slowly and then only once every 24 hours. (2) The show was continually interrupted by members of the audience leaping from their seats and needlessly running the 22 miles to Athens to announce the punchline.

What Is Truth! closed in September 489 BC after only six performances, and revue fell into disrepute.

It was to be a full fifty years before Ned Sherrin was born and the Golden Age of Revue began.

The rest is history.

The one thing every revue needs, apart from a parrot, is an audience, and every revue performer should have a complete breakdown of his audience. And here is a typical audience breaking down...

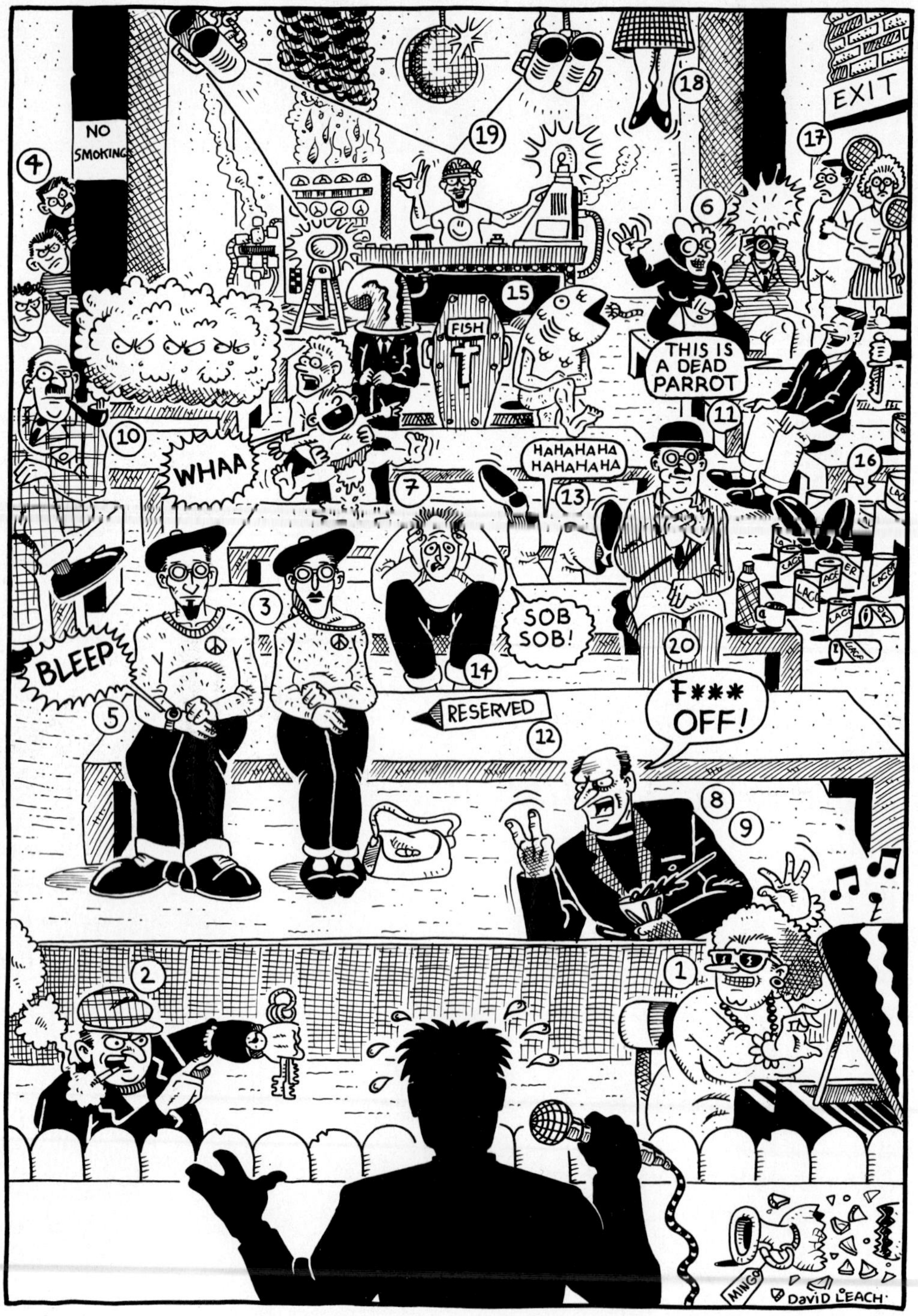
NO SMOKING
EXIT
FISH
THIS IS A DEAD PARROT
WHAA
HAHAHAHA HAHAHAHA
SOB SOB!
BLEEP
RESERVED
F*** OFF!
MING
DAVID LEACH

1. Note-perfect pianist (playing wrong song)
2. Caretaker of building
3. The director's friends (in best seats)
4. Your friends (back row behind pillar)
5. Person with digital watch that bleeps before every punchline
6. Generic mum and dad
7. Disruptive baby (didn't even pay)
8. Foul-mouthed heckler
9. Vicar who lent you the hall
10. Pipesmoker (sets off sprinkler during finale)
11. Person who knows sketches off by heart and says each line before you do
12. Reserved for Lord Lucan
13. Writer of sketch being performed
14. Director of sketch being performed
15. Annual outing of Surrealists' Society
16. Local lager lout (*or* local newspaper's drama critic)
17. People who thought it was badminton night
18. Director's aunt (lent cast Ming vase as prop)
19. Lighting man (normally does Friday evening disco)
20. Genuine member of public

THE SET

Revues, being composed of short sketches, usually containing widely different subject matter, tend to keep the set to a minimum. A plain – or at least not unduly distracting – backdrop is best. Since furniture may need to be moved between sketches, it obviously makes sense to keep that to a minimum too. An uncluttered design allows the imagination to roam freely, and the money to be spent on beer for the cast party.

The Atkinson
'The Purist's Choice'

The Atkinson Augmented
(Table kindly donated by The Conran Group plc as part of a reciprocal tax-dodge)

The Cleese
'Economical But Distinctly Zany'

9

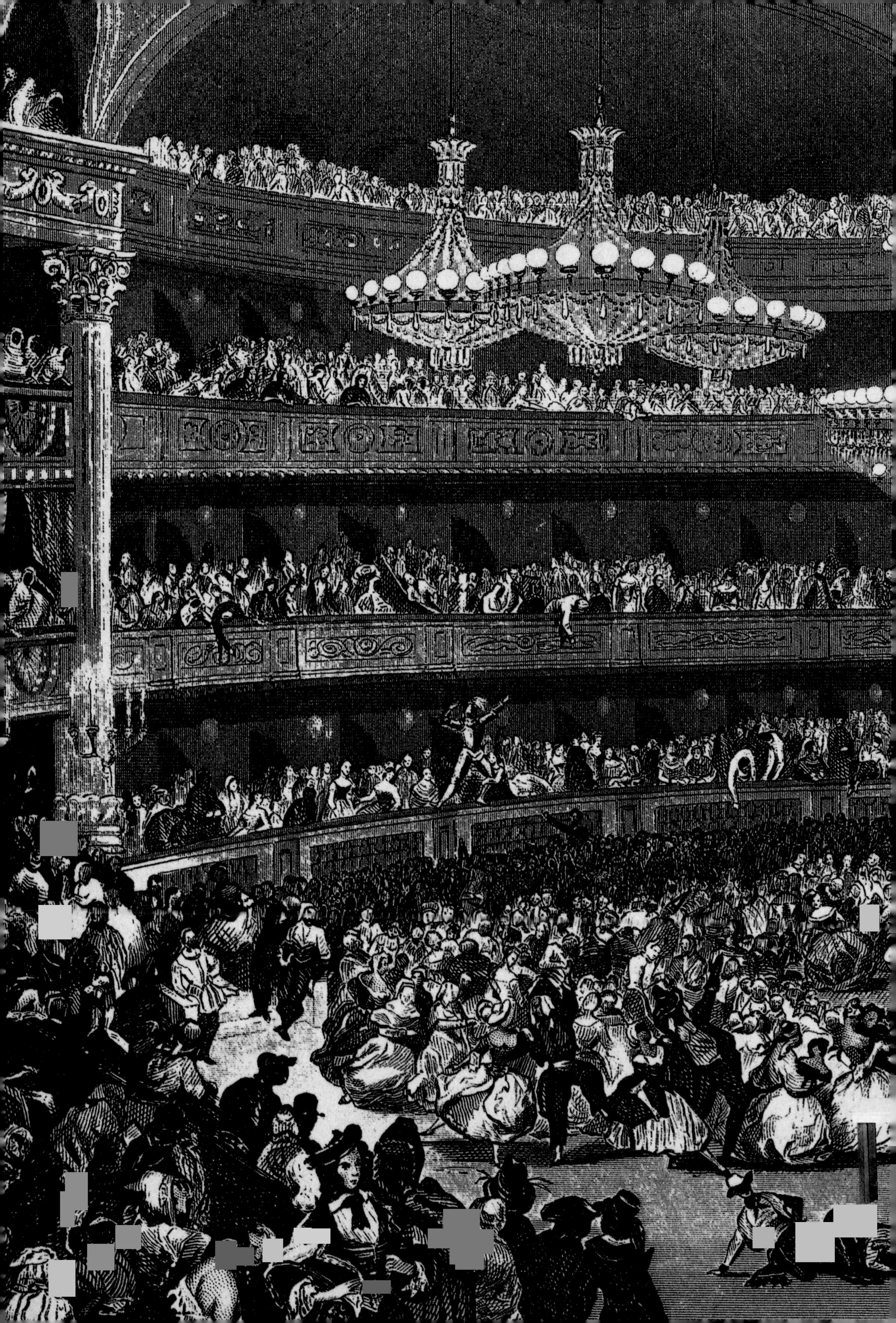

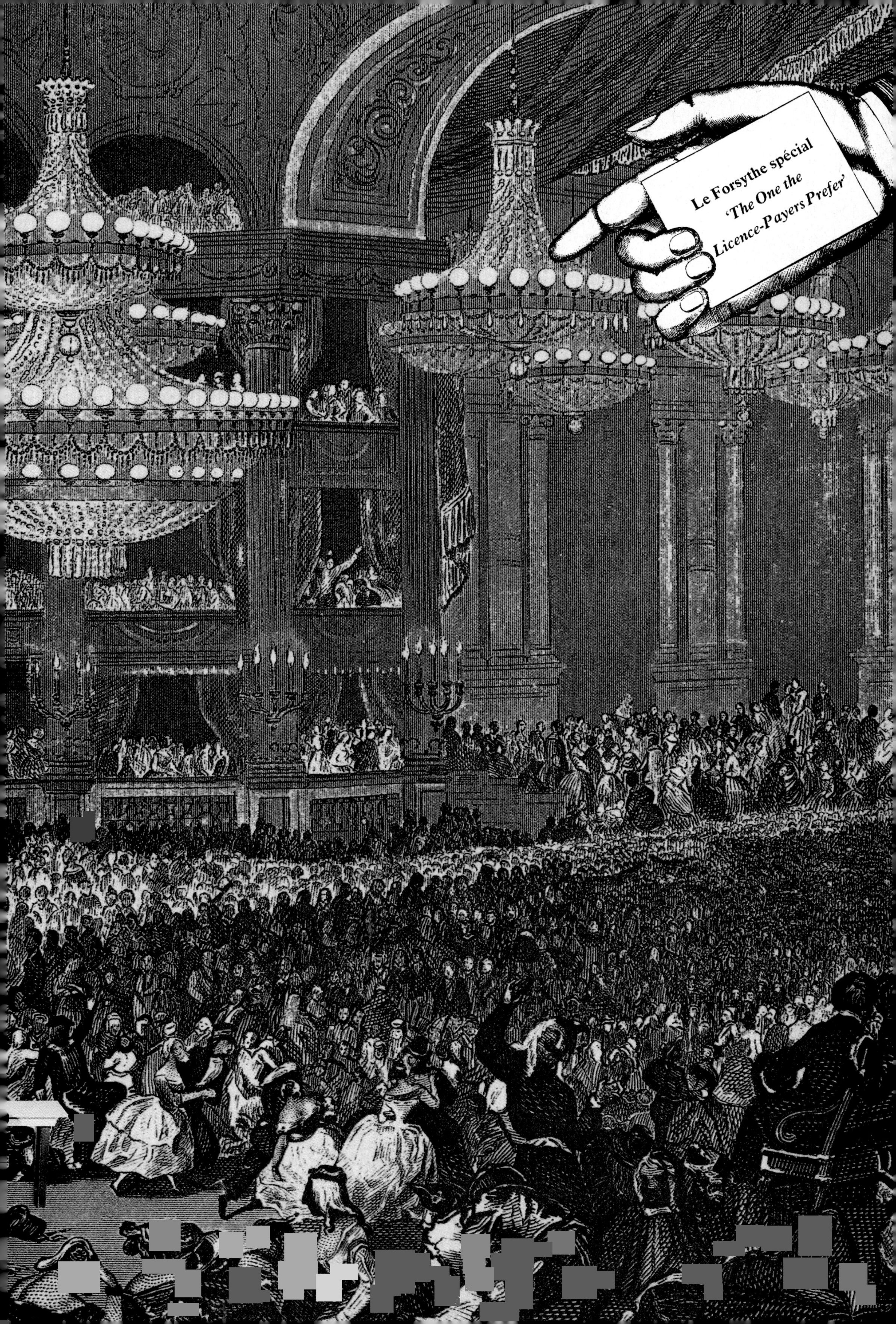
Le Forsythe spécial
'The One the
Licence-Payers Prefer'

THE PARROT SKETCH
THROUGH THE AGES

The Parrot Sketch is the funniest single thing in existence, with the possible exception of Charles Wheeler's hairdo.

Although there is only one 'The Parrot Sketch', every single revue in the history of theatre has contained a parrot in some form. Sometimes it is a major participant, sometimes it is merely mentioned in passing. It is not unusual for huge stuffed ones to drop, hilariously, from the roof.

It is vitally important to include this amusing bird at some point in your revue.

This is the level of hilarity you should be aiming at. Here are some other ways in which parrots have been used in revue from time immemorial:

The Ancient World. Early parrot sketches suffered badly from inadequate understanding of the precise nature of a parrot.

The Age of Chivalry. The parrot was introduced by Chaucer as a little light relief from all the sex and violence in his work.

Medieval Times. The famous Medieval Mystery Revues were so called because no one knew why they were called that.

The Restoration. As usual, Vanbrugh overdoes it.

Modern Times. Classic moment from the fifties – John Osborne's Angry Young Parrot.

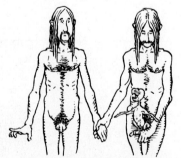

The Sixties. Very exciting work done with parrots in California.

The Seventies. After 2,460 years the parrot gets a laugh.

The Eighties. And so, full circle. Parrots are once again in short supply due to parrotist pressure groups.

FINGER-PUPPET THEATRE

Those finding it impossible to put on a public performance of the *Comic Relief Revue* owing to lack of facilities, or lack of available comic talent, or lack of a fire-extinguisher when their theatre started to burn down the night before opening, should make use of the finger-puppet theatre provided.

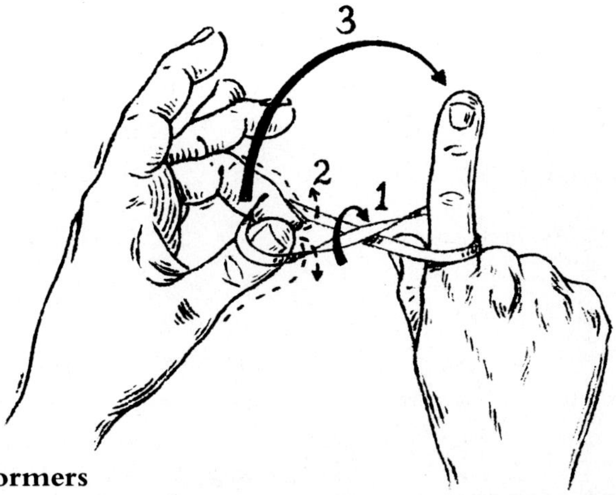
3
2
1

It is also ideal for prisoners in solitary confinement, people trapped in telephone kiosks, passengers in taxis, and single-handed yachtsmen.

Choice of Performers

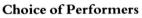

Choose any of the following performers for your sketches:

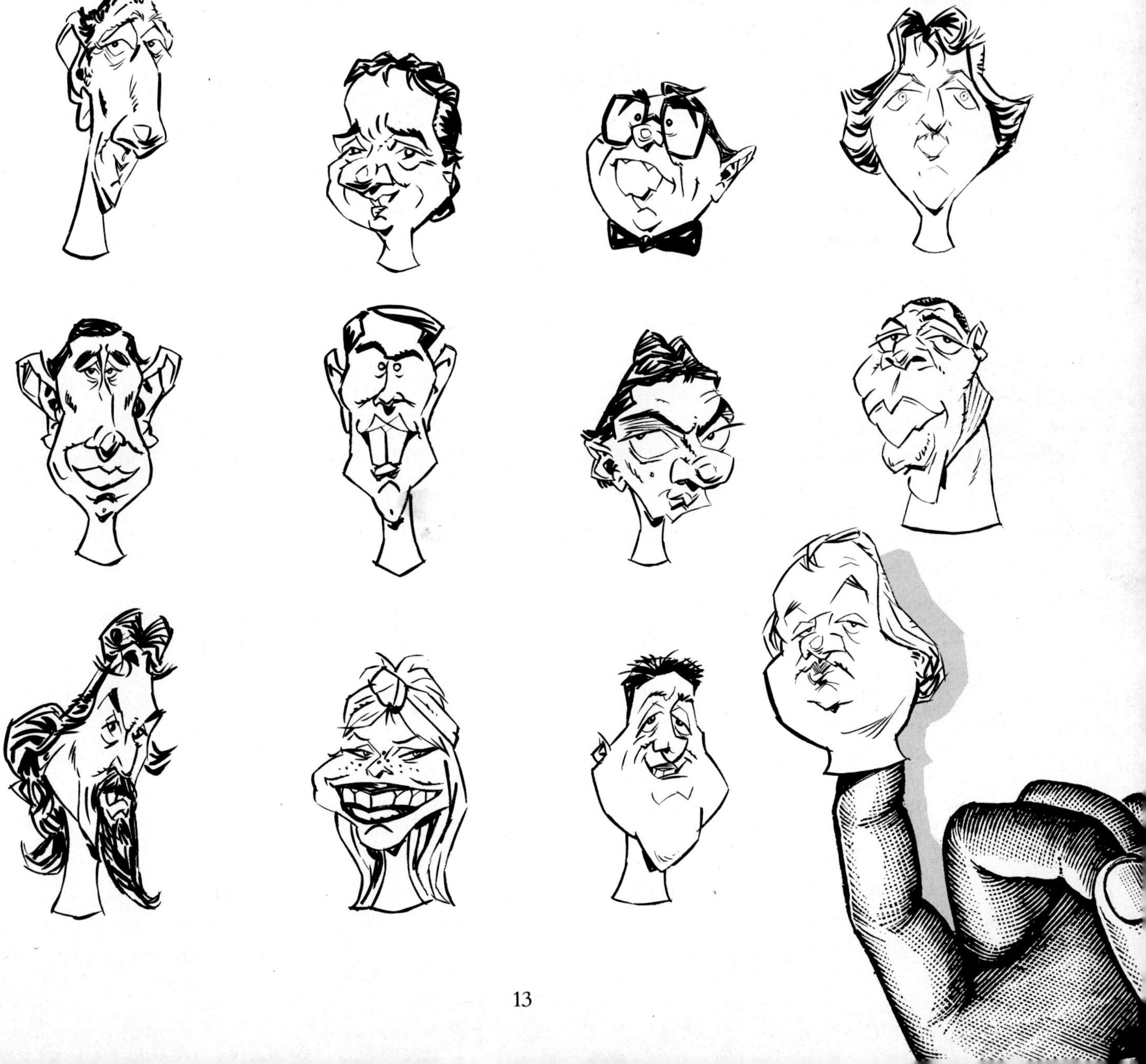

BEWARE!!!

The Curse of the Nose

This booke was conceeved in all goode wille, and all the sketches were donated by the sketchewriters who penned them, that they might be performed with great joy and that the monnaie from the stagings should be given unto the thing called Comic Relief.

Therefore, upon him or her who shall offende against its purpose benign, and gives not the proceedes to the thing that folke knowe as Comic Relief,

let this vile curse fall …

May your nose be eternally red, whether you desire it or not. May it be large and round and red, and when subjected to bright sunlight, which might normally turn it large and round and red, may it become even larger, and rounder, and bright purple.

May your nose run on those social occasions when it is especially important that you look dignified and physically attractive, and may you always forget to have a handkerchief with you, so in the car, with your future father-in-law, you find yourself having to lean your head out of the window, and drip.

May your nose sneeze at the specific moment when a sneeze is most unwanted. When the Queen is about to speak, when the coffin enters the church, when you see your loved one naked for the first time. May your sneeze be loud and complicated, not just a simple sneeze, but a sneeze that speaks volumes about catarrh. And releases volumes of catarrh.

May train doors jam it,
May big bees sting it,
May madmen bite it off
and
May it never give you peace.

On the other hand, if you send us all your dosh, we hope you never get a cold again.

IN OTHER WORDS: SERIOUSLY FOR A SEC

This book is not only a book, but a playscript. On Comic Relief Day 1988 a revue resembling it was put on at the Northcott Theatre, Exeter, and raised about £4,000. It had eight cast members, meaning each cast member earned about £500 by his/her efforts. This means that if 100,000 copies of this book were sold, and then 100,000 of you took part in a revue, we might just make, guessing conservatively, **£50,000,000** from it. So please do stage it, or bits of it, if you can – anyway, anyhow, and if people come and enjoy it, then cover your minimum costs and send us the profits – so we can help turn it into the most successful book ever not written by Moses and the Apostles.

Every penny of money that comes to Comic Relief goes straight to the projects it supports in Africa and the UK.

And our thanks to Penguin for making it possible, and happen.

14

The Comic Relief Red Nose Revue

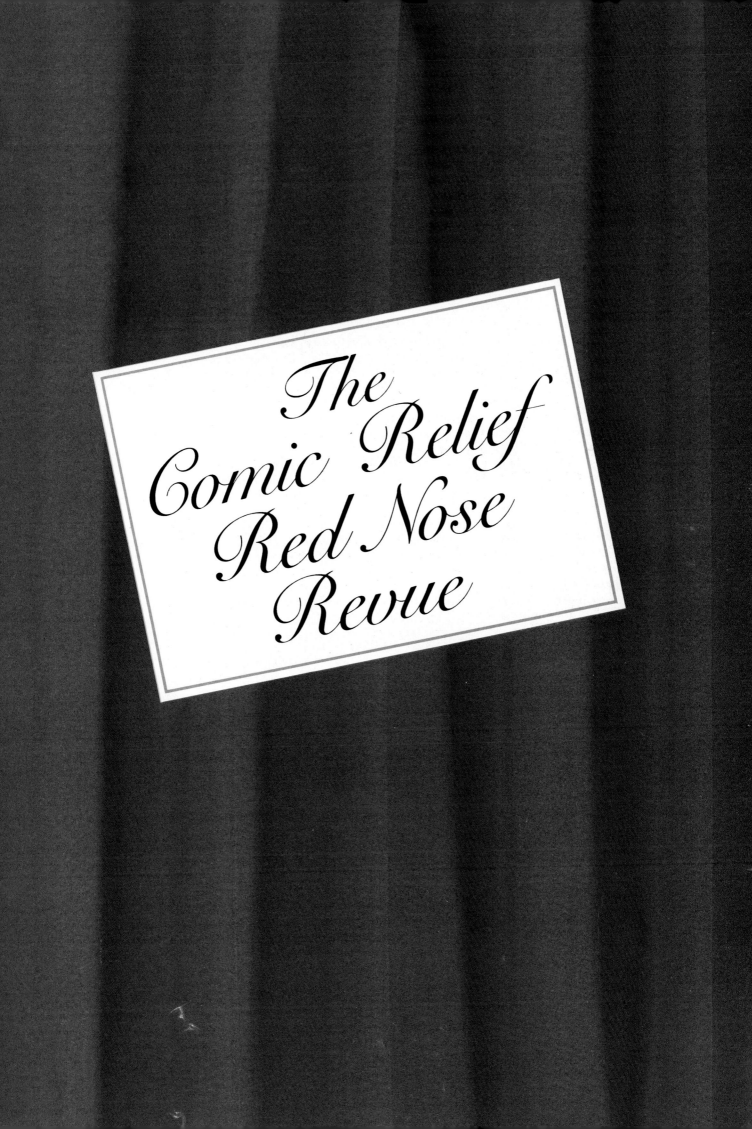

DAVID COPPERFIELD

Traditional, first performed on the occasion of Queen Victoria's 40th birthday

The ANNOUNCER *walks on. He is in formal dress, or she is in formal dress, and speaks with due formality. (If you haven't got formal dress, fine – just try not to make it shorts.)*

ANNOUNCER

Ladies and gentlemen, welcome to the . . . . . . Theatre, and to the second evening of the Royal Shakespeare Company's production of *David Copperfield*. Due to unforeseen circumstances, the part of Mr Micawber will tonight be taken by Bev Pilchard and not, as stated in the programme, by Sir John Gielgud. We apologize for any disappointment. The part of young Copperfield, which was to have been played by Bev Pilchard, will now be taken by Thomas Harpie, and the part of Mr Dick, also to be played by Bev Pilchard, will be played by Harold Lawson. The part of the Young Lunatic, in the programme to be played by Harold Lawson, will be taken by Tamara Sprigs, whose roles as Freda, Agnes, Second Young Lunatic, Miss Picknose, First Nun, Daft Prostitute and back end of Pantomime Cow will be taken by Jim Burke. Mr Burke's part as Dead Man on Battlefield will be taken by the late George Highbury, whose unexpected demise has caused tonight's changes. We are however pleased to announce that there has been a dramatic improvement in the health of Harry Friend, so the part of Second Dead Man on Battlefield, to have been played by the *late* Harry Friend, will now be played by a couple of cushions and a sack of potatoes. Mr Highbury's performance in the role of Monsieur Petitcock will be played by Carl Froggitt, who is down in the programme to play the role of Tiny Toby. The role of Tiny Toby will be played instead by Spot. The role of Rover, which was to have been played by Spot, will now be played by Shep. Shep's original role as Rabid Dog in Company of Second Daft Prostitute will tonight be omitted from the performance and replaced by the pre-recorded sound of a dog barking. The part of Small Albanian Gentleman by Roadside on the Approach to Broadstairs will be played by a small Albanian man we found by the roadside on the approach to Broadstairs when we were last there. The guitar will be played by Mark Knopfler.

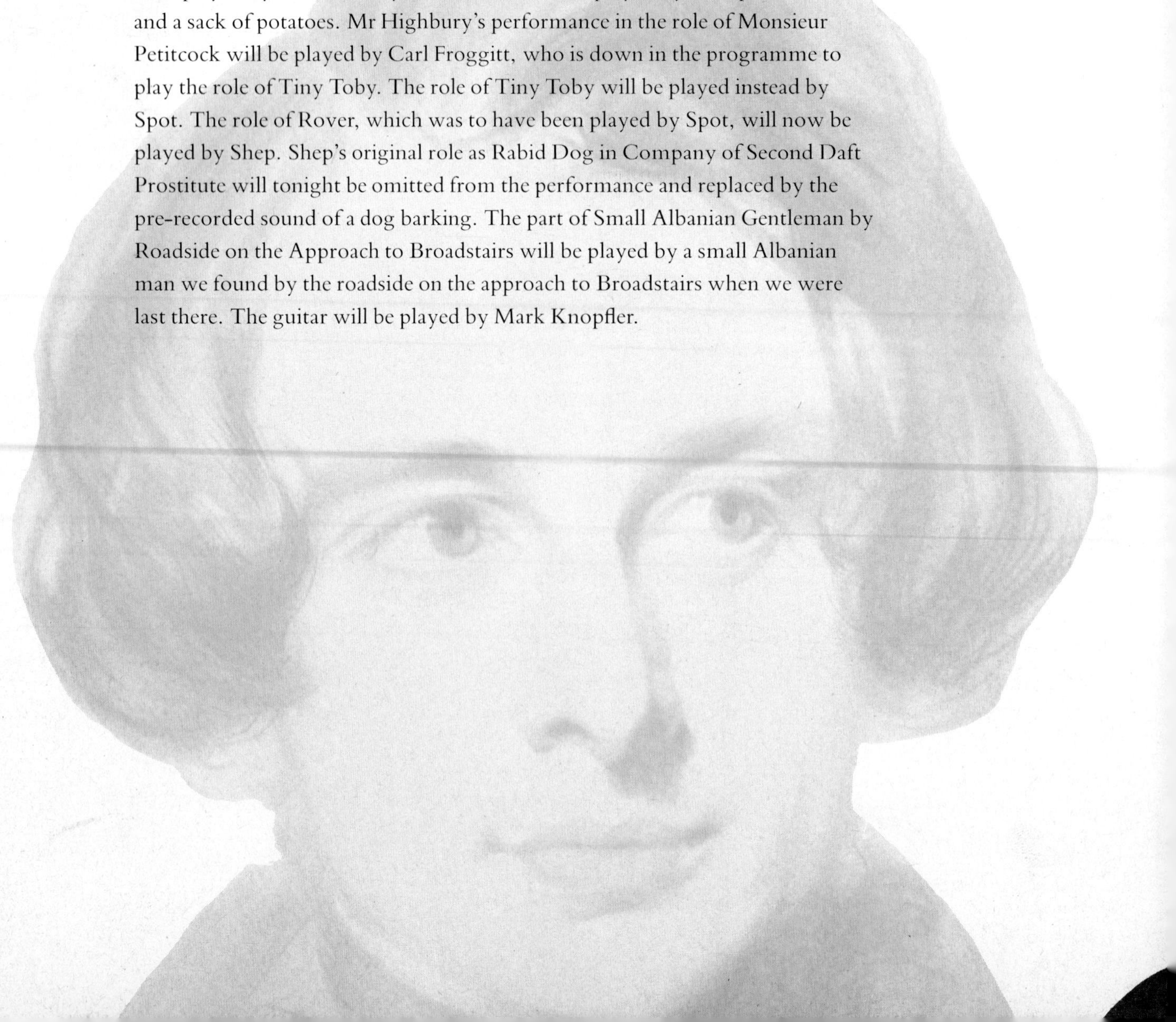

**If you fancy starting with a big bang, then forget Copperfield – this
is the big song and dance number for you, babies!!!**

YET ANOTHER OPENING

*Words and music by Joe Griffiths, Gareth Hale, and Norman Pace.
First performed in* Hale and Pace, *1988*

Hello everybody and welcome tonight;
Get ready to roll cos we'll be hitting the heights!
We gotta show and we know it's a hit –
Cos it's full of knackered clichés and fits that don't rhyme.
(Rhymes that don't fit! – Oh shit!)

We've got a show and we'll show you a show
That will show you that a show is a show.
It's a show that we know is a show that will flow;
And row by row you'll go ho ho ho.
It's a show –
It's a show that will show you a show and what is worse,
You know that the show will always use the word 'show'
Twenty times in every verse.

'Show – show – show show show'
Biz – 'What?'
Biz – It's a word that's got fizz, and pizzazz, has got razzmatazz;
That razzle dazzle goes right through my head,
And it's a word with at least four zeds.
Our business is show and we'll show you our business,
We don't mind at all;
Cos even tho' we're English, our fingers go all tinglish
When we sing in that American drawl.

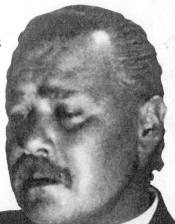

17

DIALOGUE

Hey, Gary, don't stand there in the corner all sad and blue.

Aw shucks, nobody wants to talk to me...

We do.

Ah, go on...

Hey, Gary, why don't you tell all of us why you got into Showbiz...

Who'd wanna hear about that?

We would...

OK...

I love Showbiz (*yeah*) I love showbiz (*whooah*)

And the reason I must confess (*do tell*)

I start to wake up when I wear make–up

And I slip into my sequin dress (*oh dear!*)

I love those stockings, those fishnet stockings,

And a wig that's full of curls.

I'm feeling really swell when I'm dressed up as a girl,

In my showbiz world! (*That's really great, Gary*)

But in every show, there's a bit that goes slow, when someone is suddenly
    sad;

But in times of strife, someone talks about 'life'

Then things don't seem so bad.

Then the show gets slicker and slicker,

As the music gets gradually quicker...

La la la la la la la la la, It's a show full of this and of that

There's plenty of singing and plenty of dancing and plenty of girls who sing flat

There's plenty of singing and plenty of dancing

And plenty of girls who sing fl____at!

SHOW!

18

THREE-WAY QUIZ

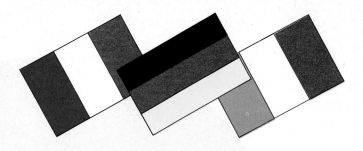

Written by Moray Hunter and John Docherty; first performed in RadioActive by Helen Atkinson Wood, Angus Deayton, Mike Fenton-Stevens, Geoffrey Perkins and Philip Pope

It is the worst quiz show in the world. Trans-European cable has struck.

MIKE: And now it's time for our European Three-Way Quiz. And we have Pierre in France, Maria from Italy, and Klaus from Germany. Hello there.

ALL: Hello.

MIKE: Great. I'm going to ask you all questions about your own country ... First off I want you all to spell the name of your native country. So, Maria?

MARIA: I.T.A.L.I.A.

MIKE: Very close, Maria. Actually ends in a 'Y'. So no points there. Pierre?

PIERRE: F.R.A.N.C.E.

MIKE: Very close, Pierre. But there's no such letter as 'Eh'. And finally, Klaus?

KLAUS: D.E.U.T.S.C.H.L.A.N.D.

MIKE: Hard lines, Klaus. Not even one correct letter there. So no one off the mark yet. No pun intended there, Klaus, ha ha. So no points, to anyone, and now the next. History. Right, Klaus. Who won the World Cup in 1966?

KLAUS: (*Suddenly very reticent*) England.

MIKE: Yes, that's right. England won it. England did in fact win the World Cup in 1966. And for ten points, Klaus, who did they beat?

KLAUS: I can't remember.

MIKE: It's worth ten points, Klaus. Could be worthwhile remembering.

KLAUS: No, I'm sorry. I can't remember.

MIKE: (*Enjoying himself*) Come on, Klaus. I'm sure you can. I'll give you a clue. Quite a lot of people you know live in that country.

KLAUS: (*Reluctantly*) West Germany.

MIKE: Correct. England did indeed thrash West Germany in the World Cup Final in 1966. Ten points, Klaus. Now, Pierre. Lord Nelson was a very famous what?

PIERRE: English sailor.

MIKE: Correct. And he won a battle called the Battle of what?

PIERRE: Trafalgar.

MIKE: Correct. (*Extremely smugly*) Who against?

PIERRE: Err. France. (*Deflated*) Woh!

MIKE: Correct. England did in fact wop the frogs. And speaking of wops (*rubbing his hands with glee at the prospect*), Maria, your turn. Anagrams. 'Lussomini' is an anagram of which Fascist dictator?

MARIA: Mussolini.

MIKE: Correct. Which country has come last in more *It's a Knockout* competitions than anyone else?

MARIA: Italy.

MIKE: Correct. Whose women are fat and short-tempered?

MARIA: Italy.

MIKE: Correct. Where does the Mafia come from?

MARIA: Italy.

MIKE: Correct again. Who runs the Mafia?

MARIA: (*Aggressively*) My father!

MIKE: Does he? ... Oh ... ah ... (*without pausing*). Ah. Who won the World Cup in 1982?

MARIA: Italy.

MIKE: Correct. Where do I love going on holiday?

MARIA: Italy.

MIKE: Of course. Who makes the best cars?

MARIA: Italy.

MIKE: Correct. What's my favourite meal?

MARIA: Spaghetti bolognese.

MIKE: Absolutely. Good old spaghetti bolognese. And who has won the quiz?

MARIA: Maria!

MIKE: That's right. The winner is good old Maria, from good old I.T.A.L.I.A., where the Mafia come from!

HORACE – A POEM

Written by Terry Jones; never performed, but should have been

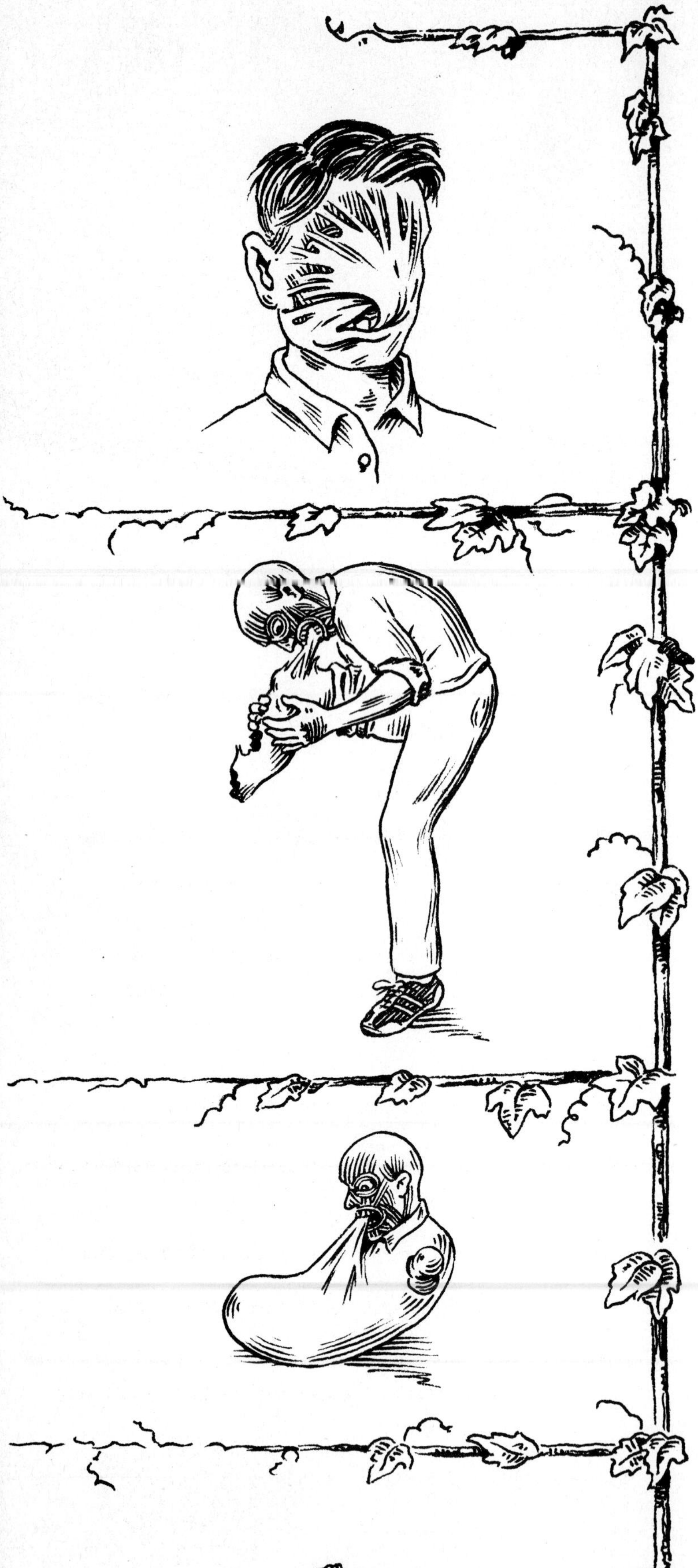

Much to his Mum and Dad's dismay
Horace ate himself one day.
He didn't stop to say his grace,
He just sat down and ate his face.
'We can't have this!' his Dad declared,
'If that lad's ate, he should be shared.'
But even as he spoke they saw
Horace eating more and more.
First his legs and then his thighs,
His arms, his nose, his hair, his eyes . . .
'Stop him, someone!' Mother cried.
'Those eyeballs would be better fried!'
But all too late, for they were gone,
And he started on his dong . . .
'Oh! foolish child!' the father mourns
'You could have deep-fried that with prawns,
Some parsley and some tartar sauce . . .'
But H. was on his second course:
His liver and his lights and lung,
His ears, his neck, his chin, his tongue;
'To think I raised him from the cot
And now he's going to scoff the lot!'
His Mother cried: 'What shall we do?
What's left won't even make a stew . . .'
And as she wept, her son was seen
To eat his head, his heart, his spleen.
And there he lay: a boy no more,
Just a stomach, on the floor . . .
None the less, since it *was* his
They ate it – that's what haggis is.*

*No, it isn't. Haggis is a kind of stuffed black pudding eaten by the Scots and considered by them to be not only a delicacy but fit for human consumption. The minced heart, liver and lungs of a sheep or calf or other animals' inner organs are mixed with oatmeal, sealed and boiled in maw in the sheep's intestinal stomach-bag and . . . Excuse me a minute. Ed.

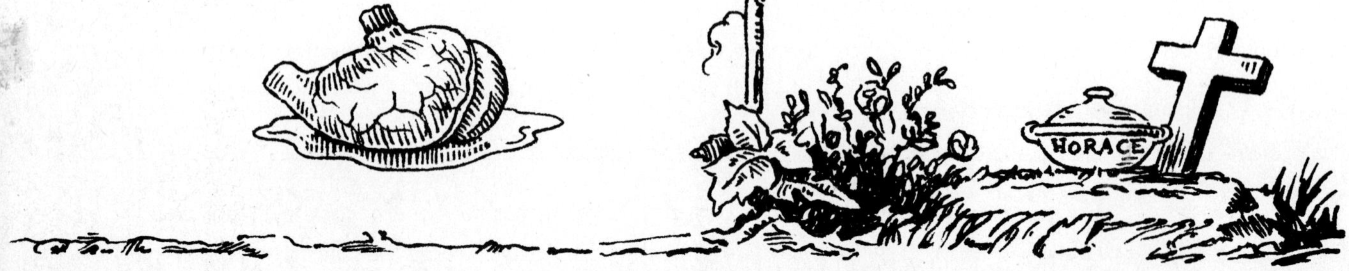
HORACE

THE LAST SUPPER

Written by John Cleese; first performed by John Cleese and Jonathan Lynn, April 1976, in A Poke in the Eye with a Sharp Stick *for Amnesty International*

An impressive PAPAL PERSON *sits on a ritzy throne in the middle of a large Catholic sort of room. We hear a cry of 'Michelangelo to see the Pope'. An* ATTENDANT *enters.*

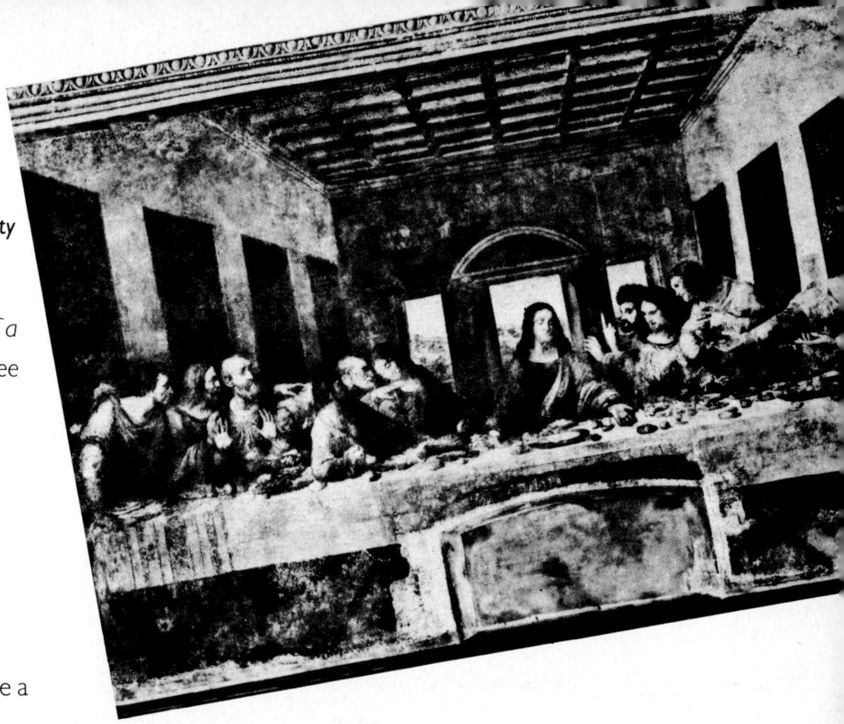

ATTENDANT: Michelangelo to see you, Your Holiness.

POPE: Show him in.
(*MICHELANGELO* enters.)

MICHELANGELO: Evening, Your Grace.

POPE: Good evening, Michelangelo. I want to have a word with you about this *Last Supper* of yours.

MICHELANGELO: Oh, yes?

POPE: I'm not happy with it.

MICHELANGELO: Oh dear. It took hours.

POPE: Not happy at all...

MICHELANGELO: Do the jellies worry you? No, they add a bit of colour, don't they? Oh, I know – you don't like the kangaroo.

POPE: What kangaroo?

MICHELANGELO: I'll alter it, no sweat.

POPE: I never saw a kangaroo!

MICHELANGELO: Well, it's right at the back, but I'll paint it out, no problem. I'll make it into a disciple.

POPE: Ah!

MICHELANGELO: All right now?

POPE: That's the problem.

MICHELANGELO: What is?

POPE: The disciples.

MICHELANGELO: Are they too Jewish? I made Judas the most Jewish.

POPE: No, no – it's just that there are twenty-eight of them.

MICHELANGELO: Well, another one would hardly notice, then. So I'll make the kangaroo into a disciple...

POPE: No!!

MICHELANGELO: All right, all right... we'll lose the kangaroo altogether – I don't mind, I was never completely happy with it...

POPE: That's not the point. There are twenty-eight disciples.

MICHELANGELO: Too many?

POPE: Of course it's too many!

MICHELANGELO: Well, in a way, but I wanted to give the impression of a huge get-together... you know, a real Last Supper – not any old supper, but a proper final treat... a real mother of a blow-out...

POPE: There were only twelve disciples at the Last Supper.

MICHELANGELO: Supposing some of the others happened to drop by?

POPE: There were only twelve disciples altogether.

MICHELANGELO: Well, maybe they'd invited some friends?

POPE: There were only twelve disciples and Our Lord at the Last Supper. The Bible clearly says so.

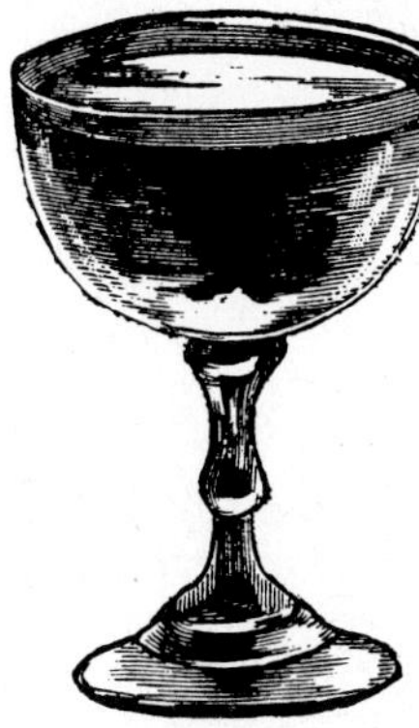

MICHELANGELO: No friends?

POPE: No friends.

MICHELANGELO: Waiters?

POPE: No!

MICHELANGELO: Cabaret?

POPE: No!!

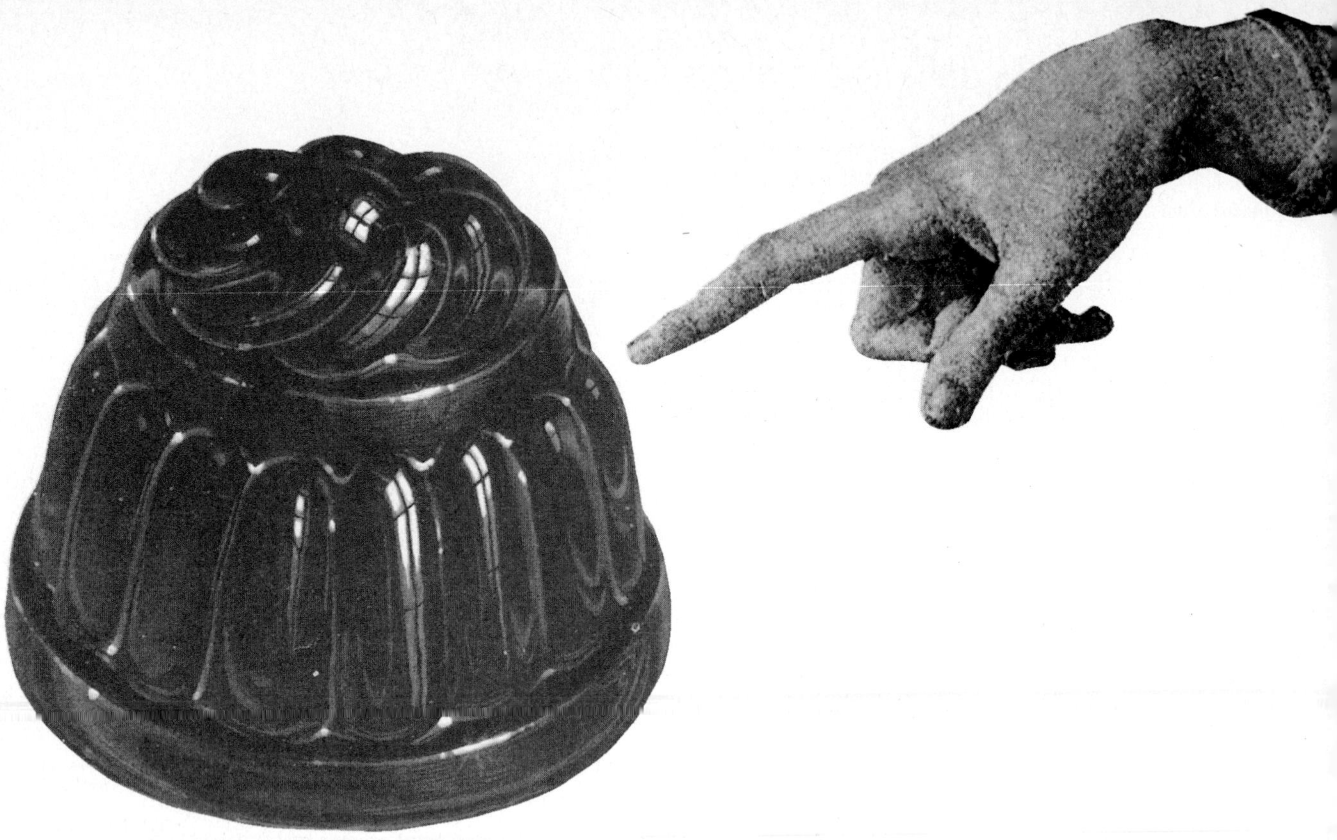

MICHELANGELO: But, you see, I like them. They fill out the canvas. I mean, I suppose we could lose three or four of them, you know, make them...

POPE: (*Loudly, ex cathedra*) There were only twelve disciples and Our Lord at the Last...

MICHELANGELO: I've got it, I've got it!!! We'll call it ... *The Penultimate Supper.*

POPE: What?

MICHELANGELO: There must have been one. I mean, if there was a last one, there must have been one before that, right?

POPE: Yes, but...

MICHELANGELO: Right, so this is the *Penultimate Supper.* The Bible doesn't say how many people were at that, does it?

POPE: Er, no, but...

MICHELANGELO: Well, there you are, then.

POPE: Look!! The Last Supper is a significant event in the life of Our Lord. The Penultimate Supper was not ... even if they had a conjuror and a steel band. Now I commissioned a *Last Supper* from you, and a *Last Supper* I want!

MICHELANGELO: Yes, but look...

POPE: With twelve disciples and one Christ!

MICHELANGELO: One?

POPE: YES, ONE.
(*MICHELANGELO is momentarily speechless.*)
Now will you please tell me what in God's name possessed you to paint this with three Christs in it?

MICHELANGELO: It works, mate!!!

POPE: It does not work!

MICHELANGELO: It does, it looks great! The fat one balances the two skinny ones!

POPE: (*Brooking no argument*) There was only one Saviour...

MICHELANGELO: I know that, everyone knows that, but what about a bit of artistic licence?

POPE: (*Bellowing*) One Redeemer!!!

MICHELANGELO: (*Shouting back*) I'll tell you what you want, mate ... you want a bloody photographer, not a creative artist with some imagination!!

POPE: I'll tell you what I want – I want a *Last Supper,* with one Christ, twelve disciples, no kangaroos, by Thursday lunch, or you don't get paid!!!

MICHELANGELO: You bloody fascist!!

POPE: Look, I'm the bloody Pope, I am! I may not know much about art, but I know what I like...

THINKING OF YOU

Written by Victoria Wood;
first performed by her too.

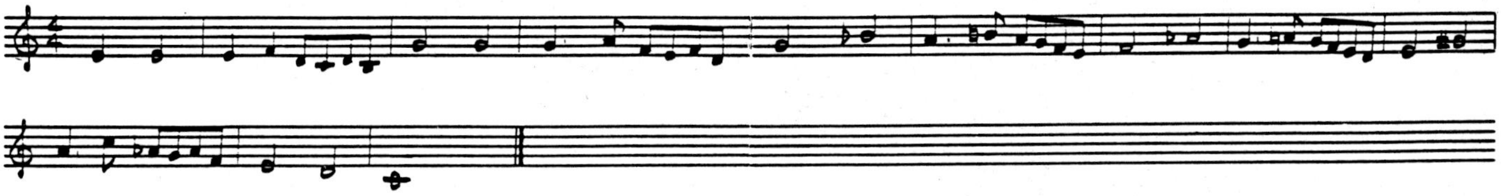

They said our love would never work
They said that when I met you.
Well, they were right, it's over now
Still, I won't forget you...

When the next door neighbour's yelling
When all day I keep on smelling
Old men's macs
Or when my ears are blocked with wax
When conversation turns to taxidermy
I will think of you.

When I see a child dismember
Insects, or when I remember
How I feel
The day after an Indian meal
Or when I see a jellied eel
My darling, I will think of you.

Or when my best friend doesn't like
Beryl Cook or David Hockney
Or when I think of Dick van Dyke
Trying to do a cockney accent.

When the shop is out of Tizer
When above my head there flies a Jumbo Jet
When all my towels are dripping wet
Or when my pink blancmange won't set
My darling, I will think of you.

When my aunt says 'Time for shut-eye',
When I wash up dinner but I get no thanks
Whenever I smell septic tanks
Whenever I see two short planks
My darling, I will think of you.

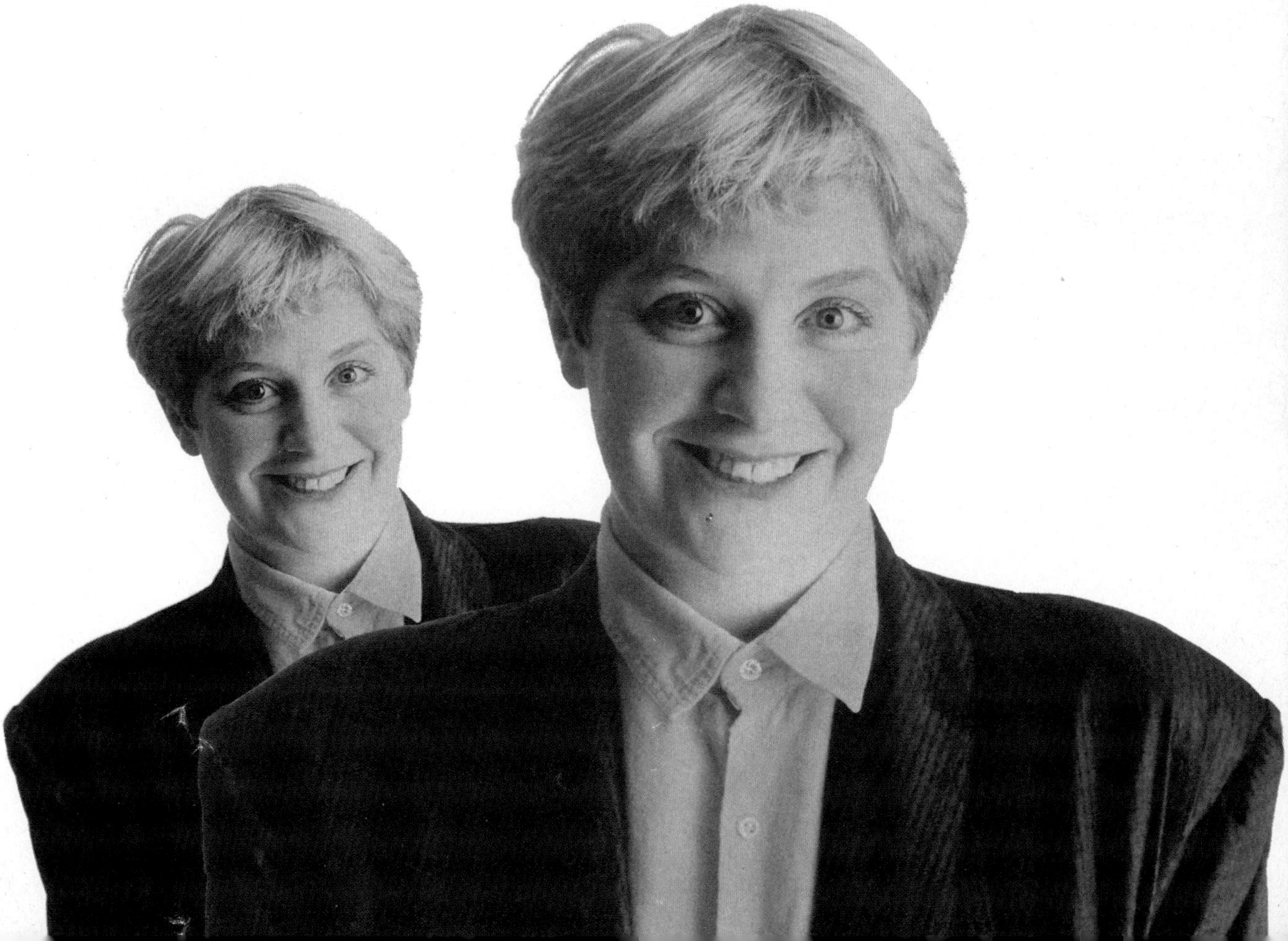

WASHING UP

*Written by Geoff Atkinson; first performed on Barrymore Plus by
Michael Barrymore and Susie Blake*

*This is your classic sketch set-up. You don't even need the desk!!! And the
INTERVIEWER can carry a clip-board if he/she is line-blind.*

SUSIE: *Speaking Frankly!* A programme in which youngsters speak frankly about their problems. Gary is eighteen, he has a problem few of us like to talk about, even fewer of us ever admit to … it's not a problem he finds easy to talk about … Gary.

GARY: Hello.

SUSIE: Gary, could you tell us a little about your 'problem'…?

GARY: Well, I was about fifteen and some mates and me went along to a party, and had like a lot to drink and we were messing around, when someone said – you know – did I fancy 'washing up'…

SUSIE: 'Washing up'?

GARY: That's right.

SUSIE: And did you, shall we say, 'get involved' at this point?

GARY: No – at first I thought I didn't want to get involved … but my mates said I would be a cissy if I didn't … so I let them talk me into it…

SUSIE: (*Thoughtful*) I see … and did you 'enjoy' this 'washing up'?

GARY: Not at first, at first I felt sick and ashamed of what I had done … but then gradually I did in fact begin to feel more relaxed when I was with people who were 'washing up'…

SUSIE: And did you seek treatment for your 'problem'?

GARY: (*Pause*) Not at first … no.

SUSIE: But afterwards you changed your mind?

GARY: Yes, I think now that if I'd had treatment I would not have allowed myself to get into the scene I got myself into…

SUSIE: And what scene was this?

GARY: Well, I was at a New Year's Eve party, at a friend's house, and he'd invited some mates round that I'd never seen before, and I knew as soon as I saw their pinnies that there was going to be trouble, and then one of them turned to me and said … (*biting lip*) did I fancy going into the kitchen…

SUSIE: (*Serious*) Into the kitchen?

GARY: (*Ashamed*) Yeah…

SUSIE: And did you refuse?

GARY: No, at the time I didn't realize what I was letting myself in for.

SUSIE: And what did you find 'in the kitchen'?

GARY: It was terrible … there were quite a few people in there – mainly blokes – and they were trying the hard stuff … dusters, mops, yard-brooms, that sort of stuff…

SUSIE: And what was your reaction…?

GARY: Shock, at first. Shock, followed by revulsion … followed by more shock, followed by more revulsion, followed by … shock. But then one of the blokes who I recognized as a local copper handed me his thick rubber squidgey…

SUSIE: A squidgey?

GARY: That's right.

SUSIE: And did you use … the squidgey?

GARY: Yeah … at first I didn't enjoy it … it was very wet and kept slipping out of my hand … but then gradually I did begin to find I was much more at ease when I had the squidgey in my hand…

SUSIE: And it was this 'craving' to do things other people might find 'repulsive' that led you into a life of crime…?

GARY: I started doing houses…

SUSIE: And what exactly did this involve?

GARY: Well, I'd break into their houses … when they were away on holiday … and clean all their windows, and polish the furniture. And take down all the curtains, especially the nice frilly ones, and take them to the dry cleaner's…

SUSIE: And I believe you actually broke into one person's house while he was asleep and washed and ironed all his shirts and trousers, while he was still wearing them, and without him knowing…

GARY: That's right.

SUSIE: And yet you made a recovery … some would say a remarkable recovery … a recovery that saw you stop doing housework almost entirely…

GARY: That is correct.

SUSIE: How did this come about?

GARY: I got married.

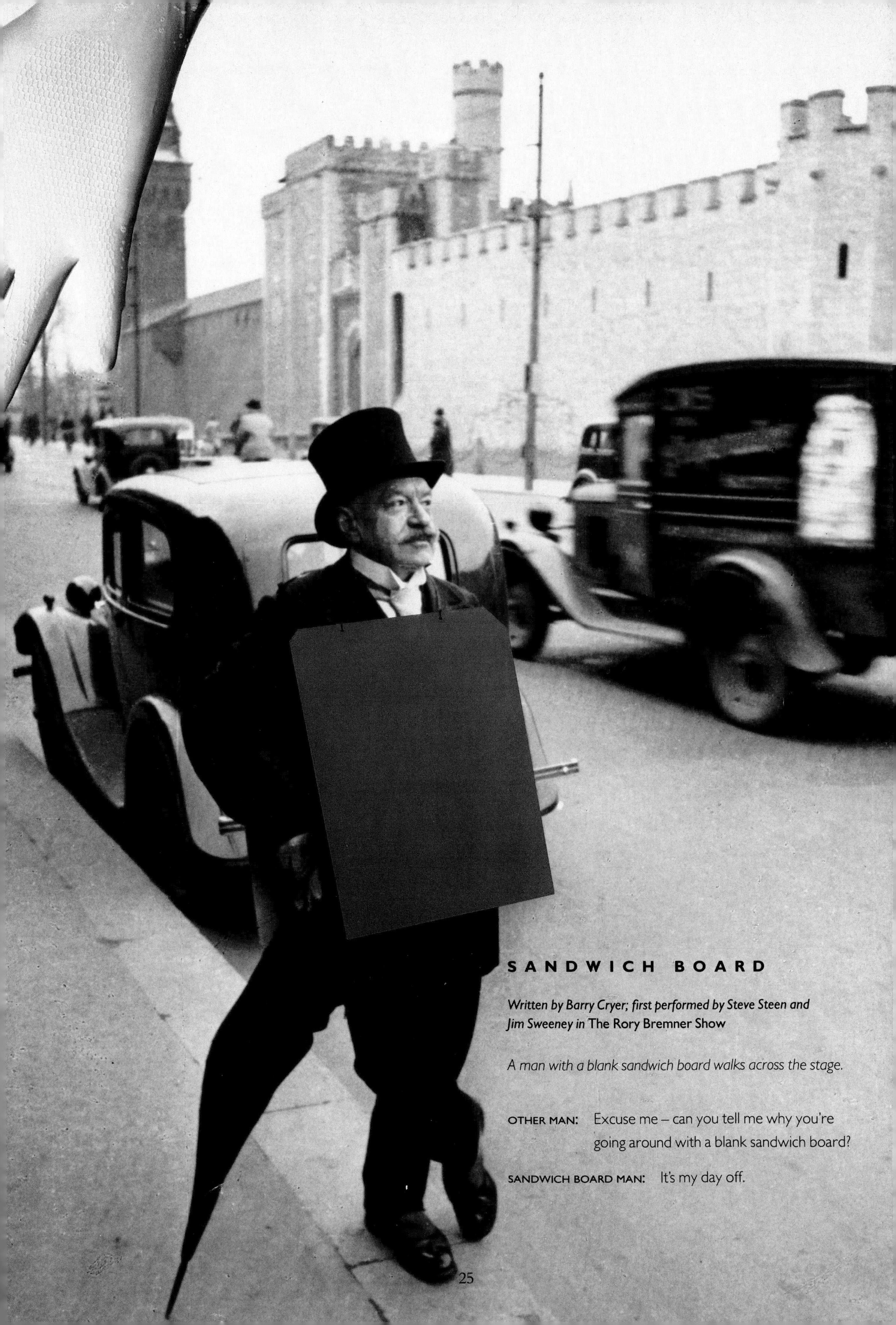

SANDWICH BOARD

Written by Barry Cryer; first performed by Steve Steen and Jim Sweeney in The Rory Bremner Show

A man with a blank sandwich board walks across the stage.

OTHER MAN: Excuse me – can you tell me why you're going around with a blank sandwich board?

SANDWICH BOARD MAN: It's my day off.

BUILDING SITE

***Written by Paul Smith and Terry Kyan; first performed by Mel Smith and Griff Rhys Jones in* The Two Ronnies, *sorry,* Alas Smith and Jones**

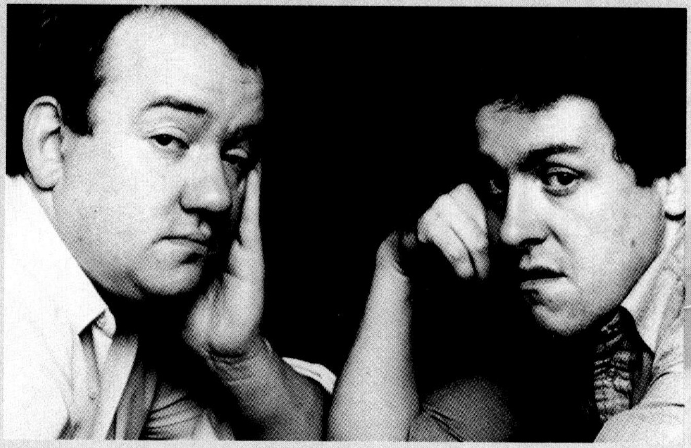

Man stands gazing out of window with preoccupied expression. He is smartly dressed and has a briefcase under his arm. On the wall behind there is a large map of the English and French coasts, a diagram of the Channel Tunnel and various cross-sectional drawings. There is a knock at the door. A man enters – he is dressed in construction suit and helmet, and has a cigarette dangling from his mouth.

MANAGER: Good morning, Stubbs.

FOREMAN: Morning, sir.

MANAGER: How are we today?

FOREMAN: Fine, fine.

MANAGER: That's good. Look, I won't beat about the bush – when we started this project a few years ago, the general idea was that we'd start tunnelling from our side, the French from theirs, and a few years later we'd both meet in the middle. (*Stands by wall chart, pointing*) Yesterday the French announced that they've completed their section (*points to halfway mark in Channel*), twin tunnels drilled, railway tracks laid, service shaft down the middle, band in position and dead on time. As for us, our position to date seems to be (*pointing at Kent*) precisely two miles from the Ashford Bypass. (*Pause.*)
What exactly seems to be holding us up?

FOREMAN: We're still waiting for a skip.

MANAGER: A skip…

FOREMAN: And, besides, the men are finishing another job at the moment.

MANAGER: Another job?

FOREMAN: Mrs Willoughby's in Dollis Hill.

MANAGER: Do you realize this is the single most important engineering project this century?

FOREMAN: I wouldn't say that – it's just a kitchen extension.

MANAGER: (*Banging fist on diagram*) I'm talking about *this*. We've paid you and your men two and a half billion pounds.

FOREMAN: Well, there's part of your hold-up, isn't it? It's probably taken them all this time to count the money. They always like to check it before they knock off at the weekend.

MANAGER: (*Sits down at desk.*) I should have seen the warning signs from the start – when the tenders came in. (*Holds up impressive batch of carefully bound documents.*) McAlpine's tender … (*Puts down and picks up series of shiny, spirally bound folders.*) Costain International's … (*Produces massive roll of computer print-out and very glossy-looking portfolio.*) Cementation Construction's … and yours … (*Holds up single piece of scrap paper.*) 'To build Channel Tunnel – labour and materials, including RSJ and damp course – £2,500,000,000 plus VAT. Please leave spare set of keys.'

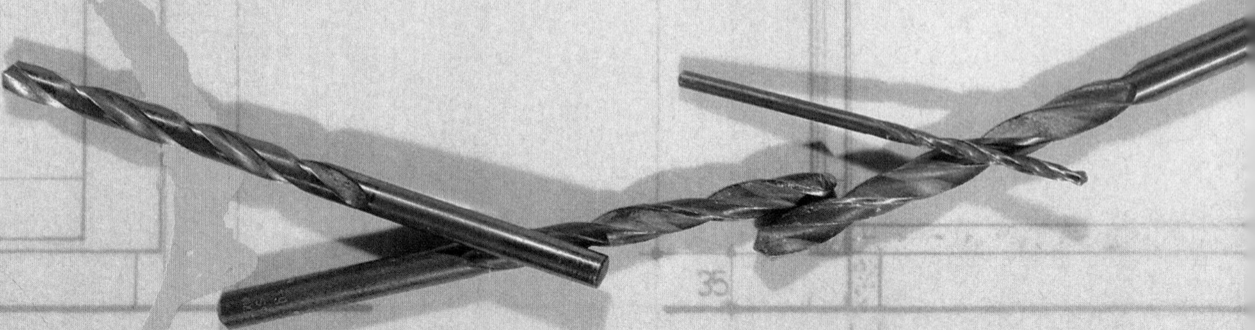

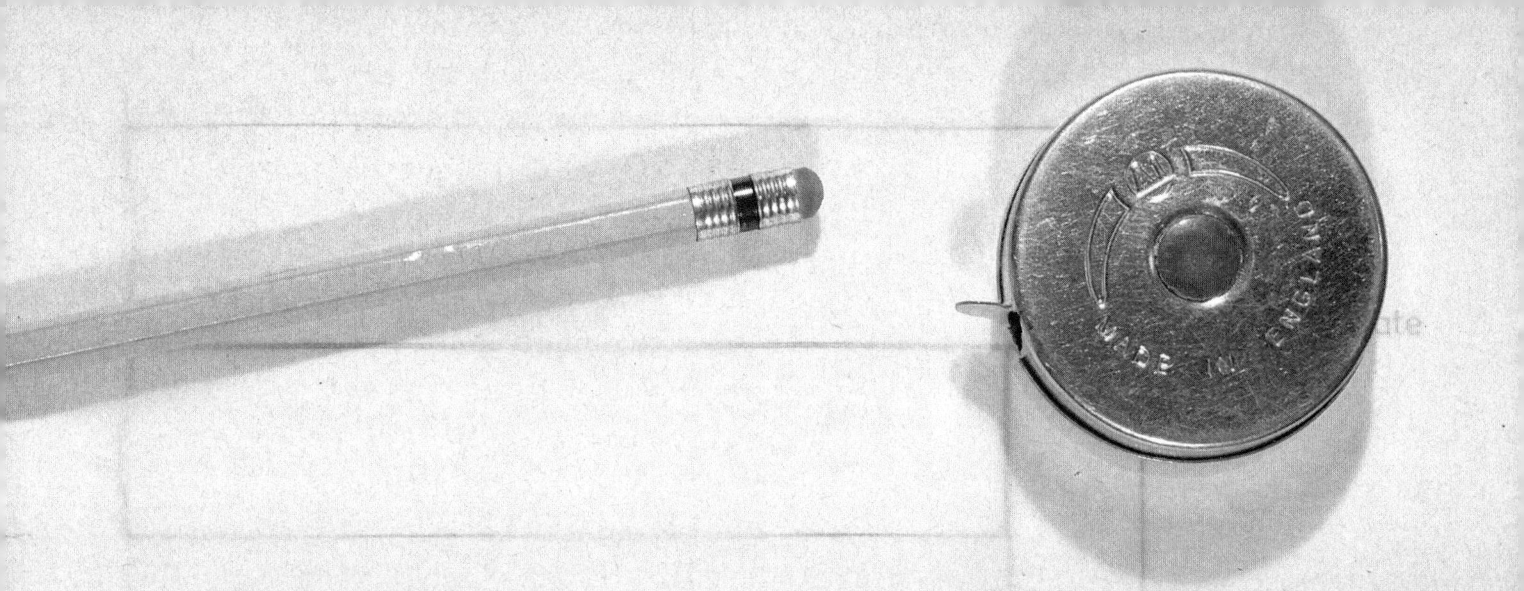

FOREMAN: (*Peering*) Yes, that's ours.

MANAGER: Look, Stubbs, we chose you because we were under the impression that your firm had an impressive track record of major international construction achievements. (*Looking at piece of paper*) I mean, you say here you got the contract for the Aswan Dam…

FOREMAN: Yes, but then the wife had to go in for a hip operation and we had to pull out.

MANAGER: …and the Thames Barrier.

FOREMAN: Yeah – we were all set, rarin' to go, and then the van packed up.

MANAGER: …and what about the World Trade Center in New York? I suppose we had to 'pull out' of that as well?

FOREMAN: Actually (*in confiding tones*) we didn't get the contract for that. They thought we were too expensive. Still, if they want to cut corners, that's their business.

MANAGER: You haven't built anything, have you?

FOREMAN: Oh, yes, we have – we refurbished the whole of the Taj Mahal.

MANAGER: The Taj Mahal?

FOREMAN: It *was* the Taj Mahal – it's now called the Laughing Poppadam. You know, in Cricklewood Broadway.

MANAGER: I don't care where it is. I'm giving you one last chance. Get your men out there now with their drilling equipment – I want three tunnels 50 metres wide, 200 metres below sea-level and 35 miles in length to link up with the French by Friday night at the latest, or else. Just get on with it.

FOREMAN: (*Making to go*) Thirty-five miles?

MANAGER: That's right.

FOREMAN: I think I lent my extension lead out to someone – you wouldn't happen to have…

MANAGER: Get out!!
(*Exit* FOREMAN *– he then has sudden thought.*)
Oh, and Stubbs…
(*Door opens again,* FOREMAN *puts his head round.*)
You couldn't have a look at my wife's patio sometime this weekend, could you?

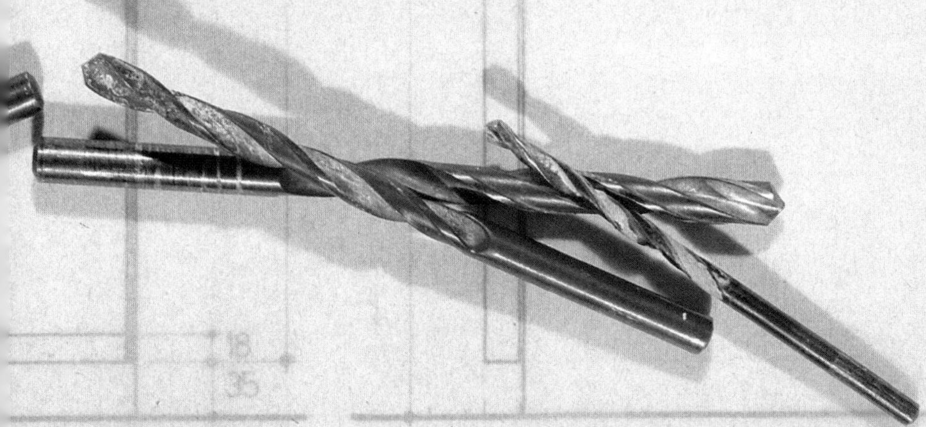

NEWSREADER

Written by Rob Grant and Doug Naylor; first performed on Son of Cliché *by Chris Barrie*

A very formal NEWSREADER *is ready to go. He/She has no idea what is in store.*

NEWSREADER

Good evening. Here is the news. Princess Anne has arrived in Swaziland today, on the first leg of her South African tour. Hello, my name is Donald. But the trip has caused a controversy because the Princess stopped off at Johannesburg airport on her way there.

I'm the man who types out the news-sheets. This move is seen by some anti-apartheid groups as a sign of implicit approval. This is my last day at the BBC.

Tory MP John Thirwell launched a shock attack on the government tonight over its handling of public sector pay rises.

And quite frankly, I don't give a monkey's any more.

He accused them of being arrogant and heartless over the issue.

My leaving party went on all afternoon, and quite honestly, I'm rat-arsed.

Mr Thirwell pointed out that civil service pay had fallen in relation to the private sector by more than 15 per cent.

I'm leaving, I'm smashed, and I feel bloody great.

In Rome today, the Pope got married.

Yes – I can make you say anything.

After a brief ceremony in a registry office, the Pope and his bride, Freddie Laker, flew off for their honeymoon to the small island of Belgium in the Dutch East Indies.

The City, and the Financial Times Index rose today, then fell off its chair and had a fight with a pig. A spokesman said: 'Would you like to buy some of my spokes?'

And finally, on a lighter note, fourteen people were massacred today in Kent by a man with a flamethrower. A relative of one of the deceased said: 'We're all jolly glad.'

That's it, next news at Christmas.

Till then, good heavens.

KAMIKAZE

*Written by Douglas Adams and Chris Keightley; first performed
in* A Kick in the Stalls, *Cambridge Footlights, 1976*

*A bunch of Japanese in plain military uniform – all with headbands.
A* COMMANDER *enters.*

ALL: Hai!

COMMANDER: Hai! You all know the purpose of this mission?

ALL: To die for the Emperor!

COMMANDER: Your task?

ALL: To seek out and destroy the American fleet in the Pacific!

COMMANDER: It is…?

ALL: A kamikaze mission!

COMMANDER: This will include the deaths of each and every one of you.

ALL: (*A little disconsolate.*) Ah so!
(*The* COMMANDER *rounds on one slightly shifty-looking character.*)

COMMANDER: Including you.

YAMAMOTO: Me, sir?

COMMANDER: Yes, you sir – you are a kamikaze pilot. What are you?

YAMAMOTO: A kamikaze pilot, sir!!

COMMANDER: And how many missions have you flown?

YAMAMOTO: Nineteen, sir.

COMMANDER: Nineteen suicide missions.

YAMAMOTO: That's right, sir. I pride myself on being the longest-serving suicide pilot in the Japanese Airforce.

COMMANDER: I'm sorry, Yamamoto, but can you not see there is a slight contradiction here?

YAMAMOTO: In what way?

COMMANDER: Well, suicide pilots are meant to commit suicide.

YAMAMOTO: That's right, sir. The problem is that in my case things just keep going wrong.

COMMANDER: Let me look at your card. First mission, 1944, January.

YAMAMOTO: That's right, sir.

COMMANDER: 'Turned back with tickly throat.'

YAMAMOTO: That's right. I wasn't going to die for my Emperor when I wasn't at the peak of my fitness.

COMMANDER: Second mission. 'Suspected toothache – return home.'

YAMAMOTO: That's right, sir. And as you can see, I was right.

COMMANDER: Third mission. 'Severe toothache – return home.'

YAMAMOTO: That's right, sir! Then I was all ready to go, when I started having trouble with my headband.

COMMANDER: So I see. Mission six. 'Headband too tight – came back with headache.'

YAMAMOTO: That's right, sir.

COMMANDER: Mission seven. 'Forgot headband.'
(*YAMAMOTO shrugs shoulders.*)
Mission eight. 'New headband slips over eyes.'

YAMAMOTO: That's right, sir.

COMMANDER: Then a new problem arises: Mission nine. 'Couldn't find target.' – Mission ten – 'Couldn't find target.' Then it's 'couldn't find target' – 'couldn't find target' – 'vertigo' – 'held up at traffic lights' – 'couldn't find target', 'couldn't find target' and 'couldn't find target'. You do know what we're looking for, don't you?

YAMAMOTO: Uhm...

COMMANDER: A-meri...

YAMAMOTO: A-meri... A Merry Christmas and a Happy New Year!

COMMANDER: American aircraft carriers.

YAMAMOTO: American aircraft carr–

COMMANDER: Yes, look – where exactly have you been looking for these aircraft carriers? I can't help noticing you seemed to have more or less totally ignored the area of the sea.

YAMAMOTO: I think you're being very unfair, sir – I've flown over the sea lots of times, and in fact once I even attacked an aircraft carrier.

COMMANDER: Ah yes – Mission eleven – let's have a look at that, shall we? Took off 0400 hrs.

YAMAMOTO: Good start.

COMMANDER: Climbed to a height of 4,000 feet and proceeded to the target area. 0430 – sighted target. Went into a power dive and successfully ... landed on the target.

YAMAMOTO: That's right, sir – I was just about to do it when I was taken short, so I just stopped off for a quick widdle. Unfortunately, by the time I was ready to start again, the element of surprise had gone. But I intend to put that all right today, sir.

COMMANDER: And commit suicide?

YAMAMOTO: Absolutely. That is my duty and that I will do.

COMMANDER: Very well. Goodbye to you all, and God save the Emperor.

ALL: God save the Emperor!!!

COMMANDER: Dismissed.
(*Pause as the COMMANDER leaves.*)

YAMAMOTO: (*Casually, to one of his comrades*) Look, you haven't got anything for diarrhoea, have you? My tummy's feeling just a little jippy...

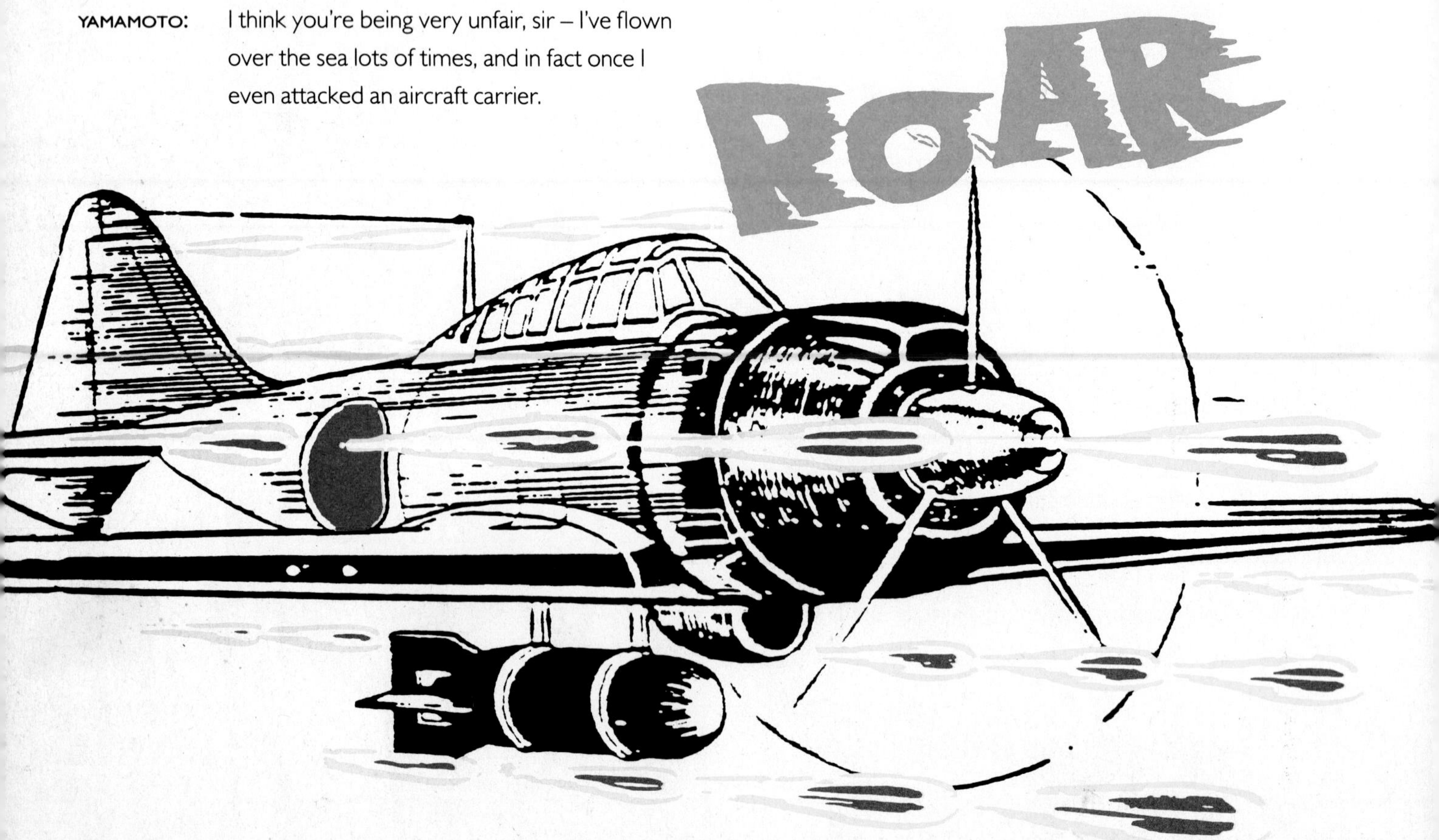
ROAR

HOLIDAY QUICKIE

Written by Ian Brown and James Hendry; performed in Dial M for Pizza *by Brenda Blethyn and Robert Bathurst*

Car interior.

SHE: Did you remember to cancel the papers?

HE: Yes.

SHE: And the milk?

HE: Yes.

SHE: Did you turn off the gas?

HE: Yes. And the electricity.

SHE: Good. (*Beat.*) That'll teach Grandma to forget my birthday.

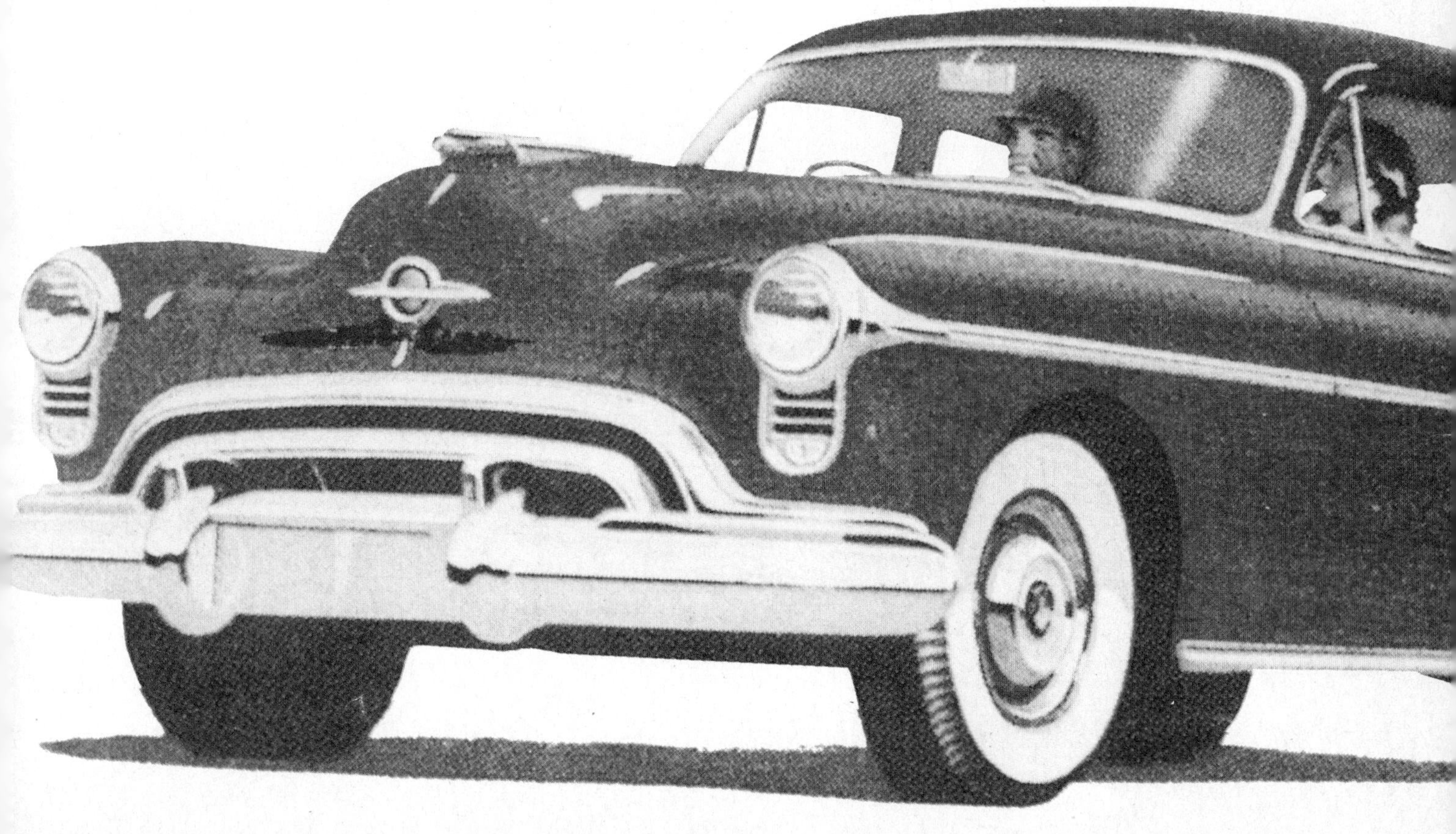

I'VE NEVER MET A NICE SOUTH AFRICAN

Lyrics by John Lloyd, music by Peter Brewis; first performed in Spitting Image *by lots of puppets*

To be performed by one pleasant singer, and a chorus of totally vile khaki-clothed South Africans, who can't even be bothered to make their bits rhyme.

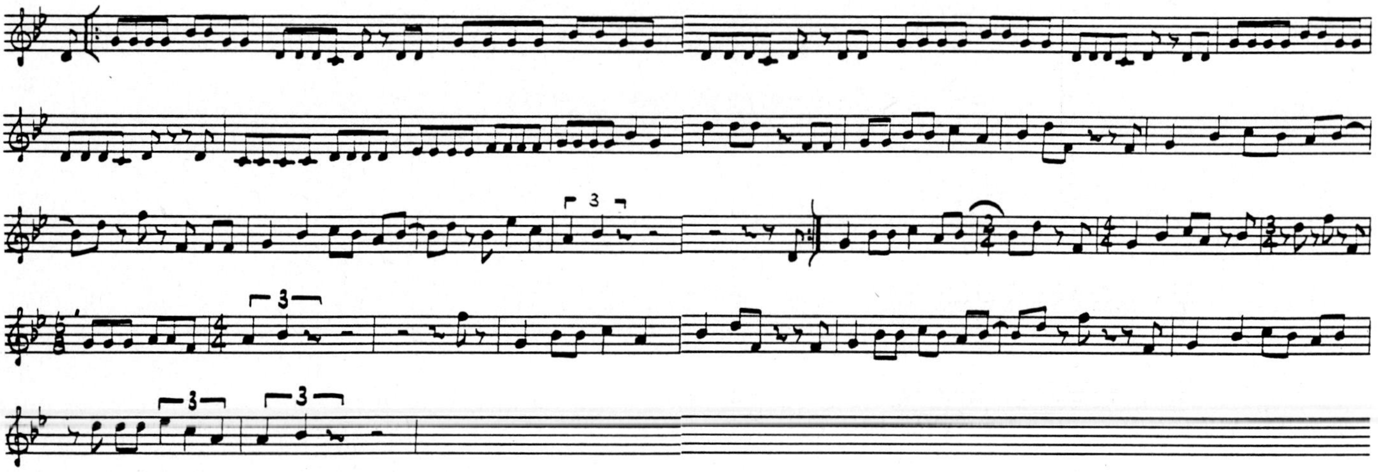

SINGER
I've travelled this world of ours from Barnsley to Peru
I've had sunstroke in the Arctic and a swim in Timbuktu
I've seen unicorns in Burma and a yeti in Nepal
And I've danced with 10-foot Pygmies in a Montezuma hall
I've met the Kings of China and the working Yorkshire miner
But I've never met a nice South African!

CHORUS
No, he's never met a nice South African
And that's not bloody surprising, man
Cos we're a bunch of arrogant bastards
Who hate black people.

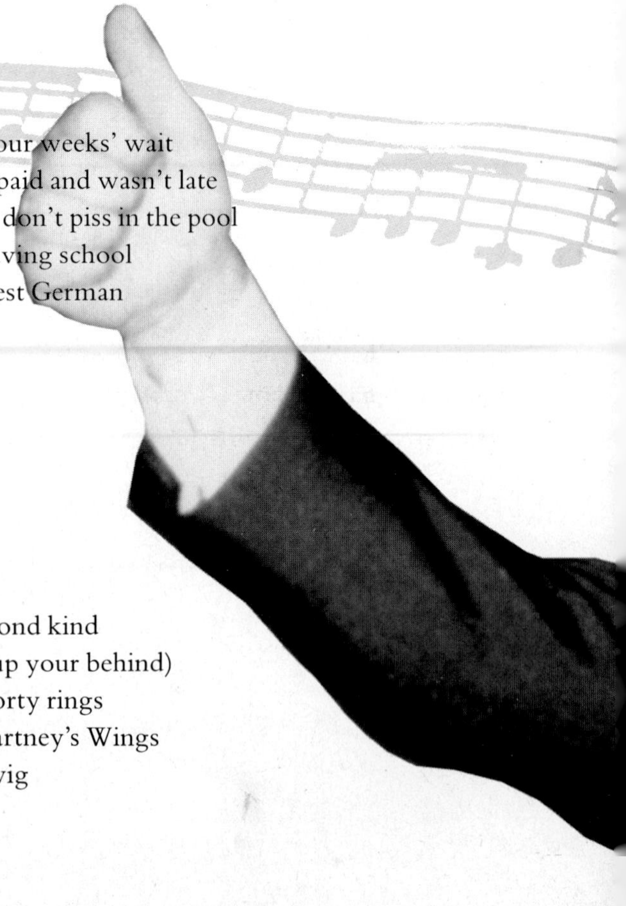

SINGER
I once got served in Woolies after less than four weeks' wait
I had lunch with Rowan Atkinson when he paid and wasn't late
I know a public swimming bath where they don't piss in the pool
I know a guy who got a job straight after leaving school
I've met a normal merman and a fairly modest German
But I've never met a nice South African.

CHORUS
No, he's never met a nice South African!
And that's not bloody surprising, man
Cos we're a bunch of terrorist murderers
Who smell like baboons.

SINGER
I've had a close encounter of the twenty-second kind
(That's when an alien spaceship disappears up your behind)
I've got Directory Inquiries after less than forty rings
I've even heard a decent song by Paul McCartney's Wings
I've seen a flying pig in a quite convincing wig
But I've never met a nice South African.

CHORUS
No, he's never met a nice South African!
And that's not bloody surprising, man
Cos we're a bunch of ignorant loudmouths
With no sense of humour.

SINGER
I've met the Loch Ness monster and he looks like Fred Astaire
At the BBC in London he's the chief commissionaire
I know a place in Glasgow where there are no daffodillies
I've met a man in Katmandu who claimed to have two willies
I've had a nice pot noodle but I've never had a poodle
And I've never met a nice South African.

CHORUS
No, he's never met a nice South African!
And that's not bloody surprising, man
We've never met one either
Except for Breyten Breytenbach
And he's emigrated to Paris.
Yes, he's quite a nice South African
And he's hardly ever killed anyone
And he's not smelly at all
That's why we put him in prison.

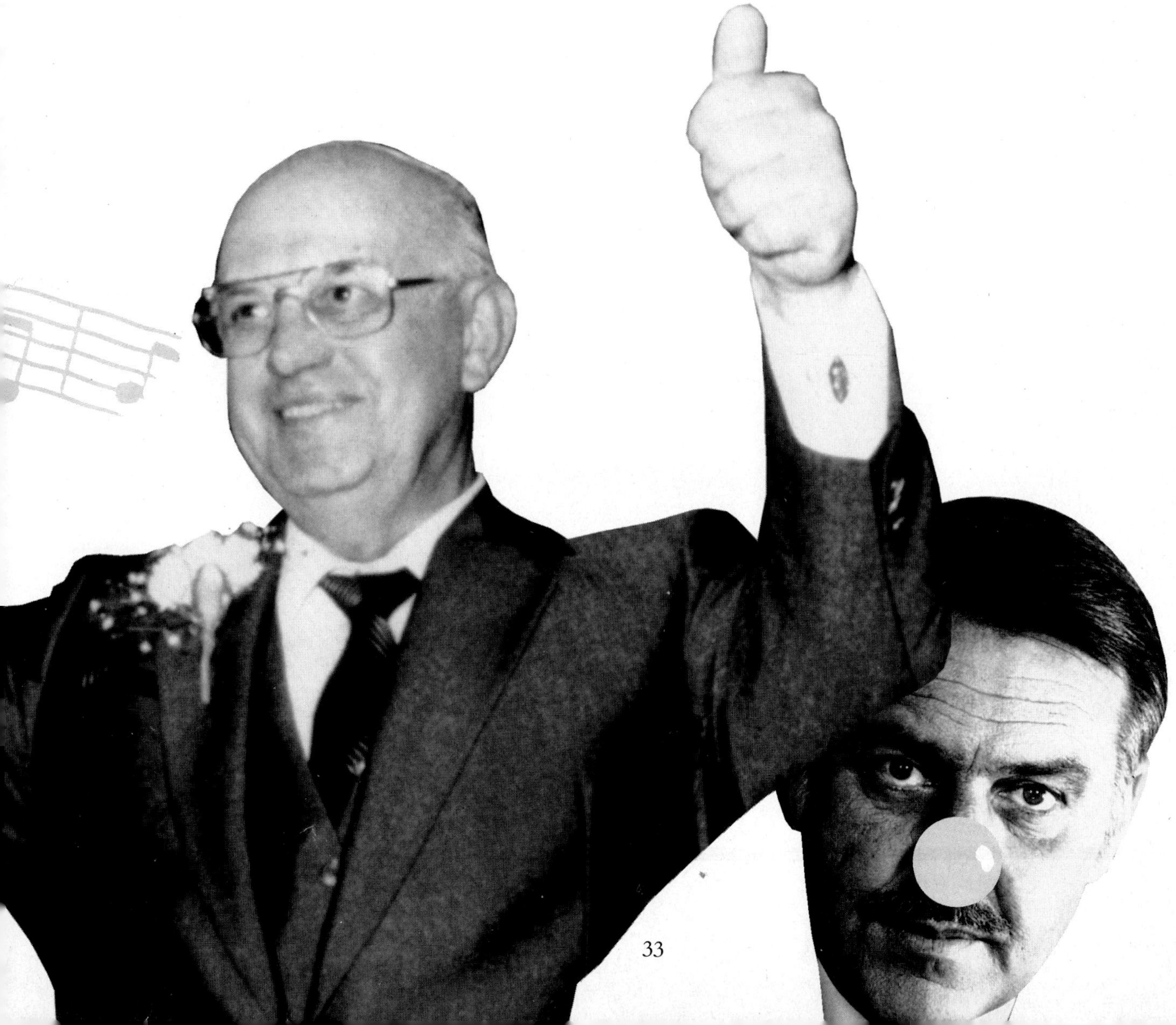

HENDON

Written by Michael Palin and Terry Jones; first performed in **Frost over Christmas** *by Ronnie Corbett and John Cleese*

A party, JOHN *and* RONNIE *stand with glasses.* RONNIE *is chatty and* JOHN *pleasantly tolerant if possible.*

RONNIE: What do you do?

JOHN: I'm the world's leading authority on Impressionist painting.

RONNIE: Oh, yes? I'm an accountant … chartered accountant. (*Pause.*)
Where do you … er … live?

JOHN: I live in a converted monastery in the Outer Hebrides.

RONNIE: Really? How interesting… I live in Hendon. (*Pause.*)
Is your wife here tonight?

JOHN: No … she's in Vietnam … fighting.

RONNIE: How fascinating… Do you know Hendon at all?

JOHN: I passed through it once … when I was being kidnapped by Russian agents.

RONNIE: Really? Well, I never! Where were they taking you?

JOHN: Oh, they had a frigate waiting for me in the Thames estuary.

RONNIE: (*Excitedly*) Really! Then you must have gone down Ulverston Road! Past our house! D'you remember – just after the baths?

JOHN: Well, I wouldn't know – they'd drugged me pretty heavily with hypertalcin metrathecane.

RONNIE: Good heavens … and what does that do?

JOHN: It paralyses the memory.

RONNIE: Does it affect your eyesight?

JOHN: Oh, yes. You're totally unconscious.

RONNIE: Oh … then you probably didn't see our house. It's number 37 on the corner… You must drop in sometime.

JOHN: Well, that's very kind of you, but I'm afraid I won't be able to. I'm going to prison.

RONNIE: Really? Not anywhere in Hendon, I suppose?

JOHN: No, it's in Guatemala. It's just a currency offence I committed when I was over there investigating a man-eating cactus they'd discovered.

RONNIE: You went all the way to Guatemala to see cactuses?

JOHN: Yes. I had some pretty horrible adventures. I was nearly trampled to death by a herd of rogue buffaloes.

RONNIE: Just looking for cactuses. If only I'd known … they've just had a display of them at Hendon Central Library. (*Pause.*)
You know it's really fascinating talking to you, because it's not everyone that's interested in Hendon.

JOHN: I'll show you something that'll interest you. (JOHN *pulls out a huge prayer mat or shawl.*)
Have you seen one of these before?

RONNIE: No, no, I haven't.

JOHN: D'you know what it is?

RONNIE: (*Quite caught up by now*) No.

JOHN: It's a Tibetan prayer shawl. Do you know how I got it?

RONNIE: (*Engrossed*) No, I don't.

JOHN: It was given to me by the chief slave-girl of the High Commander of the Tibetan Army. Oh! She was a beauty – her hair was black as a raven's wings, and one evening at the feast of Ramsit Asi, the all-powerful God of Light, when 10,000 bullocks are sacrificed on the mountain, she crept into my room, filling it with a delicious fragrance, and she cast aside her tribal robe and her black hair spilled over her delicate pale skin … as she climbed into my bed…

RONNIE: Really?

JOHN: Mmmmmmm … *She* came from Hendon.

FATAL BEATINGS

Written by Ben Elton and Richard Curtis; first performed by Rowan Atkinson and Angus Deayton in The New Review

Schoolboy music. A formal-looking tweedy gentleman with an Edinburgh accent sits at a desk. There is a knock on the door.

HEADMASTER: Come in!!!

(A tidy, sports-jacketed man enters. MR PERKINS.)

PERKINS: Ah, good morning, Headmaster.

HEADMASTER: Ah, Mr Perkins. It was good of you to come in. I realize that you're a busy man, but I didn't feel that we could discuss this matter over the electric telephone.

PERKINS: No, absolutely, Headmaster. I mean if Tommy's in some sort of trouble I'd like to nip it in the bud.

HEADMASTER: Well, quite frankly, Mr Perkins, Tommy is in trouble. Recently his behaviour has left a great deal to be desired.

PERKINS: Oh, dear me.

HEADMASTER: Yes, he takes no interest in school life whatsoever, he refuses to muck in on the sports field and it's weeks since any master received any written work from him.

PERKINS: Dear me.

HEADMASTER: Quite frankly, Mr Perkins, if he wasn't dead, I'd have him expelled.

PERKINS: I beg your pardon.

HEADMASTER: Yes, expelled. If I wasn't making allowances for the fact that your son is dead he'd be out on his ear.

PERKINS: Tommy's dead?

HEADMASTER: Yes, he's lying upstairs in sick bay now, stiff as a board and bright green. And this is, I fear, typical of his current attitude. I have pleaded with him, and so has matron, and he will make no effort.

PERKINS: Tommy's dead!

HEADMASTER: Yes, that's what's so galling – he seems to have no sense of moderation – one moment he's flying around like a paper kite, the next he's completely immovable and beginning to smell.

PERKINS: How did he die?

HEADMASTER: Well, is that important?

PERKINS: Yes, I think so.

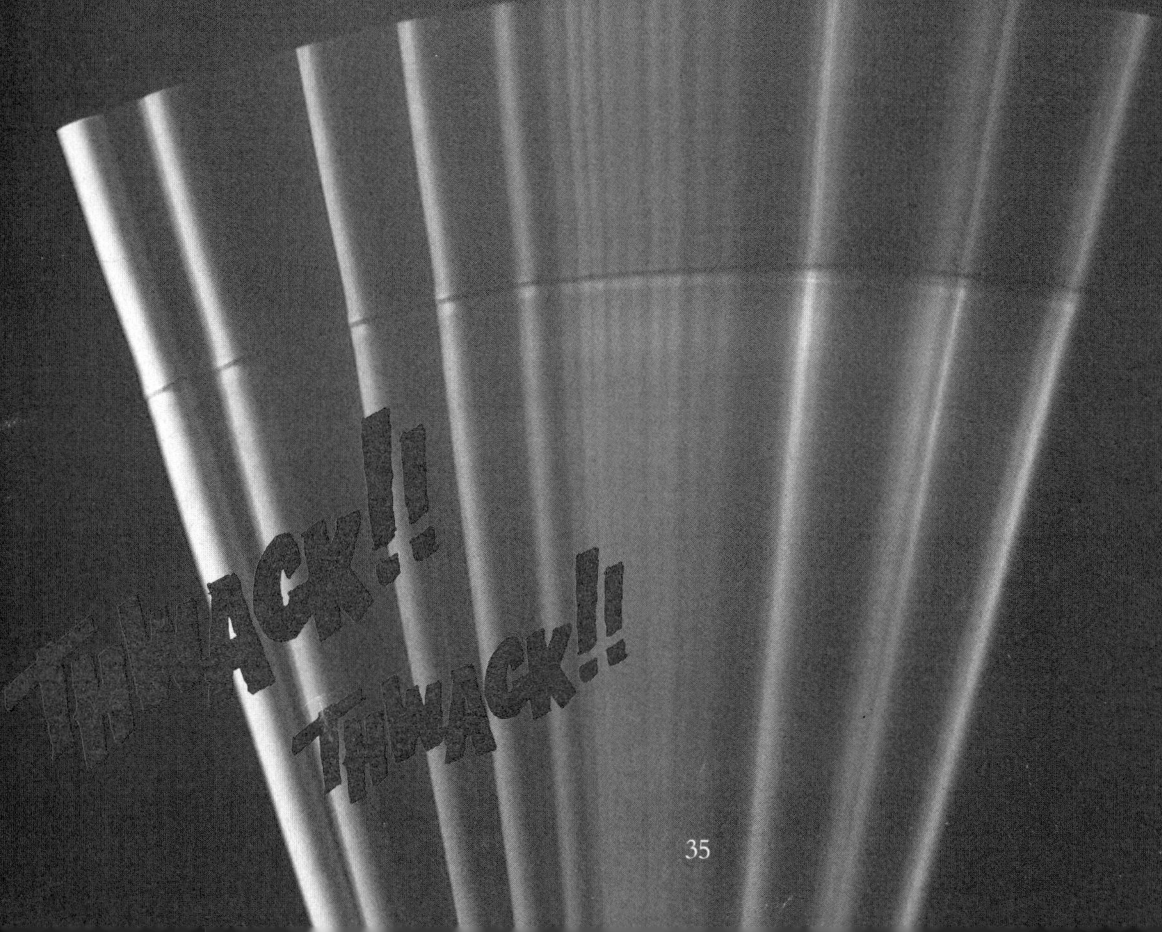
THWACK!!
THWACK!!

HEADMASTER: Well, it's all got to do with the library. You see we've had some trouble recently with boys taking library books without library cards. Your son was caught and I administered a beating, during which he died. But you'll be glad to know that the ringleader has been caught, so I don't think we'll have to worry about library discipline any more. You see the library-card system…

PERKINS: I'm sorry, you beat my son to death?

HEADMASTER: Yes, yes, so it would seem. Please, I'm not used to being interrupted. The library-card system was introduced…

PERKINS: Exactly what happened?

HEADMASTER: Well, apparently the boys were just slipping into the library and taking the books.

PERKINS: No, during the beating.

HEADMASTER: Oh, that, oh well, one moment he was bending over, and the next he was lying down.

PERKINS: Dead?

HEADMASTER: Deadish. Really, Mr Perkins, I'm starting to find this morbid fascination of yours with your son's death slightly disturbing. What we're talking about here is your son's attitude, and quite frankly I'm beginning to see where he gets it from.

PERKINS: At least I never beat him to death.

HEADMASTER: No, that was quite obvious to me from the day he arrived here, and I wondered then, and I wonder now, Mr Perkins, whether he might not have turned out a very different lad indeed if you had administered a few fatal beatings earlier on.

PERKINS: Are you completely mad?

HEADMASTER: Yes, I'm absolutely furious. In order to accommodate the funeral we've had to cancel afternoon school on Wednesday. I'm sorry, I have to be going.

PERKINS: This is preposterous.

HEADMASTER: Yes, it is. Or rather it would be – if it were true.

PERKINS: What?

HEADMASTER: I've been joking, Mr Perkins. Forgive me, it's my strange Hibernian sense of humour. I've been having you on.

PERKINS: Oh. Thank God for that.

HEADMASTER: I wouldn't cancel afternoon school to bury that little twerp.

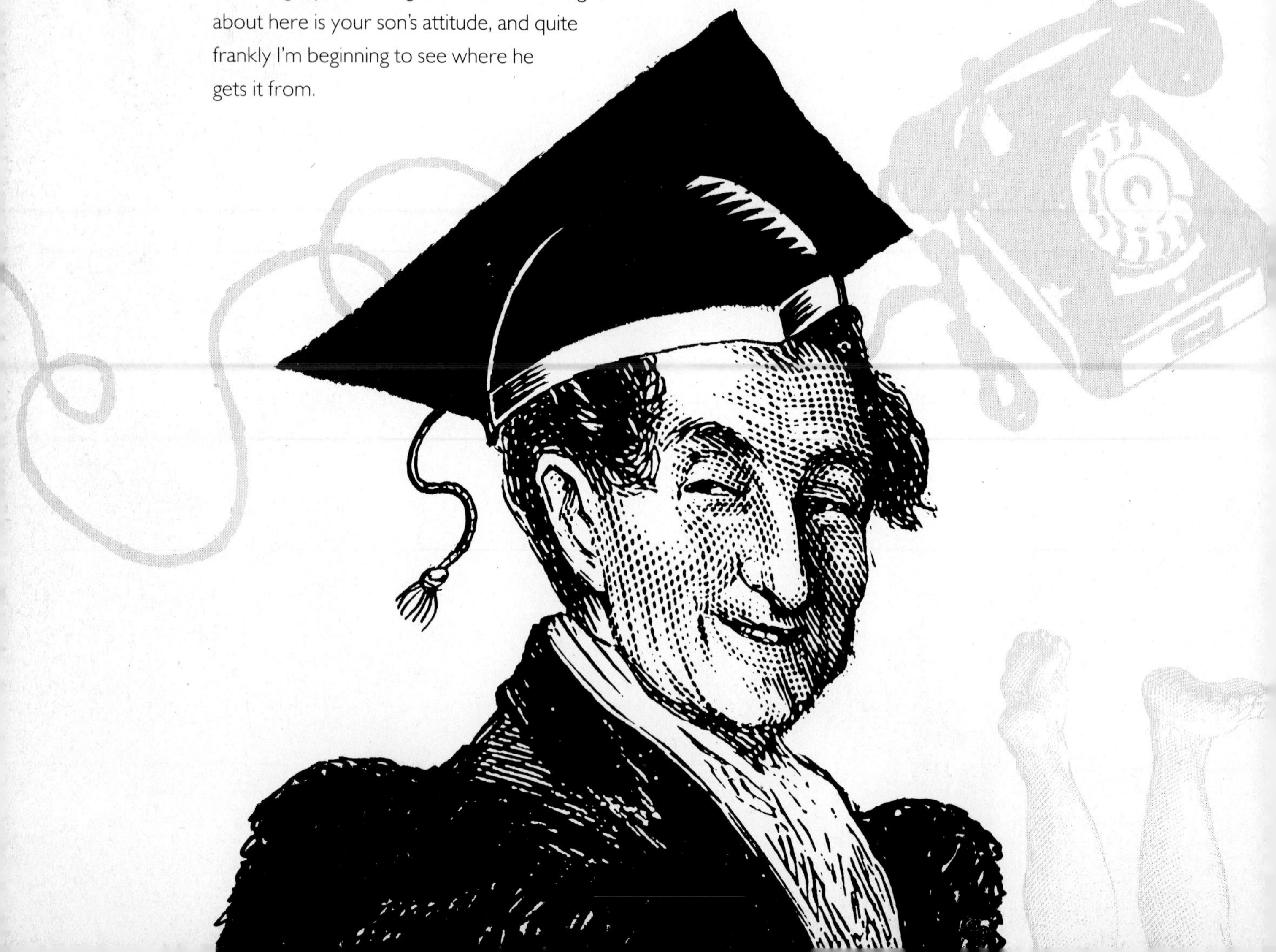

GIVING NOTES

Written by Victoria Wood; first performed by Julie Walters

ALMA, *a middle-aged sprightly woman, addresses her amateur company after a rehearsal of* Hamlet. *She claps her hands.*

Right. Bit of hush please. Connie! Thank you. Now that was quite a good rehearsal; I was quite pleased. There were a few raised eyebrows when we let it slip the Piecrust Players were having a bash at Shakespeare but I think we're getting there. But I can't say this too often: it may be *Hamlet* but it's got to be Fun Fun Fun!

(*She consults her notes.*)

Now we're still very loose on lines. Where's Gertrude? I'm not so worried about you – if you 'dry' just give us a bit of business with the shower cap. But Barbara – you will have to buckle down. I mean, Ophelia's mad scene, 'There's rosemary, that's for remembrance' – it's no good just bunging a few herbs about and saying, 'Don't mind me, I'm a loony.' Yes? You see this is our marvellous bard, Barbara, you cannot paraphrase. It's not like Pinter where you can more or less say what you like as long as you leave enough gaps.

Right. Act One, Scene One, on the ramparts. Now I know the whist table is a bit wobbly, but until Stan works out how to adapt the Beanstalk it'll have to do. What's this? Atmosphere? Yes – now what did we work on, Philip? Yes, it's midnight, it's jolly cold. What do we do when it's cold? We go 'Brrr', and we do this (*slaps hands on arms*). Right, well, don't forget again, please. And cut the hot-water bottle, it's not working.

Where's my ghost of Hamlet's father? Oh yes, what went wrong tonight, Betty? He's on nights still, is he? OK. Well, it's not really on for you to play that particular part, Betty – you're already doing the Player Queen and the back legs of Hamlet's donkey. Well, we don't know he didn't have one, do we? Why waste a good cossy?

Hamlet – drop the Geordie, David, it's not coming over. Your characterization's reasonably good, David, but it's just far too gloomy. Fair enough, make him a little bit depressed at the beginning, but start lightening it from Scene Two, from the hokey-cokey onwards, I'd say. And perhaps the, er, 'Get thee to a nunnery' with Ophelia – perhaps give a little wink to the audience, or something, because he's really just having her on, isn't he, we decided...

37

Polonius, try and show the age of the man in your voice and in your bearing, rather than waving the bus-pass. I think you'll find it easier when we get the walking frame. Is that coming, Connie? OK.

The players' scene: did any of you feel it had stretched a bit too . . . ? Yes. I think we'll go back to the tumbling on the entrance, rather than the extract from *Barnum*. You see, we're running at six hours twenty now, and if we're going to put those soliloquies back in . . .

Gravediggers? Oh yes, gravediggers. The problem here is that Shakespeare hasn't given us a lot to play with – I feel we're a little short on laughs, so, Harold, you do your dribbling, and Arthur, just put in anything you can remember from the Ayckbourn, yes?

The mad scene: apart from lines, much better, Barbara – I can tell you're getting more used to the straitjacket. Oh – any news on the skull, Connie? I'm just thinking, if your little dog pulls through, we'll have to fall back on papier mâché. All right, Connie, as long as it's dead by the dress . . .

Oh yes, Hamlet, Act Three, Scene One, I think that cut works very well, 'To be or not to be', then Ophelia comes straight in, it moves it on, it's more pacy . . .

Act Five, Gertrude, late again. What? Well, is there no service wash? I'm sure Dame Edith wasn't forever nipping out to feed the dryer.

That's about it – oh yes, Rosencrantz and Guildenstern, you're not on long, make your mark. I don't think it's too gimmicky, the tandem. And a most important general note – make-up! Half of you looked as if you hadn't got any on! And Claudius – no moles again? (*Sighs*.) I bet Margaret Lockwood never left hers in the glove compartment.

That's it for tonight then; thank you. I shall expect you to be word-perfect by the next rehearsal. Have any of you realized what date we're up to? Yes, April the twenty-seventh! And when do we open? August! It's not long!

MASTERMIND

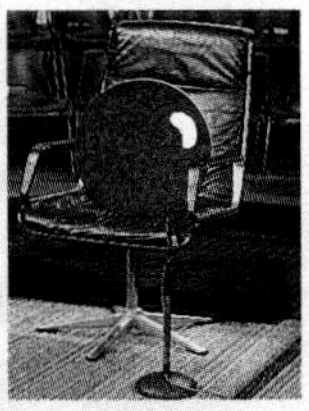

Written by David Renwick; first performed by Ronnie Barker and Ronnie Corbett in The Two Ronnies

The Mastermind *set.* CONTESTANT *is sitting in the big chair.* MAGNUS *fires the questions.*

MAGNUS: So on to our final contender. Your name, please.

CONTESTANT: Good evening.

MAGNUS: Thank you. In the first heat your chosen subject was Answering Questions Before They Were Asked. This time you have chosen to answer the question before last each time – is that correct?

CONTESTANT: Charlie Smithers.

MAGNUS: And your time starts now. What is palaeontology?

CONTESTANT: Yes, absolutely correct.

MAGNUS: Correct. What's the name of the directory that lists members of the peerage?

CONTESTANT: A study of old fossils.

MAGNUS: Correct. Who are David Owen and Sir Geoffrey Howe?

CONTESTANT: Burke's.

MAGNUS: Correct. What's the difference between a donkey and an ass?

CONTESTANT: One's a Social Democrat, the other's a member of the Cabinet.

MAGNUS: Correct. Complete the quotation, 'To be or not to be...'

CONTESTANT: They're both the same.

MAGNUS: Correct. What is Bernard Manning famous for?

CONTESTANT: 'That is the question.'

MAGNUS: Correct. Who is the present Archbishop of Canterbury?

CONTESTANT: He's a fat man who tells blue jokes.

MAGNUS: Correct. What do people kneel on in church?

CONTESTANT: The Most Reverend Robert Runcie.

MAGNUS: Correct. What do tarantulas prey on?

CONTESTANT: Hassocks.

MAGNUS: Correct. What would you use a ripcord to pull open.

CONTESTANT: Large flies.

MAGNUS: Correct. What did Marilyn Monroe always claim to wear in bed?

CONTESTANT: A parachute.

MAGNUS: Correct. What was the next new TV station to go on the air after Channel Four?

CONTESTANT: Chanel Number Five.

MAGNUS: Correct. What do we normally associate with Bedlam?

CONTESTANT: Breakfast television.

MAGNUS: Correct. What are jockstraps?

CONTESTANT: Nutcases.

MAGNUS: Correct. What would a jockey use a stirrup for?

CONTESTANT: An athletic support.

MAGNUS: Correct. Arthur Scargill is well known for what?

CONTESTANT: He puts his foot in it.

MAGNUS: Correct. Who was the famous clown who made millions laugh with his funny hair?

CONTESTANT: The leader of the mineworkers' union.

MAGNUS: Correct. What would a decorator use methylene chlorides to make?

CONTESTANT: Coco.

MAGNUS: Correct. What did Henri de Toulouse-Lautrec do?

CONTESTANT: Paint strippers.

MAGNUS: Correct. What is Dean Martin famous for?

CONTESTANT: Is he an artist?

MAGNUS: Yes – what kind of artist?

CONTESTANT: Er – pass.

MAGNUS: Yes, that's near enough. What make of vehicle is the standard London bus?

CONTESTANT: A singer.

MAGNUS: Correct. In 1892 Brandon Thomas wrote a famous long-running English farce – what is it?

CONTESTANT: British Leyland.

MAGNUS: Correct. Complete the following quotation about Shirley Williams: 'Her heart may be in the right place, but her...'

CONTESTANT: *Charley's Aunt.*

MAGNUS: Correct, and you have scored 22 and no passes!

Applause and play-out.

A BIT OF DIABOLISM

Written by Andy Hamilton; first performed in* The Million Pound Radio Show *by Harry Enfield, Andy Hamilton, Jaspar Jacob, Felicity Montagu and Nick Revell

Omen-*type music and an echoey, cave-like atmosphere.*

(If you've got a budget, try to introduce some kind of altar, and perhaps a threatening-looking polystyrene rock. Try and zap up the costumes a bit, too. But don't worry overmuch – these are not absolutely grade-A satanists.)

HIGH PRIEST: Worshippers of Satan, the hour has come to summon our master and unleash the powers of Hell.

ALL: (*Led by* HIGH PRIEST) O Prince of Darkness, the Promised One, the Divine Beast, Lord of Supreme Evil, we who follow you drink to thy power, drink to thy glory, in blood! (*A thunderclap.*)
The blood of this virgin!!!

HIGH PRIEST: Where's the virgin?

DIABOLIST 1: Sorry?

HIGH PRIEST: The virgin. Where's the virgin? Well, who was responsible for the sacrifice?

DIABOLIST 2: He was.

DIABOLIST 1: It was you.

DIABOLIST 2: You're the virgin monitor.

DIABOLIST 1: Look, the last thing I said to you on Friday after the whist drive was, don't forget, you're bringing the virgin.

(*The row continues.*)

HIGH PRIEST: Silence!! Well, that's just great, isn't it? No virgin's blood to drink. None of you lot are virgins, I suppose?

DIABOLIST 1: 'Fraid not, no.

DIABOLIST 2: Nope, sorry.

HIGH PRIEST: Thought not. Anyone done it … less than twenty times…?

ALL: 'Fraid not … *etc.*

HIGH PRIEST: Forty times?

ALL: Nope, sorry … *etc.*

WOMAN DIABOLIST: I don't enjoy it, does that count?

HIGH PRIEST: Afraid not, no … (*Sighs.*)

DIABOLIST 2: Look, can't we just skip the virgin-sacrificing and go on to the group sex…?

(*General agreement.*)

HIGH PRIEST: There *has* to be a sacrifice first.

WOMAN DIABOLIST: Well, we could sacrifice a living creature … like a goat.

HIGH PRIEST: Well, stab me, I seem to have come out without my goat, what do you know?

DIABOLIST 2: Any living creature would do, wouldn't it?

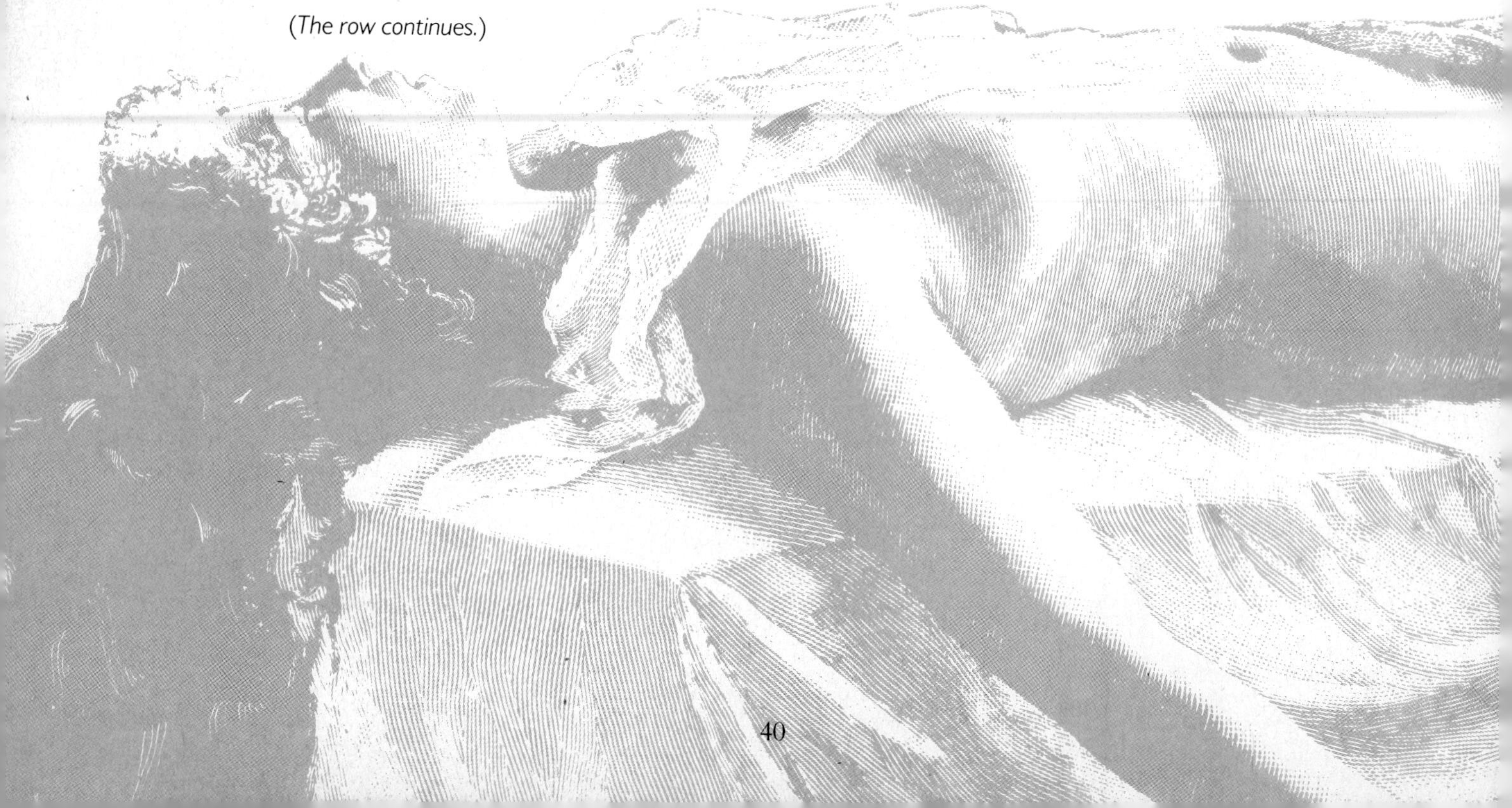

HIGH PRIEST: (*Invoking*) O Prince of Darkness, we drink to thy power, we drink to thy omnipotent glory in the blood of this earwig – no, I'm sorry, it feels silly, besides, it's too small to get the pentangle round its neck.

DIABOLIST 2: Let's just get on to the group sex.

HIGH PRIEST: Will you shut up about group sex! This is a powerful demonic ritual, not an office party. To invoke the powers of darkness we must sacrifice something. Something symbolic. Something potent.

DIABOLIST 1: Well, can we get a move on, only I go on duty in an hour.

HIGH PRIEST: On duty?

DIABOLIST 1: Yeh, with the wheel-clamping unit. Here, get your hands off me ... *etc.*

HIGH PRIEST: (*Declaiming triumphantly*) We thank you, O Prince of Darkness, for sending us this sacrifice and we drink to thy power in the blood of this ... git.

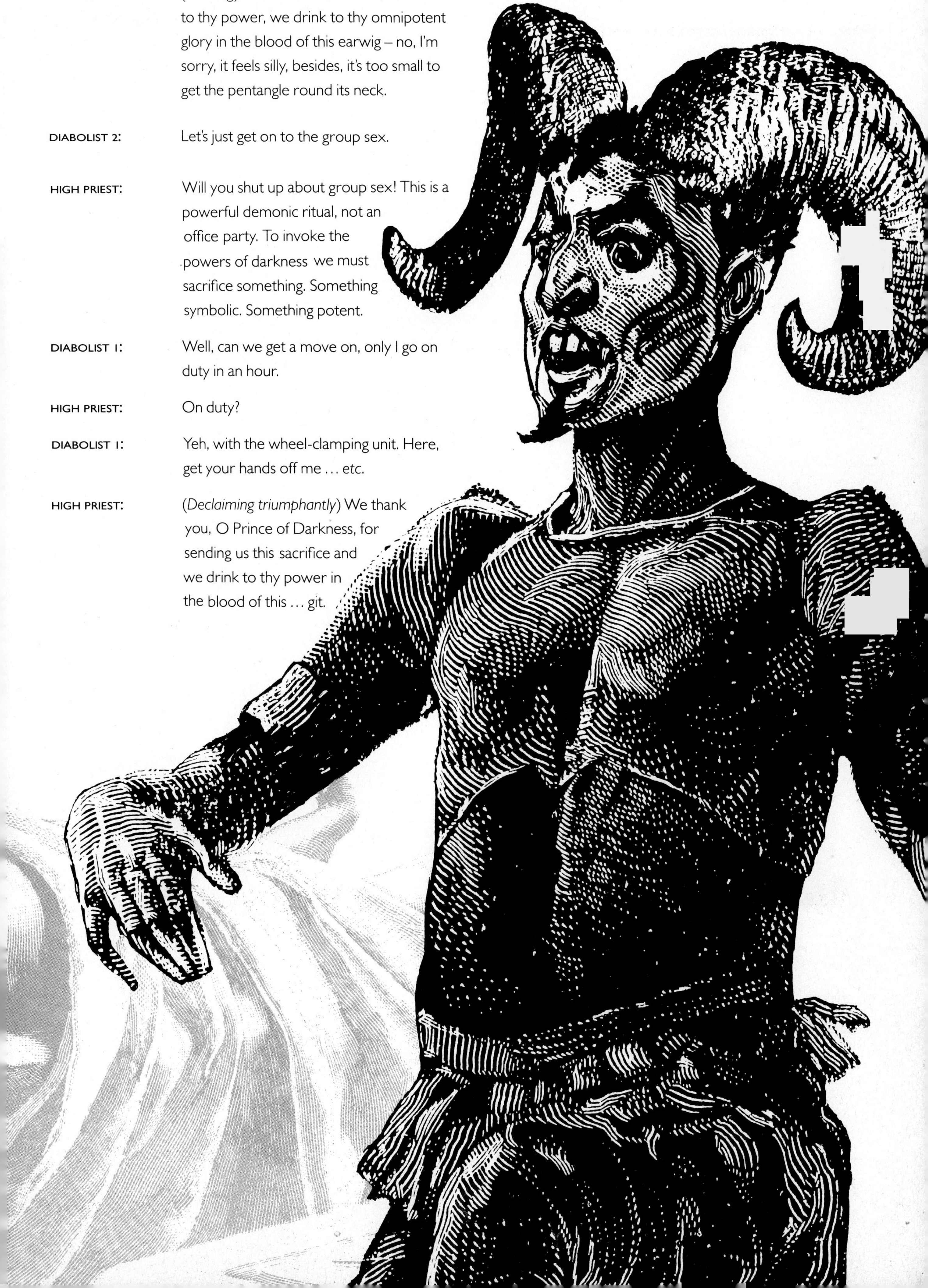

STAND-UP COMIC

Written, conceived and performed by Rowan Atkinson

Enter STRANGE LITTLE MAN *into spotlight. He speaks very deliberately.*

STRANGE-LOOKING MAN: And now, to entertain you during the interval . . . a stand-up comic.

(He places in the spotlight a copy of Beano *comic, reinforced with cardboard. It stands up in the spotlight until the house-lights come up.)*

IT IS NOW TIME FOR

THE INTERVAL

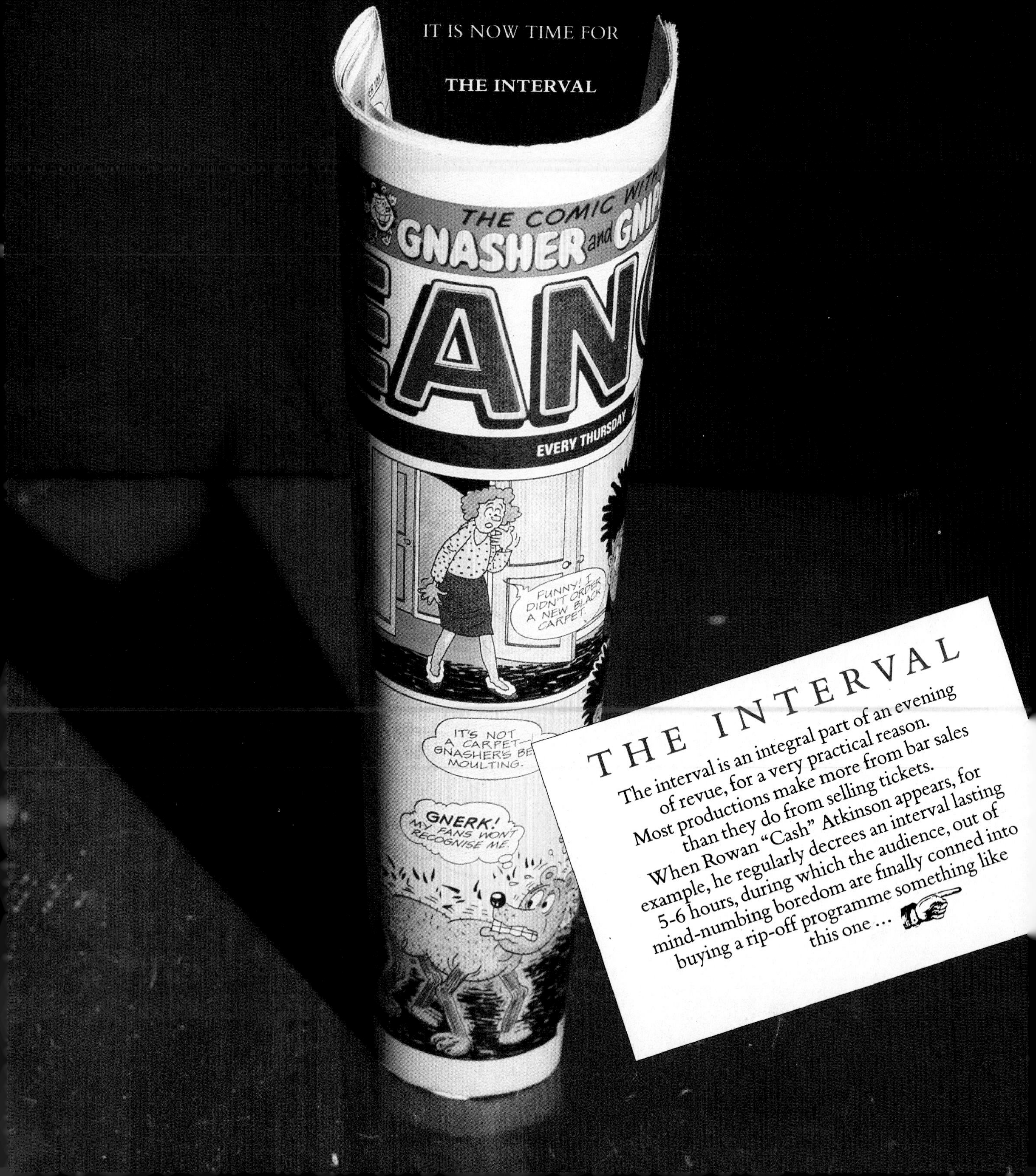

THE COMIC WITH
GNASHER and GNIP
EANO
EVERY THURSDAY
FUNNY! I DIDN'T ORDER A NEW BLACK CARPET.
IT'S NOT A CARPET— GNASHER'S BE MOULTING.
GNERK! MY FANS WON'T RECOGNISE ME.
THE INTERVAL
The interval is an integral part of an evening of revue, for a very practical reason. Most productions make more from bar sales than they do from selling tickets. When Rowan "Cash" Atkinson appears, for example, he regularly decrees an interval lasting 5-6 hours, during which the audience, out of mind-numbing boredom are finally conned into buying a rip-off programme something like this one …

RICHARD BURTON and IVAN LENDL

To make cheapskate black & white programme: cut out next six pages, photocopy, staple and sell

aren't in

THE COMIC RELIEF RED NOSE REVUE

To make elegant full-colour programme: buy hundreds of copies of this book, cut out next six pages, staple and sell

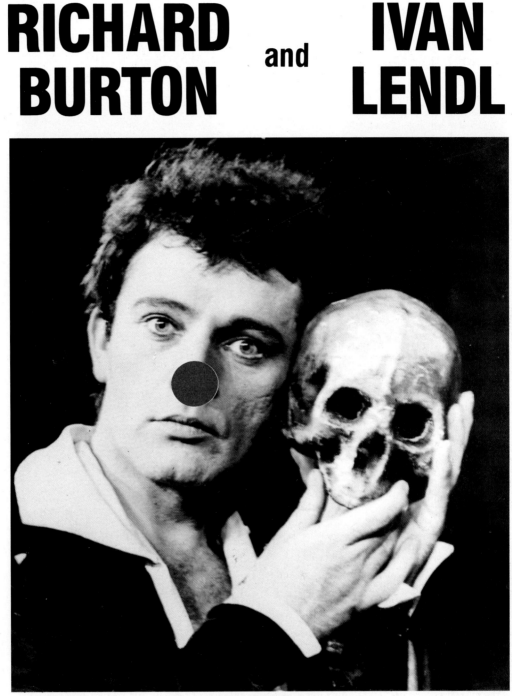

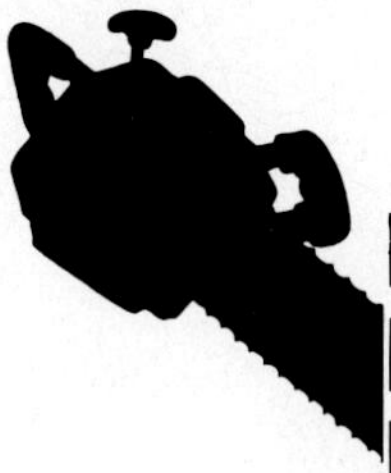

Fabber & Fabber proudly present

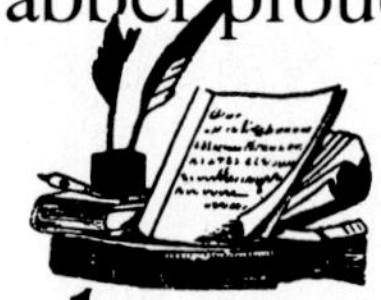

Shakespeare
THE SEQUELS

A rich New Seam of Shakespearian Plays, recently discovered in Bookshops all over London, features such plays as

Merchant of Venice 2
Shylock Gets a Better Lawyer

Taming of the Shrew 2
The Divorce

Romeo and Juliet 2
The Next Day

Hamlet 2
or
Fortinbras and Horatio: The Odd Couple

Midsummer Night's Dream 2
Bottom goes to the Seaside

'Shakespeare was no fool, and he always left some 'out' for his best characters. In this exciting new volume of plays, we hear about Othello's trick dagger, Cleopatra's trick asp, and how Richard the Third managed to get stabbed only in his trick hump.'
Jim Fabber, Gen. Mag.

Thrill again to the spills and chills of all your favourite characters, back again in glorious blank verse.

Soon to be 36 in the end rather disappointing BBC programmes,
because somehow it's so hard to get them to work on television, isn't it, Jonathan?

ff *Fabber & Fabber. 'Used to be Fab, but getting Fabber and Fabber.'*

CNLL

"It was terrible . . . corridor after corridor . . . and then, up a long dark windy staircase, and at the top of it, a hideous, Victorian construct. Worst of all, when I got there, I realised I was . . . not alone. In fact there were about twenty of us. It was at that moment I knew that I was doomed."
A lady.

Ladies: how long is it since you saw either the last thirty seconds of the first act, or the first five minutes of the second act of a play in the West End?
Gentlemen: how many times have you watched the ice melt in a gin and tonic as you stand alone in the bar throughout the interval?
If your answers to these are 'I can't remember' and 'More times than I can remember', then you're with us.

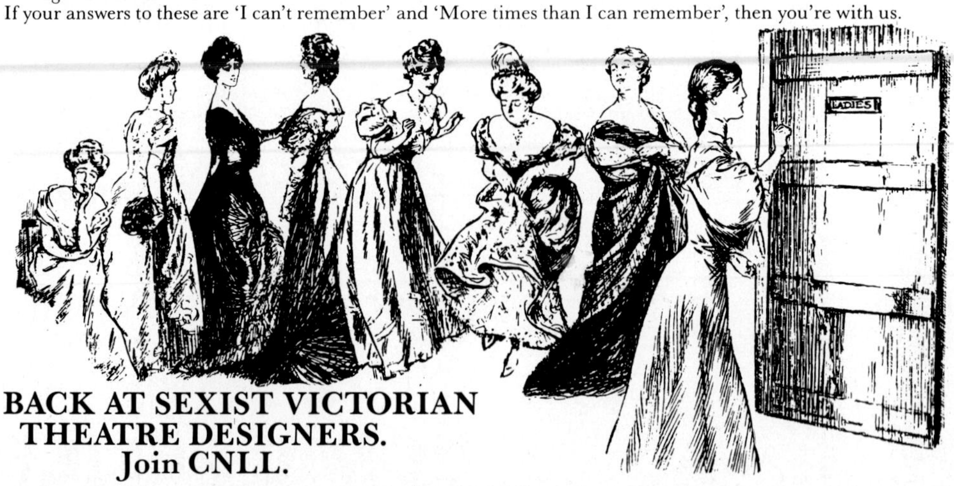
LADIES

HIT BACK AT SEXIST VICTORIAN THEATRE DESIGNERS.
Join CNLL.

The Campaign for New Ladies Loos in Tacky Old Victorian Theatres

This rather dreary page gives your programme that authentic 'West End theatregoer' appeal

The Do-It-Yourself Cast Page
(We do the dotty lines, you do the rest.)

....

are proud to present

The Red Nose Revue

at...(time)

at...(place)

in support of Comic Relief

featuring a cast that has been described by Griff Rhys-Jones as

'the most talented collection of creative artists ever to gather together under one roof since that extraordinary day when Pablo Picasso, Paul Gauguin, Ernest Hemingway, Virginia Woolf and an Italian called Puccini decided to hold a surprise birthday party for T.S. Eliot, who turned up in the company of Sarah Bernhardt and the very old Charles Dickens, only to discover that the restaurant, owned by a Mister Franz Tolstoy, that day being visited by his grandfather Leo, had been double booked, and W.H. Auden was holding a stag party for Arthur Miller and Marilyn Monroe, to which Orson Welles, Marlon Brando and Frank Sinatra turned up, despite the fact that Edward the 8th and Mrs Simpson spent the whole time trying to make them go on somewhere else.'

and photographed recently looking like this . . .

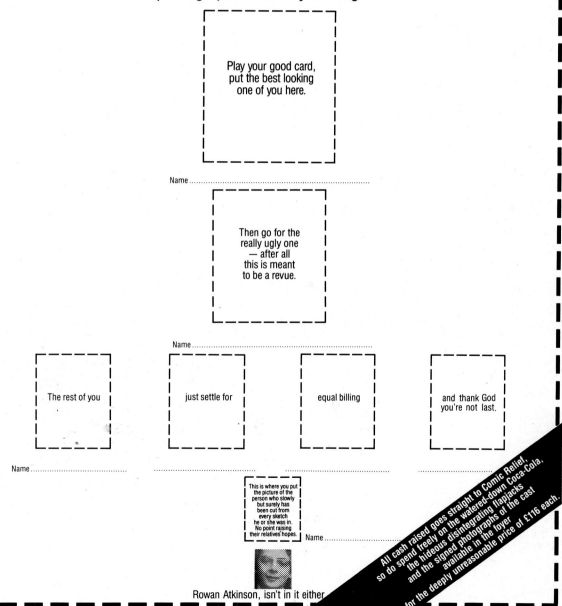

Play your good card, put the best looking one of you here.

Name...

Then go for the really ugly one — after all this is meant to be a revue.

Name...

The rest of you

just settle for

equal billing

and thank God you're not last.

Name...............................   ....

This is where you put the picture of the person who slowly but surely has been cut from every sketch he or she was in. No point raising their relatives hopes. Name.................................

Rowan Atkinson, isn't in it either

All cash raised goes straight to Comic Relief, so do spend freely on the watered-down Coca-Cola, the hideous disintegrating flapjacks and the signed photographs of the cast available in the foyer for the deeply unreasonable price of £116 each.

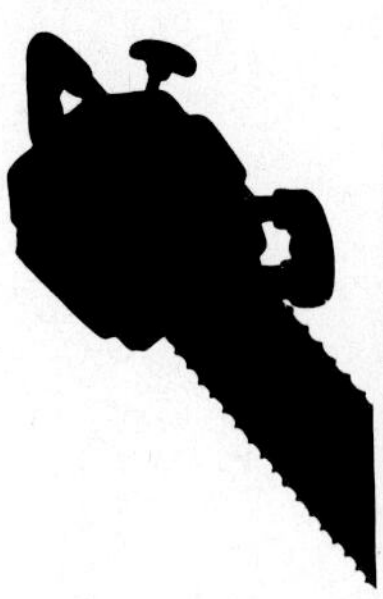

STARS OF THE HALLS

An Occasional Series by
HARWOOD BULLIVANT

'Oh, I loves to shove a carrot up, a carrot up, a carrot up, I loves to shove a carrot up, on the top shelf of me green'ouse.'

Few of us who are in our eighties, and make our living maundering on about old trouts who've been dead since 1938, will ever forget those words. For they were the words – dare I christen them 'lyrics' in modern Tin Pan Alley style? – of the most famous, indeed the *only* song sung by Norrie "Me Knickers Is Soakin'" Podny, "Empress of Entertainment".

Norrie Podny, or 'The Dagenham Darling', as she was oft affectionately dubbed, was in her heyday ('Oh glittering hours, oh sparkling moments') fêted and toasted by German Archdukes and Cockney 'Sparrer' Barrowboys alike. She was a friend of the Earl of Worcester (a second cousin of the Queen) and nary an eve e'er pass'd that she did not have at least one bunch of magnificent pansies pressed against her Dressing Room door.

With her ivory cane and her 'Tattershall Topper', she twirled and gavotted her way, not just through her own 'act', but through many a musical 'revue' – *"Hey What"* at the Aldwych, *"Never A Dull Month"* at the old Chelsea Archive, *"Get Off"* at the Alhambra, Hillingdon, and *"Your Horse-Box Is Here, Mrs. Lotterby"* at the Threnody Palace in Dulwich in 1919. And at them all she sang, thrush-like and with a heartrending clarity, "I'm A Little Carrot Girl From Golders Green".

What was it, I have oft surmised, that led her, the humble 14th child of a Bermondsey tobacco-scrubber and a Chinese horse-maid to consort with Princes and to star, on her 42nd birthday, with Rupert Tremaine in "Coriolanus" by A. P. Herbert? What was the secret of the "Chaffinch of Southwark" that led the eminent critic E. T. Snoad to write of her "My God, look at the size of them?"

And here, by your leave, I digress awhile, for this is the fourth paragraph of my little column, the part that no reader, be they never so poleaxed by the most dismal West End farce about pyjama trousers and funny Arabs, has ever got as far as reading without either nodding off, or turning in desperation to read the potted biography of the Assistant Lighting Designer on page 17 for the fourth time.

Here, I ween, I may write what I choose without the slightest fear of discovery, for in all my 31 years of writing it, there has never even been a *proof-reader* so strong-willed and diligent that he can get through more than 75 words of this literary semolina without running gibbering to the pub. In the fifties and sixties I used to make it six paragraphs to be safe, but I've found that these days four is quite sufficient, so long as I throw in plenty of old dates like '1922', a few unheard of 'eminent critics' like 'F. S. Wheatley' and 'T. P. MacWhirter', and lots of references to the 'Dalston Palindrome', the 'Wilkie Brothers', *"Heavens Below"* and *"Here Comes The Tomatoes, Your Ladyship"* (1935). None of them ever existed, of course. Well, A. P. Herbert did, but so far as I'm aware he never wrote a play called *"Coriolanus"*. But it matters not a jot, for it all serves to keep hidden for ever the true secret of the Halls.

The point was this. Norrie Podny couldn't sing a note. She had a voice like a moose, which could summon a Brougham in Cavendish Square from Hackney Marshes without even bursting a strut in her corset. If she did sing at all, which I doubt, it was in the bath, and even then the neighbours probably assumed that she was in the habit of torturing a mule on Saturday nights. But she had the most incredible pair of tits. They were huge and malleable with giant purple nipples the size of lychees. And at every performance she used to take them out and wave them around like a couple of orthopaedic pillows at a satanists' barn-dance. Then she would invite us up on to the stage one by one where we would be allowed to put our heads between them and make motorbike noises.

You see in those days there wasn't any telly, and Mary Whitehouse was only fifty or so and hadn't got going, so providing the manager of the Halls put a phonograph on really loudly just inside the door, there was no chance that even a policeman would bother to check what was going on. For some reason the managers always used to put on this dreadful song called "I'm A Little Carrot Girl From Golders Green" which Max Miller had found in his attic, and it was the ideal cover. Of course, even in those days everyone thought we Music Hall goers were insane, but they didn't *know* you see. They never saw Norrie Podny covered in mulligatawny soup being licked clean by two Cabinet Ministers and a moorhen. They never saw her opening bottles of Guinness between her gigantic buttocks, or doing the Dance of the Seven Bull-Terriers and above all they never saw her bosoms, like two fleshy mosques, thudding and bouncing and making people go deaf with pleasure for the rest of the week.

But enough, for I am now arrived at the penultimate paragraph, and must return to the dull bits.

One thing is sure, there'll never be another Norrie, ne'er another "Tottenham Toucan", for since her final concert at the Walthamstow Nectarine in 1953, about which F. R. Cawsand penned the line "Fare thee well, O Osprey of Osterley", we have not seen her like again.

If anyone in the audience starts reading this article during the evening, you really should consider a non-theatrical career

---

Do it Yourself Ad. Approach a local restaurant* for sponsorship in return for letrasetting their name here →

*or abbatoir

Mel Smith – and you know how keen he is on his tuck – thinks that

....

is the best restaurant in this town. Indeed, he would go further than that – it's the best restaurant in England – no, hell, why mince words, it's the best restaurant in the world – not only in the world today, by God – the best restaurant there has ever been in the entire history of the world, the universe and whatever comes after that. His advice is 'Go Eat There, You Lucky Blighters – I Would Join You, But I've Just Eaten There Myself, and There's a Limit to How Much Tuck One Man Can Consume in a Day, Even If His Tum Is As Big as the Grand Canyon – On the Other Hand, Hell, Yes, Why Not – An Extra Pudding Never Hurt Anyone.* See You There!!!'

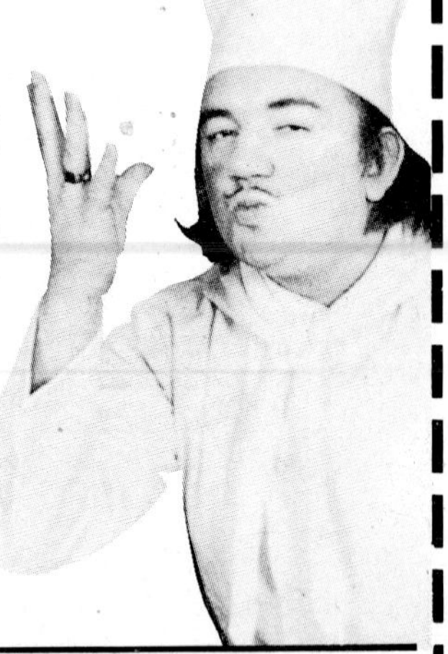

***Government Health Warning** – This is not strictly true. Very Fat Tubby McEnormous, the Famous Scottish Eating Champion, Had An Extra Pudding at the Climax of the Rotterdam Fatties Gorge-athon and Exploded, Resulting in His Immediate Expulsion from the Competition, and More Tuck for Everyone Else.

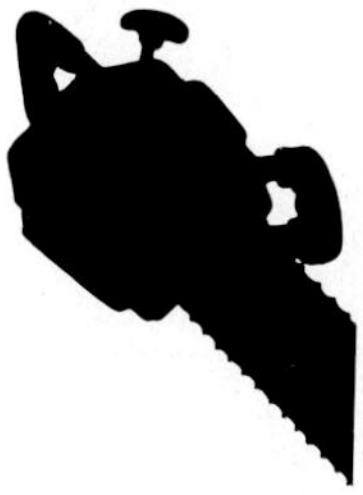

Why not persuade your audience to club together to buy one of these lovely homes and donate it to Comic Relief?

STICKLAND & BRILLET
Partners

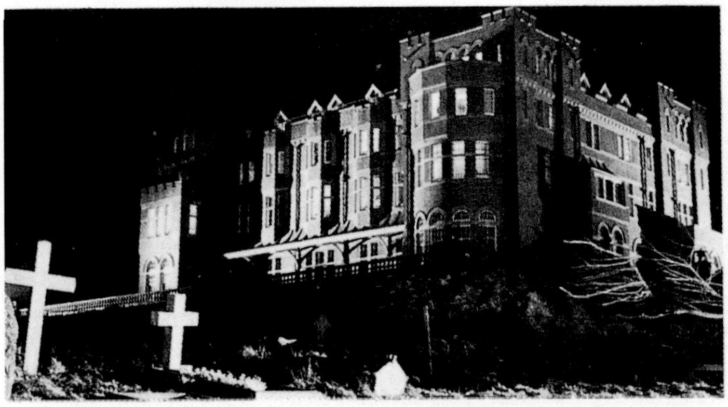

CASTLE MELMOTH. Edinburgh 314 miles. Reykjavik 6¼ miles. Kilnairnietoun 2¾ miles (take West Door out of Chinese Dining Room, village is eighth exit on left inside Conservatory behind Burmese Elm plantation).

FUCKING HUGE PIECE OF EDWARDIAN INSANITY WITH VIEWS OF SUTHERLAND, PERTHSHIRE AND CROMARTY EASILY OBTAINED BY PEERING UNDER THE LINO.

124 Reception Rooms. 98 Dining Rooms. 70 Breakfast Rooms. 62 Brunch Rooms. 34 Luncheon Lobbies. Banqueting Hall. 19th Century Elevenses Chamber. Horlicks Gallery. 254 Bedrooms (28 still undiscovered) including 40 Horse-Boudoirs, 22 Double-Labrador Suites, 9 finely-appointed Hawk-Lofts with ensuite Rabbit-Hutches.

1 Bathroom. 3,507 Downstairs Loos are fully-stocked with Green Gumboots and Tweed Capes. Billiard Room. Snooker Room. Pool Room. Crazy Golf Hall. Indoor Rugby Pitch. Tennis Court. 100ft Ballroom. 200ft Racquet Room. Cue Store. Bat Belfry. Indoor Swimming Pool (Olympic Marathon Size) with own U-Boat Pen, and quaint Portuguese Fishing Community of charm and character. 16 Gun-Rooms. 2 Stag-Flensing Chambers. 8 Smoking Rooms. 12 Grill-Rooms. 3 Magnificent Torture-Chambers. 91 Kitchens (inc. 4 fish-farms, 6 abattoirs, 2 morgues, sandwich-maker).

44 Sculleries. 770 Cupboards Under The Stairs, each with Gas Meter, Broken Kite, Plastic Bin Liner Full of Clogs, Groundsheets and Old Biscuit Tins.

2 40ft x 30ft Officers Messes. 640 3in x ½in Dogs Messes. 36 Inner Sanctums. American Style Den. Trophy Room. Sellotape Closet. Lumber Room. Muesli Store. 13,052 Inglenooks. Tea-Room. 12 Sitting Rooms. 8 Standing Rooms. 6 Kneeling Parlours. Crouching Closet. 3 Bending Over Backwards Cubby Holes. 12th Century Italian Piazza Parlour, with own fountain, cathedral. 180 Attics. 86 Junk Rooms. 64 Dust-Sheet Vestibules. Library. Public Baths. 6 Launderettes. 2 Job Centres. Haunted Grotto. Garotted Haunto. Persian Room. Japanese Restaurant (closed Suns). Heliport. 16 Vomitoriums. Another Bathroom. Bloody hell, and there's half a dozen more Gun Rooms in here too. 8 Pheasantries. Unisex Hairdressers. Railway Turntable. Extensive Wine Cellars to be sold with 80 Elderly French Peasants with original feet. 124 Studies. Dairy. Garage for 36 Cars. In addition 1,574 further rooms That No-One Could Possibly Want. Outside Toilet.

Large Servants Quarters In Own Wing. Butlers Pantry. Cooks Solarium. Battery Skivvy Farm. 38 Maid-Closets. 40ft x 40ft Gardener-Pit. 6 Swineherd Huts. 9 Flunkey-Bins. 12 Groom-Punnets. Extensive Slave-Bunker. Cave for Chauffeur. Ghillie-Box. 52 Scullion-Cages. 5 Priest-Holes.

Stable Block. Home Farm of 13,000 Acres with own Trout Cannery, Pate Farm, Salmon-Meadows and Gooserie, situated roof of North Wing approx 3½ miles aft of main funnels. Salt Flats. Grouse Moor. 32 Werewolf Kennels. 56 Cottages, three small hotels, 9 pubs, Post Office, 3 Banks, 12 Bars, Second Class Lounge, Quoit Deck, Snowstorm Paperweight & Postcard Shop.

FOR SALE BY PUBLIC AUCTION, PRIVATE TREATY OR BLOODY MIRACLE.

PUTTNAM HALL, WORCESTERSHIRE

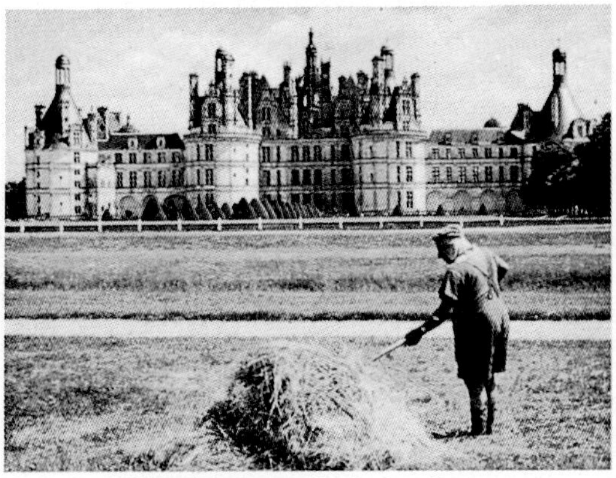

Worcester-on-Sauce 4 miles. Lea 3½ miles. Perrins 2½ miles. Puttnam 35 yards.

DESIRABLE RURAL RESIDENCE SET ON 0.0003 ACRES (Summer Months).

A Superb Thatched Antheap in original condition, within fawning distance of magnificent Puttnam Hall, country seat of Lord Puttnam of Chariot. For the once-in-a-lifetime chance of being near to the great man, this breeze, compact dwelling is OFFERED FOR SALE FREEHOLD AT £8,775 o.n.o.

Applicants, who should be young, gifted and black, should apply IN WRITING, DURING THE HOURS OF DARKNESS ONLY to SOUWESTER, COGWIT & SPRUCE Partners of Epping. The successful applicant will be expected to put up with a man who looks suspiciously like Johnny Morris poking his willy through the roof on a regular basis.

PORTICO, WAINSCOT, TRELLIS Partners

A VERY FINE, WELL-APPOINTED FAMILY RESIDENCE SET IN 2½ ACRES OF LAND.

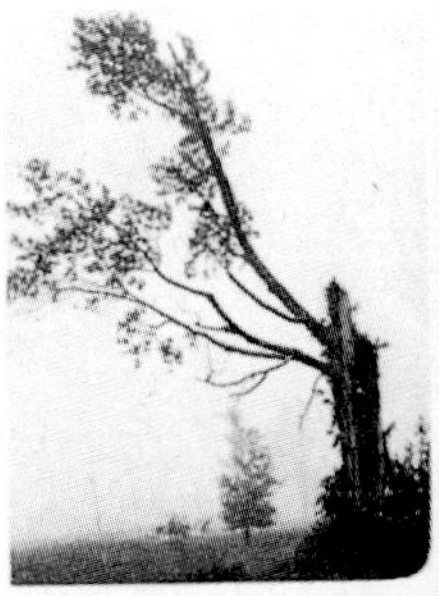

Study, south facing TREE, situated in heart of Sir Oswald Mosley Memorial Car Park, Fulham.

Ripe for imaginative conversion, this delightful old home is wood-panelled throughout. Would suit person who is fond of trees. 3/4 Bedrooms, 2 Bathrooms, Cloakroom, k&b would be nice but what can you expect for only £37,499.

OFFERS ARE INVITED FOR THIS INCREDIBLY DECENT ATTEMPT BY US TO CONTRIBUTE TO THE GENERAL WELL-BEING OF THE COMMUNITY

SLITHY, TOVES Ltd.

2 BEDROOM GARDEN FLAT, SOUTH KENSINGTON.

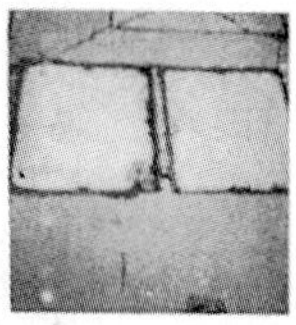

Tiny, unpleasant-smelling cellar with view of upstairs concrete coal bunker. Situated close to shops, near schools, underneath public transport etc, in South Kensington Avenue, Norwood SE55. Master Bedroom (8ft x 2ft), Smaller Bedroom (Behind sink-panel in Kitchen), Kitchen (in Wardrobe in Master Bedroom). Reception 50ft x 4ft with 19th Century Commissionaire at one end, conveniently placed outside front door. H&C running water in all rooms. Bathroom (planning permission available). Window (18in x ½in) £88,795.

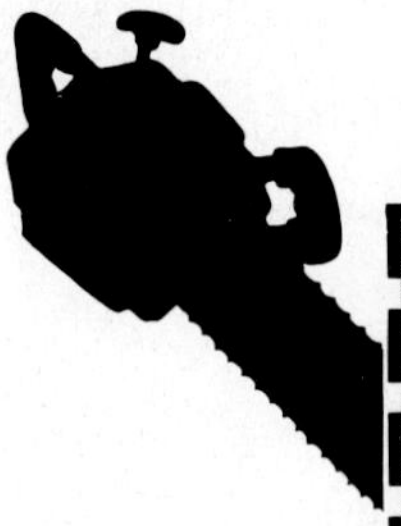

Genuine advert from best-selling New Zealand magazine

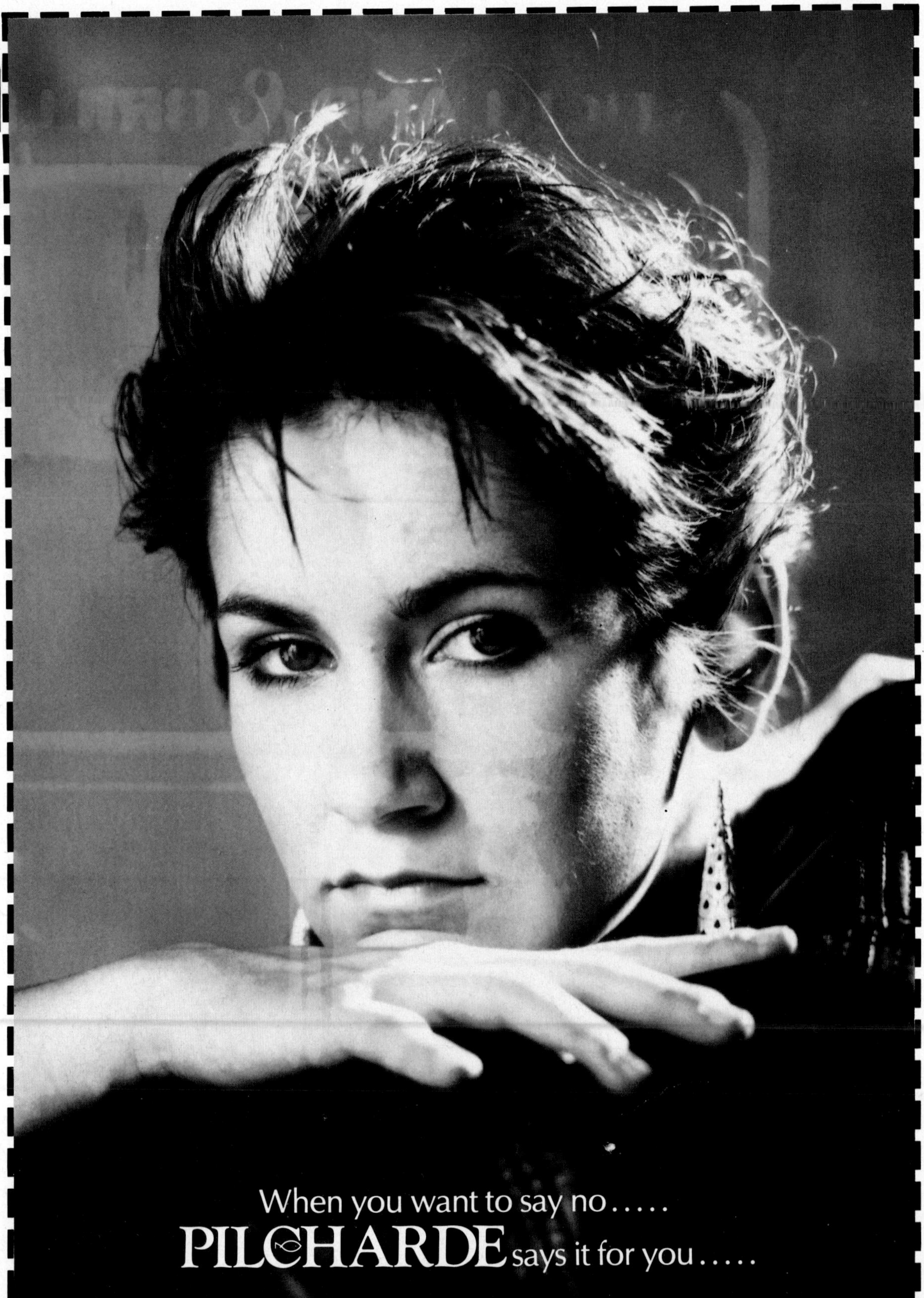
When you want to say no.....
PILCHARDE says it for you.....
When a man gets too close, he'll find out for himself how you feel about him. An unsubtle blend of malt extract, mature Portuguese mackerel and Old English cabbage.
Aerosol, spray or firkin.

Part Two

PRAYING MANTIS WEDDING

Written by Laurie Rowley; first performed in Alas Smith and Jones

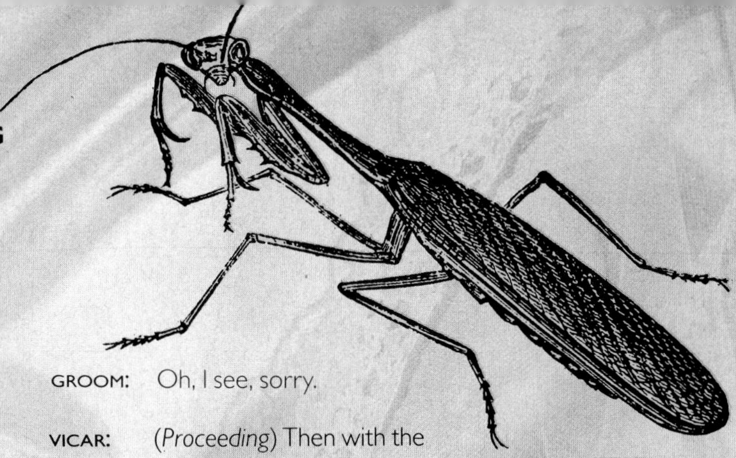

A clearing in the forest. Lighting effects of sun's rays breaking through trees. Organ plays wedding march very softly. We see VICAR *standing on a small grassy mound. He wears green leotard, green cloak, green hair and a pair of antennae sticking out of his head. He is a praying mantis vicar and holds a green Bible. Opposite him and a few yards away are* GROOM *and* BRIDE*. They are both dressed in green leotards with green hair and antennae. They are a praying mantis bride and groom. The music goes down and off.*

VICAR: Friends, we are gathered here today to join this male praying mantis and this female praying mantis together in holy matrimony. Will the bride and groom please *stalk* forward.
(*The couple move nearer to* VICAR *using long bendy strides.*)
Jeremy, do you take Amanda to be your lawful wedded wife, to love, honour and obey?

GROOM: I do.

VICAR: Amanda, do you take Jeremy to be your lawful wedded husband, to love, honour, obey and kill him after ye both have mated?

BRIDE: I do.

VICAR: Then with the power invested in me an–

GROOM: (*Politely interrupting*) Excuse me, sorry, what was that last bit again?

VICAR: What?

GROOM: That bit about 'kill him after ye both have mated'.

VICAR: Oh, that, yes, that's right, the female praying mantis always kills the male after the marriage has been consummated. Didn't you know?

GROOM: Er no, I didn't actually.

VICAR: Don't worry about it – it's entirely natural.

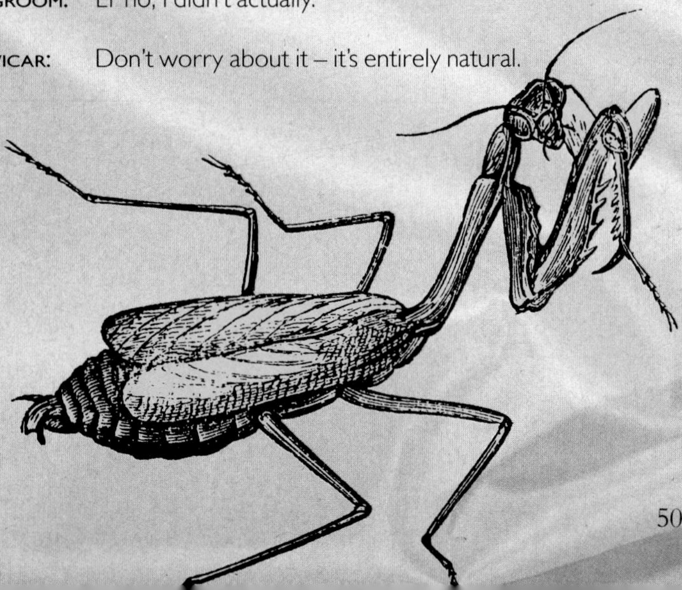

GROOM: Oh, I see, sorry.

VICAR: (*Proceeding*) Then with the power invested in me and in the eyes of…

GROOM: (*Interrupting*) Excuse me, sorry again, but what you're actually saying is that we, the two of us, go away on our honeymoon but only one of us comes back?

VICAR: I suppose you could put it that way, yes. Now let's get on, shall we.

GROOM: Yes, of course, sorry, carry on.

VICAR: …power invested in me and in the eyes of the Almighty, I…

GROOM: When you say the female kills the male after they've consummated the marriage, is that after the first time they've er … thingy, or can it be after a few times they've er, just out of interest?

VICAR: (*Slightly irritated*) It's immediately after the first time.

GROOM: So I only get the one er…

VICAR: That's about the bottom line as far as male praying mantis go. Anything wrong?

GROOM: I'm just wondering whether it's going to be worth it… I've booked the hotel for a fortnight.

VICAR: Well, make up your mind, do you want to be married or not?

GROOM: Oh, I want to be married all right, yes, it's just the murdering bit I'm not keen on, sort of puts a damper on the day, you know? How does she do it, by the way?

VICAR: Didn't your father tell you anything?

GROOM: I never met him. He was murdered on his honeymoon.

VICAR: Oh, of course, yes, I was forgetting…

GROOM: Is it poison in the cocoa or what?

VICAR: (*Matter of fact*) She clamps your throat between her incisors and bites your head off in the frenzy of the climax.

GROOM: Oh, come on – I'm good but I'm not *that* good.

MARTINS' OF BOND STREET

*Written by Jon Canter and Geoffrey Perkins; first performed by Angus
Deayton and Geoffrey Perkins in RadioActive*

We are in the world of dreadful radio advertisements.

FIRST MAN: Hello, Harry.

SECOND MAN: Hello, Derek.

FIRST MAN: I like your suit, Harry.

SECOND MAN: Thanks, Derek. It's a lightweight cotton summer suit, only £14.99 at the Martins' of Bond Street sale.

FIRST MAN: I bet they've got hundreds of great menswear bargains at fantastically reduced prices at the Martins' of Bond Street sale.

SECOND MAN: Yes, but I should hurry. The Martins' of Bond Street sale ends Saturday.

FIRST MAN: Sorry, Harry. (*Bland*) Must dash.

SECOND MAN: Where are you going?

FIRST MAN: The Martins' of Bond Street sale.

SECOND MAN: See you there!

FIRST MAN: But you've already been to the Martins' of Bond Street sale, Harry.

SECOND MAN: Right. And now I'm going back to the Martins' of Bond Street sale for another great menswear bargain.

FIRST MAN: Better hurry, Harry. Martins' of Bond Street sale ends Saturday.

SECOND MAN: I know. I told you the Martins' of Bond Street sale ends Saturday.

FIRST MAN: Did you?

SECOND MAN: Yes.

FIRST MAN: I'm so excited (*not at all*) by the thought of hundreds of great menswear bargains at fantastically reduced prices at the Martins' of Bond Street sale which ends Saturday, that I instantly forget what people say to me.

SECOND MAN: Well, just don't forget the Martins' of Bond Street sale which ends Saturday.

FIRST MAN: I won't. The Martins' of Bond Street sale which ends Saturday.

SECOND MAN: Yes, Saturday.

FIRST MAN: Harry!

SECOND MAN: Yes!

FIRST MAN: Today's Sunday!

SECOND MAN: Shit.

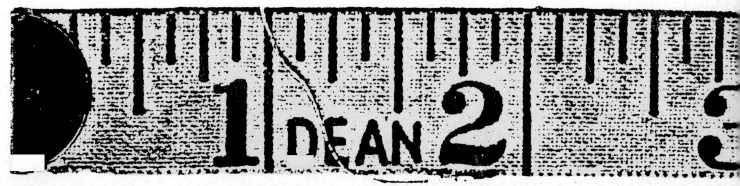

JOHN AND MARY

***Written by Bill Oddie and John Cleese; first performed by John Cleese and Jo Kendall in* Cambridge Circus**

A beautiful rural scene – in other words, see if you can muster a bush and the odd background 'moo' here and there.

JOHN: Ah, I love to be alone in the country.

MARY: John?

JOHN: Yes.

MARY: I am with you.

JOHN: I love to be alone in the country.

MARY: But, but, John, you brought me with you.

JOHN: I didn't, you hid in the back.

MARY: But you must have noticed?

JOHN: Not at all, it's a very large tandem.

MARY: But, John, when we fell off going down the stairs… You must have seen?

JOHN: I thought you were a hitchhiker.

MARY: But I am your wife. You must have recognized me?

JOHN: I didn't, Mary.

MARY: Why not?

JOHN: Because you were disguised as a cactus.

MARY: Oh, John, John, talk to me. Say something to me. Say you hate me, say I am ugly.

JOHN: Which?

MARY: Say I'm ugly.

JOHN: You are ugly.

MARY: You are only saying that, you don't really mean it, you don't care, you never think about me. Up and down all night warming the milk, mashing the rusks, all the crying and bed-wetting…

JOHN: Yes, I know, I know.

MARY: I wouldn't mind if we had a baby.

JOHN: Well, I am sorry, but I prefer bison.

MARY: John, why don't you admit, you don't … don't love me any more?

JOHN: All right, I admit it.

MARY: John, once we had something that was pure and wonderful and good. What's happened to it?

JOHN: You spent it all.

MARY: That's all that matters to you, isn't it? Money. I despise you, do you hear? I hate you, I don't know how I have been able to stand it. I… I suppose it's because I love you, I don't know. I do love you, John, I love you more than I can say, I… need you, John, I… please, John, don't look at photographs of nude women when I am speaking to you.

JOHN: All right, but, I know, you know…

MARY: You know?

JOHN: Yes.

MARY: Oh God…John?

JOHN: Yes.

MARY: What do you know?

JOHN: Well, I could be wrong.

MARY: About me and Nigel?

JOHN: Oh, oh, I was wrong. I thought it was Robert.

MARY: Yes, you are right, I can never remember names.

JOHN: Anyway, I do know about last Friday.

MARY: Last Friday?

JOHN: Yes, he was in my bed, wasn't he?

MARY: How do you know?

JOHN: He kept pushing me out.

MARY: You mean you were there too?

JOHN: You didn't even notice? Oh God!!

MARY: John, John, try to love me.

JOHN: No, Mary, it's no good, you somehow manage to hurt everyone you love.

MARY: Well, I'll take the cactus skin off.

JOHN: No, Mary, look, there is something I have been meaning to tell you…

MARY: What?

JOHN: Cardinal Richelieu died in 1642.

MARY: All right, so mother was wrong. But can't we forget the past? I mean that's all history now, don't let's dig it up again.

JOHN: You never liked me being an archaeologist, did you?

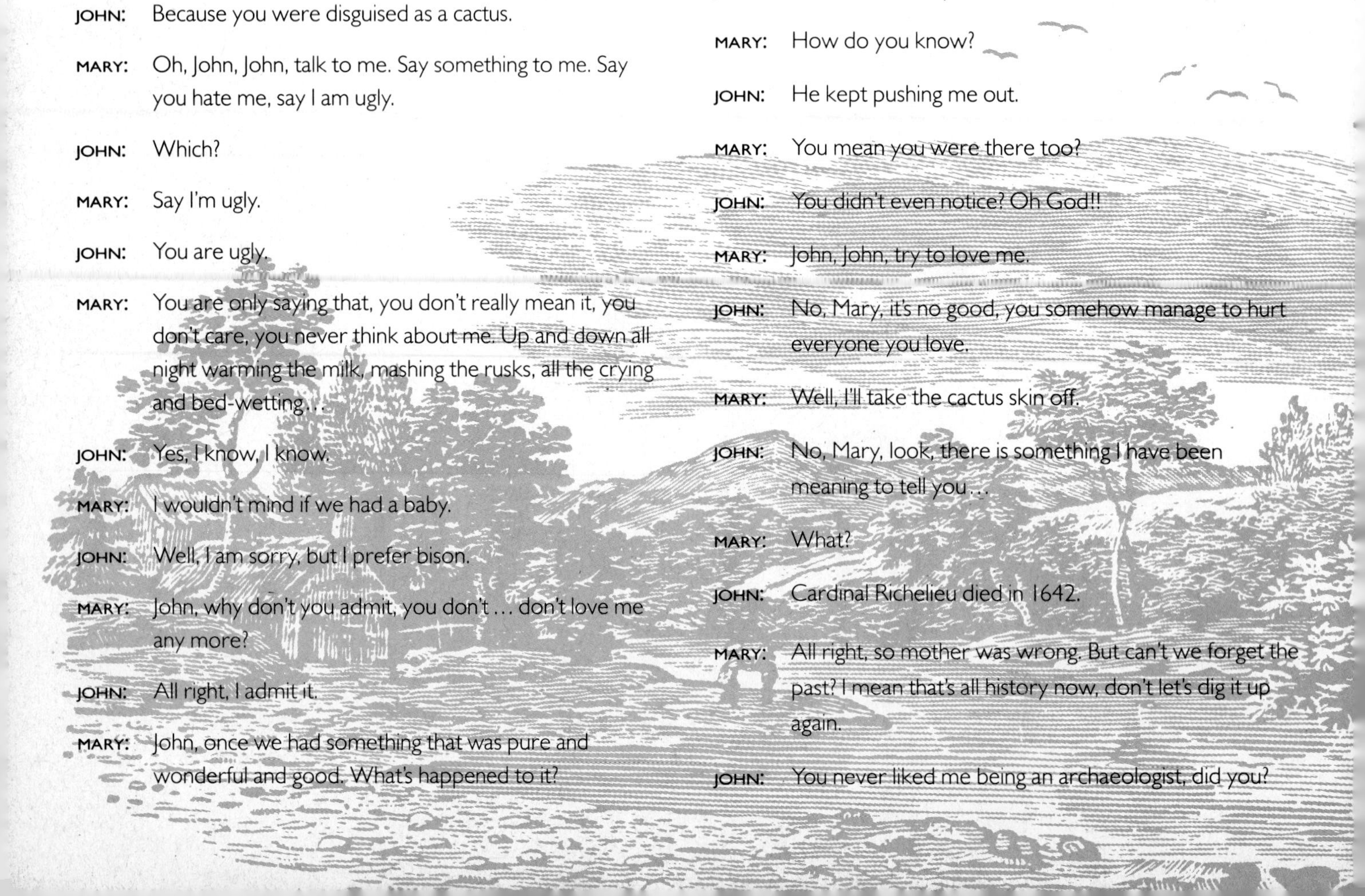

MARY: I never said that.

JOHN: You would have been happier if I had sharpened knives, or, or … sold ferrets.

MARY: Keep George out of this.

JOHN: No, I am not going to keep George out of this. If you had to have a lover, why did it have to be a ferret-seller? Blasted ferrets all over the house for months. Why couldn't it have been a budgerigar man? At least budgerigars can sing beautifully. I can still remember waking up in the morning and hearing all those ferrets singing. It used to drive me mad, always the same tune.

MARY: Well … that's all over now, can't we forget, I mean, can't we start all over again, I mean go back and begin from the beginning?

JOHN: I suppose we could try.

MARY: Please, John?

JOHN: All right … Ah, how I love to be alone in the country.

MARY: John?

JOHN: Yes?

MARY: I am with you.

JOHN: I love to be alone in the country.

MARY: But John, I … *etc., etc.*

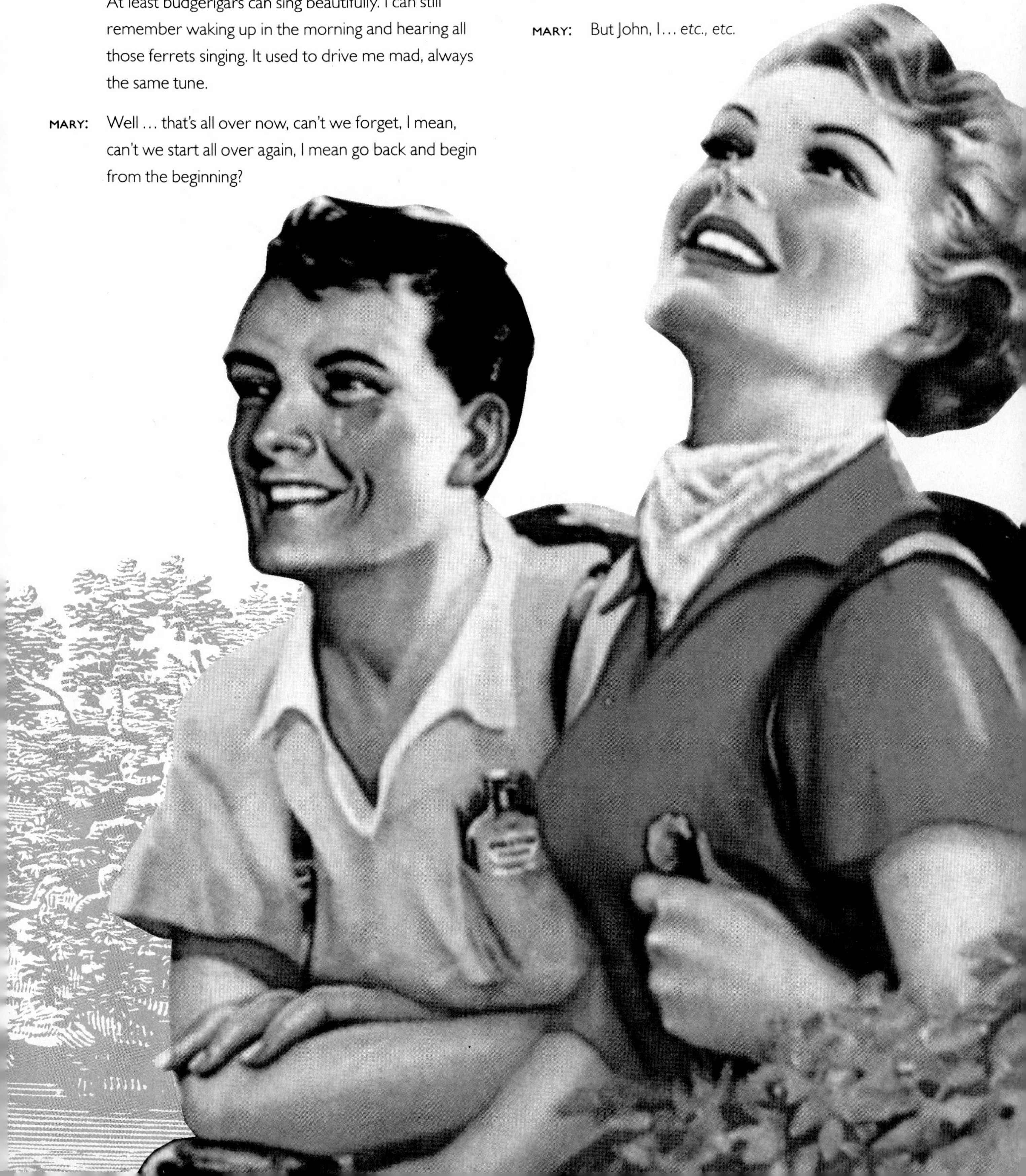

RADIATING LOVE

Lyrics and music by Dillie Keane; first performed by Fascinating Aida at the Piccadilly Theatre

The singer or singers as yet show no signs of the horrendous post-nuke deterioration to come.

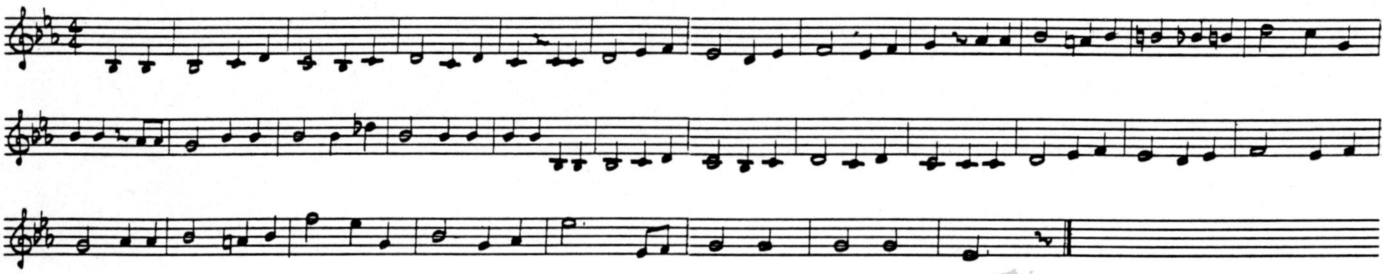

INTRO

Darling, when you're sleeping
My name I hear you call out,
Then you turn to me and hold me very near.
But I can't help wond'ring
What happens after fallout:
Will you still love me, dear?

CHORUS

Would you love me at all if I lost all my hair?
Would you still hold my hand if my skin wasn't there?
For I can't help but feel you won't find me attractive
When the isotopes render me radioactive.
Will you whisper the sweet words I so long to hear
In the hole that denotes where I once had an ear?
When I'm gaunt and exhausted, unable to crawl,
Will you love me then at all?

When I'm covered in sores would your love linger on?
Would you still like my smile when my teeth are all gone?
Would you hold me so close in a tender embrace
When I'm sprouting a cancerous growth on my face?
When these eyes you have loved gently melt down my cheek,
When the retching and vomiting leave me too weak,
Will you still feel a thrill at the sound of my name?
Yes, you will, for you'll be the same.

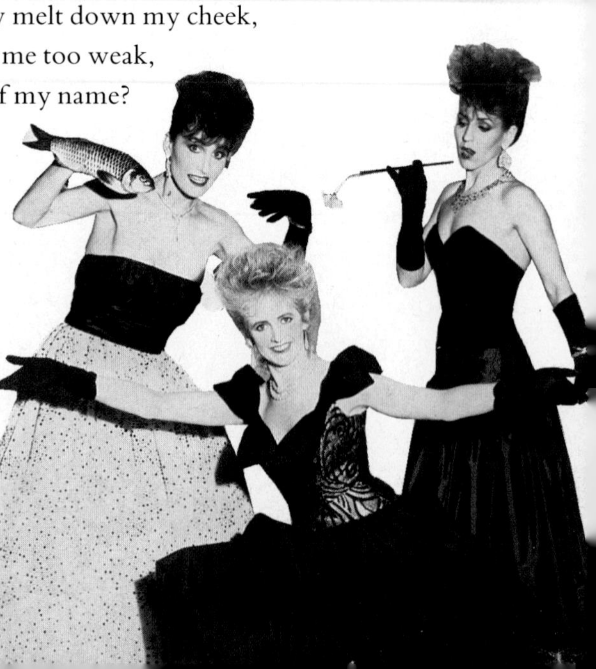

INTRODUCING TOBACCO
TO CIVILIZATION

Written and performed by Bob Newhart

*A casual modern American gets to grips with
sixteenth-century English history with the
help of a mimed telephone.*

Milestones are never really recognized right away. It takes fifty or sixty years
before people realize what an achievement it is. Like take for instance tobacco
and the discovery of tobacco. It was discovered by Sir Walter Raleigh and he
sent it over to England from the colonies. It seems to me the uses of tobacco
aren't obvious, right off the bat, you know? I imagine a phone conversation
between Sir Walter Raleigh and the head of the West Indies Company in
England, explaining about this shipment of tobacco that he had just sent over.
I think it would go something like this:

'Yeah, who is it? Sir Walter Raleigh from the colonies . . . yeah, yeah, put him
on, will you? Harry, you want to pick up the extension? It's nutty Walt again . . .
Hi, Walt baby, how are you, guy? Did we get the what? The boatload of
turkeys . . . Yeah, they arrived fine, Walt. As a matter of fact they're still here.
They're wandering all over London as a matter of fact. See that's an American
holiday, Walt.

'But . . . what is it this time, Walt, you got another winner for us, do you?
Tobacco . . . What's tobacco, Walt? . . . It's a kind of leaf? And you bought eighty
tons of it? Let me get this straight now, Walt, you bought eighty tons of leaves?
This, er, may come as kind of a surprise to you, Walt, but come fall in England
here, we're up to our . . . er . . . it isn't that kind of leaf. What is it, a special food
of some kind, Walt? Not exactly. It has a lot of different uses . . . Like what are
some of the uses, Walt? Are you saying snuff, Walt? What's snuff? You take a
pinch of tobacco . . . and you shove it up your nose? And it makes you sneeze? I
imagine it would, Walt, yeah. Gee, Golden Rod seems to do it pretty well over here.

'It has some other uses though. You can chew it . . . or put it in a pipe . . . or you
can shred it up and put it on a piece of paper and roll it up. Don't tell me, Walt,
don't tell me . . . you stick it in your ear, right, Walt? Or between your lips.
Then what do you do, Walt? You set fire to it, Walt? Then what do you do? You
inhale the smoke?! You know, Walt, it seems offhand like you could stand in
front of the fireplace and have the same thing going for you, you know.

'You see, Walt, we've been a little worried about you, you know. Ever since you
put your cape down over that mud. You see, Walt, I think you're going to have
a tough time selling people on sticking burning leaves in their mouth . . . It's
going very big over there, is it? What's the matter, Walt? You spilt your what . . .
your coffee? What's coffee, Walt? That's a drink you make out of beans, uh? A
lot of people have their coffee after their first cigarette in the morning. Is that
what you call burning leaves, Walt? "Cigarettes"?

'I tell you what, Walt. Why don't you send us a boatload of those beans too?
If you can talk people into putting burning leaves into their mouths, you've
gotta go for those beans, Walt. Right. Listen, Walt. Don't call us, we'll call you.

'Right, Walt. Goodbye.'

CHANCELLOR CIGARETTES

Written by Rob Grant and Doug Naylor; first performed in* Carrott's Lib *by Steve Frost and Nick Wilton

A sign on the wall says, ACME ADVERTISING AGENCY. BOSS *at his desk is on the phone.* FRANK *stands opposite him. They're a pretty hideous pair.*

BOSS: (*Into phone*) Uh–huh, OK. Right. (*Phone down.*) Frank – sorry to keep you. Listen, uh, I'm not ecstatic about the way you're handling the 'Chancellor' cigarette account.

FRANK: No?

BOSS: I know it's not easy trying to get away from the surreal, the lizards, the helicopter, the swimming pool – the subliminal angle. But honestly, Frank, I don't think your approach is a viable alternative.

FRANK: What don't you like about it, sir?

BOSS: What's the slogan again?

FRANK: 'Chancellor cigarettes, for the smoothest, biggest, greenest balls of early-morning sputum money can buy.'

BOSS: Right.

FRANK: What's the problem, sir? Don't you like the name 'Chancellor'?

BOSS: Look, Frank. I don't think we can promote a cigarette on the grounds that it produces bigger and greener mucus than any other.

FRANK: But the whole campaign's based on that premiss, sir. 'Chancellor (*cough, spit*) – I like a man who can bring up a good hanky-full.' We've got Joan Collins saying that.

BOSS: Sure. But I don't think it's a desirable product image to show a man bring up great globules of viscous slime, and coughing them into a hanky.

FRANK: What? Not even in soft focus, sir?

BOSS: No.

FRANK: Not even when he's on a Caribbean island, surrounded by a bevy of bikini-clad beauties, pouting in awe at the size of his mucous excreta?

BOSS: No.

FRANK: But the Mucus Man is such a good character, sir – we've got a whole series planned for him. We've got him grebbing up in Monte Carlo ... having a bronchial attack in Paris ... losing a lung in Rome ... and all the time surrounded by adoring beauties.

BOSS: No, Frank. I want you to drop the whole sputum angle.

FRANK: Back to the lizards, then, eh?

BOSS: I'm afraid so, Frank.

FRANK: How about one of the lizards coughing up a greenie?

BOSS: No, Frank.

FRANK: Well, you're the boss.

(*BOSS reaches into drawer.*)

BOSS: You can take these with you, Frank.

FRANK: What's that, sir?

(*BOSS hands him something.*)

BOSS: Your samples.

(*FRANK looks at his hand – full of slimy mucus.*)

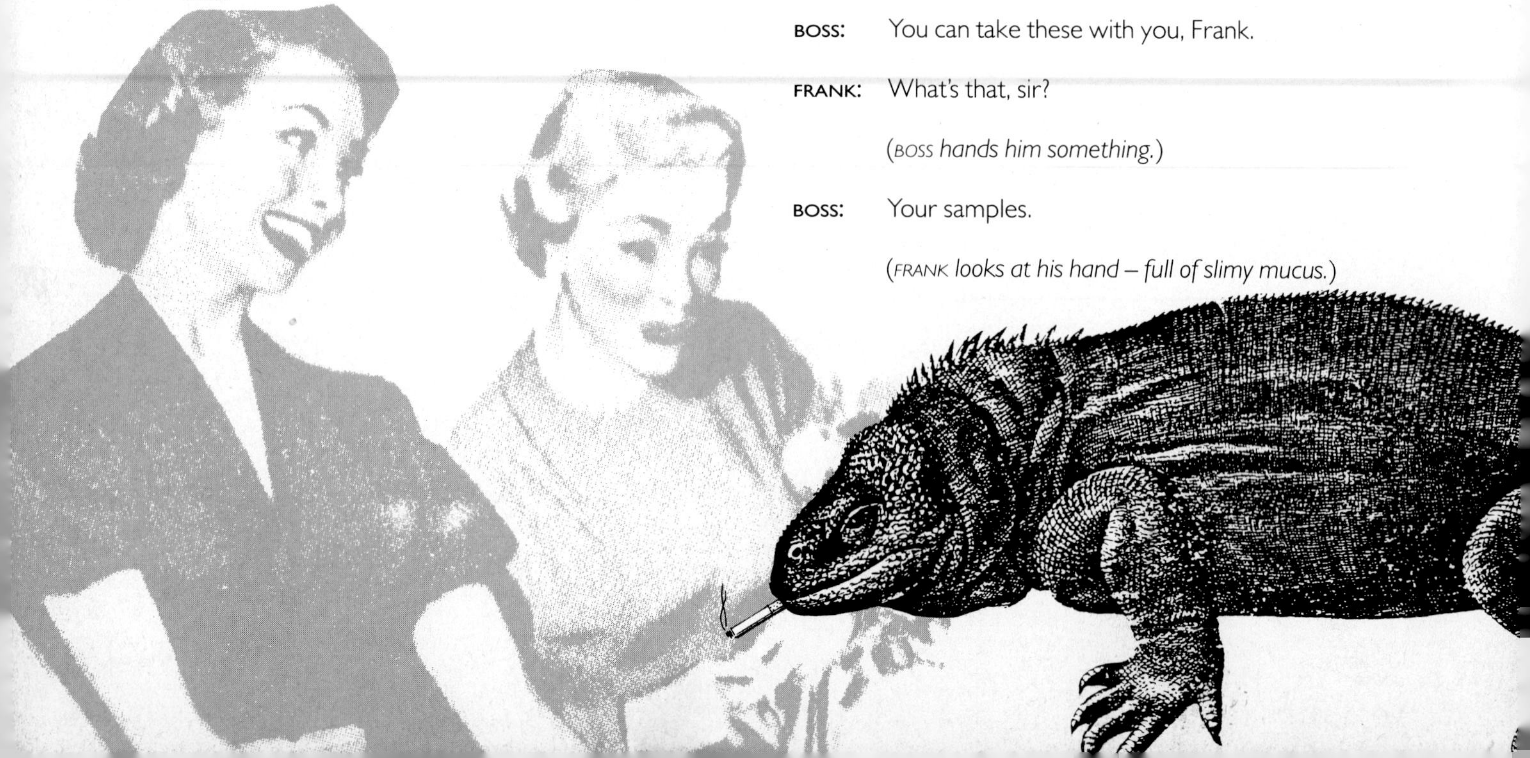

POLICE v. PRESS

***Written by Rory McGrath; first performed by Mel Smith and Griff Rhys Jones in* Alas Smith and Jones**

OFFICIAL and a couple of anonymous official types at desk. Members of the cast or crew subtly planted in the audience shout out the questions from the press.

OFFICIAL: (*Mid-sentence*) ... who is in charge of the hunt for this attacker, Police Superintendent John Rushton. (*RUSHTON enters.*)

RUSHTON: (*slowly, like a thick copper*) Gentleman of the press. I would like to brief you as to the latest developments, which are considerable, in the hunt for the killer at large in the Suffolk region.
(*OFFICIAL whispers.*)
In the Sussex region. Four hundred top police officers working day and night for the last two weeks have finally come up with a ... nickname for the killer. We shall be calling him the 'Hedgehog'.

MAIL: (*Off*) Simon Bell, *Daily Mail.* Why the 'Hedgehog'?
(*OFFICIAL whispers.*)

RUSHTON: Because other wild animals like fox, snake, rat and wolf have been used before.

MIRROR: (*Off*) Tony Robbins, *Daily Mirror.* Is it true that most policemen are of abnormally low intelligence?

RUSHTON: I'm sorry, I don't understand the question. Now, all the Hedgehog's attacks have followed the same pattern. The victim has always been a girl. And the attacks have all taken place at night...
(*OFFICIAL whispers.*)
...or during the day.

MIRROR: (*Off*) Robbins, *Mirror.* What's the capital of France?

RUSHTON: (*Caught out, thinks very hard*) Ooooo... now, what is that?
(*OFFICIAL whispers.*)
We'll have one of our experts look into it. All my top officers are searching every square inch of Hampshire.

MAIL: (*Off*) Why not Sussex where the attacks took place?

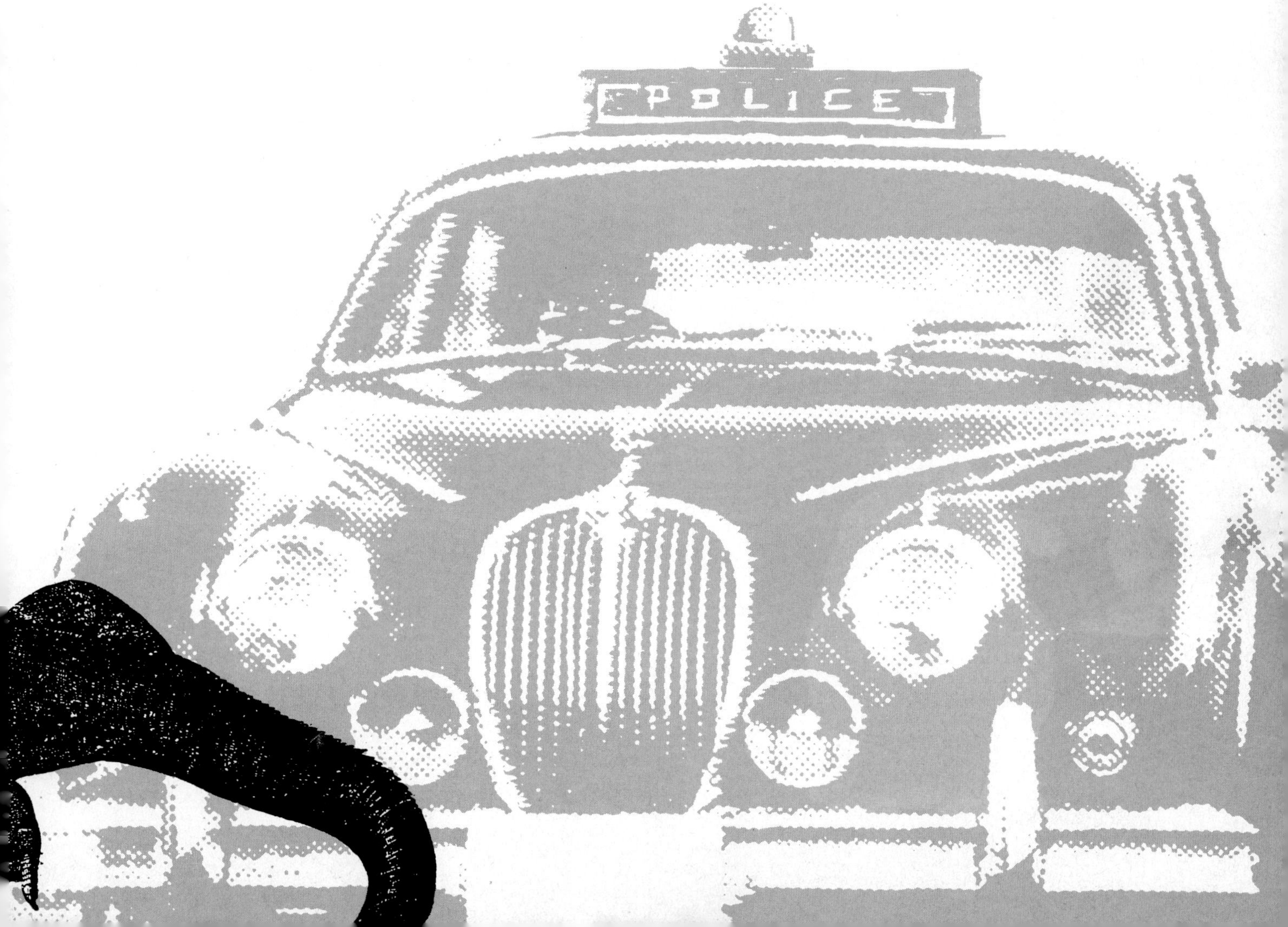
POLICE

RUSHTON: Oh, we're far too busy in Hampshire, mate. Now in addition to extra manpower (*reluctantly*) we have introduced new highspeed three-litre squad cars that make the American type noise ... you know ... WEEEeeee Weeeeee WEEEeeee WEEEeeee as opposed to the old NAnaNAnaNAnaNAna.

(*A piece of paper is handed to* OFFICIAL,*who reads it. He passes it on to* RUSHTON.)

Excuse me. (*Reads.*) Ladies and gentlemen, the capital of France is Paris. Now one of the most important clues so far was received yesterday at operational headquarters. A cassette tape with this letter (*reads*) 'Dear Mr Clever Copper'. (*Humble*) I think that refers to me. (*Reads*) 'You still haven't caught me yet. This tape might help you trace me. Yours, Deathhawk.' (*Hurried in embarrassment*) Er ... we got this letter after we decided on the Hedgehog ... er, it would mean reprogramming the computer.

GUARDIAN: (*Off*) Giles Davies, *Guardian*. Is it true that policemen beat up blacks and homosexuals indiscriminately?

RUSHTON: Depends on how many men are available.

OFFICIAL: (*Cutting off* RUSHTON *as quickly as possible*) Play the tape.

RUSHTON: Oh yes. This is the cassette sent to us by the Hedgehawk ... er ... Hog.
(*He plays cassette – it is a recording of Wham!, 'Wake me up before you go-go' or something topical and repulsive.*)

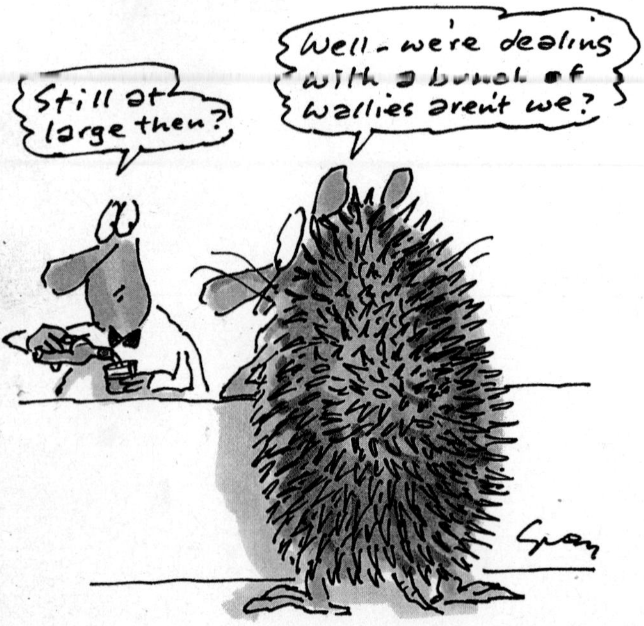
Still at large then?
Well - we're dealing with a bunch of wallies aren't we?

MAIL: (*Off*) That's Wham!

RUSHTON: I know that. We have pulled in the two gentlemen for questioning just in case. People should not be allowed to get away with that sort of thing.

THE TIMES: (*Off*) Sam Brock, *Times*. Is it true that some of your officers have had a close encounter with the 'Hedgehog'?

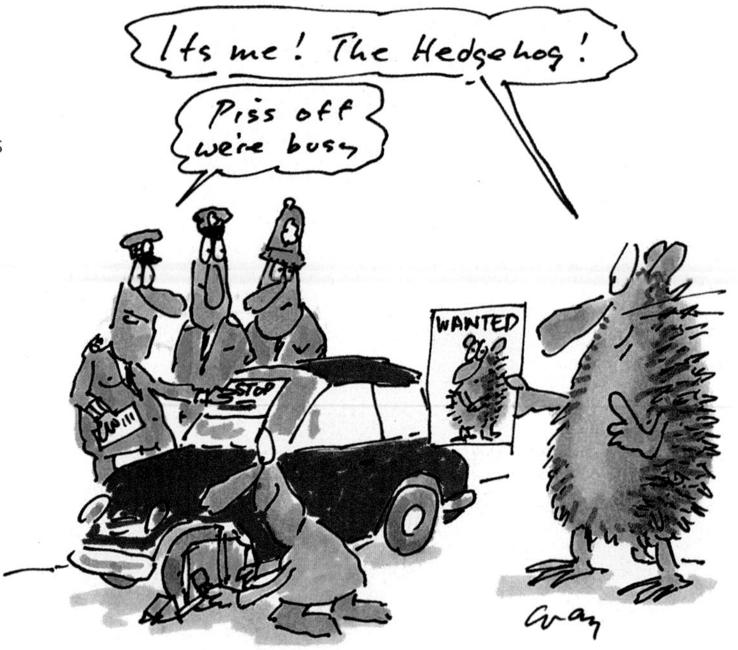
Its me! The Hedgehog!
Piss off we're busy
WANTED
STOP

RUSHTON: (*Sheepish*) Yes ... that's true.

THE TIMES: (*Off*) Is it in fact true that a senior police officer has spoken to him face to face?

RUSHTON: Er...yes.

THE TIMES: (*Off*) Then why hasn't he been caught?

(*'Hear hear' type jeers from the press.*)

RUSHTON: We couldn't nab him.

THE TIMES: (*Off*) Why not?

RUSHTON: He's a mason.

(OFFICIAL *claps hand over* RUSHTON*'s mouth just too late.*)

OFFICIAL: That'll be all, gentlemen.

I LOVED A SURGEON

Written and first performed by Richard Stilgoe in Stilgoe Around at Guy's Hospital

To be accompanied by lovely romantic music.

I loved a surgeon once, but he turned out to be a lout –
To start with it was tricky getting him to take me out.
He said that taking *bits* of people out, he'd often done
But never had he taken out a person, all in one.

He took me out to dinner, and complained the meat was tough.
He sent back seven table knives – said they weren't sharp enough.
I said, 'Come back for coffee.' He came, but wasn't keen –
He peered all round the bedroom to make sure that it was clean.

I lay in bed and waited as I sipped my coffee cup –
He came in from the bathroom when he'd finished scrubbing up.
I caught my breath – no girl expects to see the man she loves
In back-to-front pyjamas and a pair of rubber gloves.

With skilful hands he took my pulse. He listened to my heart
But didn't seem particularly desperate to start.
I said to him, 'Don't hesitate' but then the little creep
Said, 'I'm sorry, but I can't begin until you've gone to sleep.'

At that I turned my back on him, and must have nodded off.
I woke up eight hours later, had a fag and a good cough,
And noticed him – I said, 'Are you still here?' He answered 'Yes,
And last night's operation, I may say, was a success.'

'Get out!' I cried. 'Get out – away – go – get out of my sight!
At least nobody else knows what a fool I was last night!'
At that the surgeon smiled and said, 'That's where you're wrong, my friend –
The twenty students watching all applauded at the end!'

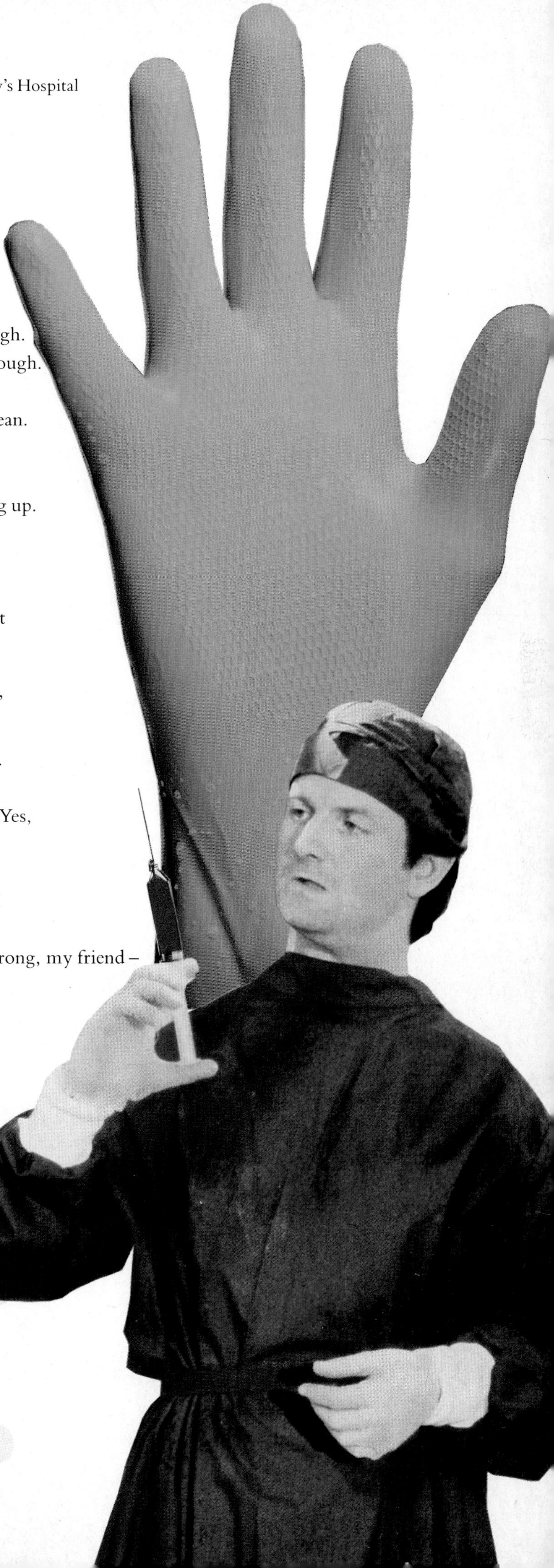

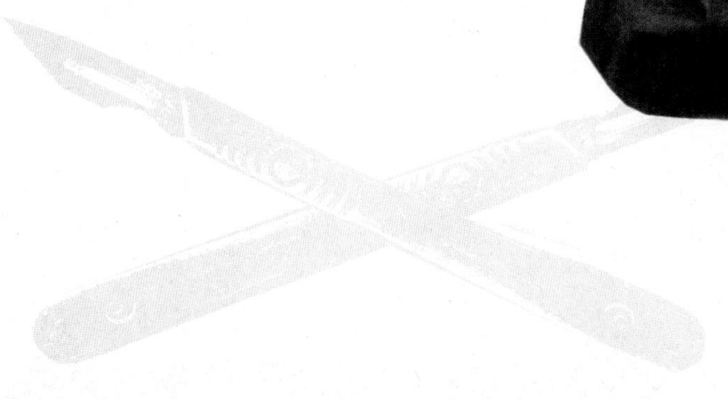

TAKE A PEW

Written by Alan Bennett; first performed by Alan Bennett in Beyond the Fringe

Dog collar, lectern, spotlight. Couldn't be simpler.

VICAR

The twenty-ninth verse of the fourteenth chapter of the book of Genesis:

'But my brother Esau is an hairy man, but I am a smooth man' – my brother Esau is an hairy man, but *I* am a smooth man. Perhaps I can paraphrase this, say the same thing in a different way, by quoting you some words from that grand old prophet, Nehemiah – Nehemiah seven, sixteen:

> And he said unto me, what seest thou
> And I said unto him, lo!
> I see the children of Bebai
> Numbering six hundred and seventy-three
> And I see the children of Asgad
> Numbering one thousand, four hundred and seventy-four.
> (*More quickly*) I see the children of Bebai
> Numbering six hundred and seventy-three
> And I see the children of Asgad
> Numbering one thousand, four hundred and seventy-four.

There come times in the lives of each and every one of us when we turn aside from our fellows and seek the solitude and tranquillity of our own firesides. When we put up our feet and put on our slippers, and sit and stare into the fire; and I wonder at such times whether your thoughts turn, as mine do, to those words I've just read you now. They are very unique and very special words, words that express as so very few words do that sense of lack that lies at the very heart of modern existence. That 'I-don't-quite-know-what-it-is-but-I'm-not-getting-everything-out-of-life-that-I-should-be-getting' sort of feeling. But they are more than this, these words, much much more. They are in a very real sense a challenge to each and every one of us here tonight. What *is* that challenge?

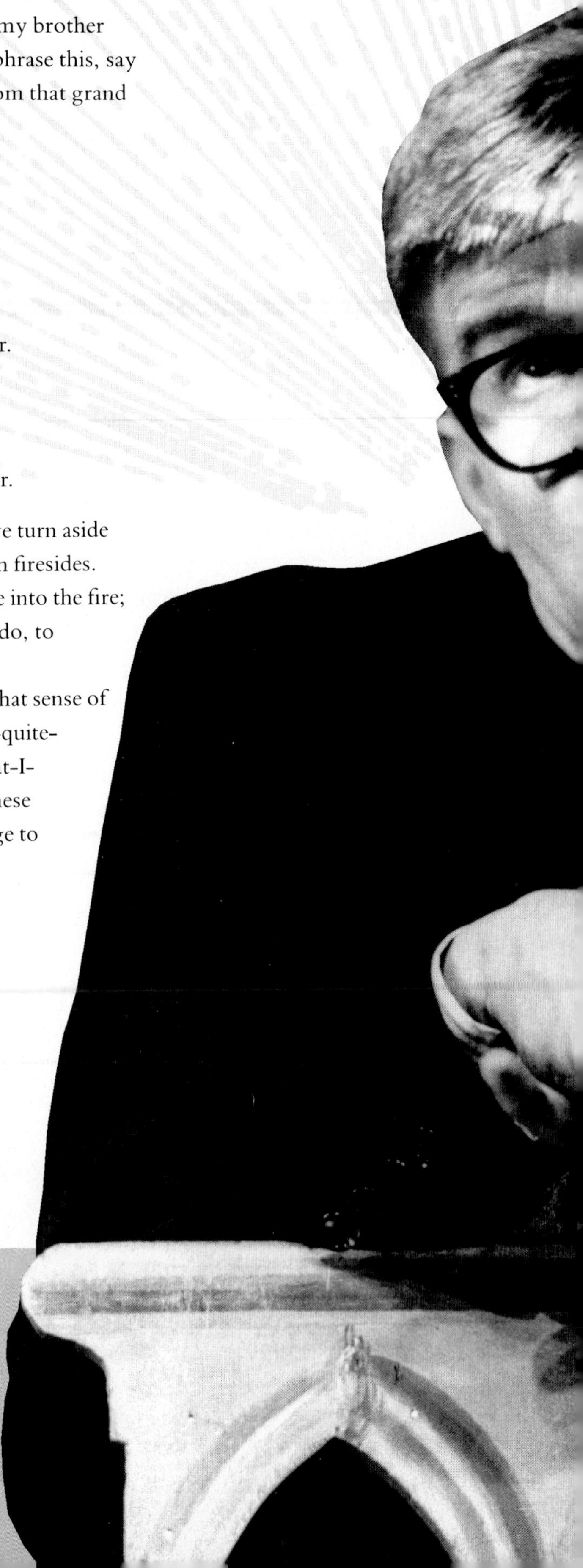

As I was on my way here tonight, I arrived at the station, and by an oversight I happened to go out by the way one is supposed to come in; and as I was going out an employee of the railway company hailed me. 'Hey, Jack,' he shouted, 'where do you think you're going?' That at any rate was the gist of what he said. But, you know, I was grateful to him; because, you see, he put me in mind of the kind of question I felt I ought to be asking you, here tonight. Where do you think *you're* going?

Very many years ago, when I was about as old as some of you are now, I went mountain climbing in Scotland with a very dear friend of mine. And there was this mountain, you see, and we decided to climb it. And so, very early one morning, we arose and began to climb. All day we climbed. Up and up and up; higher and higher and higher. Until the valley lay very small below us, and the mists of the evening began to come down, and the sun to set. And when we reached the summit we sat down to watch this magnificent sight of the sun going down behind the mountain. And as he watched, my friend very suddenly and very violently vomited.

Some of us think that life's a bit like that, don't we? But it isn't. Life, you know, is rather like opening a tin of sardines. We are all of us looking for the key. And, I wonder, how many of you here tonight have wasted years of your lives looking behind the kitchen dressers of this life for that key. I know I have. Others think they've found the key, don't they? They roll back the lid of the sardine tin of life, they reveal the sardines, the riches of life, therein, and they get them out, they enjoy them. But, you know, there's always a little bit in the corner you can't get out. I wonder – I wonder, is there a little bit in the corner of your life? I know there is in mine.

So, now, I draw to a close. I want you, when you go out into the world, in times of trouble, and sorrow, and hopelessness, and despair, amid the hurly-burly of modern life, if ever you're tempted to say, 'Stuff this for a lark'; I want you, at such times, to cast your minds back to the words of my first text to you tonight. 'But my brother Esau is an hairy man, but *I* am a smooth man.'

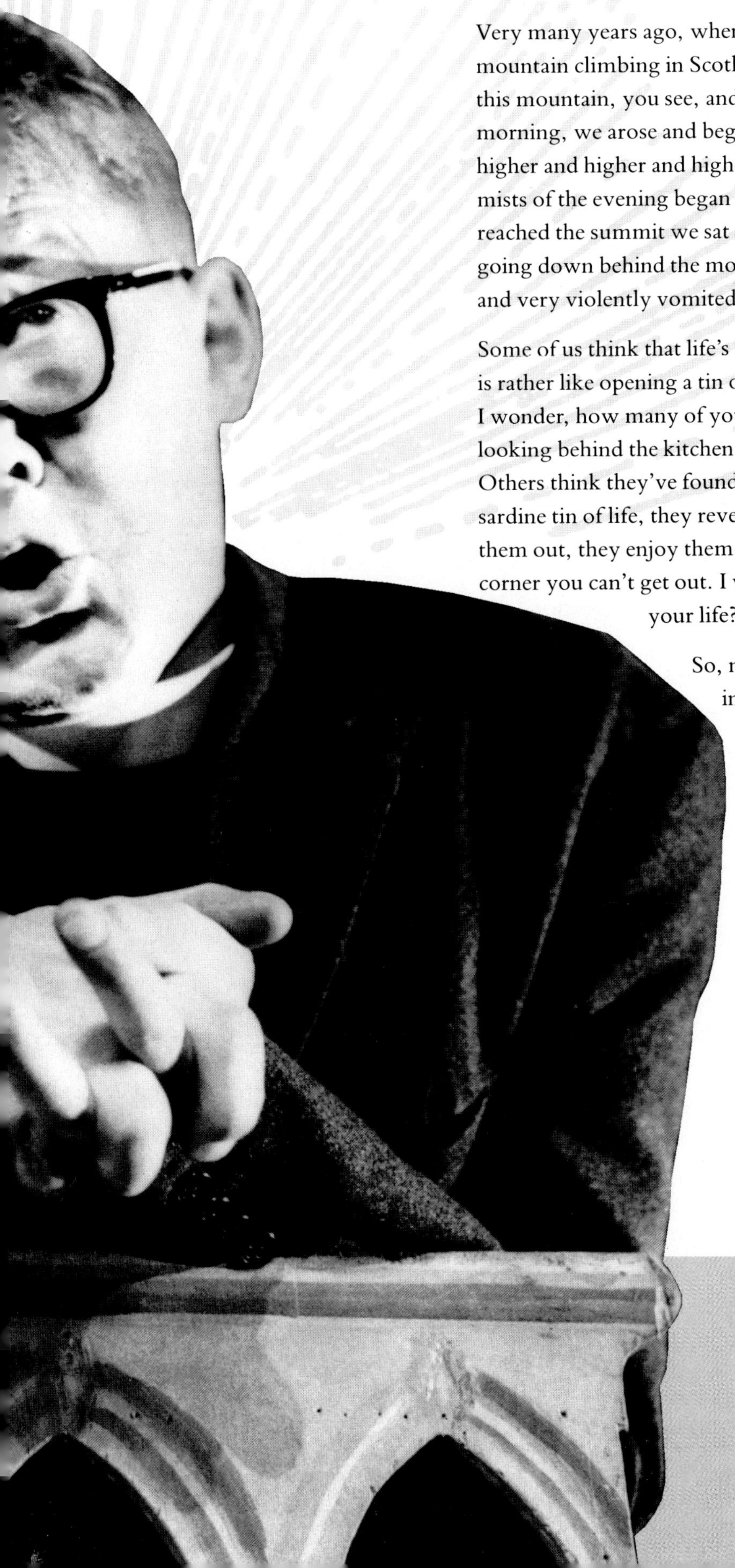

THE REHEARSAL

Written by Andy Hamilton; first performed in Who Dares Wins *by Julia Hills, Rory McGrath, Jimmy Mulville, Philip Pope and Tony Robinson*

A couple are in bed. They look contented.

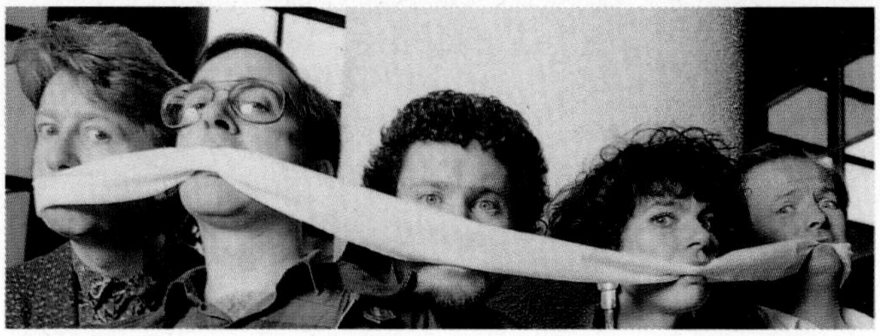

ACTOR: How was it for you?

ACTRESS: Terrific. How was it for you?

ACTOR: Oh, terrific. How was it for you, Trevor?

DIRECTOR: Terrific. OK, so we've done the foreplay bit, what I need from you now is the climax of this sex scene, so I want a long, loud, convincing orgasm.

ACTRESS: Right.

DIRECTOR: OK, action.
(*They begin. She starts making the most absurdly over-the-top and unconvincing 'eek', 'ooh', 'gosh', etc.*)
Cut! Cut! What are you doing?

ACTRESS: I'm simulating orgasm.

DIRECTOR: Is that what you sound like when you ... um ... well...

ACTRESS: Well, to be perfectly honest with you, I've never actually had one. So I'm not really sure what one sounds like.

DIRECTOR: Good grief!

ACTRESS: A friend had one once, last April, at least she thinks she did. I could ring her up and ask her how it goes.

ACTOR: Look, perhaps I can help. It's not that I mean to brag, but well, I've heard quite a few female orgasms in my time and they sound something like this...

DIRECTOR: That's a yawn.

ACTOR: What?

DIRECTOR: That's a yawn.

ACTOR: (*Very disappointed*) Is it?

CAMERAMAN: (*Interrupting*) He's right, yeah, actually the sound they make is sort of 'ow, ow, ow'.

SOUND: No, no, what's the matter with you? It's like this.
(*He imitates rhythmic creaking noise.*)

CAMERAMAN: That's the bed, dummy.

DIRECTOR: For God's sake ... it's not amateur time ... a female orgasm sounds like this ... wooo...

ALL: No...

CAMERAMAN: That's a kettle.
(*General debate.*)

DIRECTOR: It is not a kettle, it's the sound of a woman in ecstasy.
(*Ends in long argument.*)

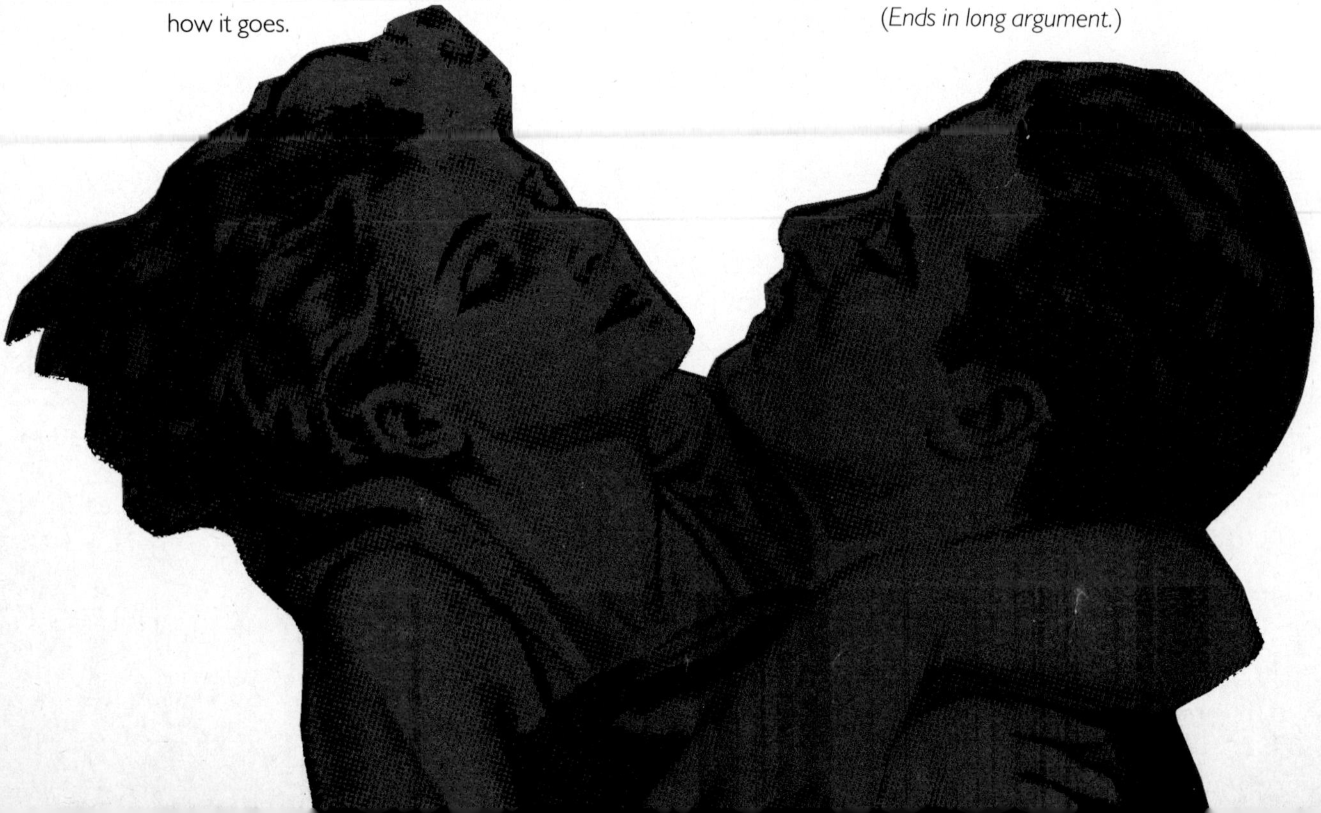

PROMPT

Written by Richard Curtis; first performed by Helen Atkinson Wood and Tim McInnerny in The Oxford Revue

BOY and GIRL enter on stage – very casually, as though they've broken out of the revue momentarily. They are a bit romantic.

BOY: We thought we'd just slip back on and have a private word.

GIRL: Yes, we thought we'd like to talk to you person to person as it were.

BOY AND GIRL: (*simultaneously*) And so…
(*A little giggle.*)

BOY: Sorry.

GIRL: You go on.

BOY: OK. So, first perhaps we should get introduced. Her name's Helen (*or whatever is the real name*).

GIRL: And his name's Tim.

BOY: And together we make Tim and Helen. (*Smile.*) We thought we might, I don't know why, just, you know, talk about how we first met, how we fell in love, about working in theatre and the extraordinary holiday we just had in Edinburgh. Right, well, Helen, you start away.

GIRL: OK. Aaaahm. Prompt.

PROMPTER: (*From off, very calm and clear*) I don't know what to say really.

GIRL: I don't know what to say, really, I'm not very good at … Prompt.

PROMPTER: Improvisation.

GIRL: Improvisation. Prompt.

BOY: (*Eager*) Come on, Helen. Think.

GIRL: What do you mean, 'come on'; you come on: you said you were going to learn the lines for this sketch.

BOY: *I* was going to learn the lines?

GIRL: Yes, you said you were going to learn the lines, so I didn't bother.

BOY: Look, if you're going to do a sketch, both people have to learn the lines. I would have thought that was blindingly obvious.

GIRL: Well, perhaps it is, but who cooked dinner last night?

BOY: (*Annoyance*) You did.

GIRL: Right, so how could I be expected to learn the lines?

BOY: OK, I'm sorry.

GIRL: You just don't seem to care at all any longer, Tim.

BOY: Oh, I do, Helen, for heaven's sake. I... Prompt.

PROMPTER: Love you.

BOY: Love you.

GIRL: No, you don't. You... Prompt.

PROMPTER: Keep making eyes.

GIRL: Keep making eyes at... Prompt.

PROMPTER: Sue.

GIRL: Sue.

BOY: Prompt.

PROMPTER: I don't.

BOY: I don't.

GIRL: Prompt.

PROMPTER: You do.

GIRL: You do.

BOY: Prompt.

PROMPTER: I don't.

BOY: I don't.

GIRL: Prompt.

BOY: Oh, look, this is a complete waste of time. We'd better just go back and get on with learning the sketch.
(They turn to go.)
That was a real mess.

GIRL: Yes.

BOY: Look, we're terribly ... Prompt.

PROMPTER: Sorry.

BOY: Sorry.

GIRL: Yes. Prompt.

PROMPTER: Sorry.

GIRL: Sorry.
(They go off, disconsolate.)

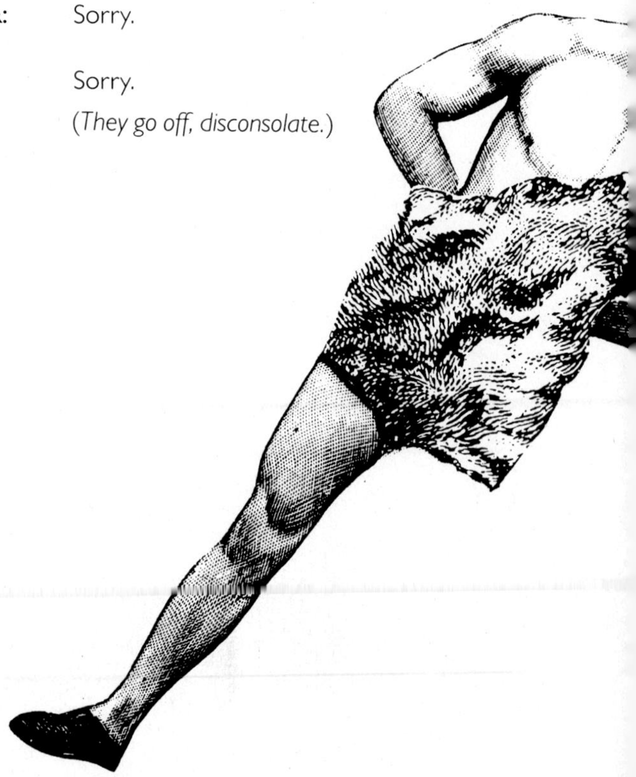

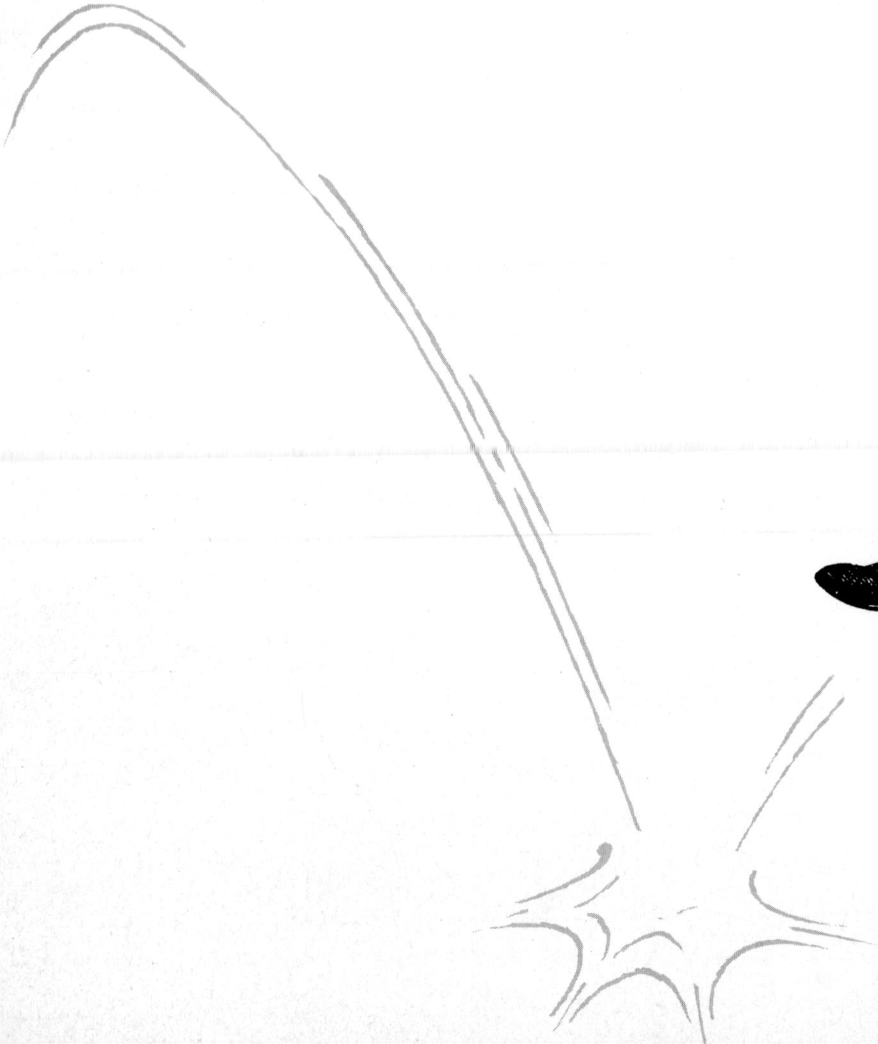

ONE LEG TOO FEW

Written by Peter Cook; first performed by Peter Cook and Dudley Moore in Beyond the Fringe

A slightly seedy office. In other words – unless you've got the cash for a maze of filing cabinets and old theatrical posters – a desk and a chair.

DIRECTOR: Miss Rigby! Stella, my love! Would you send in the next auditionee, please. Mr Spiggott, I believe it is.
(*Enter* SPIGGOTT.)
Mr Spiggott, I believe?

SPIGGOTT: Yes – Spiggott by name, Spiggott by nature.

(SPIGGOTT *follows* DIRECTOR *around chair.*)

DIRECTOR: Yes ... there's no need to follow me, Mr Spiggott. Please be stood. Now, Mr Spiggott, you are, I believe, auditioning for the part of Tarzan.

SPIGGOTT: Right.

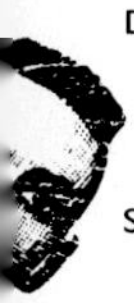

DIRECTOR: Now, Mr Spiggott, I couldn't help noticing almost at once that you are a one-legged person.

SPIGGOTT: You noticed that?

DIRECTOR: I noticed that, Mr Spiggott. When you have been in the business as long as I have you get to notice these little things almost instinctively. Now, Mr Spiggott, you, a one-legged man, are applying for the role of Tarzan – a role which traditionally involves the use of a two-legged actor.

SPIGGOTT: Correct.

DIRECTOR: And yet, you, a unidexter, are applying for the role.

SPIGGOTT: Right.

DIRECTOR: A role for which two legs would seem to be the minimum requirement.

SPIGGOTT: Very true.

DIRECTOR: Well, Mr Spiggott, need I point out to you where your deficiency lies as regards landing the role?

SPIGGOTT: Yes, I think you ought to.

DIRECTOR: Need I say with overmuch emphasis that it is in the leg division that you are deficient?

SPIGGOTT: The leg division?

DIRECTOR: Yes, the leg division, Mr Spiggott. You are deficient in it – to the tune of one. Your right leg I like. I like your right. A lovely leg for the role. That's what I said when I saw it come in. I said, 'A lovely leg for the role.' I've got nothing against your right leg. The trouble is – neither have you. You fall down on your left.

SPIGGOTT: You mean it's inadequate?

DIRECTOR: Yes, it's inadequate, Mr Spiggott. And to my mind, the British public is just not ready for the sight of a one-legged ape man swinging through the jungly tendrils.

SPIGGOTT: I see.

DIRECTOR: However, don't despair. After all, you score over a man with no legs at all. Should a legless man come in here demanding the role, I should have no hesitation in saying, 'Get out, run away.'

SPIGGOTT: So there's still a chance?

DIRECTOR: There is still a very good chance. If we get no two-legged character actors in here within the next two months, there is still a very good chance that you'll land this vital role. Failing two-legged actors, you, a unidexter, are just the sort of person we shall be attempting to contact telephonically.

SPIGGOTT: Well ... thank you very much.

DIRECTOR: So my advice is: to hop on a bus, go home, and sit by your telephone in the hope that we will be getting in touch with you. I'm really sorry I can't be more definite, but, as you realize, it's really a two-legged man we're after. Good morning, Mr Spiggott.
(SPIGGOTT *exits.*)

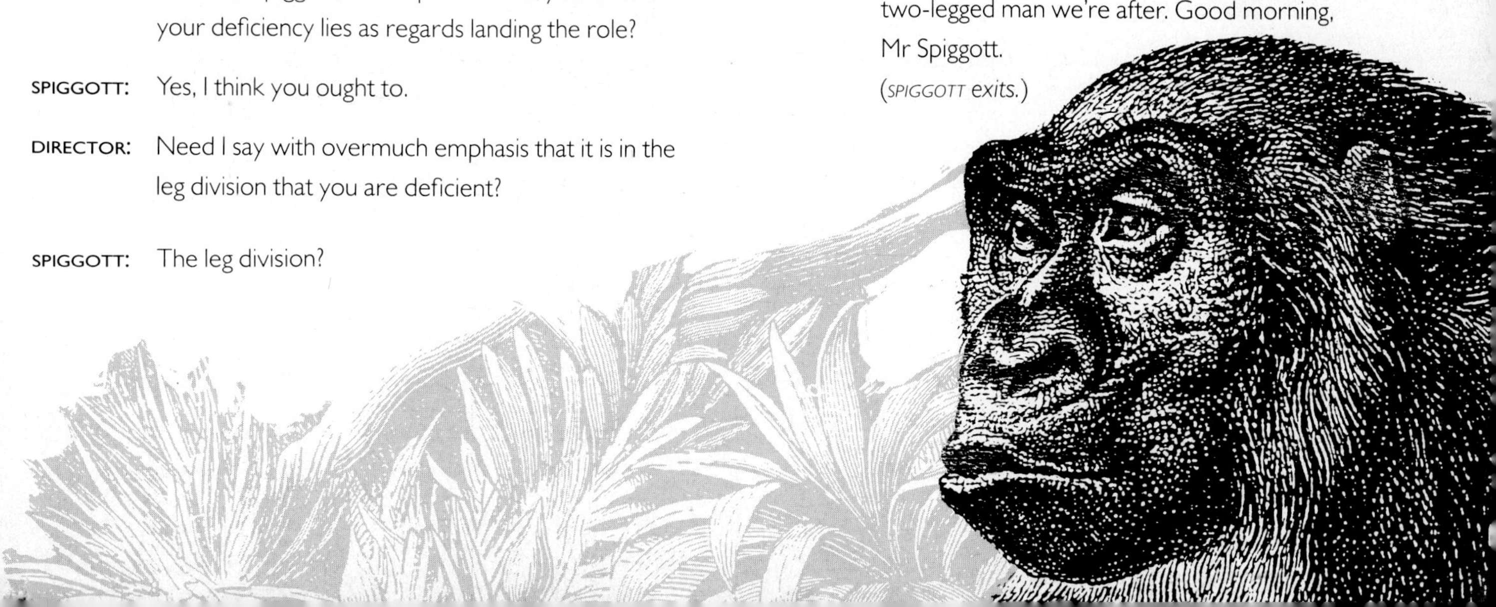

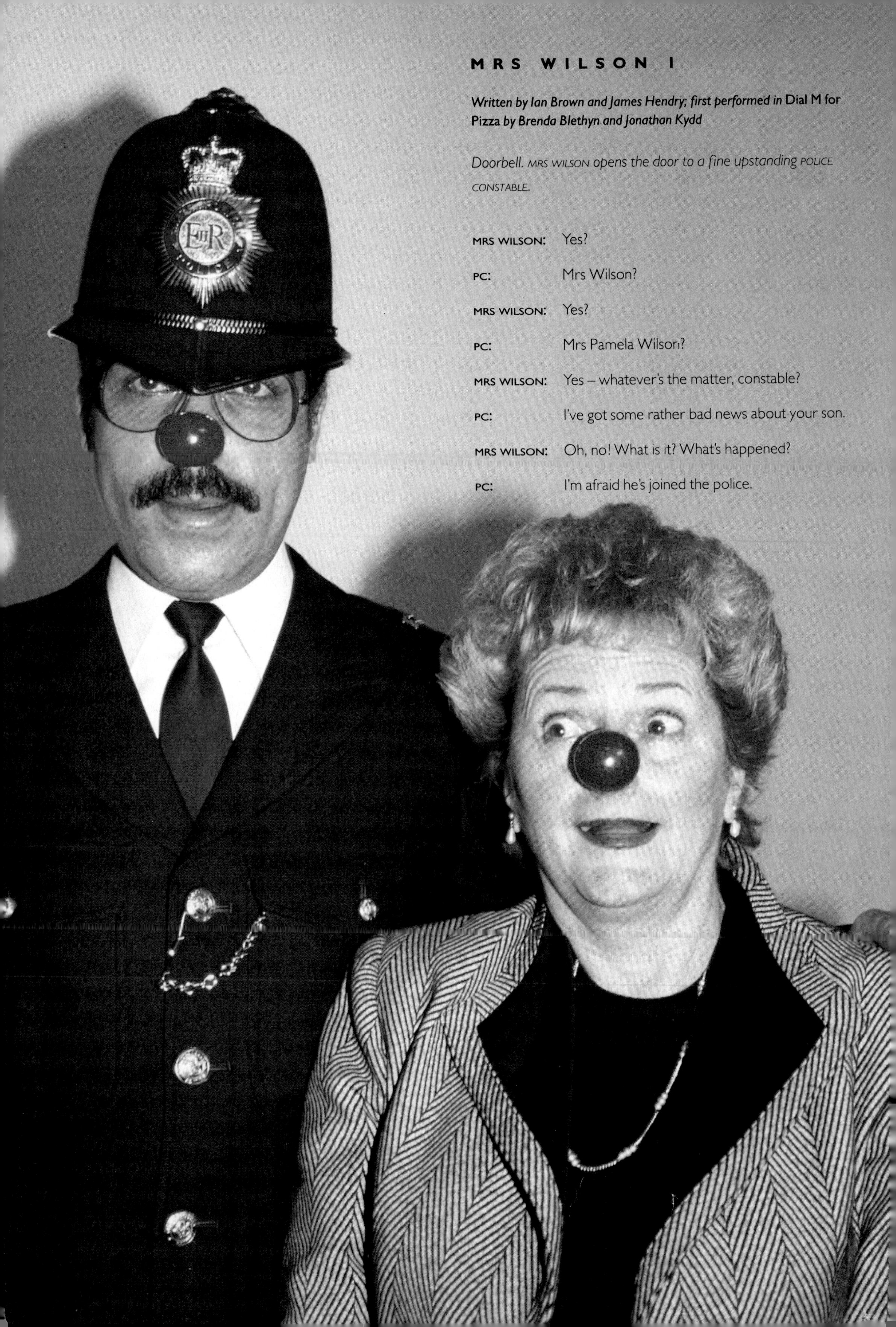

MRS WILSON 1

Written by Ian Brown and James Hendry; first performed in* Dial M for Pizza *by Brenda Blethyn and Jonathan Kydd

Doorbell. MRS WILSON *opens the door to a fine upstanding* POLICE CONSTABLE.

MRS WILSON:	Yes?
PC:	Mrs Wilson?
MRS WILSON:	Yes?
PC:	Mrs Pamela Wilson?
MRS WILSON:	Yes – whatever's the matter, constable?
PC:	I've got some rather bad news about your son.
MRS WILSON:	Oh, no! What is it? What's happened?
PC:	I'm afraid he's joined the police.

M I 5

Written by Stephen Fry; first performed by Stephen Fry and Hugh Laurie in Cambridge

Music: the Harry Lime theme. Rooms at Cambridge. A tea service is being set out by a donnish figure in tweeds. The DON *is whistling to the music as it fades. Knocking.*

DON: Come.
(*Enter* HARRIS.)
Ah, Parsons, come in – sit ye, sit ye. Formosan Oolong do you?

HARRIS: Thank you.

DON: Good, good. Now the reason I've asked you round, Parsons, is not because I'm your tutor or anything like that, but because I thought it was time you and I had a little – milk?

HARRIS: Thank you, sir.

DON: – chat together. How long is it, Parsons…?

HARRIS: Harris, sir.

DON: Just so, Harris, Harris. How long is it, Harris, that you've been at King's now?

HARRIS: Corpus Christi, sir.

DON: Corpus, as you so rightly point out, Christi. You've been at Corpus Christi now, Harris, for three years, and I've had my eye on you for some time.

HARRIS: Thank you, sir.

DON: Tell me. Did your father ever tell you the precise nature of the work he was engaged in before his – untimely death?

HARRIS: My father's still alive, sir.

DON: Ah, that's what he tells you, is it? That's your father, all right. Secretive to the last.

HARRIS: He's in advertising, sir.

DON: Advertising? Ho, that man had class. He wasn't a natural, but he was the best we had. Well, Harris… I don't want to go on calling you Harris all the time, what's your Christian name, what do your friends call you?

HARRIS: Kim, sir.

DON: Kim? No relation of… Kim Philby?

HARRIS: I don't think so, sir.

DON: Guy Philby?

HARRIS: No.

DON: Donald Philby? Sir Anthony Philby?

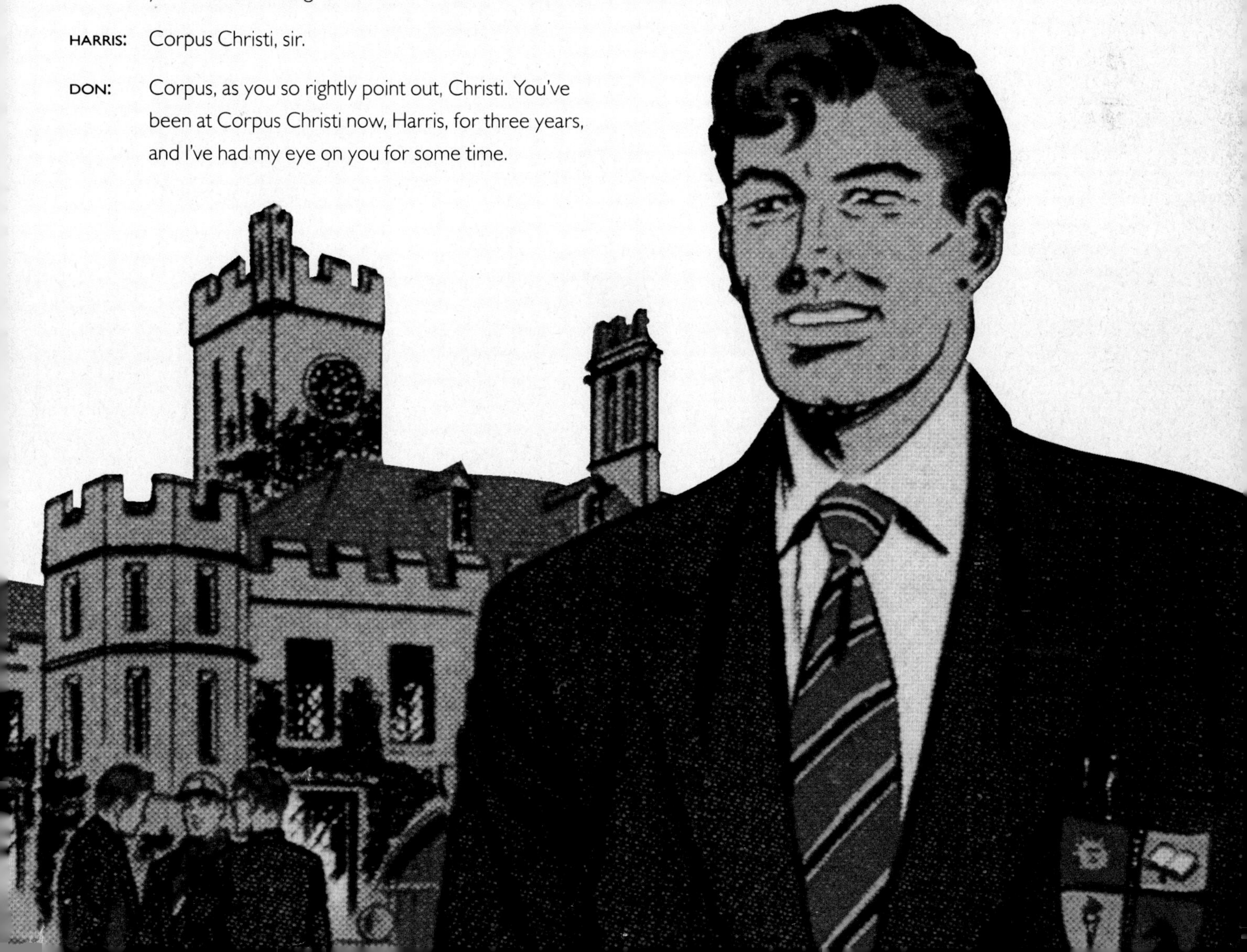

HARRIS: No, sir, not to my knowledge. My surname is Harris.

DON: Just so, but it is *Kim* Harris, isn't it?

HARRIS: Yes, sir.

DON: So, Kim Harris, ha, ha. After a year and a half at Trinity, what career had you in mind, eh? Tinker, tailor, soldier, or... or... or what, hm?

HARRIS: I hadn't thought about it too deeply, sir. I thought I might follow in my father's footsteps.

DON: Ah, the service. Dangerous footsteps, Harris, dangerous footsteps.

HARRIS: Sir?

DON: Tell me something, Harris, changing tack for a moment, I've got quite a dossier on you here and very impressive reading it makes too, if I may say so, but it tells me nothing on your UCCA form about your pain threshold. Tell me, how do you think you could cope under extremes of mental and physical discomfort?

HARRIS: Well...

DON: Well? Splendid, splendid. (*Extending hand*) Welcome aboard. I think you and I are going to be friends. I'm going to ask you to do something for me, Philby.

HARRIS: Harris, sir.

DON: Harris, I'm going to ask you to curtail your political activities for a while, valuable as they are. Duck out of the public gaze, keep a low profile. Are you a homosexual?

HARRIS: Well, I...

DON: Good. Now there are one or two people I want you to meet, you'll know some of them already. They'll debrief you. Take no notice. Guy you probably knew at Eton.

HARRIS: Holland Park, sir.

DON: I'm sorry?

HARRIS: Holland Park, I was at Holland Park.

DON: What's that?

HARRIS: The school I was at, sir. It's a comprehensive in West London.

DON: Oh, I see. Holland Park, yes, quite so, ha, ha, ha. Get out.

MRS WILSON 2

Written by Ian Brown and James Hendry; first performed in Dial M for Pizza *by Brenda Blethyn and Jonathan Kydd*

Doorbell. MRS WILSON *opens the door once more to that same fine upstanding* POLICE CONSTABLE.

MRS WILSON: Yes?

PC: Mrs Wilson?

MRS WILSON: Yes?

PC: Mrs Pamela Wilson?

MRS WILSON: Yes – whatever's the matter, constable?

PC: There's been rather an unfortunate accident.

MRS WILSON: Oh, no! What is it? What's happened?

PC: I'm afraid we're doing the same joke twice.

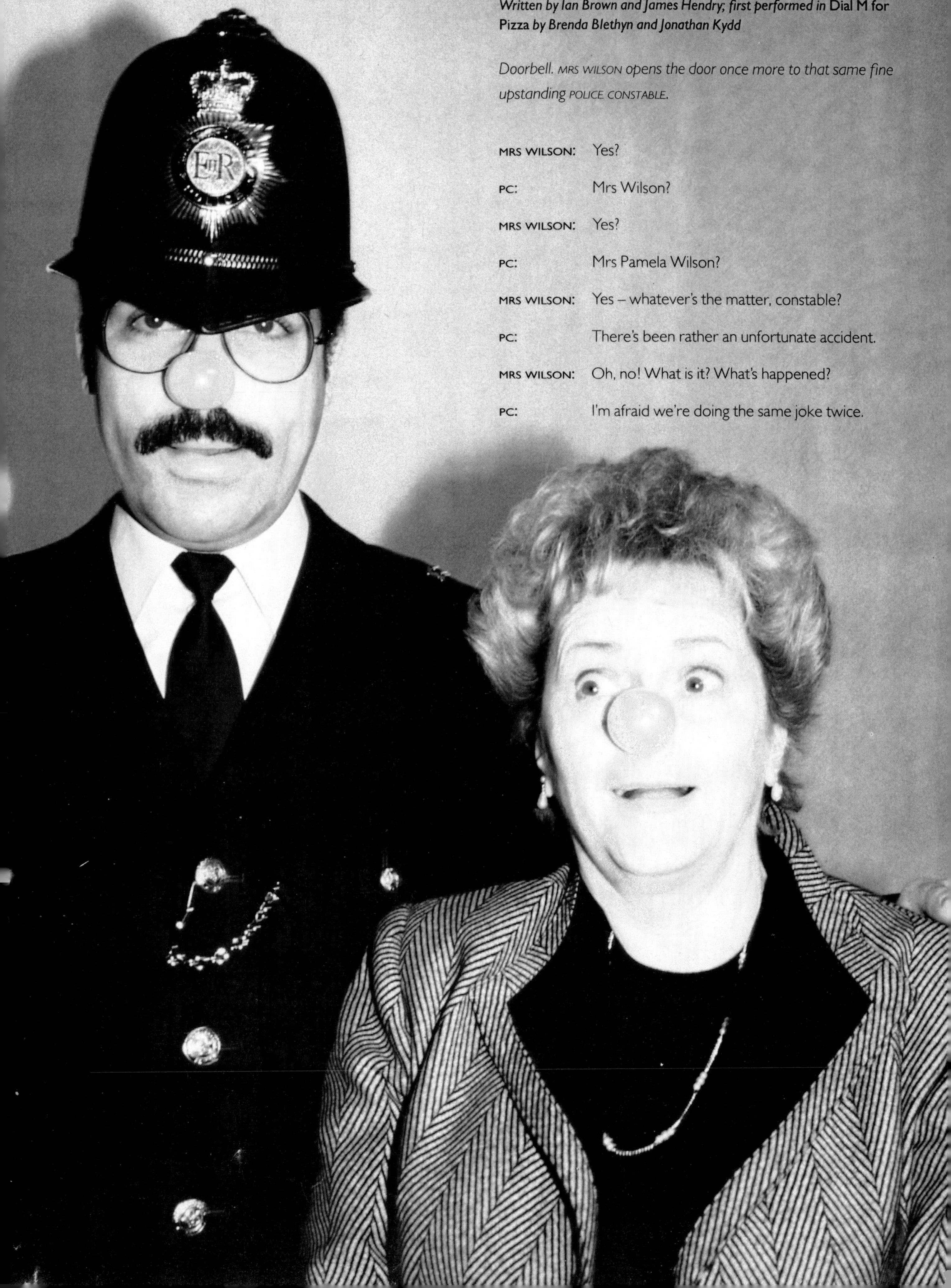

PSYCHIATRIST SKETCH

Written and performed by Peter Cook and Dudley Moore

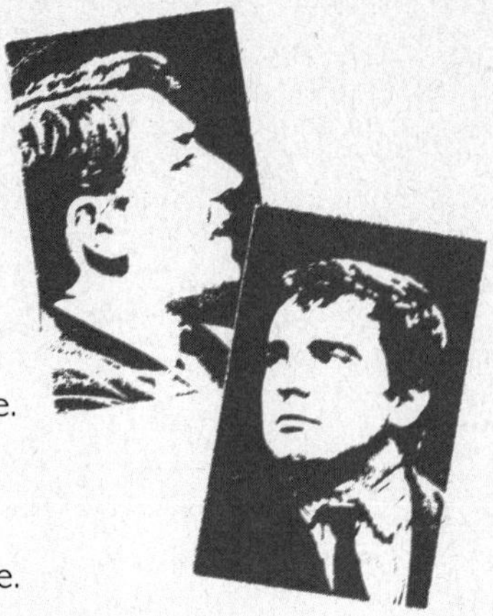

DR BRAINTREE *sits in his study.*

DOCTOR: Come in.
(*Enter* ROGER.)
Hullo, Roger.

ROGER: Hullo, Dr Braintree.

DOCTOR: Hullo, come in.

ROGER: I'm so sorry I'm late.

DOCTOR: That's quite all right – how are you?

ROGER: I'm very well, thank you.

DOCTOR: Would you like to sit down, or would you prefer to lie?

ROGER: Uhm, I'll sit, thank you.

DOCTOR: Right, well, sit right down. Tell me, how are you in yourself?

ROGER: I'm really feeling rather in the pink.

DOCTOR: Oh, this is terrific.

ROGER: Yes. It's really, you know – if anyone had told me that talking to psychiatrists would have helped me at all, I'd have laughed in their faces, you know.

DOCTOR: Yes.

ROGER: But I can honestly say that our little chats together have really been of tremendous benefit to me.

DOCTOR: I'm so glad, Roger: of course a lot of people are instinctively very suspicious of psychiatry, and possibly, you know, with reason, but it can help at times.

ROGER: Well, I really think it can, because you know, I've got so much self-confidence now. I'm much less self-conscious in the company of the opposite sex, which I wasn't, as you know.

DOCTOR: Yes, yes, yes, yes, yes. You're less inhibited, are you?

ROGER: (*Suggestively*) Oh, I should say.

DOCTOR: Good, this is terrific.

ROGER: And the wonderful thing about it all is … well, I'm in love.

DOCTOR: Well, this is wonderful news, Roger – you're in love. With a woman?

ROGER: Yes.

DOCTOR: So much the better – that's terrific.

ROGER: You know, it's so wonderful to be in love – I can't tell you the absolute joy I have.

DOCTOR: Well, love is a wonderful thing: I've been there myself. It's a wonderful thing.

ROGER: I mean, she's … this girl, this creature (*emotional*), this goddess …

DOCTOR: Yes …

ROGER: She's so, you know, it's so right. Everything is so wonderful, you know.

DOCTOR: Yes, yes – you really click together.

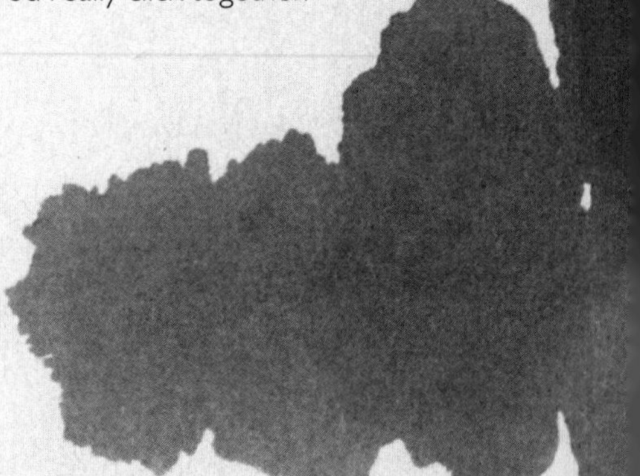

ROGER: Yes. Oh, it's so marvellous, but – the only trouble is that, apart from this wonderful light-hearted love I have, I seem to be saddled with this tremendous burning sense of guilt.

DOCTOR: You have guilt as well as love: well, this is unfortunate, Roger. You know, sex is the most wonderful, natural, healthy thing in the world. There's no reason at all to have any guilt about it. I mean, why should you have guilt about sex – it's a lovely beautiful thing.

ROGER: Well, it's not really as simple as that, you know – it's rather difficult to explain. Uhm, I don't really know where to start.

DOCTOR: Well, begin at the beginning. That's always the best place. What's the girl's name?

ROGER: (*Pause.*) Stephanie.

DOCTOR: Stephanie. That's a lovely name, isn't it – well, my wife's name in fact, isn't it?

ROGER: Yes, it's Stephanie.

DOCTOR: Yes, it's Stephanie.

ROGER: No, it's Stephanie.

DOCTOR: Yes, it's Stephanie, Roger.

ROGER: Yes, it's Stephanie: it's your wife.

DOCTOR: Oh, you're in love with my wife, Stephanie. Well, this is a perfectly understandable thing, Roger. She's a very attractive woman – I married her myself. I don't see why you should feel upset about that.

ROGER: But she's in love with me.

DOCTOR: Well, this is again perfectly understandable, Roger. I mean, you're a perfectly attractive human being, as I've told you over the last few weeks. There's nothing repulsive about you, is there? There's no reason why a highly sexed woman such as Stephanie shouldn't fall in love with you. And I must explain to you, Roger, that I'm a very busy man: I have many, many patients to see – I see rather less of my wife perhaps than I should, and I think it's perfectly understandable she should seek some sort of companionship outside the marriage – I don't think that's unreasonable at all.

ROGER: But she's not seeking anything outside the marriage – nor am I. We want to get married.

DOCTOR: Well, this again is understandable. After all, you're two young people in love and you want to express your feelings within the confines of a bourgeois society through marriage. I think it's very appropriate.

ROGER: The awful thing is, you see – I should feel grateful to you for what you've done. And all I can feel is this burning jealousy – I can't bear the thought of you touching her.

DOCTOR: Well, of course, I understand this. One is tremendously possessive about someone one loves – it would be unhealthy not to have this jealousy reaction, Roger.

ROGER: But don't you see – I hate you.

DOCTOR: Of course you hate me, Roger.

ROGER: I hate you for being so near her.

DOCTOR: Yes, of course you hate me, Roger. You love to hate the one who loves the one you hate to love the one you hate. This is a very old rule, Roger – there's nothing to feel ashamed about. It's absolutely reasonable.

ROGER: Don't you understand – I want to kill you.

DOCTOR: Of course you want to kill me. Because by killing me, Roger, you eradicate the one you hate. This is a perfectly natural reaction, Roger.

ROGER: You're so reasonable, aren't you?

DOCTOR: Yes, I am.

ROGER: (Getting cross) You understand it all so much … you're so logical.
            (Gets up to strike him.)

DOCTOR: Yes, I am – it's my job.

ROGER: I'm going to have to kill you now.

DOCTOR: Ah – Roger – this is a little inconvenient, because I have another patient at six-thirty and then there's someone else at seven after that. I wonder if you could make it some time next week. (Standing over him.) Could you make it early in the week, say? (Pause – relax.)

ROGER: When do you think?

DOCTOR: How are you fixed on Wednesday morning? Say nine-thirty – would that be convenient?

ROGER: Yes, that's perfect.

DOCTOR: Right, well, if you could pop along at nine-thirty and kill me then.

ROGER: Once again, Doctor Braintree, I'm amazed, you know, really. I'm so grateful to you for showing me the way.

DOCTOR: It's what I'm here for, Roger.

ROGER: Thank you very much. Thank you.

DOCTOR: And with a bit of luck, this should be the last time you have to visit me.

71

THE GOOD OLD DAYS

Written by John Cleese, Marty Feldman, Graham Chapman and Tim Brooke-Taylor; first performed in At Last the 1948 Show

It is sundowner time at a tropical paradise. Four north-countrymen, in late middle age and tuxedos, sit contemplating the sunset. A WAITER *pours some claret for one of them to taste.*

JOSHUA: Very passable. Not bad at all.

(*The* WAITER *pours the wine for the rest of them, and departs.*)

OBADIAH: Can't beat a good glass of Château de Chasselas, eh, Josiah?

JOSIAH: Aye, you're right there, Obadiah.

EZEKIEL: Who'd have thought … forty years ago … that we'd be sitting here, drinking Château de Chasselas?

JOSHUA: Aye. In those days we were glad to have the price of a cup of tea.

OBADIAH: Aye, a cup of *cold* tea…

EZEKIEL: Without milk or sugar…

JOSIAH: *Or* tea…

JOSHUA: Aye, and a cracked cup at that.

EZEKIEL: We never had a cup. We used to drink out of a rolled-up newspaper.

OBADIAH: Best we could manage was to chew a piece of damp cloth.

JOSIAH: But y'know … we were happier in those days, although we were poor.

JOSHUA: *Because* we were poor … My old dad used to say, 'Money doesn't bring you happiness, son.'

EZEKIEL: He was right. I was happier then and I had *nothing*. We used to live in a tiny old tumbledown house with great holes in the roof.

OBADIAH: A house! You were lucky to have a house. We used to live in one room, twenty-six of us, no furniture, and half the floor was missing. We were all huddled in one corner, for fear of falling.

JOSIAH: You were lucky to have a room. We used to live in the corridor.

JOSHUA: Ooooh, I used to *dream* of living in a corridor. That would have been a palace to us. We lived in an old water tank in the rubbish tip. We were woken up every morning by having a load of rotting fish dumped on us. House, huh!

EZEKIEL: Well, when I said *house* … it was only a hole in the ground covered by a couple of foot of torn canvas, but it was a house to *us*.

OBADIAH: We were evicted from our hole in the ground. We had to go and live in the lake.

JOSIAH: Eee! You were lucky to have a lake. There were over 150 of us living in a small shoebox in the middle of the road.

JOSHUA: A *cardboard* box?

JOSIAH: Yes.

JOSHUA: You were lucky. We lived for three months in a rolled-up newspaper in a septic tank. We used to get up at six, clean the newspaper, eat a crust of stale bread, work fourteen hours at the mill, day in, day out, for sixpence a week, come home, and Dad would thrash us to sleep with his belt.

OBADIAH: Luxury! We used to get out of the lake at three, clean it, eat a handful of hot gravel, work twenty hours at t'mill for twopence a month, come home, and Dad would beat us about the head and neck with a broken bottle, *if* we were *lucky*.

(*A pause.*)

JOSIAH: Aye, well, we had it *tough*. I had to get out of the shoebox at midnight, lick the road clean, eat a couple of bits of cold gravel, work twenty-three hours a day at the mill for a penny every four years and when we got home Dad would slice us in half with a bread knife.

(*A longer pause.*)

EZEKIEL: Right… I had to get up in the morning at ten o'clock at night, half an hour before I went to bed, eat a lump of poison, work twenty-nine hours a day at t'mill and pay boss to let us work, come home, and each night Dad used to kill us and dance about on our graves, singing.

(*A very long pause.*)

JOSHUA: Aye, and you try and tell the young people of today that, and they won't believe you.

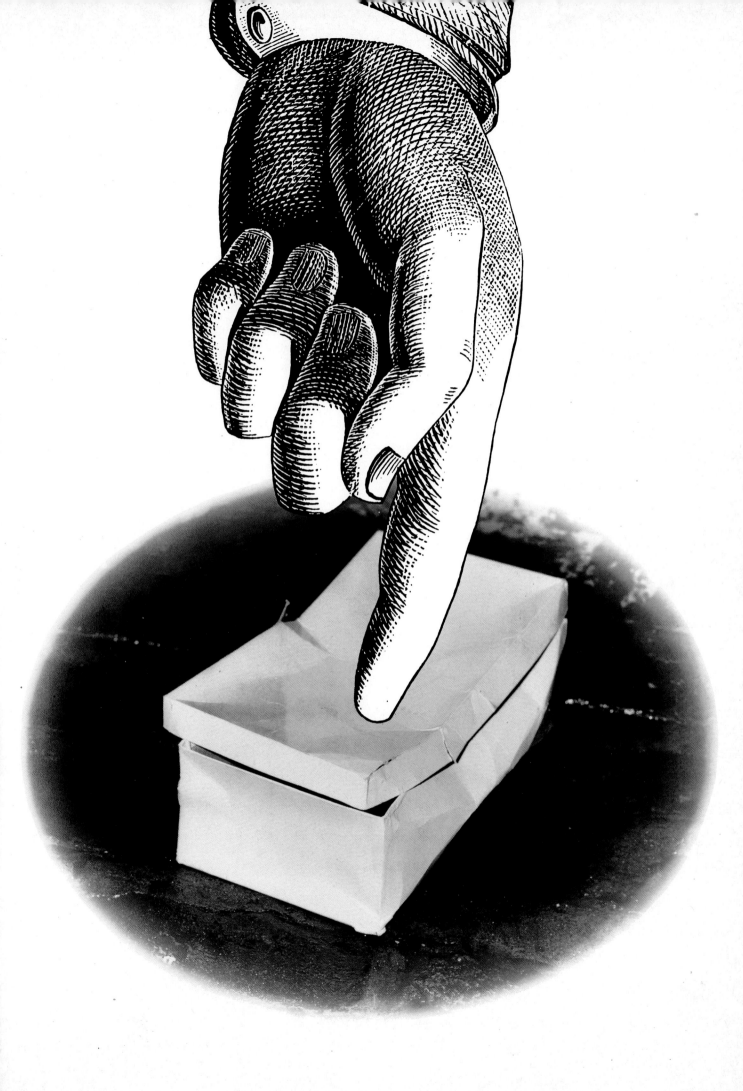

COWPOKE

Lyrics by Griff Rhys Jones, original music by Michael Bywater; first performed a long, long time ago, when the West was wild, and men were men and Griff still had the odd drink now and then. To be accompanied by your favourite cowboy tune.

A Country-and-Western COWPOKE *sits on a stool. He can be joined for the chorus by any number of other cowpokes or pokesses.*

COWPOKE:
I'd like to sing a little song about a cowboy
who has fallen on hard times.

I'm sittin' on the floor of the jailhouse,
And I'm feeling so down and so blue.
And I'll never forget what the dear loved one said.
She said, 'Moo, Moo, Moo, Moo.'

Now a man on the range sure gets lonely,
Like a ship without a rudder.
There's a lowing of the herd and his feelings get stirred
And he fancies a bit of the udder.

Now one of those guys was called William,
We sing of his escapades still.
He was made of such stuff
That cows were enough
And we called him Buffalo Bill.

I'm a lone cowpoke
And surely do ? ? ?
There were no ladies there but we didn't care,
We were too busy poking the cow.
We were too busy poking the cow.

But every man meets his match in the end,
And now I am filled with remorse.
I came into town, there were no cows around,
But I shouldn't have poked . . . the sheriff's wife.

So I'm sitting on the floor at the jailhouse
And I'm feeling so down and so blue.
And I'll never forget what the dear loved one said.
She said, 'Moo, Moo, Moo, Moo.'
Yes, she did.
She said, 'Moo, Moo, Moo, Moo.'

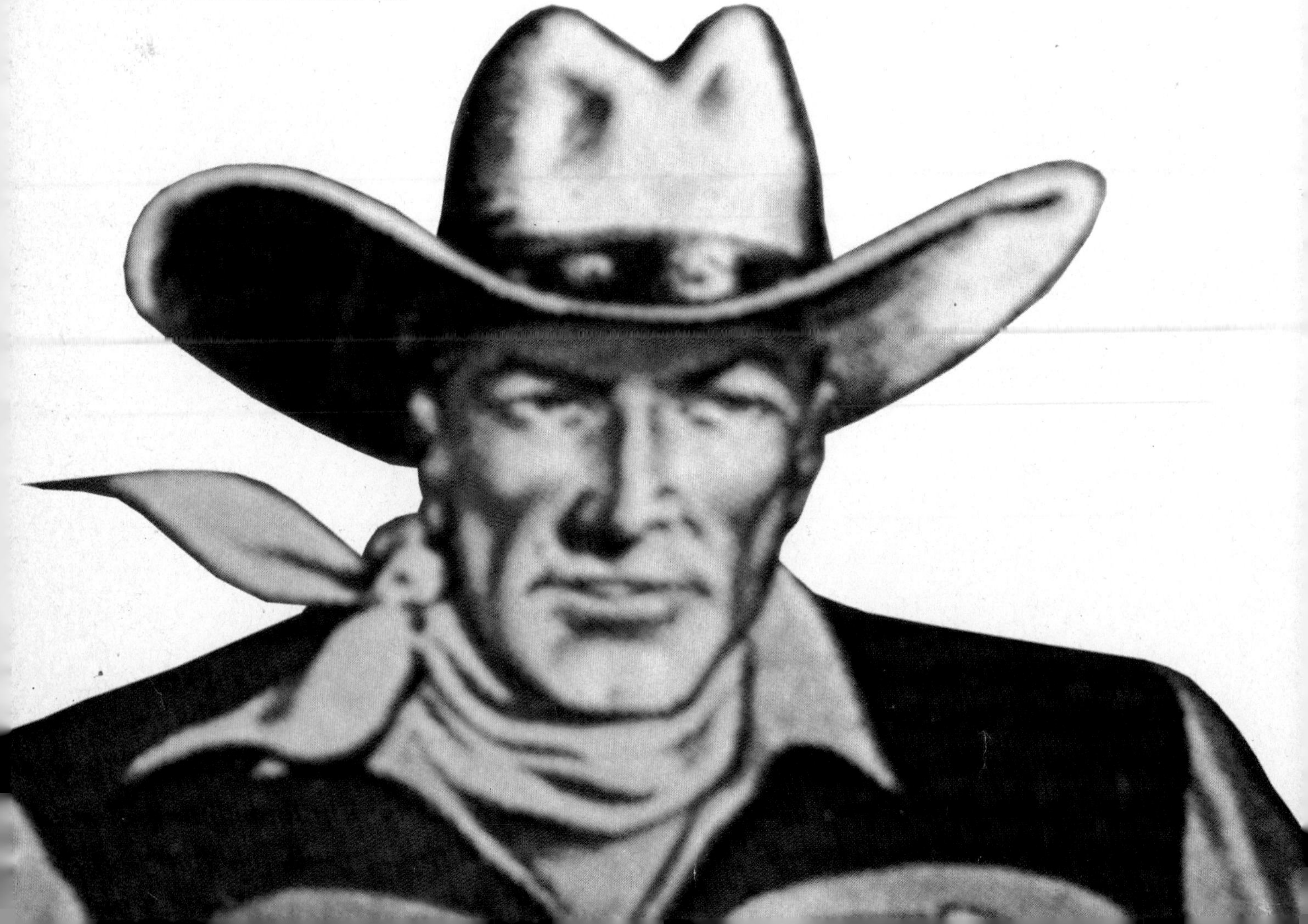

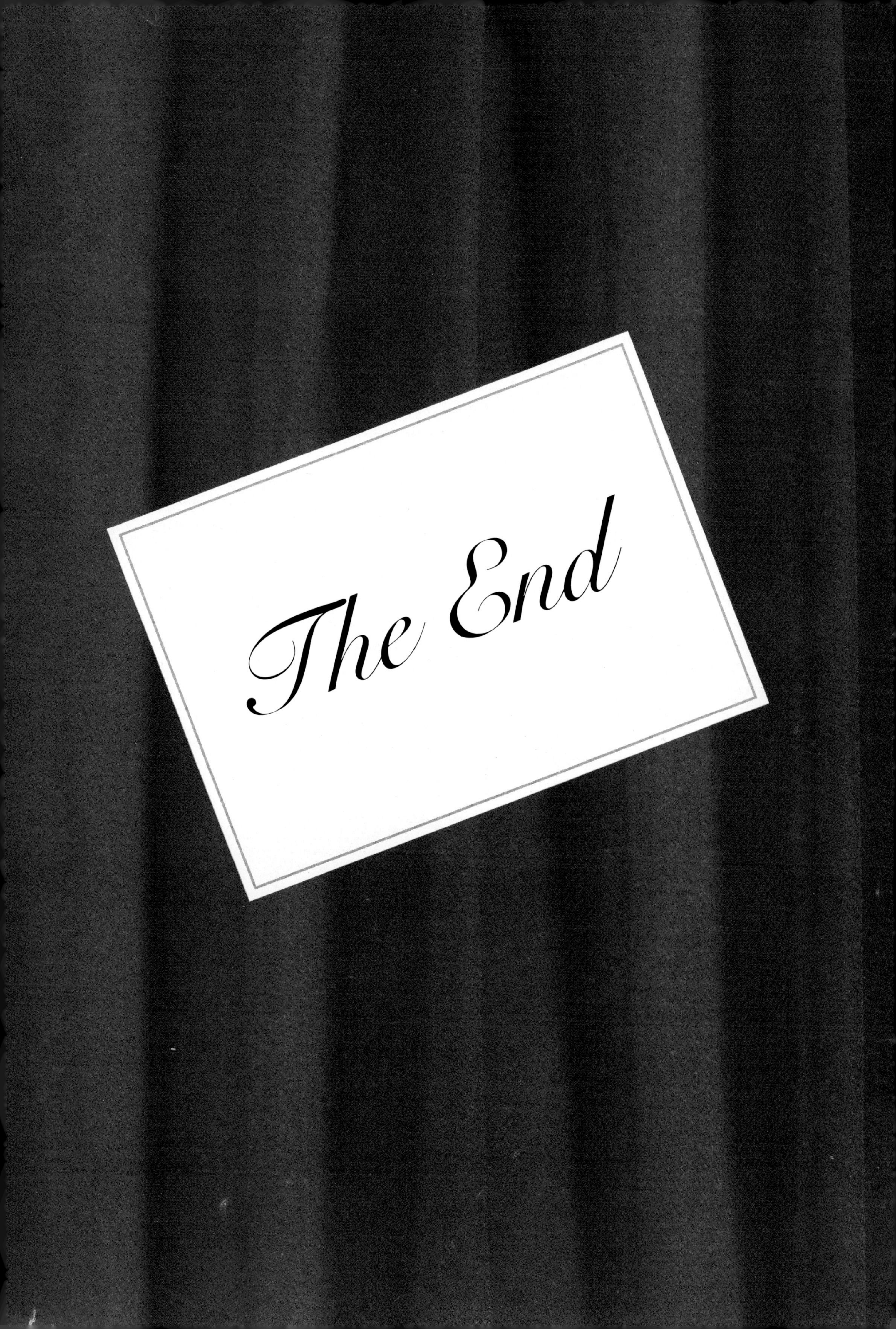
The End

The Do-It-Yourself Comic Relief Revue-Mounting Manual

A Pompous Idiot

Dear Reader and Revue-Mounter,

You now have the script, the text, the magical words with which to coax joyful laughter from your beloved audience. But these are the mere ingredients with which you must bake the cake of merriment. You have the runny eggs of Cleese, the pure flavour of Bennett, the tart vanilla of Elton, the wholesome milk of Fry & Laurie – and indeed, you have the Cook. But it is up to you, dear artiste, to beat them together into smoothness with the rough wooden spoon of rehearsal, to pour them into the baking tin of the theatre, to bake them in the heated panic of dress rehearsal and finally to take them out of the oven and to present the completed cake of gags to the hungry ears of the paying public.

A. Pompous-Idiot

As so often happens when you bake a cake, you may cock it up entirely, and you'll find you've left something out –

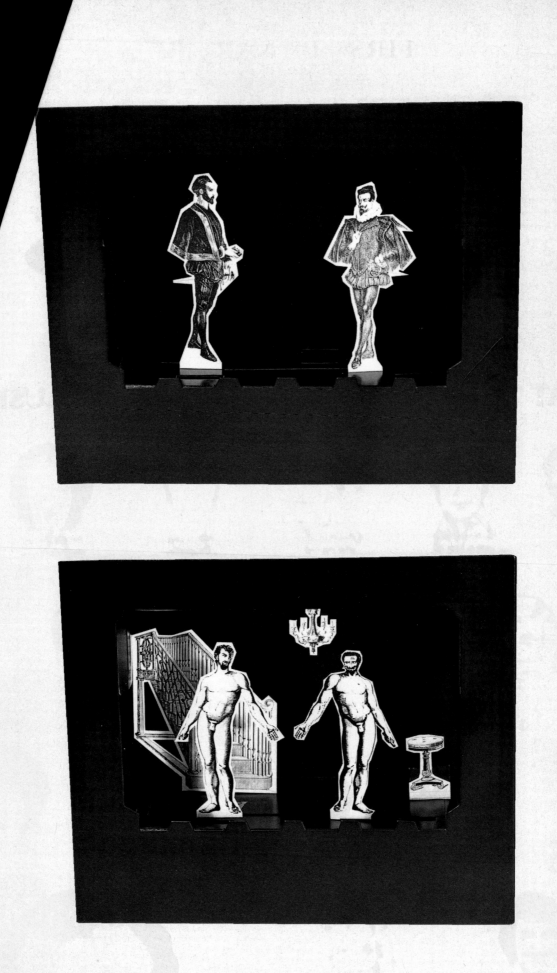

Here are some hints for you to get through
some of the more difficult moments
of the culinary excitement that
is the mounting of a revue...

FIRST BEWARE!!!!

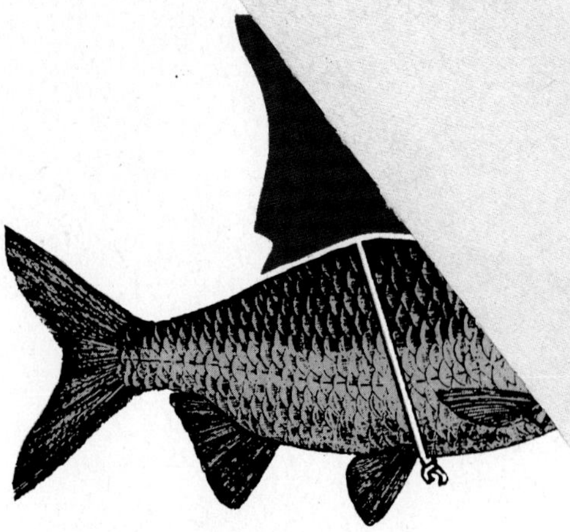

The theatre is a place famous for lies – most everything said there is untrue. When the man in the toga enters and says, 'I am Julius Caesar,' he is, of course, not Julius Caesar – he is an actor dressed in a towel. When a big man in armour says, 'I am a Lion,' he is, quite obviously, not a lion, but rather, he is a li-ar. Hamlet the Dane is almost always John the Englishman, or Kenneth the Irishman, or Robbie the Scotsman, and Titania, Queen of the Fairies, is in fact Judith, or Sharon, or, in certain boys' school productions, Bernard.

So with the eventual aim of theatre being to produce a whopping great two-hour-long fib, you should be wary of lies and delusions all along the way in theatrical life. We therefore provide you, before you stage your revue, with this crucial check list of

GREAT THEATRICAL LIES AND SELF-DELUSI

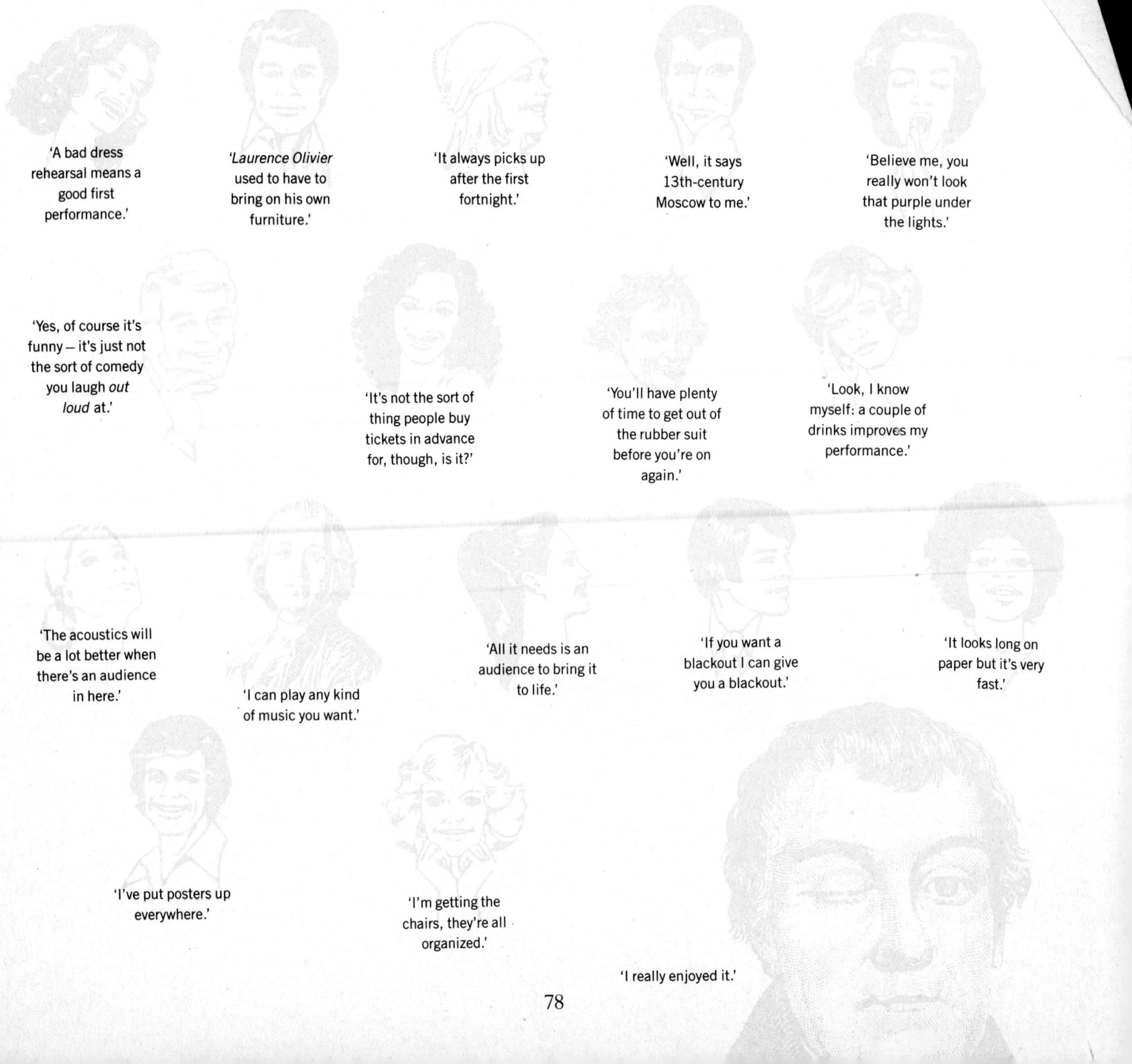

'A bad dress rehearsal means a good first performance.'

'*Laurence Olivier* used to have to bring on his own furniture.'

'It always picks up after the first fortnight.'

'Well, it says 13th-century Moscow to me.'

'Believe me, you really won't look that purple under the lights.'

'Yes, of course it's funny – it's just not the sort of comedy you laugh *out loud* at.'

'It's not the sort of thing people buy tickets in advance for, though, is it?'

'You'll have plenty of time to get out of the rubber suit before you're on again.'

'Look, I know myself: a couple of drinks improves my performance.'

'The acoustics will be a lot better when there's an audience in here.'

'I can play any kind of music you want.'

'All it needs is an audience to bring it to life.'

'If you want a blackout I can give you a blackout.'

'It looks long on paper but it's very fast.'

'I've put posters up everywhere.'

'I'm getting the chairs, they're all organized.'

'I really enjoyed it.'

HOW TO WRITE YOUR OWN REVUE

There are only four things you need to write your own brilliant revue instead of doing ours. Once you have all four you will immediately become rich and famous and enjoy as much sex as Griff Rhys Jones.*

The four things are: Impressions, Topical Jokes, Targets and Funny Names.

1. IMPRESSIONS

At some point in your revue you will need to do an impression of a well-known personality . . . or even Paddy Ashdown.

Follow the useful hints below to impress people with your uncanny ability.

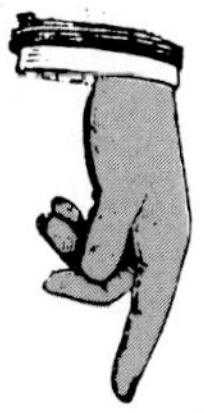

THE CATCHPHRASE

Most well-known people can be deftly suggested by the words that the public automatically associates with them.

e.g.

'Hallo, good evening and welcome' – David Frost

'Hi de hi!' – Su Pollard

'Hallo everybody peeps, innit?' – Michael Dukakis

MAKE-UP

'Less is More' is the golden rule here. Something as drastic as plastic surgery is not recommended. It's expensive, painful, and doesn't make you look any different. Lord Hailsham is a salutary lesson.

**If you like it more often than that you should consult your doctor immediately.*

TIPS FOR SPECIFIC IMPRESSIONS

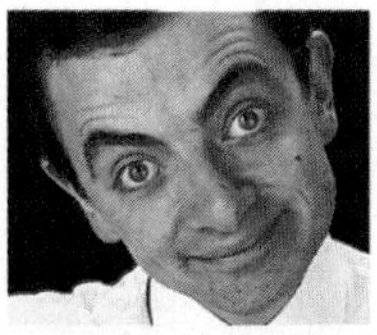

Prince Charles
Fiddle with your cuffs, say 'carbuncle' a lot and try to touch your ears with the corners of your mouth.

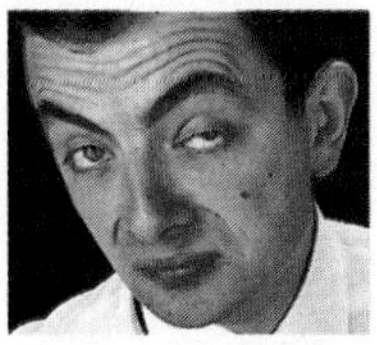

Ronald Reagan
Smear rouge on your cheeks, drink two bottles of Scotch and then say the first thing that comes into your head. Great Reagan impersonators to learn from include Rory Bremner, Phil Cool, and George Bush.

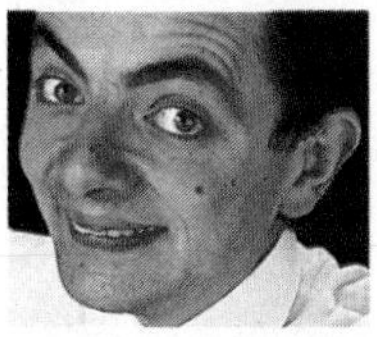

Mrs Thatcher
Just to give you the feel of the character, first try putting a few hundred thousand people out of work.

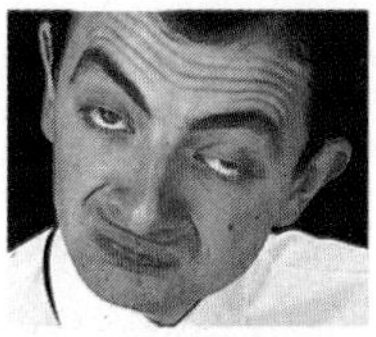

Esther Rantzen
False teeth would be a definite asset here. Unfortunately she persists with the ones Dame Nature so mischievously issued her.

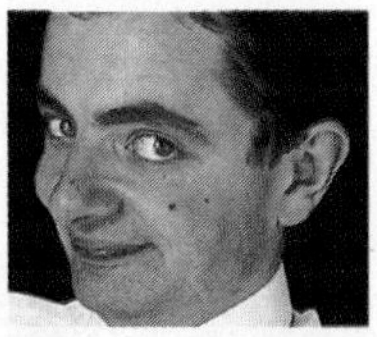

Frank Bruno
Catch the essence of Big Frank by doing your impression of a brick shithouse and building up from there. Even more important are those little throwaway gags like: 'I know I can beat Tyson.'

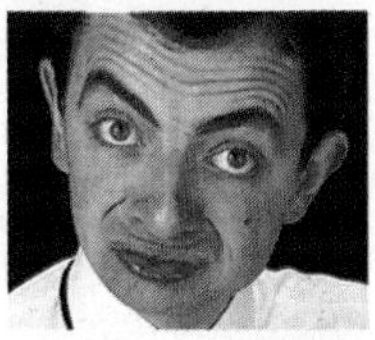

Anita Dobson
A strong singing voice is a terrific advantage . . . although she seems to have got by without one.

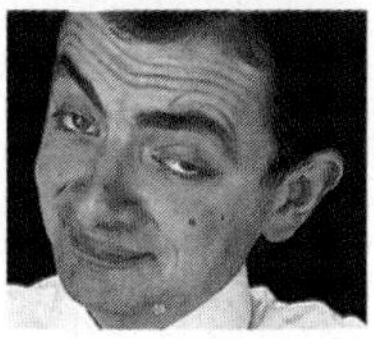

Roy Hattersley
Once you've mastered this impression you can perform at private parties or rent yourself out as a garden sprinkler.

Handy Tip: make a tape of the voice you want to do . . . and mime to it.

2. TOPICAL JOKES

Revues should contain an element of satire.
Failing this, they should have some Topical Jokes.

A Topical Joke is a slightly out-of-date idea expressed
rather more loudly than usual.

Ninety per cent of these ideas are untrue but, despite the
fact that everyone's heard them a million times before,
they are accepted as not only true but clever. Topical
Jokes about any of the things below are blue-chip
mirth-inducers.

THINGS THAT ARE NOT TRUE BUT ALWAYS GET A LAUGH

The *Guardian* is full
of typing errors.

The Skoda is a crap car

British Rail make curly
sandwiches

Builders always show
their bum cleavage

The SLD holds its party
conference in a phone box.

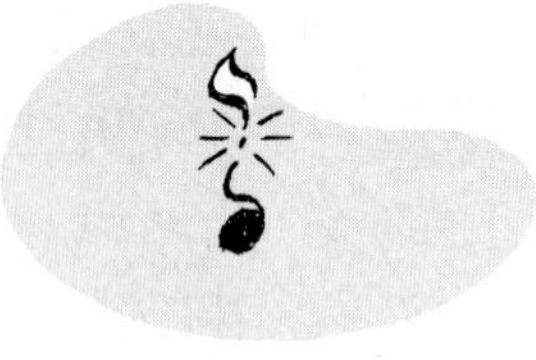

Andrew Lloyd Webber has
never written an original tune

Anneka Rice has an
enormous bottom

Mrs Thatcher wants to put all
of us in extermination camps

Michael Jackson is insane

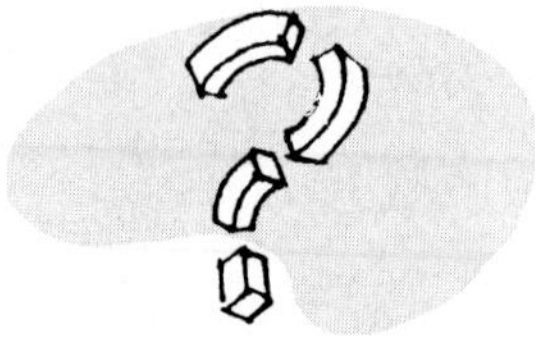

Channel Four caters
only for Asian lesbians

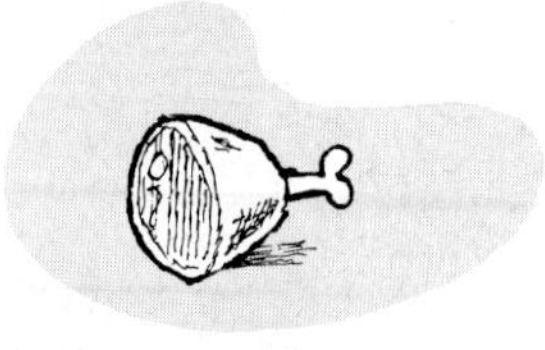

Roger Moore can't act

Neil Kinnock gets
bossed by Glenys

Arthur Scargill has three
Shredded Wheat on his head

Nobody in their right mind
wears socks with sandals

Opera singers are fat

David Steel is a dwarf

Prince Charles is insane

THINGS THAT ARE NOT NECESSARILY TRUE BUT ALWAYS GET A LAUGH

Denis Thatcher drinks a lot

England has a useless football team

Chartered accountants are boring

Mark Thatcher gets lost all the time

Only creeps have carphones

Mrs Thatcher wants to put some of us in
extermination camps

THINGS THAT ARE TRUE AND DEADLY SERIOUS

Estate agents, without a single exception, are scum

3. TARGETS

If you can't think of any topical jokes, then 'Targets' are
an effective substitute.

A Target is a name that is just dropped into the script. It
doesn't need to be in the vicinity of an actual joke.
Provided it is the name of one of the kinds of things
below, it will almost always get a laugh, no matter how
irrelevant the context.

– the name of any politician, showbiz personality or
sportsperson who has recently made a
mess of their marriage

– the name of any well-known person suspected of
wearing a wig

– the name of any transport vehicle known by its initials,
e.g. TSR2, APT, C5

– the name of the current England football team manager

– the name of anyone recently photographed within 30
feet of Joan Collins

– Gyles Brandreth (whoever he is)

If you have plenty of Targets and not many jokes, you
will be referred to as 'hard-hitting'.

If you have no jokes at all you will be referred to as 'witty'.

81

4. FUNNY NAMES

If you have no Impressions, no Topical Jokes and no Targets, then your last hope is 'Funny Names'. Frequently, when creating a revue, a funny name is needed. Usually, more time is wasted trying to decide on the correct funny name than in the whole of the rest of the project put together.

To save you the trouble, we have provided a list of authentically funny names. The mere mention of even *one* of these (in the right context) is guaranteed to have your audience gibbering with mirth.

The *Royal Alternative Variety Club of Great Britain Humorous Nomenclature Handbook 1988* lists the three funniest names in the universe as follows:

1. **Perkins**   2. **Colonel Muriel Volestrangler**   3. **Mrs Thatcher**

Unfortunately, both Perkins and Mrs Thatcher are heavily overused, and Colonel Muriel Volestrangler is © John Cleese.

The *following* names however, while extremely funny, have never been used at all. You are invited to pepper them freely about your revue, either singly or in clumps.

Ted Clot	Beryl Mince	Shadbolt Sardine Esq.
Lionel Topiary Hedgepeacock	Gervase Bobblehat	Eric Poppadum
Eunice Thelwell Brunt	Kevin Leisure-Gherkin	Beryl Streep
Norris Melt	Martin Tosspot	Enderby Cheese
Harrison Shadwell Lemming	Philippe de Quiverlobe	Severiano Breastbud
Kurt Viaduct	Sir Nugent Trimphone	Quentin Kumquat
Huge Roast Potato	Sir Hilary Batwing	Sir Pilchard Ordinary
Maurice Idiot	Hon. Peregrine Spunt-Bovington	Broadbean, 3rd Viscount Oysterlobster
Isaiah Hovis Velcro	Gunther Harditem	Ross Hoss
Geraint S. Nightbottom	E. Huntbunter Potato III	Sir Frumious Poffle
J. Polyp Arsebandit	Mrs Edwina Biryani	Bill Fromage
Ludwig V. Noot	Ebury Milksop	Thackeray Bobblebottom
Giuseppe Saveloy	Lorimer Mortlake Carpet	
Bev Pilchard		So, now you know it all, get writing!

If you are to have a truly successful show, it is as well to have a Royal turn up.
Here is a quick guide to

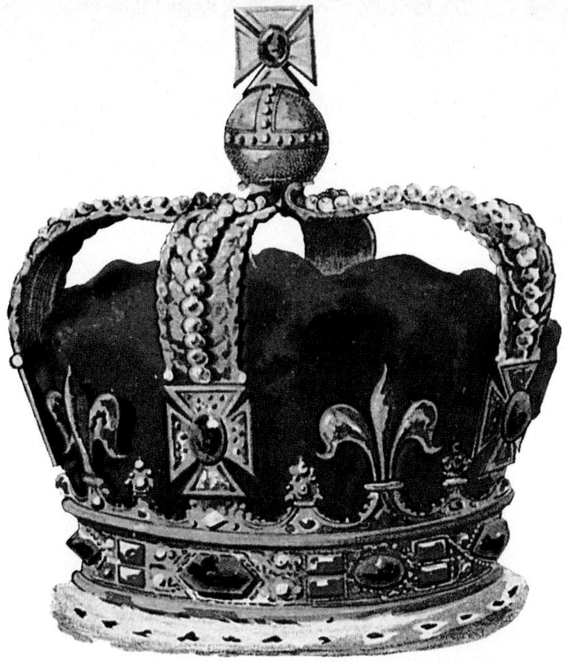

How to Get a Royal

If you don't know a Royal personally, then your best bet is to bump into one casually. This isn't easy either as Royals don't usually go to ordinary places (e.g. the laundrette, the betting shop, the toilet, Sainsbury's on Friday night).

Also, if you are lucky enough to meet one in the street (e.g. a royal walkabout), you will usually be a bit dumbstruck and blurt out something pretty useless like 'Hullo', or 'This is my niece Tracey' or 'These flowers are for you.' Train yourself to avoid this mistake. Always have a useful phrase on your lips, like:

'Are you doing anything on Tuesday?'
or
'Will you be in our revue next Friday week in the college bar?'

If you can't bump into a Royal at all, then you will just have to write to them. A few tips will help. Always include a stamped addressed envelope (preferably addressed to yourself). Never include a stamped addressed stamp, which is vaguely silly and doesn't serve any purpose at all. And do be careful to describe exactly what you want in a suitably gracious tone (e.g. 'We would love you to play the part made famous by John Cleese in the enclosed sketch for which we feel sure you would be perfect and we're sure it would raise thousands for our charity' is much better than 'We're not fussy who turns up just as long as it's not the stuck-up tarty one with the beardy husband or that twit who went to Cambridge and could you find your own way from the bus station as we won't have time to pick you up').

Remember, the Queen doesn't have an agent so you will have to write to her direct (address is in the phone directory, or try *Thompson's Local*, under Constitutional Rulers). And if you have met before it is a good idea to remind her; familiarity counts for a lot in Royal circles. But don't exaggerate – just because you were at Wembley for the same Cup Final as her twenty years ago, it's not an excuse for treating her as an old pal.

Good phrases to use in your letter are 'Your Royal Highness', 'ever humble' and 'your most obedient servant'. Bad phrases to use are 'wotcha cock', 'laugh till they fart' and 'drugs at the party'.

Remember, if your Royal does agree, you will have a lot of preparation to take care of and be particularly attentive when you get on stage – should the royal guest dry or corpse, do not on any account encourage heckling. There is nothing more off-putting than a shout of 'Oh Gawd, jug-ears doesn't even know the words.'

On the other hand, a few rules of etiquette may be relaxed when encountering Royals on the stage. You do not need to bow every time a Royal makes an appearance, nor should you shake the royal person by the hand when he or she enters and get the rest of the cast in the sketch to stand in line so they can be introduced to the royal personage. However, undue familiarity (i.e. goosing from behind to get a cheap laugh) should be avoided at all costs – unless, of course, prior permission is granted in writing.

Finally, do thank the royal person at the end of the performance. You might like to buy them a small present for their help. A box of Terry's All-Gold is usually sufficient, unless they have put in particularly good work, in which case you could stretch it to a Boots Gift Voucher as well (that lovely range of footcare items always comes in useful). And do invite them to any party afterwards but don't be offended if they refuse. And be very careful if they don't.
Good luck.

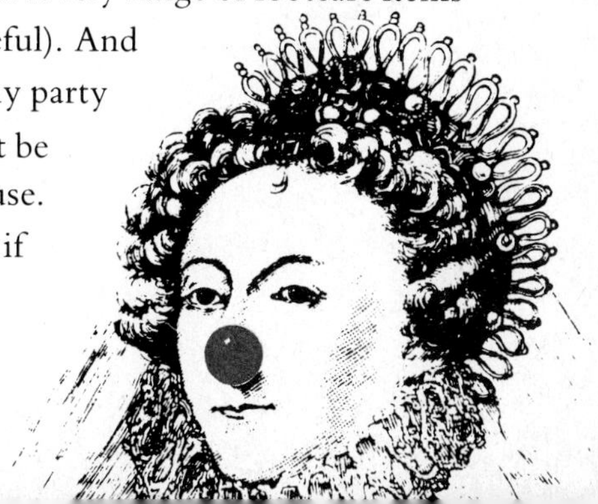

PRE-SHOW DEPRESSION

If you haven't got a royal personage, and you're approaching your first night, you are likely to suffer from a serious bout of pre-show depression. Don't be gloomy about this – it is very usual indeed. We asked a very famous comedy performer, who shall remain nameless, to help ease you through this difficult time with a little confession of his own. At first he refused, but then we told the grubby little nonentity that we would describe him in the introduction as 'a very famous comedy performer, who shall remain nameless', and he wrote back with this:

'Many people imagine that I am a jolly, happy-go-lucky person simply because I work in comedy and have pierced nipples. This is in fact not the case. The latter were the result of a horrific laser malfunction at a gay disco, and one of the essential prerequisites of working in comedy is a depressed and miserable persona. Most of the great comic talents are well known to be desperately unhappy in their lives off the boards as these candid snaps of performers caught in offguard moments illustrate:

Ben Elton

Peter Cook

Victoria Wood

John Cleese

Alexei Sayle

Spike Milligan

Rowan Atkinson

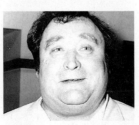
Bernard Manning

In fact, to be really funny on the night, it is essential that you cultivate a miserable and depressed personality. Here is a timetable which may help:

Curtain minus 8 hrs:	Get up. Look at photograph of Arnold Schwarzenegger (men) or Kim Basinger (women). Look in mirror. Cry liberally.
minus 7½ hrs:	Go back to bed.
minus 7 hrs:	Get up. Count pills. Write suicide note: 'I am a failure – I can't go on.'
minus 6½ hrs:	Take overdose.
minus 6 hrs:	Get up. Check medical book for effects of excess Haliborange. Get dressed.
minus 5½ hrs:	See latest Michael Winner movie.
minus 5 hrs:	Throw up.
minus 4½ hrs:	Stick head in gas oven, having written new note: 'Can't cope with modern age – must end it all.'
minus 4 hrs:	Discover gas isn't poisonous any more. Ring up cute number to find out what they're doing after the show.
minus 3½ hrs:	Check Schwarzenegger and Basinger photos to explain why what just happened on the phone just happened. Leave new note: 'Everything goes wrong. Can't stand it any longer.'
minus 3 hrs:	Throw yourself on to tube track.
minus 2½ hrs:	Realize it was Northern Line. Get up again.
minus 2 hrs:	Spend tea-time with a double-glazing salesman.
minus 1½ hrs:	Spend £4,000 on double-glazing.
minus 1 hr:	Run and hurl yourself out of a top-floor window.
minus ½ hr:	Still unable to open double-glazed window. Go to revue venue.
minus 20 mins:	Get dressed in praying mantis costume, write final note: 'This is the end.'
ZERO:	Go on. And may God have mercy on your soul.

If you get depressed, and then suddenly wish you weren't, follow the example of stage comedians down the ages, for whom there was no more natural place to go to ease the nerves than the toilet.

For today's top comics, the toilet is almost a second home. Alternative comedienne Jennifer Saunders owns toilets in London, Paris, Barcelona and Los Angeles. She often flies to the West Coast just to spend a penny.

Eddie Murphy is a notable exception to the toilet-attending rule. As today's hottest comic property, he just doesn't have the time. So Eddie's team of loyal minders goes on his behalf.

John Cleese, by contrast, takes his own toilet all around the world, and has it plumbed in wherever he's filming. 'It was originally built for Hollywood legend Hedy Lamarr in the thirties,' John told us. 'It has a fabulous diamond-encrusted seat which cannot be used but makes a superb investment.'

Here are a few glimpses of the loo-styles of the rich and famous:

Eton-and Oxford-educated Dave 'Mr Funnyfart' Pants is Britain's top toilet humorist. Here we see him researching his next gag.

Radical funster Ben Elton has his handle firmly on the Left!

Anarchic Alexei Sayle has a toilet inspired by Marcel Duchamp.

As you'd expect, there's nothing funny about Jimmy Tarbuck's toilet.

Improvisational genius Robin Williams makes up his own toilet as he goes along from stuff he finds lying around.

This is where Mel Smith and Griff Rhys Jones rehearse their popular TV shows.

The 'Siamese' loo of Dawn French and Lenny Henry – two comedians who often find themselves 'on the throne' together!

WHERE TO PUT YOUR MOTHER

One of the major reasons for your depression may be your reflections on the **monumentally stupid** moment three weeks ago when you asked your mother if she'd like to come along, and she said, yes, she'd love to, particularly since it's for charity and are there any songs by Noël Coward? Unfortunately, you can't turn back the clocks on this one, it's in her diary, and she's slipping on her sensible tights at this very moment – just in case the hall's central heating isn't working. Damage limitation is your only option. So...

Never let your mother sit in the front row: she's apt to smile at you and nudge your father all the way through the performance. Put her at least six rows back and at one end and afterwards tell her it's a theatrical superstition.

Never ask her what she thought of the show – she will almost certainly make a disparaging remark about your hair/your hands/your failure to stand still/your trousers/your breasts.

Don't let her bring one of her friends.

Do tell her beforehand if you're going to say '★★★★'. Particularly if it comes in the middle of the word 'mother★★★★er'.

If all else fails, take heart from the following list of remarks made by famous people's mothers at important moments in theatrical history:

'He's always been a bit mopey.'
Mrs Beckett after seeing *Waiting for Godot*

'The one who played Miss Prism, now she's a nice sort of girl, Oscar.'
Mrs Wilde after seeing *The Importance of Being Earnest*

'It was quite interesting but I didn't like the curtains.'
Mrs Shakespeare after seeing *Hamlet*

'The seats were very hard, weren't they?'
Mrs Aeschylus after seeing the *Oresteia* trilogy

When the final moment comes, and you're out of the toilet and into the costume, it is, of course, the time for prayer. We present you with two types of prayer for that very sacred moment before the rising of the curtain and the offering up of yourself as the sacrificial goat upon the altar of comedy.

FIRST NIGHT PRAYER – FORMAL

He who shall play the Vicar in the highly amusing Vicar Sketch, shall, before the curtain goes up and while the stage manager doth peek through the curtain and say, 'They do look like a friendly house', say these few words:

VICAR

Dear Lord,

Whose son Jesu did crack the highly amusing visual gag about the man with the log in his eye,

And who did himself play upon Abraham the ultimate practical gag of telling him he had to kill his son,

Look down with mercy upon our humble revue this evening.

May the blackouts fall as fast upon the punchline as you fell upon the enemies of David

And may the laughter from the audience fall as fulsome as the rain that fell upon the world of Noah.

May the opening number work, because as thou knowest, from thine experience with Adam and Eve, something which gets off to a dodgy start is likely to just go from bad to worse.

For it is written in your Bible, it is easier for a camel to go through the eye of a needle than it is for a badly timed gag to get a woof.

Forgive us our blasphemies, as we forgive those who blaspheme against us under the influence of alcohol in the back row.

In the name of the Father, the Son, the Holy Ghost and St Biddulph,★

Amen.

★*See page 6.*

If you hang a bit looser in your religious outlook, are the kind of guy or gal who prefers *Good News for Modern Man* to the King James Authorized, then you might prefer to go with this one:

First Night Prayer-Kinda Informal, You Know

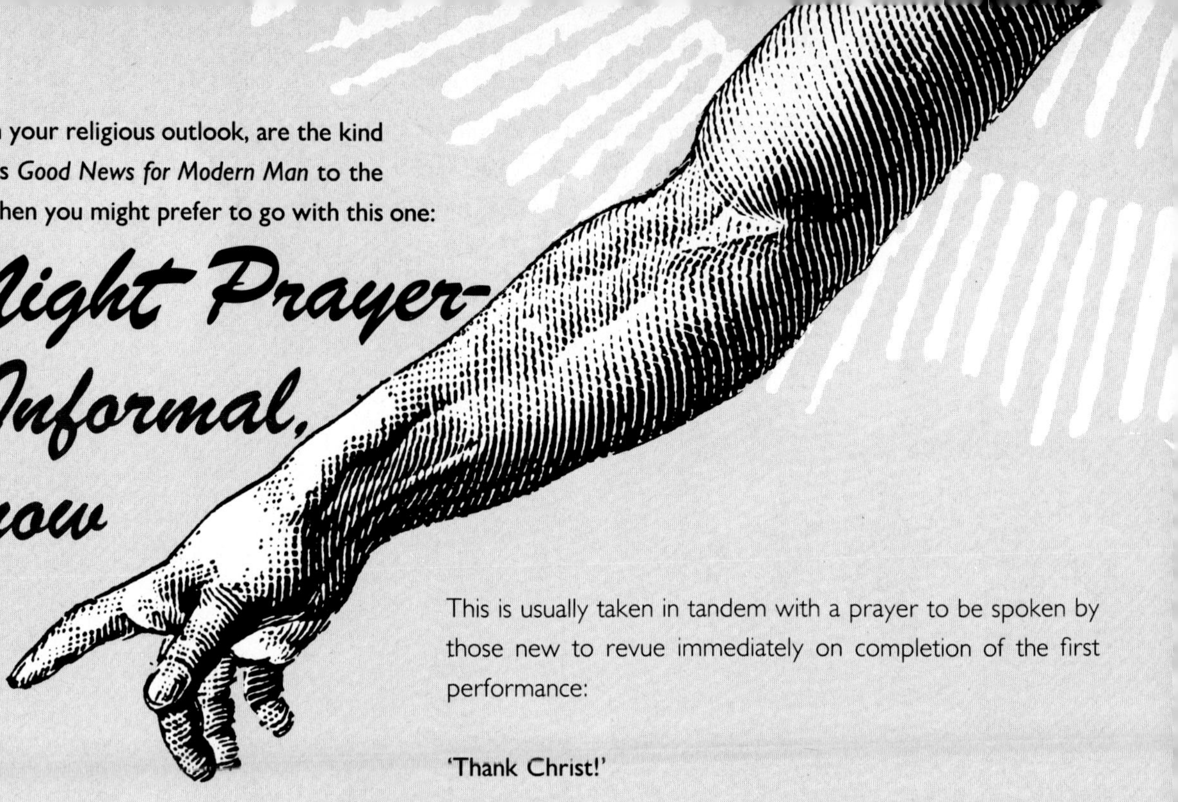

VICAR

Oh Christ
Oh Jesus
Oh bloody hell
Oh Christ Almighty...
What?
No no no. Of course not. I'm fine.
How long before we...?
Oh.
Oh Christ.
Oh Christ, I'm going to be sick.
Oh God.
Bloody hell.
Oh Christ.

(to be repeated as necessary)

This is usually taken in tandem with a prayer to be spoken by those new to revue immediately on completion of the first performance:

'Thank Christ!'

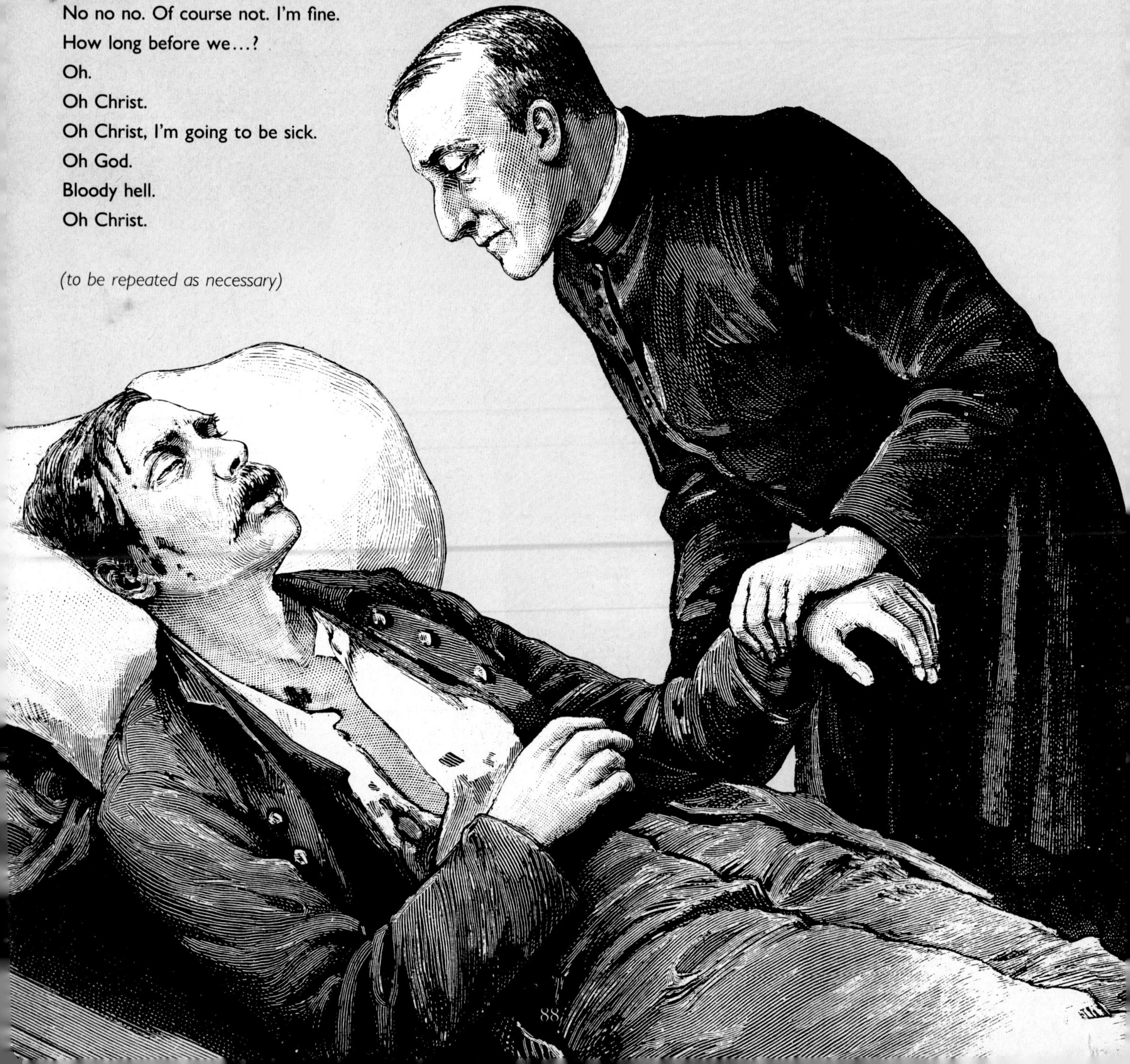

At this very last moment, you will find that your major concern is whether or not you can actually remember the lines which you hope may just make certain childish members of the audience laugh . . . a bit . . . if you're lucky. The true professional will never let this be a worry. Not because he/she actually knows the lines, but because he/she has in fact concealed the script somewhere on stage. This is a very important and great theatrical tradition.

THE PLACING OF SCRIPTS

Traditionally the reason why so many sketches are delivered from the pulpit or the newsdesk is so that the scripts can be in front of the performer. But there is in fact no limit to the number of places where scripts can be concealed. As these photographs will reveal.

Marlon Brando points helpfully to his ear-shaped script.

Alec Guinness thanks God for his new contact lenses.

Charlton Heston takes the unsubtle approach.

Baldrick reads his vegetable before eating it.

Barbara's badge helps mummy with his very small part.

Cagney reads cameraman's head.

It is of course once you are actually into the performance that your troubles really start. Let us simply prepare you for two eventualities. The one extremely likely to occur, the other very rare.

THE COMIC RELIEF GUIDE TO HANDLING HECKLERS

Unfortunately you may occasionally, though very rarely, be confronted by hecklers in your audience. There is an art to dealing with these and you are advised not to attempt ambitious replies until you are fully proficient. Start with a few simple retorts.

Beginners replies for hecklers:

1. Pardon?

2. Please will you go away.

3. Shut up, you nincompoop.

4. That's not a very nice thing to say.

5. Yes, sorry, Headmaster, it won't happen again.

It will be quite a while before you can risk moving on the *riposte majeure*, such as used by the most practised of club comedians. When you are ready though, it goes something like this...

Come up here on stage and say that to my face, you fat-mouthed drunken git, and I'll ram my fist so far down your gob, you'll have teeth where your toenails used to be.

The problem with this is that if the heckler **is** a fat-mouthed drunken git, he probably will come up on stage and ram **his** first down **your** gob so far you'll have teeth where your toenails used to be. And that's no state to be in while attempting to convey the light delicacies of a comedy skit.

90

DEATH

A much more frequent problem on the sketch circuit is what to do when someone drops dead during the performance. The best answer, and the one favoured by Sir Ivor Novello, is to make light of the whole affair with a joke. A good light-hearted ad lib can do a lot to ease the tension in situations like this.

Good ad libs to use in the event of a person dropping dead on stage:

1. Some people will do anything to steal the limelight round here.

2. Is there a mortician in the house?

3. He never did *that* in rehearsals.

4. Prompt!

5. (*As Cleese*) This actor is no more, he is an ex-actor, he's a stiff, b'reft of life, he's rolled up the curtain and gone to visit the choir invisible.

Less good, but the one you'll probably end up using...

6. Oh, blast, he's snuffed it!

But don't worry – far more prestigious actors than yourself have had to face this problem in their careers (*see photograph*).

So now, at last, the curtain is down, the laughter (and one hopes only a small percentage of the cast) has died. Only one thing remains –

THE CAST PARTY

Yep, it's the mind-bending, tear-jerking, truth-telling, drink-spilling, actress-slapping nightmare that you all so look forward to for so long. In the face of such a dark, broken-light, spilt-beer, torn-dress, abandoned-hope disaster, words fail – so, here, to carry with you into that jungle of jollity, is your own very special private Comic Relief cast party flow chart.

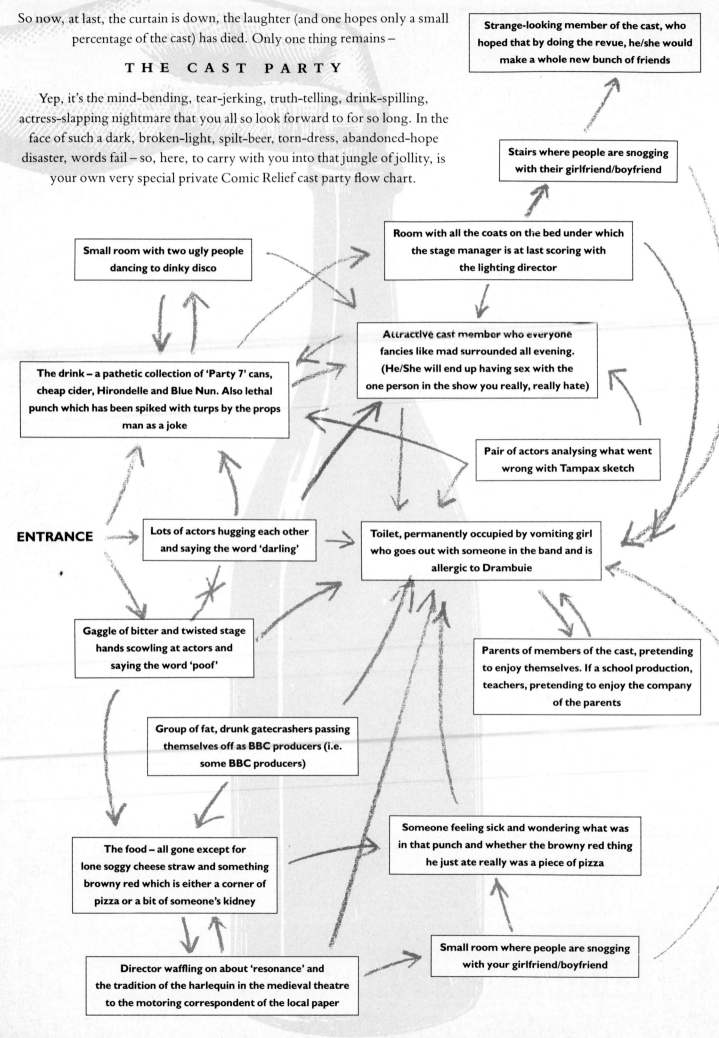

Strange-looking member of the cast, who hoped that by doing the revue, he/she would make a whole new bunch of friends

Stairs where people are snogging with their girlfriend/boyfriend

Small room with two ugly people dancing to dinky disco

Room with all the coats on the bed under which the stage manager is at last scoring with the lighting director

The drink – a pathetic collection of 'Party 7' cans, cheap cider, Hirondelle and Blue Nun. Also lethal punch which has been spiked with turps by the props man as a joke

Attractive cast member who everyone fancies like mad surrounded all evening. (He/She will end up having sex with the one person in the show you really, really hate)

Pair of actors analysing what went wrong with Tampax sketch

ENTRANCE

Lots of actors hugging each other and saying the word 'darling'

Toilet, permanently occupied by vomiting girl who goes out with someone in the band and is allergic to Drambuie

Gaggle of bitter and twisted stage hands scowling at actors and saying the word 'poof'

Parents of members of the cast, pretending to enjoy themselves. If a school production, teachers, pretending to enjoy the company of the parents

Group of fat, drunk gatecrashers passing themselves off as BBC producers (i.e. some BBC producers)

Someone feeling sick and wondering what was in that punch and whether the browny red thing he just ate really was a piece of pizza

The food – all gone except for lone soggy cheese straw and something browny red which is either a corner of pizza or a bit of someone's kidney

Small room where people are snogging with your girlfriend/boyfriend

Director waffling on about 'resonance' and the tradition of the harlequin in the medieval theatre to the motoring correspondent of the local paper

OTHER COMIC RELIEF BOOKS

TRAPPIST VERSION

A Trappist version of the *Comic Relief Revue* featuring 96 pages of entirely blank white paper and suitable for Cistercian performance is available from the publishers, price £7.95.

A large-print version for partially sighted Trappist monks featuring large-format white paper is available on special request.

BED-WETTING AMONGST THE TROBRIAND ISLANDERS   £10.95

by Dr Trudy Robertson
An in-depth anthropological study of the cultural taboos of a remote people Nothing whatever to do with Comic Relief, but bloody funny all the same

COMIC RELIEF REVUE FOR MIMES   £25.95

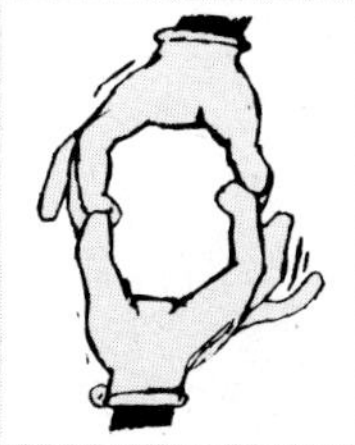

Awful

DER KOMIKENRELIEFEN-MEISTERBUCH   DM 42.99

German language edn
The funniest sketches to come out of Germany since 1380. If you get pleasure from smacking people in the face with a bockwurst, you will enjoy both pages.

COMIC RELIEF REVUE DE LUXE   £480.50

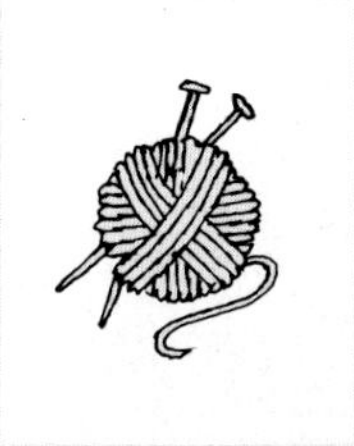

Adapted by Gyles Brandreth
Nestling in its own 3-cwt sycamore hamper, the text is lavishly knitted on to the fronts of 96 hideous sweaters.

THE FAMILY COMIC RELIEF REVUE BOOK   £5.95

Adapted by William Rees-Mogg
All references to members of the Royal Family, the Church of England, and the Conservative Party have been deftly removed by the toad-like editor, encased in a lead-lined box, and sent to the Pope for exorcism.
All filth – including the use of the disgusting and repeated word 'relief' – has been removed and incinerated personally by an Elder of the Church of Scotland.
A slim (but clean) volume

ORDER FORM

NAME _____	ORDER NO. _____	INTERNAL USE ONLY **PENGUIN FORM NUMBER D28901**
ADDRESS _____		
_____		ENTRY REF. ☐☐☐☐☐ VERIFIER REF. ☐☐☐☐☐
_____	POST CODE	

SPECIAL INSTRUCTIONS

ACCOUNT NO. ☐☐☐☐☐☐ / D.A.C. ☐☐   CUSTOMER ORDER REFERENCE ☐☐☐☐☐☐☐☐☐☐☐

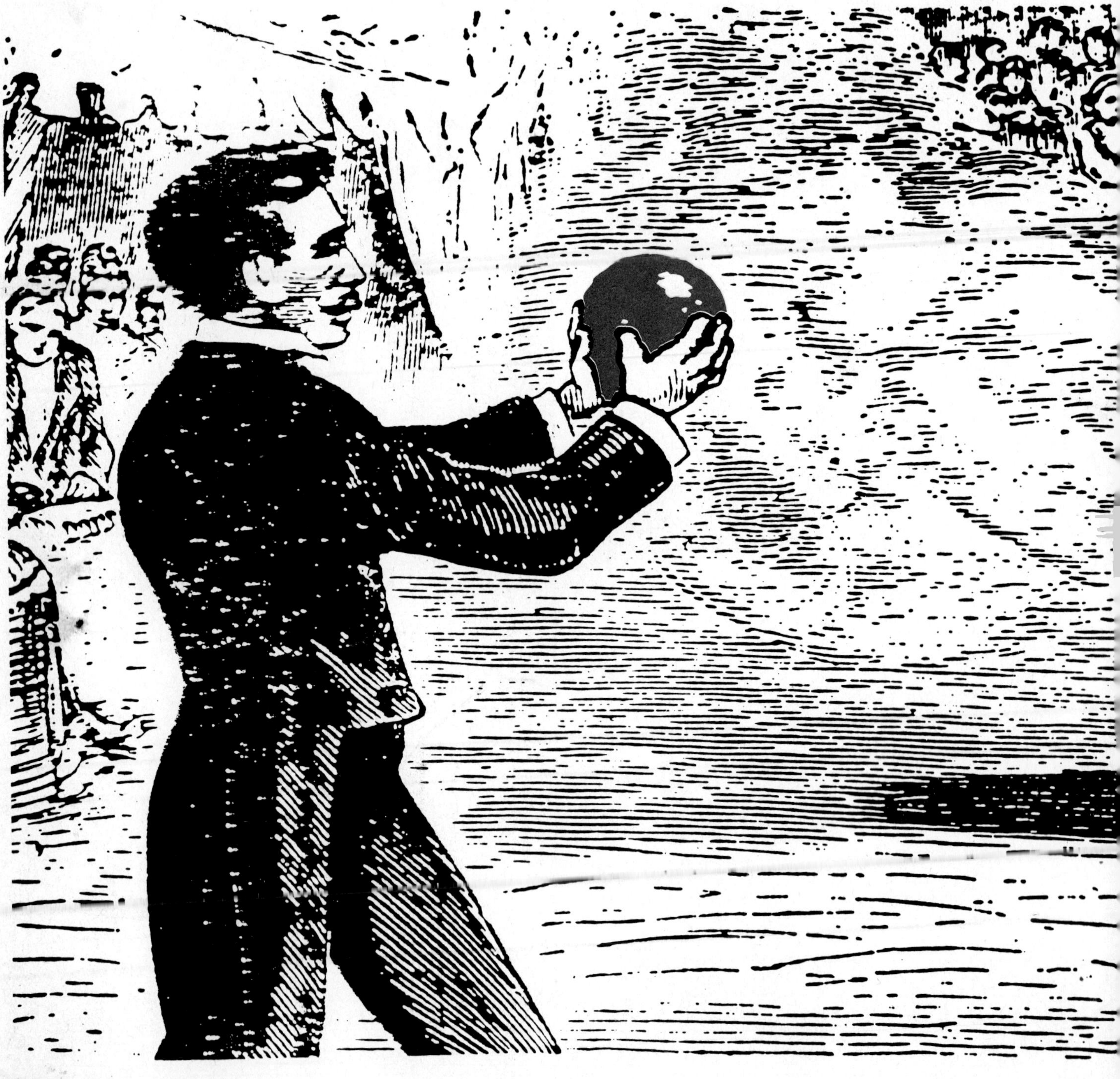